FUTURE SURVEY ANNUAL
1985

A Guide to the Recent Literature of Trends, Forecasts, and Policy Proposals

Edited by
Michael Marien

with
Lane Jennings

Volume 6 in a Continuing Series

World Future Society
Bethesda, Maryland U.S.A.

The World Future Society, an association for the study of alternative futures, is a non-profit educational and scientific organization founded in 1966. The Society acts as an impartial clearinghouse for a variety of different views, and does not take positions on what will happen—or ought to happen—in the future. The criteria for selecting items, and the opinions expressed in the introduction, are those of the Editor, and do not necessarily reflect the position of the World Future Society or any of its officers.

The Future Survey Annual Series
Edited by Michael Marien, with Lane Jennings

Volume 1. **Future Survey Annual 1979** (Items 1/1603) 255 pages.
Volume 2. **Future Survey Annual 1980-81** (Items 1604/3090) 268 pages.
Volume 3. **Future Survey Annual 1981-82** (Items 3091/4457) 260 pages.
Volume 4. **Future Survey Annual 1983** (Items 4458/5597) 240 pages.
Volume 5. **Future Survey Annual 1984** (Items 5598/6464) 209 pages.
Volume 6. **Future Survey Annual 1985** (Items 6465/7299) 208 pages.

$25.00 each from: World Future Society
Book Service
4916 St. Elmo Avenue
Bethesda, MD 20814
U.S.A.
301/656-8274

Copyright ©1986 by World Future Society

ISBN: 0-930242-29-7

Future Survey Annual 1985
Table of Contents

"If anything is important, it is the future. The past is gone, and the present exists only as a fleeting moment. Everything that we think and do from this moment on can affect only the future. And it is in the future that we shall spend the rest of our lives. But growing complexity and the glut of information, much of which is irrelevant, have made it extremely difficult to obtain the information required for wise decisions."

– Edward Cornish

"The rise and fall of images of the future precedes or accompanies the rise and fall of cultures. The image of the future can act not only as a barometer, but as a regulative mechanism which alternately opens and shuts the dampers on the mighty blast-furnace of culture. It not only indicates alternative choices and possibilities, but actively promotes certain choices and in effect puts them to work in determining the future. A close examination of prevailing images, then, puts us in a position to forecast the probable future. The task before us is to re-awaken the almost dormant awareness of the future and to find the best nourishment for a starving social imagination."

– Fred Polak

"It is natural and necessary for us to have visions of the future. But the mind is by no means inclined to contemplate a large variety of possible futures, and tends rather to attach itself to the futurible (a possible descendant from the present state of affairs) that appears to be intellectually the most probable or affectively the most desirable. Man is fortunate when the desirable and probable coincide. The case is often otherwise. We are forever making forecasts—with scanty data, no awareness of method, no criticism, and no cooperation. It is urgent that we make this natural and individual activity into a cooperative and organic endeavor, subject to greater exigencies of intellectual rigor. We need a forum in which forecasts are proposed and debated, and it is vital that a large number of competing propositions be offered."

– Bertrand de Jouvenel

"Competition of ideas is fundamental to a free society. If it is to remain free, a society cannot permit itself to be dominated by one strain of thought. Public policy derives from the ideas, speculation, and theories of thoughtful men and women. Policy makers themselves rarely originate the concepts underlying the laws by which we are governed. They choose among practical options to formulate legislation, governmental directives, regulations, and programs. If there is no testing of ideas by competition, public policy decisions may undermine rather than bolster the foundations of a free society. Assuring effective competition in the arena of idea formation is the principal objective of AEI."

– American Enterprise Institute for
Public Policy Research

"The sociological imagination . . . in considerable part consists of the capacity to shift from one perspective to another, and in the process to build up an adequate view of a total society and of its components. It is this imagination, of course, that sets off the social scientist from the mere technician. Its essence is the combination of ideas that no one expected were combinable, and a truly fierce drive to make sense of the world, which the technician as such usually lacks."

– C. Wright Mills

"The really creative breakthroughs will be made when our researchers start to merge their ideas, flowing them over into the next or related discipline, where they can pick up knowledge they didn't have within their own discipline, and meld them together."

– Edgar Mitchell

"We worry about the future as we have never worried before. And we have reason. We are in trouble as a species. If we are to recover our confidence, it will have to be the confidence of maturity. And it will have to be built, as all mature confidence is built, on a willingness to face problems forthrightly and on some reasonable success in coping with them. That is hard, but adulthood is hard. The advantages of pluralism are diminished if the various elements of the society are out of touch with one another. A society that is capable of continuous renewal will have effective internal communication among its diverse elements. We do not have that today. We are drowning in a torrent of talk, but most of it serves only to raise the noise level."

– John W. Gardner

INTRODUCTION

Future Survey Annual is prepared for a variety of people in education, business, and government. Such people may be known by a variety of titles: futurist, futures researcher, policy analyst, planner, policymaker, researcher, teacher, student, or political activist. All of these people seek to "scan" the environment—to get a broad view of what is happening and who is thinking what. And many of these people hope to shape a better future for their organizations, communities, governments, and perhaps the entire world.

This guide is a tool for the multiple purposes of these multiple users. In the most general sense, it seeks to enhance understanding of major problems and possibilities: what is changing (trends), what may happen (forecasts), and what ought to be done (policy proposals, prescriptions, ideas for the future). To attend to all of these matters in a variety of problem areas, **Future Survey Annual** necessarily crosses the barriers to understanding that have been established between academic disciplines and professions, between specialized academicians and popular journalists, between book and periodical formats, and between various ideologies or worldviews: liberal and conservative, establishment and anti-establishment.

The diversity of worldviews in this guide may be confusing to many readers. To some, it may even be offensive. But this reflects the real world—which, if anything, is even more complex, confusing, and contentious than suggested by the abstracts assembled here. Attempts to picture our world as less complex than it is have doubtlessly led to many of our problems. Conversely, assembling the major alternative views of what our problems are and what should be done about them may, it is hoped, help promote more rational analysis, thus encouraging a genuine dialogue between all informed points of view, and wiser decisions in the global public interest.

Scope of the Guide

This **Annual** integrates abstracts of 835 books, reports, and articles that first appeared in the monthly issues of *Future Survey* between October 1984 and September 1985. It adds to the 6,464 items brought together in the five previous **Future Survey Annuals**, for a total of 7,299 items. The slightly smaller number of abstracts in this **Annual**, compared with the 867 items in **Future Survey Annual 1984**, does not reflect any decline in worthy futures-relevant books and articles (which, very roughly estimated, have been constant over the past seven years). Rather, it reflects greater attention to depth over breadth, and thus longer abstracts filling limited space.

● Criteria for Selection. The literature cited here has been selected by scanning the output of more than 150 book publishers, a score of research institutes, several dozen general interest magazines, leading newspapers, and more than 200 scholarly and professional journals. Criteria for selection include breadth, originality, authoritativeness, and importance to the public interest.

● Time Frame. This guide encompasses books and articles published largely in 1984 and 1985. The literature under survey is widely scattered among a great variety of publishers and periodicals, so some important books and articles have doubtlessly been overlooked. Other appropriate items from the 1984-1985 period may have already been published in **Future Survey Annual 1984** or will be published in **Future Survey Annual 1986.**

● Linguistic Limits. Coverage is confined to English-language materials, most of which were written by Americans, published in the US, and concerned with US problems and interests. This is not in any way to suggest that American views of world problems are necessarily superior to non-American views; rather, one must begin with the material at hand (and there is an abundance of it) and set realistic limits. An ideal survey of futures-relevant literature would be global and multi-lingual, and it would also cover fictional works as well as non-fiction. **Future Survey Annual** may evolve toward this ideal, but such coverage would require many abstractors, rather than the effort of a single editor, as at present.

● Emphasis on Broad and Long-Term Views. Items have been chosen that are broad and long-term in their implications, rather than immediate and narrow. Overviews of problem areas are especially favored, as are books and articles that might be of interest to readers in more than one field. Criticisms of general policies are included, especially policies (such as Star Wars) with broad implications. But items dealing with specific and relatively narrow policy decisions are not included, nor has much attention been given to short-horizon situations (such as US policy in Central America) which are subject to considerable change over brief time periods.

Futures Research?

The literature documented in this guide can in a very broad sense be seen as "futures research" or "futures studies," in that all of the items herein are explicitly or implicitly concerned in some way with possible or desirable futures. However, few of the authors view themselves as futurists or futures researchers, so it would thus be misleading to suggest that this literature, drawn from many disciplines and sources, constitutes anything resembling a "field," let alone a discipline. It would also be misleading to consider any of this literature, let alone all of it, as "futurology" (which suggests some organized field of study with pretensions to being a science).

Similarly, much of the literature herein can be broadly seen as "policy studies," because it is relevant in some way to public policy. Yet, parallel to the above situation, few of the authors view themselves as "policy analysts," although a fair number are social scientists of one sort or another.

It is best to modestly characterize this literature simply as "futures-relevant" and "policy-relevant," so as to avoid any misleading labelling.

Four Purposes of this Guide

Future Survey Annual seeks to promote progress toward four broad goals, which might also be seen as integrative frontiers for the loose "multi-fields" of futures studies and policy studies.

● **To Consider Both Hopes and Fears**. Major hopes and fears covered in this guide are summarized in **Chart 1**. Any serious survey of present problems and future possibilities should encompass both plausible hopes and plausible fears. Yet there is a widespread tendency to take the extremist positions of either Pollyanna or Cassandra. The pessimism of Cassandra is immobilizing, and keeps us from taking positive action. But the naive optimism of Pollyanna is even more widespread (see **FSAnnual 1979,** #1504), and keeps us from facing our many problems. There is reason for hope, and many good suggestions for positive action in this guide, but we need a tough-minded optimism if we are to make genuine progress.

● **To Bridge Global and National Perspectives**. A global society is forming in many respects, bringing global problems—especially economic and environmental—which require concerted action among nations. And there are many problems such as unemployment and crumbling infrastructure which are shared by all nations, and could be alleviated by better sharing of information across national boundaries. **Chart 2** shows the intertwining of global and domestic conerns, enabling those with a broad worldview to relate their concerns to domestic issues, and those who focus on domestic policy to add a much-needed global dimension to their thinking.

● **To Identify and Combine Multiple Perspectives**. This guide seeks to illustrate the multitude of perspectives that can be brought to a variety of problems and issues. One might think that contemporary standards of rational thought would insist that all facets of every problem be identified, and that all proposed solutions should be carefully weighed, debated, refined, and—where possible—combined. Such a scholarly ideal is virtually the antithesis of the parochial chaos of contemporary thought. The two appendices illustrate this problem of fragmentation. **Appendix 1** outlines 100 impacts of computers and other new information technologies. **Appendix 2** lists 325 futures-relevant and policy-relevant journals, suggesting the difficulty—if not impossibility—of conducting a serious dialogue on any issue. This glut of information is aggravated by our industrial era intellectual infrastructure, dominated by the major research universities, and their lack of orientation toward identifying and combining these multiple perspectives in any coherent way.

Appendix 1, on the impacts of information technologies, is appearing in **Future Survey Annual** for the first time. Similar appendices in recent years include "60 Paths to US and Global Security" and "75 Paths to Economic Health" in **Future Survey Annual 1984** (pp.185-188), and "55 Ways to End the Energy Crunch" in **Future Survey Annual 1980-81** (p.vii). These compilations have not been updated because relatively little has been added to them in the past year. The peace and national security debate, has been largely displaced by the Star Wars issue, thinking about economic alternatives has been placed on hold by Graham-Rudman, and energy alternatives are not of interest so long as oil supplies appear abundant.

● **To Reconcile Realists and Idealists**. One way to divide the many perspectives brought together in this guide is to distinguish between realists and idealists. Realists tend to be "establishment" thinkers with either liberal or conservative leanings, anchored by respectable social science findings and employing a relatively narrow-focused, short-term, technologically-oriented, and putatively value-free view of the future. Realists tend to call themselves policy analysts. If they consider the future in any conscious way, they tend to project the most likely future (often based on problematic assumptions), rather than considering alternative futures—especially desirable or prescriptive futures. Idealists are more prone to call themselves futurists or futures researchers, and to be innovative, non-establishment thinkers with a global perspective that is relatively broad, long-term, and oriented to human needs and ecological concerns. Such views are often identified politically as "beyond right and left."

Both realists and idealists seldom acknowledge each other's thinking. When they do, it is frequently in a superficial and disparaging manner. This guide seeks to encourage a much-needed dialogue. Realists must broaden their worldviews in time and space, reconsider their assumptions, and develop some notion of preferable futures. It is equally important for idealists to come down to earth to some greater degree, to focus on the ideas that are presently in power and how they got there, and to specify how their more appropriate paradigms are superior to those that guide present policy.

For both groups, as well as for people who are in-between or simply confused, this guide to recent trends, forecasts, and policy proposals should amply demonstrate that amid the complexities of the human condition—the broader and more truthful reality—there are many worthy ideas competing for attention. Let them all be heard!

Chart 1
Major Hopes and Fears, 1985:
A Longer and Broader Alternative to Economic Indicators

Significant hopes and fears are outlined below, to serve as an introductory overview of major problems and possibilities, and as a much broader and longer alternative to the narrow and short-term picture that is given by economic and demographic indicators. Roughly summarized, the general trend between 1984 and 1985 is one of **no change in the ratio of hopes and fears**. Despite the resurgence of optimism in some parts of America, the number and severity of fearful long-term problems continues to outweigh many plausible hopes. This is not a brief for pessimism, but for facing our problems in a mature and responsible manner. If we were to do so, we could have a positive hope/fear ratio.

Some hopes and fears are, of course, strongly disputed. The economy is robust to some observers and on the verge of collapse to others (H1,F2). Biotechnology and the new communications technologies offer undiluted promise to some but largely threats to others. High-tech solutions in defense (H3) and agriculture (H10) promise salvation to some, but a deepening of our problems to others. These differences should be seriously debated at length, but they aren't. Suffice it to say that any attempt to look at all of the informed thinking and to honestly balance both hopes and fears would probably find contemporary fears outweighing hopes. That, at least, is my conclusion from preparing this guidebook.

Hopes and fears are listed here in rough order of their imminence and importance. Items with identification numbers ranging from #5598 through #6375 are to be found in **Future Survey Annual 1984**. Items with numbers from #4515 to #5491 are in **FS Annual 1983**.

HOPES
Favorable Trends and Plausible Hopes

H1. ECONOMY: recent growth and lowered inflation, emerging super-industrial high-tech world economy (6806,5979,4916/4920); a robust entrepreneurial economy (6847,6906,6908, 6055/6066). [NOTE: But fears still linger—see F2.]

H2. INFORMATION AGE: spread of ever-improving computers and telecommunications [NOTE: see Appendix 1 for positive impacts.]

H3. EFFECTIVE SDI DEFENSE: "Assured survival" through Star Wars technologies (6631/6636,5762). [NOTE: Intensely disputed—see 6638/6652.]

H4. BIOTECHNOLOGY: genetic engineering enabling new and improved species, better human health (7198,7211,7231,6376/6377,5430/5436) [NOTE: Also a threat—see F15.]

H5. HEALTH: new drugs and technologies (6231/6235); new out-of-hospital services (6225/6228); holistic practices and emphasis on prevention (7005/7006, 7035/7036,7039,5208/5214) possible lifespan extension (5262); gene therapy (7201/7202); potential for healthy public policy (6999/7001); child survival potential (6495). [NOTE: Offset by growing finance problems—see F11.]

H6. ROBOTS: various applications in manufacturing, pollution cleanup, security, and helping people (7232,6318,6392,5063/5064).

H7. OUTER SPACE: exploration, industrialization, migration (7215/7223,6385/6390,5445/5450); superpower cooperation (6652/6653).

H8. WORK: flattened hierarchies, humanized conditions (6902/6904,6085/6097,5075/5087). [NOTE: For others there is no work—see F4.]

H9. NEW THINKING: futures research (6417/6427); broader perspectives (6403/6406,5491,4402); participatory development (6556,5921,5700/5703); coproduction of services (6137/6138); global models (7247,5480/5487), new scientific worldview? (7180).

H10. AGRICULTURAL TECHNOLOGY: new machinery and crops, more efficiency, computerization and management skills (6749,5922,5937/5938,4505/4908). [NOTE: Hotly disputed—see 5929/5936,5939/5942, 4911/4915.]

H11. ENERGY: new sources and technologies, opportunities for conservation (6686/6697,5840/5856, 4767/4778). [NOTE: Another oil crisis still a threat—see F14.]

FEARS
Unfavorable Trends and Plausible Fears

F1. WAR/NUCLEAR WINTER: escalation of arms race (6613/6623,5765/5803,4684/4717); Star Wars destabilization threat (6638/6652)

F2. ECONOMIC COLLAPSE: global monetary instability and possible depression (6540/6545, 5673/5689,4515/4541); US deficit (6817/6819, 6031/6038).

F3. ENVIRONMENTAL CONCERNS: general 6474,6482,6701); climate change (6707,5880, 5460/5461); soil loss (6716); global deforestation (6708,5887/5896); disappearing species (6708, 4804/4814); toxic waste (6723,5902,4848/4860); acid rain (6728,4861/4864,3597). [NOTE: Gloomy view strongly disputed—see 5598.]

F4. UNEMPLOYMENT: In US and worldwide (6482, 6885,6893,6084,5668,5036/5048).

F5. WORLD POPULATION: long-term growth and problematic resource base (6482,6492/6493, 5633/5637,4493/4496).

F6. WATER SUPPLY: misuse, pollution (6482,6699, 6715,6719,6734/6736,5906/5913,4865/4873).

F7. PUBLIC WORKS: infrastructure disrepair, requiring billions to rebuild (6784,6022,5043).

F8. INEQUALITY: widening rich-poor gap in US, and shrinking of middle class (6768,6867,6056, 5336,5032,5014,4956).

F9. JUSTICE SYSTEM: rising litigation, crowded courts, irrational corrections (6947/6948,6972 /6980,5164/5197); illicit drugs (6182); corruption of politics (6803,6060/6063).

F10. AIDS: possibility of "acquired immune deficiency syndrome" as world health disaster (7024).

F11. HEALTH CARE COSTS: disproportionate rise in medical costs; monitarization of health care (7009/7020,6209/6224).

F12. CHILDREN: neglect, abuse, disappearing childhood (7058,6101,6247/6249,5277/5285).

F13. COMMUNICATIONS: information overload (6296/6301); surveillance threat (6991/6992); centralized control within US, and US domination (6289/6290,5401/5402,4545). [NOTE: see Appendix 1 for negative impacts.]

F14. ENERGY: threat of a new oil crisis (5813/5820, 4748/4753); fuelwood shortage in Third World (6675); electricity shortage in US? (6681).

F15. BIOTECHNOLOGY: potential to create harmful species and tamper with human gene pool (7198,6372/6375,5437/5441). [NOTE: For upbeat view, see H4.]

vii

Worldview: The Intertwining of Global and U.S. Concerns

American concerns and world concerns are increasingly intertwined. **Future Survey Annual** attempts to balance both perspectives. In some instances, the distinctions between the two perspectives are obvious; in others, they may not be. In some instances, the two levels of concern are in separate sections of the guide; in other instances, they are best viewed together within a section. Items with identification numbers ranging from #5598 through #6370 are to be found in **Future Survey Annual 1984**. Items with numbers from #4481 to #5526 are in **FS Annual 1983**.

	GLOBAL PERSPECTIVES	U.S. PERSPECTIVES
● **Population**	World population (6491/6495,5633/ 5636,4491/4496)	US population; illegal immigration (6497, 5637/5642,4933/4935)
● **Societal Directions**	World regions and nations (Section III); sustainable societies (6482/8484,5628)	General US Directions (Section VII)
● **Energy**	Global surveys (6672/ 6676,5829,4758/4761)	US surveys and issues (6678/6692,5830/5838, 4764/4765)
● **Resources**	World resources (6482/ 6485,6707/6718,5882/ 5893,5598/5602)	US resources (6730/6740,5905/5914)
● **Food**	World food problems (6141/6147,5915/5924, 4880/4893)	US food and agriculture (6748/6752,5926/5936, 4894/4915)
● **Economy**	Global economy (Section II)	US economy (Section VIII)
● **Work**	Global unemployment (6526,4496); technology and work (6893/6894)	US unemployment (6846,6885/6890, 5968,5036/5048)
● **Corporations**	Multinationals (6565 6528,6074,4481/4488)	Corporate innovation (6905/6921); corporate/ government relations (6057/6073)
● **Environment**	International cooperation (6699/6706,5867,4799/4825); climate change (6474, 4826/4828)	Domestic issues (6719/6729, 5897/5983, 4830/4879)
● **Science/Technology**	Technology transfer (6369/6370,4590/4592) for development (6565,4586/4590, 4344/4383)	Domestic issues (6719/ 6729,6353/6368,5417/5429)
● **Education**	Global learning needs (7059/7060,6261/6265)	US learning needs (7062/7071,6251/6260,5293/5301)
● **Communications**	New World Information Order (7108/7119,6289/ 6293,5356/5360); world markets (6325/6328,6288,5404)	Information Society issues (7121/7130, 6294/6301,5343/5355)
● **Health**	World health strategy (6495,6999-7001)	US issues (7007/7024)
● **National Security**	Section IV	Section IV

Highlights of Future Survey Annual 1985

As a form of introductory overview, or partial executive summary, the following items
are recommended by the editor for their breadth, importance, and/or originality.

***6465 World Futures: A Critical Analysis of Alternatives** (Hughes, Johns Hopkins). Examines the bases of difference in alternative world views, competing theories, and contradictory data, concluding that each of the major models or paradigms has weaknesses as well as strengths, and that we may evolve to a greater synthesis of world views.

***6467** *Charting the Way the World Works* (Meadows, *Technology Review*). Describes the methods and philosophies of global modelers, and some common findings such as the growing gap between rich and poor, the finiteness of physical capital, and the failure to meet human needs due to mismanagement rather than scarcity.

***6474 The Coevolution of Climate and Life** (Schneider /Londer, Sierra Club Books). The social and technological juggernaut is resulting in a radical shift of the balance between climate and life; creating a sustainable future will require policies that recognize and deal with climatic risks and opportunities.

***6475 The Parable of the Tribes: The Problem of Power in Social Evolution** (Schmookler, U of California). The major trends in the transformation of human society have increased competitive power; threatened tribes must become like their foe or be destroyed. There is no turning back, but there may be a way forward if we recognize this parable and act responsibly.

***6481 Human Betterment** (Boulding, Sage Publications). The scholarly study of human betterment is possible and desirable, and the payoffs are likely to be enormous. Chapters explore the meaning of human betterment, the nature of significant change, decision-making skills, development of peace and riches, and the doing of good.

***6482 GAIA: An Atlas of Planet Management** (Myers, ed., Anchor/Doubleday). A guide to a planet in transition, with more than 100 contributors providing overviews of tropical forests, soil, oceans, mineral reserves, the fuelwood crisis, the destruction of genetic diversity, health and unemployment, the world market, technology transfer, and costs of militarism.

***6483 The Global Possible: Resources, Development, and the New Century** (World Resources Institute). A statement and an agenda for action, derived from a May 1984 meeting near Washington; the central theme is that it is possible to build a world that is more secure, more prosperous, and more sustainable—if we attain new levels of cooperation.

***6495 The State of the World's Children 1985** (Grant, Oxford U Press). Drastically improved child health and survival are now possible by using four simple and inexpensive methods: oral rehydration therapy, growth monitoring, breast feeding, and \$5 worth of immunization. These techniques could save about 7 million children per year—and, in turn, help reduce birth rates!

***6556 People-Centered Development** (Korten/Klauss, eds., Kumarian Press). Selected readings on participatory development projects in the Third World: mechanisms to empower people, which have emerged as theoretically desirable and practically feasible alternatives to centrally planned development programs.

***6566 Canadian Cultural Futures: Options for Living Together** (Spraakman/Becher/Wilde, eds., Canadian Association for Futures Studies). Papers from a 1982 CAFS conference on the values and beliefs that will determine how Canadians will live together; the conclusion surveys constant and transforming factors in both world and Canadian culture.

***6569** *Political Risk Analysis for Canada and Mexico* (Drobnick, *Technological Forecasting and Social Change*). A two-round Delphi inquiry on socio-economic change and business contingencies. Critical trends for Canada include growing resentment of US culture and rising environmental concern; major trends for Mexico include rising nationalism, and a sharp rise in unemployment and illegal migration to US.

***6571 The Caribbean Basin to the Year 2000: Demographic, Economic, and Resource-Use Trends in Seventeen Countries** (Graham/ Edwards, Westview). Assuming no great change in trade, aid, or population policies, total population in the Caribbean basin will increase by almost 50%, from 52 million in 1982 to 77 million in 2000; urban population will likely grow at an even faster pace.

***6600 Strategic Requirements for the Army to the Year 2000** (Kupperman/Taylor, eds., Lexington Books). Essays on the world political-military environment of the 1990s, trends that are likely to have an impact on the US Army, and strategic requirements for each of five regions in the world.

***6605 Thinking About the Unthinkable in the 1980s** (Kahn, Simon and Schuster). An update of the late Herman Kahn's 1962 book, seeking to eliminate certain irrelevant or foolish assertions from the national security debate; includes five categories of "not implausible" outbreak scenarios, and a proposal for a long-range anti-nuclear policy.

ix

*6613 ***Militarization in the United States and the Soviet Union: The Deepening Trends*** (Thee, *Alternatives*). Militarization centers on the acquisition of arms, the use of force, and the expansion of military influence; interrelated factors leading to militarization in both superpowers are described, as well as economic, social, and cultural impacts.

*6625 **Beam Weapons: The Next Arms Race** (Hecht, Plenum Press). A clearly-written, authoritative, and fair-minded overview of the emerging technology behind Star Wars, concluding that laser weapons show signs of promise, but that there are very real technological limitations and uncertainties.

*6652 ***Forging Missiles Into Spaceships*** (Deudney, *World Policy Journal*). The Star Wars plan of beating swords into shields is fundamentally illusory, and likely to set off a major arms race; instead, a peace strategy for US-USSR space cooperation is proposed, which would transform the superpower relationship and create a common security system.

*6672 **Energy in the Global Arena: Actors, Values, Policies, and Futures** (Hughes *et al.*, Duke U Press). An overview of the global energy system and the transition away from oil, categories of actors (nation-states, interest groups, NGOs, etc.), energy values motivating actor behavior, policy-making approaches for short- and long-term payoffs, and forecasting alternative energy paths.

*6677 ***A Soft Energy Path for Canada*** (Friends of the Earth Canada, *Alternatives*). Summary of a 1983 FOE study of the potential for energy conservation and renewable energy, concluding that Canada in 2025 could use 12% to 34% less energy than it did in 1978 despite a 50% increase in population and a 140% to 200% rise in GDP. Also discusses strategic issues, implementation, priorities, and research needs.

*6699 **State of the World 1985: A Worldwatch Institute Report on Progress Toward a Sustainable Society** (Brown *et al.*, Norton). The second in a series of annual reports, introducing the notion of population-induced climate change, whereby the collective actions of nearly 5 billion people now appear capable of causing continental and even global changes in natural systems.

*6701 **Environment and the Global Arena: Actors, Values, Policies, and Futures** (Dahlberg *et al.*, Duke U Press). An overview of environment as a global issue, with chapters on basic concepts for understanding the environment, governmental and non-governmental actors at global and national levels, prominent environmental values, and designing a global alternative future.

*6705 **Sustaining Tomorrow: A Strategy for World Conservation and Development** (Thibodeau/ Field, eds., U Press of New England). Essays on sustainable development and the World Conservation Strategy, promoted since 1980 by the International Union for Conservation of Nature and Natural Resources, the UN Environment Program and the World Wildlife Fund.

*6706 **Environmentalists: Vanguard for a New Society** (Milbrath, State U of New York Press). The results of a three-nation comparative study of environmental beliefs and values, conducted in 1980 and 1982 by the Science Center in Berlin, the University of Bath in England, and the Environmental Studies Center at SUNY-Buffalo. Findings show a substantial movement away from the dominant social paradigm.

*6719 **State of the Environment: An Assessment at Mid-Decade** (Conservation Foundation). An overview of progress and problems in the US, with chapters on underlying trends, environmental contaminants, the state of natural resources, identifying issues, risk assessment, cross-media pollutants, water resources, and intergovernmental relations and environmental policy.

*6723 **Superfund Strategy** (Office of Technology Assessment). Estimates that 10,000 or more toxic waste sites may require cleanup, in contrast to the EPA estimate of 2,000 sites. A sensibly paced effort to clean up these sites could take up to 50 years and cost several hundred billion dollars. Underestimating national cleanup needs could lead to future environmental crisis.

*6757 ***Project Outlook: Social Issues*** (Enzer, *New Management*). A 1984 poll of planners and futurists by the USC Center for Futures Research on the probability of 28 social issues occurring over the next 20 years, e.g. a single six-year term for the US President, National Health Insurance, prayer in the public schools, strict enforcement of US immigration law. (Also see #7231 on sci/tech developments.)

*6761 **The Trouble With America** (Crozier, U of California Press). A long-time French observer writes that America in the 1980s wants to forget history and dream of happy days, although the era of the frontier is over; the system has drifted off into trivia and appearances, with underinformed and misinformed citizens. From a broader perspective, America is frozen in place.

*6774 **Mandate for Leadership II: Continuing the Conservative Revolution** (Butler/Sanera/Weinrod, eds., Heritage Foundation). An update of the 1980 **Mandate**, designed as a road map to steer the nation into a sound future guided by conservative principles. This update utilizes more than 150 experts and offers some 1,300 proposals for domestic and foreign policy agencies, as well as ways to implement them.

*6775 **Future 21: Directions for America in the 21st Century** (Weyrich/Marshner, eds., Devin-Adair). Essays by conservative leaders on such issues as an international gold standard, a new America First nationalism, the conservative opportunity society, reconsidering the US relationship with the UN, confronting the communists, policies to support the traditional nuclear family, and fortifying conservative values by promoting high-tech.

*6779 **Window of Opportunity: A Blueprint for the Future** (Gingrich, TOR Books). A conservative Congressman argues that America can create a bright future if we reform the government and the welfare state. Many ideas are offered, such as more space exploration, promoting lifelong learning, streamlining the legal system, ending pork barrel politics in the Pentagon, and merit pay in public bureaucracies.

*6783 **Beyond Reagan: Alternatives for the '80s** (Gartner/Greer/Riessman, eds., Harper & Row). Essays on economics for people, democratizing investment, attacking poverty, revisioning public responsibility, restructuring national defense policy, immigration policy, a new voter registration strategy, bottom-sideways democratic planning, and expanding political participation.

*6784 **Rebuilding America** (Vaughan/Pollard, Council of State Planning Agencies). The decay of the US infrastructure—roads, bridges, water systems, etc.—is a major concern, especially because the rate of investment in public capital has declined by nearly 50% in the past decade. This study seeks to help state and local officials to think strategically about the problem.

*6791 **Strong Democracy: Participatory Politics for a New Age** (Barber, U of California Press). Argues that we suffer from too little democracy, and that strong democracy is the only viable form that modern democratic politics can take. Strong democracy seeks to revitalize citizenship by encouraging participation of all the people in some public matters at least some of the time.

*6833 ***Unexplored America: Economic Rebirth in a Postindustrial World*** (Branfman, *World Policy Journal*). We are in the early stages of transformation to a global civilization, and must now shift from today's high-consumption/high-debt economy to one that places its highest priority on savings and investment. National modernization must replace short-term growth as the key principle of American politics.

*6845 **America's Economic Future: Environmentalists Broaden the Industrial Policy Debate** (Hamrin, Natural Resources Defense Council). Seeks to widen the industrial policy debate by proposing five principal goals: a sustainable global economy, a healthy US economy that seeks quality of life for all, sustaining the US resource base, total employment, and widespread participation in economic and political decisions.

*6846 **Revitalizing Western Economies** (Ackoff *et al.*, Jossey-Bass). The postindustrial transformation involves a basic change in social priorities, shifting attention to improving quality of life through more and better services. Unemployment must be solved by debureaucratizing and demonopolizing both public and private services.

*6873 **Time to Care: A Report Prepared for the Swedish Secretariat for Futures Studies** (Lagergren *et al.*, Pergamon Press). Final report of the Care in Society project, concluding that continuing the old ways of the welfare state will be disastrous. Welfare problems must be solved nearer the source, with citizens assuming more responsibility in caring for each other and overseeing professional care.

*6883 **The Self-Help Revolution** (Gartner/Riessman, eds., Human Sciences Press). Essays on various self-help groups as alternatives to costly and ineffective service bureaucratization, collaborative models for professionals and self-help groups, self-help groups as a way to revitalize professions, and questions of evaluation and assessment.

*6893 **The Future of Work: A Guide to a Changing Society** (Handy, Basil Blackwell). For better or worse, new patterns of work are on their way: full-employment society becomes the part-employment society, muscle jobs yield to finger and brain jobs, services are growing, bureaucracies are going out and networks and partnerships are coming in, and many people will have shorter working lives.

*6908 **Innovation and Entrepreneurship: Practice and Principles** (Drucker, Harper & Row). In the past 10-15 years, the most significant event is the emergence of a truly entrepreneurial economy in the US; it may be a major turning point in history. Chapters describe how innovation and entrepreneurship can be organized as systematic work.

*6911 **Leaders: The Strategies for Taking Charge** (Bennis/Nanus, Harper & Row). Leadership is the key to successful organizations, and the need for leaders has never been so great. The authors interviewed 90 public and private leaders, finding that all embodied four major competencies: the ability to create an agenda, to communicate the vision, to implement the vision, and to maintain positive self-regard.

*6939 **The Future of Urban Form: The Impact of New Technology** (Brotchie *et al.*, eds., Croom Helm/Nichols). Essays on changes in industrial and living patterns, the dynamics of urban change, impacts of teleshopping, the growing roles of the informal sector and self-help, forces for decentralization, and communication/transport interactions.

*6944 **The Future of State and Local Government as Seen in the Futures Literature** (Hitchcock/Coates, Academy for State and Local Government). Summarizes a wide variety of trends and issues such as steadily rising costs, growing citizen demand for services, an aging and more diverse population, infrastructure and environmental problems, Federal vs. state/local responsibilities, and regulation vs. deregulation.

*6950 **No Place to Hide: Crisis and Future of American Habitats** (Marti, Greenwood Press). On the basic factors likely to structure the future evolution of buildings and communities, with many future possibilities suggested. Increased integration of technology into edifices has caused a relative dehumanization; in the future, there may be no place left to retreat to.

*6962 **The Future of the Automobile: The Report of MIT's International Automobile Program** (Altshuler *et al.*, MIT Press). An intensive four-year study of the next 20 years, involving experts in the seven auto-producing nations. World demand for new autos is expected to grow from 41 million in 1979 to 51 million in 1990 and 67 million in 2000, with total vehicle ownership rising from 396 million to 679 million (1979-2000).

***6975 Sense and Nonsense About Crime: A Policy Guide** (Walker, Brooks/Cole). Crime policy is intellectually bankrupt, with both liberals and conservatives guilty of peddling nonsense such as preventive detention, selective incapacitation, mandatory sentancing, use of the death penalty, gun control, etc. A genuine anticrime program can only begin by creating real economic opportunity.

***6976 American Violence and Public Policy: An Update of the National Commission on the Causes and Prevention of Violence** (Curtis, ed., Yale U Press). Reiterates that the criminal justice system merely reacts to crime and cannot do much to prevent it. Massive new investments will not reduce our historically high levels of crime. Rather, a focus is needed on neighborhood, family, and employment.

***6999 Improving World Health: A Least Cost Strategy** (Chandler, Worldwatch Institute). The WHO goal of "health for all by the year 2000" can only succeed by using limited resources in the most efficient way possible: maternal and child care for the poor, clean drinking water and sanitation facilities, diet education, control of tobacco products, primary health care, and basic research for low-cost cures.

***7001 Beyond Health Care: Proceedings of a Conference on Healthy Public Policy** (*Canadian Journal of Public Health*). Papers on the principles of a healthy public policy, social obstacles to health, health megatrends, the WHO goal of "health for all by the year 2000," healthy workplaces and communities, health and empowerment, and recommendations for action.

***7006 Alternative Medicines: Popular and Policy Perspectives** (Salmon, ed., Tavistock Publications). Scholarly chapters on scientific medicine since the late 19th century, homeopathy, chiropractic, traditional Chinese medicine, indigenous systems of healing, psychic healing, holistic health centers in the US, and the liklihood of a broader range of services in the new medical industrial complex.

***7039 Pharmacy in the 21st Century: Planning for an Uncertain Future** (Bezold, ed., American Assn. of Colleges of Pharmacy). Essays on alternative futures for society and health care, prospects for extending life expectancy, new access to information on drug use, new drugs and drug delivery systems, new health services in a variety of settings, new sensitivity to the full costs and benefits of new technology, etc.

***7047 Marriage and the Family in the Year 2020** (Kirkendall/Gravett, eds., Prometheus Books). Essays on social forces and the changing family, new marriage styles and family forms, mate selection in 2020, transformations in human reproduction, moral concepts in 2020, work/education/family connections, and the social consequences of life extension.

***7108 The Uneasy Eighties: The Transition to an Information Society** (Cordell, Science Council of Canada). On the shape of the new information infrastructure, new industries and new ways of doing things, solutions for the privacy issue, applications and implications of artificial intelligence, and the major reorientation of workers and institutions that will be required.

***7114 Information and the Crisis Economy** (Schiller, Ablex Publishing Co). An enormous technico-social transformation is underway, promoted by two central and interactive forces: the transnational corporation and the new information technologies. The scale of the corporation is unthinkable without the new technologies, which are mainly applied to large-scale firms.

***7131 The Information Technology Revolution** (Forester, ed., MIT Press). A massive anthology of 48 essays by US and UK authors, on such topics as artificial intelligence, the telecommunications explosion, videotex, computers in the home and school, the office of the future, the future quantity and quality of work, smart weapons, and questioning the information society.

***7135 The Intimate Machine: Close Encounters with Computers and Robots** (Frude, NAL Books). Microtechnology opens up vast new horizons and we may soon have systems that counterfeit people to some degree. The new companion machines will supplement the current image of the computer as calculator with those of counselor, colleague, and friend. But by humanizing machines, we may dehumanize people.

***7187 Citizen Participation in Science Policy** (Peterson, ed., U of Massachusetts Press). Americans feel that citizens should participate in decisions that affect them, but effective participation in many issues is difficult due to technical content. These essays explore such themes as citizen involvement in social risk assessment, public interest science, and problems of nuclear technology.

***7198 Biotechnology: A New Industrial Revolution** (Prentis, George Braziller). Describes potential applications of the new biotechnology in medicine, agriculture, energy production, and industry. The US and Japan are in the best position to benefit, with the US leading in genetic engineering and Japan ahead in technologies needed for large-scale fermentations.

***7199 Broken Code: The Exploitation of DNA** (Lappé, Sierra Club Books). Biologists have broken the code of life, and can now add or subtract genetic information to the flow of life on earth. But who will control the fruits of this new knowledge, and to what ends? Lappé seeks to defuse unwarranted fears, while pointing to unrecognized perils and the needs for some oversight.

*7211 **Future Man** (Stableford, Crown Publishers). In this new phase of human evolution, man will be able to control his own race through genetic engineering. Chapters describe new ways to combat disease, spare parts for people, controlling the life span, engineering more perfect people, control of the mind, and extensions of man such as computers and robots. Includes many striking photos, drawings, and charts.

*7215 **Out of the Cradle: Exploring the Frontiers Beyond Earth.** (Hartmann/Miller/Lee, Workman Publishing Co). Chapters on the need for space exploration, the evolution of shuttles to space cities, robot astronauts, the exploration of Mars, the outer solar system, and the search for extraterrestrial life. Includes 120 photos and paintings.

*7231 ***Project Outlook: Scientific and Technical Events*** (Enzer, *New Management*). Forecasts of a panel polled by the USC Center for Futures Research, on the possibility of developments over the next 20 years, such as usable nuclear fusion, a super battery, hydrogen energy, salt-tolerant grains, medical cures for alcoholism and obesity, 100-year average life expectancy, artificial intelligence, etc. (Also see #6757.)

*7253 **Mobilizing the Ultimate Resource** (Linstone, ed., *Technological Forecasting and Social Change* Special Issue). Papers on how to better apply the resource of the human intellect to the human crisis, covering such topics as greater citizen involvement in steering technology, redesigning the modern university, our trained incapacity, and the need for multiple perspectives.

*7281 **Ideas About the Future: A History of Futurism, 1794-1982** (Beckwith). Critical essays on the strengths and weaknesses of 25 writers: Condorcet, Saint-Simon, de Tocqueville, Marx, Bellamy, Wells, Keynes, Myrdal, Toynbee, Chase, Bell, Heilbroner, Kahn, Toffler, Naisbitt, O'Neill, etc.

Some Highlights of **Future Survey Annual 1986**
A Forecast of Outstanding Items in Next Year's Compilation

* **A Common Sense Guide to World Peace**, by Benjamin B. Ferencz (Oceana Publications, Dec 1985/112p/$15.00pb). There has been a slow movement toward a more rational world order; further progress requires greater clarification and acceptance of international law, a willingness to rely on international courts, and some sort of international peace force to enforce the laws. Ferencz describes what can and should be done to meet this goal.

* **The Electronic Oracle: Computer Models and Social Decisions**, by Donella H. Meadows and J.M. Robinson (John Wiley & Sons, May 1985/445p/$39.95). Computer models in practice have clarified and improved social decisions only in limited areas. Strengths and weaknesses of nine major computer models are examined, concluding with suggestions for improving the construction and use of such models in general.

* **An Environmental Agenda for the Future**, by John H. Adams *et al.* (Island Press, Oct 1985/155p/$5.95pb). A two-year project sponsored by the chief executives of ten major environmental and conservation organizations. Proposals cover nuclear issues, population growth, energy strategies, water resources, toxic waste, acid rain, wildlife, private lands and agriculture, protected land systems, public lands, the urban environment, and international responsibilities.

* **Future Work: Jobs, Self-Employment and Leisure After the Industrial Age**, by James Robertson (Universe Books, Dec 1985/220p/$17.50). Argues that the days of full employment are behind us, and advocates a "sane, humane, ecological society" in which work is redefined to include many forms of useful activity in addition to paid employment. The expansion of "ownwork" (paid or unpaid jobs that people control for themselves) is deemed necessary for healthy economies.

* **Megatraumas: America at the Year 2000** by Richard D. Lamm (Houghton Mifflin, Oct 1985/290p/$16.95). Colorado's governor warns that long-term problems are being ignored and that the US is heading into an era of multiple traumas. Using the device of imaginary speeches and memos prepared in the year 2000, Lamm explores such topics as lack of investment, immigration, violence, unemployment, toxic waste, entitlements, and applying systems thinking to our problems.

* **Policymaking Under Adversity**, by Yehezkel Dror (Transaction Books, Jan 1986/437p/$39.95). The second of three seminal volumes on policymaking theory, reality, and improvement. Chapters on policymaking predicaments and responses, principles for handling adversity, the need for visions and policymaking infrastructure, integrative philosophy, and redesign approaches to improve the central mind of governments.

* **Silico Sapiens: The Fundamentals and Future of Robots**, by Joseph Deken (Bantam New Age Books, Jan 1986/259p/$4.50pb). Robotics is the final step in computer evolution—the stage of autonomy where a computer life form can take independent action. The computer of the future is a robot, and three basic forms are described: microbots, midrobots, and macrobots. Robotics has the capability to deflect the course of evolution, as a new species of *Silico sapiens* arises.

* **State of the World 1986: A Worldwatch Institute Report on Progress Toward a Sustainable Society**, by Lester R. Brown *et al.* (W. W. Norton, Feb 1986/263p/$18.95;$9.95pb). This third annual assessment further analyzes the extensive deterioration of natural support systems and declining economic conditions in much of the Third World. But a new argument is added: that this

decline poses threats to national and international security that now rival traditional military threats.

* **The Third Millennium. A History of the World: AD 2000-3000**, by Brian Stableford and David Langford (Knopf, Sept 1985/224p/$20.00). Two British science fiction writers offer a lushly illustrated history of the future looking back from AD 3000, skillfully combining plausible visions of technology, politics, and personalities: e.g. politics as greens vs. greys, minimal welfare support worldwide, maglev subways, lifespans of 150 years, radically modified humans, and much, much more.

* **Work, Unemployment and the New Technology**, by Colin Gill (Polity Press/Basil Blackwell, Dec 1985/204p/$24.95;$9.95pb). A major discontinuity in economic development is underway, largely due to the computer. Chapters on the automated office, automation in manufacturing, the threat of unemployment, trade union responses in Europe and the US, and the resulting challenges that should be on the political agenda of all Western democracies.

* **World Enough and Time: Successful Strategies for Resource Management**, by Robert Repetto (Yale U Press/World Resources Institute, March 1986/147p/$16.00;$5.95pb). An optimistic summary of the 1984 Global Possible Conference, designed to complement the technical background papers in **The Global Possible**, edited by Repetto (Yale U Press, Dec 1985/538p/$45.00;$13.95pb). Sustainable development is possible if policymakers attend to least-cost basic services, use common resources wisely, price resources properly, design for efficiency, and build management capability.

* **World Resources 1986: An Assessment of the Resource Base that Supports the Global Economy**, by World Resources Institute and International Institute for Environment and Development (Basic Books, May 1986/353p/$32.95;$16.95pb). First volume in an annual series that supplies basic information and current data on world conditions and trends. Chapters on population, human settlements, food and agriculture, forests and rangelands, wildlife, energy, freshwater, oceans, the atmosphere, and policies for sound management.

I. WORLD FUTURES

A. <u>Evolutionary Trends</u>

*6465

World Futures: A Critical Analysis of Alternatives. Barry B. Hughes (Graduate School of International Studies, U of Denver). Baltimore MD: Johns Hopkins U Press, Jan 1985/243p/$25.00;$10.95pb.

During the 1970s, there was an explosion of interest in global issues and global futures, due to decreased East-West conflict allowing other issues to be given greater attention, the "other" issues becoming more important, an increasingly global data base related to these issues, the development of skills to analyze the data base, and psychological attraction to the oncoming year 2000. The clash of prophets over the last ten years has been dramatic, with images of even the fairly near future varying sharply. It is unlikely that any of the groups or individuals producing different images of the future monopolize understanding of how the world works—yet they often write as if they do, frequently with messianic fervor. This book seeks to aid those who are frustrated at the confusing array of possible futures, attempting to show how the bases of difference arise from alternative world views (or models or paradigms), competing theories and methodologies, and contradictory evidence or data. Key futures studies of the 1970s and early 1980s are reviewed (including various world models, **Global 2000**, Toffler's **Third Wave**, and Naisbitt's **Megatrends**), concluding that there is little or no evidence of any convergence toward a middle ground. Various world views are assessed (classical liberal, internationalist, radical, neotraditionalist, and modernist). Another chapter on values and political structures arranges views of the future in four categories: centralized-conflictive futures (Orwell's **1984**), centralized-cooperative futures, decentralized-cooperative futures, and decentralized-conflictive futures. Additional chapters analyze different forecasts in several issue areas: population, economics, energy, food and agriculture, technology, and the environment. Concludes that none of the major world views presented here will necessarily become dominant; each has weaknesses as well as strengths, and the global development system is so complex that analysts are in the position of the blind men and the elephant. An alternative to dominance by one world view is an evolution to a greater synthesis of world views [NOTE: also see Wagar, #6466, who postulates a theory of sequential dominance]. We do stand in a unique point in time, in the sense of recognizing the transitions before us and having more effective choices than ever before. It is increasingly up to all of us to examine our value systems and our world views, and decide what kind of global future we want. [NOTE: A most welcome social science approach to sorting out a variety of views. A similar British work by Freeman and Jahoda, **World Futures: The Great Debate** (Universe, 1978; **FS Annual 1979**, #0012) is narrower in scope.]

(world views analyzed)

6466

The Next Three Futures, W. Warren Wagar (Prof of History, SUNY-Binghamton), *World Future Society Bulletin*, 18:6, Nov-Dec 1984, 12-19.

The author of **The City of Man** (Houghton Mifflin, 1963) and many other books and articles on the history of futures thinking reviews the development of his own thinking since the 1960s. He concludes that establishment futurists expect the glorious consummation of capitalism, radical futurists expect a victory for the workers, and eco-decentralist futurists expect some form of ecotopia—and they may all be right, if they are willing to wait their turn. The capitalist world economy is probably good for one or even two more Kondratieff long waves of 40 to 50 years each (radicals who foresee its imminent collapse are victims of wishful thinking). The seed within the capitalism fruit is socialism, and the informal corporate world order will be followed by a socialist world republic. After the building of socialism over many generations, a powerful new counter-culture will arrive, shaping a world order "as if people really mattered," restoring full self-government to communities, and promoting a simpler and more self-reliant economy. This third future of mankind will mark the end of the collectivist era, and the beginning of what Engels once termed "the kingdom of freedom." Having unified and saved the world, socialism will some day become redundant, and the scaffolding it has erected can be allowed to crumble.   **(capitalism, socialism, eco-decentralism)**

*6467

Charting the Way the World Works, Donella H. Meadows (Dartmouth College), *Technology Review*, 88:2, Feb-Mar 1985, 54-62.

Co-author of **The Limits to Growth** (Universe, 1972) and **Groping in the Dark: The First Decade of Global Modelling** (Wiley, 1982; **FS Annual 1983**, #5480) describes the methods and philosophies of global modelers. Despite great diversity, the models suggest some common conclusions: 1) existing resources and known technologies can support all the needs of the world's people for some time to come—needs are unmet because of mismanagement, not scarcity; 2) population and physical capital cannot grow forever on a finite planet—scarcity does not now exist, but can be generated if rapid growth continues; 3) no reliable or complete information is available about the degree to which the earth's environment can absorb the wastes created to meet human needs (soil erosion, groundwater pollution, radioactive waste); 4) if continued, present policies will lead to a growing gap between rich and poor—further operation of the world economic system will not eliminate poverty; 5) technology can help, but is not the answer (e.g., providing infinite, cheap energy would exacerbate inequality, population growth, and environmental problems); 6) interdependence among people and nations is much greater than commonly imagined; 7) policy changes made soon are likely to have more impact with less effort than the same changes made later; 8) many complex international programs and agreements are based on inconsistent assumptions. Concludes that global models will probably never provide the key to full understanding of our complex world, but they can and have served as a creative irritant, forcing us to look at complexity and to keep confronting it.   **(global models: common findings)**

6468

The New State of the World Atlas. Michael Kidron and Ronald Segal. A Pluto Press Project. NY: Simon & Schuster, Sept 1984/$19.95;$10.95pb.

Update of the 1981 edition, with 57 maps of the world arranged in 12 sections. 1) **The Aggressive State**: countries by proportional population, territorial claims on Antarctica, national claims on the oceans; 2) **Arms and the State**: foreign military installations worldwide, military spending as a proportion of GNP, actual and potential members of the nuclear club, wars in the past ten years; 3) **Natural Resources**: producers of major minerals, major energy producers and consumers, importers and exporters of food; 4) **Economy**: use of nuclear power, exports and share of world trade, states largely dependent on a single product for export income, per capita GNP; 5) **Government**: form of government, government share of GDP, ratio of military expenditures to public health expenditures ("harmworkers and healthworkers"), state oppression and torture, world refugee flows; 6) **Holds on the Mind**: language of rule and countries with a significant linguistic conflict, religion of rule and sites of recent religious conflict; 7) **Business**: bank assets, location of biggest industrial companies; 8) **Labor**: importers and exporters of labor, ratio of agricultural workers to industrial workers, ratio of female wage-earners to male wage earners, degree of trade union independence, unemployment rates; 9) **Society**: incomes of a country's top 5% compared with the bottom 20%, calories available per capita, hospital beds and life expectancy, illiteracy, radios and telephones, crimes; 10) **Environment**: air and land pollution, urban population as proportion of total, bioclimatic zones and areas of high and moderate risk, protected areas; 11) **Intimations of Mortality**: acceleration or deceleration in industrial growth rate, average inflation rate in 1970s, debtor nations, gold holdings as proportion of national reserves; 12) **The Name of Action**: states with green movements, legal status of abortion, gays, minorities, degree of popular pressure on state regimes. In the Introduction, the authors warn of a decline in the standards of data provided by the UN and other international organizations. [NOTE: Fascinating and original maps showing various inequities in the world, but data not provided.]

(57 maps of world conditions)

6469

This World of Man. Pekka Kuusi (Helsinki). Oxford UK and Elmsford NY: Pergamon Press, Jan 1985/283p/$28.00. [First published in Finland in 1982.]

Attempts to combine biological and humanistic knowledge in developing a general picture of the changes the human species must make in order to live within the processes of nature. Chapters are devoted to the evolution of man, man as a part of nature, the need for a new world concept viewing man as one of nature's animals, agrarian culture, the transition to scientific-technological culture, the transition from self-regulated to directed evolution as a prerequisite for survival, regulating the size of the human population, food and energy in a sustainable world system, and protecting man against himself. The problem of human existence will become more pronounced as more people use more natural resources in an increasingly intricate social system. By 2050, four essential changes must occur in the behavior of the human species: terminating the population increase, shifting to a sustainable energy system, shifting to equalizing joint regulation of natural resources, and withdrawing from the practice of war. Cooperation, leading to an interdependence between all members of the species, must be our guiding symbol and goal. If the capitalistic and socialistic countries cease to fear each other and begin purposeful cooperation, the whole development of mankind could start on a new solid foundation. Concludes with the hope that the young people will transform the peace movement into an all-embracing movement for survival.

(directed evolution)

6470

Staying Alive: The Psychology of Human Survival. Roger Walsh (Prof of Psychiatry, U of California-Irvine). Boulder CO: Shambhala/New Science Library, Sept 1984/124p/$5.95pb.

We have reached a critical time in our history that may decide the fate of both our species and our planet. For the first time in our evolution, all the major threats to our survival are human-caused. Problems such as nuclear weapons, pollution, and ecological imbalance stem directly from our behavior. The state of the world is thus a creation and expression of our own minds, and it is to our minds that we must look for solutions. After a brief review of global threats to human survival, Walsh provides an overview of psychological factors that contribute to our difficulties: beliefs and assumptions, reinforcement and social learning, the three poisons (addiction, aversion, and delusion), perceptual tendencies of dualism and fragmentation, defense mechanisms, fear, immaturity, and inauthenticity. Concludes that the growing up that is demanded of us is a form of evolution. [NOTE: Thoughtful, but at a superficial level that fails to suggest the complexity of our problems.]

(psychology and world problems)

6471

Before It Is Too Late. Aurelio Peccei (deceased, 1984; President, Club of Rome) and Daisaku Ikeda (past President, Soka Gakkai International). Tokyo: Kodansha International (dist. in US by Harper & Row), Dec 1984/154p/$14.95.

Essays by Peccei and by Ikeda, and dialogues between the two, on man and nature, the cultural crisis, global deforestation, religion and world view, spiritual values, democracy, peace, outmoded national states, grass roots movements, obligations and rights, and education and learning. The authors stress that adequate human response to the threats and challenges that have arisen at this perhaps decisive turn in history must not be delayed much longer. The overall world situation is not getting better, and the danger that current crises may become much graver is very real. It is within our power to turn the tide, and we must do whatever we can to adopt a new course before it is too late. **(world problems)**

6472

Environment and Population: Problems of Adaptation. An Experimental Book Integrating Statements by 162 Contributors. Edited by John B. Calhoun (National Institute of Mental Health). NY: Praeger Special Studies, 1983/486p/$60.00.

The undergirding premise is that, if one understands how a single human brain interrelates ideas, it should be possible to take ideas from many individuals and sequence them in the manner of a single brain. Calhoun attempted to do so by asking 162 authors to write about an important researchable problem within a broad domain suggested by the words adaptation, population, and environment. About a dozen contributors (examples in parentheses) are arranged in each of 13 chapters on roles and functions in life processes, adaptation and policy (Lynton Caldwell on environmental policy), acquired adaptations, negentropy enhancement as the core of evolution, ecosystem complexity (Kenneth E.F. Watt on the ability of the human mind to cope with complexity; Jerzy A. Wojciechowski on knowledge as a source of problems), social systems evolution (Richard L. Meier on ultra-modern industrialization), group organization and stress (Yona Friedman on questions arising from communication difficulties), the built environment, models of inquiry (Robert Plutchik on universal problems of adaptation), global policy for survival (Ervin Laszlo on developing a credible concept of global society; Amitai Etzioni on creative adaptation to a world of rising shortages), health and human needs, crowding and stimulus overload, and development. Calhoun manipulates these contributions in various ways, including 1625 "generic concept nodes" and an elaborate 66-page "concept associational index." [NOTE: The experiment is rather pretentious, for the resulting product can simply be seen as a large guidebook and/or anthology, albeit one that is interesting and potentially useful, in that many of the contributors have at least one foot on the ground of human reality.] (**environment/adaptation guidebook**)

6473

The World as a Total System. Kenneth E. Boulding (U of Colorado). Beverly Hills CA: Sage Publications, April 1985/183p/$25.00.

A view of the earth as a general system in the evolutionary pattern and as a complex structure of many different systems. Chapters discuss the types of systems that we can perceive in our minds (essentially an introduction to general systems theory), and the world as a physical system, a biological system, a social system, an economic system, a political system, a communication system, and an evaluative system. The future of the biosphere is very uncertain because humans represent a real "system break" in the evolutionary process, due to their enormous capacity for learning and for producing artifacts. There are probably now more species of human artifacts all over the planet than there are biological species. Indeed, the total mass of human artifacts (buildings, automobiles, roads, furniture, etc.) may be substantially larger than the total mass of all living organisms. Concludes that the greatest cause for pessimism at the moment is the apparent stability of the set of valuations that leads into violence, national defense, and the eventual destruction of the human race in historic time by nuclear war. [NOTE: Offers a very broad framework for understanding the human situation; the companion volume (# 6481) offers an equally broad framework for taking action to improve this situation.]
(**world as system**)

*6474

The Coevolution of Climate and Life. Stephen H. Schneider (National Center for Atmospheric Research, Boulder CO) and Randi Londer (NYC). San Francisco CA: Sierra Club Books, May 1984/563p/$25.00.

Climate and life have coevolved, exerting fundamental controlling influences on each other. Today, the balance of mutual influence between climate and life is shifting radically, as mankind's social and technological juggernaut results in climate modification. Considerable evidence suggests that we are modifying climate at a rate faster than we can understand, with consequences that we cannot predict. The book explains the vast sweep of climate history; the mechanisms of climate change; relationships between climate, food production, water supplies, energy use; and the political and ethical implications of climatological discoveries. Concludes that creating a sustainable future will depend on society permitting policies that recognize and deal with climatic risks and opportunities. Some principles for living with climatic change include:

1) Beware of generalizing from short-term records, because climatic fluctuations can occur over many time scales; 2) Build diversity in food, water, and energy sources to provide stability; 3) Breed and stockpile many varieties of genetic resources as a hedge against climatic trends; 4) Maintain sufficient reserves and distribution systems to see us through some degree of climate-induced risk; 5) Charge true costs and internalize externalities; 6) Match agricultural practices to crop-climate timetables; 7) Improve end use efficiency by stressing conservation; 8) Maintain good international rapport among nations in order to solve global commons problems; 9) Reduce the inventory of nuclear arms to lessen the risk of a "nuclear winter" effect on climate. [NOTE: Authoritative and readable.]
(**living with climate change**)

*6475

The Parable of the Tribes: The Problem of Power in Social Evolution. Andrew Bard Schmookler (Bethesda MD). Berkeley CA: U of California Press, May 1984/400p/$19.95.

History's acceleration has made manifest what has been true from the beginning of civilization: the structure of life has been constantly subject to profound changes as new cultural ways are developed to replace the old. But what determines the direction in which civilization evolves? To many people, change seems explicable by a commonsense theory of social evolution, assuming that history is about progress and that civilization is The Great Ascent. But this benign model of social evolution cannot explain why human life under civilization has not been better. Schmookler proposes a perspective on social evolution quite different from the commonsense view, arguing that the major trends in the transformation of human society have had the effect of increasing competitive power. Imagine a group of tribes living within reach of one another. If all choose the way of peace, then all may live in peace. But if one tribe is ambitious for expansion and conquest, the threatened tribes must become like their foe or be destroyed or absorbed. This parable of the tribes shows that power is like a contaminant, which inexorably becomes universal in the system of competing societies. What is viable in a world beset by the struggle for power is what can prevail. What prevails may not best meet human needs, and thus the continuous selection for power has closed off many humane cultural options. The parable of the tribes presents a tragic picture of human destiny: a paradox that changed man's liberation from the ways of nature into bondage to the ways of power. There is no turning back, but there may be a way of moving forward, creating a new order that requires an end to the intersocietal anarchy that has been the overarching context of civilized life. An ideal cultural system for humanity would be determined by values rooted in a a profound vision of the meaning of human life. The parable of the tribes encourages us to see all mankind as subject to the same distressing circumstance, and help us to act responsibly to shape the future. It is a message to liberate the human spirit, by driving a wedge between us and the power systems that rule our lives. [NOTE: An original and sweeping analysis; unfortunately, in order to promote the tragic view, the idea of progress is casually dismissed, and major writers on the subject, such as J.B. Bury, Robert Nisbet, and W. Warren Wagar, are ignored. More important, no prescriptions of any substance are offered to seriously liberate us from the tragic condition that is portrayed.]
(**parable of the tribes**)

6476

The Evolution of Cooperation. Robert Axelrod (Prof of Political Science, U of Michigan). NY: Basic Books, March 1984/241p/$17.95.

The theory of biological evolution is based on the struggle for life and survival of the fittest. Yet, cooperation is common between members of the same species and even members of different species. Before 1960, accounts of the evolutionary process largely dismissed cooperative phenomena as not requiring special attention. Evolutionary theory now pays attention to the manifest existence of cooperation and related group behavior. If we understood the process better, we could speed up the evolution of cooperation. To enhance this understanding, Axelrod invited professional game theorists to participate in a computer tournament based on the famous Prisoner's Dilemma, which formulates the problems involved in promoting cooperation. It was found that TIT FOR TAT, a straightforward strategy of reciprocity, exhibited features of fundamental importance to successful cooperation. These findings provide new grounds for hope in the arena of international politics, where independent, egoistic nations face each other in a dangerously disorganized world system. The advice to national leaders, as well as players of the prisoner's dilemma: don't be envious, don't be the first to defect, reciprocate both cooperation and defection, and don't be too clever. **(promoting cooperation)**

6477

The Synergism Hypothesis: A Theory of Progressive Evolution. Peter A. Corning (Human Biology Program, Stanford U). NY: McGraw-Hill, June 1983/492p/$19.95; $12.95pb.

About the origin and nature of human societies and how they have evolved, using the "interactional paradigm" as an analytical framework. Natural selection and teleonomic selection have played a central role in the progressive evolutionary trend toward more complex, hierarchically organized systems. The key to this trend has been functional synergism—combinatorial or cooperative effects that have had positive consequences in relation to the problem of survival and reproduction. This synergism hypothesis provides a framework for a general theory of progressive evolution. These theoretical foundations are concluded with a general theory of politics. Corning sees in the present trend of events the hope of a reconciliation and synthesis between reductionist and holistic views of life, and between scientific and humanistic ways of understanding man and society. [NOTE: Heavy going, but perhaps rewarding to the specialist in this mode of thought.] **(synergism in evolution)**

6478

Ever-Expanding Horizons: The Dual Informational Sources of Human Evolution. Carl P. Swanson (Prof Emeritus of Botany, U of Massachusetts - Amherst). Amherst MA: U of Massachusetts Press, May 1983/162p/ $13.50;$7.50pb.

Explains the analogy between organic and cultural evolution, applying what is known of organic evolution to human culture. Evolution is cumulative change through time, with sufficient direction to be detected as other than random fluctuations. All systems that evolve do so because of instabilities inherent within themselves or imposed from without. Under the rubric of general evolution, four major levels of change are recognized: cosmic, chemical, organic or biological, and cultural. As the number of evolving components and possible states of a system increase, diversity within the system will also increase. Plasticity of behavior is an inherited phenomenon that achieves its highest expression in the human species, aided by the invention of increasingly sophisticated symbolic and technological devices for the retention and management of that which has been learned. As concepts are tinkered with, cultural evolution became the latest branching fork along the course of universal evolution. [NOTE: As Schmookler (#6475) might note, this is a conventionally benign view of evolution that considers culture completely outside of any modern sociopolitical context; a pleasantly innocuous exercise.]

(organic and cultural evolution)

6479

English: Out to Conquer the World (Special Report), *U.S. News & World Report*, 18 Feb 1985, 49-59.

English has become to the modern world what Latin was to the ancients, dominating the planet as the medium of exchange in science, technology, commerce, tourism, diplomacy, and culture. The language initially spread with the British empire; after WWII, English with the twist of American jargon was boosted by US economic and political power. It has now captured the lead in the information explosion: English is the medium for 80% of information stored in computers around the world. Some 345 million people use English as their first language, and an additional 400 million as their second. It is the native language of 12 countries, an official or semiofficial tongue in 33 others, and widely studied in the schools of at least 56 additional countries (in the Soviet Union, more than half of the secondary-school students study English). Stuart Berg Flexner (Editor-in-Chief, Random House dictionaries) observes that, if the Soviet Union does not come to dominate world politics, it is quite conceivable that American English will become almost universal as a second language around the world, although there would be regional dialects. James Alatis (Dean, School of Languages, Georgetown U) views the growth of the English language as "ineluctable, inexorable and inevitable."

(English as world language)

6480

The State of the Language: English Observed. Philip Howard (Literary Editor, *The Times*, London). NY: Oxford U Press, Feb 1985/180p/$14.95.

The recent wave of worry about the state of the English language has been rolling for about 20 years. But reports of the death of English are an exaggeration. The language is going through a phase of rapid change, probably more rapid than any it has gone through before, but this change is healthy, manageable, and on the whole beneficial. Chapters are devoted to the registers of the language (the two major ones are written and spoken English), slang, jargon (with comments on Psychobabble and Computerese), dialect, cliché, euphemism, spelling, and punctuation (the language is changing towards having shorter sentences and more full stops). Concludes with the guess that English will hang together as a world language, with a strong central core surrounded by a rich profusion of dialects and jargons, all largely unintelligible to outsiders. Even if the pessimists are right, it is not the end of the world, if one looks at the rich things that grew out of the fragmentation of Latin. [NOTE: A jolly good read; as Howard notes, "It is possible to be serious without being either solemn or incomprehensible."] **(changes in English language)**

B. Toward a Better World

*6481

Human Betterment. Kenneth E. Boulding (U of Colorado). Beverly Hills CA: Sage Publications, Feb 1985/ 224p/$25.00.

We should not be ashamed of wanting to save the world, or wanting to improve it. Never perhaps in the history of the planet has there been such a vast array of possible futures, ranging from total catastrophe to a much better world with stable peace, diminishing poverty, stronger communities, and a greater realization of human potential. But unless we think such a better world is possible, it will not happen. The thesis of this essay is that normative analysis and the study of human betterment by the methods of the scholarly community is possible, even if it may not always be wholly successful. The payoffs from careful normative analysis are likely to be enormous, and it is surprising that so little human energy and intelligence go into it. Chapters in this volume—"intended only as a preface, a door opening on a large and too little explored field of activity for the human mind"—consider the meaning of human betterment, the nature of significant change, the role of human decision, the development of decision-making skills, the development of riches, the development of justice and freedom, the development of peace, development as the learning of quality, and the doing of good.

(potential of normative analysis)

*6482

GAIA: An Atlas of Planet Management. Edited by Norman Myers (Oxford UK). Garden City NY: Anchor Press/Doubleday, Nov 1984/272p(8x11")/$29.95;$17.95pb.

In ancient Greece, Gaia was goddess of the earth. A group of space scientists discovered the phenomenon of the self-sustaining biosphere and named it Gaia—the living planet. Since then, we have begun to learn about the planetary life-support systems which rule our lives. Gaia went its creative way for several billion years, becoming steadily more diverse, complex, and fruitful. In the last few seconds of life's "evolutionary day," *Homo sapiens* appeared, and is now experiencing exponential growth in numbers, energy consumption, mobility, production of information, and consumption. Overtaxing the Earth's ecosystem leads to a variety of breakdowns and human conflicts. This guide to a planet in transition, involving more than 100 contributors, is arranged in 7 sections: 1) **Land**: tropical forests, the disappearing soil, a new agriculture; 2) **Ocean**: pollution, law of the sea, the polar zones; 3) **Elements**: the freshwater reservoir, mineral reserves, the fuelwood crisis, energy efficiency; 4) **Evolution**: genetic resources, the destruction of diversity, conserving the wild; 5) **Humankind**: the work famine, the literacy chasm, managing numbers, health for all; 6) **Civilization**: the world city, the world market, technology transfer; 7) **Management**: the family of nations, the cost of militarism. Concludes in a brief epilogue that our ignorance is vast, for we still know little about the workings of the Earth's ecosystem, the true rates of soil loss and pollution, the extent of hunger and workless populations, and the various degradative processes that are underway. Yet there are signs of hope that we are making a start on the road toward sensible stewardship of our planet. [NOTE: A slick coffee-table book with scores of striking photos and charts; should also prove useful as an introduction and a reference to the "global problematique," and as a companion to the Worldwatch Institute's **State of the World Report** (**FS Annual 1984**, #5601), the Club of Rome's **Making It Happen** (**FS Annual 1983**, #5595), and the more politically-oriented **New State of the World Atlas** (#6468).]

(living planet guidebook)

*6483

The Global Possible: Resources, Development, and the New Century. Global Possible Conference, World Resources Institute.Washington DC: WRI Publications (1735 New York Ave, NW), 1984/37p/$3.50pb.

A statement and an agenda for action produced at a May 1984 meeting near Washington, involving 75 leaders of science, government, industry, and citizen groups from 20 countries. The central and emphatic message is that it is possible to build a world that is more secure, more prosperous, and more sustainable both economically and environmentally. This global possible will require new levels of cooperation, a global partnership between developed and developing countries, and peaceful cooperation to remove the threat of nuclear war. International security is at stake: if we allow world population to grow, the increasing pressure of people on resources will lead to rising political tensions and conflict, waves of "ecological refugees," disputes over scarce land and water, and increasingly isolationist trade and foreign policy. The actions suggested in the following agenda would make an enormous difference in the world's welfare over the next 10 to 30 years. 1) **Population, Poverty, and Development:** adopt labor-intensive economic development strategies, expand greatly the educational and employment opportunities available to women, reduce death rates by making sanitary services and simple health care widely available, double access to family planning services in the Third World over the next decade, increase capital flows for development assistance; 2) **The Urban Environment:** slow migration rates into large cities with policies that decentralize industries and provide rural employment, encourage neighborhood self-help improvement initiatives, raise international awareness of mounting urban problems and their implications; 3) **Fresh Water:** charge rates to water users that reflect costs and encourage efficiency, achieve sharp increases in irrigation efficiency, manage fertilizers and pesticides to protect surface- and ground-waters; 4) **Biological Diversity:** complete a comprehensive international network of protected areas for conservation of genetic resources, develop national conservation strategies within the World Conservation Strategy framework, raise the level of awareness of the nature and importance of biological diversity; 5) **Tropical Forests:** a new international fund to subsidize protected forests, lay the groundwork for large-scale fuelwood planting in the 1990s, encourage private-sector participation in tree farming; 6) **Agricultural Land:** promote intensified production on good lands, improve existing irrigation works and promote smallholder agriculture, reduce impact of livestock overgrazing, increase soil conservation programs; 7) **Living Marine Resources:** promote an ecosystem conservation principle, accelerate aquaculture development, prevent pollution and destruction of critical habitats; 8) **Energy:** promote rapid gains in conservation and energy efficiency as the highest priority through raising oil and gas prices to international levels, promote renewable energy sources; 9) **Non-Fuel Minerals:** insure adequate flows of investment capital to LDCs, reduce the vulnerability of producing countries to market fluctuations, restore mining sites and prevent offshore pollution; 10) **Atmosphere and Climate:** develop long-term energy strategies to meet the real energy needs of all countries while avoiding the grave risks of carbon dioxide buildup, prepare for adverse climate change by pursuing anticipatory responses such as more resilient crop strains, adopt the proposed Framework Convention to Protect the Ozone Layer; 11) **International Assistance and the Environment:** greater support to decentralized projects providing services to all, greater emphasis on agrarian reform and improved productivity of small agriculture; 12) **Assessment of Conditions, Trends, and Capabilities:** agree on key environmental indicators, fully develop the Global Environment Monitoring System, undertake an international scientific research program; 13)**Business, Science and Citizens:** support efforts to help business managers understand more fully the environmental and social impacts of their actions, develop appropriate constraints on economic activity when external social costs of production must be internalized, organize a series of international events to attract wide attention to key issues, strengthen international scientific organizations. [NOTE: An important and concise statement; unfortunately, the conference was not attended by any representative of the Soviet Union or its allies.]

(Global Possible Conference)

6484

The Second Biennial Conference on the Fate of the Earth: Conference Policy and Action Statement. Center for Innovative Diplomacy. Palo Alto CA: CID (644 Emerson St, #30), Sept 1984/12p/free.

A statement signed by 18 Nobel Laureates and 162 leaders of arms control/disarmament and environmentalist organizations, designed to raise public awareness of threats to human survival and to provide a tool for building political support. The statement is divided into three parts: 1) **Restoring Rationality to National Security**: elimination of all strategies for surviving and winning so-called limited nuclear wars, substantial worldwide reductions in nuclear and conventional weapons, an international treaty to demilitarize space and ban beam weapons, sound conversion programs to retrain defense workers and retool plants, stronger policies to halt the potential spread of nuclear weapons to non-nuclear nations, democratic global organizations to adjudicate international conflicts in a non-violent manner; 2) **Promoting a Sustainable Global Economy**: savings from disarmament to be reinvested in programs to help LDCs, policies to reverse the growth rate of human population, vigorous international programs of pollution control, a halt to the destruction of irreplaceable genetic resources, all governments adopting a policy of living within the carrying capacity of their own ecosystems; 3) **Making a New Commitment**: new and enlightened leadership within all nations (especially the US), each of us educating and inspiring action.

The statement is supplemented by a "United States Legislative Action Agenda," specifying American action in each of the three areas: 1) **National Security**: moratoria on destabilizing weapons, a nuclear freeze, Congressional hearings on deep cuts, replacing nuclear exports with a sunbeams for peace program, ratify outstanding international law treaties, funding for a non-aligned verification system, hearings on U.N. reform; 2) **Sustainable Development**: increased US foreign assistance, substantial expansion for population programs, strengthen programs to reduce pollution and protect biological diversity; 3) **A New Commitment**: establish a global foresight capability in the US government, expand public participation in strategic planning, increase support for global education programs, increase support for the Peace Corps and exchange programs, create a US Peace Academy.

(Fate of the Earth Conference policy statement)

6485

Global Solutions: Innovative Approaches to World Problems. Edited by Edward Cornish (President, WFS). Bethesda MD: World Future Society, 1984/160p(8x11")/ $6.95pb.

Most of the world's problems can be solved—if we make the proper effort, and abandon the myth that nothing can be done to change the future. These essays from *The Futurist* include James Dator on images of global governance, Harold S. Becker on scenarios of the future US-USSR balance of power, Lester R. Brown on how the food connection might transform US-USSR relations, Robert Rodale on the search for a sustainable agriculture, Ralph E. Hamil on macroengineering projects that may begin in the next few decades, Frank P. Davidson on political problems in undertaking macroengineering projects, Jesco von Puttkamer on transcending the limits to growth by the industrialization of space, Charles L. Gould and C. R. Gerber on raising global productivity through space communications, Orville L. Freeman and William Person on how multinational corporations can bring hope for the poorest nations, Don Larson on nitrogen-fixing shrubs as an answer to the world firewood shortage, Bruce Stokes on do-it-yourself housing, Frank Meissner on unconventional foods, Trevor Hancock on public policies to create a healthy future, and Kimon Valaskakis on the conserver society as emerging paradigm.

(solutions to world problems)

6486

The Crucial Epoch: Essential Knowledge for Living in a World in Transformation, Ervin Laszlo (UNITAR-NYC), *Futures*, 17:1, Feb 1985, 2-23.

The era of technological-industrial civilization, with its global interdependence and growing vulnerability and inequity, is coming to a close. Something else will take its place, which is up to us to decide. The system that we have put into place since WWII cannot be indefinitely sustained. We are now about to enter an era of critical instability which will not be locally confined—a crisis of unprecedented dimensions. There will be a rupture, and trends will turn around or break off. Some general guidelines are suggested for preparation and action: 1) when a major perturbation challenges the basic structures of a system, the system has options to select a new path for its evolution or extinction; 2) initiate foresightful action in every setting of society and in all societies; such action will be greatly amplified when the system enters the phase of active transformation; 3) make self-reliance under a wide range of conditions the cornerstone of plans and activities.

(era of critical instability ahead)

6487

Toward a Global Infrastructure, Masaki Nakajima (President of the Board, Mitsubishi Research Institute), *Technology in Society* (Pergamon), 6:1, 1984, 85-94.

Emotional responses to the fear of nuclear holocaust are not enough; it is necessary to find a more systematic and constructive approach to decelerating the arms race. At the same time, the world economy today faces its gravest crisis since WWII, and needs a bold vision and policies to dispel its stagnation. Allowing the world economic system to follow a peaceful and steady course, without excessive dependence on military expenditure, requires public investment on a global scale. A Global Infrastructure Fund (GIF), first proposed in 1977, could be a key to the simultaneous solution of the persistent problems that face the world today. The goal of this "Global New Deal" is to generate a fund of $500 billion to pursue the long-range goal of peaceful construction for humanity. The GIF would encourage both the free world and the socialist bloc to pool their resources for Third World development through mutual effort. The fund could be collected through an export levy for major exporters (which would amount to only 2% or 3% of the current annual arms expenditures, worldwide). Some potential macroprojects for GIF include: 1) greening of the deserts in the Sahara, the Sinai, and the Arabian peninsula; 2) a large-scale installation for collecting solar energy in a remote part of the world; 3) construction of a second Panama Canal and an additional Atlantic-Pacific canal in Nicaragua; 4) a dam across the Bering Strait, making the North Pacific climate more temperate; 5) construction of nine dams and seven artificial lakes across the Amazon and the Orinoco [NOTE: see #6717, which questions the value of large dams]; 6) a modern "Silk Road" superhighway from central Europe to China; 7) a trans-Europe North-South motorway from Gdansk to Athens; 8) a bridge/tunnel between Morocco and Spain; 9) a global network of superports; 10) a global communications network of satellites and ground stations for various media. Each macroproject would cost about $10 billion, and once completed would be designated as a non-bombardment object. This GIF approach would enable people worldwide to learn the value of cooperative, large-scale, and peaceful ventures.

(Global Infrastructure Fund)

6488

The 2025 Report: A Concise History of the Future, 1975-2025. Norman Macrae (Deputy Editor, *The Economist*). NY: Macmillan, Dec 1984/258p/$15.95.

A scenario of how and why the tumultuous history of the past half-century has come about, as written in 2025. Soviet-American collaboration began during the administration of President Hart in 1989. The much-maligned antimissile initiative of 1983 bore fruit in 1999, when President Kemp and Prime Minister Berisov put on a TV show during which the Soviets launched unarmed missiles from Siberia and computer messages telecommuted from the US made them crash back on the site they took off from. This demonstration of a telecommuted beam led to a declaration that the nuclear nightmare was over. Subsidiary nuclear powers like Britain and France destroyed their warheads, allowing the US and USSR to act as global policemen. In 2004, Roberta Kennedy was elected US President by a landslide, and she ushered in an age of genuine pluralism, choosing small central government and dispersal into small communities, while participating in the international Centrobank—the last great act of government before governments grew much less important. This new central bank relied largely on a computer program, authorizing it to print enough new foreign exchange called bancor for any applicant country to allow its economic growth to proceed at the fastest possible noninflationary pace. Performance contracts were put out, allowing firms to draw money from Centrobank if they transformed life in Third World villages by introducing fuller employment with appropriate, labor-intensive technology. Other chapters are devoted to the steady rise in importance of the telecommunications-computer terminal (the TC), the dispersal of telecommuting brainworkers in the TC age, the TC and education, food gluts as a result of the genetic engineering revolution, gluts of energy and minerals as a result of biotechnology, amnesiac and memory-enhancing drugs, multinational HMOs that qualify for Centrobank payments to keep people healthy, competitive crime prevention corporations paid on performance contracts (also communes taking in convicted criminals, receiving $20,000 for

each year that they do not commit an offense against anyone), and internationalized taxes for people above certain income levels to keep them from moving out of high-tax areas. [NOTE: An upbeat view of a high-tech, decentralist/ libertarian future. The superficial and rambling narrative obscures the wisps of some possibly useful ideas such as Centrobank and widespread performance contracts.]

(a happy, high-tech future)

6489

Historical Generations and Generation Units: A Global Pattern of Youth Movements, Richard G. Braungart (Prof of Sociology, Syracuse U), *Journal of Political and Military Sociology*, 12:1, Spring 1984, 113-135.

Former Research Director of the 1970 President's Commission on Campus Unrest examines youth movements worldwide over the past 170 years, identifying four historical generations (Young Europe, Post-Victorian, Great Depression, and 1960s) representing 41 generational movements and 82 sets of generational units such as SDS and YAF in the US. The study distinguishes between spontaneous and sponsored units on the political left and right. Concludes that cycles of intergenerational conflict represent barometers of social and political change, often bound up with local, national, and global struggles. Generational movements show every indication of continuing into the future and contributing to a new international political culture. The challenge to modern societies around the world is not to inhibit or destroy this creative social impulse for change and revitalization, but to move it from a volatile arena to a more rational political forum where competition over ideas can be negotiated peacefully.

(world youth movements since 1815)

C. Population and Human Rights

6490

Mexico City Declaration on Population and Development, United Nations International Conference on Population, *The New York Times*, Thursday, 16 Aug 1984, A10.

The Conference met on August 14 to appraise the implementation of the World Population Plan of Action, adopted at Bucharest in 1974. It reaffirmed the validity of the principles and objectives of the Plan, and adopted additional recommendations for action, noting that the number of people living in absolute poverty has increased over the past decade. Experience over the past ten years shows the necessity of: 1) full participation by the entire community and grass-roots organizations in the design and implementation of policies and programs; 2) political commitment of heads of state and other leaders; and 3) international cooperation, which can be notably successful. It is also important to understand that population and development policies reinforce each other when they respond to individual, family, and community needs.

(UN population conference)

6491

Reflections on Population. Rafael M. Salas (Executive Director, UNFPA). Elmsford NY: Pergamon Press, July 1984/240p/$30.00.

A sequel to **International Population Assistance: The First Decade** (1979), in which Salas described the concepts governing the United Nations Fund for Population Activities. This book describes the work of the UNFPA up through 1984, with chapters on fertility and the status of women, morbidity and mortality, population distribution and migration, population growth and structure, promotion of knowledge and implementation of policies and programs, and international cooperation in population matters. Concludes with the five most recent annual reports on the State of World Population, and various selected statements.   (**UN views on world population**)

6492

The Crowded Earth: People and Politics of Population. Pranay Gupte. NY: W. W. Norton, Sept 1984/349p/ $17.95.

Former *New York Times* correspondent traveled through 50 countries and presents his notes, observations, and anecdotes about various government birth control policies. China's campaign against its population growth has been remarkably successful (the rate having dropped into the range of many Western countries), but this poses a harsh dilemma for Western values oriented toward voluntary birth control. China is seen as the first of what promises to be a parade of Third World countries that will also find ways of further restricting the procreative freedom of individuals. On the other hand, many countries will have difficulty in coping with their mounting population pressures, especially because Western support for family planning shows signs of flagging. Contrary to some smug observers, the global "population bomb" has not been defused; its fuse is long and still burning. (**population control policy**)

6493

Time Bomb or Myth: The Population Problem, Robert S. McNamara (former President, World Bank), *Foreign Affairs*, 62:5, Summer 1984, 1107-1131.

Population growth rates in most LDCs fell significantly in the 1970s, leading many to believe that there are no more serious population problems, and that efforts to deal with such problems can thus be relaxed. But if actions are not taken to accelerate the reductions in the rate of growth, world population (now 4.7 billion) will not stabilize below 11 billion, and certain regions and countries will grow beyond the limits consistent with political stability and acceptable social and economic conditions. Nations facing population-induced instability will be more and more tempted to impose coercive measures of fertility regulation, and invididual families in these nations will move to higher levels of abortion and female infanticide. There is much humane action that can be taken to encourage couples to desire smaller families and to provide them with the contraceptive means to implement that desire. If immediate and much more effective action is not initiated, the penalties to poor individuals and nations will be enormous. And the ripple effects—political, economic, and moral—will inevitably extend to the rich as well.

(**need to accelerate population programs**)

6494

Births, Deaths, and Taxes: The Demographic and Political Transitions. A.F.K. Organski (U of Michigan), Jacek Kugler (Vanderbilt U), J. Timothy Johnson (Centers for Disease Control, Atlanta), and Youssef Cohen (U of Pennsylvania). Chicago, Ill: U of Chicago Press, Oct 1984/ 161p/$18.00.

Argues that the growth of government power, as measured by increases in taxation, finds direct expression in the number of children born and the number of people dying in a given population: the larger the scale of government, the lower the rate of childbearing and the lower the rate of mortality. Because mortality rates decline first, state growth in recent decades precipitated a population explosion. But continued state growth, along with social and economic development, is now causing a drop in fertility as well. This relationship, if confirmed by further scholarly inquiry, has profound implications for the field of development, which has heretofore assumed that improvements in only economic and social conditions will bring about a drop in population growth. Moreover, the future should differ from current expectations about developing and developed countries. The present political topography has emerged from the growth of US and USSR preeminence. The findings in this book, however, suggest that in the decades ahead the distribution of power in the world is likely to change again, with China emerging as a contender for power with the other two colossi. It is not at all inevitable that China will succeed, but her chances of success are enhanced by her political control over the vast majority of her people. As China has demonstrated, bringing the population explosion under control has come about not from a rise in economic productivity as everyone supposed, but from a rise in what is really political productivity. [NOTE: An intriguing analysis, although the "child survival revolution" advocated by UNICEF (#6495) appears far more promising as a way to quickly limit population growth.]   (**government and population growth**)

*6495

The State of the World's Children 1985. James P. Grant (Executive Director, UNICEF). Published for UNICEF. NY: Oxford U Press, March 1985/131p(8x10")/$7.95pb.

In 1984, the lives of half a million children were saved by oral rehydration therapy (ORT). Less than 15% of the world's families are using this revolutionary low-cost technique for preventing and treating diarrhoeal dehydration—the biggest single killer of children in the modern world. Previously, dehydration could only be treated intravenously by medical personnel in clinics. Now it can be prevented orally by parents at home, using mass-produced ten-cent sachets of pre-packed salts or the even cheaper home-made solutions of sugar, salt, and water. UNICEF believes that ORT can become available to half the world's families in the next five years, saving the lives of some 2 million young children a year. ORT is the most dramatic of several simple and inexpensive methods for protecting children; the others are growth monitoring, breast-feeding, and a full $5 course of immunization against diseases that kill 5 million young children a year and leave 5 million more disabled. These basic strategies of the child survival revolution represent major advances because they are not dependent only on the extension of health services, they are very low cost, they are universal in their relevance, and they do not depend on changes in values. Drastically improved child health and survival are thus made realistic by shifting the operational center of gravity from health institutions to the family itself.

If the child survival revolution is to be a revolution for a majority, it must depend more on ordinary families than on medical institutions. Empowering mothers with the knowledge and techniques of child protection is the key to the revolution in child health. But the responsibility for turning that key rests with the whole of society, through three kinds of support for women: female education, family spacing, and food supplements. An elementary safety net of minimum food entitlements, primary health care, elementary education, safe sanitation, and clean water could be put in place by most developing nations. An even more basic, modest, and immediate goal is the basis of this report: a few specific tasks which most nations could achieve in the next few years. All families could be enabled to use ORT, all children could be immunized, all mothers could become aware of the importance of breast-feeding, and almost all parents could have the means and the knowledge to prevent malnutrition by monitoring their children's growth. The political and economic costs are absolutely minimal in relation to the benefits such protection would bring.

These low-cost techniques have the potential to save the lives of about 7 million children each year. But would this result in a surge in world population? To the contrary, all the evidence suggests that a reduction in the number of child deaths would help to bring a greater reduction in the number of child births, because: 1) the death of an infant means the end of breast-feeding and of the contraceptive protection which breast-feeding provides; 2) the greater the chance of a child's survival, the less the parents need to insure against loss by bearing more children than they want; 3) rising levels of female education—a key to the child survival strategy—are also strongly associated with falling birth rates; 4) any change which reinforces the confidence of parents in their own ability to improve their circumstances would in turn make the acceptance of family planning more likely. For all these reasons, reducing child deaths is likely to cause population growth to slow down and stabilize at an earlier date and at a lower level than would otherwise have been the case. To illustrate, Sri Lanka has achieved a revolution in child survival; if every developing nation attained similar infant death rates and birth rates, there would be 7.5 million fewer child deaths each year—and 35 million fewer births. [NOTE: An important and genuinely hopeful development!]

(child survival revolution and world population)

6496

Adolescent Fertility: Worldwide Concerns. Judith Senderowitz and John M. Paxman. *Population Bulletin*, 40:2, April 1985/51p/$4.00 single copy.

Teenage fertility rates are declining almost everywhere, like those of older women. But there is growing concern over the adverse health, social, economic, and demographic effects of early childbearing. Illness and mortality rates are significantly higher for mothers under 20 and their infants than they are for older mothers. Early childbearing contributes to rapid population growth, due to larger completed family sizes, truncated education, lower future family income, and shorter timespans between generations. Future world population growth will be particularly affected by teenage fertility in LDCs, which contain 82% of the 245 million women aged 15-19 in 1985, with the number projected to rise to 320 million by 2020. In most LDCs, early marriage and childbearing are still the norm. Abortion and out-of-wedlock childbearing are increasing among teenagers in many developed and fast-urbanizing developing countries. This reflects more and earlier premarital sexual activity, fostered by the lengthening gap between puberty and marriage, diminished parental and social controls, and increasing peer and media pressures to be sexually active. Though generally still controversial and inadequate, sex education in school and teenagers' access to birth control services are increasing. Concludes that the march into the 21st century has eroded many traditional rites of passage and moral values related to sexuality and the adult role of parenthood. Given the changing biological and social realities of our time, new rites of passage must be found, and new guidance must be provided about values. Both are now missing. [Also see #6497, on teenage fertility in the US.]

(teenage fertility worldwide)

6497

Teenage Pregnancy in Developed Countries: Determinants and Policy Implications, Elise F. Jones (Alan Guttmacher Institute) *et al.*, *Family Planning Perspectives*, 17:2, March-April 1985, 53-63.

Summarizes the results of a comparative study of adolescent pregnancy and childbearing in 37 developed countries. These rates have been declining in the US and in virtually all the countries of Europe, but teenage fertility is still considerably higher in the US than in the majority of other developed countries. There is a large differential within the US between the rates of white and black teenagers, but even if only whites are considered, the US rates are still much higher than in most other countries. Levels of adolescent sexual activity in the US are not very different from those in countries with much lower teenage pregnancy rates. Increasing the legitimacy and availability of contraception and sex education is likely to result in declining teenage pregnancy rates. That has been the experience of many countries in Western Europe, and there is no reason to think that such an approach would not also be successful in the US. But a well-defined expression of political will is needed.   **(high US teen pregnancy rate)**

6498

The Makings of a New Contraceptive: An Effective, Safe, Reversible Implant Protects for Five Years, Lynn Landman, *RF: An Occasional Report on the Work of the Rockefeller Foundation* (1133 Ave of the Americas, NYC), Jan 1985, 9-10.

Over the next several years, hundreds of thousands of women around the world will use a new implanted contraceptive, named Norplant (a trademark owned by the Population Council), as quickly as the device can be mass-produced by its Finnish manufacturer, Leiras. The implant in the upper arm consists of six narrow tubes, each measuring about 1.3 inches long and 0.1 inch in diameter. The silicone rubber tubing serves as a matrix through which a progestin hormone is released at a daily rate for a five-year period. At this point, the implant appears to be as close-to-perfect a contraceptive method, short of sterilization, as is possible. In one- and three-year trials in nine countries (perhaps the most extensive clinical trials taken with any contraceptive), the annual pregnancy rate was less than 1 per 100 users. Continuation rates—how long a woman will continue to use it—are reported to be high in a variety of cultural and religious settings. The initial public sector cost is about $2.50 a year, but as demand for the product grows, the price should decline so that it becomes comparable to that of the Pill (about $1.45 a year).

(new 5-year contraceptive)

6499

Sex and Destiny: The Politics of Human Fertility.
Germaine Greer. NY: Harper & Row, May 1984/$19.95.

The much-touted "population explosion" is a temporary demographic bulge that the overprivileged Western societies have used an an excuse to impose their idea of appropriate family size on the rest of the world. The West's declining fertility is not due to an increase in enlightenment, but to the systematic downgrading of motherhood and the birth experience, creating a sterile, consumption-oriented society that uses most of the world's resources. Traditional cultures have always practiced family planning, but their non-pharmaceutical methods have been scorned and discredited by Western specialists. [Also see *Breast Feeding*, by R. V. Short (*Scientific American*, April 1984, 35-41), who argues that "lactational amenorrhea" is at least as good as any modern contraceptive; breast feeding is nature's contraceptive, but this function has not been appreciated by physicians, scientists, and birth control advocates. Many Third World women are abandoning breast feeding for bottle feeding, resulting in a rising rate of population growth and poorer infant health.]

(politics of world fertility)

6500

Toward the Understanding and Prevention of Genocide. Edited by Israel W. Charny (Tel Aviv U). Boulder CO: Westview, Aug 1984/c400p/$31.00.

Proceedings of the 1982 International Conference on the Holocaust and Genocide, covering such topics as scenarios of past and future genocide, dynamics of genocide, international alerts and campaigning against genocide, a program of action for the UN, international law and prevention of genocide, an applied science approach to a genocide early warning system, a World Genocide Tribunal to supplement the early warning system as a preventative measure, and the lessons of the Holocaust. [Also see Charny, **How Can We Commit the Unthinkable? Genocide: The Human Cancer** (Westview, 1982; **FS Annual 1983**, #4500).]

(genocide prevention)

6501

The Transformation of the Jews. Calvin Goldscheider (Hebrew U of Jerusalem) and Alan S. Zuckerman (Brown U). Chicago, Ill: U of Chicago Press, Oct 1984/272p/$24.95.

In the 19th century, three-quarters of the world's Jews lived in Europe; by 1980, two-thirds were in Israel and the US. The authors examine the radical transformation of Jewish religious observances, social organizations, and education, as well as the various waves of migration and the terror of the Holocaust. They conclude that the upheavals of modernization did not destroy Jewish cohesion, but created new kinds of communal ties.

(Jewish transformations over 200 years)

6502

Freedom in the World: Political Rights and Civil Liberties, 1984-1985. Raymond D. Gastil (Director, Comparative Survey of Freedom). Westport CT: Greenwood Press, Feb 1985/438p/$35.00.

The 12th year of the Comparative Survey and the 6th edition in a series of annual reports, measuring political rights and civil liberties on a 7-point scale in each of 216 countries and territories. Since the last survey, the outstanding events were Nigeria's return to military rule and the completion of Argentina's return to democracy. These events symbolized two of the most important trends of recent years: the erosive decline of freedom in most of Africa and the progress of freedom in the Americas. Still, at the end of 1984, most countries remained without working democracies. Since the first Survey in 1973, the percentage of people living in freedom worldwide and the percentage of free nations has not changed noticeably. The best chance for democratic advance appears to be in those societies that are coming increasingly to participate in the modern world.   **(12th world freedom survey)**

D. International Relations

6503

Nation Against Nation: What Happened to the U.N. Dream and What the U.S. Can Do About It. Thomas M. Franck (Prof of Law, NYU). NY: Oxford U Press, April 1985/384p/$19.95.

The former Director of Research at UNITAR acknowledges that the American public has become increasingly disenchanted with the UN. He examines the record, confirming that the UN often operates in a way that undermines respect for individual human rights and hampers conflict resolution. But the fault often lies with the US itself, which helped form the UN with wildly unrealistic views of what it could do. As the wishful thoughts proved false, they were often replaced with new fantasies designed to bring their own disappointments. For a decade or more the US was able to use the UN essentially as a tool and adjunct to its foreign policy, and Washington failed to predict and plan for the inevitable shift of power at the UN led by the newly emergent Third World nations. If realism compels the US to start from a scaled-down expectation of the UN's potential, it also requires us to accept that the institution exists and that it mirrors some disagreeable but true aspects of the contemporary world. Although the UN is nowhere near as noble and efficacious as was once hoped, neither is it as venal or useless as some now claim. The US can still win on some issues at the UN, and could probably win more often if it was willing to do the necessary long-range strategic planning, deploy seasoned personnel, and take the UN seriously as a place for politics. At some point, the balance of US national interest may well make it more prudent to leave than to stay. Contemplating such an alternative future should encompass three imperatives: 1) the US must not pull out of the UN without a full and informed public debate, at least on the order of the one which preceded entry in 1945; 2) the US should act only in concert with principal friends and allies, including non-Europeans; if it leaves, let it leave in good company; 3) the US must have ready at hand a credible plan for an alternative forum in which to conduct multilateral diplomacy, so that it does not drift into isolationism. Concludes that the UN system is not about to be reformed, except in the most marginal ways. The realistic choice presented to the US is to understand it and operate as effectively as possible within it, or to get out—in part, or altogether. For now, the US national interest is better served by a "hard-ball" strategy of staying in.

(US should stay in UN)

6504

The U.N. at 40: A Supporter's Lament, Edward C. Luck (President, UN Assn of the US), *Foreign Policy*, No 57, Winter 1984-85, 143-159.

The 40th birthday of the United Nations in 1985 provides cause for sober reassessment. Its performance has inevitably fallen short of its founding vision. As its ideals have withered, the UN has tended to reflect international discord. Buffeted by competing visions of its role in the world, the UN is searching for an identity. Trying to be all things to all people, it has ended up disappointing most and disaffecting some (most importantly, the US). Three basic visions exist today regarding the UN's purpose beyond its role as a universal political forum: 1) performing functional activities such as UNICEF and WHO (which offers the least risk but chances political irrelevance); 2) promoting systemic change (which offers high risk and polarization with little chance at achievement); 3) implementing collective security (high risk but much potential gain). To become a stronger organization, the UN will have to make a difference to the central issues of peace and security facing humankind, as well as maintain its useful functional activities. Sweeping efforts at systemic change must be left for future agendas and more propitious climates. The UN can rebuild its credibility and vitality by aiming for concrete, constructive, but unspectacular achievements. All countries have a stake in making the UN system work, and each needs to contribute to turning the system around. The UN is an instrument, not an ideal, that must be used and cared for through good times and bad.

(strengthening the UN)

6505

Issues Before the 39th General Assembly of the United Nations, 1984-1985. Edited by Donald J. Puchala (Prof of Government, U of South Carolina). Published for the United Nations Association of the USA. Lexington MA: Lexington Books, Oct 1984/185p/$20.00.

An annual publication of the UNA/USA, this volume offers sections on dispute settlement and decolonization, arms control and disarmament, economics and development, global resource management, human rights and social issues, legal issues, and administration and budget. In his preface, Puchala notes that the UN certainly appears to be politically stagnating at present, as reflected in almost every section of this book. The lesson in world politics that this inactivity teaches is that effective international cooperation follows only from consensus among states; when governments disagree, international organizations cannot act. The UN's current lack of decisiveness and impact may also tell something about its present historical context. A long era—the age of the great European empires—has recently ended, and the UN contributed to its passing. Now a new phase in world history is beginning, and the values and institutions that will shape it are in dispute. What some call stagnation in the UN may thus be more revealingly identified as the early stages of a great debate about the foundations of the 21st century world order: the forms of political and economic organization that will best serve mankind, the modes of international organization that will best support global peace, entitlements to the earth's resources, the proper relationship of people to the natural environment, the definition of human decency and human rights, and the status of women, children, races, and refugees. Yearly editions of **Issues** will update the global debate as it evolves.

(emerging great debate on world order)

6506

A World Without a U.N.: What Would Happen If the United Nations Shut Down. Edited by Burton Yale Pines (VP, Heritage Foundation). Foreword by Ambasssador Charles M. Lichenstein. A United Nations Assessment Project Study. Washington: The Heritage Foundation, 1984/176p/$8.00pb.

In September 1983, US Ambassador Lichenstein told a UN committee that if UN members did not like the way they were being treated in the US, they should seriously consider removing the UN from America. This view expresses the feeling of great numbers of Americans who see the UN as an organization out of control. The UN has become exceedingly anti-US, anti-West, and anti-free enterprise; it has betrayed the spirit and substance of its Charter; it has not helped the poor and needy of the world; it has failed as a peacekeeper and protector of human rights; it distorts reality like a house of mirrors (exaggerating some things, diminishing others, and obscuring most); it globalizes issues that should remain local and regional.

The Heritage Foundation asked experts to review the UN record in nine key areas: disarmament, economic development, peacekeeping, environmental protection, health, food and agriculture, education, human rights, and the UN role as a safety valve to reduce international tensions. Their conclusions, discussed in this volume, vary in the specifics, but in general confirm that politicization and other problems of the UN increasingly prevent it from fulfilling even partially the tasks outlined in its Charter. Among the reforms for continued US membership which Washington should consider demanding: 1) the UN technical agencies should once again deal exclusively with technical matters; 2) the UN should stop funding the PLO, SWAPO, and similar terrorist groups; 3) the General Assembly's stature must be reduced because it is dominated by an intolerant majority; as long as the General Assembly refuses to function responsibly, the US could downgrade its delegation. If these reforms are not accepted, or if they fail, the US and other democratic nations should consider withdrawing from the UN. If this prompts its dissolution, the world would be no worse off. It would remain a world filled with multinational bodies. Probably all of the UN's specialized agencies would still function and be funded independently. Indeed, the technical and specialized agencies would benefit if freed from their association with the UN. World leaders could meet in a "Town Meeting of the World," convened annually in different capitals. Diplomats could meet informally, as they now do, in the world's great capitals such as London, Paris, or Washington. This all could function as well as it now does without the UN's costly Secretariat, its cronyism, legions of bureaucrats, high salaries, and anti-Western ideology. A world without the UN would be a better world. [NOTE: A provocative and plausible "scenario" from the conservative think tank that nurtured the Star Wars idea.]

(a better world without the UN?)

6507

The United States and Multilateral Diplomacy: A Handbook. Norman A. Graham, Richard L. Kauffman, and Michael F. Oppenheimer (The Futures Group). Dobbs Ferry NY: Oceana Publications, May 1984/266p/$35.00.

Global conferences proliferated during the last decade and were frequently dominated by North-South conflict. Such conferences will continue as a principal instrument of developing country diplomacy in addressing issues on energy, industrialization, technology, and debt. These conferences will present an important opportunity for US diplomacy to shape a reasonable accommodation with LDC demands and to strive for a cooperative approach to global problems. The risks of opting out are far greater than those of active participation and leadership. Yet, the US has often not been able to exploit multilateral diplomatic opportunities: positions taken at one conference have often contradicted those at others, bureaucratic competition and a general absence of policy have delayed the preconference articulation of US interests, and the US has embarassed itself by making commitments that were subsequently negated. The US approach to multilateral conferences has been further compromised by the attitudes that US interests cannot be promoted through such conferences, and that successful conference representation requires no special negotiating skills or accumulation of experience.

This handbook, prepared for the US Department of State, offers chapters on the context of US participation in global conferences (postures of various countries and regions), the structure and characteristics of global conferences, managing preparations for a conference, selecting and preparing members of US delegations, managing the delegation at the conference, negotiating problems and strategies, and managing the follow-up to the conference. A 60-page section of the book provides summaries of 13 selected global conferences: Conference on the Human Environment (Stockholm, 1972), World Population Conference (Bucharest, 1974), World Food Conference (Rome, 1974), the Law of the Sea Conferences, HABITAT (Vancouver, 1976), ILO World Employment Conference (Geneva, 1976), UN Water conference (Argentina, 1977), UN Conference on Desertification (Nairobi, 1977), UN Conference on Technical Cooperation among Developing Countries (Buenos Aires, 1978), UN Conference on Science and Technology for Development (Vienna, 1979), Conference on New and Renewable Sources of Energy (Nairobi, 1981), World Assembly on Aging (Vienna, 1982), and The Second UN Conference on the Exploration and Peaceful Uses of Outer Space (Vienna, 1982). Each summary describes the diplomatic setting, conference dynamics, key issues, influential participants, and conference results. Concludes

6508

The Expansion of International Society. Edited by Hedley Bull (U of Oxford) and Adam Watson (U of Virginia). NY: Oxford U Press, July 1984/480p/$39.95.

Describes the floodtide of European expansion that began in the 16th century and united the world into a single economic and political unit, the process whereby the non-European states came to take their place as members of the same society, the repudiation of outside domination by states and peoples of the Third World, and the new international society that has emerged. Concludes with a discussion of whether the geographical expansion of this society has led to a contraction of consensus about common interests, rules, and institutions.

(new international society)

6509

Democracy Must Work: A Trilateral Agenda for the Decade. David Owen (MP and former Labour Foreign Secretary), Zbigniew Brzezinski (Columbia U), and Saburo Okita (former Japanese Foreign Minister). A Task Force Report to the Trilateral Commission. Triangle Papers:28. NY: New York U Press (dist by Columbia U Press), July 1984/88p/$12.50.

A truly global world system is emerging, but dangers of a truly global dimension now confront mankind. If the world is to prosper, and if the democracies are to flourish,

the national governments—particularly of the main trilateral countries (the US, Japan, and Western Europe)—will have to take more account of the interdependence of their decision-making. Closer coordination of macroeconomic policies is called for along some of the lines attempted at the annual economic summits. A coordinated program can only be developed, though, if plans are laid for two or three summits in sequence. Economic coordination is by itself insufficient: it has to go wider and involve security issues. Such a comprehensive summit should henceforth be called Strategic or Policy Summits. [NOTE: For an alternative view from "The Other Economic Summit," see #6526.] This study analyzes the major challenges of the next decade, with chapters on employment and equity, interdependence and growth, and cooperation or fragmentation. Concludes by suggesting six critical tasks. Three call for action by particular trilateral countries or regions: reduction of the US budget deficit, larger international responsibilities for Japan, and European revitalization to cope with its technological backwardness and persistently high unemployment. Three require action by all: coordination of economic policies for sustained growth, a more equal sharing of defense costs, and coping with the international debt problem.

(trilateral tasks)

6510

The European Challenge: From Atlantic Alliance to Pan-European Entente for Peace and Jobs. Andre Gunder Frank (U of Amsterdam). Westport CT: Lawrence Hill & Co, 1984/104p/$6.95pb.

Examines the growing economic rivalry between the major Western powers, the need to avoid nuclear war, the disarray and discontent within the Atlantic Alliance, and political and economic problems in the Soviet Union and Eastern Europe. A solution for the problems of both East and West may be found in a pan-European alternative: an economic and political alliance between Western and Eastern Europe. Such a rapprochement could offer possibilities for a European denuclearized zone and open the way for world peace and a disarmament agreement. The US would then be liberated from a major basis of its all-consuming obsession with Soviet power and its supposed threat, and freed to shift its economic and political attention more to a Pacific Rim strategy. **(pan-European entente?)**

6511

Grave New World. Michael A. Ledeen (CSIS, Georgetown U). NY: Oxford U Press, April 1985/244p/$17.95.

The current international crisis has been made more perilous by the failure of the two superpowers to design and conduct intelligent and effective foreign policies. The increased risk of war in the world has resulted from a lack of control by the superpowers, stemming from their incoherence and unpredictability. The increasingly aggressive actions of the Kremlin stem from a structural crisis of great magnitude that has no obvious solution, at least in the immediate future; American social, political, and economic structures are solid enough, but there seems little chance that the national elite can design and conduct an effective foreign policy. Soviet policy is conducted seriously, but made against the background of internal crisis; American policy is conducted against the background of relative calm, but is not serious. The remedy for the Soviet malady is abandoning communism for a workable system. The remedy for the US is the creation of a policy elite that is better informed about the world and thus prepared to fight for our vital interests. Ledeen prefers a relatively aggressive US policy in support of the democratic revolution around the world, because it is in keeping with American traditions and most likely to strike at the evils and weaknesses in the Soviet system. [NOTE: For a completely opposite view, see below.] **(superpower incoherence)**

6512

Reason and Realpolitik: U.S. Foreign Policy and World Order. Louis René Beres (Prof of Political Science, Purdue U). Lexington MA: Lexington Books, 1984/143p/ $20.00;$9.95pb.

If the lessons of history teach us anything at all, they point to the futility of America's strategy of realpolitik—a strategy founded upon the very principles that have ensured the oblivion of other great states. We must recognize the false premises that continue to shape our search for a durable and just world peace. In making anti-Sovietism the centerpiece of its policy, the US has accepted an orientation to global affairs that is inherently self-defeating. During the next few years, the victims of US-supported repression throughout the world will begin to overthrow their oppressors, creating anti-American successor governments as in Vietnam and Cuba. This development would be avoidable if the US remained true to its doctrinal foundations, opposing all tyrannical regimes. The US must fashion its foreign policy on a new set of premises, consonant with the constraints of planetary conditions and national survival. American national interest must be defined from the standpoint of what is best for the world system as a whole. The new definition of national interest must do away with the ethic of social Darwinism. By supplanting competitive self-seeking with cooperative self-seeking, the US can move forward to the kind of global renaissance that is so desperately needed. The underlying point of contention between the superpowers is not ideological or economic, but a groundless rhetoric reinforced by self-serving elites, who may have more in common with each other than with their respective populations. The rivalry between the US and USSR is now essentially a contrivance of the elites and their defense community handmaidens, supporting each other while they undermine the security of both countries. **(US national interest redefined)**

6513

Our Own Worst Enemy: The Unmaking of American Foreign Policy. I. M. Destler (Institute for International Economics), Leslie H. Gelb (*New York Times*), and Anthony Lake (Amherst College).NY: Simon & Schuster, Aug 1984/ 319p/$17.95.

American society and government has been breaking down over the past 20 years, with Vietnam destroying an already crumbling policy consensus. Nothing has arisen to take its place, which accounts for the difficulties that the US now has in framing and sticking to a coherent global policy. Policy has become increasingly infused with politics, and the Reagan Administration has now put politics over policy. The twin American illusions of omnipotence and total responsibility for other nations raised people's expectations and tempted would-be Presidents to promise great international accomplishments at little risk and low cost.The new "professionals" have become polemicists, polarized by ideological differences and concerned more with defending the purity of their positions than with accommodating them to political reality. Compounding this difficulty is the fact that those who are in authority tend not to stay there for very long. Although impossible to resurrect the old foreign policy consensus, it is possible to restore the stabilizing functions of that consensus so

that there would be less of a tendency to swing from one policy extreme to another. This should be done by encourging a greater reliance upon career personnel. **(US foreign policy questioned)**

6514

Endless Enemies: The Making of an Unfriendly World. Jonathan Kwitney (*The Wall Street Journal*). NY: Congdon & Weed, Aug 1984/435p/$19.95.

No matter who has been in office over the past 30 years, America's efforts overseas have become more and more remote from the true interests of its people. US foreign policy has left the nation in constant peril of war with a seemingly unending list of enemies. The US makes enemies in the Third World by suppressing democracy and free enterprise as thoroughly as the Russians do.This is because the US foreign policy agencies—overt and covert— have chosen to see the globe as polarized by a contest between Communism and Americanism. The common pattern is one of a shallow intellectual approach to the diversity of societies and cultures, the momentum of covert action (which increases to justify its existence), and the greed of local leaders and foreign businessmen who take immoderate profits from Third World economies, paving the way for governments that are antithetical to capitalism and democracy. **(US foreign policy questioned)**

6515

Roots of Failure: United States Policy in the Third World. Melvin Gurtov (U of California-Riverside) and Ray Maghroori. Westport CT: Greenwood Press, Dec 1984/ 224p/$27.95.

The expansion of international influence through military or political intervention is a central objective of US policy, particularly with regard to the Third World. The overriding negative costs of US foreign policy "successes" suggest the need to develop alternative foreign policy goals that will take human needs and the well-being of the entire planet into account. Continuing a policy of confrontation with some Third World governments and fragile partnerships with others undermines America's national interests and threatens global security.

(US foreign policy questioned)

6516

To Promote Peace: U.S. Foreign Policy in the Mid-1980s. Edited by Dennis L. Bark (Hoover Institution). Stanford CA: Hoover Institution Press (Publication 294), 1984/298p/$19.95.

Companion of **To Promote Prosperity** (#6828) and a follow-on to **The United States in the 1980s** (Hoover, 1980/868p; **FS Annual 1980-81**, #2232), designed as background for a Republican administration. In this volume, Melvyn Krauss argues that the transfer of income from the have to the have-less countries is no substitute for economic growth; Alain Besancon and L. H. Gann warn that differences between what totalitarian regimes say and what they do warrant careful attention and that the church must recognize this point to retain its credibility on the peace issue; Ronald I. McKinnon proposes new standards to prevent sudden fluctuations in monetary exchange rates; Edward Teller advocates increased development of coal and nuclear-generated electricity; L.H. Gann scolds the peace movement for possibly threatening peace because of its destabilizing effect on the will to maintain a credible defense; Melvyn Krauss asserts that "defense free-riding" by the Japanese and West Europeans is no longer justifiable; Robert Wesson encourages reforging the community of the Americas; Ramon H. Myers analyzes the principal economic and political problems that threaten to destabilize the Pacific Basin's current prosperity; Peter J. Duignan urges the US to foster self-reliant economic development in Africa and to contain Soviet aggression; H. Joachim Maitre warns that the USSR is moving closer to its objective of removing the US military presence from Western Europe and establishing hegemony over the entire continent; William R. Van Cleave criticizes Reagan Administration opponents who reject increased defense spending to keep pace with continually expanding Soviet military power, and Arnold Beichman stresses the need to rebuild the US intelligence system. [NOTE:It is not made clear how these ideas serve "to promote peace," for they are based on quite different premises than the many books and articles that give serious attention to the problems of promoting peace (e.g., see below). Nevertheless, these essays deserve close consideration, because this is the type of worldview likely to influence the Reagan Administration.]   (**Hoover Institution on attaining peace**)

6517

We Need a New Relationship With the Russians, Richard M. Nixon, *The Washington Post*, Sunday, 13 May 1984, C8.

How can the US make progress in building peace in the world? The super hawks point out that the Soviets lie, cheat, and are out to do us in, and that our only policy is to build up military superiority and squeeze them economically. The super doves say that the Soviets arm because we do, and we can only convince them that we are for peace by reducing our armaments—but, as we cut back on our weapons systems in the late 1970s, they increased theirs. Instead of these two extreme views, we must convince the Soviets that they cannot win a war, and that the rewards of peace are infinitely greater. Russians and Americans can be friends, but the governments of the US and the USSR can never be friends. However, we cannot afford to be enemies. The most and the least we can hope to do is to develop a process in which we negotiate our differences and resolve them where possible. There are four basic pillars in building this detente (or peaceful competition or cold peace). 1) military power: it is vital that the US restore the military balance of power; 2) economic power: trade in nonstrategic items as a tool to implement foreign policy; 3) hardheaded diplomacy: revive the practice of annual summits between the leaders of the US and USSR, and set up an agreement on rules of engagement which will prevent our differences from exploding into war; 4) ideological power: making it clear to the people of the Third World that we are for a better way in which they can progress toward a better life.

(**Nixon's four pillars of peaceful competition**)

6518

Why Trust the Soviets? Richard J. Barnet (Institute for Policy Studies), *World Policy Journal* (World Policy Institute, NYC), 1:3, Spring 1984, 461-482.

A lack of trust between the superpowers has been both a cause and a consequence of the serious deterioration in US-Soviet relations. The question we should ask is not "Can we trust the Russians?" but "In what way is it prudent for us to trust them, for what, and how far?" The security of the US cannot be improved by inducing greater insecurity and mistrust in the USSR, and vice versa. The following actions are proposed to encourage greater trust: 1) the US should renounce the illusions about nuclear weapons that have guided its national strategic planning; 2) the US should make it unmistakably clear that the Soviet Union is and will be treated as a legitimate superpower with rights and responsibilities commensurate with those of the US; 3) each superpower must convince the other that the avoidance of nuclear war is its principal goal, and that its strategy for accomplishing this is to reduce the military threat to the other; 4) the superpowers should agree to acquire no new foreign military bases and to initiate a process of withdrawal from bases that they presently occupy (most US bases ringing the Soviet Union were acquired before the era of transcontinental bombers and missiles); 5) both superpowers should unilaterally halt arms shipments to governments fighting nationalist insurgencies, and take other steps to demilitarize the Third World; 6) the superpowers should spell out a set of shared objectives and a framework within which individual agreements can be reached. Concludes that fundamental changes in public attitude, along with the increasingly unmanageable technological and economic demands of the arms race, are clearing the way for a bold initiative. An historic transformation in US-Soviet relations is now possible; nothing less can lift the lengthening shadow of nuclear war. [Also see **Deadly Gambits: The Reagan Administration and the Stalemate in Nuclear Arms Control** by Strobe Talbot of *Time* magazine (NY: Knopf, Oct 1984/380p/$17.95), who chronicles the recent breakdown of US-Soviet relations.]

(**building trust in US-Soviet relations**)

6519

US/USSR Bi-National Research Park in the Bering Strait, Walter Orr Roberts (President Emeritus, University Corporation for Atmospheric Research), *Co-Evolution Quarterly*, No 43, Fall 1984, p70.

Proposes that the US and Soviets designate as a research preserve the region of about 175 x 110 miles centered on the Bering Strait and extending about 50 miles inland on both continents. Within the zone, joint research could be conducted on environmental, atmospheric, oceanographic, and anthropological aspects of this unique region. Doing so would have great symbolic power, while offering no national security hazards for either nation.

(**US-Soviet research park?**)

6520

Peace With China—and U.S.S.R., John Marks (Search for Common Ground, Washington) and David Landau, *The Los Angeles Times,* Tuesday, 1 May 1984, Part II.

The obstacles to a fundamental shift in Soviet-American relations are formidable. Yet, in 1971-72 a "paradigm shift" took place in relations of the US and China: the shifting was not so much Chinese behavior as the prism through which Americans viewed China. If the US and China have come so far, could not the Americans and Soviets do the same? Soviet and American leaders would seem to be no more or less prisoners of their own ideologies than were the Americans and the Chinese. The Chinese-American shift could provide a model for how two dedicated foes can alter the very fabric of relations.

(**peace with China as model**)

II. INTERNATIONAL ECONOMICS

A. The World Economy

6521

World Development Report 1984. The World Bank. NY: Oxford U Press, July 1984/286p (8x11")/ $20.00; $8.00pb. [24p Summary free from World Bank Publications, Box 37525, Washington DC 20013.]

Seventh in an annual series examining economic and population policy. Part I on economic performance concludes that the 1980-83 recession was not an isolated event, but relates to rigidities steadily built into economies from the mid-1960s onward, e.g. inflexible arrangements for setting wages and prices, and for managing public finances. Two basic scenarios are presented for the world economy in 1985-1995: 1) The Low Case, in which nothing is done to improve economic performance: GDP growth averages 2.5% per year in the industrial countries and 4.7% per year in developing countries; 2) The High Case, where GDP growth averages 4.3% per year in the industrial countries and 5.5% a year in developing countries. [NOTE: No recession or collapse is considered: is the Low Case unreasonably high?]. Part II on population emphasizes three themes: rapid population growth is a development problem, there are appropriate public policies to reduce fertility, and policy does make a difference. The evidence seems conclusive that poverty and rapid population growth reinforce each other. [Also see **World Economic Survey 1984: Current Trends and Policies in the World Economy**, prepared by the UN Dept of International Economic and Social Affairs (NY: United Nations Publications, 1984/109p [8x11"]/$11.00), which assesses trends in world economic conditions, international trade and payments, and growth in the world economy.]   (**world economic surveys**)

6522

World Economic Growth: Case Studies of Developed and Developing Nations. Edited by Arnold C. Harberger (Distinguished Service Professor, U of Chicago). San Francisco CA: ICS Press (Institute for Contemporary Studies), Dec 1984/508p/$22.95;$9.95pb.

Twelve studies of individual countries, addressing the question of whether "good" economic policy can be associated with "good" economic results. Developed countries studied include Britain, Japan, Sweden, West Germany, and the US. Developing countries studied include Tanzania, Ghana, Indonesia, Jamaica, Taiwan, Mexico, and Uruguay. Concludes with some principal "lessons" associated with successful growth policy: 1) avoid false technicism in economic policymaking (in too many countries, the task of economic planning has been conceived as that of making projections of future progress, thus distracting people from attacking real policy problems); 2) keep budgets and inflationary pressures under reasonable control; 3) take advantage of international trade; 4) make tax systems simple, easy to administer, and as neutral as possible (the best tax for accomplishing these purposes is the value-added tax, which has come to be the most important source of revenue in close to half the non-Communist world); 5) avoid excessive income tax rates, which distort behavior and create large disincentives to economic activity while yielding little revenue; 6) avoid excessive use of tax incentives to achieve particular objectives. [NOTE: The spirit of this book is much like that which seeks to identify "good" or "effective" schools (#7076) and "excellent" corporations (**FS Annual 1984**, #6463).]

(**successful growth policy**)

6523

Worlds Apart: Technology and North-South Relations in the Global Economy. Sam Cole (Dept of Environmental Design and Planning, SUNY-Buffalo) and Ian Miles (Science Policy Research Unit, U of Sussex). Brighton UK: Harvester Press/Wheatsheaf Books and Totowa NJ: Rowman & Allanheld, Oct 1984/283p/$18.95. [Brief version, **Development, Distribution and the Future**, in *Futures*, 16:5, Oct 1984, 471-493.]

Explores four alternative strategies for global development, their implications for national and international distribution of income in the early 21st century, and the trade-offs demanded of different actors in the world system. 1) The Status Quo view, supported by the stronger OECD countries, the Trilateral Commission, and international banks: advocates an extended international division of labor and new technologies as central to a revitalized world economy. 2) The New International Economic Order proposals, favored by many Third World countries: view the present crisis to be of great magnitude, requiring a series of international mechanisms to reduce instabilities in the system and ensure that world markets operate fairly. 3) Collective Self-Reliance, favored by a few Third World governments and individuals in political parties and in international organizations: questions whether industrial countries would agree to a NIEO, and looks for a more independent development path by Southern countries as a whole. 4) Human Needs Orientation: restructure international links to further national domestic basic needs requirements; structure production systems so that a more equitable distribution is achieved through the market, providing a basis for long-term sustained growth. These strategies are synthesized with a computer model and a scenario describing a possible future history of world development up to 2020, where a sequence of policies is implemented with different degrees of success. Concludes that a global human needs strategy could abolish the worst extremes of poverty and substantially reduce global inequalities. But such a strategy is unlikely to be implemented in the foreseeable future without large-scale change in international relations and attitudes. [NOTE: Rather technical, and worlds apart from other analyses both in style and substance.]   (**four global development alternatives**)

6524

World Financial Curbs Eased By Technology and Ideology, Nicholas D. Kristof, *The New York Times*, Sat, 26 Jan 1985, p1.

A wave of financial deregulation is sweeping business centers worldwide, spurred by a spreading free market ideology and by advances in microprocessing and satellite communications that make it possible to access markets all over the world. Interest rates are being freed from government regulation. Withholding taxes are being eliminated on the foreign purchase of domestic securities. Domestic financial markets are being opened to foreigners. Financial institutions are being allowed to enter new businesses. (One analyst foresees the emergence of "world-class financial institutions" over the next ten years, with headquarters in three or four cities.) As these changes gather momentum, they are eroding economic boundaries and providing new opportunities for international investment, but also frustrating national economic policies. Deregulation has pushed interest rates higher for Latin American countries, and made it more difficult for industrialized countries to control their money supply. Among the beneficiaries of deregulation are corporations, which are now able to raise money more flexibly and probably more cheaply. **(world financial deregulation)**

6525

The Age of Interdependence: Economic Policy in a Shrinking World. Michael Stewart (Reader in Political Economy, University College, London). Cambridge MA: MIT Press, March 1984/192p/$15.00.

Governments make macroeconomic decisions in a myopic way, looking at the effects of their decisions only on their own country and only two or three years ahead. Stewart explores the growth of interdependence in the world economy over the past 10 to 15 years, the deflationary bias in the working of the world economy as a whole, and the two basic strategies to avoid this bias: the de-linking of countries from each other by imposing import and exchange controls, or closer coordination of macroeconomic policies. A strategy of de-linking is not consistent with the extensive international cooperation that will be needed to deal with environmental problems. Concludes that if the seven OECD countries represented at the periodic economic summits can agree on coordinated policies of expansion, the rest of the world will be pulled along in their wake. **(macroeconomic coordination needed)**

6526

The Other Economic Summit: Report and Summary. London: TOES (42 Warriner Gardens), 1984/40p/$3.50. [Additional copies $1.00 each; Conference Papers, $15.00. Distributed in US by Intermediate Technology Development Group, Box 337, Croton-on-Hudson, NY 10520.]

The TOES conference was held in London in June 1984 to highlight the irrelevance of the Economic Summit held by the seven major developed countries (see #6509 on Trilateral Commission ideas for future summits). The conference was convened to promote the view that economic growth, as conventionally understood, is no longer a dependable policy option. Real growth is now proving elusive, and only seems attainable at the cost of huge indebtedness. Such growth is also proving to be jobless growth, and it makes no attempt to address the problems of resource depletion, environmental deterioration, and the misallocated expenditure on the arms race. The conference papers include Manfred Max-Neef on human needs and their satisfiers, James Robertson on the redefinition of work and employment, Anne Miller on a Basic Income Guarantee scheme to weaken the link between employment and income distribution, Guy Dauncey on the regeneration of local economies, Jeremy Seabrook on the market creation of dependency and its counterfeiting of human needs, David Fleming on a New Mixed Economy that combines both formal and informal economies, Ward Morehouse on a General Stock Ownership Plan to achieve a basic income for all, Willis Harman on the new corporate role of thinking beyond the bottom line, Anila Graham on broad directions for world development (involving reform of international financial institutions, the new concept of collective self-reliance among LDCs, and a new framework for trade), Her-

man Daly on how the pursuit of economic growth is economically and environmenally unsound, Ken Penney on increasing local economic self-reliance, and Fred Harrison on land value taxation to end land speculation and increase public access to land. TOES plans additional annual conferences to serve as a shadow to the Economic Summits. In sum, it seeks to promote a New Economics based on personal development and social justice, satisfaction of the whole range of human needs, sustainable use of resources, and conservation of the environment.

(The Other Economic Summit)

6527

International Political Economy Yearbook. Volume 1: **An International Political Economy**. Edited by W. Ladd Hollist and F. LaMond Tullis (both Brigham Young U). Boulder CO: Westview, Dec 1984/ c250p/ $30.00; $12.95pb.

Essays on alternative perspectives for conceptualizing the global political economy, historical development of the global political economy, the state in advanced market economies, class relations, the politics of commodity trade, alternative views of the political economy of transnational corporations, the politics of money and international debt, the global crisis of hunger, and the future of the field of international political economics.

(world political economy)

6528

Triad Power: The Coming Shape of Global Competition. Kenichi Ohmae (Managing Director, McKinsey & Co-Tokyo). NY: Free Press, April 1985/220p/$19.95.

The pace of technological changes is exploding. With Japan's emergence as an industrial power, the combined GNP of Japan and the US accounts for 30% of the Free World's total. The figure reaches 45% by adding the four key countries of the European Community (UK, West Germany, France, and Italy). Global enterprises established mainly in the 1960s are now faced with discrepancies between their traditional approach and these new realities. Ohmae challenges the one-world concept of the multinationals and focuses on cross-cultural alliances. Capturing markets in all three parts of the Triad is often the only way to achieve the economies of scale world-class automated plants demand in order to pay for themselves. There is an emergence of the Triadians or OECDites, with cross-national similarities in basic demand patterns, especially among the younger generation. But despite consumers' loss of national identity in the OECD countries, protectionist pressures are mounting. This necessitates that any global enterprise must become a true insider, or honorary citizen, in each of the Triad regions.

(new global competition)

6529

The U.S. and the World Economy: Policy Alternatives for New Realities. Edited by John Yochelson (CSIS, Georgetown U). Boulder CO: Westview, Nov 1984/c120p/ $12.95.

Essays on structural change in the US economy, the US and new technological competition, trade policy in the 1980s, linkages between trade and foreign policy, exchange-rate disequilibrium, Third World debt, and the role of the private sector. **(US and world economy)**

6530

The Global Repercussions of U.S. Monetary and Fiscal Policy. Edited by Sylvia A. Hewlett, Henry Kaufman, and Peter B. Kenen. Sponsored by the Economic Policy Council of the United Nations. Cambridge MA: Ballinger Publishing Co, Oct 1984/c270p/$25.00.

Bankers, labor leaders, economists, and industrialists urge the US to formulate policy outside of a "domestic vacuum," and offer new insights into how domestic divisions and massive global problems can be minimized through better policies. Contents focus on US stabilization policies in an international context, linkage effects, international indebtedness, exchange rate regimes, monetary targeting, trade implications of US monetary and fiscal policy, new factors in the world economy in the wake of the debt crisis, and the economic policy mix in an evolving economy.   (**US monetary and fiscal policy**)

6531

Automate, Emigrate, or Evaporate: America's Choices in the Global Economy, Charles McMillion (Industrial Policy & Employment Project, US House of Representatives Small Business Committee), *The Futurist*, 19:2, April 1985, 45-47.

The global economy has undermined the assumption of a closed economy, or at least an economy immune to external disruption. With its open economy, additional demand in the US does not require additional production in the US. The American lifestyle makes it a wonderful place to live and to sell goods and services, but the US has an extremely uncompetitive economic structure in which to employ workers and to produce. The costs of maintaining health and safety standards and environmental protection laws add to the costs of employment. The US can successfully compete in the global economy only when it regains a substantial lead in productivity. One approach to encouraging this improvement would be an Extension Service for Productivity, a central service for the broad dissemination of information modeled after the Agricultural Extension Service.   (**US need to improve productivity**)

6532

The Great Depression, 1929-1938: Lessons for the 1980s. Christian Saint-Etienne (OECD). Stanford CA: Hoover Institution Press, 1984/134p/$19.95.

New studies have appeared in the last 20 years attempting to explain some of the policy mistakes during the Great Depression. Saint-Etienne draws on these sources in arguing that the Great Depression did not result from a combination of apocalyptic forces, but from ineptitude, demogoguery, and lack of courage in political decision-making. Technical expertise has now replaced the ineptitude of the 1930s, but the difficult questions of the modern period are not being addressed. Three general conclusions follow from this study: there is a need for pervasive adjustment in reducing deficits, Third World nations need something on the scope of a Marshall Plan for their development needs, and the good times are over. Three conditions are necessary for future growth: protectionism cannot be allowed, the international banking system must be reformed, and the monetary policies of the major industrial countries must be coordinated.   (**lessons from Great Depression**)

6533

A Monetary System for the Future, Richard N. Cooper (Prof of International Economics, Harvard U), *Foreign Affairs*, 63:1, Fall 1984, 166-184.

A new Bretton Woods conference is wholly premature, but it is not premature to begin thinking about how we would like international monetary arrangements to evolve. By 2010, the world will be very electronic. Reliable, high-speed, and low-cost communications over the globe will permit management control of production in many places. Lower transportation costs will encourage trade. But real movements in exchange rates will be highly disruptive of profits, production, and employment in any particular location. If we are to preserve an open trading and financial system, we will need a system of credibly fixed exchange rates. Rates can be most credibly fixed if they are eliminated altogether by use of a single currency. Cooper proposes the creation of a common currency for all of the industrial democracies, with a common monetary policy and a joint Bank of Issue to determine the monetary policy. Free trade would be a natural but not entirely necessary complement to these macroeconomic arrangements. This scheme is far too radical for the near future, but some such scheme will be necessary 25 years from now. A single world money is not feasible, though, because it is highly doubtful that democratic countries could ever allow autocratic regimes to vote on monetary policy. Moreover, negotiating a single currency for all may be impossible. It would be relatively easier to begin with a common currency for the US, Japan, and members of the European Community. Other democracies would be free to join, but none would be obliged to do so. Such an arrangement would be of value even to nonmembers, by providing a stable monetary environment against which to frame their economic policies.

(**common currency for US, Japan, & EC?**)

6534

The Past as Prologue: Prospects for a New Bretton Woods, Joanne Gowa (Dept of Political Science, U of Pennsylvania), *Orbis*, 28:2, Summer 1984, 329-339.

Appeals for a fundamental reform of the international monetary system, comparable to that accomplished in 1944 at Bretton Woods NH, are no surprise. Given the difficult decade that followed the collapse of the Bretton Woods system in the early 1970s, it is understandable that policymakers might seek to resurrect a system like the previous one, or at least to organize a conference that might lead to such a system. But such attempts have little prospect of succeeding: 1) the 1944 conference rested on a constellation of international power that has long since vanished; 2) the Bretton Woods regime itself, although laboriously negotiated, proved to be much more mythical than real; 3) grand international conferences seeking to reform the international monetary system have a poor track record: the successful conference of 1944 was preceded by two failures and followed by two failures and one meeting of marginal importance; 4) the inability of negotiators in the past to anticipate economic developments of central importance to their negotiations suggests a large element of irreducible uncertainty. There are, however, a variety of low profile but useful arenas for discussing and occasionally resolving problems of monetary relations, e.g. the Bank of International Settlements, the executive board of the IMF, and meetings of officials from OECD finance ministries. Reliance on these less formal arenas may be optimal for present times and problems.

(**global monetary conference a poor prospect**)

B. Debt Crises

6535

Debt Crisis Is Waning In Developing Nations, But It May Hit Again, S. Karene Witcher, *The Wall Street Journal*, Tuesday, 26 March 1985, p1.

Many developing countries are growing again, and many bankers now view the international debt crisis as less threatening. But the respite from the cliffhanging days of 1982 and 1983 may prove brief. Many economists argue, and some bankers privately agree, that major problems could abruptly resurface. Experts expect 1985 to be relatively quiet, but some think that the financial problems of developing countries, including Mexico and Brazil, may worsen in 1986. By then, it will be obvious that many Third World countries cannot fuel strong economic growth and handle debt payments simultaneously. Their inability to do both at once may reignite the political and financial tensions of the early 1980s. If the governments of debt-burdened countries pay the banks and further slash living standards, their political stability could be threatened, and they might be replaced by authoritarian regimes. Many economists expect Latin American exports to slow, especially if the US economy slows down. Protectionism against Latin American goods is growing in industrialized countries. And if US interest rates rise, Latin American debt costs will surge. **(debt crisis in 1986?)**

6536

Third World Debt: The Bomb Is Defused, Gary Hector, *Fortune*, 18 Feb 1985, 36-50.

Evidence is building that the international debt crisis is over. The largest debtor countries, notably Mexico and Brazil, have made stunning economic progress in the past year, posting strong real growth and large trade surpluses. With Mexico leading the way, the debtor countries and their lenders are working out realistic long-term schedules for repaying the huge loans. Still, a feeling of hard times pervades the major Latin American countries. A jump in interest rates, a drop in commodity prices, or a sudden slowdown in the world economy could bring fresh setbacks. But while a year ago it seemed that the problems of a single large country might spark an international financial calamity, the danger now appears remote. Officials at banks, international agencies, and government finance ministries are now confident they can anticipate and avert new crises. **(debt crisis over?)**

6537

The Debt Crisis: Why System-Wide Reform Is Critical, George Soros (Soros Fund Management, NYC), *The New York Times*, Sunday, 19 Aug 1984, F2.

The ability of the debtor nations to service their debt has improved, but their willingness to do so has become increasingly doubtful. A transformation is occurring in the relative bargaining position of lenders and borrowers. The debtor countries have built up their currency reserves, while the position of the banks has been eroding. Incentives to expand bank credit are stronger than ever, and volume has become increasingly important to reduce the proportion of doubtful loans. The seeds of a recession in 1985 are now being planted, and unless something is done the credit system will run out of control. A new international lending institution can and should be formed to take over the collective lending function from the banks. If such a systemic reform is not implemented, we are headed for major problems in the world banking system.
(new international lending bank needed)

6538

On the Consequences of Muddling Through the Debt Crisis, Rudiger Dornbusch (Prof of Economics, MIT), *The World Economy*, 7:2, June 1984, 145-161.

Bankers and policymakers have discouraged thinking about global solutions to the debt crisis. But muddling through is poor policy because, in the near-term, it does not return the debtor economies to reasonably functioning market-oriented economies. Instead, it has created siege economies. The only constructive alternative is for governments of developed countries to remove barriers to imports, and for banks to write down some debts on interest or principal. This course is essential because there is no prospect in the next 5 or 10 years of a resumption in private resource transfers to developing countries. The only significant growth that LDCs can achieve while servicing their debts must come from export growth and import substitution. **(LDC debt crisis)**

6539

Politics and Economics of External Debt Crisis: The Latin American Experience. Edited by Miguel S. Wionczek (El Colegio de Mexico). Boulder CO: Westview, March 1985/c375p/$37.50.

Essays by Latin American experts on the Latin American debt experience and difficulties from the viewpoint of the borrowers. Topics include the world crisis and the outlook for Latin America, capital market financing to developing countries, the world monetary system and the international business cycle, and case studies of Argentina, Brazil, Mexico, Venezuela, Chile, Peru, and Central America.
(Latin American debt)

6540

The Debt Crisis, John McClaughry (Institute for Liberty and Community, Concord VT), *Resurgence*, No 107, Nov-Dec 1984, 33-34.

Former Senior Policy Advisor to President Reagan warns that the world of international finance is moving steadily toward major calamity, and the great bulk of the coming economic pain will be generously distributed among those who had nothing to do with causing the problem: the common people. All of us are likely victims of the coming economic debacle, caused by overgrown economic institutions, collaborating with overgrown national governments in the exercise of special privilege, pursuing narrowly defined economic goals that exclude the well-being of humanity, and subsidizing waste and incompetence instead of investing in thrift and industry. To counter this threat to their economic security, the common people of the West should: 1) prevent government bailouts of big banks, and stop schemes to transfer near-worthless Third World loans from the banks to the taxpayers; 2) insist that Western aid to the Third World be channeled through nongovernmental people-to-people organizations which aim to improve the economic prospects of villagers; 3) take steps to protect themselves against the probable destruction of official currencies by creating alternative currencies that can retain their worth as the value of the dollar, pound, and franc sink out of sight. In the long run, sound local economies, where local people, businesses, and financial institutions produce things of real value to people, will prove to be the salvation of humanity.

(debt crisis and the common people)

6541

Can the Debt Bomb Be Defused? André Gunder Frank (Prof of Development Economics, U of Amsterdam), *World Policy Journal* (World Policy Institute, NYC), 1:4, Summer 1984, 723-743.

The worst of the world economic crisis that began in the mid-1960s may yet lie ahead: the looming possibility of a major financial collapse which could aggravate, if not initiate, a severe worldwide Depression. The conditions that could bring about a financial crash in the 1980s were created by the apparent solution to the economic crisis of the 1970s: a constant stream of credit extended to consumers, corporations, and governments, as well as Third World countries. This debt economy has helped to sustain the world economy. But it has also produced a debt bomb whose fuse grows shorter and shorter. Some $800 billion of Third World debt overhangs the world's financial system, threatening to cause the collapse of an even larger amount of consumer, corporate, and government debt.

Perhaps the only saving grace for policymakers is that it probably matters little, if at all, what policy they now decide to pursue. For it is almost certain that no matter what they do, a new recession will come sooner or later, influencing events much more strongly than any policy. There have been over 40 recessions since the beginning of industrial capitalism around 1800, and four recessions since the beginning of the present world economic crisis in the mid-1960s. Economic policy did not significantly modify—let alone prevent—any of these recessions. But all of them affected economic policy. No responsible and informed analyst now doubts that another recession will come. The question is when, and with what force and consequences. This next recession is more ominous than previous recessions because it threatens to detonate the Third World debt bomb. It is also likely to explode the consumer credit, corporate, and government debt bombs, which are receiving much less attention than their dangers merit. Such a course of events is made all the more likely by the bunching of debt maturity in the mid-1980s. The fuse of the debt bomb is about as long as the present economic recovery, which will end in 1985, 1986, or sometime thereafter. With the advent of the next recession, the present liquidity crisis in the Third World will quickly turn into a solvency crisis. When it becomes impossible for Third World countries to service their debt, there will be a moratorium or default. Such a failure to pay may be the first domino leading to an uncontrolled chain of bank failures and a financial crash. At that point, payment stops will become a matter of policy as everyone rushes in to save his or her skin. In the North and the South, it seems difficult if not impossible to find a way of translating everyone's long-run common interest in avoiding this debacle into some short-run action. [NOTE: Frank chides William R. Cline of the Institute for International Economics for a 1983 worst case forecast of 1.3% growth in the world economy, when it is quite possible that a new recession could bring negative growth rates. If this evokes complaint, consider the World Bank's "Low Case" of 2.7% growth in the industrial countries and 4.7% in the developing countries over the next ten years (#6521). Or see #6806 below for a cautiously exuberant view. Are huge chunks of reality being ignored by some analysts?]

(debt bomb set off by likely recession?)

6542

The Second Debt Crisis Is Coming, C. Fred Bergsten (Director, Institute for International Economics), *Challenge*, 28:2, May-June 1985. (Also in *Vital Speeches*, 51:12, 1 April 1985, 358-363.)

In the world recession of the early 1980s, real interest rates soared and global demand tumbled, resulting in the LDC debt crisis. The lasting effects of this close brush with systemic disaster cannot yet be compiled, although many LDCs have already suffered a "lost decade" without any growth in per capita consumption or worse. The international position of the US is now developing in an ominous way, both qualitatively and quantitatively, similar to that of the developing countries during 1973-82. The US current-account deficit in 1984—about $100 billion—was virtually identical to the current-account deficit of all LDCs in 1981, the year before the crisis broke. By the end of 1985, the US will be the largest debtor country in the world, substantially exceeding the current leaders, Brazil and Mexico. By 1989, US debt could exceed the total external debt of all LDCs ($1 trillion), and rise by $300 billion or so annually thereafter.

Virtually all economic analysis concludes that the US dollar is overvalued by about 40% in terms of the underlying competitive position of the economy. This effectively taxes all US exports by 40%, and subsidizes all imports by a like amount. The losses in America's competitiveness extend even to its most efficient industries, including agriculture and computers. The dollar overvaluation is leading to protectionism; indeed, the Reagan Administration has adopted more import controls than any since the 1920s. Continuing erosion of the trading system seems likely, with resort to additional restrictions on a sector-by-sector basis as the pressures become unbearable at the industry level. About half the major economic forecasters foresee a new recession in the US by 1986, and the other half expect a significant slowdown. If the US dollar is anywhere near current levels when the next recession hits and unemployment moves up once again, the stage will be set for a potentially enormous disruption of world trade.

What is to be done? The main requirement is for the US to initiate a sizable, credible, and sustained program to reduce its budget deficits by about $150 billion annually by 1988. This should include a slowdown in the defense buildup, further cuts in middle-class entitlement programs, and consumption-oriented tax increases. There should also be an orderly movement toward lower exchange rates for the dollar and a substantial change in Administration policy, which seems to like the strong dollar because it finances the budget deficit and implies international confidence in economic policies. Concludes with the hope that the US will perceive the risk in time and take effective action to preempt it. "The fire brigade may not have enough water to douse this one once it ignites."

(US as world's largest debtor)

6543

America's Growing International Debt, Richard Drobnick (Center for Futures Research, USC), *The Futurist*, 18:6, Dec 1984, 18-20.

By the end of 1985, if not sooner, the US will probably become the world's largest net user of foreign savings, as a result of foreign deposits in US banks, purchase of US stocks and bonds, and direct investments in factories and real estate. The dangers in this situation are that the large trade deficits accompanying America's capital importer status result in a high loss of profits and jobs in trade-sensitive US industries. The flow of investment capital to the

US will retard economic growth and job formation in Europe and the LDCs, probably initiating a vicious circle of political instability and more capital flight to the US. By becoming a debtor, the US is mortgaging its future. At some point there will be flight from dollars by foreign and domestic investors, requiring a steep depreciation, a rise in interest rates, or exchange controls.

(US as world's largest debtor)

6544

Deficits and the Dollar: The World Economy at Risk. Stephen Marris (Institute for International Economics). Cambridge MA: MIT Press, Jan 1985/120p/$6.00pb.

The large US budget and trade deficits are of major concern both in America and around the world. Marris argues that they cannot be sustained, and examines how to get the US and the world as a whole back into equilibrium. Major changes in the mix of fiscal and monetary policies in the US and other industrial countries are essential to avoid another global recession and a new debt crisis. A cooperative policy response by America and its partners is suggested, in order to avoid such a crisis. Suggestions are also made on how to respond to a crisis if it does occur, in a way that can lead to a more stable international monetary system. **(US deficit and world economy)**

6545

The Next Four Years: The U.S. and the World Economy. William D. Eberle, Richard N. Gardner, and Ann Crittenden. NY: Aspen Institute for Humanistic Studies, 1984/17p/$3.00. (Available from Aspen Institute Publications, Box 150, Queenstown MD 21658.)

The next four years present unprecedented challenges of economic policy-making. The way in which the Reagan Administration handles these challenges will affect the world economy for years to come, in that the US is at the center of the international economic system. The essential first step in dealing with any of these issues is the need to produce a bipartisan deficit reduction package. The reduction of the US deficit is a prerequisite for restoring order to an international financial climate increasingly characterized by fragmentation and drift. The unprecedented US deficits reflect a combination of the significant tax reduction of 1981, the explosion in defense spending, the dramatic rise in debt interest payments, and automatic increases in Congressionally-mandated social programs. Payments on debt interest, defense, and mandated entitlements now account for more than 80% of the Federal budget. By fiscal 1989, according to CBO projections, these three items will exceed revenues by $64 billion—we will thus have a deficit even if we eliminate the entire apparatus of national civilian government. These figures reflect a nation living beyond its means and failing to build for its future. The US budget deficit has serious international ramifications because it is being financed by huge capital flows from abroad—money which is needed to help revive the sagging economies of Western Europe and the Third World. Concludes with two proposals for improved inter- and intra-national coordination: 1) some forum where problems of exchange rates, trade, debt, and development can be discussed and negotiated among nations (e.g., a revitalized summit process); 2) some new mechanism in the US government to integrate economic decision-making, so that domestic economic management, trade policy, and international debt and development policy are all shaped in harmony. For too long, US economic policy has been made as if the rest of the world did not exist; the US no longer has the luxury to entertain this illusion.

(US deficit a global threat)

6546

The Superdollar (Cover Story), *Business Week*, 8 Oct 1984, 164-174.

The world has not lived with a superdollar since the 1950s, when the US dominated the world economy. Although the rest of the world has caught up with the US in ability to produce goods, America rules once again because it is the mecca for investment capital. The world is again moving to a dollar standard, and the new era of dollar hegemony is reshaping the world economy. Because the dollar is so strong, relatively low inflation in the US will probably continue for years. In Europe, capital will be difficult to attract, making it hard to modernize inefficient industries. In Japan, high export-led growth will continue unless halted by protectionism. In the Third World, the oppressive burden of debt will continue. Treasury Secretary Regan predicts that it is very probable that the dollar will remain strong through the rest of the decade. The superdollar will not necessarily lead to ever-expanding trade deficits because it is attracting foreign investment into US plant and equipment, which will make the US more competitive.

(competitiveness enhanced by US dollar)

C. Trade

6547

Tinderbox for Trade (Two Parts), Charles A. Cerami, *The New York Times*, Sunday, 13 Jan 1985, F3, and Sunday, 20 Jan 1985, F3.

Two articles by the director of a trade study being conducted at the Atlantic Council of the United States. *The Looming Worldwide Job Shortage* (13 Jan) warns that the underlying global trend is for more and more persons to compete for a scanty supply of jobs. No nation has yet to recognize how the jobless hordes are building to a "critical mass" that could be harder to control than any nuclear arsenal. Much economic policy is based on the desperate hope that some technological breakthrough will somehow develop another wave of job opportunities. But it is more likely that today's wave of technology will lead to permanently higher unemployment. The world economy could, however, be reinvigorated with sufficient exertion on the part of a few major governments by a new concept of global economic growth and world trade expansion.

We Need a Marshall Plan for the 80's (20 Jan) argues that the answer to shrinking world markets is a 1980's version of the Marshall Plan, in which billions of private investment dollars and government credit is channeled to the Third World for building new enterprises and wealth. A new international conference on trade should convene with the long-range aim of pursuing growth on three fronts: 1) developing countries must get firm assurance of steady access to the markets of the advanced countries; 2) the US should urge other leading nations to join in arranging funds over and above the debt repayment needs of the Third World; 3) business in the advanced world must be encouraged to do far more direct investing in the developing countries. **(plan to expand world trade)**

6548

The Structure and Evolution of Recent U.S. Trade Policy. Edited by Robert E. Baldwin (Prof of Economics, U of Wisconsin) and Anne O. Krueger (VP, World Bank). Chicago, Ill: U of Chicago Press, Nov 1984/c504p/$53.00.

A systematic effort to analyze specific US trade policies, particularly nontariff measures. Contributors consider industry-specific trade barriers, the effect of tariff preferences and export-promoting policies, the worldwide impact of import policies, the levels of protection in developing countries, and the costs and benefits of various policies to trading nations. **(trade policy, US)**

6549

State Government Export Promotion: An Exporter's Guide. Alan R. Posner. Westport CT: Greenwood Press, Oct 1984/c168p/$29.95.

On the ways that state government agencies can promote the overseas exports of producers in their respective states, the contributions that universities can make to export promotion, export promotion services now offered by each state, specific problems and opportunities in agricultural exports, and the long-term consequences of continued US emphasis on the export of services and capital investment vs. agricultural products and manufactures. **(state export promotion)**

6550

East-West Trade and Finance in the World Economy: A New Look for the 1980s. Edited by C. T. Saunders (European Research Center, U of Sussex). NY: St. Martin's Press, Feb 1985/c304p/$32.50.

Proceedings of a 1983 meeting in Moscow sponsored by the Vienna Institute for Comparative Economic Studies, which drew together economists from East and West to discuss economic cooperation. Essays consider recent trends in East-West economic affairs, problems of indebtedness of CMEA nations, aspects of agriculture and technology transfer, various forms of buy-back and counter-trade, new elements of the international division of labor, the global impact of debt rescheduling, trade restriction as a political weapon, expectations of East-West economic relations a decade ago and actual outcome, and new instruments of trade promotion. **(East-West trade)**

6551

The Politics of East-West Trade. Edited by Gordon B. Smith (U of South Carolina). Boulder CO: Westview, Aug 1984/c267p/$32.50.

Topics include an assessment of the degree to which the Soviet economy depends on Western technology imports, the extent to which Western technology has helped or hindered Soviet economic and technological growth, the specific impact of US trade sanctions in four critical sectors (computers, energy, agriculture, and defense), the cost to the US economy of US trade sanctions against the USSR, and an integrated trade strategy for the West. [Also see **Economic Warfare or Detente: An Assessment of East-West Relations in the 1980s**, edited by Reinhard Rode and Hanns-Dieter Jacobsen (Westview, April 1985/c300p/$25.00), which concludes that East-West trade is an important stabilizing element.] **(East-West trade)**

6552

Trade, Technology, and Soviet-American Relations. Edited by Bruce Parrott (Johns Hopkins U). Bloomington IN: Indiana U Press, June 1985/400p/$35.00;$17.50.

Essays on trends in Soviet trade with the West, Soviet assimilation of Western technology, the contribution of Western technology to Soviet military programs, the impact of US-USSR trade and trade denial on the US economy, and the implications of US-USSR economic interchange for American relations with Western Europe and Japan. **(East-West trade)**

6553

As Global 24-Hour Trading Nears, Regulators Warn of Market Abuses, *The Wall Street Journal*, Mon, 11 Feb 1985, p25.

A limited form of global trading now exists, with stocks of more than 500 major US and foreign companies trading on at least one exchange outside their home country. But there is little or no coordination among international stock exchanges or securities firms. Most people in the securities industry think that global trading is inevitable. Some officials believe that, within five years, improved technology in the securities and communications industries, coupled with expanding deregulation of international financial markets, will lead to an integrated worldwide trading system. Such 24-hour trading, long an option for the professional trader, will become a reality for every investor. Officials in the securities industry predict that the US and Britain will be the first countries to come together in global trading. More than 200 US stocks already trade in London, and scores of British stocks trade on US exchanges and over-the-counter markets. Eventually, Tokyo—the second-largest stock market—will become the third leg of the market. The move toward global trading will not be simple, or without risks: US officials worry that global trading may spawn a plethora of stock market rip-offs. **(global stock trading by 1990?)**

6554

Policing the Global Trade in Dangerous Products, Lim Siang Jin and Dexter Tiranti (International Organization of Consumers Unions, PO Box 1045, Penang, Malaysia), *IFDA Dossier*, No 38, Nov-Dec 1983, 37-48.

In the industrialized countries, consumers have organized a defense against dangerous goods. Producers of such goods now look to the Third World as a market and/or dumping ground. Dumping is easy in the Third World because consumers are often illiterate, the legal machinery in most Third World countries does not act as a deterrent, and Third World governments often condone illicit trade. The global communications revolution with its containerized shipping, air freight, and telex/telephone satellites has enabled Western products to be sold in the most distant lands. For government officials on the receiving end of these imports, there is little objective and comprehensive information on the inflowing products. To address this problem, the IOCU has launched a Consumer Interpol to hasten the exchange of information on hazardous products, focus attention on generic safety problems, help build the capability of consumer groups, and support national and international efforts to control the trade in hazardous technologies and consumer products. Three cases of action are described: a consumer alert against a useless mosquito repellent, the exposure of a dangerous anti-diarrhoeal drug distributed by Ciba-Geigy (clioquinol), and identification of contaminated bandages put in first aid kits. **(Consumer Interpol)**

D. <u>Third World Development</u>

6555

Ecodevelopment: Concepts, Projects, Strategies. Edited by Bernhard Glaeser (International Institute for Environment and Society, Science Center Berlin). Oxford UK and Elmsford NY: Pergamon Press, Aug 1984/247p/$49.50.

Ecodevelopment means an alternative policy of economic development that takes care of environmental limits, is ecologically sound, satisfies basic needs (especially of the poorest) and utilizes local resources, both human and natural. Contributions include Johan Galtung on environmental politics in overdeveloped and underdeveloped countries, nutrient recycling as an alternative to shifting cultivation, ecofarming and ecodevelopment, industrial aspects, environmental goals and development needs, current agricultural developments in North America and Europe, and Ignacy Sachs on technological choices and consumption patterns. **(ecodevelopment)**

*6556

People-Centered Development: Contributions Toward Theory and Planning Frameworks. Edited by David C. Korten (Asia Regional Advisor, USAID) and Rudi Klauss (Natl. Assn. of Schools of Public Administration). West Hartford CT: Kumarian Press (630 Oakwood Ave), May 1984/333p/$32.50;$16.50pb.

A new paradigm is currently emerging from a global process of collective social invention. Its dominant logic is that of a balanced human ecology, with substantial value placed on local initiative and diversity. Citizens and planners around the world have sought to enrich individual and community life by establishing mechanisms to empower people. In the Third World, participatory development projects have emerged as theoretically desirable and practically feasible alternatives to centrally planned development programs. This anthology of 30 excerpts is organized in six parts: 1) **The Agenda for Social Transformation:** Willis Harman on key choices, Alvin Toffler on Third Wave development (Gandhi with satellites), George Land on directionality in evolution, John Platt on major evolutionary jumps; 2) **Life on a Small Planet:** Kenneth Boulding on the economics of spaceship earth, Elizabeth Dodson Gray on moving with the natural grains of life, Garrett Hardin's 1968 classic on the tragedy of the commons; 3) **Resource Competition and Poverty:** orthodox development economics, peasant perceptions of drinking water, urban bias in world development, the dynamics of dependency and marginality; 4) **Social Learning and Planning:** Edgar Dunn on the nature of social learning, David Korten on rural development programming, John Friedmann on planning as social learning, Russell Ackoff on the nature of development and planning; 5) **Planning for Equity and Self-Reliance:** frameworks for people-centered development, agropolitan development, the self-reliant city; 6) **Governance by the People:** Alvin Toffler on the crisis of democratic governance, Peter Berger and Richard Neuhaus on empowering people, Grace Goodell on a conservative perspective of political and social development, Jessica Lipnack and Jeffrey Stamps on the power and joy of networking.

(reader on people-centered development)

6557

Social Innovations for Development. Edited by Carl-Goran Heden (Karolinska Institutet, Stockholm) and Alexander King (International Federation of Institutes of Advanced Study, Paris). Oxford UK and Elmsford NY: Pergamon Press, Aug 1984/167p/$18.00.

Papers from a 1979 seminar in Sweden: Alexander King on the need for innovation, Carl-Goran Heden on catalysts for creativity, Otto Neuloh on the history and internationalization of social innovation, D. Stuart Conger on social and technical inventions in a developing world, Georges Gueron on the work of the International Foundation for Social Innovations (Paris), Stevan Dedijer on sci/tech-related social innovations in UNCSTD national papers, Aron Wiener on promoting social innovation through

international prizes, Courtney Nelson on the Institute for Scientific and Technological Cooperation (Washington), Peter S. Reid on the work of the Intermediate Technology Development Group (London), Guy Gresford on the UN System as a catalyst for science and technology, and Harlan Cleveland and Abdel Rahman on dynamism and development. Alexander King concludes that awards and incentives should be given in four main categories of social innovations that: 1) show concern for regulation and achievement of socio-economic goals (productivity growth, improving income distribution, an instrument for calculating cost-benefit in a wider sense than traditional economics); 2) maintain viable steady states in the bio sphere (reforestation, water resource management); 3) encourage participatory, effective, and decentralized decision-making; 4) innovate at the supra-national level (new forms of international cooperation, strengthen the UN system, promote the exchange of information, raise the productivity of science). Three kinds of awards could be considered: for the inventor, for the implementation, and for the best marketing program for the invention or implementation. [NOTE: If instituted properly, such a system of awards might quickly supersede the narrow and obsolete Nobel Prizes.] **(encouraging social innovation)**

6558

Unfinished Agenda: The Dynamics of Modernization in Developing Nations. Manning Nash (Prof of Anthropology, U of Chicago). Boulder CO: Westview, Sept 1984/c160p/$25.00.

An analysis of social change since decolonization in Latin America, the Middle East, and especially Southeast Asia, focusing on societies that are attempting to modernize while maintaining continuities with their traditions. Nash describes the role of education in modernization, and the general social variables that facilitate or inhibit structural transformation. **(modernization and tradition)**

6559

The Dynamics of Development and Development Administration. Kempe Ronald Hope (U of the West Indies, Jamaica). Westport CT: Greenwood Press, July 1984/128p/$27.95.

On the evolution of the concept of "development" from the inter-war years through the 1950s, when the expression "Third World" first emerged, to the 1970s and the present when holistic technology transfer and other new approaches emphasizing economic independence began to take precedence. Chapters on the history of modern development administration, the role of the development administrator, bureaucracy in government, and the dynamic interaction between development and administration.

(development administration)

6560

A Practical Development Strategy: Logic and Reality, Ervin Laszlo (UNITAR-NYC), *World Futures*, 20:1/2, 1984, 69-78.

Editor of the Club of Rome report **Goals for Mankind** (Dutton, 1977) and of various books on the New International Economic Order asserts that the nations of the world need to observe one simple but cardinal rule in their current plans and policies: one does not achieve satisfactory results unless one relates goals to levels of implementation. Some policies are best managed at the level of village or neighborhood; others call for management at the national or global level. Many processes between these levels call for regional management within individual states or among them. International regional cooperation, in particular, is optimal for the coordination and management of many processes vital to the economic security of nations and peoples. Self-sufficiency in many areas can often be achieved only on an international regional level. Cooperation with neighbors is a way toward lessening dependence on developed powers and international markets, while achieving the level of diversification required to become entirely autonomous in fulfilling basic human needs. Regional cooperation has the added advantage of increasing negotiating power of small states in international meetings. For the time being, the gap between logic and reality prevents the creation of political units that reflect balanced economic conditions. But the gap could be bridged by flexible economic arrangements that attain the same end. A new world economic system could be created in the remaining years of this decade through such a structure of international cooperation. Regional sovereignity in the economic realm may have to become the paramount goal in the 1980s and 1990s, similar in magnitude and importance to what sovereignity in the political realm was in earlier decades. A new global order can then arise from the multiple strands of interregional cooperation.

(international regional cooperation needed)

6561

Transnationals and the Third World: The Struggle for Culture. Armand Mattelart (Paris). South Hadley MA: Bergin & Garvey Publishers, Dec 1983/184p/$22.95.

On the role of transnational firms as "socio-cultural investors," with an examination of how they affect host countries through technology, foods, consumption patterns, drugs, trade-union bargaining, employment practices, television, and the role of women. Regulatory efforts to reduce the effects of transnationals and promote self-reliance are critically reviewed.   **(impact of transnationals)**

6562

Spatial, Environmental and Resource Policy in the Developing Countries. Edited by Manas Chatterji (SUNY) *et al.* Hampshire UK and Brookfield VT: Gower Publishing Co, April 1984/428p/$41.95.

The 31 papers are arranged in four parts: 1) **Planning Issues and Techniques of Analysis:** methodology of development planning, new development concepts in relation to the energy crisis, economic development and decentralization, using an integrated multiregional model; 2) **Urban and Metropolitan Growth Patterns:** technical assistance and national urban policies in Asia, urbanization and development; 3) **Population, Housing, and Land Use:** growth and spatial patterns in Indian cities, financing urban development, planning in urban areas, urbanization and labor absorption in Latin America, urban transport policy; 4) **Resources and Development:** the role of intermediate cities, current practices in technology transfer, the future development of regional science.

(spatial policy in Third World)

6563

Cultural Policies: From Model to Market. *Cultures: Dialogue Between the Peoples of the World* (UNESCO, Paris), No 33, 1983/205p/34F.

Articles on the World Conference on Cultural Policies (Mexico City, Aug 1982), cultural emancipation as a means of economic development, the return and restitution of cultural property as an issue of international justice, a comparison of cultural policies in various countries, typology and effects of cultural policies, two models of modern development and cultural expression, and promoting the arts. Concludes with *The Mexico City Declaration on Cultural Policies* (pp189-196), which lists 54 governing principles, including: 1) the assertion of cultural identity contributes to the liberation of peoples; 2) all cultures are part of the cultural heritage of mankind; 3) we must insure that the cultural identity of each people is preserved and protected, and that the equal dignity of all cultures is recognized; 4) it is vital to humanize development, and any cultural policy should restore to the development process its profound, human significance; 5) cultural democracy is based on the broadest possible participation by the individual and society in the creation of cultural goods, in decision-making concerning cultural life, and in the dissemination and enjoyment of culture; 6) a program for the democratization of culture calls for decentralization of the centers where the arts are created and enjoyed; 7) the establishment of a lasting peace is essential to the existence of human culture; 8) peace means respect for others' rights.   **(cultural policy and development)**

6564

The Gap Between Rich and Poor: Contending Perspectives on the Political Economy of Development. Edited by Mitchell A. Seligson (U of Arizona). Boulder CO: Westview, Sept 1984/c400p/$40.00;$15.95pb.

The per capita income gap between low income and industrialized countries grew from $3677 to $9648 between 1950 and 1980, and an ever-widening gap separates the rich from the poor within the developing nations themselves. But other evidence suggests that middle-income countries may be gaining on the rich countries, and that growth with equity has occurred in a number of developing nations that have committed themselves to such a policy. This volume presents the arguments for both sides of the debate, concluding with Herman Kahn's assessment of the future of the rich-poor gap.   **(growing rich-poor gaps?)**

6565

INTERNATIONAL DEVELOPMENT RESOURCES (20 Volumes). Edited by Pradip K. Ghosh (Center for International Development, U of Maryland). Westport CT: Greenwood Press, 1984.

Each volume follows a consistent four-part format of current readings (documents on issues, strategies, methods, country studies), statistical data, annotated bibliography on key literature, and a directory of information sources.

1) **Industrialization and Development** (Mar 1984/ 566p/$45.00).
2) **Urban Development in the Third World** (Apr 1984/ 546p/$45.00).
3) **Technology Policy and Development** (Apr 1984/ 593p/$49.95).
4) **Energy Policy and Third World Development** (Apr 1984/394p/$45.00).
5) **Population, Environment and Resources, and Third World Development** (Apr 1984/c600p/ $55.00).
6) **Health, Food, and Nutrition in Third World Development** (Apr 1984/c600p/$55.00).
7) **Economic Policy and Planning: A Third World Perspective** (Apr 1984/711p/$59.95).
8) **Development Policy and Planning** (Apr 1984/ 626p/$55.00).
9) **New International Economic Order** (May 1984/ 561p/$49.95).

10) **Foreign Aid and Third World Development** (Sept 1984/365p/$49.95).
11) **Multi-National Corporations and Third World Development** (Sept 1984/473p/$45.00).
12) **Economic Integration and Third World Development** (Oct 1984/407p/$45.00).
13) **Third World Development: Basic Needs Approach** (Oct 1984/436p/$45.00).
14) **Appropriate Technology in Third World Development** (Nov 1984/494p/$49.95).
15) **Development Cooperation and Third World Development** (Nov 1984/497p/$49.95).
16) **International Trade and Third World Development** (Dec 1984/569p/$49.95).
17) **Disarmament and Development** (Dec 1984/447p/$45.00).
18) **Developing South Asia** (Dec 1984/582p/$55.00).
19) **Developing Latin America** (Dec 1984/416p/$45.00).
20) **Developing Africa** (Dec 1984/435p/$45.00).
                        (development resource books)

III. WORLD REGIONS AND NATIONS

A. The Americas

*6566

Canadian Cultural Futures: Options for Living Together. Edited by Gary Spraakman, Tom Becher, and Keith Wilde. Montreal: Canadian Association for Futures Studies (3764 Cote-des-Neiges), 1984/109p(8x11")/$8.00pb. [Order copies from S Consulting and Research, 146 Clareview Road, Edmonton, Alberta T5A 3Y3.]

Papers from the 1982 CAFS conference at the University of British Columbia, on the values and beliefs that will determine how Canadians live together. Topics include improving the regime of tolerance, the search for meaning, multiculturalism as a fundamental component of Canadian culture, art as an indicator of the future, foreign policy and technology, popular images of Canada's future, Christian neo-fascism as a possible cultural future, global culture in a global cottage, the influence of the microchip on education and culture, economic association with the US, the future role of government in culture, on forgetting to remember our future, and the need for an ecology of knowledge. In a concluding chapter, Spraakman summarizes constant factors in world culture (the importance of science and technology, the desire for a high standard of material living), transforming factors in world culture (new technological breakthroughs, the lower cost of communicating, the demand for meaningful participation, emergence of eclectic paradigms), constant factors in Canadian culture (an international orientation, consciousness of land and geography), transforming factors in Canadian culture (a more pessimistic image of the future, less uniformity of values and beliefs, less economic growth), and the constant and interacting influences of Canadian subcultures. The new Canadian culture in the foreseeable future can be described by five characteristics: 1) balkanized economic sectors; 2) minimal and perhaps zero or negative economic growth (Canadians will thus feel and act deprived); 3) increasing fragmentation among sectors in Canadian society, leading to greater differences and more prevalent conflict; 4) less dominance of the big "C" Canadian culture, as world culture and Canadian sub-cultures gain dominance; 5) less integration of well-defined values and beliefs in big "C" Canadian culture. In sum, the foreseeable Canadian cultural future is not a return to "the true north strong and free." Canadians are entering a transition period where uncertainty, change, and disruption will be characteristic until the reality of the megachanges can be assessed and put to work for the betterment of more Canadians. This will likely take 20 or 30 years. [NOTE: An exemplary framework for summarizing cultural change.]

(future Canadian culture)

6567

Global 2000: Canada. A View of Canadian Economic Development Prospects, Resources and the Environment. Roger D. Voyer (Nordicity Group Ltd) and Mark G. Murphy (MGM Research Associates). Elmsford NY: Pergamon Press, Nov 1984/164p/$15.00pb.

A study commissioned by Environment Canada and sponsored by the Canadian Association for the Club of Rome. It follows **Global 2000: Implications for Canada**, an "outside view" prepared by Gerald O. Barney, the study director of the US **Global 2000 Report to the President**. This inside view takes a long-term structural perspective on issues facing Canada in the context of the international economy. Canada has a small, open economy that has grown increasingly dependent on the US economy. It has continued to depend on resource exports for economic health, and has not evolved with other industrial countries toward higher value-added industries. This phenomenon, combined with unique levels of foreign ownership, has resulted in a serious balance of international payments situation. Despite the promise of tourism, resources remain a cornerstone of the economy. But the resource sector faces deep structural problems. A strategy to guide Canada to the year 2000 and beyond should include the following elements: 1) setting in place and sustaining a long-term industrial strategy based on capturing new industrial (particularly high-tech) opportunities, import replacement, and developing goods and services related to urbanization and an aging population; 2) policies to tap Canadian capital markets more effectively and to encourage the development of Canadian-owned establishments; 3) policies to insure a sustainable resource base and to support appropriate resource and industrial development; 4) investigating new approaches to employment that maintain an acceptable standard of living, such as a shorter work week, working from the home, work-sharing, etc. Concludes that this strategy should be cast within a broader framework which recognizes "total costing" that reveals the real costs of stresses on the resource base and the environment.

(Canadian economic development)

6568

Planning Canada's Role in the New Global Economy, Clyde Weaver and Peter Richards (both U of British Columbia), *Journal of the American Planning Association*, 51:1, Winter 1985, 43-52.

Part of a special issue on planning in Canada. The authors point out that everything in Canada is colored by its corridor form of settlement and by its narrow export-led economy based on natural resources. Canadians do not cultivate this image, and Americans seldom recognize it, but it constitutes the central fact of Canadian life, making Canada profoundly different from the US in many ways. Economic planning during the Trudeau era attempted but failed to diversify export partners and the commodities Canada sells abroad. Today a fundamental restructuring of the Canadian economy is required if Canada is to establish a viable role for itself in the new global economy. The importance of triangular ties between Canada, the US, and Japan must be explicitly recognized; together, they form the backbone of a new economic axis spanning the Pacific Basin. [NOTE: See #6581.] The Canadian state does not have a unitary structure or a homogeneous constituency inclined toward consensus, as Japan does. A different form of indicative planning is called for, able to create conjuncture among actors and objectives as they are found in Canada. The key to defusing regional and class-based conflict in a progressive manner is an integrated economic decision-making system based on the principles of self-management. Such a decentralized yet coherent approach to planning, drawing in community groups and other non-governmental organizations, can allow people to cooperate in a "transactive" style.

(planning a new Canadian economy)

*6569

Political Risk Analysis for Canada and Mexico, Richard Drobnick (Center for Futures Research, USC), *Technological Forecasting and Social Change*, 26:4, Dec 1984, 315-353.

Ideas from two groups of corporate and country specialists (27 with expertise on Canada and 21 with expertise on Mexico) were obtained in mid-1982 via a two-round Delphi inquiry on socioeconomic change and business contingencies in Canada and Mexico. Critical trends for Canada include: halting the long-term decline in centralization of political power, a continuing decline of US corporate influence on the Canadian government, increasing resentment of US cultural imperialism, increasing Canadian concerns about the environment, an improved exchange rate for the Canadian dollar, and stabilized US-Canada relations. Critical events for Canada in the next 20 years include the spread of Canadianization to various foreign investments (75% probability by 2002), the political separation of Quebec (45% probability), and a 25% cut in social welfare spending by the Federal government (35% probability).

Critical trends for Mexico include increasing nationalism, a drop in the population growth rate from 3.3% per year in 1980 to 2.7% in 1990, declining cohesion within the ruling party (PRI), a substantial increase in the political influence of the military and in terrorist activity, a sharp rise in unemployment (perhaps by as much as 60% in the 1981-1990 period), a declining value of the peso (by 1990, less than 1/6 of its already substantially reduced 1983 value), a substantial increase in illegal migration to the US (perhaps by as much as 60%), and a deterioration of US-Mexico relations. Critical events for Mexico include a severe tightening of rules on new foreign investments (60% probability by 2002), terrorist attacks on foreign business as a commonplace (55% probability), leftist political parties threaten the hegemony of the PRI (60% probability), Mexico repudiates its international debts (25% probability), stringent enforcement of US immigration laws sharply reduce the flow of illegal aliens (45% probability), changes in US immigration policy produce a major diplomatic conflict (65% probability), and US armed forces intervene in a Central American country (70% probability).

The concluding consensus view of the panelists was that living conditions would be improving in the US at a noticeably faster pace than in Canada or Mexico throughout the rest of the 1980s.

(Delphi panel on Canada and Mexico)

6570

The U.S. and Mexico: Borderland Development and the National Economies. Edited by Lay James Gibson (U of Arizona) and Alfonso Corona Renturia (National U of Mexico). Boulder CO: Westview, Feb 1985/c300p/$25.00.

On the structural characteristics of the border region and the flow of goods, services, capital, and people between the US and Mexico. Includes such topics as costs and benefits of Mexican border industrialization, problems of the sea and US-Mexican political relationships, technology flow and economic independence, internationalization of industry, the welfare economics of Mexico-US migration, new policies and strategies for transnational investments in Juarez, and the political impact of recent shifts in the Mexican economy.

(US-Mexico relations)

*6571

The Caribbean Basin to the Year 2000: Demographic, Economic, and Resource-Use Trends in Seventeen Countries. Norman A. Graham and Keith L. Edwards (both of The Futures Group, Glastonbury CT). Boulder CO: Westview, Nov 1984/166p/$18.50.

The results of projection and analysis of 17 Caribbean basin countries make it clear that many of them face a long-term struggle against severe demographic and economic pressures. This view assumes no dramatic improvements in trade and aid, and no drastic policies to curb population growth. Without such policies, total population in the Caribbean basin will likely increase by nearly 50%, from 52 million in 1982 to 77 million in 2000. The most populated countries in the Caribbean basin by 2000 will be Guatemala (12.6 million), Cuba (11.6 million), Haiti (9.6 million), Dominican Republic (9.3 million), El Salvador (8.7 million), Honduras (6.9 million), Nicaragua (5.2 million), Costa Rica (2.8 million), Panama (2.9 million), and Jamaica (2.8 million). Urban population will likely grow at an even faster pace, because of continued high levels of rural to urban migration together with high fertility in cities. There is no reason to expect dramatic improvement in the income disparities and relative deprivation that characterize the populations of many of these countries. The economic strong points in the Caribbean basin are Trinidad and Tobago, and to a lesser extent the Bahamas. The countries that appear most vulnerable are El Salvador, Guatemala, Guyana, Haiti, Honduras, and Nicaragua. The combination of strong population growth pressures, weak economic performance, and in many cases a limited and diminishing natural resource base will increasingly constrain governments from promoting economic development and relieving human misery. Tourism has become a mainstay of many Caribbean economies over the past two decades, but overreliance on tourism can expose a country to changing market conditions, encourage social unrest, and provide little help to other sectors. There are significant opportunities for a constructive US role in the long-term rehabilitation and development of the region, through increased economic and technical assistance, trade, and investment.

(Caribbean basin population up 50% by 2000)

6572

The International Crisis of the Caribbean. Anthony Payne (Huddersfield Polytechnic). Baltimore MD: Johns Hopkins U Press, March 1984/192p/$18.50.

A survey of the current state of the Caribbean, the potential for future conflict in the region, and the policies that might be adopted to prevent it. Chapters consider US involvement, the role of the European powers, the emergence of Mexico and Venezuela as important regional powers, and the increasingly aggressive stance of Cuba. Payne criticizes much of the current thinking of the US and British governments, viewing the Caribbean as a battleground on which the rivalries of great and middle powers, as well as the merits of alternative ideologies and development strategies, are being fought out.

(Caribbean battleground)

6573

Puerto Rico: The Search for a National Policy. Edited by Richard J. Bloomfield (Director, World Peace Foundation). Boulder CO: Westview, Feb 1985/c220p/$30.00.

Explores the main issues surrounding Puerto Rico's political status and economic development from the point of view of the US government's reponsibility for solutions. Contributors discuss the social costs of Puerto Rico's dependent development pattern, ways in which the US and Puerto Rican governments could improve the island's economic performance, and the controversial status issue as an international problem for the US. Concludes with views from the leaders of the four major Puerto Rican political parties as to how to facilitate a transition to their preferred status for the island.

(Puerto Rico-US relations)

6574

Report on Cuba: Findings of the Study Group on United States-Cuban Relations. Central American and Caribbean Program (Johns Hopkins U). Boulder CO: Westview, June 1984/42p/$8.00.

Present US policy toward Cuba lacks long-range objectives, and a new policy of gradual engagement is proposed. Such a shift in US policy would not cause immediate or major improvements, but in the long run it would strengthen bilateral relations, allow a more constructive relationship on multilateral issues, and eventually reduce Soviet influence in Cuba. **(US-Cuba relations)**

6575

From Gunboats to Diplomacy: New U.S. Policies for Latin America. Edited by Richard Newfarmer (World Bank). Baltimore MD: Johns Hopkins U Press, Feb 1984/254p/$25.00;$11.95pb.

US relations with Latin America have entered a new and seriously misguided phase in recent years. An overemphasis on the East-West conflict has obscured the indigenous origins of much of the unrest in Latin America, while this same stress has led the US government to apply its demands for democratic principles and human rights unevenly. Essays in this volume consider US policies toward specific Latin American countries (Mexico, Nicaragua, El Salvador, Cuba, Chile, etc.), problems of Latin American refugees, US economic policy toward Latin America, the Caribbean Basin initiative, and principles for a new US foreign policy. **(US-Latin America relations)**

6576

Politics, Policies, and Economic Development in Latin America. Edited by Robert Wesson (Prof of Political Science, U of California-Santa Barbara). Stanford CA: Hoover Institution Press, Dec 1984/$24.95;$13.95pb.

Nine Latin American experts survey recent political and economic developments: free market authoritarianism in Chile, frustrations of ungovernability in Argentina, military rule and economic failure in Uruguay, political determinants of development in Brazil, military and civilian political economy in Peru, party-led development in Mexico, the National Front and economic development in Colombia, the democratic politics of petroleum in Venezuela, alternative development approaches in Jamaica, and problems of social democracy in Costa Rica.

(politics and development in Latin America)

6577

The Brazilian Economy in the Eighties. Edited by J. Salazar-Carrillo (Florida International U) and R. Fendt Jr (Rio de Janeiro). Elmsford NY: Pergamon Press, Feb 1985/c270p/$35.00.

Essays on imperfect capital mobility and exchange risk, forecasting exports and foreign debt in Brazil, benefits and costs of foreign investments in Brazil, determinants and limits of foreign indebtedness, short run economic policy in Brazil, and long-term perspectives.

(Brazilian economy)

B. The Soviet Union

6578

Areas of Challenge for Soviet Foreign Policy in the 1980s. Gerrit W. Gong (CSIS, Georgetown U), Angela E. Stent, and Rebecca V. Strode. Bloomington IN: Indiana U Press, Dec 1984/176p/$20.00;$7.95pb.

Three specialists in Soviet international behavior assess challenges to Soviet foreign policy: the West European context, prospects for the future cohesion of the Atlantic alliance, the long-term political and economic objectives of the PRC and their probable impact on Chinese-Soviet-US relations, Soviet strategic policies in the SALT era, and future prospects for arms control. **(USSR foreign policy)**

6579

Sovieticus: American Perceptions and Soviet Realities. Stephen F. Cohen (Princeton U). NY: W. W. Norton, June 1985/$12.95.

A compilation of "Sovieticus" columns from *The Nation*, arguing that the common Western image of the USSR is a caricature resulting largely from the US media's tendency to report only negatively about Russia. Achievements in the USSR are systematically ignored, such as the expanded social welfare programs, a rising standard of living, and a GNP that has quadrupled in 30 years. Attention is also given to a new generation of Soviet democratic dissidents, many in their 20s and 30s.

(negative US view of Soviets)

6580

The Vast Diversion of Soviet Rivers, Philip P. Micklin (Prof of Geography, Western Michigan U), *Environment*, 27:2, March 1985, 12-20ff.

Long-distance water transfers have been studied seriously in the USSR since the 1930s. Plans have been announced to begin construction in 1986 of diversions from rivers and lakes of the northern European USSR into the Volga Basin. Before 2000, nearly 20 cubic kilometers of water will be diverted south. Larger water diversions are expected for the first half of the 21st century, totalling 120 cubic kilometers a year, or roughly 20% of the annual flow at the mouth of the Mississippi River. Micklin discusses impacts of the Soviet river diversion, including the possibility of affecting Northern Hemisphere climate by altering the Arctic ice cover. But opinion is divided, within and outside the USSR, as to whether diversion—assuming it had perceptible effects—would increase or decrease the ice cover, leading respectively to Arctic cooling or warming. The weight of opinion presently leans toward more ice and a cooler Arctic.

(a cooler Arctic from Soviet water diversion?)

C. East Asia

6581

The Emerging Pacific Community: A Regional Perspective. Edited by Robert L. Downen (CSIS, Georgetown U) and Bruce J. Dickson (Brookings Institution). Boulder CO: Westview, May 1984/245p/$17.50.

Papers from a conference sponsored by the Center for Strategic and International Studies on the potential for cooperation among the nations of the Pacific region. Topics include US interests and the emerging Pacific Community, the future of the Pacific basin concept, political designing for Pacific cooperation, the Pacific potential and the Alaskan factor, conflict and cooperation in regional trade and investment, the role of raw materials, international implications of Chinese trade policy reforms, the security of the Western Pacific, the future of Hong Kong, and Southeast Asia refugee flows and other destabilizing factors.

(Pacific region)

6582

The China 2000 Study: A Personal View, Zheng Guanglin (Institute of Scientific and Technical Information of China, Beijing), *Futures Research Quarterly* (WFS), 1:1, Spring 1985, 7-12.

Since 1979, the People's Republic of China has shifted emphasis to economic construction, revising China's strategic objectives for the year 2000, and developing science and technology. The strategic objective for China is now to quadruple the annual gross value of industrial and agricultural production over the last two decades of this century—an increase in average real growth of 7% annually. All government organizations at all levels have begun to work out plans to achieve the nation's overall strategic objectives. But in the absence of coordination, these local efforts overlapped and lacked the comprehensive perspective and efficiency that China needs. To overcome this defect, the State Council of China proposed in 1981 that a clear picture of the future should be prepared, and directed ISTIC to begin the *China 2000* study, the first major futures research project in China. A preliminary report was published in 1983 in the form of ten research reports on population, economic development, energy, communications and transportation, cropland, water supply and demand, conserving water resources, forest resources, non-fuel mineral resources, and food supply and demand. A new study group has been organized to improve the study, encouraging the joint participation of many government agencies and hundreds of learned societies. The revised *China 2000* study will be completed by the end of 1985. Zheng offers four personal observations: 1) reaching China's grand strategic objective for the year 2000 is a very important and very difficult task, but China does have the advantage of having a superior socialist system; 2) major setbacks that China has suffered in the past were in part due to forgetting some of China's experiences and realities, e.g. holding excessively high and somewhat unrealistic expectations for quick results; 3) the strategic transition of science and technology worldwide presents a major challenge to China, but also a major opportunity to leap over outmoded technologies while avoiding serious disruptions of ecological balance; 4) what has been done so far on the *China 2000* study is only a preliminary and rather crude analysis, and futurists are requested to suggest improvements. **(*China 2000* study)**

6583

To Get Rich Is Glorious: China in the Eighties. Orville Schell. NY: Pantheon, March 1985/210p/$15.95.

Many Americans may be in danger of romanticizing or idealizing China's recent economic reforms. In the past, Western dreams of China, whether of business or revolution, have fallen terribly short of their hoped-for realization. Once again, as in the 19th century, the West is dreaming of China as an endless sinkhole for capital and goods—a billion customers just waiting to drink our Cokes, wear our jeans, and buy our weapons. It is all too easy to forget that what is actually out there is a relatively impoverished country that has historically been either economically self-sufficient or unable to buy any appreciable amount of Western goods. Recent reforms have brought some dramatic economic progress. But Schell worries about an inequitable distribution of the gains, and that in their eagerness to privatize the Chinese may throw out everything which was of value from the past, including the collective maintenance of irrigation and flood control projects. At the same time, in their zeal to acquire Western technology and luxuries, the Chinese may also inadvertently allow the development of an underworld class of young speculators and criminals.

(cautions on Chinese change)

6584

China in Transition. Edited by Marvin E. Wolfgang (U of Pennsylvania). *The ANNALS of the American Academy of Political and Social Science*, Vol 476, Nov 1984/170p/ $15.00;$7.95pb.

Essays on China's political and bureaucratic reforms, the development of Chinese law and the rapid growth of legal education, industrial reforms (although with no improvement yet in the main measures of productivity), the new course in Chinese agriculture in favor of commercialization and individual incentives, the substantial increase in population mobility, the goal of stabilizing China's population at 1.2 billion by 2000, the successful one-child campaign (which has led to a rapidly aging population), the future of Sino-Soviet relations, and the fluctuation in US-China relations from hostility to euphoria to realism.

(Chinese transitions)

6585

China Policy for the Next Decade: Report of the Atlantic Council's Committee on China Policy. Edited by U. Alexis Johnson (Chairman), George R. Packard (Rapporteur) and Alfred D. Wilhelm, Jr (Project Director). Boston MA: Oelgeschlager, Gunn & Hain, June 1984/445p/ $27.50;$12.50pb.

Papers on US China policy from an Atlantic perspective, viewpoints of US friends and allies, the national interests and objectives of the People's Republic of China, the four modernizations program, the Chinese perspective on national security, the emerging relationship with Taiwan, trade and technology transfers, and arms sales and arms control. Policy recommendations include: the US should seek enhanced cooperation with China, an economically healthy and secure China is in the national interest of the US and its friends and allies, the US should maintain a strong military presence in East Asia and the Pacific, Atlantic friends and allies should be consulted with respect to China policies, the basis of US relations with China should not rest exclusively on common opposition to the USSR, the US should not construe expected improvements in Sino-Soviet relations as necessarily adverse to our national interests, the US should actively promote the transfer of technologies that are consistent with China's economic development needs, it is in the US interest that the Chinese economy move toward modernization, and the US should avoid promoting any particular solution to the Taiwan situation in the hope that it will be worked out peacefully by the Chinese on both sides of the Strait.

(**US policy toward China**)

D. Africa

6586

Africa Projected: From Recession to Renaissance by the Year 2000? Edited by Timothy M. Shaw (Dalhousie U, Nova Scotia) and Olajide Aluko (U of Ife, Nigeria). NY: St. Martin's Press, Nov 1984/298p/$22.50.

Original essays on the Africanization of Africa, problems and prospects of regionalism, regional trends and South Africa's future, scientific and technological independence, possible futures for the OAU in the world system, the future of food and agriculture, the changing position of women in the African labor force, and the elusiveness of basic human needs in African development. Appendices include the OAU Lagos Plan of Action and the UNITAR Strategies for the Future of Africa. (**African futures**)

6587

Sub-Saharan Africa: Population Pressures on Development. Thomas J. Goliber. *Population Bulletin*, 40:1, Feb 1985/47p/$4.00 single copy.

The population of sub-Saharan Africa's 42 countries, estimated at 434 million in mid-1984, is likely to triple to 1.4 billion by 2025. Annual growth is 3.1%—up from 2.5% in the 1960s—and rising. This rapid population growth increasingly constrains government efforts to feed people adequately, preserve the land base essential for development, catch up with the demand for education and health services, and cope with exploding cities. Reducing fertility will require lower infant mortality [NOTE: see #85-427], more educational and employment opportunities for women, and family planning services specially adapted for Africa. (**rising population in Sub-Saharan Africa**)

6588

Business in the Shadow of Apartheid: U.S. Firms in South Africa. Edited by Jonathan Leape (Dept of Economics, Harvard U), Bo Baskin (NYC), and Stefan Underhill. Lexington MA: Lexington Books, Jan 1985/242p/$19.95.

Essays, largely by South Africans (academics, journalists, businessmen, and political leaders), on why Americans should care about South Africa, the prospects for change, and the opportunities for American influence. In their lengthy introduction, the editors point out that the strategy of Grand Apartheid reflects the dilemma of a white regime that conceives of itself as a "free world" democratic state while denying basic democratic rights to 80% of the population. The political weakness of the black majority results from the white regime's strategy of division and dispossession, its efforts to prevent blacks from developing economic and political institutions, and tribal and ideological conflicts among the blacks. Thus the probability of radical change through the exertion of black power or the fall of the white government is extremely small. The Afrikaners control the agenda, and for them the benefits of maintaining power through apartheid still far outweigh the costs. Americans can nevertheless have some effect on the pace of change in South Africa, through their government and US firms. Armed intervention by the US is virtually unimaginable, although the US government might impose economic sanctions. The effectiveness of these sanctions would depend on the support they receive from other countries and South Africa's capacity to adapt. The withdrawal of US firms from South Africa could have a dramatic psychological impact, but whatever the arguments pro and con, there is little chance that disinvestment will occur in the near future. Firms are, however, susceptible to pressure, which could focus their attention on community development, recognizing black trade unions, and other ways to redefine their interests to the benefit of black South Africans. Concludes with an appendix listing the addresses of some 350 US companies with subsidiaries or affiliates in South Africa.

(**US firms in South Africa**)

IV. DEFENSE AND DISARMAMENT

A. General Strategy

6589

An American Strategy of Peace: Toward a Constructive Foreign Policy In 1984 and Beyond. World Without War Council-Midwest. Chicago, Ill: WWWC-M (421 S Wabash), 1984/31p(8x10")/$2.00.

Agreement about America's strategy of peace will not emerge out of the current debate over military strategy, which is limited to questions of how much of what weapons to deploy. A strategy of peace must ask how each nation's security can be increased, and what institutions are needed to resolve conflicts. Although it is premature to spell out in detail the workings of a new global security system, general goals can be identified: 1) international processes and structures for regional and national crisis intervention and mediation; 2) reversal of the arms race and disarmament under reliable inspection and control; 3) international legal and political institutions to resolve conflict; 4) a sense of world political community to sustain these institutions and promote the observance of basic human rights; 5) acceleration of economic and political development in the Third World. As an alternative to the organized mass violence of war, a creative new departure for US foreign policy would be a fully developed strategy of initiatives toward these five goals.   **(peace strategy for US)**

6590

Trilateral Security: Defense & Arms Control Policies in the 1980s. Report of the Trilateral Task Force on Security & Arms Control to the Trilateral Commission (Gerard C. Smith, Paolo Vittorelli, and Kiichi Saeki). The Triangle Papers:26. NY: The Trilateral Commission (345 E 46th St), 1983/106p/pb.

The security of the trilateral regions (Europe, Japan, and North America) is indivisible—there is in fact a trilateral community of security interests, and a trilateral approach to meet the dangers of the 1980s offers the best chance of success. The heart of trilateral security will continue to rest indefinitely on strong survivable nuclear deterrent forces. Nuclear weapons control also remains an urgent concern. A comprehensive approach is called for, involving controls over weapons numbers and characteristics, their use, and their spread to nations other than the present nuclear five. The only path to improved security requires a more balanced combination of the two types of policy: buildup and control (which has been recently given second place to the buildup). [NOTE: No indication is given that other paths to "improved security" have been considered.]   **(trilateral security)**

6591

A Strategy for the 90's, Stansfield Turner, *The New York Times,* 6 May 1984, 38ff.

The former Director of the CIA argues that the US must find strategies to fit today's realities. In maintaining its military establishment, the US has three broad objectives: 1) to deter nuclear war or be ready to wage such war if deterrence fails; 2) to assist in the defense of Western Europe and South Korea; 3) to be able to intervene in other areas of the world if our interests require such action. Six times since WWII we have gone into combat in such areas, and we are likely to do so again. Our inadequate performance in three of these combat situations (Korea, Vietnam, and Iran) points to our lack of preparedness for this type of warfare. Our most urgent need is to be better prepared in the area where we are most likely to be challenged—in intervention around the world. Although nuclear deterrence is our most vital objective, we are already well prepared in this area.

(US need to prepare for intervention)

6592

National Security Strategy: Choices and Limits. Edited by Stephen J. Cimbala (Penn State U). NY: Praeger Publishers, June 1984/384p/$34.95.

Essays on the concept of strategy, alternative strategies, capabilities for alternative strategies, strategic policymaking, strategy as offense and defense, presidential leadership, and possible use of US military force.

(national security strategy)

6593

America Overcommitted: United States National Interests in the 1980s. Donald E. Nuechterlein (Prof of International Affairs, Federal Executive Institute). Lexington KY: University Press of Kentucky, Jan 1985/ 238p/$23.00;$10.00pb.

Whether the US remains a superpower into the 21st century depends on how it decides its international priorities in the 1980s. Seven geographical areas of the world are analyzed in terms of US interests, with the conclusion that the US is overcommitted internationally. US military forces are stretched to a dangerous degree not only in Western Europe, but also in the Middle East, Indian Ocean, and Asia. The US must face the reality that it does not have the means or the will to defend more than North America, Western Europe, Japan, the Philippines, Australia, Turkey, Israel, and Egypt in the foreseeable future. The attitude of Americans toward the world has changed fundamentally since President Kennedy said in 1961 that Americans would go anywhere and pay any price to defend freedom. We are not returning to the isolationism of the 1930s, but we are less willing to bear the defense burdens of the world than we were 20 years ago. A careful reshaping of US military strategy is not only prudent in the mid-1980s, but an absolute necessity to avoid courting disaster as an overcommitted giant.   **(US overcommitted)**

6594

Generals for Peace and Disarmament: A Challenge to US/NATO Strategy. General Gert Bastian (West Germany) *et al*. NY: Universe Books, Dec 1984/151p/ $15.00;$6.95pb.

Generals for Peace and Disarmament is a group of former NATO generals and admirals who first came together in 1981. Over the past few years, the group has made various statements on the problem of security. Winning a nuclear war is not possible, and there can be no Star Wars defense against nuclear weapons. This book discusses the Reagan Administration's policy of confrontation, NATO's nuclear plans, alternative defense concepts, and confidence building measures. Concludes with a statement on disarmament, advocating ridding Europe of all nuclear weapons by creating nuclear-free zones, prevention of the militarization of outer space, a return to detente and cooperation, the freezing of military budgets and a step-by-step decrease, etc.   **(Generals for disarmament)**

6595

Managing East-West Conflict: A Framework for Sustained Engagement. Aspen Institute International Group. Washington, DC: Aspen Institute (1333 New Hampshire Ave), Nov 1984/$5.00. [Excerpts in *The New York Times*, Tuesday, 27 Nov 1984, A14.]

A report recommending more high-level meetings between East and West, especially summit meetings. If summit meetings are more frequent, unrealistic expectations will be deflated. Also recommended: 1) a new body to be called a strategic panel, composed of a small number of US and Soviet representatives, to explore ways of reducing nuclear weapons in Europe, controlling technological innovation, improving verification and treaty compliance, and enhancing stability; 2) a network of crisis control centers linking the capitals of nuclear-weapon states. Signers of the report include Pierre Trudeau of Canada, Edward Heath and Shirley Williams of Britain, Edgar Faure of France, Saburo Okita of Japan, and Rev. Theodore Hesburgh, Jacob K. Javits, George F. Kennan, Robert S. McNamara, and Elliott L. Richardson.

(strategic panel proposed)

6596

National Security in the Third World. Abdul-Monem M. Al-Mashat (Cairo U). Boulder CO: Westview, Feb 1985/ c130p/$16.00pb.

Addresses the security problems of Third World states, arguing for new ways to define and measure national security so that the concept may be appropriately applied to the needs of developing countries. A concept of national security that focuses primarily on the international threat system while ignoring domestic well-being is inadequate on theoretical and pragmatic grounds.

(new national security concept for LDCs)

6597

National Security Crisis Forecasting and Management. Edited by Gerald W. Hopple (Defense Systems, Inc), Stephen J. Andriole (International Information Systems, Inc), and Amos Freedy (Perceptronics, Inc). Boulder CO: Westview, March 1984/211p/$23.00pb.

On the application of various analytical methodologies to the problems of forecasting crises more accurately and managing them more effectively. Topics include Soviet and US crisis management patterns, computer-based early warning, computer-based crisis management, strategic implications of terrorism, the role of technology in crisis warning and management, accelerated warfare vs. constant-speed human beings, cohesion and leadership in air/land battle 2000, and a strategy for the rapid deployment force. **(crisis forecasting and management)**

6598

Alternative Military Strategies for the Future. Edited by Keith A. Dunn and William O. Staudenmaier (US Army War College). Boulder CO: Westview, April 1985/c240p/ $24.00.

Prominent civilian and military experts (including Jeffrey Record, Edward Luttwak, and Earl C. Ravenal), representing the maritime/continental coalition, military reform, and noninterventionist schools of thought, outline changes in military strategy, policy, and force structure that the US must adopt to cope with threats to national security in the 1980s and 1990s. The authors analyze US interests and objectives, the changing strategic environment, planning for the most likely contingencies, and the proper mix of economic and military instruments for dealing with future threats. Alternatives considered here range from a strategic withdrawal from global commitments to proposals for increasing US power projection in the Third World. **(alternative US military strategies)**

6599

Revising U.S. Military Strategy: Tailoring Means to Ends. Jeffrey Record (Institute for Foreign Policy Analysis, Cambridge MA). Elmsford NY: Pergamon, Summer 1984/160p/$16.95;$9.95pb.

Addresses the central dilemma of US military strategy since the 1940s: a pronounced excess of commitments over capabilities. Contents cover containment vs. nuclear supremacy, flexible response and the two and a half war strategy, harmonizing aspirations and resources, a new transatlantic division of military labor, a closer strategic engagement of China, exploiting Soviet weaknesses, greater reliance on reserve forces, and enhanced strategic mobility. **(US military strategy)**

*6600

Strategic Requirements for the Army to the Year 2000. Edited by Robert H. Kupperman and William J. Taylor, Jr (Center for Strategic and International Studies, Georgetown U). Lexington MA: Lexington Books, June 1984/539p/$35.00.

Essays seeking to project the worldwide political-military environment of the 1990s, identify trends likely to have an impact on the US Army, suggest general directions for solutions, and to consider strategic requirements for each of five regions in the world. The chapters are written on the stated assumptions that general nuclear war and a catastrophic breakdown of the world economic order will not occur, the Soviet Union will continue to pursue its goal of world domination, and no unilateral technological breakthrough will occur to enable total dominance by any nation. Political-military violence will continue at high levels through the 1980s, but will be magnified many times in the 1990s because: 1) the Soviets will gain and maintain throughout the 1990s a solid reputation for strategic nuclear superiority; 2) the Third World will be increasingly ripe for Soviet initiatives in the 1990s; 3) the ready and increasing availability of relatively sophisticated weapons on the world market; 4) the relative weakness of supranational institutions. Vital interests of the US include commercial access to essential natural resources, military access to essential air and sea lanes, the right to maintain forward bases, a strong mobilization base, the maintenance and further strengthening of US alliance systems, the control of the proliferation of nuclear weapons, and the containment of Soviet influence. Some likely conflicts directly threatening these interests include renewed conflict between Israel and its Arab neighbors, a Soviet military attack on Iran preparatory to a move against Persian Gulf oil installations, an invasion of the Republic of Korea from North Korea, Soviet/Cuban-supported guerrilla attacks in Central America, Cuban-supported insurrection in Columbia, a Vietnamese thrust into Thailand, Soviet-supported terrorism, and psychological warfare targeted on cohesion of the US alliance structure. The most likely threats will require improved Army conventional and unconventional land-force capabilities.

Specific topics covered in this volume include the future of US foreign and defense policy (viewing the likely consequence of parsimony in defense efforts as a US failure to exercise influence in a security crisis), R&D for the future (a major problem is the growing disparity between the Army's manpower pool and the demands made upon that pool by the Army's equipment), energy technology (the prosperity of the West will continue to depend on maintenance of political stability in the Persian Gulf), Army mobilization in the 1990s, manpower and training for revised missions, the need to return to some form of obligatory national military service (a pilot program of reserves-only draft is proposed), the ample prospects for unconventional war (Clausewitz and Mao will not go out of style, and Murphy's Law will still operate), the exponential rise in terrorism (enabled by far more lethal tools for destruction, immediate and global attention of the media, and a wide range of motives for terrorist attack), Soviet proxy warfare, the world political environment in general, and prospects in the Americas, Europe, the Middle East, East Asia and the Pacific Basin (three scenarios provided, centered around the post-Marcos political regime in the Philippines), and Africa (likelihood of instability is very high over the next 20 years, but the US mood is unlikely to support direct intervention). [NOTE: Many gloomy scenarios here to sustain hawkish policy, but no consideration of the global impact of computers and telecommunications, for better or worse, or the possibility of any substantial improvements in peace-keeping.]

(US Army requirements by 2000)

6601
Supplemental Ways for Improving International Stability (SWIIS). Edited by H. Chestnut (SWIIS Foundation, Schenectady NY) *et al*. Elmsford NY: Pergamon Press, July 1984/289p(8x12")/$68.00.

Proceedings of a 1983 workshop of the International Federation of Automatic Control, held in Laxenburg, Austria. The control engineers and other specialists from 14 countries attempt to consider novel and peaceful ways to deal with some of the major disagreements in today's world, with modest expectations reflected in the notion of "supplemental ways." (Indeed, one of the significant ideas brought out at the workshop was the importance of modest expectations as a factor for success in negotiations and conflict resolution.) Sessions considered: 1) cultural, political, educational, and legal aspects of international stability; 2) techno-economic conditions for international stability (stability in the international monetary system, an alternative path to progress, superpower arms competition, etc.); 3) system analytical approaches to international stability; 4) negotiation and mediation; 5) decision-making processes. [NOTE: A possibly useful effort by well-meaning specialists, but it is difficult to pick out any viable ideas from the mass of naive pontification and arcane academic writing. An executive summary, by someone who can communicate, is needed.] **(control engineers seek peace)**

B. Visions of War

6602
The Climatic Effects of Nuclear War, Richard P. Turco, Owen B. Toon, Thomas P. Ackerman, James B. Pollack, and Carl Sagan, *Scientific American*, 251:2, August 1984, 33-43.

A restatement, based on subsequent studies, of the widely-cited "TTAPS" paper on the possibility of a nuclear winter (*Science*, 23 Dec 1983; **FS Annual 1984**, #5775). Recent findings by the TTAPS group, confirmed by others in Europe and the USSR, suggest that the long-term climatic effects of a major nuclear war are likely to be much severer than had been supposed. In the aftermath of such a war, vast areas of earth could be subjected to prolonged darkness, abnormally low temperatures, violent windstorms, toxic smog, and persistent radioactive fallout. These physical effects would be compounded by the widespread breakdown of transportation systems, power grids,

agricultural production, food processing, medical care, sanitation, and central government. Even in regions far from the conflict, survivors would be imperiled by starvation, hypothermia, radiation sickness, epidemics, and other dire consequences. In sum, the likeliest outcome of a nuclear war (e.g., the "base line" case is a 5000-megaton nuclear exchange) would be a climatic catastrophe. [Also see **The Effects on the Atmosphere of a Major Nuclear Exchange**, a report of the National Research Council (Washington: National Academy of Sciences, Dec 1984/193p/$14.50) which also finds a clear possibility of a nuclear winter despite great uncertainty. A brief summary of the first TTAPS study is provided in a 15-page "Nuclear Winter" supplement by Anne Ehrlich, *Bulletin of the Atomic Scientists*, April 1984.] **(nuclear winter studies)**

6603
Nuclear Weapons and Nuclear War: A Source Book for Health Professionals. Edited by Christine Cassel (Mt Sinai Medical Center, NYC) *et al*. NY: Praeger Publishers, July 1984/553p/$29.95;$12.95pb.

Selected readings made primarily from the point of view of medicine and human biology. Topics include medical responsibility and nuclear war, the threat of accidental nuclear war, a digest of nuclear weaponry, immediate biological effects of detonation, radiation injury, the physician's role in the post-attack period, long-term effects of radiation, long-term ecological effects, sociopsychological aspects of the arms race, economic implications of the arms race, patriotism and war, the civil defense debate, arms control proposals, and the effects of nuclear winter.

(nuclear war anthoology)

6604
Nuclear War: A Teaching Guide (Special Supplement), edited by Dick Ringler (Prof of English, U of Wisconsin), *Bulletin of the Atomic Scientists*, 40:10, Dec 1984, 32p (insert).

Brief essays on nuclear-age education, war/peace and liberal education, and approaches in the following disciplines and professions: physical sciences, engineering, biological sciences, social sciences, history, humanities, religious studies, medicine [also see sourcebook above], law, journalism, education, interdisciplinary programs, institution-wide programs, and inter-institution programs.

(nuclear war teaching guide)

*6605
Thinking About the Unthinkable in the 1980s. Herman Kahn. NY: Simon and Schuster, July 1984/250p/ $16.95.

When **Thinking About the Unthinkable** was published in 1962, not thinking about nuclear war was still an option. It no longer is. Even though the possibilities of nuclear war are remote, they are probable enough that they must be taken with deadly seriousness. But the debate over nuclear war and national security policy is often confused. Certain irrelevant or foolish assertions should be eliminated from the debate, e.g., "we should seek total world wide disarmament," "control of nuclear weapons should be pursued through an effective world government," "there should be a total nuclear freeze," "deterrence must fail eventually (nuclear weapons will probably be used sometime in the next 100 years, but their use is much more likely to be small and limited)," "a nuclear war can be limited" or "there is no possibility of a limited war." Five categories of "not-implausible" outbreak scenarios are provided in order of increasing probability of occurrence: 1) surprise nuclear attack, deliberate or inadvertent; 2) early eruption to nuclear war from an intense crisis (e.g. in Persian Gulf, East Europe, East Asia); 3) US first strike to defend Western Europe (the "classic" scenario for outbreak of nuclear war); 4) escalation to nuclear war from a protracted crisis; 5) escalation from a war of competitive mobilization. Concludes with a proposal for a "long-range antinuclear policy," which is seen as the only politically, morally, and militarily defensible policy. Such a policy should make nuclear weapons be and seem to be virtually unusable (politically or physically), prevent nuclear intimidation, decrease the prestige associated with owning nuclear weapons, be flexible enough to withstand crises, and contain a declaration of no first use. [NOTE: A useful prod to thinking, whether one agrees with the late Herman Kahn or not. Unlike most writers/analysts/critics/intellectuals who ignore or grossly distort opposing arguments, Kahn takes on all comers.]

(Kahn rethinks the unthinkable)

6606

US-Soviet Relations and Nuclear Risk Reduction, Joseph S. Nye, Jr (Prof of Government, Harvard U), *Political Science Quarterly*, 99:3, Fall 1984, 401-414.

Although the Soviet Union will remain an enigma, its nuclear capability is an inescapable fact, and there is broad public concern over whether we can manage the relationship so as to reduce the risk of nuclear war. Efforts to reduce this risk must start with an understanding of the likely paths by which a nuclear war might begin. Ranked by probability, they are: 1) escalation of a conventional war; 2) a pre-emptive attack launched in desperation in a time of crisis, because one side rightly or wrongly believes that the other intends to strike first; 3) accidental use of nuclear weapons by malfunctions of people or machines; 4) initiation by terrorist organizations or nuclear-armed nations other than the superpowers; 5) a surprise attack by one superpower on all or part of the nuclear forces of the other. A variety of measures can be taken to reduce the risk of nuclear war along each of these five paths. Measures such as improving physical communications (upgrading the Hotline) or sharing and evaluating information (such as a joint crisis center) are useful in managing a crisis that has already begun. But they may not be very significant in preventing crises from arising. A serious strategy for nuclear risk reduction should employ multiple measures addressed to the whole range of possible paths to a nuclear war. **(reducing nuclear war risk)**

6607

A Strategy for Terminating a Nuclear War. Clark C. Abt (Abt Associates, Cambridge MA). Boulder CO: Westview, April 1985/c200p/$19.50.

Both deterrence and the potential for limiting damage are strengthened by pre-war plans for a nuclear ceasefire and stalemate short of holocaust. Abt explores the feasibility of antagonists agreeing to exclude their "open cities" from nuclear targeting and to replace strategic bombardment with retaliatory invasion to create less of a hairtrigger deterrent. **(pre-war plan for ceasefire)**

6608

Future War: Armed Conflict in the Next Decade. Edited by Frank Barnaby (Prof of Peace Research, Free U in Amsterdam). NY: Facts on File, 1984/192p/$16.95.

Fifteen chapters on why wars may go on happening (wars over oil, bigger and better weapons), where wars happen, nuclear arsenals, the risk of nuclear weapons proliferation, new war technologies (the cruise missile, modern combat aircraft, military communications networks), the automated battlefield of the future (guided weapons, unmanned remotely piloted vehicles, and perhaps robot troops), the military use of the oceans, war in space (by

Jeff Hecht; see #6625), chemical and biological warfare, the potential damage of modern war, the economics of warfare, the arms trade, war games and military planning, and the relationship between armies and governments. [NOTE: Not as futuristic as promised in the title, but a good introduction to the present military situation, aided by many photographs and diagrams.]

(war potential overview)

6609

Smart Weapons and Warfare: Facing Up to Hi-Tech Vulnerability, Paul F. Walker and James C. Mihori (both Klein Walker Associates, Cambridge MA), *Environment*, 26:6, July-Aug 1984, 14-18ff.

Smart weapons, sometimes called precision-guided or homing weapons, are missiles with greatly improved kill probability on the first or second shot. They get their improved deadliness through sophisticated guidance, better reliability, longer-range capabilities, stealthy flight, and more effective warheads. Like it or not, these technologies are forcing a fundamental reassessment by armies, navies, and air forces regarding their procurements, deployments, tactics, and strategies. The short-term impact is likely to be negative, as large capital items such as surface ships are lost. The longer-term impact may be more mixed: militarized areas of the globe may stabilize due to the dominance of defensive tactics, and military budgets may decrease if expensive and vulnerable weapons are deleted. But, at the same time, the spread of small, deadly missiles may turn non-superpower warring factions, subnational groups, and terrorists into powerful forces.

(impact of smart weapons)

6610

Gene Wars, Jonathan B. Tucker (Senior Editor, *High Technology*,) *Foreign Policy*, No 57, Winter 1984-85, 58-79.

The dark side of recombinant DNA technology is the misuse of gene-splicing to develop new and more effective forms of biological warfare (BW) agents. The rapid spread of biotechnology could foster suspicions of covert BW development. Despite a 1972 treaty banning biological and toxic weapons, the potential for a renewed biological arms race seems present. In the not-too-distant future, countries throughout the world will learn how to produce an enormous variety of biological molecules, including toxins, on a scale that was previously inconceivable. A large capital investment is not needed. At least three types of BW proliferation can be envisioned: 1) poor, non-nuclear countries driven to develop a BW capability; 2) use by paramilitary organizations such as the CIA and KGB (small quantities of BW agents can be easily transported, making them effective where overt military action is not logistically or politically feasible); 3) use by terrorist organizations. Mankind's ability to manipulate the fundamental processes of life cannot be disinvented. The only way to control misuse of biotechnology is through a verifiable and enforceable arms control regime. Efforts are underway to strengthen the existing regime. The scientific community should also play a major role in confining the new biology to peaceful applications. **(new biological arms race?)**

6611

CBW: The Poor Man's Atomic Bomb. Neil C. Livingstone and Joseph D. Douglass, Jr. Cambridge MA: Institute for Foreign Policy Analysis (675 Mass. Ave.), 1984/33p/$5.00.

Warns that the danger of a terrorist group manufacturing or stealing lethal chemical or biological weapons poses a far greater threat to US national security than the widely feared prospect of terrorists acquiring a nuclear bomb. The

authors examine the nature of C/B weapons, their use by the USSR and transfer by Moscow to third parties, and their flexibility as a means of political coercion, economic warfare, and assassination.   Concludes by urging the US to take a number of preventive measures such as improved intelligence and internal security capabilities, training law enforcement officials, and enforcing stricter controls over the production, sale, and transfer of C/B agents.
(threat of chemical/biological weapons)

6612

New Modes of Conflict, Brian Michael Jenkins (The Rand Corp), *Orbis*, 28:1, Spring 1984, 5-16.

The three components of armed conflict—conventional war, guerilla warfare, and terrorism—will coexist in the future, suggesting an era of warfare quite different from that of the recent past. Governments and subnational entities will employ these modes of conflict individually, interchangeably, sequentially, or simultaneously. In the future, war may be less destructive, but also less coherent. Warfare will cease to be finite, and the distinction between war and peace will dissolve. Hostilities will be endless. Both world wars of this century reflected the industrial age: they were wars of production. The growing use of terrorism reflects the postindustrial age: political power increasingly rests on the ability to create or control information; terrorists are primitive warriors in an information war. The destruction they cause is miniscule, but they create events that appear important and are often of great political consequence. Terrorist activity will certainly persist, and may escalate because of government resistance and growing difficulty in capturing headlines. At one time it was assumed that "the bomb" would be the great equalizer among nations; this role now seems to be played by terrorism.   **(terrorism as postindustrial conflict)**

C. The Arms Race

*6613

Militarization in the United States and the Soviet Union: The Deepening Trends, Marek Thee (Editor, *Bulletin of Peace Proposals*; Senior Fellow, International Peace Research Institute), *Alternatives: A Journal of World Policy*, 10:1, Summer 1984, 93-113.

The process of militarization today centers on the acquisition of armaments, the use of force, and the expansion of military influence. Economically, it tends to distort development priorities and to contribute to economic crisis. Socially, it accustoms a society to the preferential treatment of military interests, to undemocratic reign, and to inequitable distribution of national income. Culturally, it tends to corrupt human values, advance the cult of power, stimulate nationalism, and sap the spiritual and ethical fabric of society. The US and the Soviet Union are the authors of the global balance of terror, and the driving force behind the globalization of the arms race. Between them, they account for 96% of the world's strategic nuclear forces, 70% of the world's exports of major weapons, and 50% of global military spending. The deep structures of militarization in both superpowers are the result of several interrelated factors: the historical impulse, the political-military rivalry, the action-reaction-overreaction dynamic in military competition, the autonomous momentum of military technology, the misguided effects of military doctrines and strategies, and the sustainment of these structures by powerful alliances of elites. If it is to be reversed, militarization must be countered with broad and precise strategies to address all of the above factors.

This essay is part of a Special Issue of *Alternatives* on **Militarization and Society**, edited by Robert C. Johansen and Sherill Leonard. Other essays focus on trends in Africa (militarization has increased considerably in recent years), trends in the Middle East, trends in Asia (undergoing pervasive militarization), the economic impact of global militarization, and the social effects of military autonomy in developing countries. In their introduction, the editors lament that the unrelenting spread of militarization offends common sense and morality, and exacts a staggering toll on the health, stability, and future security of societies. Governments and peoples are locked in the self-destructive, vicious, and intensifying process of military competition. The deification of the military has not only failed to lessen the imperfections of life—it has magnified them. Today it is military values and institutions themselves that most vitally threaten human survival. [Also see **Global Militarization**, edited by Peter Wallensteen, Johan Galtung, and Carlos Portales (Westview, Feb 1985/240p/$24.95).]   **(global militarization)**

6614

World Armaments and Disarmament: SIPRI Yearbook 1984. Stockholm International Peace Research Institute. London & Philadelphia: Taylor & Francis, July 1984/700p/$62.00.

The 15th Yearbook by an international staff working on neutral ground, surveying the world military sector and the success or failure of attempts to constrain military activity. Chapters are devoted to public opinion and nuclear weapons, the nuclear arms race, nuclear explosions in 1983, world military expenditure, the international arms trade and multinational weapons projects, military R&D expenditures, new technologies to strengthen conventional deterrence, developments in chemical and biological warfare, implications of genetic engineering, characteristics of ballistic missiles, the military use of outer space, nuclear weapons command/control/communications, the Honduras-Nicaragua conflict and prospects for arms control in Central America, the conference on security-building measures and disarmament in Europe, common security, multilateral arms control efforts, and arms control agreements. [NOTE: Exhaustive scholarly detail; see below for the brief version.]   **(1984 SIPRI Yearbook)**

6615

The Arms Race and Arms Control 1984. Stockholm International Peace Research Institute. London and Philadelphia: Taylor & Francis, July 1984/208p/$10.00pb.

The third short version of the SIPRI Yearbook (see above), with chapters on nuclear weapons, nuclear explosions, world military expenditure (estimated in 1983 to be US $750-800 billion at current prices), trade in major conventional weapons, ballistic missile defense, negotiations on chemical disarmament, US and Soviet allegations of breaches in arms control agreements, and the conference on security-building measures and disarmament in Europe. In the Preface, Frank Barnaby (Director, SIPRI) warns that the armaments process has gotten dangerously out of control. The acceleration of the arms race is not simply a US-USSR technological struggle, but includes the acquisition of sophisticated weapons by Third World countries.   **(SIPRI Yearbook in brief)**

6616

Nuclear Proliferation Today. Leonard S. Spector (Carnegie Endowment for International Peace, Washington). Cambridge MA: Ballinger Publishing Co, Nov 1984/496p/$25.00, and NY: Random House/Vintage Books, Oct 1984/478p/$5.95pb. (Brief version in *Bulletin of the Atomic Scientists*, 41:1, Jan 1985, 11-14.)

The first in a series of annual reports on the spread of nuclear weapons, which poses one of the greatest threats of our time and is among the most likely triggers of a future nuclear holocaust. As of July 1984, five nations are known to possess nuclear weapons: the US, the USSR, Great Britain, France, and China. Although it has never acknowledged having them, Israel is thought to have an arsenal of some 20 untested nuclear weapons. South Africa is thought to have accumulated material for about 15 nuclear devices. India detonated a single nuclear device in 1974, but is not believed to have manufactured weapons. Recent developments suggest that Pakistan will acquire the capability to assemble nuclear weapons, and India and Pakistan may be on the verge of a serious nuclear arms race. In the 12 months ending July 1984, several other nations took important steps to acquire or expand their capabilities. If Pakistan does acquire a nuclear weapons capability in 1985, the international non-proliferation regime is likely to suffer a grievous blow.

(nuclear proliferation report)

6617

Resource Paper on the U.S. Nuclear Arsenal (Special Supplement), William M. Arkin (Institute for Policy Studies), Thomas B. Cochran (Natural Resources Defense Council), and Milton M. Hoenig, *Bulletin of the Atomic Scientists*, 40:7, Aug-Sept 1984, 15p.

A condensation and updating of the **Nuclear Weapons Databook** (Ballinger, 1984/340p), describing the current and proposed US stockpile of nuclear weapons. The number of warheads in the US arsenal peaked in 1967 at just over 32,000, declining to about 24,000 in the 1978-1982 period. There are now 26 types of warheads deployed in 28 different delivery systems. Under current plans, about 21,000 new warheads will be added to the stockpile between 1983 and 1993. In the absence of significant arms control agreements, the size of the stockpile will further increase in the 1990s. Concludes that, aside from a vision of nuclear superiority, the Reagan Administration has no coherent plan for the future of the US nuclear arsenal. The new additions will result in smaller weapons, greater accuracy, and higher yield-to-weight ratios. The buildup is moving forward irrespective of existing and proposed weapons control limitations, in that the Administration does not view arms control as a practical means to improve US security. "If arms control didn't exist, it is hard to imagine how the existing weapons acquisition process would be any different." [NOTE: Highly detailed.]

(guide to US nuclear weapons buildup)

6618

Soviets Said to Lead U.S. by 8,000 Warheads, Richard Halloran, *The New York Times*, Monday, 18 June 1984, A8.

A new estimate, prepared under the auspices of Richard L. Wagner (Asst to the Secretary of Defense for Atomic Affairs), shows that the Soviet Union overtook the US in nuclear warheads more than five years ago. It now has about 34,000 nuclear warheads in comparison to 26,000 warheads in the US. Until now, both government and private estimates have reported the US with a greater stockpile of nuclear warheads, and the USSR with a larger number of means of delivery, primarily in missiles. However, William A. Arkin (Institute for Policy Studies; see above) and Jeffrey I. Sands (National Resources Defense Council) assert that the Defense Department has inflated the figures to create a "warhead gap." They estimate the Soviet stockpile of warheads to range from 21,400 to 41,250 (about half of them built since 1979), with the higher figure reflecting an assumption that all Soviet missiles able to carry multiple warheads are armed to the limit, and that all silos able to be reloaded have warheads available for reloading. The Pentagon responded that it used other, top secret sources of information to arrive at its estimate. [NOTE: In whom should we trust?]

(Soviet warhead estimates)

6619

Myths That Drive the Arms Race, Franklyn D. Holzman (Harvard Russian Research Center; Tufts U), *Challenge*, 27:4, Sept-Oct 1984, 32-36.

There is considerable evidence that US estimates of Soviet and Warsaw Pact military expenditures are incorrectly calculated and misleadingly presented. Several factors explain the distorted view: 1) the widespread quotation of CIA annual estimates of total USSR military spending without deducting 15% of Soviet expenditure devoted to the Chinese front (removing this expenditure roughly halves the "spending gap"); 2) the CIA restricts its estimate to comparing military expenditures of the US and USSR; if contributions by our allies and the Soviet allies are factored in, the imbalance between NATO and Warsaw Pact military spending is sharply reversed; 3) as acknowledged by the CIA, dollar cost calculations tend to overstate Soviet defense activities relative to those of the US (e.g., we value the 4.5 million Soviet military personnel on the basis of US pay scales, which are much higher). The Reagan Administration contends that the Soviets are far ahead of the US; if they are not, it hardly makes sense to throw more dollars into US defense at the expense of so many civilian priorities. [NOTE: Of course it makes "sense," if one values ideology more highly than veracity. Also see ***Now a "Warhead Gap"*** by Robert T. Scott (*Bulletin of the Atomic Scientists*, 40:9, Nov 1984, 43-44), which describes questionable Pentagon estimates of the Soviet Union surpassing the US in the size of its nuclear stockpile.]   **(US-USSR spending gap questioned)**

6620

We Always Exaggerate Soviet Power, Jonathan Steele (*The Guardian*, London), *The Washington Post*, Sunday, 25 Dec 1983, B2.

The US rarely seems interested in serious analysis of the USSR; in the last 10 years there has been an astonishing decline in Russian studies and the availability of professional expertise. Many Western decision-makers insist that the only basis for Western policy toward the USSR should be the nature of Soviet capabilities—not what Moscow is likely to do, but what it can do. This inevitably encourages pessimism, if not paranoia, and leads to a "worst case" analysis. But the image of a remorselessly expanding Soviet Union, formed in the 1940s under the Stalin regime, is no longer valid in the 1980s. Within the continuing context of a missionary ideology and a publicly proclaimed faith in the eventual triumph of socialism, the Kremlin's perceptions of the world have undergone important changes. Soviet policymakers have to operate in an international context overwhelmingly suspicious of their intentions. This constraint has gradually created a pattern of activity that differs from what it might be in their ideal world.   **(USSR threat inflated by US)**

6621

The Threat: Inside the Soviet Military Machine.
Andrew Cockburn (NYC). NY: Random House, June 1983/
338p/$16.95.

Shows the difference between the Soviet armed forces
as they really are and as they are portrayed by the US
military and its allies abroad. The difference can be accounted for by a deliberate and continuous inflation of the
threat by the US, resulting in the emergence of a war
economy, a high rate of defense spending, and an ongoing
atmosphere of fear. Despite what Soviet and American
generals claim, the Soviet nuclear forces are no more capable of fighting and winning a nuclear war than those of
the US. Soviet soldiers are ill-trained, and USSR military
industries operate with gross inefficiencies.

(USSR threat inflated by US)

6622

American Arms Supermarket. Michael T. Klare (Institute for Policy Studies, Washington). Austin TX: U of Texas
Press, Dec 1984/312p/$24.50;$10.95pb.

Examines the policies, procedures, and goals that have
governed US arms programs over the past 20 years, and
how these programs actually performed in a number of
key countries and regions. The US is the world's leading
supplier of arms and military services. Arms transfers are
an increasingly important instrument of US foreign policy
because of a decline in the more traditional expressions of
military power. But these arms transfers have also decisively and irrevocably altered the world political-military
environment, transforming many once-powerless Third
World nations into major military contenders. The arms
trade is rapidly slipping out of control, as sales continue
to rise (albeit at a somewhat slower rate in recent years),
as sales of sophisticated weapons account for an ever-larger
share of US military exports, as the number of clients
proliferate, and as sales of arms-making technology and
military skills also proliferate (enabling more and more
countries to produce and export arms on their own). Increased US sales have been matched by the Soviet Union
and other major suppliers, thereby fueling regional arms
races. Contrary to the belief that arms transfers advance
America's interests, there is a growing body of evidence to
suggest that they are unreliable instruments of policy and
can actually diminish US influence. An alternative policy
framework should seek the following: 1) prudent arms exports that attempt to lower the risk of violence; 2) arms
transfers at all times subordinated to basic foreign policy
goals; 3) significant changes in the present decision-making system which tends to favor sales rather than caution;
4) an improved enforcement capacity to insure that equipment is delivered to intended recipients and used exclusively for purposes specified by US law; 5) promotion of
international restraint. **(arms export policy)**

6623

*Here The Superpowers Go Again: Costly New Arms,
No New Security*, Edward L. Warner III (Rand Corp,
Washington), *The Washington Post* (Outlook Section), Sun-
day, 10 Feb 1985, D1.

The resumption of arms control talks by the two superpowers in no way signifies a pause in the strategic arms
race. Even if they reach new agreements, both the US and
the USSR will almost certainly continue building and de-
ploying large numbers of new strategic weapons. The coming generation of offensive weapons is not more of the same
thing. The next round of new deployments on both sides
will involve weapons with improved accuracy and increased versatility. None of the weapons now under development offers the prospect of significantly shifting the
balance of power, or of enhancing either superpower's relative security. New weapons now on the horizon are enu-
merated: new ICBMs, new active and passive decoys to
serve as "penetration aids," improved submarine-launched
missile capacity, adapting older bombers and building
new ones that add significant capabilities, new ground-
launched cruise missiles, etc. These new weapons appear
destined to perpetuate the assured retaliation stalemate
and the rough parity in intercontinental nuclear attack
forces. **(arms race renewal)**

6624

NATO's Improved Conventional Weapons, Michael T.
Klare (Five Colleges Prof of Peace and World Security,
Amherst MA), *Technology Review*, 88:4, May-June 1985,
34-40.

The past five years of NATO's history were dominated
by a debate over nuclear weapons; the next five are likely
to be dominated by a debate over conventional weapons.
The Western nations have accelerated programs to develop
a new generation of precisely-guided nonnuclear missiles,
bombs, shells, and other weapons, relying on the ability
of computers and other electronics to deliver them on
target. But the longer-range and more powerful of these
weapons raise serious dangers of igniting a nuclear war,
and of triggering a new round in the conventional arms
race. There are two broad alternatives to acquiring high-
tech conventional weapons: negotiating a reduction in
Warsaw Pact forces and acquiring an array of defensive
measures that would not lead to escalation, e.g. training
and equipping large numbers of civilian reservists to attack
invading forces with short-range precision-guided muni-
tions. **(new conventional weapons)**

D. Star Wars Pro and Con

*6625

Beam Weapons: The Next Arms Race. Jeff Hecht
(Boston MA; co-founder, *Lasers and Applications*
magazine). NY: Plenum Press, Feb 1984/363p/$17.95.

President Reagan's March 1983 "Star Wars" speech was
the first Presidential-level recognition of an on-going
research program to develop beam weapons. This new
technology is being drawn into the arms race, as military
planners seek dramatic new capabilities moving toward the
ideal weapon. A high-energy laser would shoot a beam of
light moving at 180,000 miles per second. A particle-beam
generator would shoot subatomic particles or atoms, accelerated almost to the speed of light and carrying large
amounts of energy. In theory, both would seem more potent
than guns, artillery, or missiles. If demonstrations work out
well, a large development effort will follow—but success is
far from certain. Hecht devotes chapters to weapon system
design, the long history of beam weapons in legend and
fiction, high-energy laser technology, beam and fire control,
the X-Ray laser, particle-beam technology, high-power
microwaves, countermeasures and counter-countermea-
sures, high-tech warfare, defense against nuclear attack,
antisatellite weapons, battlefield beam weapons, and
strategic arms control. Concludes that beam weapons are
very immature, but they show signs of promise, and at least
some of the technology (most likely infrared, visible, and
ultraviolet lasers) has a reasonable chance at working sometime in the next few decades. The pessimists [e.g. Tsipis,
#6649] are so determinedly pessimistic that they are largely

shrugged off by most people active in laser weapon development. On the other hand, proponents of crash development programs ignore the very real technological limitations and uncertainties present in all beam weapon concepts. Without carefully planned experiments performed in a logical sequence, billions of dollars could be wasted in exploring blind alleys. Laser technology will not go away, and progress is continuing around the world; it would thus be foolish to walk away from its opportunities. On the other hand, there are no good reasons for a crash-priority major program. If beam weapons are merely another round in the arms race, they will be followed by countermeasures, and bigger beam weapons, and so on. The best we can hope for is not that beam weapons will end the arms race, but that they will buy the time to end it. There is little alternative but to continue working on beam weapons; at the same time, the US and USSR must both strive to build the mutual understanding and respect that can lead to a genuine peace. [NOTE: A very clear, authoritative, and fair-minded overview of a highly controversial emerging technology, although a bit weak on the politics and high strategy involved, which prompts others to call for a ban. But, as suggested by Hecht, is it possible to stop this technological thrust? And the idea of defending against nuclear weapons has a strong appeal to some, especially in the Reagan Administration. The "Star Wars" issue may thus be only in its early stages.]   **(beam weapons explained)**

6626

Space-War Era: It's Already Here, Robert A. Kittle, *U.S. News & World Report*, 17 Dec 1984, 28-32.

The militarization of space is happening at a quiet but rapidly accelerating pace. Experts say that the military thrust into space is so advanced that, if war were to erupt tomorrow between the US and USSR, the heavens would be a crucial battleground. The nearly 250 US and Soviet military satellites operating around the globe are indispensable to fighting and avoiding a conflict. In any future conflict, the first blow is likely to be struck in space: by knocking out an enemy's critical satellite links, an aggressor could leave the opponent deaf, mute, and sightless before the first battle was fought on earth. By 1990, even more dramatic developments are expected: 1) in early 1985, the first US space shuttle mission devoted entirely to military pursuits; at least 16 Defense Department shuttle flights are scheduled to be flown by 1989; 2) a network of 18 US satellites to be operational in 1988, allowing aircraft, ships, and soldiers in the field to pinpoint their exact locations; 3) a laser communications satellite may soon enable US submarines to communicate from the ocean's depths (at present, they must rise close to the surface to receive messages); 4) the Soviet Salyut 7 space station will place heavy emphasis on ocean reconnaissance; 5) a much larger Soviet space station, housing 6 to 12 cosmonauts, will be used for military surveillance and for R&D of space-based weapons; 6) a US antisatellite system superior to the Soviet killer satellite launched in 1982; 7) the invention of directed-energy weapons by both superpowers.

(rapid space militarization under way)

6627

Star Wars: The Soviet Thrust, *U.S. News & World Report*, 18 Feb 1985, 34-35.

A close examination of Soviet military plans reveals that the USSR is pursuing its own version of Star Wars in an ambitious drive to develop lasers and other exotic weaponry for a space-based defensive shield. The Defense Department believes Moscow might be able to launch the first prototype of a space-based laser antisatellite system in the late 1980s or early 1990s. Even more worrisome for

the US in the short run is a related Soviet project to create an earth-based missile defense system. Expert opinion is far from unanimous, though, on whether the Soviet program surpasses or even matches US capabilities.

(USSR Star Wars program)

6628

'Star Wars' Research Forges Ahead, William J. Broad, *The New York Times*, Tuesday, 5 Feb 1985, C1.

Defenders and detractors may fight over the feasibility of Star Wars, and Congress may blanch over its vast budgetary implications. But at laboratories around the country, there is little hesitancy as thousands of scientists push technology to the limit "in what is being envisioned as the biggest research project of all time." The proposed 5-year $26 billion effort, known as the Strategic Defense Initiative, is said by Pentagon officials to dwarf research for both the Manhattan Project and the Apollo moon program. In recent months, scientists have succeeded in shooting laser beams through the earth's turbulent atmosphere without distortion, destroying a mock warhead in space with a "smart" projectile, and testing nuclear weapons that channel their explosive energy into deadly beams. Critics say that the effort is ultimately futile because the Soviets could easily outwit any defense with simple countermeasures such as attacking the shield, protecting the skin of offensive missiles, or overwhelming the defense with decoys.   **(Star Wars research program biggest ever)**

6629

Star Wars Science Expected to Spawn Peaceful Inventions, Malcolm W. Browne, *The New York Times*, Tuesday, 2 April 1985, C1.

Of the $100 million the government is expected to spend on Strategic Defense Initiative research in the coming year, most will go for projects having little immediate bearing on peaceful applications. Critics of the initiative argue that the money would be better spent directly on civilian research. Defenders see gains for medicine and industry. Military designers are interested in building an X-ray laser to deliver vastly more destructive energy to a distant target in space than is possible with conventional lasers. Aside from its weapons applications, the X-ray laser has excited biologists, chemists, and physicists because of its possible use in a super microscope capable of taking holographic 3-D movies of the genetic code of a living cell. The development of death ray technology could also lead to safer fruits and vegetables by using a very intense X-ray beam to irradiate food products (thus replacing chemical fumigation used on many crops). Astronomy is also expected to benefit from the offshoots of weapons research: laser weapons would require precision mirrors, which may significantly enhance the quality of future astronomical telescopes. [NOTE: But do these benefits begin to outweigh the direct and indirect costs?]

(peaceful dividends of Star Wars research)

6630

Star Wars Plan Spurs Defense Firms to Vie for Billions in Orders, Tim Carrington, *The Wall Street Journal*, Tuesday, 21 May 1985, p1.

For defense contractors across America, the Star Wars program is more than a new strategy for national defense: it is "the business opportunity of a generation." The scramble for the pot of gold is on, with dozens of large military contractors setting up special divisions to snare business from the Strategic Defense Initiative Office of the Department of Defense. The industry is also starting to mobilize its fabled lobbying apparatus to build political support for what critics charge could become the greatest Federal pork-barrel project ever. The cost of Star Wars is officially estimated at $26 billion in the first five years. If the research leads to a fully deployed system, "it has the potential to be the first trillion-dollar weapons project," according to former Defense Secretary Harold Brown. [Also see *The Star Warriors* (Cover Story), *Newsweek*, 17 June 1985, 34-45, which focuses on prominent individuals involved in Star Wars research.]

(Star Wars: biggest pork barrel ever?)

6631

A Star Is Born: Strategic Defense Has Unconditional Support, *Policy Review*, No. 33, Summer 1985, 94-96.

A *Policy Review*/Sindlinger Poll conducted in May 1985 surveyed 2,318 Americans in proportion to the population of the 48 contiguous states. It found that 68% of respondents did not trust the Soviet Union most of the time, and 57% felt that the US could not protect itself now from incoming nuclear missiles. It asked if the development of Star Wars would make the US more secure, with 73.1% responding that it would do so, 8.7% expecting less security, and 18.2% not sure or seeing no difference. Respondents were then asked: "Even if a perfect defense cannot be developed, would you favor and support developing a system which protects most of our population, even if it cannot protect everyone?" The answer: 84.7% yes, 2.4% no, and 12.9% not sure. "Would you favor development of a Star Wars system for the US, even if it meant that the US would have to renegotiate or withdraw from our existing arms control agreements with the Soviet Union?" The answer: 69.1% yes, 6.7% no, and 24.2% no opinion. [NOTE: A most interesting strategy for the "pro" side of the Great Star Wars Debate, although a quite different set of answers might follow from a different set of leading questions.]

(73% see US more secure with Star Wars)

6632

Defense In Space Is Not 'Star Wars,' Zbigniew Brzezinski (Columbia U), Robert Jastrow (Dartmouth College), and Max M. Kampelman, *The New York Times Magazine*, 27 Jan 1985, 28ff.

The idea of basing our national security on the ability to defend ourselves deserves serious consideration. New weapons technology is shaping an increasingly precarious US-Soviet relationship. We thus must consider some form of Strategic Defense Initiative. Major issues to be addressed are whether such a defense is technically and budgetarily feasible, whether it enhances stability and the prospects for arms control, and the implications for our relationship with the Soviet Union. The simplest and most appealing strategic option is comprehensive arms control, but such a future is not likely, based on the Soviet record of compliance with previous accords. The second traditional alternative, mutual assured destruction, cannot be an acceptable long-run option, although it is necessary in the absence of any better choice. Thus a new third option, the Strategy of Mutual Security, must be explored as preferable. With development and some additional research, we can now construct and deploy a two-layer or double-screen defense, which can be in place by the early 1990s at a cost of roughly $60 billion. A conservative estimate of the effectiveness of each layer would be 70%; the combined effectiveness of the two layers would be over 90%. A three- or four-layer defense may become a reality by the end of the century. If such an advanced system appears practical, "its deployment may well boost the efficiency of our defense to a level so close to perfection as to signal a final end to the era of nuclear ballistic missiles." A research program

offering such enormous potential gains in finding a way out of the current maze of world terror must be pursued. [NOTE: An appealing argument by an important trio of authors: the former national security adviser to President Carter, the founder of the Goddard Institute for Space Studies, and the head of the US delegation to the new arms control talks with the USSR.]

(Strategic Defense Initiative defended)

6633

Toward a Defense Strategy, Kenneth L. Adelman (Director, US Arms Control and Disarmament Agency), *The New York Times* (Op-Ed), Sunday, 10 March 1985, E23.

The starting point for any rational discourse on the Strategic Defense Initiative is a large dose of modesty in predicting what science can offer in the future. How many times in our history has human ingenuity overcome human expectations and even expert predictions? The President should have options—not just one button. If another button to destroy incoming nuclear weapons might be feasible, shouldn't we look into that possibility? There are three other reasons to move toward a defensive strategy: 1) defensive technology has progressed markedly over the past decade or so and holds considerable promise; 2) the ethical dimension: if we find that some defensive systems can reduce the risk of war, then morality should drive us hard in the direction of moving the world away from nuclear weapons; 3) strategic defense research is a prudent hedge against the vigorous Soviet research program underway for some years. Our strategic defense research efforts are fully consistent with our treaty obligations, particularly the ABM treaty. Concludes that we must scrupulously guard against a vicious cycle in which defensive efforts spur the other side on to more offensive efforts. The future of arms control is envisioned in three phases: deterrence continuing to rest almost exclusively on offensive nuclear retaliatory capabilities (perhaps for 10 or 15 years), a second phase in which we move toward an ever-greater reliance on defense, and a final period bringing the complete elimination of nuclear arms. This evolution will depend on cooperation by Washington and Moscow.

(Star Wars defended)

6634

The Case for Strategic Defense, Lewis E. Lehrman (Chairman, Citizens for America), *Policy Review* (Heritage Foundation), No 31, Winter 1985, 42-46.

Today our nation can be destroyed in hours if not minutes by Soviet nuclear weapons. Our only defense is the threat of massive, brutal retaliation, or Mutual Assured Destruction. No strategic defense system can be perfect, but even a less than perfect defense would radically change the present strategic equation. A defense system 90% to 95% effective would represent an enormous improvement upon our present vulnerability. By comparison, an effective nuclear freeze would merely leave the Soviets and Americans still in possession of all the weapons of mutual destruction. No current arms control proposals—even the most optimistic—envisage such a dramatic reduction of offensive weapons. Moreover, the beauty of this particular form of arms control is that it does not depend on bilateral agreement and unattainable trust. "Indeed, strategic defense is the practical equivalent, and much more, of a nuclear freeze." Critics insist that US deployment of strategic defenses will intensify the arms race and heighten tensions. This is always possible, but if there is to be an intensified arms race, better that it be a race for peace and survival. A near leakproof defense probably cannot be deployed until the 1990s. However, an effective program can start immediately using existing technology for civil defense, air defense, and ABM defense. This would fulfill the oath and duty of the President to take all measures to defend and protect the US and its citizens.

(Strategic Defense Initiative defended)

6635

Assured Survival: Putting the Star Wars Defense in Perspective. Ben Bova (former Editor, *Omni*). Boston MA: Houghton Mifflin, Oct 1984/343p/$15.95.

The alternative to MAD (Mutual Assured Destruction) is a policy of Assured Survival, a concept perhaps first used by Jerry E. Pournelle. This idea rests on the possibility of defending the nation against nuclear attack. For four decades, the arms race has emphasized development of more destructive weapons of attack. Each attempt to negotiate an end to the arms race has only exacerbated it. But the tools for "warfare suppression" are being developed today in both the US and USSR. These defensive tools (high-powered lasers, drone aircraft and missiles, new computers) are not enough, and must be matched by new developments in our political outlook. Like MAD, Assured Survival must be mutual if it is to work. The only way to make the transition from offensive weaponry to defensive is to make certain that neither of the superpowers perceives its interests to be threatened by such defenses. The way to assure mutual survival is to make the development of space-based defenses a worldwide effort. A scenario of warfare suppression might involve the following: 1) the Western allies create a multinational space-based defense system; 2) the Soviets follow suit with their orbital ABM satellites; 3) East-West tensions ease and the two systems function more and more cooperatively; 4) capitalizing on this momentum, Third World nations create an International Peacekeeping Force of satellites, smart weapons, and a small cadre of personnel to direct the system (which seeks to prevent aggression across international borders); 5) gradually, many nations realize they can reduce their national defense burdens and rely on the IPF to protect them. Scenarios are also provided describing how the IPF wards off a Soviet invasion of Poland and thus prevents WWIII, and how a "good strong roof" over the US consisting of some 250 satellites armed with 25-megawatt chemical lasers almost completely stops an enemy attack in 1999. Concludes that there is no doubt that orbital weaponry will be built; the question is whether we have the political sense and moral courage to create a true IPF to make war impossible. [NOTE: A major breakthrough in the nuclear arms impasse, or the ultimately naive technological fix? Also see **High Frontier: A New National Strategy** by Lt. Gen. Daniel O. Graham (Washington: High Frontier, 1982), a major study supported by the Heritage Foundation. **American Military Space Policy** by Colin S. Gray (Cambridge MA: Abt Books, 1983/128p/$28.00) argues that there is no policy choice regarding space as a potential battlefield; the only question is whether the US will be able to defend its interests in space effectively. **The New High Ground: Strategies and Weapons of Space-Age War** by Thomas Karas (NY: Simon & Schuster, 1983/224p/$14.95) asserts that space technology will not resolve our frustrating strategic stalemate with the USSR.]

(Star Wars defense can suppress war)

6636

For a Limited Missile Defense, Martin Anderson (Hoover Institution), *The New York Times*, Monday, 29 Oct 1984, A23.

Former advisor to President Reagan admits that a full-scale strategic-missile defense is decades away—and we may never be able to fully protect the US from an all-out attack by thousands of Soviet nuclear missiles. But a limited missile defense, designed to intercept and destroy a handful of nuclear missiles, could be built now and could guarantee complete protection from the accidental firing of a single missile or a deliberate attack by a few missiles. The likelihood of a planned nuclear attack by one superpower on the other is very remote, but the chance of a single missile being fired increases daily because of growing threats of accidental launch, terrorist attack, or small nations acquiring nuclear capability. In June 1984, the US Army demonstrated that a dummy nuclear warhead could in fact be disintegrated in outer space with no nuclear explosion. Putting aside the complex arguments of a comprehensive Star Wars defense system, the protection of even one city from accidental destruction or from terrorist attack would justify a limited defense. If we can clearly distinguish between a comprehensive defenseand a limited defense against a few missiles, we should encourage the Soviet Union to do the same. If the US and Soviets both had the capacity to prevent accidental destruction of any major city, the road to strategic arms reduction might be smoother. [NOTE: A brilliant compromise or a pernicious foot-in-the-door to introduce Star Wars systems? In any event, this adds an important dimension to the debate.]

(defense against a few missiles proposed)

6637

From H-Bomb to Star Wars: The Politics of Strategic Decision Making. Jonathan B. Stein (CSIS, Georgetown U). Lexington MA: Lexington Books, 1984/118p/$20.00; $9.95pb.

A detailed analysis of President Truman's hydrogen bomb decision of 1950, and a preliminary assessment of President Reagan's space-based ballistic missile defense decision of 1983, probing the relationship between politics and technology. Contrary to widespread opinion, Stein contends that politics drives technological development in the strategic arena. The decisions by Truman and Reagan are similar in many ways. In both cases, the basic technologies needed to build the conceived weapons systems were not in place before each President focused national attention on these projects. In both instances, a military solution was preferable to a diplomatic or political solution (with proponents declaring that their concept would eliminate once and for all hostile threats aimed at the US). In both instances, a technical fix was sought, as it often is by those faced with a particularly vexing political challenge. Stein concludes that the Strategic Defense Initiative must be viewed as part of an administrative pattern of strategic decisions favoring arms acquisition over arms control. The strategic consequences, however, are a retreat from arms control and an acceleration of various trends that worsen crisis stability. The arms race in space promises to be exponentially more dangerous than the strategic posturing to date, because the Soviet Union will respond to our space-based defensive systems in the same manner it has responded to our first generation of hydrogen bombs. As an alternative, the time is ripe to pursue a two-tiered approach to offensive and defensive arms control that fits into the emerging strategic environment of the 1990s and beyond. We have no choice but to force the strategic relationship into one of stable deterrence at increasingly lower levels of offensive arms. In the process, we will strengthen US and international security for the next generation of strategic decision-makers.

(arms control as Star Wars alternative)

6638

The War for Star Wars, George W. Ball (former Undersecretary of State), *The New York Review of Books*, 32:6, 11 April 1985, 38-44.

President Reagan's abrupt announcement of the SDI on 23 March 1983 was "one of the most irresponsible acts by any head of state in modern times." The idea to develop some sort of antiballistic missile system was first debated more than 30 years ago, but was renounced in the 1972 ABM treaty. Reagan's announcement to provide "new hope for our children in the twenty-first century" was made after the most cursory consultation and preparation. Although the Heritage Foundation-supported "High Frontier" study of Lt. Gen. Daniel O. Graham, former director of the Defense Intelligence Agency, was reviewed and rejected by the Pentagon and the Office of Technology Assessment, the study appears to have influenced the President. After his announcement, the Administration closed ranks and supported Reagan.

The President's defense initiative is a fantasy that nuclear danger can be eliminated by a new technology. Unless Congress substantively reduces the requested appropriation, we shall be committed to a new stage of weapons competition that will further drain the resources of both the US and the USSR, while creating new vested interests in continuing weapons development. Quite conveniently, we may thus give validity to the current faddish but foolish contention that arms control is no longer achievable. After wasting vast resources on an ephemeral project, we are almost certain to discover that our country is in greater danger than ever, as the pendulum of advantage swings with increasing speed from offense to defense and back again, giving a relentless dynamic to the arms race. And so we may unwittingly confirm the President's assertion that his Star Wars proposal "holds the promise of changing the course of history."

(Star Wars: to change the course of history?)

6639

The Real Meaning of Star Wars, E.P. Thompson (VP, Committee for Nuclear Disarmament), *The Nation*, 9 March 1985, 273-275.

British historian warns that, ideologically, Star Wars represents the ultimate breakdown of deterrence theory—an attempt by the US nuclear establishment to return to the womb of Hiroshima. The Star Wars ideological delirium is attuned to all the worst traditions of American right-wing populism: with astonishing simplicity it combines isolationism ("They can't get us") with external menace. It combines the faith that whatever America does must be moral with the American preference for fixing things by technological means rather than political resolution. We should not dismiss this as mere politicians' talk. When the most powerful nation on earth crawls back into an ideological womb, it means that an epoch is coming to an end. It is a terrifying signal of our human predicament. This combination of material avarice (the arms lobbby) and ideological self-delusion may prove to be the terminal dementia of the nuclear age. There will never be an impermeable shield against nuclear evil; the only shield against chaos is that of the human conscience, and it is time to put it in repair. **(Star Wars: "ideological delirium")**

6640

Star Wars: Bad Even If It Works, Charles L. Glaser (Avoiding Nuclear War Project, Harvard U), *Bulletin of the Atomic Scientists*, 41:3, March 1985, 13-16. **(Longer version in** *International Security*, Fall 1984.)

Strategic defense and the prospect of invulnerability to nuclear attack have undeniable appeal. But no one should be romantic or unrealistic about the world that would result from highly effective defenses—strategic defense cannot return us to a prenuclear world. The arguments for not dramatically altering the nuclear status quo are much stronger than those favoring strategic defense. 1) **Sensitivity to Small Improvements**: a situation in which both superpowers deployed nearly inpenetrable defenses would be extremely sensitive to small improvements in one country's ability to penetrate; by contrast the addition of new warheads to the redundant assured-destruction capabilities of the superpowers does not significantly alter the nuclear situation; 2) **Pressure to Improve**: in a world of nearly impenetrable defenses, nations would feel tremendous pressure to try to defeat the adversary's defenses and to improve their offense; 3) **Uncertainty**: the effectiveness of the defenses would be uncertain, and neither the US nor the USSR would ever feel adequately defended; 4) **Suitcase Bombs**: the ability to defend effectively against airborne bombs could greatly increase the importance of clandestinely delivered nuclear weapons placed on Soviet ships and commerical airplanes or carried into the US by Soviet agents (such deliveries are now possible); 5) **Conventional War**: nearly impenetrable defenses could increase the probability of superpower conventional wars; 6) **Allies**: if strategic defense were believed to increase the probability of conventional war, tremendous resistance by European allies should be anticipated; 7) **Pressures Against Cooperation**: conditions of reduced vulnerability would make a political environment in which cooperation between the US and USSR is far more difficult to establish than under conditions of assured destruction. **(Star Wars questioned)**

6641

'Star Wars'—Costly, Futile, Henry Bienen (Prof of Politics, Princeton U) and Jeremiah P. Ostriker (Chairman, Astrophysical Sciences Dept, Princeton U), *The New York Times*, Sunday, 13 Jan 1985, E25.

The strategic defense initiative, or Star Wars, is futile, dangerous, and costly. The stark fact must be stated: we cannot protect most of our people from nuclear attack. Cities are vulnerable to low-flying cruise missiles, submarine-launched missiles, and nuclear weapons detonated by terrorists. Star Wars would not protect us from any of these weapons systems. Moreover, a Star Wars defense would undoubtedly create an incentive for yet another multiplication of offensive missile systems. Based on the recent history of bargaining, Star Wars cannot be used effectively as a bargaining chip either. Research on Star Wars should be continued to avoid being surprised by a Soviet technical breakthrough, but we should not proceed beyond research to a major arms buildup. The nuclear airplane and high altitude bomber, despite heavy initial spending, were stopped when their technical deficiencies were exposed. It is not too late to drastically scale back the Star Wars program. **(Star Wars questioned)**

6642

The President's Choice: Star Wars or Arms Control, McGeorge Bundy, George F. Kennan, Robert S. McNamara, and Gerard Smith, *Foreign Affairs*, 63:2, Winter 1984-85, 264-278.

The central flaw in President Reagan's proposed Strategic Defense Initiative, popularly known as "Star Wars," is that it cannot be achieved. The overwhelming consensus of the US technical community indicates no prospect whatever that science and technology can, at any time in the next several decades, make nuclear weapons impotent and obsolete. It is fanciful in the extreme to suppose that the prospect of any new US deployment to undermine the effectiveness of Soviet missiles will not be met by a determined response. Even if a 100% leak-proof defense could be achieved against missiles, there would remain the difficulty of defense against bomber aircraft and the clandestine introduction of warheads. The last thing Americans want or need is an astronomic bill for a vastly intensified nuclear competition, sold under a false label. The Anti-Ballistic Missile Treaty of 1972, which outlaws any Star Wars defense, should be reaffirmed, and efforts made to broaden its coverage and tighten some of its language. There should also be a further exploration of the possibility of an agreement that would safeguard the peaceful uses of space—uses that have much greater value to us than to the Soviets. [This argument is countered by Senator Jake Garn (R-Utah), who asserts that the Strategic Defensive initiative will reduce the threat of nuclear war, and that the Soviets need no stimulus from the US to prompt a military buildup (*New York Times* Letter, 16 Dec 1984, 12E).]   **(Star Wars questioned)**

6643

Star Wars and the State of Our Souls. Patricia M. Mische (Co-Founder, GEA). Whole Earth Papers No. 20. East Orange NJ: Global Education Associates (552 Park Ave), Sept 1984/76p/$2.50pb.

Two essays arguing that the Star Wars proposals offer no real breakthroughs in strengthening US or world security. The tragedy is that in a Faustian fascination with doing what is technologically possible, we may sell our souls. Three clusterings of weapons are reviewed: 1) anti-satellite weapons (ASATs) aimed at destroying an opponent's satellites; 2) the Star Wars anti-ballistic missile (ABM) systems, involving high-energy lasers and particle beams; and 3) the multi-layered "High Frontier" proposal of Lt. Gen. Daniel O. Graham (including a spaceborne filter of 432 orbiting battle stations, a second layer to intercept missiles that make it through the first layer, a ground-based system to intercept any additional leakages, and a passive fourth layer of civil defense). Concludes that if we are to make outer space the first frontier for peace, we need a comprehensive ban on all space weapons in the immediate future.

This pamphlet ends with a brief proposal by Robert M. Bowman (President, Institute for Space and Security Studies, Potomac MD) for a Deep Freeze: a comprehensive agreement ending development, production, and deployment of all strategic systems, nuclear weapons, delivery systems, space weaponry, directed energy weapons, chemical weapons, and biological weapons. Such a freeze would end the race toward an elusive superiority which neither the US or USSR can achieve. Although a single comprehensive agreement cannot be attained immediately, a list of positive steps is offered that the US could take without risk (e.g., ratify SALT II, establish a Peace Academy, re-establish scientific and education relations with the USSR).   **(Star Wars questioned)**

6644

Star Wars Means Only Trouble, Stanley Hoffman (Chairman, Center for European Studies, Harvard U), *The New York Times* (Op-Ed), Monday, 25 Feb 1985, A17.

The main attraction of the Strategic Defense Initiative or Star Wars is the eventual return to America's historic invulnerability. But most experts believe that such defense is extremely distant and doomed to imperfection. Once the public realizes this, will it be willing to pay the enormous cost of a dubious defense program? Just as we have developed new weapons aimed at penetrating or overwhelming every defense the USSR has devised, the USSR is likely to concentrate on ways of keeping our nuclear forces vulnerable. And they are unlikely to consent to the drastic reduction of offensive weapons we seek, unless we scrap or drastically constrain our defensive program. As the superpowers continue to seek ways to make each other's nuclear forces vulnerable, the Europeans would look with dismay at the destruction of arms control possibilities and the resulting political tensions between the superpowers that increase the chances of a conventional war in Europe. In the foreseeable future, defensive buildups would at best only supplement deterrence; far from contributing to its stability, they would make it even more uncertain than has the recent development of offensive technologies by both sides. The line between deterrence and provocation would be even more blurred. The spiral of insanity driven by a combination of shortsighted military logic and political illusions would spin more giddily than ever.

(Star Wars questioned)

6645

It's Still Star Wars (Editorial), *The New York Times*, Sunday, 24 Feb 1985, 18E.

President Reagan and his aides have been selling Star Wars on four different, incompatible grounds: 1) It is the only moral defense in the nuclear age (but any defense paired with an offense would be highly provocative to the USSR); 2) It is only research for our grandchildren (but no program proclaimed with trumpets from the Oval Office will be "research" in Soviet eyes); 3) It will soon be useful, even if imperfect (but the Soviets can keep up with US defense technology); 4) It is really just a bargaining chip and a stimulus to arms control (but the President says that Star Wars is not negotiable). Concludes that if Star Wars is not practical to defend cities, not necessary to defend missiles, too grandiose to be just research, and not even a bargaining chip, what is it? "Whatever the President may call it, it's still Star Wars, the most far-fetched yet least considered venture of the nuclear age."

(Star Wars questioned)

6646

Directed Energy Missile Defense in Space. Ashton B. Carter (MIT). Prepared for the U.S. Office of Technology Assessment. Washington: USGPO, 1984/98p/$4.50pb.

A physicist who formerly worked for the Pentagon's Office of Program Analysis and Evaluation examines the Star Wars proposal, concluding that the prospect of a perfect or near perfect defense from the emerging technologies "is so remote that it should not serve as the basis of public expectation or national policy." No final judgment is made about the utility of less capable defense systems.

(Star Wars questioned)

6647

SDI In Search of a Mission, Peter A. Clausen (Union of Concerned Scientists), *World Policy Journal*, 2:2, Spring 1985, 249-269.

The Strategic Defense Initiative has created the first serious prospect of territorial US missile defenses since the 1972 Anti-Ballistic Missile treaty banned such weapons systems. The strategic arguments for the SDI rest on two fundamentally flawed premises: an unfounded technological optimism about the effectiveness of space-based missile defenses, and a striking lack of realism about Soviet reactions to the program. Given the likely Soviet responses, the SDI can only lead to an increased threat to US security and a less stable and predictable strategic environment. Little time may be available to avoid the strategic risks and costs of the SDI. While the program is inherently long-term, the negative consequences of SDI will be felt in the very near future—long before actual deployment. If the SDI proceeds on its present course for just a few years, the ABM treaty will be fatally compromised and Soviet reactions will be set in motion. Only by its early demise can the SDI support US security goals. The SDI must be transformed from a strategic imperative to a genuine research program. Washington must change its characterization of the program, sharply cut SDI funding to levels appropriate for a research program, and support the additional arms control measures that are needed to preserve the integrity of the ABM program. A continued rejection of these constraints can only encourage the perception that the overriding US objective remains not arms control, but the illusory pursuit of military superiority.

(short-term negative effect of SDI)

6648

Negotiate a Ban On Space Weapons, Howard Ris (Executive Director, Union of Concerned Scientists, Cambridge MA), *The New York Times* (Op-Ed), Friday, 30 Nov 1984, A31.

Americans rely more on satellites than do the Soviets, so an arms race in space is probably more dangerous to US interests. A self-interested US strategy would aim at banning the testing and use of space weapons. The "Star Wars" program presents an obstacle to control of antisatellite weapons and nuclear arms.   (**ban space weapons**)

6649

Anti-Satellite Weapons: The Present Danger, Kosta Tsipis and Eric Raiten (both MIT), *Technology Review*, 87:6, Aug-Sept 1984, 54-63.

Anti-satellite (ASAT) weapons could not stop a nuclear attack, and might trigger one. Because of its technological sophistication, the US could probably develop an ASAT capable of destroying satellites in geosynchronous orbit before the USSR can do so. But the Soviets would undoubtedly follow suit. Once they do, they will retain an everlasting advantage because the US depends far more on satellites than does the USSR. It is thus in the US interest to keep the Soviets from improving their ASATs, and the only way to do so is through a treaty that bans further testing and deployment of all ASAT weapons. There seems to be no reason why such a test ban could not be verified with reconnaissance satellites and space-surveillance facilities.

(anti-satellite weapon ban needed)

6650

Space-Based Ballistic-Missile Defense, Hans A. Bethe (Cornell U), Richard L. Garwin (IBM Fellow), Kurt Gottfried (Cornell U), and Henry W. Kendall (MIT), *Scientific American*, 251:4, Oct 1984, 39-49.

Based on a book by a group associated with the Union of Concerned Scientists (**The Fallacy of Star Wars: Why Space Weapons Can't Protect Us**, edited by John Tirman. NY: Vintage, Fall 1984/$4.95pb), warning that powerful groups in the governments of both superpowers act as if the aggressive exploitation of anything technology has to offer is critical to the security of the nation they serve. But does the President's Star Wars proposal hold the promise for a secure and peaceful world? Or is it a grandiose illusion that science can re-create the world that disappeared when the first nuclear bomb was exploded in

1945? If attempts are made by the US and USSR to implement a space-based system aimed at thwarting a nuclear attack, several factors will have a significant impact: 1) the new technologies will at best take many years to develop; 2) both sides are already engaged in "strategic modernization" programs to further enhance their already awesome offensive forces; 3) the ABM treaty, already under attack, will fall by the wayside. These factors will accelerate the arms race and diminish the stability of the deterrent balance in a crisis. A defense that could not fend off a full-scale strategic attack, but might be effective against a weak retaliatory blow following an all-out preemptive strike, would be particularly provocative. If the Strategic Defense Initiative were to be pursued, its questionable performance, the ease with which it could be overwhelmed or circumvented, and its potential as an antisatellite system would cause grievous damage to US security. The path toward greater security lies in the opposite direction of making every effort to negotiate a bilateral ban on the testing and use of space weapons at all altitudes.

(space weapon ban needed)

6651

Reassess the Focus of Star Wars, Senator Albert Gore Jr (D-Tenn), *The New York Times* (Op-Ed), Monday, 3 June 1985, A19.

Star Wars has already gained enough momentum to pose a serious challenge to the future of arms control. The initiative has been questioned, but often for the wrong reasons. Opponents argue that we should abandon or defer the President's proposal for a leakproof defense, but concede the feasibility of a more limited defense of our missile silos. They also argue that, despite the flaws in the President's vision, we should vigorously pursue research on strategic defenses because the Soviets are doing so. Both of these propositions should be challenged, because the likely result of a partially effective defense combined with a powerful offense would be perceived by the other side as a threatening first-strike capability. We should choose a different course. If Star Wars is a genie out of the bottle, we should insist that the research program remain focused and confined to ground-based facilities. Once Star Wars research is introduced into space, we shall have passed beyond research into a gray area at the threshold of weapons development. A mutual ban on research activities in space would reinforce the dividing line between research and development, and this ban could be verified. Such an agreement defining permissible research would be a first step toward greater realism on both sides.

(ban Star Wars research in space)

*6652

Forging Missiles Into Spaceships, Daniel Deudney (Fellow, World Policy Institute), *World Policy Journal*, 2:2, Spring 1985, 271-303.

The Star Wars plan is not just another major weapons program. In addition to moving the arms race into space, it poses a fundamental—and deeply misleading—alternative to America's post WWII strategy of nuclear deterrence combined with arms control. The seductive appeal of a defensive transition is the promise of providing national security without the politically taxing necessity of getting along better with the Soviet Union. The Star Wars plan, marketed as a program of "beating swords into shields," offers the prospect of uniting those who fear the Soviets with those who fear the bomb. But this vision is fundamentally illusory. Such a system promises to be technically implausible, fantastically expensive, easily countered militarily, provocative to the USSR, politically destabilizing, and likely to set off an offensive arms race of unprecedented proportions.

This article sets forth a peace strategy for space co-operation. The peace movement will not be able to counter Star Wars with the same arguments it has used against nuclear weapons. Instead, it must develop what it has often lacked—a strategy and a set of principles. To compete with the seductive appeal of Star Wars, the peace movement must lay aside its antitechnological ethos and its ad hoc methods. It must steer rather than brake technology. A positive agenda is needed, calling for large-scale cooperation between the US and the USSR in the manned exploitation of deep space and multilateral efforts to secure earth by making better use of space technologies. Such a two-part agenda could help transform the US-Soviet relationship and create a common security system, thus achieving more security than even the most successfully implemented defensive weapons system could promise. A program for space cooperation is not a panacea for the security predicament, but in the short term it does provide the opportunity to avert another confrontational arms race and to create openings for conciliatory diplomacy. In the long term, it offers the possibility of a fundamental reshaping of the US-USSR relationship. The choice before us is not whether to build space weapons, but how our species will evolve into space. The space movement and the peace movement are natural—even if unrecognized—allies. They need each other in order to achieve their objectives. [NOTE: An important proposal.]

(space cooperation as Star Wars alternative)

6653

Star Trek: A Positive Alternative to Star Wars, Daniel Deudney (World Policy Institute), *New Options Newsletter* (Box 19324, Washington DC 20036), No. 19, 29 July 1985, 1-2.

A brief, updated version of Deudney's essay on ***Forging Missiles Into Spaceships*** (#6652), warning that Star Wars promises to be technically implausible, fantastically expensive, easily countered militarily, and likely to set off an unprecedented race to develop new offensive weapons. Supporters of Star Wars have gained the upper hand because the peace movement continues to use the same old arguments against nuclear weapons, which will not be able to counter the appeal of Star Wars. The peace movement must lay aside its anti-technological ethos, and develop a positive agenda for the cooperative use of space technology. This Star Trek agenda would involve the US and USSR in three basic activities: 1) cooperative deep-space pioneering—a long-term commitment to jointly explore and colonize the moon, Mars, and asteroids; 2) earth habitability studies—using space technology for integrated studies of the earth and its environment; 3) information security—using satellites to verify compliance with arms control agreements. In the long term, this agenda offers the possibility of a fundamental reshaping of the US-Soviet relationship and the whole global security system.

(Star Trek alternative to Star Wars)

6654

Defense-Protected Build-Down, Jack N. Barkenbus and Alvin M. Weinberg (both Institute for Energy Analysis, Oak Ridge TN), *Bulletin of the Atomic Scientists*, 40:8, Oct 1984, 18-23.

Most observers will agree that a defense-oriented world is safer and generally preferable to an offense-oriented one, and that assured survival is preferable to assured destruction. But many arms control experts regard defensive weapons systems as undesirable because their deployment will touch off yet another expensive round of technological development, and no one has shown how to avoid the instability of transition to a defense-oriented

world. These concerns can be overcome by adopting a strategy that combines deployment of defensive weapons with a concomitant and compensating reduction of offensive weapons. Such a defense-protected build-down does not depend on the effectiveness of space-based Star Wars weapons. What is new in this proposal is the insertion of symmetry (and hence stability) into the transition process. Defense-protected build-down offers a means of reducing nuclear armaments without political and strategic risks, it can be initiated unilaterally, and it is not inimical to the strategic interests of the Soviet Union. [NOTE: A middle-of-the-road proposal.] **(defense-protected build-down)**

6655

The Strategic Defense Initiative: Perception vs. Reality, Wolfgang K.H. Panofsky (Director Emeritus, Stanford Linear Accelerator Center), *Physics Today*, 38:6, June 1985, 34-45.

Former President of the American Physical Society argues that the nuclear arms race has been fueled by permitting nuclear weapons to become symbols of political strength, thereby deflecting attention from their great danger. This triumph of perception over technical reality has kept US and Soviet decision-makers from addressing the fateful question, "When is enough enough?" We must not permit this to happen again with Star Wars, or we will embark on another upward spiral in the arms race. Despite the lack of a solid technical basis for SDI, a situation of enormous danger has evolved that includes a threat to strategic stability and the viability of the ABM treaty, a threat of new major military expenditures, and a threat of distorting technical manpower and financial priorities both within the military and the entire Federal budget. There is no technical or strategic justification for any action beyond a limited research program designed not to promote a project but to insure against technological surprise.

This article is coupled with ***SDI: The Politics and Science of Weapons in Space*** (pp24-32) by Gerold Yonas (Chief Scientist, Strategic Defense Initiative Organization), who describes four phases of SDI: 1) a research phase from now until the early 1990s, after which decisions can be made on whether to begin development; 2) a systems development phase, when prototypes can be designed and tested; 3) a transition phase when both the US and USSR begin to deploy their defenses in sequential, incremental ways while making significant reductions in offensive missile forces; 4) the final phase when ballistic missile defenses are fully in place and offensive missiles are at a negotiated low point. [NOTE: Other Star Wars pro and con couplings include Colin S. Gray and Harold Brown in *The Christian Science Monitor* (9 Aug 1985, 16-17) and Ben Bova and Antonia Handler Chayes in *The New York Times* (25 July 1985). In none of these instances has there been a genuine debate, where each advocate addresses the arguments of the opposing advocate. One would think that the gravity of the Star Wars decision deserves widespread and extensive public debates, rather than segregated side-by-side arguments, each untouched by any criticism.]

(Star Wars pro and con)

6656

Pie in the Sky—or Space Defense? *The New York Times* (Op-Ed), Tuesday, 12 Feb 1985, A19.

Two opposed essays on Star Wars. In ***Even Half Way Is Wrong*** by Richard L. Garwin (IBM) and Kurt Gottfried (Cornell U), it is argued that an interim missile defense system in orbit by the early 1990s would be a house of cards: the Soviets could easily demolish the two "shields" that are envisioned. The second essay, ***If Star Wars Works*** by Ben Bova (National Space Institute), argues that every revolutionary idea invokes three reactions: it's impossible, it's possible but not worth doing, and it was a good idea all along; if the new defensive technologies of Star Wars breaks the stalemate of mutual assured destruction, today's critics will insist that it was a good idea all along.

(Star Wars pro and con)

6657

Science Fiction Authors Choose Sides in Star Wars, William J. Broad, *The New York Times*, Tuesday, 26 Feb 1985, C1.

Science fiction writers are split into camps that either vigorously support the Strategic Defense Initiative or urge alternatives such as cooperation in space with the Soviet Union. They are speaking out, writing broadsides and books, signing petitions, founding and quitting societies, and lobbying on behalf of their chosen views. Recently the authors Robert A. Heinlein and Jerry Pournelle have been promoting the "High Frontier" proposed by Lt. Gen. Daniel O. Graham, in which hundreds of orbiting battle stations would be used to shoot down enemy missiles. On the other side of the debate is Arthur C. Clarke, who has testified in Congress against Star Wars, calling plans for a space shield "technological obscenities." Isaac Asimov recently quit the board of governors of the L-5 Society, a space lobbying organization, because it would not take a firm stand against missile defense. Frederick Pohl worries that most of the authors supporting Star Wars are not cold warriors, but people who want to trick the military into spending money on space.

(sci-fi authors split on Star Wars)

E. Seeking Peace

6658

Surviving: The Best Game on Earth. Norie Huddle (Alexandria VA). Foreword by Studs Terkel. NY: Schocken Books, July 1984/281p/$16.95.

A "Studs Terkel approach" to national security, offering interviews centered around the questions of how we can make the US and the world more secure, how we can create a positive vision of the future, and how we can stop and reverse the arms race. **Paul Green** (The Committee on the Present Danger) views the Russians as intent on world domination, and does not answer any of the basic questions. Admiral **Elmo Zumwalt** (Arlington VA) argues that countervailing power is needed in the absence of a world rule of law, and that US military inferiority has led to serious consequences. **Pat Mische** (Global Education Associates) confides that her marriage to Gerald Mische was dedicated to building world unity, and emphasizes the need to educate people to find alternatives; the infrastructure for a world security system is potentially there if we have the political will to develop it. **Melor Sturua** (former Washington Bureau Chief, *Izvestia)* insists that it is meaningless to say who has military superiority because both sides have the capacity for overkill. Retired Rear Admiral **Gene La Rocque** (Center for Defense Information) thinks that our overemphasis on weapons R&D has provided us with the best weapons in the world, but creates a constant instability in the balance of power. **Lester Brown** (Worldwatch Institute) argues for greater appreciation of the real threats to our national and global security: the need to develop renewable energy sources, increase food supplies, control inflation, etc. **Richard Falk** (Princeton U) focuses on the need for a better sense of appropriate human limits, such as not relying on technologies which,

if they fail, inflict irreversible catastrophes. **Hazel Henderson** warns that an economic crisis is developing from hyped-up military budgets that deplete the economy and destroy jobs, leading to increasing rates of inflation. **Edgar Mitchell** (Jupiter, Fla) views battling to the death as an obsolete concept from primitive times, and advocates working toward a cooperative model of human relations. **Edward Teller** (Hoover Institute) insists that we must choose between either giving up and forgetting about freedom, or being prepared to defend it and extend it to everyone; to maintain freedom, more US technology in warfare will be needed. **Harvey Cox** (Harvard Divinity School) stresses that we need a fundamental redefinition of what makes people secure, and a sense of what an alternative security system would be. **Buckminster Fuller** reiterates his oft-stated view that humanity needs a design science revolution so selfishness becomes unnecessary and war obsolete. **Yuri Antipov**, formerly with the Soviet delegation to the UN, states that the momentum for the arms race is dictated by the US, or at least by the Soviet perception of what is going on in the US, and that the main problem is the fear we have of each other. **Ina May Gaskin** (The Farm) points to the need for women's communications skills. **Robert Muller** (Assistant Secretary-General, UN) views the human species as very mature in scientific and technological fields, but requiring progress in improving the way we live together. Huddle concludes that creating communion and the commitment to each other's well-being is truly the Best Game on Earth. [NOTE: Mildly interesting, but not illuminating, for most of the interviews do not get beyond stating well-worn positions and superficial cliches; this promising format fails to evoke any new content.] **(interviews on security)**.

6659

Alternative Defense (Special Issue). Edited by Jan Oberg (Peace Research Institute, Lund U). *Journal of Peace Research,* 21:2, 1984, 95-192.

Jan Oberg introduces the essays by highlighting the need for constructive efforts to rethink and redefine what a civilized society means by such terms as "defense," "security," and "peace." **Kenneth Boulding** (U of Colorado) views the most important conflict in the world today as that between national defense organizations of the world and the human race itself, concluding that the only national defense that is now feasible is stable peace. **Barry Buzan** (U of Warwick) argues that security is a more comprehensive concept than either "power" or "peace" for understanding the basic problems of international relations. **Johan Galtung** (Berghof Stiftung, West Berlin) emphasizes that the most important distinction in the range of possible reactions to an attack is between offensive and defensive means of defense, and urges "transarmament" toward defensive defense. **Wilhelm Agrell** (Lund U) discusses a high technology territorial defense as a possible strategy for small and medium-size countries. **Dieter S. Lutz** (U of Hamberg) outlines steps toward realizing a regional European System of Collective Security. **Samuel S. Kim** (Monmouth College and World Policy Institute) proposes five "principled processes" for transition to a just, peaceful, and humane world order: a nonviolent revolutionary praxis, an ongoing dialectic between preferred futures and the unfolding present, a systemic process, a coalition building process working into all the key decision-making points, and recognizing transition as a protracted process. **(rethinking defense and security)**

6660

There Are Alternatives! Four Roads to Peace and Security. Johan Galtung (International Peace Research Institute, Oslo). Nottingham UK: Spokesman Press, May 1984/221p/$35.00;$11.95pb. (Dist. in US by Dufour Editions, Box 449, Chester Springs PA 19425.)

The four roads that governments and movements can try to travel so as to arrive at peace are: 1) conflict resolution; 2) a stable balance of power where both sides can agree that enough is enough; 3) disarmament, or pursuing a negative arms race; and 4) alternative security policies (transarmament from offensive to defensive defense, decoupling from the superpowers, national self-reliance and inner strength, and being useful to other countries so that belligerents will leave one alone). Chapters are devoted to each of these four approaches, with the conclusion that all have to be pursued in a meaningful way at the same time. A major difficulty in doing so is the traditional division of labor among these four components: conflict resolution and balance of power have been seen as the task of governments, while disarmament and alternative defense are left to popular movements. Good peace politics would make all four paths both governmental and non-governmental. A special department or Ministry of Peace should be established in all countries, so as to permit an integrated view and perhaps some integrated action. And why not a United Nations Peace Program, combining functions that are today divided? **(roads to peace)**

6661

Defence Without the Bomb. The Report of the Alternative Defence Commission. London: Taylor & Francis Ltd, 1983/311p/$9.00pb. (Available in US from Taylor & Francis, 242 Cherry St, Philadelphia PA 19106.)

The Commission proposes that Britain should get rid of its own nuclear weapons and secure the removal of nuclear weapons and bases from British territory. It believes that nuclear disarmament by Britain and Western Europe would reduce the danger of nuclear war and of a major war in Europe, especially if accompanied by moves to secure political settlements and wider measures of disarmament. A constructive stress upon unilateral initiatives is more likely to lead to agreement than the policy of "negotiation from strength" which in fact has tended to reinforce the arms race. The military posture generally favored by the Commission is one of "defensive deterrence," or having the capacity to inflict heavy losses on any invading force. Chapters of the Report are devoted to defense policy, Britain and NATO, military options for non-nuclear defense, strategies against occupation, and the process of transition from a nuclear to a non-nuclear strategy during the presumed five-year term of office of a British government committed to nuclear disarmament.

(British nuclear disarmament proposed)

6662

The Abolition. Jonathan Schell (*The New Yorker*). NY: Knopf, June 1984/173p/$11.95.

Author of **The Fate of the Earth** (Knopf, 1982; **FS Annual 1981-82,** #3349) points out the anomalies and deficiencies of the deterrence concept, which relies on the threat to perpetuate an unparalleled atrocity as retaliation to a nuclear strike. He proposes "deterrence once removed," involving a global agreement on abolition of nuclear weapons while recognizing they cannot be uninvented. Instead of growing arsenals of increasingly accurate warheads, we need a "nuclear weaponless" deterrence with nations permitted to hold themselves in a state of readiness for nuclear rearmament. Supplementing this nuclear weaponless state would be agreement on limited and balanced conventional forces and antinuclear defenses. With such a "defensive emphasis" strategy, deterrence would not depend on each nation's ability to destroy the other's population. **(nuclear weaponless deterrence)**

6663

Peace-Ways: 16 Christian Perspectives on Security in a Nuclear Age. Edited by Charles P. Lutz (Office of Church in Society, American Lutheran Church) and Jerry L. Folk (Augustana College). Minneapolis MN: Augsburg Publishing House, 1983/224p/pb.

Essays arranged in four parts: 1) The Nuclear World: our nuclear situation as a challenge to believers, the case for deterrence, why arms control isn't working, what other Believers are saying; 2) Arms and Justice: the arms race and economic security, the theft from those who hunger, war and sexism in the nuclear age; 3) Biblical and Theological Perspectives: biblical paths to peacemaking, the case for pacifism, the search for a "just security" ethic; 4) Aids for Peace Action: casting out the nuclear demon, political tools for peacemaking, the challenges for US churches, local actions for global peace.

(Christian perspectives on security)

6664

Ambassadors for Peace, Jim Garrison, *Resurgence*, No. 104, May-June 1984, 16-18.

Track One diplomacy—government to government—is blocked. Track Two diplomacy involves side-stepping our governments and creating our own diplomacy with the Soviets. The only hope for achieving peace is for people to take control over their own lives and insist that peace happen so strongly that they are willing to go around their governments and make contact with the other side. Organizations active in Track Two diplomacy include the Esalen Institute Soviet/American Exchange Program and the Institute for Soviet American Relations. [NOTE: Seeds of hope or a naive and dangerous delusion?]

(people-to-people diplomacy)

6665

Beyond the Hotline: How Crisis Control Can Prevent Nuclear War. William L. Ury (Director, Harvard Nuclear Negotiation Project). Boston MA: Houghton Mifflin, March 1985/187p/$14.95.

Today the nations of the West and the nations of the East face a similar danger. Each side has marshaled enormous military forces poised to strike at any moment. An uneasy truce has lasted for 40 years; yet, at any time, a regional conflict, a terrorist act, or an accident could suddenly ignite a deadly superpower confrontation. A system to control nuclear crises would loosely resemble other crisis control systems that protect us from fires, floods, and medical emergencies. Like fires, crises are endemic; some are accidental, others are caused deliberately. In either case, they can be effectively stopped before they go out of control. A joint US-Soviet crisis control center, located both in Washington and Moscow and linked by instant teleconferencing, could monitor possible dangers and stand ready to help defuse a crisis. In some ways we already have such a system. The Hotline between the Pentagon and Moscow has been used since 1963, and the Incidents at Sea Agreement was signed by the superpowers in 1972. We can create a full-fledged crisis control system from these two initial building blocks. Because it is common sense, crisis control is common ground. It is in no way a substitute for arms reductions, improved relations, or deterrence. But it is an essential complement to all three, dealing with the most likely way war might occur: people making mistakes in a time of crisis. [Also see **Crisis Behavior** by psychiatrist Lester Grinspoon of the Harvard Medical School (*Bulletin of the Atomic Scientists*, April

1984, 25-28), who warns that common sense is unlikely to prevail during a time of rising international tension or amid the panic following a nuclear attack.]

(crisis control center needed)

6666

A Risk Reduction Center, Nunn-Warner Working Group on Nuclear Risk Reduction (Senators Sam Nunn and John Warner, *et al.*), *Bulletin of the Atomic Scientists,* 40:6, June-July 1984, 28-29.

An increasing number of circumstances could precipitate the outbreak of nuclear war in ways that neither the US nor the USSR anticipated or intended, possibly involving other nuclear powers or terrorist groups. The two great powers need to initiate discussions aimed at establishing an explicit and comprehensive system for the prevention and containment of nuclear crises. To begin, they might agree to establish separate national nuclear risk reduction centers in their respective capitals, perhaps with liaison officers in the counterpart center or jointly manned centers in the two capitals (alternatively, a single center at a neutral site might be staffed by representatives of both nations). The potential roles of the centers might be: 1) discussing procedures to be followed in the event of possible incidents involving the use of nuclear weapons; 2) maintaining close contact during incidents precipitated by nuclear terrorists; 3) exchanging information on events that might lead to nuclear proliferation; 4) establishing a dialogue about nuclear doctrines and activities.

(nuclear risk reduction centers)

F. Defense Spending and Organization

6667

The Defense Reform Debate: Issues and Analysis. Edited by Asa A. Clark IV *et al.* (Dept of Social Sciences, US Military Academy). Baltimore MD: Johns Hopkins U Press, May 1984/400p/$30.00;$12.95pb.

Presents opposing views on strategy, reforming the military establishment, doctrinal issues, force structure, modernization and weapons acquisition, the organization of defense policy making, and the outlook for defense reform.

(defense reform)

6668

The Defense Program: Buildup or Binge? Richard Stebbing (Prof of Public Policy, Duke U), *Foreign Affairs*, 63:4, Spring 1985, 848-872.

Former Deputy Chief of the Office of Management and Budget's National Security Division asks whether significant military improvements are being attained, or whether our money is being squandered after $330 billion of real growth in Pentagon spending since 1980. The defense budget for 1985 is 50% greater, after inflation, than in 1980—yet our military force structure is almost identical to 1980. Nor are we producing anywhere near 50% more weapons than in 1980. Nor do we appear to be 50% more combat-ready. There are many familiar reasons for the inefficiency of the US defense effort: cost overruns, political interference, counterproductive military service rivalries, and gold-plated weapons. Less familiar causes have to do with management and leadership. While perceptions in the US have been of an aggressive Soviet military buildup, the real source of danger has been the internal managerial problems which sap our strength, leaving us spending an ever-increasing portion of our budget on defense with far too few improvements for the effort. Current proposals for more effective defense spending include reforming the

Joint Chiefs of Staff, reexamining the fighting doctrines of the military services, reforming the defense budget process, increasing competition in defense purchasing, and reexamining manpower requirements and military pay and retirement systems. Such positive changes require strong leadership. **(US defense spending questioned)**

6669

Defense Facts of Life: The Plans/Reality Mismatch. Franklin C. Spinney (Dept of Defense) and James Clay Thompson (U of North Carolina-Greensboro). Boulder CO: Westview, April 1985/c262p/$35.00;$16.00pb.

Originally presented as a Pentagon staff report by Spinney, and edited for clarity by Thompson, this study shows how the desire for high technology drives costs ever-higher and affects long-term behavior. Short-term decisions to increase procurement budgets in order to modernize with costly weapons have resulted in severe cuts in operating budgets, creating a very low level of readiness in US forces. At the same time, the complex equipment that is being bought is so expensive to operate and maintain that ever-smaller numbers can be afforded, resulting in a steady shrinkage in the size of US forces. The long-term consequences of short-term decisions have resulted in a mismatch between plans and reality. Even with an increased defense budget, US defense problems may worsen if past spending patterns are not changed.

(impact of costly weapons)

6670

The Pentagon and the Art of War: The Question of Military Reform. Edward N. Luttwak (CSIS, Georgetown U). NY: Simon & Schuster, Feb 1985/333p/$17.95.

The symptoms of US defense system ailments are the failure in virtually every military engagement undertaken since Vietnam, as well as the continuing inability to match Soviet military strength with a properly balanced array of nuclear and conventional forces. The key reform is to provide a central military staff that can present the true choices of national military strategy for the policy decisions of the President and Secretary of Defense. The rank and file of such a National Defense Staff would provide an integrated strategic overview all the way down the chain of command, overcoming the problem of interservice rivalry. **(National Defense Staff proposed)**

6671

The Key West Key, Morton H. Halperin (Center for National Security Studies) and David Halperin, *Foreign Policy*, No 53, Winter 1983-84, 114-130.

In the years following WWII, a series of agreements were made to divide US military functions among the armed services. The first and most important of these agreements was negotiated in 1948 at Key West. Although these agreements have clarified service responsibilities and missions, they have contributed to some of the most glaring failures of US policy in the postwar era, e.g., Vietnam and the 1980 hostage rescue attempt in Iran. Considering current policy issues, the Key West structure insured that the worthy idea of basing the MX missile on small submarines off US shores was never taken seriously because the Navy has a virtual monopoly on sea-based forces, while the MX belongs to the Air Force. If the US seeks to meet its military objectives, it must replace the Key West structure and follow the principle that no branch of the military should have to rely on other branches to carry out its duties.

(debilitating division of military)

V. ENERGY

A. Global Outlooks

*6672

Energy in the Global Arena: Actors, Values, Policies, and Futures. Barry B. Hughes (U of Denver), Robert W. Rycroft (GWU), Donald A. Sylvan (Ohio State U), B. Thomas Trout (U of New Hampshire), and James E. Harf (Ohio State U). Global Issues Series. Durham NC: Duke U Press, Jan 1985/188p/$10.75pb.

Energy is a global issue because it is characterized by an incapacity for autonomous decision (thus exemplifying the worldwide trend toward proliferating numbers and types of actors), it possesses a present imperative that impels actors to press for resolution that requires policy action, and it is an essential component of human development and survival. **Hughes** describes the current global energy system and the transition away from oil. **Rycroft** sketches six categories of actors: nation-states, international governmental organizations, international nongovernmental organizations, national interest groups, government subunits, and subnational interest groups and individuals (e.g., Amory Lovins is credited with having altered the entire energy debate). **Harf**, **Sylvan**, and **Trout** examine six energy values that categorize the motivations behind actor behavior: supply reliability, advantageous cost, economic and regional equities, environmental safeguards, regime maintenance, and national and corporate autonomy. **Rycroft** considers three policy-making approaches (political, economic, technical) that address three basic functions (production, distribution, and consumption) for both short-term and long-term payoffs. **Sylvan** discusses the forecasting of energy futures and alternative energy paths: a decentralized solar future, a high coal future, and a nuclear future. [NOTE: An excellent overview and introduction.]   (**energy as global issue**)

6673

Energy: A Global Outlook. The Case for Effective International Cooperation. 2nd Edition. H.E. Abdulhady Hassen Taher (General Petroleum and Mineral Organization, Saudi Arabia). Elmsford NY: Pergamon Press, Winter 1984-85/430p/$46.00;$22.00pb.

First published in 1982 (**FS Annual 1983**, #4758), this new edition has been extensively revised and updated. Contents include historical evolution of the international oil industry, the global energy supply and demand balance, the rationale for OPEC, impact of structural changes on the international energy industries, the North-South energy dialogue, an international energy development program, statistics on global primary energy, and energy scenarios for 1985, 1990, and 2000.

(**global energy scenarios**)

6674

Energy Productivity: Key to Environmental Protection and Economic Progress. William U. Chandler. Worldwatch Paper 63. Washington: Worldwatch Institute, Jan 1985/62p/$4.00pb.

Studies of energy futures help define the state of the world by exploring where current trends will lead, and influencing research, development, and investment. A sanguine outlook again pervades the energy community, as forecasters draw curves of growing demand (some suggest a tripling by 2025). If these visions become reality, the world will pay an enormous economic and environmental price. Among the consequences of using much more energy would be greater risk of acid rain, carbon-dioxide-induced climate change, species extinction, nuclear weapons proliferation, human dislocation, capital shortages, and debt. Most models of global energy demand do not consider the potential for conservation, which has barely been tapped. Conservation should be seen as a way to maintain a nation's competitive position in the world economy, to improve trade balances by reducing imports or freeing up fuel for export, and to promote economic growth by cutting capital requirements for energy. Chandler discusses this potential in terms of increased industrial efficiency, saving oil in transportation, and improving buildings and appliances, and presents scenarios to contrast with those of the US Department of Energy.

(**high energy demand future questioned**)

6675

Fuelwood: The Energy Crisis That Won't Go Away. Erik Eckholm, Gerald Foley, Geoffrey Barnard, and Lloyd Timberlake. London and Washington: Earthscan/International Institute for Environment and Development (1717 Massachusetts Ave), Fall 1984/105p/$7.00pb.

The poorer half of humankind still relies on our most ancient fuel for cooking and home heating. The world fuelwood crisis began to receive wide attention in the mid-1970s; since then, the situation has become steadily worse. In most countries, virtually every rural family relies on wood for all or part of its cooking and heating. Because poor people cannot afford alternatives, wood remains the main fuel even where forests are rapidly disappearing. As traditional wood supplies become inaccessible, villagers switch to inferior-burning shrubs and trees. The role of firewood gatherers in causing deforestation, however, has often been exaggerated; the spread of agriculture is usually by far the major cause of forest clearing. A 1980 FAO study estimates that 100 million people in 26 countries already face acute fuelwood scarcity, while another 1.3 billion people live in deficit areas and face a looming crisis. Coping with the fuelwood crisis will require a combination of activities: village woodlots, increased tree growing on private land, better forest management, rational use of crop residues, more fuel-efficient cookstoves, and genuine popular participation in decisions about community forestry.

(**LDC fuelwood crisis**)

6676

The European Energy Challenge: East and West. George W. Hoffman (Prof of Geography, U. of Texas). Durham NC: Duke U Press, Dec 1984/c250p/$30.00.

Examines the problem of establishing a reliable energy supply base in western Europe through structural changes and alternate and substitute energy sources. Covers such topics as lessons of the 1970s, energy efficiency and conservation in Eastern and Western Europe, security problems arising from increasing reliance on Soviet energy, North Sea supplies of gas and oil, international energy cooperation, and dangers of inaction.   (**energy in Europe**)

*6677

A Soft Energy Path for Canada: Can It Be Made to Work? (Special Report), Friends of the Earth Canada, *Alternatives: Perspectives on Society, Technology and Environment* (Faculty of Environmental Studies, U of Waterloo, Ontario), 12:1, Fall 1984, 48p insert.

A summary of the 1983 Friends of the Earth soft energy path (FOESEP) study of the potential for energy conservation and renewable energy in Canada to 2025. The full report, **2025: Soft Energy Futures for Canada**, was submitted to the Federal government and published in 12 volumes (a national report and 11 provincial/territorial reports) by the Department of Energy, Mines and Resources in Ottawa. All 12 volumes are available for free. A popularized version, **Life After Oil: A Renewable Energy Policy for Canada**, by Robert Bott, David Brooks, and John Robinson, has been published by Hurtig Publishers Ltd. in Edmonton.

This Special Report summarizes the impact and implementation issues raised by the FOESEP study and discussed at a Fall 1983 workshop at the University of Waterloo. A soft energy path policy would encourage energy technologies that are renewable, diverse, flexible and easy to use and understand, of appropriate size and location, matched in quality to end-use needs, and environmentally and socially benign. The FOESEP study was based on the judgments that energy demand forecasts are an increasingly unreliable basis for decision-making, and that, in a time of uncertainty when significant choices are possible, it is more important to try to explore the range of choices and their impacts than to try to predict which choice is more likely. The study concludes that Canada in 2025 could use 12% to 34% less energy than it did in 1978, in spite of a 50% increase in population and a 140% to 200% rise in GDP. Over the 47-year period, reliance on renewable forms of energy would rise from 16% to 77%-82%. This would involve more job creation potential and geopolitical security, and less environmental worries, than with the fossil and nuclear fuels on which Canada presently depends. Overall energy use would peak around 2000 at just above 1978 levels, then decline through 2025, provided cost-effective energy conservation measures are implemented at a reasonable rate. The mix of future energy supply sources was determined for each province and territory on the basis of availability through the study period, cost competitiveness, and technical feasibility.

The Waterloo workshop discussed key economic problem areas (full social cost pricing, the characteristics of a desirable future economy, the lack of delivery systems for soft energy technologies), implementation priorities (end-use efficiency standards, energy service centers, energy pricing reform, providing economic incentives for key renewables), strategic issues, and research needs. Concludes that any argument in favor of soft energy futures must concretely address the environmental, socio-economic, and political dimensions and be linked explicitly to the evolution of other sectors and fields. The soft energy strategy should be integrated directly into the more general Conserver Society proposal first enunciated by the Science Council of Canada (**FS Annual 1979**, #0767/0769).

(soft energy path for Canada)

B. U.S. Issues

6678

Principles for Electric Power Policy. Technology Futures Inc. and Scientific Foresight Inc. (both Austin, Texas). Westport CT: Greenwood Press/Quorum Books, Oct 1984/448p/$49.95.

An extensive NSF-supported technology assessment conducted within the context of six scenarios: the "Average Future Scenario" (a limited but growing role for nuclear and a dominant role for coal), "Nuclear Resurgence" (high demand and increasing acceptability of nuclear while disenchantment with coal grows), "Mega-plant" (high demand, with supply by unconventional sources such as solar power satellites), "Small Coal Plants" (high demand met by relatively small coal-based facilities), "Post Industrial Scenario" (low demand, as business activity is dominated by services and very high-tech manufacturing), and "Economic Malaise" (low demand satisfied by plants similar to those now used). Two underlying principles of the assessment are that electric power policies are inexorably interrelated with most public policies and many facets of society, and that these policies typically have long-term implications and are difficult to modify. Seven principles are synthesized from the study: 1) the importance of electric power to the US will continue to grow in the foreseeable future; 2) projections of the long-term size and distribution of electric power demand will be increasingly uncertain; 3) the range of practical electric power generation sources may expand dramatically over the next three decades; 4) the roles, structures, and procedures of electric utilities could change significantly in the relatively near future; 5) the means, extents, and purposes of electric utility regulation could change significantly in the near future; 6) it will be increasingly difficult for electric power policy to strike acceptable balances among efficiency, equity, and risk; 7) the single most efficient means of achieving flexibility in electric power policy is through broad-based, long-term research, development, and demonstration programs to confront a future that promises to be mercurial, diverse, and surprising. [NOTE: An interesting chapter on "Potentials for Regret: Policy/Future Mismatches" explores the consequences for society of electric power policy that anticipates a future that does not come to pass. Despite apparent thoroughness, though, this study contrasts sharply with the declining demand view of Flavin (#6687) and the Canadian soft energy path study (#6677).]

(electric power scenarios)

6679

Present and Future Perspectives for Electric Utilities, J. Sherman Fehrer *et al* (Electric Power Research Institute), *Environment*, 26:10, Dec 1984, 14-20ff.

The 500-some EPRI members represent investor-owned, municipal, cooperative, and Federal utilities. The Eighth Industry Survey, conducted in late 1983, assesses the concerns, needs, and priorities of 65 major utilities producing 60% of US electricity. The utilities reported their most pressing problems (financial concerns, environmental issues, and nuclear plant construction), their greatest research needs (most important is acid rain), and their perception of certain technical concerns (acidic deposition and disposal of ash and scrubber sludge are given a high likelihood of being important issues after 1994). Respondents indicated that they would not invest in any new nuclear plants, but would maintain a high interest in protecting the investments they have already made. By 1992, over 20% of electricity is expected to be generated by nuclear plants, up from 13% in 1983. **(electric utility survey)**

6680

Forecasting U.S. Electricity Demand: Trends and Methodologies. Edited by Adela Bolet (CSIS, Georgetown U). Boulder CO: Westview, April 1985/c230p/$23.50.

Forecasting methodologies and assumptions vary widely, and forecasters differ in their institutional perspective depending on whether they are private consultants or affiliated with the government, the utility industry, or academia. Based on a series of workshops designed to establish a dialogue between these groups, this volume assesses forecasting methods in the areas of industrial, commercial, and residential electricity use, and analyzes recent trends and forecasts. Topics include the changing structure of industrial energy use, least cost analysis of industrial electricity demand, factors affecting least cost demand forecasting results, commercial sector electricity consumption to 2000, and residential load forecasting. [NOTE: This book exemplifies the technocratic proclivity to get lost in the trees and lose sight of the forest. A fundamental difficulty of attention solely to forecasting method is that it ignores the articulation of desirable and attainable futures and thus, consciously or unconsciously, reinforces the status quo. The Canadian FOESEP study (#6677) illustrates a possible attractive future for electricity that would never be considered by energy forecasters. This is no small matter: on such visions of the future rests the fate of nations.] **(energy forecasting methods)**

6681

The Coming Electric Crisis, Peter Navarro (Harvard U), *The Wall Street Journal*, Wed, 17 Oct 1984, p30.

Author of **The Dimming of America: The Real Cost of Utility Regulation** (Ballinger, Nov 1984/152p/$25.00) argues that the market costs of generating electricity have risen at a faster pace than regulated electricity prices. This benefits consumers, but utility executives adapt to this rate suppression by minimizing capital expenditures. Once the current agenda of "hard path" power-plant construction is finished, utilities are likely to cease any further major construction. As a result, the dimming of America is now a real possibility, resulting in a stagnant economy. National averages suggest that we have substantial extra electricity capacity, but they disguise wide regional disparities, and there is no national grid at present to link the supply-poor and supply-rich regions. At greatest risk is the rapidly growing Sun Belt and states in the Upper Midwest. [NOTE: Not mentioned here is the prospect that cogeneration(#6696) and inducements for conservation (#6690) might compensate for the shortfall in supply.] **(electricity shortages coming?)**

6682

Energy Use: The Human Dimension. National Research Council (edited by Paul C. Stern and Elliot Aronson). NY: W.H. Freeman, April 1984/237p/$28.95;$15.95.

Although it is comforting to believe that US energy problems are well on their way to solution, a serious disruption in oil supply is always possible, with grave consequences for the US. Most analyses of energy production and use have ignored the important aspect of the human dimension: the cultural practices, social interactions, and human feelings that influence the behavior of individuals and institutions. This study by the NRC Committee on Behavioral and Social Aspects of Energy Consumption and Production offers chapters on the four different views of energy widely held in the US (energy as a commodity, an ecological resource, a social necessity, and a strategic material), problems of energy information, five views of the individual as energy user (as investor, consumer, social group member, expression of personal values, and problem avoider), the variety of energy emergencies, and issues affecting local energy action. Three characteristics of the national energy system were found to be central: the diversity of the US energy system and the ways that people and experts think about it, the uncertainty among policy makers and endemic mistrust among users, and the issues of individual and community control. Concludes with 29 recommendations, such as: 1) government and utilities should use the best knowledge of communication processes in presenting information to energy users; 2) energy information should be distributed through sources that are trusted; 3) Federal and private agencies should develop simple and understandable indices of energy efficiency; 4) more informative utility bills should be developed; 5) governments should provide energy information in disaggregated fashion for diverse users; 6) organizations should develop separate budgets of energy costs and form units to monitor energy use; 7) experiments should be conducted to share costs and benefits of energy efficiency investments between building owners and renters; 8) the Federal government should develop a broad organizational structure for energy emergency preparedness, linked with complementary structures at regional and local levels; 9) the Federal government should consider "stockpiling" information for an emergency, such as prepackaged news releases and TV spots; 10) research should be sponsored to evaluate the success or failure of local energy activities, how they begin, and how they are transformed.

(human dimensions of energy use)

6683

Research and Development: Widening the Energy Horizon, Joel Darmstadter (Resources for the Future), Hans H. Landsberg (RFF), and Herbert C. Morton (US Bureau of Labor Statistics), *Environment*, 26:3, April 1984, 25-37.

An overview of the role that R&D has played and can play in widening energy options. Until the advent of nuclear energy, R&D was carried out largely by energy producers and consumers, or the academic community. The 1973 oil shock broadened the scope of government R&D. Specific areas of energy R&D are discussed: nuclear energy (more efficient instrumentation, better personnel training), synthetic liquid fuels, coal combustion, and solar technology. Concludes that nuclear power research has increased its primacy in recent years, while solar, geothermal, fossil fuels, and conservation R&D are likely to lose ground, at least for a while. [NOTE: A tepid discussion that avoids consideration of how to choose wisely among alternate energy sources and research options.]

(energy R&D)

6684

Current Issues in Energy Policy: A Symposium. Edited by Richard L. Ender and John Choon K. Kim (U of Alaska-Anchorage). *Policy Studies Journal*, 13:2, Dec 1984, 303-431.

Articles on organizational learning and energy policy, political constraints on developing alternative energy sources, deregulation and energy conservation, state energy preparedness policy, renewable energy policy and politics, the natural gas industry, implications for petroleum refining from competition on the outer continental shelf, energy policy and boom/bust cycles, and a study of hard-path vs. soft-path advocates. **(energy policy)**

6685

State Energy Policy: Current Issues, Future Directions. Edited by Stephen W. Sawyer (U of Maryland) and John R. Armstrong (Minnesota Dept of Energy). Boulder CO: Westview, June 1985/c250p/$23.50.

The states are now in the forefront of energy policy in the US. Randolph's inventory of current state activities (see above) serves to introduce these essays on appropriate Federal-state roles, what states should and should not do to stimulate local initiatives, the state role in creative financing, redefining the roles of public utility commissions, state energy conservation programs, energy extension services, the residential conservation service, weatherization and other low-income assistance programs, experience in promoting renewable energy development, the costs and benefits of renewable energy tax incentives, and identifying the most inadequately addressed needs.

(**state energy policy**)

C. Alternative Sources and Technologies

6686

Renewable Energy at the Crossroads: Today's Contribution, Tomorrow's Potential. Christopher Flavin (Worldwatch Institute). Washington: Center for Renewable Resources (1001 Connecticut Ave, #638), Jan 1985/ 20p(8 1/2 x11")/$5.00pb.

Co-author of **Renewable Energy: The Power to Choose** (Norton, 1983; **FS Annual 1984**, #5841) notes that since 1978, US energy use has fallen 10%, oil consumption has dropped 20%, and oil imports are down by 35%. Most of this improvement comes not from coal or nuclear power, as the "experts" had predicted, but from a 23% boost in the efficiency of the US economy (better home insulation, more efficient cars, etc.). Renewable energy sources have a major role to play in the more efficient economy now developing in the US. Since 1979, the renewable share of energy supply has risen from 6% to 9%, with wood fuel and hydropower accounting for most of the growth. Important advances in windpower and photovoltaics are not yet visible on national energy charts, and the stage is set for at least a half dozen renewable energy technologies to move from the laboratory to the marketplace. Unfortunately, today's energy marketplace is still rigged against small-scale renewable technologies. This serves to cripple US energy security, as well as leadership in industries with stiff international competition. Sections of this brief report are devoted to developments in biomass energy, hydropower, solar thermal energy, photovoltaics, geothermal energy, and windpower. [NOTE: A handsome pamphlet offering an introductory overview and an update to the author's authoritative book.]

(**renewable energy**)

6687

Electricity's Future: The Shift to Efficiency and Small-Scale Power. Christopher Flavin. Worldwatch Paper 61. Washington: Worldwatch Institute, Nov 1984/ 70p/$4.00pb. (Brief version in *The Futurist*, April 1985, 36-44.)

Electric power has largely supplanted oil as the most controversial energy issue of the 1980s. Soaring costs, high interest rates, and environmental damage caused by large power plants have wreaked havoc on the once-booming industy. Electricity's future role is more uncertain than at any time since the first commercial power plants opened in 1882. Nuclear energy has suffered a series of setbacks undermining public confidence. Coal plants are a major cause of air pollution and are implicated in acid rain. Many

in the power business maintain that new demands will keep electricity use growing. But more efficient appliances and industrial equipment make this unlikely. Amid the confusion of muddle-through strategies, many planners have missed the most important development in the early 1980s: large central power plants no longer entirely dominate electricity planning, and a variety of small-scale power projects are being developed. This rush to small-scale power (including a mix of cogeneration, biomass, small hydropower, windpower and geothermal energy) has been largely ignored or actively obstructed by the utility industry. With the right incentives, opportunities for improving electricity efficiency and using decentralized technologies are enormous. The future will likely bring a combination of large utility grids, smaller mini-grids, and many independent households and industries. Though complicated, such a mixed system could be easily run and monitored by computer. Whether complete decentralization ever occurs, moving in this direction is the best way to contain electricity costs and improve the environment.

(**electric power in US**)

6688

Energy Developments: New Forms, Renewables, Conservation. Edited by F. A. Curtis (U of Regina). Elmsford NY: Pergamon Press, Spring 1984/1050p/ $170.00.

Proceedings of ENERGEX '84: The Global Energy Forum, held in Saskatchewan in May 1984, exploring international concerns on the technical, economic, and human dimensions of energy developments. Contents cover such topics as coal gasification and liquefaction, oil sands and shales, tidal power, biomass energy, geothermal energy, photovoltaics, energy conservation, and government incentive programs. [Also see **Hydrogen Energy Progress V**, edited by T. N. Veziroglu and J. B. Taylor (Pergamon, Summer 1984/2000p in 4 vols/$250.00), offering the proceedings of the 5th World Hydrogen Energy Conference, held in Toronto in July 1984.]

(**conferences on renewable energy**)

6689

Renewable Energy for Industrialization and Development. David John Jhirad (Brookhaven National Laboratory, NY). Boulder CO: Westview, Nov 1984/c200p/ $20.00.

Assesses solar thermal, solar photovoltaic, wind, biomass conversion, small-scale hydro, and ocean energy technologies for industry, transportation, the electric power sector, architecture, agriculture, and rural systems in the energy plans of developing nations. Special attention is paid to the economic, social, and financial costs of renewable energy systems in comparison with conventional energy options, drawing on examples from Asia, Africa, and Latin America.   (**renewable energy in Third World**)

6690

Economic Incentives for Energy Conservation. Peter N. Nemetz and Marilyn Hankey (U of British Columbia). NY: Wiley-Interscience, March 1984/324p/$45.95.

The 1973-1983 period represents a watershed in North American energy policy as the era of inexpensive energy disappeared, perhaps forever. Government policy reponses to increasing world energy prices and uncertain supply have been weak and diffuse. Only recently has a concerted effort been undertaken to apply appropriate economic mechanisms such as incentives. This book seeks to examine recent experience with incentives for influencing energy demand, and to offer prescriptions for future energy policy. Chapters discuss utility costs, electricity pricing, alternative rate structures, load management, residential energy conservation in California, and conservation incentives in Oregon and Wisconsin. Concludes by suggesting nine positive elements of policy design: ease of participation, significant monetary incentives, extensive information diffusion, consultation and participation of industry and community leaders, ease of enforcement, high coverage and impact, the need for mandatory elements, the need for follow-up monitoring, and the need for quality control. Conversely, the deficiencies of many current conservation programs include inadequate monetary incentives, inadequate prior consultation, poor dissemination of information, and poor targeting of program respondents.

(incentives to save energy)

6691

Energy Conservation Programs: A Review of State Initiatives in the USA, John Randolph (Virginia Polytechnic Institute), *Energy Policy*, 12:4, Dec 1984, 425-438.

Few states had any energy planning and policy experience prior to the 1973 oil embargo. Since 1976, state government has played an increasingly important role in defining and providing a clear national direction in energy. Their activities lie in three areas: administering a number of Federal energy conservation programs, broadening utility regulation, and initiating their own programs to promote conservation and renewable energy. These initiatives include tax incentives for energy investments, grant and loan programs, energy standards and regulations, and R&D. Randolph reviews the involvement of each of the 50 states in these activities and identifies innovative approaches. Few evaluation studies have been conducted to assess the effectiveness of these programs, and there is a wide variation among the states in the extent to which these programs have been implemented.

(state energy programs)

6692

Eclipse of Solar Power Leaves a Burning Need, Charles K. Ebinger (CSIS, Georgetown U), *The Wall Street Journal*, Monday, 29 Oct 1984, p32.

The stage is being set for a major crisis in the electric power sector within the next 10 years. Much attention has been paid to the economic problems of nuclear power and the environmental problems of coal. But a third alternative to greater dependence on imported oil has also foundered: the promise of renewable energy from the sun and wind is not materializing as rapidly as hoped. President Carter's vision of 20% of US energy coming from solar power by 2000 is only a distant memory. Photovoltaic power still costs about 10 times more than electricity generated by oil. Some large companies such as Exxon and Texas Instruments have been backing out of solar power. The industry for wind power has grown, not from energy or cost advantages, but from tax advantagers. As a society, we should not give up on solar and other renewable sources, especially because US electricity use is up by 6% in 1984—a figure far greater than anticipated. But we must view the prospects of renewables in a sober manner, while allowing the market to operate so as to power a healthy economy in the 1990s. **(faded promise of solar)**

6693

Solar Power: The Promise Fades, Roger Pollak (*Renewable Energy News*), *The Progressive*, 48:9, Sept 1984, 32-35.

"The sun has set on hopes for a radical solar future." Today, many of renewable energy's leading advocates are conservatives. The hippies and activists who started companies have become more corporate, or they have been bought up and moved out. Many activists were unrealistic about how a solar transition would take place, assuming that solar technology itself, once widespread, would make our energy system and America more egalitarian. But it turned out that renewable energy systems are not as simple, inexpensive, and easily controlled as many had supposed. They are ill-suited to producer cooperatives and worker-owned businesses. In such highly capital-intensive industries as photovoltaics, the participation of small business may already be a thing of the past.

(faded promise of solar)

6694

A Cloudy Forecast for Solar Cells, Colin Norman, *Science*, Vol 226, 19 Oct 1984, 319-320.

In 1981, the infant US photovoltaic industry was not unduly concerned when the Reagan Administration cut back on Federal programs in solar energy. Today, the industry is in trouble, and the US may lose its dominance in the field, primarily to Japan (which has a government-supported program called Project Sunshine). Although costs have been dropping steadily, current state-of-the-art solar cells are still very expensive. Over the past 25 years, the cost of producing and installing cells capable of generating 1 watt of power has fallen from about $1000 to $8 to $12. But costs will have to get below $2 per watt before the market takes off. To get to that point will require a change in technology, from today's cells made of crystalline silicon to some less materials-intensive process, probably cells made of amorphous silicon. (One manufacturer predicts that amorphous silicon cells can be produced for less than 50 cents a watt by 1990.) Although profits are still limited, worldwide sales of solar cells have expanded fivefold in the past three years and non-US firms have taken a growing share of the market (from 10% in the late 1970s to about 40% today). Japanese firms are already producing amorphous silicon cells in substantial quantities, and they are appearing on the market in solar-powered calculators and wristwatches. Faced with the threat of foreign competition and the difficulties of raising capital for development, many in the US photovoltaic industry are now looking for assistance from the Federal government. The industry's chief goal is to extend and expand tax credits for the purchase of solar cells. According to one recent study, if the tax credit is allowed to expire at the end of 1985, the US will lose its dominant position in the market to Japan by 1990. **(Japan as solar leader?)**

6695

America's Plentiful Energy Resource, David Osborne, *The Atlantic Monthly*, March 1984, 86-102.

The ideal energy resource is methane or natural gas, which is well on its way to becoming the world's primary source of energy. It is clean, efficient, and economical, but we have heard little about it because many energy experts in the late 1970s believed we were running out of natural gas. Although gas exploration is still in its infancy, the US is now experiencing a glut of gas so severe that producers are capping wells by the thousands. Respected authorities now estimate that the US has a 75-year reserve, while visionaries speak in terms of hundreds of years. Present forecasts of the Office of Technology Assessment perpetuate the errors of underestimation by excluding vast quantities of gas in tight-sand formation, in coal seams, and in Alaska. The key to stimulating use of our abundant gas supplies is to keep prices somewhere near the costs of exploration and production—and thus below the price of OPEC oil. In the anticompetitive gas industry, any of three measures might be used: 1) set prices at the cost of production plus a fair rate of return; 2) use Federal antitrust powers to force genuine price competition among producers; 3) establish a government energy corporation to compete in all sectors of the industry. Besides going a long way toward resolving our energy problems, natural gas is also an answer to environmental problems. In the long run, the wisest solution to the acid rain problem may be full or partial substitution of natural gas for high sulphur coal, and conversion of partially-completed nuclear plants to gas. [Also see a similar argument by Barry Commoner in *The New Yorker*, 2 May 1983; **FS Annual 1984**, #5842.]

(natural gas as world's primary fuel?)

6696

Cogeneration Jars the Power Industry, Stuart Diamond, *The New York Times*, Sunday, 10 June 1984, F1.

Cogeneration is a simple and inexpensive system for harnessing waste heat that otherwise escapes as electricity is generated. In 1900, primitive cogenerators produced 50% of US electricity, but this activity declined as America turned to big utilities and power grids. This old technology is now enjoying a new boom, as a result of sharply rising electricity bills, new technology making cogeneration equipment cheaper and more efficient, and a Supreme Court ruling in 1983 requiring utilities to buy surplus power generated by businesses and even individuals. In 1984, cogeneration is likely to produce 7% of US electricity, up from 5% in 1983 and 3% in 1981. Industry experts estimate that it will produce 15% of US electricity by 2000. Cogeneration is of primary interest to such large, energy-intensive industries as paper and pulp, oil refining, chemicals, primary metals, and food processing. These concerns are being increasingly joined by schools, hospitals, hotels, banks, and restaurants (e.g, McDonald's is studying cogeneration for its franchises). The declining cost of cogeneration may even make it economic for private homes. Some utilities are fighting cogeneration because of the loss of customers and revenue, and the fear that a few cogenerators may someday turn out enough extra electricity to compete as power utilities themselves. Other utilities, especially in areas of high energy growth, are advocates of cogeneration.   **(growth of cogeneration)**

6697

The Man-Made Sun: The Quest for Fusion Power. T. A. Heppenheimer (Fountain Valley CA). Boston MA: Little, Brown / An Omni Press Book, March 1984/347p/ $19.95.

Author of **Colonies in Space** (Stackpole, 1977) and **Toward Distant Suns** (Stackpole, 1979) describes the three decades of big science research in the US, USSR, and elsewhere to duplicate the fusion processes that are the sources of the sun's energy. This fusion power, which does not rely on splitting atoms apart but on fusing them together, is much less dangerous than nuclear power, and may well be mankind's ultimate energy source in the 21st century. There are two major and competing approaches to solving the most important problems of fusion: the magnetic-mirror approach being tried at the Lawrence Livermore Laboratory in California, and the tokamak reactors at Princeton University. Most of the book is devoted to describing the politics of these projects.

(fusion power projects)

6698

Nuclear Follies (Cover Story), James Cook, *Forbes*, 135: 3, 11 Feb 1985, 82-100.

"The failure of the US nuclear power program ranks as the largest managerial disaster in business history, a disaster on a monumental scale." The US utility industry has already invested $125 billion in nuclear power, with an additional $140 billion to come before the decade is out. Only the blind or the biased can think that most of the money has been well spent. It is a defeat for the US consumer, the competitiveness of US industry, the utilities, and the private enterprise system. Without recognizing the risks, the US electric power industry undertook a commitment bigger than the space program or the Vietnam War, and, in little more than a decade, transformed what elsewhere in the world is a low-cost and reliable form of energy into one that is high in cost and unreliable. Nuclear power was not killed by the obstructionist tactics of its opponents, but by its friends: the Federal government and the Nuclear Regulatory Commission, the equipment manufacturers, the contractors and subcontractors, the utility executives, and the state regulatory commissions. The failure of the US nuclear power program is changing the economic geography of America (weakening regions where power costs will go sharply higher), and the threat of bankruptcy has become a reality for at least a handful of major electric companies. Problems and possibilities for reviving the nuclear option are discussed, concluding that they cannot be implemented without sacrificing consumer, corporate, and state interests. [Also see ***Nuclear Power's Ever-Darker Future*** (*New York Times*, 20 Jan 1985, F6), which reports the advice of many energy analysts to abandon plants that are less than 80% completed.]

(US nuclear power a "managerial disaster")

VI. ENVIRONMENT AND RESOURCES

A. Global Overviews

*6699

State of the World 1985: A Worldwatch Institute Report on Progress Toward a Sustainable Society. Lester R. Brown (President, Worldwatch Institute) *et al.* NY: W. W. Norton, Feb 1985/301p/$18.95;$8.95pb.

The second in a series of integrative annual reports. Each edition covers the same basic issues—energy, environment, food, population, and economic trends—but from a different perspective. The first report (**FS Annual 1984**, #5601) focused on the components of sustainable development. This report introduces the notion of population-induced climate change. In the initial chapter, Brown warns that the world has been lulled into a false sense of security by recent progress in slowing population growth and reducing dependence on oil. The collective actions of a world population approaching five billion now appear capable of causing continental and even global changes in natural systems. As human pressures build, the relationship between people and their natural support systems can cross key threshholds, leading to a breakdown. Nowhere is this breakdown more tragically evident than in Africa, where famine is spreading across the continent. Population growth in Africa—the fastest of any continent in history—may be indirectly reducing rainfall by decreasing the land's vegetative cover. There are no developments in prospect on either the agriculture or the family planning side of the food/population equation that will arrest the slide in African per capita food production. In contrast, China's per capita grain production has risen 30% since 1970, due to halving the rate of population growth and launching extensive agricultural reforms. As the scale of human impacts on natural systems becomes evident, governments will be forced to make difficult choices. For many Third World countries, the choice is between an abrupt lowering of birth rates or a possible malnutrition-induced rise in death rates. In much of Africa, reversing ecological deterioration and economic decline may require international collaboration greater than any since the Allies mobilized during WWII.

Other sections in this report focus on reducing hunger, managing freshwater supplies, world fisheries, protecting forests from air pollution and acid rain, conserving biological diversity, increasing energy efficiency, renewable energy, stopping population growth, and rethinking the future (restoring soils, reforesting the earth, recycling materials, and responsible policy replacing ideology).

(**progress toward sustainability?**)

6700

A Condensed Version of the Next Century, Jeannie Peterson, *Ambio*, 13:3, 1984, 202-205.

Summarizes a special issue of *Ambio* on the world environment in the 21st century. Overall, the likely picture is one with a human population that has more than doubled, higher global temperatures than the Earth has known for millions of years, food supplies at variance with population distribution, a mega-spasm of species extinctions, a drastic increase in the proportion of older people, armies of unemployed and unemployable, and expanses of ruined land no longer capable of supporting agriculture. Other articles in this issue focus on global population projections to over 10 billion, managing water under conditions of scarcity, climate, the possibility of deserts doubling in size, future food supply, the fuelwood shortage, species extinction (by Norman Myers), major health problems in the next century, the employment situation, climatic change and policy (by Thomas C. Schelling), and the need for attitudinal change and technological choices.

(**bleak view of 21st century**)

*6701

Environment and the Global Arena: Actors, Values, Policies, and Futures. Kenneth A. Dahlberg (Western Michigan U), Marvin S. Soroos (North Carolina State U), Anne Thompson Feraru (California State U-Fullerton), James E. Harf (Ohio State U), and B. Thomas Trout (U of New Hampshire). Global Issues Series. Durham NC: Duke U Press, Jan 1985/188p/$10.75pb.

One in a series of textbooks on contemporary issues in the global arena, with each issue addressed within a systematic and integrated framework common to all. Other volumes deal with energy (#85-247), food, population, and the new global agenda; each volume deals with actors, values, policies, and futures.

Environment is a global issue because, by definition, it transcends the traditional boundaries of the nation-state. **Dahlberg** describes basic concepts for understanding the environment (ecosystem, carrying capacity, and tragedy of the commons), the evolution of global threats to the biosphere, and problems of evaluation and forecasting (inadequate data, delayed impacts of many environmental processes, the fragmented and specialized nature of most of our institutions). **Feraru** considers governmental and non-governmental environmental actors at the global, regional, national, and sub-national level. **Soroos** outlines the most prominent environmental values: controlling pollution, preserving genetic diversity, conserving natural resources, and limiting population growth. He also describes environmental policies (restraints, restrictions, taxes, enclosures, and public monopoly) and approaches to designing a global alternative future (international regimes, steady-state economics, centralized political authority, local self-reliance, global equity, and new technology such as space colonies). [NOTE: An excellent overview and introduction.]   (**environment as global issue**)

6702

Global Science: Energy, Resources, Environment. Second Edition. John W. Christensen (Cherry Creek High School, Englewood CO). Dubuque, Iowa: Kendall/Hunt Publishing Co, 1984/355p (8x11") pb.

A textbook for high school students by a teacher of global science, with chapters on spaceship earth and the ecosystem concept, basic energy/resource concepts, energy and society, population and food, energy supply and demand, energy for the future, mineral resources, impacts of energy consumption, the economics of resources and environment, and policy issues.   (**global science high school text**)

6703

Long-Term Ecological Research, James T. Callahan (NSF), *BioScience*, 34:6, June 1984, 363-367.

Research in ecology has traditionally been funded for short periods of time and performed at single sites—conditions not conducive to projects addressing much greater time and geographic scales. Some ecologists assert that the development of a unified-theoretical base for the science has been severely retarded by the lack of comprehensive and comparable information on a broad diversity of ecosystems. Support by NSF for long-term ecological research should lead to new and improved ecological theories, and better diagnoses for solving the growing array of fundamental ecological problems.

(**long-term ecological research needed**)

6704

Deep Ecology. Edited by Michael Tobias (Los Angeles). San Diego CA: Avant Books (3719 Sixth Ave), Dec 1984/ 296p/$12.95pb.

The shallow approach to the natural world is contrasted with the "deep ecology" approach, introduced by Arne Naess (Prof of Philosophy, U of Oslo) in 1973. Serving as the foundation for a new school of ecological thought, deep ecology transcends the merely utilitarian, and regards as intrinsic values the diversity of nature and the human need to be fully integrated in the natural world. Essays include George Sessions on ecological consciousness and paradigm change, Norman Myers on the challenge of disappearing species, William R. Catton Jr on the world's finite carrying capacity and the destiny of human lemmings, Herman E. Daly on the need for a steady-state society, Roderick Nash on the ethical extension of the American Revolution to include the new ecology, Garrett Hardin on discriminating altruisms, Murray Bookchin on the bases for an ecological ethics, Arne Naess on the process of identification as a source of deep ecological attitudes, and a dialogue with Paolo Soleri on complexity, Arcosanti, and survival. (**"deep ecology" essays**)

*6705

Sustaining Tomorrow: A Strategy for World Conservation and Development. Edited by Francis R. Thibodeau and Hermann H. Field (both Dept of Urban and Environmental Policy, Tufts U) Hanover NH: University Press of New England, Dec 1984/186p/$22.50; $12.50pb.

In 1980, the International Union for Conservation of Nature and Natural Resources (IUCN) launched the World Conservation Strategy in cooperation with the UN Environment Program and the World Wildlife Fund. [See **FS Annual 1981-82**, #3564/3565.] The aim of the Strategy is to maintain essential ecological processes and life support systems on which human survival and development depend, to preserve genetic diversity, and to insure the sustainable utilization of important species and ecosystems. The main obstacles to conservation are the belief that living resource conservation is a limited sector rather than a process that cuts across and must be considered by all sectors, the failure to integrate conservation with development, inadequate legislation and lack of enforcement, and a lack of support for conservation due to an inadequate awareness of its benefits. The Strategy recommends anticipatory environmental policies, an integrated method of evaluating land and water resources, reviews of legislation concerning living resources, increased training of personnel, greater public participation in planning and decision-making concerning living resource use, international action to support and coordinate national action, and a more comprehensive international conservation law.

The three initiating organizations have continued to develop and implement the goals of the Strategy at the international level. And more than 30 countries are preparing national strategies modeled on the World Conservation Strategy. This book is intended to bring the context of an international overview to conservation thought and action at the regional and local level. Essays focus on the World Conservation Strategy, ecological processes and life support systems, preserving genetic diversity, sustainable use of species and ecosystems, national and regional conservation strategies, environmental planning and rational use, building support for environmental education, conservation-based rural development, environmental policy and law, managing the global commons, tropical forests and genetic resource areas, regional strategies for managing the oceans, and food and population. A concluding chapter on sustainable development by Jean-Claude Faby (UNEP) outlines four basic prerequisites: 1) appropriate methodological frameworks to evaluate alternatives (involving cost-benefit analysis, risk management, environmental impact assessment, and technical guidelines); 2) appropriate institutional frameworks to facilitate decision-making and action; 3) formulation of concrete alternatives for technologies, processes, practices, and products; 4) education and training, and dissemination of environment-related information. (**World Conservation Strategy**)

*6706

Environmentalists: Vanguard for a New Society. Lester W. Milbrath (Director, Environmental Studies Center, SUNY-Buffalo). Albany NY: State U of New York Press, Sept 1984/180p/$29.50;$9.95pb.

Today's society needs new prophets who understand how the world works physically and socially, and who have the breadth and depth of vision to develop a new ethical belief structure to enable humans to guide their affairs. A new group of leaders known as environmentalists are beginning to develop a new environmental paradigm (NEP) to challenge the dominant social paradigm (DSP). The key characteristics of the environmentalists' world view are their high valuation of nature, sense of empathy toward other species and peoples, desire to carefully plan so as to avoid risks to humans and nature, and recognition that there are limits to growth. These reformers in the vanguard place a high valuation on a safe and clean environment and are strong advocates of social change. In contrast, the rearguard defenders of the DSP place a high valuation on economic growth.

This book presents the results of a three-nation comparative study of environmental beliefs and values, conducted by the Science Center in Berlin, the University of Bath in England, and the Environmental Studies Center at SUNY-Buffalo in 1980 and in 1982. Several thousand people, including various elites (business and labor leaders, elected officials, environmentalists) and the general public, were surveyed by means of a lengthy questionnaire. The findings show a substantial movement away from the DSP toward the NEP. Nearly 20% of the US public agrees with the rearguard DSP and 20% with the vanguard NEP, with most of the public falling near the middle of the two polarized groups. In England, 9% of the public is in the rearguard and 24% with the vanguard. In Germany, about 30% of the public are found on each end of the dimension. The rearguard is dominated by people in the production section of the economy and is almost totally dominated by males. The vanguard is made up of people in the service sector and has a substantial representation of females. Across countries, the Germans seem substantially more environmentally oriented than the Americans, with England falling in-between. Concludes that the vanguard is clearly not strong enough at present to contend successfully against the rearguard. Many people have departed from some of the central beliefs of the DSP, but they will not give societal leadership to the vanguard as long as the DSP continues to perform reasonably adequately. If the DSP is not sustainable, as the environmentalists argue, physical and societal events will painfully force people to continue the relearning process. [NOTE: A fascinating and important look at what may be the major underlying force in the politics of the future.]

(environmental paradigm in 3 countries)

B. Global Resources

6707

Anticipating Climate Change: Implications for Welfare and Policy, Thomas C. Schelling (Harvard U), *Environment*, 26:8, Oct 1984, 6-9ff.

Recent estimates, less alarming than those of the late 1970s, point to a 2% annual increase in the worldwide use of fossil fuels, and at least a doubling in accumulated carbon dioxide levels by 2000. A comprehensive framework is offered for outlining policy choices that address future climatic changes. The framework includes five categories of analysis and choice: 1) the background against which potential changes are to be judged (without a CO_2 effect, would global temperature rise or fall, by how much, and with how much certainty in the estimate?); 2) reducing CO_2 production (decrease energy use, reduce deforestation); 3) removing CO_2 from effluents or the atmosphere (e.g. by reforestation); 4) countervailing modifications (enhance precipitation, change the cloud cover, build dams and canals); 5) adapting to increased CO_2 (migration, compensating losers, changed agriculture policies, better water use efficiency). **(climate change and policy)**

6708

The Primary Source: Tropical Forests and Our Future. Norman Myers (Oxford UK). NY: W.W. Norton, 1984/399p/$17.95.

Author of **The Sinking Ark** (Pergamon, 1979; **FS Annual 1979**, #0615) and **A Wealth of Wild Species** (Westview, 1983; **FS Annual 1983**, #4804) argues that tropical forests are over-exploited but under-used. Compared to settled agriculture and plantation forestry, human exploitation of tropical forests betrays the outmoded sensibility of the hunter-gatherer societies of 10,000 years ago. Less than 1/20th of tropical forests come under any sort of management program whatever, and reforestation is minimal. Northerners still fail to recognize that tropical forests are the basic stabilizing factor in global climate and that mass species extinction squanders a valuable resource that we have not begun to tap. Rational steps require: 1) a systematic research effort underwritten by developed nations to stabilize wasteful activities in developing nations; 2) making secondary forests hubs of activity in agriculture and forestry so as to relieve the pressure on virgin forests; 3) more plantations for commercial timber and fuel wood; 4) agricultural advances to enable small-scale farmers to practice intensive and stable cultivation; 5) many more parks and other protected areas. [Also see **Dreams of Amazonia** by Roger D. Stone (Viking, Jan 1985/$17.95), which questions schemes to exploit the fragile Amazon Basin, and **In the Rain Forest** by Catherine Caufield (Knopf, Jan 1985/$16.95), which reports on threats to the world's tropical forests.]

(saving tropical forests)

6709

Neptune's Revenge: The Ocean of Tomorrow. Anne W. Simon (NYC). NY: Franklin Watts, Oct 1984/222p/$15.95.

Neptune was the god of the ancients who protected the sea. Neptune's control has been seized by our society, with the growing power to intrude on the sea. Expanding numbers in the world want more of the ocean's resources: more fish for protein, more oil from undersea rock, more minerals, and more room to get rid of growing piles of waste, be it toxic chemicals, radioactive discards, or sewage. Our trident is technology, making new uses of the ocean possible, but risking pollution and overfishing. All over the world, people are making new uses of the ocean, and the ocean responds by changes that are just beginning to be noticed and understood. The ocean has deteriorated. Parts of the sea are dying, and no one is certain if ocean functions are retrievable or ocean deterioration is reversible. As marine life deteriorates further, it will become less valuable to man. Then life on earth, deprived of ocean support, will also deteriorate; Neptune will have his revenge. This worst-case scenario is predicated on today's facts. If there is a long-range chance of such an ocean holocaust, we must do what we can now to reverse it. Putting the ocean first is a rigorous discipline, requiring us to think far ahead and to make long-term decisions.   **(ocean deterioration)**

6710

America Looks to the Sea: Ocean Use and the National Interest. Douglas L. Brooks (former Executive Director, National Advisory Committee on Oceans and Atmosphere). Boston MA: Jones and Bartlett Publishers (20 Park Plaza), Sept 1984/266p/$19.95.

Since WWII, land people have invaded the sea in a surging rush, resulting in a pervasive transformation of seagoing enterprises. Many old values are threatened, and many new opportunities are promised. Chapters are devoted to oceanography, the politics of oceans, fisheries, world shipping, energy from the sea, waste disposal, coastal zones, military uses, and the Law of the Sea Treaty. Concludes that the importance of the oceans has been consistently overlooked, and the means to realize the national interest in effective use of the sea misunderstood. Most fundamentally, we need to recognize that the sea is a great commons, requiring the increasing number of users of the sea to act as nurturers rather than exploiters. Renewable resources, sustainable yields, and long-term returns on investment should take precedence over extractive uses yielding only short-term payoffs. [NOTE: A good overview of ocean-related issues.]   **(ocean management)**

6711

World Fisheries Face Change and Challenge, J.E. Carroz (FAO), *Mazingira*, 8:3, July 1984, 17-21.

The annual world fish catch grew from less than 20 million tons in the late 1940s to more than 65 million tons by 1970, not only due to the growth of demand, but aided by synthetic fiber fishing nets, mechanical gear handling systems, and the introduction of freezing at sea. As a result of this rapid expansion in catching capabilities and the resulting catch, several important fish stocks were overexploited and some collapsed. The present world fish catch of about 75 million tons (of which 55 million tons are directly consumed as human food) represents a slow growth since 1970. World demand for fish as food will grow to some 90 to 95 million tons per year by 2000. To bridge the potential gap between supply and demand, world fisheries will have to: 1) make better use of currently exploited resources through improved management and waste reduction; 2) find ways to increase production from neglected or under-used marine resources; 3) promote greater output from inland waters and aquaculture. The recent extension of national jurisdiction over fisheries creates an opportunity to improve fisheries management. [Also see companion article, *Aquaculture Expansion and Environmental Considerations*, pp 24-28.]

(**managing world fisheries**)

6712
The World's Beaches Are Vanishing, John Gribbin, *New Scientist*, 10 May 1984, 30-32.

A global survey sponsored by the International Geographical Union has discovered that beaches have been shrinking quickly over the past 100 years. More than 70% of the total length of sandy coastline around the world has retreated at a rate of at least 10 cm. per year in recent decades. Less than 10% of the world's sandy coast is growing, and the rest has stayed much the same. Many seaside resorts are losing their sandy beaches, coast roads are being undermined, and buildings destroyed as the coastline retreats. One of the major contributing factors to the rapid increase in beach erosion is the construction of artificial structures such as sea walls, jetties, and dams. On the other hand, suggestions that the global increase in erosion may be due to a rise in sea level do not stand up.

[Also see the "Living with the Shore" series of more than 20 volumes, edited by Orrin H. Pilkey, Jr (Duke U) and William J. Neal (Grand Valley State College), to be published by Duke U Press. Each volume will describe the dynamics of shoreline change, and include shore-specific guidelines for building and buying. The first three volumes have been published: **Living with the East Florida Shore** (Oct 1984/c200p/$24.75;$11.75pb), **Living with the West Florida Shore** (Nov 1984/c180p/$24.75;$11.75), and **Living with the Alabama-Mississippi Shore** (Nov 1984/c190p/$24.75;$11.75pb). Other volumes in the series will discuss the shorelines of the Eastern US, Western US, and the Great Lakes. Pilkey is the co-author (with Wallace Kaufman) of **The Beaches are Moving: The Drowning of America's Shoreline** (Anchor/Doubleday, 1979).]

(**beach erosion**)

6713
External Costs of Coastal Beach Pollution: An Hedonic Approach. Elizabeth A. Wilman (U of Calgary). A Resources for the Future Book. Baltimore MD: Johns Hopkins U Press, Dec 1984/c168p/$15.00pb.

Estimates of economic damages from oil spills and other incidents are necessary for efficient management of coastal zones, especially the decision of whether the benefits of developing offshore oil outweigh the costs. Wilman develops a methodology for imputing a monetary value to the loss in beach recreational services resulting from a hypothetical oil spill. (**beach pollution costs**)

6714
World Water '83: The World Problem. Institution of Civil Engineers. London: Thomas Telford Ltd (26-34 Old St), 1984/218p.

Proceedings of a July 1983 conference in London, with presentations on the scale of the world problem, assessment of water supply investment priorities in developing countries, World Bank operations and finance, other sources of finance and generation of income from water projects, training, the role of the consultant and NGOs,

river basin management, groundwater development, dealing with leakage, urban waste disposal problems, sanitation and health, water and food production, and appropriate technology. (**world water problems**)

6715
Water: Rethinking Management in an Age of Scarcity. Sandra Postel. Worldwatch Paper 62. Washington: Worldwatch Institute, Dec 1984/65p/$4.00. (Also in **State of the World 1985**, #85-231.)

If current trends continue, fresh water may in many areas become a constraint on economic activity and food production over the coming decades. Increasing competition for limited supplies and the rising economic and environmental costs of traditional water strategies demand a new approach to the management of fresh water. But few governments have recognized the need for such a reevaluation, much less begun to design policies for the future. Much of the profligate waste and inefficiency in today's use of water results from policies that promote an antiquated illusion of abundance, such as keeping people from paying the true cost of water they use. Most governments continue to expect traditional dam and diversion projects to relieve regional water stresses. Yet the engineering complexities of these projects, threats of ecological disruption, multibillion-dollar price tags, and 20-year lead times all leave little hope that water will be delivered in time to avert projected shortages. Measures to conserve, recycle, and reuse fresh water may in many cases make the resource available at lower cost and with less environmental disruption than developing new supplies. Conservation and better management can free a large volume of water—and capital. Thus far, we have seen only hints of their potential. (**water conservation needed**)

6716
Soil Erosion: Quiet Crisis in the World Economy. Lester R. Brown and Edward C. Wolf. Worldwatch Paper 60. Washington DC: Worldwatch Institute, Sept 1984/49p/$4.00.

Over the past generation, world food output has more than doubled. But some of the agricultural practices enabling this increased output have also led to excessive soil erosion. As the demand for food climbs, the world is beginning to mine its soils, converting a renewable resource into a nonrenewable one. The loss of topsoil affects the ability to grow food by reducing the inherent productivity of the land and by increasing the costs of food production. It is a quiet crisis that is not widely perceived. Projections of world food supply made in the early 1970s did not anticipate the slowdown in growth of output over the last decade, perhaps due to ignoring the effect of soil erosion on food production. To remedy this shortcoming, the authors make a rough estimate of the worldwide loss of topsoil from cropland: because of population growth, they project a 19% decline in cropland per person between 1984 and 2000. But if current rates of soil erosion continue, the amount of topsoil per person will decline by 32% in the same period. This estimate is not highly refined and by no means final, but it does provide some sense of how fast soils are being lost, which is necessary to mobilize the resources to save them. Although agriculture is the foundation of the global economy, few countries, industrial or developing, are responding effectively to this emerging threat to economic sustainability. Eager to maximize food output today, we are borrowing from tomorrow, raising profound questions of intergenerational equity. In the absence of successful efforts to stem the loss of topsoil, the social effects of erosion will probably first be seen in Africa, in the form of acute food shortages and higher mortality rates, particularly for infants. Even in the US, the loss of soil through erosion exceeds tolerable levels on some 44% of the cropland. [NOTE: A major reason for failing to appreciate the problem of soil erosion may be the pervasive hope of technological fixes: better and cheaper fertilizers, computerized management, and new plant varieties that can grow in poor soil. Will these compensations (not mentioned by Brown and Wolf) substitute at all for the loss of soil (a factor that the high-tech advocates seem to ignore)? Which is the higher research priority: stemming soil loss or new technology?]   (**32% less topsoil per person by 2000?**)

6717

Large-Scale Dams: A Special Report, Edward Goldsmith and Nicholas Hildyard, *The Ecologist*, 14:5-6, 1984, 206-231.

Four articles and a 16-page Briefing Document insert summarizing a three-volume study by Goldsmith and Hildyard, **The Social and Environmental Effects of Large Dams** (**FS Annual 1984**, #5907). Today's modern technology enables the building of large and complex dams. By 1990, a total of 113 dams over 150 meters in height is expected worldwide, of which 49 will have been built during the 1980s. Even more ambitious schemes are planned for the future, as a result of the political prestige resulting from dams and the lure of cheap hydro-power and irrigated agriculture. But the negative impacts are rarely revealed: 1) massive resettlement of residents from flooded areas, frequently on inferior land and with little or no compensation; 2) the loss of good agricultural land in flooded areas; 3) the loss of wildlife; 4) loss of water from a dam's reservoir in hot and dry areas; 5) increased incidence of waterborne diseases, notably malaria and schistosomiasis; 6) pressure applied to often fragile geological structures by the vast mass of impounded water can give rise to earthquakes; 7) the building of flood control embankments actually increases the severity of floods; 8) the reservoir of a dam sooner or later fills up with silt and other detritus; 9) irrigation schemes result in increased salinization and waterlogging. Some observers argue that if certain conditions are rigorously followed, the benefits of large dams will far outweigh the costs; in practice, the benign super-dam is a myth—all large dams are inevitably destructive. In sum, large-scale dams are a recipe for massive land degradation and inevitable starvation for millions of peasants in the decades to come. We have become trapped on a technological treadmill, with an increasingly desperate search for new technological fixes. The "think big" mentality is too firmly entrenched in Third World governments to expect their water development schemes to be abandoned. The only way to prevent large dams is to appeal to donor governments, development banks, and international aid agencies without whose financial help the schemes could not be built. Funds for all large-scale water development schemes should be cut off, regardless of how advanced these schemes might be. [NOTE:A potentially important technology assessment without being labeled as such.]
(**large dams questioned**)

6718

The Doomsday Myth: 10,000 Years of Economic Crises. Charles Maurice and Charles W. Smithson (both Dept of Economics, Texas A&M University). Foreword by Phil Gramm. Stanford CA: Hoover Institution Press, Fall 1984/142p/$16.95.

Societies have experienced resource shortages throughout history, many as bad or worse than the petroleum shortages in the 1970s. If markets are given the freedom to respond, people will react to shortages and the resulting increases in prices with substitution and/or technological change, thereby eliminating the crisis. Markets work to eliminate shortages, so forecasts of doom or collapse based on shortages are groundless, and the "doom merchants" such as the Club of Rome are wrong. Earlier resource crises are described: the crude rubber crisis during WWII, the US timber crisis in the early 20th century, the whale oil crisis of the mid-19th century, the English timber crisis of the 16th century, the timber crisis in ancient Greece, and the prehistoric crisis in hunting/gathering that resulted in the agricultural revolution. Concludes that there are several areas in which we might experience shortages over the next few decades—especially petroleum and water. But if the marketplace is permitted to function, any future shortages will be eliminated. Any government involvement, though, could change a normal shortage into a crisis; doomsday could arrive, but only if we invite it. [NOTE: A simple, one-sided argument that strikes persuasively at the major blind spot of "limits to growth" pessimists, but less persuasively at advocates of foresight and action.]
(**resource scarcity doomsayers are wrong**)

C. <u>U.S. Environment Issues</u>

*6719

State of the Environment: An Assessment at Mid-Decade. A Report from The Conservation Foundation. Washington: The Conservation Foundation, June 1984/ 586p/$16.00pb.

Environmental policy at mid-decade is suspended between old problems and new, between progress and retrogression, between cooperation and polarization. The US has made significant progress in many environmental areas where laws and institutions have been explicitly devised to address specific problems. Quantitative indicators of environmental quality show a picture similar to that depicted in **State of the Environment 1982** (**FS Annual 1983**, #4830). Air quality has continued to improve, and water quality on balance has remained constant. These findings, however, are based on traditional measures of pollution, and do not take into account pollution from toxic substances. The status of wildlife in the US is mixed, but reliable information on many species is not available. The progress that has been made should not obscure the many points of controversy and vulnerability in on-going environmental programs. Budget cuts at both Federal and state levels over the past few years have weakened these programs. Environmental monitoring and research are inadequate to evaluate existing programs or to identify new problems. Many potentially harmful toxic substances are not adequately monitored, and thus there is no way to assess their risks. The acid rain problem demonstrates the need for new approaches to management: rather than an aberration, it is probably the prototype of the new environmental problems that we will increasingly confront. It is typical because causes and effects cannot be delineated with precision, the possible costs of either action or inaction are very large, and existing laws and institutions are not adequate to deal with the problem.

This assessment is divided into eight chapters: 1) **Underlying Trends**: US population growth rate continues to fall and the pattern of economic growth has the potential for reducing environmental stresses, but US expenditures for pollution control are falling; 2) **Environmental Contaminants**: available information indicates that at least some regulatory efforts have been successful, but knowledge about potential hazards of many substances is extremely limited; 3) **Natural Resources**: water, land, croplands, forests, wildlife, energy, recreation; 4) **Identifying Issues**: confronted with an assortment of issues, we need an overall sense of what must be done and what priorities should be set (a list of 47 major environmental problems is distilled from six studies); 5) **Risk Assessment and Risk Control**: government today is being asked to control many more risks than in the past, but almost all risk assessments are plagued by inadequate data; 6) **Controlling Cross-Media Pollutants**: many pollutants move from one medium to another, causing damage in each (e.g. leaking landfills contaminate air and water); the cross-media approach examines release from a source, waste management, cycling, and exposure of human and environmental receptors; 7) **Water Resources**: US water policy has entered a period of fundamental change, as the nation moves from an era of water development to an era of water management; 8) **Intergovernmental Relations and Environmental Policy**: the inherent tension of intergovernmental relations is exacerbated by the uneven distribution among governments of the costs and benefits of various programs; greater realism in the planning and overseeing of environmental programs would make the programs more effective and enhance intergovernmental relations. [NOTE: An essential foundation for understanding environmental problems and prospects, and an exemplary model for overviews of other problem areas.]

(**environmental progress mixed**)

6720
Clues to the Future Environmental Agenda, 1985-2020: An Environmental Foresight Study. Vary T. Coates, Joseph F. Coates, and Lisa Heinz. Washington: J.F. Coates, Inc (3738 Kanawha St NW), Dec 1984/78p.

A report submitted to the Office of Exploratory Research of the US Environmental Protection Agency, suggesting an agenda of environmental problems that will demand action over the next few decades. The ten highest priority problems include toxic chemicals in the environment (a widespread problem likely to affect any region or community), groundwater contamination, depletion of surface water and groundwater (conflicts over water rights and competing uses of water are likely to increase significantly), unanticipated side effects of biotechnology, soil erosion and declining productivity of agricultural lands, acid rain, infrastructure problems (water and sanitation systems, roads, bridges, etc.), disruption of basic ecological systems (which may have critical long-range effects that have not yet been recognized), problems related to nuclear energy, and synergistic or cross-media problems (substances otherwise harmless that interact with other substances to become toxic). Problems of second order importance include beach erosion, dams, desertification, noise, ocean pollution, municipal solid waste management, atmospheric carbon dioxide, ozone, pipeline spills, non-ionizing radiation, and indoor air pollution. Concludes that concern will increasingly focus on health effects of pollutants, and the largest source of new environmental concerns will be new materials (plastics, composites, specialty chemicals) with unfamiliar characteristics and side effects. A large number of potential problems should be monitored systematically, with exploratory studies and assessments undertaken at appropriate stages in their development. [Also see **Toxics '95: The Outlook of Factors and Trends for Toxic Chemicals**, by Vary T. Coates et al. (J.F. Coates, Inc., May 1984/215p), a report prepared for the EPA Office of Pesticides and Toxic Substances.]

(**future environmental agenda**)

6721
Bid the Devil "Good Morning!": Anticipating Environmental Hazards and Risks, Vary T. Coates, Joseph F. Coates, and Lisa Heinz (J.F. Coates, Inc, Washington), *Futures Research Quarterly* (WFS), 1:1, Spring 1985, 37-46.

The Irish say "Don't bid the devil good morning," meaning that if you worry about things that will never happen, you may be inviting trouble. But such a philosophy has meant that we are continually taken unaware by environmental disasters, or by the long accumulating harmful consequences of decades of inattention. We need better ways to foresee the emergence of new and potent environmental issues. Even if we cannot thereby avoid them entirely, we can at least develop strategic plans for reducing and managing them. As resources for environmental protection (money, authority, and the will to act) become ever more scarce, the need to use those resources effectively makes environmental foresight ever more desirable. This paper suggests some simple search instruments, in the form of concepts, checklists, and criteria, that are useful in the attempt to identify in advance the environmental agenda that must be addressed in coming decades. Five types of search instruments, or sets of diagnostic questions, are outlined: 1) sources of environmental problems (new technologies, new uses of familiar technologies, disappearance of a natural control mechanism, changing social values); 2) the scale or nature of potential cost or loss (frequency, severity, and immediacy of risk to human life or health); 3) the nature or locus of risks (whose life or health is put at risk, how, when, where, and by whom); 4) tractability of the problem (whether it is recognized and mechanisms exist to control it); 5) long-range social trends converging on the problem: global trends (greater demands to exploit resources), domestic trends (changes in values and expectations, depletion of water supplies, dispersion of pollution problems).

(**anticipating environmental issues**)

6722
Environmental Ignorance Is Not Bliss, Robert W. Crandall (Brookings Institution), *The Wall Street Journal*, Monday, 22 April 1985, p28.

Author of **Controlling Industrial Pollution** (Brookings, 1983) observes the 15th anniversary of Earth Day by claiming that there now seems to be little interest in the issues of smog and dirty rivers. Some argue that this change has occurred because the government has successfuly attacked the problems of air and water pollution, and is now preparing to tackle the greater problem of toxic substances. In fact, there is little evidence that Federal environmental policy has made US air and water appreciably cleaner. We do not know whether our environmental policies have worked at all, despite spending at least $50 billion a year on pollution abatement. What is most alarming is that no one in Congress or the Reagan Administration seems to care. Congress seems to have enacted a set of environmental statutes that bear much more oppressively on new and growing industries than on older, dying ones. The EPA cannot provide a very solid scientific basis for the standards it sets for most air or water pollutants. And the EPA has little idea as to who is discharging what and in what amounts, nor does it enforce its standards in a thorough, systematic manner. Congress seems more interested in exploiting new scares at Love Canal or the Union Carbide plant in West Virginia than in designing an environmental policy that really would work at a reasonable cost.

(**environmental ignorance**)

*6723

Superfund Strategy. U.S. Congress, Office of Technology Assessment. Washington: USGPO, May 1985/282p/$10.00 (S/N 052-003-00994-3). Summary copies available free from OTA.

The Environmental Protection Agency estimates that about 2,000 toxic waste sites should be placed on the National Priorities List, qualifying them for a permanent cleanup. OTA estimates that 10,000 sites—or more—may require cleanup. The EPA low estimate can be traced to a lack of detailed planning for the program, optimism about the number of sites requiring cleanup, and optimism about the effectiveness of cleanup technologies.

With Superfund's existing resources, it is not technically or economically possible to permanently clean up even 2,000 sites in less than several decades. Only 30% of the 538 sites now on the NPL are receiving remedial cleanup attention, which tends to be impermanent. Some sites are getting worse, and repeated costs are almost inevitable. Environmentally, risks are often transferred from one place to another, and to future generations. Underestimating national cleanup needs could result in environmental crisis years or decades from now. Costs to Superfund could easily be $100 billion—out of total costs to the nation of several hundred billion dollars—and a sensibly paced effort could take up to 50 years to clean 10,000 sites. A two-part strategy is proposed: 1) in the near term (the next 15 years), a focus on identification and assessment of potential NPL sites, preventing the sites from getting worse, permanent cleanups for some especially threatening sites, and developing institutional capabilities for a long-term program; 2) over the long term, a focus on more extensive site studies and on permanent cleanups (when technically feasible) at all sites that pose significant threats to human health and the environment. Federal support can help in obtaining more information on health and environmental effects, developing specific national cleanup goals, demonstrating permanent cleanup technologies, providing increased support for EPA, increasing support for training and education, and supporting public participation in decisionmaking. [NOTE: EPA Administrator Lee Thomas still estimates that about 2,000 toxic waste sites need cleanup, and that most of this cleanup "will be behind us" by 1995 (*U.S. News and World Report* 8 July 1985, p.41).]

(**toxic waste cleanup underestimated**)

6724

Superfund, Superbust, T. Lawrence Jones (President, American Insurance Association), *The New York Times* (Op-Ed), Friday, 24 May 1985, A25.

In nearly five years, the EPA's Superfund has had $1.6 billion available to it, but it has produced little cleanup. Instead, Superfund has triggered a seemingly endless series of lawsuits, which attempt to determine who did what in creating a hazardous waste site and to fix liability for the cost of cleaning up the site. [NOTE: Jones' trade organization represents casualty insurance companies.] Many sites contain waste from many businesses. Some users may no longer be in business. Some may have deposited very little waste; others a great deal. Much waste is not toxic; some is. But the government sues as many users as are accessible, claiming that each is liable for the total cost of cleanup if no one else contributes. The US urgently needs to review its attitude towards waste management and toward the laws that govern environmental liability. Superfund is a good idea, but major changes are needed in interpretation and enforcement.

(**toxic waste cleanup mishandled**)

6725

The Health Detective's Handbook: A Guide to the Investigation of Environmental Health Hazards by Nonprofessionals. Edited by Marvin S. Legator, Barbara L. Harper, and Michael J. Scott (all U of Texas Medical Branch-Galveston). Baltimore MD: Johns Hopkins U Press, June 1985/304p/$27.50;$12.95pb.

The Environmental Protection Agency estimates that 90% of a possible 50,000 hazardous waste sites in the US pose a potential threat to human health, owing to improper location or poor management. The problem is extremely serious not only because of the number of sites, but also because those sites are usually located near places where people live and work. If an individual suspects his or her neighborhood to be affected by hazardous wastes or other dangerous pollutants, what can be done? This book is based on the premise that motivated citizens can and should help themselves. Indeed, according to Legator, the so-called amateurs at Love Canal—the homeowners—did a far better job of evaluating the health of the community than did the professionals of the NY Health Department. The key to solving pollution problems in communities is strong neighborhood organization. Such organizations should engage in three tasks: 1) conduct a detailed community survey to determine how many people are affected by pollution and in what ways; 2) tabulate the information into an incontrovertable statement that local, state, and Federal officials will be unable to brush aside; 3) push, push, and push until the problem is solved.

(**community groups and toxic wastes**)

6726

Beyond Dumping: New Strategies for Controlling Toxic Contamination. Edited by Bruce Piasecki. Foreword by Rep. James Florio. Westport CT: Greenwood Press, 1984/239p/$35.00.

Americans can now treat, rather than dump, the bulk of US hazardous waste. Piasecki describes regulatory reforms and market incentives that can shift US industries beyond the land disposal of their high-priority toxic wastes, outlines new approaches at Federal and state levels, analyzes the lessons learned from past managerial efforts to secure and contain leaking landfills, and reports on new market conditions and technological advances that render treatment cost-effective. Concludes with an annotated bibliography.

(**toxic waste treatment**)

6727

Emissions Trading: An Exercise in Reforming Pollution Policy. T. H. Tietenberg (Prof of Economics, Colby College). Baltimore MD: Johns Hopkins U Press, Feb 1985/238p/$22.50.

Emissions trading is the first large-scale attempt to use economic incentives in US environmental policy. It allows plants to accumulate credits for reducing emissions beyond the levels dictated by the EPA, and to sell or trade those credits to other plants whose pollution control costs are higher. Tietenberg finds that the cost savings actually achieved by the program are considerably less than might have been expected, because current regulations are inconsistent with cost effectiveness. Concludes with recommendations for improving emissions trading, which promises to remain an integral part of US air pollution control policy.

(**emissions trading reforms**)

6728

Acid Rain and Transported Air Pollutants: Implications for Public Policy. U.S. Congress, Office of Technology Assessment. Washington DC: USGPO, June 1984/$9.50 (S/N 052-003-00956-1). Summary copies free from OTA.

Acid rain, ozone, and fine particles such as airborne sulfate are endangering US resources. These air pollutants have harmed lakes and streams, lowered crop yields, damaged manmade materials, decreased visibility, and may be threatening forests and even human health. Acid deposition, commonly called "acid rain," occurs when sulfur dioxide and nitrogen oxides—released primarily from burning of fossil fuels— return to the earth as rain, snow, fog, dew, and as dry particles and gases. Ozone is produced when nitrogen oxides interact with hydrocarbons, and is estimated to cause a 6% to 7% loss of US agricultural productivity. Sulfur pollutants accelerate the deterioration of economically important materials (such as iron and steel, zinc, paint, and stone), and sulfate particles in the air are the greatest single factor in reducing visibility in the Eastern US. Controlling these pollutants will involve substantial costs. Scientific uncertainty about many aspects of the problem complicates the decision of whether and when to control, and additional research will not provide an unambiguous answer in the near future. Approaches for action by Congress include mandating emissions reductions, liming lakes and streams, and modifying Federal research programs to provide more timely guidance. [Journalistic accounts of the problem include **Acid Rain** by Robert H. Boyle and R. Alexander Boyle (Schocken Books, July 1983/146p/$14.95;$8.95pb), **Troubled Skies, Troubled Waters** by Jon R. Luoma (Viking, Jan 1984/178p/$12.95), and **A Killing Rain: The Global Threat of Acid Precipitation** by Thomas Pawlick (Sierra Club, Oct 1984/224p/$14.95).]　**(acid rain; ozone pollution)**

6729

Environmental Planning and Management. John H. Baldwin (Director of Environmental Studies, U of Oregon). Boulder CO: Westview, Oct 1984/c310p/$42.50;$18.50 pb.

A textbook offering an overview of the causes and interrelationships of environmental problems, the economic and ecological functions of the land, the flow of resources from acquisition through disposal, water quality and quantity, toxic and solid wastes, economic costs of environmental controls, environmental impact statements, and the practice of community environmental planning and management.　**(environmental management textbook)**

D. U.S. Resources

6730

Renewing America: Natural Resource Assets and State Economic Development. William E. Nothdurft. Foreword by Gov. Scott M. Matheson (D-Utah). Washington DC: The Council of State Planning Agencies, 1984/198p/$14.95pb.

Brings together three bodies of thought—about the economics of resource scarcity, investment theory, and state development policy—to illuminate the role of renewable natural resources in economic development of US states. Natural resources, along with financial capital, physical infrastructure, and a well-trained and motivated workforce, are important economic building blocks. But years of waste, neglect, and inadequate investment have left many of these critical national assets in short supply or in an advanced state of deterioration: 1) astonishing quantities of agricultural soils are eroding faster than replacement takes place; 2) thousands of acres of irrigated cropland have become salt-laden and useless; 3) soil compaction is an increasing problem; 4) surface waters are oversubscribed, and groundwater is being "mined"; 5) rangelands are overgrazed in many areas; 6) many of the most prized commercial fish species are near collapse; 7) most of the virgin timber is gone, and failure years ago to ensure reforestation of timberlands poses the prospect of shortages in future decades; 8) domestic mineral and energy production have been declining steadily for years. These concerns tend to be thought of as environmental issues, but they are fundamentally economic. By failing to make needed maintenance investments in natural resources, the nation foregoes important opportunities for industrial expansion, new business development, job creation, revenue enhancement, increased supply stability, and sustainable growth. The Federal government has yet to develop a coherent investment program to improve resource capital supplies; indeed, a pattern of disinvestment is increasingly apparent. The private market also fails to insure adequate investment, because it seeks primarily to achieve maximum profits in relatively short planning horizons. States are therefore stepping into the void. To gain greater control over their economic futures, they can audit their economies, target their tax and regulatory policies to achieve long-term goals, influence the flow of private capital, create quasi-public financial institutions to fill gaps in the marketplace, and guide the private marketplace to needed investments in resource-based enterprises.　**(natural resources and state economies)**

6731

Regions and Resources: Strategies for Development. David Kresge (VP, Union Pacific Corp) *et al.* Cambridge MA: MIT Press, June 1984/264p/$27.50.

A state or region that is rich in valuable resources can design innovative long-range policies that improve the welfare of residents and provide a cushion for boom and bust cycles of the future. The authors construct a model and apply it to Alaska's experience following development of its North Slope petroleum, projecting trends of growth under different scenarios to 2000. They analyze the effects of specific policy actions, such as direct distribution of oil revenues, income tax cuts, public investment programs, manpower training programs, and subsidies for new industries.　**(state resource planning)**

6732

Natural Resource Administration: Introducing a New Methodology for Management Development. Edited by C. West Churchman (U of California-Berkeley), Spencer H. Smith (formerly US Fish and Wildlife Service), and Albert H. Rosenthal (U of New Mexico). Boulder CO: Westview, Oct 1984/c160p/$20.00.

Successful natural resource administration demands the ability to deal with the interests of many actors—including the public and wildlife—in a balanced, constructive way. Such an approach to management constantly searches for creative compromises that protect today's wildlife for future generations while maximizing present social and economic benefits. Topics considered here include the interaction of human management of wildlife with natural regulation of wildlife, the need for sound R&D programs, the importance of public participation in managing natural resources, and the political and administrative context in which resource management takes place.　**(natural resource management)**

6733

This Land Is Your Land: The Struggle to Save America's Public Lands. Bernard Shanks (Phoenix, Arizona). San Francisco CA: Sierra Club Books, Oct 1984/ 310p/$19.95.

Public lands are the source of the largest welfare program in America. Laws subsidize livestock grazing and timber harvesting, encouraging overgrazing and overcutting. Federally financed water projects obliterate fishing and wildlife habitats for the profit of a few. The public lands are the most tangible resources for our future generations, and protecting them is a sacred public trust. We must keep the lands public because arid areas are most suited to well-managed multiple use, the Federal lands are a capital resource of enormous magnitude, and the public lands are objects of irreplaceable beauty. There has never been a rational and balanced public land management policy. A superagency oriented toward the public interest should set a unified policy and integrate the work of the present agencies. The frontier ethic that has guided the US for centuries is no longer appropriate, nor is "multiple use" that disguises plundering of public lands for private profits. A democratic public lands policy would return a fair market price to the public. A share of revenues from public lands leasing should be allocated to a perpetual trust fund to sustain public land productivity, support soil conservation and land reclamation, and develop new parks and recreation areas.   **(public lands management)**

6734

Protecting the Nation's Groundwater From Contamination. U.S. Congress, Office of Technology Assessment. Washington DC: USGPO, Oct 1984/$7.50 (S/N 052-003-00966-8). Summary copies free from OTA.

Groundwater is used for drinking by about one-half of the US population. But contaminants are being found, with increasing frequency, in the groundwater of every state. Many of these substances are linked to human health hazards, and they can also have serious social, economic, and environmental impacts. Despite increased Federal and state efforts in recent years, our ability to protect groundwater is limited because there is no explicit national legislative mandate to protect it, and relevant programs and institutions are not coordinated. Better protection of groundwater quality requires a broadening of laws and programs to include sources of contamination, contaminants, and users of groundwater not now covered. Adequate and sustained Federal support to the states is also required, including Federal funds earmarked for groundwater, support for training programs, development of technically sound criteria for detection and correction, and efficient information exchange.   **(groundwater pollution)**

6735

Measuring the Benefits of Clean Air and Water. Allen V. Kneese (Senior Fellow, RFF). A Resources for the Future Book. Baltimore MD: Johns Hopkins U Press, Oct 1984/ 104p/$5.95pb.

The current economic situation has caused many to question whether costly environmental regulations are affordable or even necessary. Kneese discusses methods for quantitatively estimating the benefits derived from maintaining or improving air and water quality, centered on two broad approaches: 1) methods based, however indirectly, on observed human behavior with respect to environmental goods (e.g. travel to recreational opportunities, prices paid for houses in different locations); 2) questioning respondents about their willingness to pay for various hypothetical changes in environmental quality. Other tools of

benefits assessment include bidding games, wage differentials, risk reduction evaluation, and mortality and morbidity cost estimation.   **(air/water benefits assessment)**

6736

Funding Clean Water. Edited by H. Clyde Reeves (Lincoln Institute of Land Policy). Lexington MA: Lexington Books, March 1984/226p/$36.00.

The future of US water is very much in doubt, and may soon develop into a crisis. Chemical pollutants and overconsumption aside, the core of the problem is the nation's water infrastructure: delivery systems and wastewater facilities. Many of these systems are inadequate or in a state of decay, and will soon need extensive rehabilitation or replacement at a price tag of $2 trillion to $4 trillion—at a time when the US seems ill-equipped to take such action. These papers from a 1982 conference sponsored by the Tax Policy Roundtable of the Lincoln Institute consider the general questions of the infrastructure financing gap between what is needed and what will be raised, winners and losers as a result of government subsidies for clean water, the Federal role in funding, and state and local roles. Case studies are provided of funding clean water in Illinois, Kentucky, Maryland, Michigan, New York, South Carolina, Utah, Washington, and Wisconsin.

(US water infrastructure)

6737

Municipal Water Demand: Statistical and Management Issues. Clive Vaughan Jones (Economic Data Resources, Inc) *et al*. Boulder CO: Westview, June 1984/ 170p/$24.50.

The US water industry faces the need for massive capital investment to maintain existing structures and to provide further services, especially in the growing sunbelt. These needs must be assessed for cost-effectiveness within a context of policy alternatives, including measures to manage water consumption. The authors describe statistical methods for forecasting municipal water demand (including case studies of the Seattle and Denver water systems), and address such issues as the factors influencing water use, estimating demand by customer class, evaluating the reliability of forecasts, and applying these models to planning.   **(forecasting water demand)**

6738

U.S. Vulnerability to an Oil Import Curtailment: The Oil Replacement Capability. U.S. Congress, Office of Technology Assessment. Washington DC: USGPO, Sept 1984/$5.50.(S/N 052-003-00963-3.) Summary copies free from OTA.

Current US oil demand is 15.8 million barrels per day, of which 4.8 MB/D are net imports. If a large and protracted US oil supply shortfall begins in the next few years, the US has the technical and manufacturing capability to replace up to 3.6 MB/D of oil with other energy supply and demand technologies within five years after the onset of the shortfall. Technologies that can replace the largest amounts of oil are those that substitute alternative fuels for oil and increase the fuel efficiency of vehicles. In the longer term, declining domestic oil production will increase US vulnerability to an oil shortfall, even if all stationary uses of fuel oil are replaced. The US can significantly reduce its vulnerability in the next few decades by 1) relying more heavily on coal and biomass for chemical feedstocks; 2) increasing efficiency of transportation and natural gas use; 3) producing synthetic transportation fuels; 4) accelerating the replacement and conservation of stationary uses of oil.   **(reducing US oil shock vulnerability)**

6739

Strategic Materials: Technologies to Reduce U.S. Import Vulnerability. U.S. Congress, Office of Technology Assessment. Washington: USGPO, Summary, Jan 1985. Copies free from OTA. [Full report not yet available.]

The nations of southern Africa are the major suppliers to the US of chromium, cobalt, manganese, and platinum group metals, all essential to defense and the civilian economy. There is almost no domestic production of any of these metals. A stockpile of strategic materials is maintained for defense applications, but the non-defense economy remains vulnerable to supply disruptions. A combination of actions, specific to each metal, must be undertaken. An overall strategy would encompass three approaches: 1) diversify the supply of strategic metals by developing known deposits and exploring for new deposits; 2) decrease demand by improving manufacturing processes and recycling; 3) identify and test substitutes and develop new materials with reduced strategic material content (e.g., improved ceramic and composite materials may become important alternatives to chromium and cobalt alloys). A range of policy options for the government are explored. **(strategic materials vulnerability)**

6740

The Death of Mining (Cover Story), *Business Week*, 17 Dec 1984, 64-70.

The economic recovery of 1983-84 largely bypassed producers of copper, iron ore, nickel, lead, zinc, and molybdenum. These companies are reeling from chronic problems of shrinking markets, huge debt, and depressed prices. This may exemplify an industrial megatrend: the inexorable shift of the production and processing of all basic materials from the industrial countries to the Third World. In 1980, metals mining in America was an $8.9 billion enterprise; by 1983, it had shrunk to $5.9 billion. Mining employment has declined from 109,000 in 1981 to 45,000 in early 1984, and could fall a further 30% in the next 2 to 3 years. The mining industry is hobbled by a worldwide excess capacity that shows no signs of abating. Despite disappointing demand, Third World countries, eager to exploit their natural resources, keep opening giant new mines that incorporate the latest recovery techniques. Another broad-based US recession in 1985 or 1986 would probably sound the death knell for a North American industry that is already permanently bedridden.

(mining in decline)

E. Food and Agriculture

6741

The Politics of Starvation, Nevin S. Scrimshaw (Institute Professor, MIT), *Technology Review*, 87:6, Aug-Sept 1984, 18-27ff.

By World Bank estimates, at least 800 million persons in the Third World have a diet so limited that they do not have the energy for routine physical activities. WHO estimates that another 300 million children are retarded in growth and mental development as a result of malnutrition. In some poor countries, 70-80% of the children grow up with their genetic potential impaired. In most LDCs, the amount of food is not the limiting factor; rather, large portions of the population do not have access to land or enough money to buy food. At the heart of the problem are government policies that promote inequitable land tenure systems and do not provide adequate access to education and health services. For the last three decades, the US response to hunger has been governed by two largely erroneous beliefs: that economic growth will eventually trickle down and reduce poverty, and that chronic hunger can be cured simply by supplying food. Indeed, aid from developed countries may be counterproductive when substituted for national efforts to improve food production and distribution. The principal factor behind every success story in eliminating hunger and malnutrition (e.g., China, Costa Rica, Cuba) is a government that cares about its people. Conversely, foreign financial assistance is futile for many LDCs unless accompanied by dramatic changes in government policies. The US should not provide direct assistance to countries unwilling to invest in such policies, except during periods of acute emergency.

(caring government needed to end hunger)

6742

Food Crisis Detection: Going Beyond the Balance Sheet, Peter Cutler (Food Emergencies Research Unit, London School of Hygiene and Tropical Medicine), *Food Policy*, 9:3, Aug 1984, 189-192.

The state of the art of famine analysis and the actual practice of food crisis forecasting differ markedly. Balance sheet data expressing food needs in terms of tonnages are difficult to collect and interpret. Some countries regularly cry wolf in an effort to maximize aid above regular donations. Other countries sometimes minimize their emergency needs because of unwillingness to court dependence on "imperialist" countries. The solution to better crisis prediction is seen by many as better crop forecasting to produce better balance sheets. But a cheaper and more precise early warning technique is careful monitoring of selected markets for foodgrains, livestock, and labor.

(food crisis forecasting)

6743

A Five-Point Plan for Action, Jean Mayer (President, Tufts U), *Newsweek*, 26 Nov 1984, p58.

Each new famine, such as the present one in Africa, is dealt with as if it were a completely new phenomenon. In fact, we can in most cases predict famines and prevent them—or, if this fails, at least cope with them in much more effective ways than at present. Five basic steps should be taken. 1) Establish an Early-Warning System: survey crop prices in threatened areas and bring together data on weather and economic conditions; 2) Mobilize Grain Reserves: the rich countries that import grain could establish sufficient reserves to meet a temporary shortage, enabling the diversion of ships to a famine region; 3) Settle the Population: keep local populations in place by creating additional first-aid stations as a form of reassurance; 4) Centralize Relief Efforts: uncoordinated activities of voluntary agencies lack effectiveness; 5) Improve Agricultural and Population Planning: the greatest need in the countries threatened by famine is for effective agricultural extension services and available tools of birth control.

(basic steps to prevent famine)

6744

New Crops for Arid Lands, C. Wiley Hinman (U of Arizona), *Science*, Vol 225, 28 Sept 1984, 1445-1449.

Recent decades have witnessed an apparent increase in the rate of desertification of agricultural land (more than one-third of our planet's land is now arid). The two most important reasons for desertification are denuding of the land through deforestation and overgrazing, and heavy irrigation over long periods which increases soil salinity in many areas. As a result of these compounded problems, the deserts advance and farming of cotton and food crops becomes increasingly expensive. We cultivate only about 100 species on a large scale (with about 90% of our food coming from a dozen crops), and none of the significant crops grown today are xerophytic (adapted for life with limited water supply). Five plants are described that could be grown commercially under arid conditions: 1) Jojoba, a shrub of the Sonoran desert with seeds containing about 50% oil; 2) Guayule, a shrub producing rubber that is virtually identical to that of the rubber tree; 3) Buffalo Gourd, a perennial vine producing a large crop of seeds rich in oil and protein; 4) Bladderpod, an oilseed producer that is a potential source of chemicals; 5) Gumweed, which produces a sticky resin that might not only prove to be an ideal substitute, but may provide completely new resins. Concludes that commercialization of these plants will most likely occur through multicompany efforts, or cooperation between government and the private sector.

(arid land commercial crops)

6745

Livestock for the Landless, Noel Vietmeyer (National Academy of Sciences), *Ceres*, 17:2, No 98, March-April 1984, 43-46.

Computers are getting smaller and becoming more personal, but few people have considered the possibility of microlivestock for home use. Yet, with "personal livestock," even the landless in the Third World could raise their own meat in their dwellings. The almost universal use of chickens shows how vital small and easily managed livestock can be to poor people. Other examples of home livestock are less well known: 1) Guinea Pigs, the main source of meat for many Indians in Bolivia, Ecuador, and Peru; they are prolific, tractible, and easy to feed and house; 2) Domestic Rodents, such as the grasscutter in Ghana and the giant rat in Nigeria, which sell for more than beef, pork, or lamb; 3) The Blue Duiker, a small African antelope that stands about 30 cm. high (there are about 80 other kinds of duikers found in Africa that are often kept as pets and can feed an average family at one meal); 4) Dwarf Pigs, found in northern India; 5) Reptiles, such as iguanas and other lizards; 6) Pigeons and Quail; 7) Snails (Nigerians have been raising edible snails in small pens). Many of these small species are undomesticated and almost unstudied; given a little attention, some of them may prove to be remarkably important. Microlivestock makes sense where refrigeration is not available, and such animals can be raised on kitchen scraps and weedy vegetation.

(microlivestock for Third World poor?)

6746

Tropical Aquaculture: Need for a Strong Research Base, Roger S. Pullin and Richard A. Neal (Aquatic Resources Management Center, Makati, The Philippines), *Marine Policy*, 8:3, July 1984, 217-228.

The potential for contributions to human nutrition through aquaculture is enormous, e.g.: a 1976 FAO Conference concluded that a five- to ten-fold increase would be possible in the next three decades. In spite of its underdeveloped state, aquaculture in 1980 contributed about 9% of the world's supply of fishery products. But with few exceptions (such as trout, catfish, oysters, and carp), its technologies are poorly developed in comparison to animal husbandry of poultry and mammals. It is now clear that certain groups of finfish (tilapia, carp, mullet, milkfish, and catfish), molluscs, and crustaceans can become prime food commodities of international significance, comparable to major livestock commodities. But the basic research essential for expansion of aquaculture in developing countries is being neglected. A global aquacultural research center is proposed, to tackle basic research problems beyond the capability of existing institutions.

(unfilled potential of aquaculture)

6747

Agricultural Development in the Third World. Edited by Carl K. Eicher and John M. Staatz (both Dept of Agricultural Economics, Michigan State U). Baltimore MD: Johns Hopkins U Press, June 1984/512p/$37.50;$16.50pb.

Essays on agricultural policies and strategies needed to deal with problems of poverty, inequality, and malnutrition. Topics include models of agricultural development, the political economy of rural development in Latin America, developing a food strategy, food price policy and income distribution, the role of the US in alleviating world hunger, food security in LDCs, exports and economic development of LDCs, the role of land reform, policy issues involving rural small-scale industry, agricultural credit projects and policies, the economics of agricultural research, benefits and obstacles in developing appropriate agricultural technology, long-term development and equity in rural Africa, and facing up to Africa's food crisis.

(food and agriculture in LDCs)

6748

U.S. Food and Fiber—Abundance or Austerity? Staff of Resources for the Future (Washington DC), *Resources* (RFF), No 76, Spring 1984, 2-20.

A special issue based on a RFF report to USDA, examining the future of US agriculture primarily over the next two decades, with a more general assessment to 2020. The conclusions are admittedly upbeat, stressing the world's potential to feed a 6.1 billion population in 2000 moderately better than it fed 4.3 billion in 1980. Some 85% of projected production increases will depend on greater productivity of resources, and only 15% on expanding the cultivated land base. Long-term planning for agriculture should be predicated on a 70% to 100% increase in effective global demand by 2020 for US food and fiber, at real prices close to those of recent years. American agriculture will depend increasingly on the export market, resulting in greater instability and uncertainty for US producers and consumers. The productive capacity of US agriculture has expanded a great deal in recent decades, and the process can be further expanded through various combinations of improved management of resources and technologies now employed, expanded use of resources, and new or improved technologies to enhance resource productivity. [NOTE: Remarkably, no mention is made of the soil erosion problem in the US or the world, which preoccupies the Worldwatch report, above. Is RFF too much the Pollyanna, or is Worldwatch too much the Cassandra?]

(global demand for US food by 2020)

6749

Farm Recession Spurs Radical Restructuring of Agriculture in U.S., Jeffrey Zaslow, *The Wall Street Journal*, Friday, 9 Nov 1984, p1.

American agriculture is in the midst of a radical restructuring. The unforeseen length and severity of the current farm recession, which began in 1980, have accelerated the trend dramatically, forcing basic changes that are only now becoming clear. Big farms are getting bigger, traditional medium-size farms are vanishing, and small farms are hanging on because their operators frequently work in factories as well as fields. With the advent of professional farm managers, the concept of farming as strictly a family enterprise is increasingly outdated. There is a similar divergence of fortunes among those who serve farmers: old line farm equipment makers are troubled after years of depressed demand (farm equipment dealers have declined by 22% in the past five years). But scores of newer businesses, catering to the upscale appetite for technology and expertise, are thriving. One study predicts that 30% of farmers will own computers within five years, up from 3-5% in 1984. All of these developments bode well for consumers, who are likely to continue to get relatively cheap food. [Also see *New Breed of Farmers Focus on Bottom Line and Defy Traditions* (*Wall Street Journal*, 13 Nov 1984, p1), on the new, specialized, entrepreneurial, high-tech farmer.] (**big US farms getting bigger**)

6750

Fat of the Land. Fred Powledge. NY: Simon & Schuster, April 1984/287p/$15.95.

Of the nearly $300 billion Americans spent in 1982 on domestically produced food at the retail level, about one-fourth went to farmers, with the rest going to middlemen. Americans are becoming increasingly removed from their food sources, resulting in higher prices for lower quality. We are locked into a system that unnecessarily transports food thousands of miles, and encourages concentration in retailing to the detriment of consumers. Consumers can improve the quality of their food by forming food co-ops with friends and neighbors, and by establishing contacts with local farmers. (**US food system questioned**)

6751

Agricultural Policy Issues. *Agriculture and Human Values* Newsletter (Humanities and Agriculture Program, U of Florida), 1:1, Winter 1984, 1-27/free.

Five essays on social issues of agricultural policy, derived from a pilot program funded by the W. K. Kellogg Foundation to restore to the liberal arts curriculum a concern for learning what an educated person needs to know about the modern practice of agriculture, so as to participate in informed disussions about policy and to provide leadership. [NOTE: A splendid idea that should be extended to all areas of public policy!]. **Lawrence Busch** and **William B. Lacy** (U of Kentucky) outline 12 issues, including the collapse of the farm programs of the 1930s, the splintered farm bloc, the decline of the farm sector (from about 25% of the population in the 1930s to less than 3% today), an uninformed public that takes agriculture for granted, concentration in the food industries, the vagaries of international markets, the physical abuse of the natural resource base, and the lack of a long-term agricultural policy. **Katherine L. Clancy** (Syracuse U) describes the two faces of US malnutrition: hunger and the diseases related to overconsumption. **Don F. Hadwiger** (Iowa State U) argues that governments of the developed countries are inclined to abuse their agriculture. **H.O. Kunkel** (Dean, Texas A&M College of Agriculture) notes that there has been little scholarship in agricultural ethics and values. **William Aiken** (Chatham College) considers value conflicts in agriculture, and advocates unbiased dialogue between critics and defenders of agribusiness.
 (**values and agriculture**)

6752

Bioshelters, Ocean Arks, City Farming: Ecology as the Basis for Design. Nancy Jack Todd and John Todd (Falmouth MA). San Francisco CA: Sierra Club Books (dist by Random House), June 1984/210p/$25.00;$10.95pb.

The co-founders of the New Alchemy Institute and Ocean Arks International describe designs for human settlements that incorporate principles inherent in the natural world. The emerging precepts of biological design are: the living world is the matrix for all design, design should follow the laws of life, biological equity must determine design, design must reflect bioregionality, projects should be based on renewable energy resources, design should be sustainable through integrating living systems, design should be coevolutionary with the natural world and should help to heal the planet, and design should follow a sacred ecology. Chapters focus on bioshelters and solar villages [NOTE: described in greater detail in the Todds' **Tomorrow is Our Permanent Address**, Harper & Row, 1980; **FS Annual 1980-81**, #2540], redesigning communities, ocean arks (a new kind of low-cost vessel which can be built mostly from local materials and fulfills a Third World need for a versatile craft), urban agriculture of the future (e.g., transforming abandoned buildings into multi-tiered farmsteads), and agriculture based on stewardship and sustainability. The text is accompanied by idealized sketches such as a neighborhood sewage treatment facility, a roof top farm and park, sidewalk gardening, bus stop aquaculture, and a solar-powered train. (**ecological design**)

VII. SOCIETY AND GOVERNMENT

A. Major U.S. Trends

6753

Forecast 2000: George Gallup, Jr., Predicts the Future of America. George Gallup, Jr (President, Gallup Poll, Princeton NJ), with William Proctor (NYC). NY: William Morrow & Co, July 1984/179p/$12.95.

A significant degree of prediction is possible through the identification and analysis of the powerful Future Forces in our midst. Four basic methods are used here to forecast likely developments: the voice of the people (attitudes and expectations from broad-based surveys—the American public has invariably been ahead of political and legislative leaders), the future direction of present trends, the youth factor (values and attitudes about life are largely fixed by the late teens), and expert opinion (a poll among 1,346 national opinion leaders). Nine dominant Future Forces are selected that will shape our lives for better or worse by 2000. 1) **Wars, Terrorism, and the Nuclear Threat**: the threat of some terrorist group using nuclear weapons is especially worrisome; to reduce the threat we must limit the proliferation of nuclear arms, negotiate reductions with the Soviet Union, and help the Third World countries develop a vested interest in the international economy so they will be less inclined to encourage violence. 2) **Overpopulation**: as other areas of the world begin to suffer more from population problems—even the Chinese population continues to grow out of control—it is inevitable that the US will feel the impact; to meet the challenge, we must improve food distribution, limit world population, and reduce population concentrations (voluntary, government-funded relocation of welfare families from urban ghettos to areas where living conditions and job opportunities are better is viewed favorably by the public). 3) **Economic Pressures**: in the minds of opinion leaders, the US economic situation takes precedence over all other forces; inflation is likely to head up again, and we must worry about the deficit and unemployment (still, the outlook is generally bright). 4) **The Two-Edged Sword of Technological Progress**: computerization will bring sweeping changes in business, the home, education, government, and health care; but we must not overlook the dark side of privacy invasion, crime, and threats to national security. 5) **The Environmental Emergency**: we must be aware of the destruction of our environment, the threat to the water supply, air pollution, and acid rain; the actions we take by 2000 could be decisive for the future of healthy human life. 6) **Crime and Violence**: crime is a growing problem, but there is reason to be somewhat optimistic if peace-loving citizens can band together and work as a community to resolve these problems. 7) **The Faltering Family**: pressures on the family include alternative lifestyles, dramatic attitude changes toward sexual morality, economic necessity forcing women to work outside the home, and grassroots feminist philosophy (which has brought great benefits to many while also working against traditional family ties). 8) **Drug and Alcohol Addiction**: despite the concern with physical fitness, there is a growing trend to drug use among youths and adults. 9) **American Politics**: we face a curious mixture of frustration, apathy, and activism; important legislation likely to be enacted in the next two decades as a result of mounting public pressure includes Federal funding of Congressional election campaigns, a limit on terms of office in Congress, reform in the Presidential primary system, national referendums on major issues, compulsory national service (80% of opinion leaders and 70% of the general public favor requiring all young men to give one year of service to the nation), a single six-year Presidential term, abolition of the Electoral College, requiring business firms to provide on-the-job training for 16- to 18-year-olds, a constitutional amendment to balance the Federal budget, enactment of the Equal Rights Amendment, stricter handgun laws, and statehood for Puerto Rico. Concludes that we can influence these forces for better or worse through improved education, mature commitment, and the volunteer tradition in America to band together and make things happen. [NOTE: A mix of naive analysis and astute insight; overall, a useful companion and counterbalance to hyperoptimistic writers e.g.#6762 and #6906.]   (**nine Future Forces**)

6754

Future Forces: An Association Executive's Guide to A Decade of Change and Choice. David Pearce Snyder (Bethesda MD) and Gregg Edwards (Washington DC). Washington: The Foundation of the American Society of Association Executives (1575 Eye St NW), Nov 1984/108p/$30.00pb ($20.00 for ASAE members).

A guide to the "knowable future"—the inevitable demographic, economic, and technological realities that will characterize the near-term future—for the associations that serve US industries, trades, and professions. The forces, which should serve as a checklist to promote sound planning assumptions, include the baby boom generation and its implications, the continued dominance of information work (the single most important economic reality between now and 1995), implications of the emerging electronic info-structure, industrialization of the Third World ("we can reasonably expect to clothe, house, and feed" the earth's 11.5 billion people anticipated in about 100 years), the primary objective of increasing productivity, explosive increases in the demands for training programs and training personnel (education seems certain to become America's largest industry, with adult training as the largest component), worldwide demand for developmental and replacement capital sustaining double-digit interest rates, the shift from wage-work to entrepreneurship, footloose industries and mobile resources, new ways to do practically everything through new hard technologies (structures and materials) and soft technologies (institutional arrangements), industrial automation and robotics, the automated office, collaborative workplace arrangements, and electronic health delivery. [NOTE: A more sober style than Naisbitt, and somewhat more meat (the forecast for education is noteworthy); but similar to Naisbitt, there is a curious omission of any "Negatrends," notably the arms race, the US budget deficit, and environmental deterioration. In short, roughly half of the "future forces" are omitted!]

(**trends in work and technology**)

6755

The Year Ahead: 1985. John Naisbitt and The Naisbitt Group (Washington DC). NY: AMACOM/American Management Association, Feb 1985/63p/$6.95pb.

Ten trends that will affect the work and life of most Americans in 1985 and beyond: 1) the beginning of labor shortages as we move toward full employment (redefined as 93% to 94% of the workforce employed); 2) the US Hispanic population outnumbering blacks by the end of 1985 (the number of Hispanics is doubling every ten years as a result of immigration and a high birth rate); 3) the retraining of managers, not workers, in the reinvented corporation; 4) educational technology to transform the classroom; 5) bypass giving new definition to businesses (developing ways to get around monopoly service providers to save time and money; e.g., helicopters to bypass congested airports, in-house telecommunications networks, electricity cogeneration); 6) the San Antonio-Austin corridor as the US biotechnology capital; 7) the eruption of food pollution as an environmental issue (due to growing perception of pesticides, herbicides, hormones, and antibiotics in the food chain); 8) 24-hour stock trading as we move toward a single unitary global economy; 9) announcement of the marriage of computers and telephones; 10) home delivery by doctors, druggists, and Kentucky Fried Chicken. [NOTE: Some interesting assertions, including the introduction of one "Negatrend" (#7); but most have little or nothing to do with the immediate "year ahead," and all are presented with awesome superficiality. That's entertainment.] **(more Naisbitt trends)**

6756

America's Changing Social Agenda: Measuring Its Impact on Business, Lawrence Kaagan (Vice Pres., Yankelovitch, Skelly and White), *New Jersey Bell Journal* (540 Broad St, Newark NJ), 7:3, Fall 1984, 25-34.

Changes in public attitudes and social climate in the post WWII period indicate how trends were shaped. In the immediate post-war years, there was a climate of a nearly universal commitment to an economic agenda for the US. In the 1960s, a live-for-today orientation evolved (with a quest for more quality and self-fulfillment in one's life), and a new social agenda came to replace the economic focus. The late 1970s and early 1980s buffeted America with an infectious strain of self-doubt. By 1983, a subtle but important shift away from the dominant trends of the late 1970s had begun, and a national mood of assertiveness become evident. The new national goal appears to be a blending of social and economic agendas. Five themes are expected to dominate the social and policy-making climate for the rest of the decade: 1) tempering of traditional American optimism; 2) an emphasis on cost-effectiveness of personal and institutional activity; 3) a strategic posture to leverage resources and win; 4) a search for quality and excellence; 5) a focus on the local and grassroots activism. The policy climate is more complex now, and no single ideology will provide the rationale for policy-making as in earlier decades. Rather, this complex new policy climate will be marked by shared responsibilities, multiple tools, and new criteria for evaluating performance. The social climate of the 1980s will expect social responsibility from businesspeople, as well as profitability. The rest of this decade will be characterized by a pro-business set of social attitudes and policy orientations, granting companies more freedom to do what business does best. But the line will be drawn when these freedoms become license.

(changing US social climate)

*6757

Project Outlook: Social Issues, Selwyn Enzer (Project Director), *New Management*, 2:4, Spring 1985, 35-39.

Once a year, the USC Center for Futures Research polls a large panel of planners and futurists concerned with the future environment of business. This "Club of 1000" shares its forecasts of 150 possible social, political, economic, and technological events. Each panelist selects those few future events on which he or she has the most information. For each item selected, panelists forecast the probability of its occurrence over the next 20 years. The Winter 1985 issue of *New Management* published a poll of scientific and technical events (#7231); the Summer 1985 issue will publish a poll of global events. The following selected possibilities are from a 1984 poll on 28 social issues:

1) Boards of Directors of corporations held personally liable for product safety and pollution (45% median estimate by 2004; 25% to 60% Inter-Quartile range of estimates);

2) National Health Insurance program adopted in US, providing general coverage for all (50% median estimate down from 90% in 1979; 25%-75% I-Q range);

3) US adopts a program to maximize recycling of non-renewable materials (50% median down from 75% in 1979; 25%-70% I-Q);

4) US creates a comprehensive national program to reduce oil consumption (40% median down from 50% in 1979; 20%-70% I-Q);

5) A major program to develop effective intracity mass transport systems in all large US cities (25% median down from 40% in 1979; 10%-50% I-Q);

6) Stringent enforcement of US immigration law to reduce illegal aliens (30% median; 15%-60% I-Q);

7) Office of the US President restructured to a single six-year term (20% median; 10%-30% I-Q);

8) Voluntary simplicity: consumers make dramatic reductions in their demand for products and services (20% median down from 70% in 1979; 5%-50% I-Q);

9) Sharp decline in percent of high school graduates attending college (30% median down from 70% in 1979; 20%-60% I-Q);

10) Prayer permitted in the public schools (50% median; 30%-75% I-Q);

11) Catholic Church permits all forms of birth control (10% median down from 60% in 1979; 8%-45% I-Q).

[NOTE: Assuming a constancy in the panelists consulted, the shifting image of the future on many of the above issues (e.g, #8 and #9) deserves notice.]

(social developments by 2004)

6758

Post-Industrial Society. Edited by A. Bruce Boenau and Katsuyuki Niiro (Gettysburg College, PA). Lanham MD: University Press of America, Dec 1983/502p/$18.75pb.

Essays from the 1982-83 Gettysburg College Senior Scholars Seminar, arrayed in three parts: 1) **Technology and Post-Industrial Society**: the effect of robotics on US employment, implications of electronic funds transfer for monetary policy, family farms and the future, the effects of post-industrial technology on defense; 2) **Post-Industrial Society and the World**: democratizing the US corporation, industrial policy for a post-industrial society, the Third World and interdependence, the New International Information Order demanded by the Third World; 3) **Society and Culture in the Post-Industrial Era**: poverty and democracy in America, the American family, communications and privacy, a case for computer literacy in public schools, the relevance of a liberal arts education in a post-industrial society, Christ and post-industrial society, inter-religious dialogue in an era of communications, the danger of future dehumanization, visions of limits to progress in science fiction literature.

(essays on post-industrial society)

6759

On Nineteen Eighty-Four. Edited by Peter Stansky (Prof of History, Stanford U). NY: W. H. Freeman, March 1984/226p/$17.95;$10.95pb. (First published as part of *The Portable Stanford* series in 1983.)

After three introductory essays on George Orwell and his famous book, 19 additional contributions, all by Stanford faculty members, are arranged in three appropriate categories: 1) **War Is Peace**: triangularity and international violence, newspeak and nukespeak, the economics of **1984**, population and environment, the world food economy of 1983 as economic doublethink, the politics of technology and the technology of politics, the biomedical revolution and totalitarian control; 2) **Ignorance Is Strength**: lawspeak and doublethink, why the survival of humanity depends on the responsible use of language, Orwell's view of women, television and telescreen, Smokey the Bear as Big Brother; 3) **Freedom Is Slavery**: the sexual politics of **1984**, totaliterror, the functions of Big Brother, the psychological reality of mind control. [Also see *1984* **Revisited**, edited by Irving Howe (Harper & Row, Sept 1983/$10.95;$3.50pb), and **The Future of Nineteen Eighty-Four**, edited by Ejner J. Jensen (U of Michigan Press, 1984/209p), which offers humanistic essays largely by U of Michigan faculty.]　　(**1984 essays**)

6760

The Minimal Self: Psychic Survival in Troubled Times. Christopher Lasch (Prof of History, U of Rochester). NY: W. W. Norton, Nov 1984/317p/$16.95.

A sequel to **The Culture of Narcissism** (Norton, 1979; **FS Annual 1979**, #779), arguing that narcissism is not synonymous with mere selfishness or indifference to others, but implies a weak or "minimal" self prone to festering feelings of vulnerability that are often overcompensated for by outbursts of megalomania. Our culture of narcissism reflects the dominant personality of our time, shaped by the character-forming agencies of family, school, and work, and our dependence on technology. The strategy of psychic minimalism reflects political despair, for through political action we could order our condition along saner lines. Lasch attacks the helping professions for undermining the family's authority, neo-conservatives for their piety, and feminist and radical theorists for advocating an ecstatic oneness with the world (an ego-less merging with all things that is a perfect state of mind for a consumer). The preferred alternative is a locally-rooted form of democracy in which work and politics can serve as character-forming disciplines.　　(**psychic minimalism**)

*6761

The Trouble With America. Michel Crozier (Director, Centre de sociologie des organisations, Paris). Translated by Peter Heinegg. Foreword by David Riesman. Berkeley CA: U of California Press, Dec 1984/156p/$16.95.

A long-time student and friend of America, who has taught at Michigan, UC-Berkeley, and Harvard, found on a 1980 revisit that the dream had faded, leaving nothing but empty rhetoric. University communities and young people were demoralized, decision-makers had lost their grip on reality, and information was buried in an avalanche of computer printouts. The America of the 1980s wants to forget history and dream of happy days. Such happy days will not come back; innocence is out of reach for adult nations as much as for adult human beings. The country is getting closer and closer to a public relations dictatorship, with its citizens unquestionably underinformed and misinformed. The system has drifted off into trivia, appearances, and spectacular immediacy. A highly adaptive, nonstop society does not have the time to examine the implications of all the little adjustments it makes on short notice. Distracted by the immediate hustle and bustle, it fails to see that from a broader perspective it is frozen in place. American politics must be recivilized, requiring an immense educational effort so the public can draw closer to the national elites and so that the elites can break out of their complacency, arrogance, and insularity. The moral crisis that America is going through today grows out of the discovery that the limits to a development thought to be unlimited have now been reached—a time of saturation. The era of the frontier is over, and Americans can hold on to their values only if they learn to accept the existence of other values that can enrich them. Prolonged success always brings decline; one society after another has been trapped in the same fallacy of exceptionalism. No one would dare use the American case today as the lab for the future; Americans may still achieve many firsts, but their patent on exploration has expired. More than any other people in the civilized world, Americans overemphasize action; it may be better that they act less and think more. Their new frontier is no longer political or even social; it is the frontier of the mind. To overcome its present impotence, the US has no other course than to invest in knowledge and understanding, and the institutions which make this possible. Present-day America worships "celebrities," but basically it rejects leadership. There will not be commitment and care without the assertive power of individual leaders willing to run the risk of failure. [NOTE: Subtle insights from an observer who may well deserve the mantle of the new de Tocqueville.]　　(**American malaise**)

6762

The Good News Is The Bad News Is Wrong. Ben J. Wattenberg (American Enterprise Institute; Co-Editor, *Public Opinion*). NY: Simon & Schuster, Oct 1984/431p/$17.95.

The intellectual panic-mongering that brings messages of despair and failure are wrong and dangerous. We live in a nation that in most respects never had it so good. The bad news of the environmentalists is often wrong news. We are living longer, healthier lives. Many new products make our lives less risky, while others make life pleasanter. Our population is not exploding, and resources are not disappearing. We have not abandoned nature and we are not a bunch of crass slobs. The quality of our lives is not eroding. Poverty was halved in the 1960s, then halved again in the 1970s. Unemployment will be lower in the long-run future, and we are probably heading into an era of labor shortages. The percentage of Americans living in owner-occupied dwellings is rising, and there will be a housing boom in the 1980s. Worldwide, life expectancy at birth is rising in the low income nations, the daily per capita calorie supply is rising, the percentage of literate adults in the LDCs rose from 39% to 56% from 1960 to 1980, and GNP per capita is rising.

America has not lost its nerve; rather, too many people in high places were told it had, and this self-deluding prophecy was for a while self-fulfilling. Why, then, all the bad news? Because of the bad news bias of the media. Bad news is big news; good news is no news. Journalists are negative because of their left-of-center and anti-establishment tilt. [NOTE: A breezy, cocky style buttressed with much census data. A tough argument—but not without omissions and distortions—and a marked contrast to Crozier's pessimism (above).]　　(**bad news bias of media**)

6763

America in the Age of Enlitenment, Robert Garfield (Advertising Columnist, *USA Today*), *The New York Times* (Op-Ed), Sat, 20 Oct 1984, p23.

A "rant" about our society having its substance vacuumed out of it. We have lite beer, lite breadsticks, lite TV dinners, lite pancake syrup, light manufacturing and light rock music. We have light sociology in **Megatrends**, and light business administration in **The One-Minute Manager**. We have a light President who sent light convoys to Grenada to wage a light war. We are witnessing a transformation in the needs and desires of an entire culture. Lite is easier, enabling us to escape from structure and to be free of burden. [NOTE: Also see a suspiciously similar argument, *When Litening Strikes*, by Jim Fergus (*Newsweek*, 24 Dec 1984, p10), who adds that Ronald Reagan defines our age, as it defines him, and that the Lite Age is the final triumph of style over substance. In any event, it gives us an interesting notion to think about a bit.]   (**the lite age**)

6764

The Malling of America: An Inside Look at the Great Consumer Paradise. William Severini Kowinski. NY: William Morrow & Co, Feb 1985/411p/$17.95.

In the past 15 years, at least 4,700 new malls have appeared around the US, mostly dominated by large and generally nonlocal corporations. The theme behind their design and management is a three-part principle of enclosure, protection, and control. Malls and television have reinforced each other by preprogramming the Baby Boom generation to get on with the great American pastime of shopping, which has become the chief cultural activity in our "united states of shopping." The mall has become the new town center, magnet, and exemplar. Toting the tricks that they learned in suburbia, mall builders are arriving back downtown, greeted by inner-city aldermen and mayors who are eager to offer favorable sites and tax breaks. [Also see **Roadside Empires: How the Chains Franchised America,** by Stan Luxenberg (NY: Viking, 1984/313p/$17.95).]   (**malls in America**)

6765

Paying for Culture. Edited by Patricia A. McFate (President, American-Scandanavian Foundation, NYC). *The ANNALS of the American Academy of Political and Social Science*, Vol 471, Jan 1984/157p/$7.95pb.

Essays on the past and future of US cultural philanthropy, the price of government funding of culture, the public and the arts, changing public attitudes toward funding the arts, how corporations can help, the future of Federal support for the arts, cultural policy in Norway, indirect aid to the arts, growth and change of arts funding in the 1963-1983 period, and notes on the Presidential Task Force on the Arts and Humanities and President's Committee on the Arts and Humanities.   (**US cultural policy**)

6766

The Democratic Muse: Visual Arts and the Public Interest. Edward C. Banfield (Prof of Government, Harvard U). A Twentieth Century Fund Essay. NY: Basic Books, Feb 1984/256p/$15.95.

Examines art education in the public schools, the typical art museum, and the activities of the National Endowment for the Arts. All of these institutions tend to misrepresent the nature of art by presenting it as something other than aesthetic experience—e.g., as entertainment, history, or psychotherapy. Concludes that, for the artist as well as the citizen, there are strong reasons for leaving art in private hands.   (**US cultural policy**)

6767

Gambling: America Takes a Chance, John Dillon, *The Christian Science Monitor*, 8-12 & 15-17 July 1985.

An eight-part series on the rapid spread of lotteries in the US. Housewives, truck drivers, and businessmen spent $6.8 billion on state-run lotteries in fiscal 1984—an increase of 32% over the previous year. The biggest lottery of all, in California, is set to begin on Labor Day 1985. The most effective argument for gambling is that it is a painless tax. Other arguments include taking money away from illegal gambling, and keeping it from going to another state where gambling is legal. The new state lotteries are encouraging gambling behavior among people who have never bet before—especially women. At least two million Americans are now addicted to gambling, and experts say it is getting worse. Some Congressmen now want to launch a national lottery which, they claim, could quickly raise several billion dollars a year. A 1984 Gallup Poll shows 56% approval and 35% disapproval of such a lottery among men; 48% approval and 38% disapproval among women. Lottery opponents seek to halt or at least demand truth in lottery advertising, stiffen tax laws on lottery winnings, and begin new education programs especially emphasizing that lotteries hurt the poor.   (**state lotteries growing**)

6768

What's Happening to the Middle Class? McKinley L. Blackburn and David E. Bloom (both Dept of Economics, Harvard U), *American Demographics*, 7:1, Jan 1985, 18-25.

Recent assertions about the decline of the middle class have lacked documentation. The authors compared data from the March 1969 and March 1983 Current Population Surveys, finding that the middle class has indeed declined. The US has moved in the direction of becoming a nation of "haves" and "have nots," with less in-between. The share of families with middle-class incomes fell from 27.4% in 1969 to 23.1% in 1983, while the share of upper-middle families fell from 14.4% to 14.2% and lower-middle families fell from 20.6% to 18.6%. During the same period, the number of upper income families increased from 8.2% to 12.8%, while lower income families rose from 29.4% to 31.4% Explanations for the growth of the lower class include the growing number of single-person households (from 22.5% in 1969 to 32.7% in 1983) and the large number of low-wage younger workers entering the labor force. The growth of upper income families is best explained by the growth of two-earner families (in 1983, 25.7% of families with two or more earners were in the upper class, compared with only 7.7% of one-earner families). Concludes that any further decline in the middle class is likely to be small, if it occurs at all. Unemployment rates are expected to continue their downward trend, and the earnings of baby boomers will increase. The growth of two-earner families is likely to slow, because labor force participatioon rates of women are getting close to those of men. On the other hand, the middle class will not recoup all the losses it has suffered during the past 15 years, because unemployment rates are unlikely to fall to earlier levels and the proportion of single-person households will stay at present levels. And it is hard to imagine that the growth of two-earner families will reverse itself, with women returning to the home.

(**decline of middle-class**)

6769

The Fastest Growing Minority, Leon F. Bouvier and Anthony J. Agresta (both Population Reference Bureau), *American Demographics*, 7:5, May 1985, 30-33.

The Asian-American population grew by 142% between 1970 and 1980, and is expected to double by 2000 to 8.1 million. This population is growing rapidly because Asian countries are home to most of the world's population, and Asians now account for 40% of immigrants to the US. California was home to about one-third of all Asian-Americans in 1980, while New York was home to 9%. The Japanese were the largest Asian ethnic group in the US from 1910 to 1970. By 1980, the Chinese were the largest Asian ethnic group, accounting for 22% of Asian-Americans. By 1990, the Filipinos will outnumber the Chinese. By 2000, Koreans will surpass the Japanese to become the third largest Asian ethnic group. By 2010, the number of Vietnamese and Asian Indians in the US will also surpass the number of Japanese. Asian-Americans, now about 2% of US population, will represent 3% of US population by 2000. By 2050, projections show that they will be 6.4% of Americans—one part of an increasingly diverse US population in which one in three Americans will be black, Hispanic, or Asian.

(Asians as fastest-growing US ethnic group)

6770

Texas, California and Florida Show Major Population Gains Since 1980, John Herbers, *The New York Times*, Sunday, 28 April 1985, p30.

According to mid-decade estimates, half the 11 million growth in population since the 1980 US Census has occurred in just three states: Texas (2.2 million), California (2.1 million), and Florida (1.3 million). Highest growth rates were in Alaska (28.1%), Texas (15.2%), Oklahoma (13.3%), and the Mountain States (12.3% collectively). Negative growth rates were posted by Michigan (-0.7%), Iowa (-0.7%), and Ohio (-0.3%). The Middle Atlantic region improved markedly from the 1970s. In every region, the greatest growth appears to be taking place around the big-city suburbs and in small metro areas. [Also see ***Population's Rise in the Northeast Reverses a Trend*** (*The New York Times*, Sunday, 7 April 1985, p1), which describes a reversal of population losses in the 1970s despite earlier forecasts to the contrary; New England turned the corner first, unexpectedly followed by the Middle Atlantic region. The Middle Atlantic resurgence reflects in part the transition of New York City to an economy based on information flows.] **(US population growth since 1980)**

6771

The Great Oil Era Ends in Texas, Robert Reinhold, *The New York Times*, Sunday, 16 Sept 1984, F1.

Some 47 billion barrels of oil have been pumped out of Texas since the early 1900s, leaving only about 7.5 billion barrels that can be recovered profitably, even if oil prices double. Texas provided 32% of all US oil and gas in 1983, and may continue its leadership as two other major producers—Oklahoma and Louisana—also watch their reserves dwindle. As the wells begin to dry up in Texas, the state faces a rapid and painful transition to a post-oil economy. It is problematic whether the emerging high-tech economic order can generate the vast personal fortunes and the jobs that the old order did, because Texas is now entering an economic arena in which it has few natural advantages. Scores of new ventures in medical technology, the space industry, scientific research, and movie-making (the world's largest motion picture sound stage is being built near Houston) are representative of the effort to diversify the Texas economy. But economist Bernard L. Weinstein (The John Gray Institute, Beaumont) warns that a major impediment to modernization is the Texas educational system. In the next few years, Texas will have to make the hard decision to raise taxes to improve education and other services, or see its economy slip irreversibly.

(post-oil economy in Texas)

6772

Survival of the American Frontier, Frank J. Popper (Urban Studies Dept, Rutgers U), *Resources* (Resources for the Future, Washington), No 77, Summer 1984, 1-4.

Frederick Jackson Turner's famous 1893 essay for the US Census Bureau, ***The Significance of the Frontier in American History***, argued that the frontier and the pursuit of its land had shaped much of America's development and character, and that the disappearance of the frontier marked a transition to a new national era. Nearly a century later, the declaration looks odd and premature. The 1980 Census reveals 143 western counties with less than two people per square mile. The frontier counties (mostly in Alaska, Idaho, the Great Basin in Nevada and Utah, and the Great Plains from Montana to Texas) comprise about one-quarter of the US land area, but have a total population of only 572,000, or one American in 396. We do not know what to make of the surviving frontier because it is off the beaten path; at best, a place to fly over. The future may see renewed Sagebrush Rebellions, perhaps some strengthening of water technologies that would allow more agriculture, and possibly some emergency use of the lands (perhaps after a major West Coast earthquake). But the most likely vision is that, centuries from now, most of the frontier will be roughly what it is today: purple mountain majesties that lack the fruited plain. In sum, we no longer are a frontier nation, but we still are a nation with a frontier. [NOTE: An interesting argument, albeit one that twists the definition of "frontier."] **(America's frontier counties)**

B. Conservative Visions

6773

The Reagan Record. Edited by John L. Palmer and Isabel V. Sawhill (Co-Directors, Urban Institute Changing Domestic Priorities Project). Cambridge MA: Ballinger, Fall 1984/412p/$28.00;$12.95pb.

The capstone of a 3-year Urban Institute project that has examined recent changes in Federal policy and their impacts on the US economy, state and local governments, nonprofit institutions, families, and individuals. The Reagan Administration vision of a better America based on less government and more individual enterprise has been revolutionary in purpose but evolutionary in practice. Reagan sought a reduction of more than one-quarter in domestic spending, which would have eliminated the hallmarks of the Great Society. But this full-scale retreat from the welfare state was only partially successful. And the administration has done little to date in reforming spending, tax, and regulatory policies. The Reagan Administration has implemented a substantial shift in national priorities and sparked a fresh debate about the purposes of government. But its policies have often failed to produce the promised results, and the process of shrinking government has simply substituted one set of beneficiaries for another.

The Changing Domestic Priorities project also held six conferences in the latter half of 1983. The critiques of the discussants and the conference summaries are being published by the Urban Institute Press: 1) **The Social Contract Revisited: Aims and Outcomes of President Reagan's Social Welfare Policy**, edited by D. Lee Bawden ($10.95pb), considers the trend of poverty, income losses in a recession, the fairness of Reagan's budget cuts, and welfare dependency. 2) **Federal Budget Policy in the 1980s**, edited by Gregory B. Mills and John L. Palmer ($15.95pb), covers the severity of the large deficits, the defense budget, health care financing, Federal aid to state and local governments, tax policy, and budget making. 3) **The Reagan Regulatory Strategy: An Assessment**, edited by George C. Eads and Michael Fix, focuses on regulatory reform, and federalism and regulation. 4) **Natural Resources and the Environment: The Reagan Approach**, edited by Paul R. Portney ($9.95pb), offers sections on natural resources, environmental policy, energy policy, and agricultural policy. 5) **The Legacy of Reaganomics: Prospects for Long-Term Growth**, edited by Charles R. Hulten and Isabel V. Sawhill ($14.95pb), analyzes international competition and US economic growth, Federal spending priorities and long-term growth, and the legacy of current macroeconomic policies. 6) **The Reagan Presidency and the Governing of America**, edited by Lester M. Salamon and Michael S. Lund ($12.95pb), discusses White House policy development, policymaking for private sector initiatives, the Reagan impact on the Civil Service, intergovernmental reform, and the limits of privatization.

Summaries of these six volumes, and the initial overview chapter of **The Reagan Record**, appear in *The Urban Institute Policy and Research Report*, 14:1, Aug 1984, 1-27.
(Reagan domestic policy assessed)

*6774

Mandate for Leadership II: Continuing the Conservative Revolution. Edited by Stuart M. Butler, Michael Sanera, and W. Bruce Weinrod. Washington: The Heritage Foundation, Dec 1984/566p/$23.95;$14.95pb.

The first **Mandate for Leadership** report (**FS Annual 1981-82** #3712/3713), released just before Ronald Reagan's inauguration, was designed as a detailed road map to help the fledgling Administration steer the nation into a sound future guided by conservative principles. In the Foreword to this new report, Edwin J. Feulner Jr (President, The Heritage Foundation) claims that, by the end of the President's first year in office, nearly two-thirds of **Mandate's** more than 2,000 specific recommendations had been or were being transformed into policy. He also claims that President Reagan said that **Mandate** gave him and his Administration "special substantive help we'll never forget."

This new **Mandate** marshalls the talents and experience of more than 150 experts and offers nearly 1,300 specific proposals to make the Federal government leaner, the economy stronger, the nation safer, and the individual American freer. In prescribing policies for domestic issues, **Mandate II** is guided by the basic principles of restructuring incentives to encourage the efficient use of resources, returning control of government programs to those most directly affected by them, expanding the economy, and turning a myriad of government services over to the private sector. In foreign policy and defense issues, the guiding convictions are that the US must develop a defense that actually defends the nation (i.e., the Strategic Defense Initiative), US alliances must be strengthened, democratic pluralism must be promoted in the Third World and in Soviet-Dominated states, and the Soviet Union must be challenged ideologically, diplomatically, and politically.

Contributions are arranged in four sections: 1) **Domestic Agencies**: Agriculture, Commerce, Education, Energy, EPA, Health and Human Services, HUD, Interior, Justice, Labor, Transportation, Treasury; 2) **Defense and Foreign Policy Agencies**: Department of Defense, Department of State, the Intelligence Community; 3) **Institutional Reforms**: the Congressional budget process, the Federal regulatory process, the Social Security system, defense assessment, regaining control of the Department of State, the war powers resolution; 4) **Implementing the Mandate**: the environment of the political executive, internal and external constraints on policy-making, techniques for managing policy change, case studies in public administration. [NOTE: An exemplary format for articulating a program of specific changes, and perhaps one of the best predictors of the political winds in the next few years, for better or worse. While others fuss and stew in vague, fragmented, and academized efforts, the Heritage Foundation apparently has learned how to deliver an atlas of policy prescriptions.] **(conservative agenda)**

*6775

Future 21: Directions for America in the 21st Century. Edited by Paul M. Weyrich (President, Free Congress Research and Education Foundation) and Connaught Marshner (Chairman, National Pro-Family Coalition). Greenwich CT: Devin-Adair, Nov 1984 / 248p/ $16.95.

Essays by conservative leaders on steps America must take to survive beyond 2000. 1) **Economic Issues**. Lewis E. Lehrman (Lehrman Institute) advocates an international gold standard as the least imperfect of monetary institutions by which the US can establish sound money, wipe out inflation, and promote a long-term investment boom. Patrick J. Buchanan describes the New International Economic Order as the second sacking of the West, and advocates a new America First nationalism and rejection of the IMF, the World Bank, and the UN. 2) **Defense and Foreign Policy Issues**. Lt. Gen. Daniel O. Graham (U.S.A., ret.) outlines his High Frontier proposal for strategic defense to replace the failed doctrine of Mutual Assured Destruction with Assured Survival (also see **FS Annual 1984**, #5762). Congressman Newt Gingrich and James A. M. Muncy propose the exploration and development of space as a key to the conservative opportunity society. Burton Yale Pines (VP, Heritage Foundation) calls for a reappraisal of the US relationship with the United Nations, which is seen as supporting terrorists, promoting a double standard that overlooks the outrages committed by the socialist and communist nations, and crusading against free enterprise (especially multinational corporations); even with changes, the US should consider withdrawing from the UN and asking it to vacate its Manhattan headquarters—a world body that has achieved so little is not going to be missed very much. Major Gen. John K. Singlaub (U.S.A., ret.) advocates a comprehensive total strategy to confront the communists who have been waging a one-sided war against the free world. Charles A. Moser (Prof of Slavic, GWU) views communist tyranny as the primary threat in the world and urges an offensive US foreign policy. 3) **Social Issues**. Connaught Marshner notes that the predictions of the "future-terror advocates" (e.g., talk of the population bomb) have been disproved, and advocates natural law ethics as a substitute for situation ethics. Allen C. Carlson (The Rockford Institute) proposes a conservative educational agenda that includes the rebuilding of a distinct sense of American Civilization, deregulation and defederalization of the educational enterprise, radical deconsolidation of the public schools, and a joint program of tuition tax credits and vouchers. Connaught Marshner argues that the traditional nuclear family is the only environment in which children will receive the care they need, and that public policy must support motherhood and responsible parenthood. Ronald F. Docksai addresses the problems of health care reform, which can best be met by policies that force us to accept more responsibilities for the health insurance we purchase, and that place greater emphasis on health promotion and disease prevention. John C. Grunden views the promotion of computerization and high-tech society as a focal point for sweeping in changes that fortify conservative values. 4) **Institutional Issues**. Paul M. Weyrich explores the problems of bureaucracy. Patrick B. McGuigan, director of the Free Congress Foundation's Judicial Reform Project, describes approaches to reining in judicial activism. Paul M. Weyrich concludes by advocating state and national voter initiatives by which the people themselves can decide directly upon issues of vital importance. [NOTE: Well-written, provocative, right-wing radicalism: a distinctively different alternative future, a few pieces of which are now being assembled by the Reagan Administration.]

(**conservative policies**)

6776

Beyond the Status Quo: Policy Proposals for America. Edited by David Boaz (VP, Cato Institute) and Edward H. Crane (President, Cato Institute). Washington: Cato Institute, Jan 1985/292p/$8.95pb.

The mission of the Cato Institute is to illuminate policy options consistent with the traditional American principles of peace, limited government, and the free market. The ideas in this book seek to move forward in new directions with new agendas, "as the tired liberal-conservative debates of the past become increasingly less relevant." James Dale Davidson argues for the Balanced Budget Amendment to the constitution. Jule R. Herbert Jr. offers principles for reform and simplification of the tax system. Peter J. Ferrara calls for reforming Social Security with a new Super IRA program, gradually allowing younger workers to opt out of a system that will be bankrupt in the long term [also see **FS Annual 1983**, #5019]. Bruce Bartlett argues that a renewed appreciation of the role of the entrepreneur is essential, and proposes reforms to encourage entrepreneurship. Murray L. Weidenbaum decries the costs of current US trade barriers and proposes strategies to move toward free trade. Earl Ravenel warns about the costs and dangers of the US commitment to NATO. Thomas Gale Moore discusses regulatory reforms that the Reagan Administration has so far failed to take up, especially a more cost-effective approach to the Clean Air Act and the abolition of natural gas regulations. Catherine England urges sweeping reforms of the antitrust laws so that they no longer discourage competition. Milton Mueller advocates a move toward private property and free markets in communications and information. Clint Bolick blames the rising costs and declining quality of the public schools on their monopoly nature. Joan Kennedy Taylor argues for deregulating the poor by such actions as repealing the minimum wage law and exempting people below the poverty level from income taxes. Terry Anderson charges that pollution and the misuse of natural resources are caused not by market failure, but by a failure to establish markets and define property rights in resources. And Bernard H. Siegan argues that the responsibility of the Supreme Court is to protect the liberties of the people and the constitutional structure of government—but not to legislate.

(**Cato Institute policy agenda**)

6777

Constitutional Economics: Containing the Economic Powers of Government. Edited by Richard B. McKenzie (Clemson U and The Heritage Foundation). Lexington MA: Lexington Books, March 1984/254p/$27.50.

An intellectual movement is afoot that promises more radical reforms of government than those ever attempted by Keynesian and supply-side economics. Rightfully dubbed constitutional economics, and following in the tradition of Thomas Jefferson, it promises to reconsider the constitutional constraints on the fiscal, monetary, and regulatory powers of the Federal government. Constitutional economics is fundamentally concerned with the framework for social processes—the structure of and interrelationships among political and economic institutions. It has emerged out of the work of such scholars as James Buchanan, Milton Friedman, Friedrich Hayek, and William Niskanen. In an open-ended democracy, in which government powers are unchecked, businesses will be led by an invisible hand to subvert market forces through the use of unchecked governmental powers. Constitutional economists' see much government regulation leading to reduced competition and reduced economic growth. The government may very well have grown beyond the consent of the governed. Because of the growth in the technology of taxation, regulation, and deficit financing, additional auxiliary precautions must be considered. Constitutional economics offers such a theory of fiscal, monetary, and regulatory bounds on government. Essays in this volume discuss sources of opposition to constitutional reform, the monetary powers of government, fiscal powers of government, the regulatory process, and practical problems of constitutional reform. [NOTE: Perhaps some important change brewing here, as McKenzie hopes.]

(**limiting government**)

6778

A Populist Conservative Platform for the 1980s. Populist Conservative Tax Coalition. Falls Church VA: PCTC (7777 Leesburg Pike), 1984/56p(4x9")/free.

The Populist Conservative Tax Coalition was launched in April 1984 by Richard A. Viguerie (Publisher, *Conservative Digest*) and others, as a national organization to speak up for working Americans who are frustrated with the ever-increasing burden of taxation. The Coalition plans a national convention in August 1985, and seeks to recruit a million members by the end of 1986. It supports a flat rate 10% income tax, military superiority over the Soviet Union, the High Frontier space-based defense system, free enterprise in space, the balanced budget amendment to the Constitution, education vouchers, a return to the gold standard, requiring the UN headquarters to be located in a communist country at least six months a year, the sale of public housing to its occupants at prices they can afford, a significant reduction in Federal spending, a crackdown on illegal drugs and pornography, reconfirmation of Federal judges every ten years, a program to sell protected forest areas to conservation groups for nominal prices, etc. The Coalition opposes all tax increases, forced busing, racial and gender quotas, corporate welfare, elitist controls on the use of land by private owners, funding for the Corporation for Public Broadcasting, etc. [Also see **The Establishment vs. The People: Is a New Populist Revolt on the Way?** by Richard A. Viguerie (American Populist Institute, 7777 Leesburg Pike, Falls Church VA) and Viguerie's prediction that a permanent new party, seeking to restore the principles of Jeffersonian democracy, will appear by 1986 (*The State of the Union: A Populist View*, *Vital Speeches of the Day*, 50:15, 15 May 1984, 474-480). Viguerie is an expert in direct mail: "a very populist method of communication."] (**populist conservative platform**)

*6779

Window of Opportunity: A Blueprint for the Future.
Rep. Newt Gingrich (R-Georgia). NY: TOR Books (dist by
St. Martin's), Sept 1984/272p/$14.95.

Chairman of the Congressional Space Caucus announces
that there is a window of opportunity through which Americans can look, and—with luck and hard work—create a
bright and optimistic future. Reaching this optimistic future will require reforms of the government and the welfare
system. It also requires a bold dream: we not only have a
right to dream, but we have an absolute need to do so. The
power of dreams gives us energy for a better future. When
those who dream are ignorant of technology, they envision
only a limited future of declining resources, a limit to
growth, and a need for massive bureaucracy to spread the
misery equally. But we can find hope to motivate us for
the next several generations through activities in space:
spending more on civilian space programs, increasing the
speed with which we commercialize space, involving our
allies and our Third World friends in the development of
space, and developing a tourism program for the American
people—the beginnings of populism in space. The single
most appropriate millennium project would be the opening
on January 1, 2000, of a lunar research base for the whole
free world.

The right direction for the US in the 21st century will
involve a shift back toward traditional values and conservative basic principles such as work, thrift, and a strong
criminal justice system. The major principles of an "opportunity society" will all oppose the underlying concepts of
the welfare state: 1) the world must be understood holisti-
cally (the greatest weakness of the welfare state has been
its infatuation with reductionism); 2) examine proposals
systemically, within the context of the system they will
affect; 3) use models of organic life, rather than mechanistic
life (the welfare state is infatuated with the instant gratification models of the industrial society); 4) promote long-
term considerations vs. short-term expediency; 5) set
priorities for leadership in a complex and unstable world,
and be very cautious about where and when we commit
ourselves; 6) constantly strengthen our citizens by encouraging them to relearn the habits and skills of self-government; 7) re-emphasize the importance of ethical and
honorable behavior, and instill the importance of spiritual
commitment; 8) wherever possible, develop government
services and programs at the least centralized and most
human level possible; 9) in almost every field, we must
focus on reigniting the spirit of free enterprise, which once
made America so dynamic.

Progress toward the opportunity society requires innovative reform of major bureaucratic structures: 1) **The Legal
System**: deemphasize courtroom activity and expand the
use of mediators and arbitrators, simplify the intricate
processes of the legal profession which have so infused
government, excise the cost-raising legal fees now built
into the American business system; 2) **Health Care**: focus
on preventive medicine, decentralize decision-making so
we can move more rapidly to new technologies and procedures, rely more on patients and their friends and families
instead of health professionals, change the third-party payment system so the individual is once again involved in
market costs; 3) **Rethink Education**: shift our focus from
teaching to learning, promote lifetime learning in our information society, focus on discipline and the fundamentals,
re-establish apprenticeship systems, use mass media and
computers for learning, challenge higher education and
debate alternative ways of organizing learning, promote
an intellectually open academe ("the modern academic
world tends to be as ideologically monolithic as a Republican country club," and is filled with left-wing ideological

biases serving as a barrier to truth), promote action research and a reality-based approach to knowledge; 4) **Welfare**: give cash and credit vouchers directly to the poor,
generous services to the very neediest, day care centers to
enable welfare mothers to work, people paying something
for every health service (even if only fifty cents), turn public
housing into condominiums which poor people can buy
through sweat equity, consider a nutrition program making basic foodstuffs available free or at nominal cost (thus
eliminating the much-abused food stamp program), re-
shape child support laws so that parents are forced to
support their children, make non-violent offenders perform
acts of restitution; 5) **Military Reform**: end the pork barrel politics and mindless micromanagement which makes
it impossible for the Pentagon to run efficiently, reform
military purchasing; 6) **Public Bureaucracies**: combine
technology with a system of merit pay and idea bonuses,
give the President a line-item veto as a step toward a
balanced budget. In sum, the opportunity society calls not
for a laissez-faire society in which the economic world is
a neutral jungle, but for forceful government intervention
on behalf of growth and opportunity.

Concludes with a discussion of America's increasingly
incoherent foreign and military policy. The Right and Left
wings of US political and intellectual thought are in conflict
about the nature of the world, and both have much truth
on their side: the Right warning of tyranny and the Left
warning of nuclear annihilation. The Right must address
issues of a less conflict-ridden and dangerous world, while
the Left must confront the realities of Soviet interventions.
We must educate both our news media and our elected
politicans. We should move to less vulnerable offensive
weapons, shift away from ballistic missles toward recalla-
ble systems, develop a "star wars" active defense against
ballistic missles, move toward serious civil defense,
strengthen our conventional forces, and promote the doctrines of Mutual Assured Survival and Defense Protected
Buildown. [NOTE: An ill-organized jumble of provocative
ideas, unfortunately with no index. Gingrich, a former college professor with a PhD in history, combines historical
comments with popular anecdotes and references to Alvin
Toffler, Peter F. Drucker, John Naisbitt, and Thomas Peters and Robert Waterman (authors of the best-seller, **In
Search of Excellence**). Although starry-eyed about space
and the information society ("the information revolution
will raise the quality of life for all of us, and it will allow
the entire Third World to participate in a richer and more
exciting world"), he does offer some fresh and insightful
ideas for health, education, and welfare. His appeals to
dreaming and big thinking are welcome, but he pays no
attention to environment and resources, the international
economy, and promoting peace. In all, like it or not, Gingrich goes well beyond the banalities found in most books
by politicians.]   **(Gingrich's opportunity society)**

C. Liberal Visions

6780

America's Future: Transition to the 21st Century.
William H. Boyer (Prof Emeritus of Education, U of
Hawaii). NY: Praeger Publishers, 1984/168p/$24.95

In a new, emerging view, people are in charge of social
futures. Trends do not shape history; rather, social,
economic, and political aspects of life are seen as having
been invented by people. The future can be the result of
intentional democratic social planning. Boyer seeks to explain how basic changes are possible in the social systems

that threaten human survival—the macrosystems that result in war, ecocide and poverty. A strategy is proposed for integrated transition planning toward a 21st century with significantly greater human rights and a high quality of life. Long-range goals based on a set of value priorities are necessary for transition planning; for example, guiding values might include survival, social justice, and quality of life. An ecological economics of the 21st century should be compatible with nature, reliable for delivery of basic needs, and accessible for employment so everyone can participate. **(integrated transition planning)**

6781

Welfare Capitalism—and After. Bert Cochran (Research Institute on International Change, Columbia U). NY: Schocken Books, Jan 1984/227p/$18.95.

The US economy is caught in a spiral of decline. Familiar welfare state remedies are now irrelevant, while the neoconservative fiscal remedies are part of the problem, not the solution. The afflictions periodically besetting late capitalism are due to become more acute and less manageable, aggravated by three developments that did not have to be reckoned with in the crisis of 50 years ago: the emergence of ex-colonials as independent states, the rise of the Soviet Union as the second world superpower, and energy depletions and environmental impediments that raise costs and clog circuits to production growth. Society has passed the point of no return in permitting natural resources and public funds to be treated as inexhaustible. The era of crises points to the inescapable need to shape the economic undertaking. This can be envisioned only with the introduction of central planning and government takeover of more functions. But this should not suggest the abomination of Soviet planning. Both theory and practice suggest that authentic national planning need not entail Soviet-style takeovers of all economic activities. Moreover, those industries brought under social ownership will not necessarily function under the central state authority, but by municipal and district authorities. The final national plan will not be in the form of a decree issued from on high, but the product of the proposals and wishes of great numbers. It will also be vastly more realistic in scheduling inputs, drawing up production schedules, and ensuring internal consistency than Soviet performance at its ultimate best. Multinational corporations need not face dissolution under the regimes of ascendent states; one can see arrangements in which transmogrified multinationals are fitted into the emergent collectivities similar to the nationally owned British Petroleum. The formation of transnational blocs can be envisaged around several central states which will become the effective clearinghouses to coordinate economic tasks and regularize international exchanges. **(need for national planning)**

6782

Alternatives: Proposals for America From the Democratic Left. Edited by Irving Howe. NY: Pantheon, May 1984/137p/$6.95pb.

Essays by "perma-progressives" (Robert Lekachman, Bob Kuttner, Barbara Ehrenreich, Frances Fox Piven, Gordon Adams, and Michael Harrington) deploring Reaganomics and advocating full employment, universal health insurance, tax and welfare reforms, and deep cuts in the profligate spending of the Pentagon. Harrington views the system created by the New Deal as incapable of coping with the sweeping transformations by the world division of labor, the technological revolution, and the internationalization of capital. National economic planning is needed that goes far beyond the New Deal as the New Deal went beyond Herbert Hoover.

(need for national planning)

6783

Beyond Reagan: Alternatives for the '80s. Edited by Alan Gartner, Colin Greer, and Frank Riessman. A *Social Policy* Book. NY: Harper & Row, May 1984/347p/$15.50.

Essays by authors who share the imperative to remake society free of the barriers of prejudice, privilege, and distorted commitments to defense, prestige, and morality. Participation is the wellspring of democratic energy, and all of these essays emphasize the theme of participation, whether it means the achievement of full inclusion in society for previously excluded groups, citizens playing new roles in the economy as well as the polity, including previously excluded isses in public discourse and policymaking, or citizens involved in the decision-making process. Contributions are in four parts: 1) **Economic Visions**: the reconstruction of finance and implications for industrial policy, economics for people, democratizing investment, attacking poverty; 2) **The Future of Human Services**: the case for income support, the consumer as a hidden resource, Theodore R. Sizer on a new kind of school system that will evolve by the 1990s (defended as an alternative but ultimately a replacement, it will reward student initiative, use home-based technologies, and adhere little to the traditional curriculum), bilingual education, revisioning public reponsibility; 3) **National Security**: restructuring national defense policy, a labor-oriented perspective on immigration policy, economics and the environmental movement; 4) **Political Participation**: the new voter registration strategy, Ralph Nader on the future of the consumer movement, Bertram Gross and Kusum Singh on the bottom-sideways approach to democratic planning (empowering the majority of the population to articulate their common interests and guide their collective future), expanding political participation, transforming the Democratic party, and Harry C. Boyte on a communitarian-populist view of the American dream. **(expanding participation)**

*6784

Rebuilding America (Two Volumes). Roger J. Vaughan and Robert Pollard. Washington DC: The Council of State Planning Agencies, 1984/182p and 234p/$14.95pb(each).

The decay of the US infrastructure—roads, bridges, water supply and treatment systems, ports, terminals, etc.—is a major public policy issue. The rate of investment in public capital, both on new projects and on maintenance, has declined by nearly 50% in the last decade. Large expenditures will be needed, especially in areas where the expansion of employment and population has outstripped the capacity of transportation networks and water treatment plants. In addition, new types of public facilities must be built to provide safer and more efficient disposal of industrial and municipal waste, and to accommodate the rapidly growing demands for telecommunications. A broad public investment strategy is required, encompassing 8 basic elements: 1) redesigned engineering standards and improved maintenance procedures, to allow money to be spent on high priority projects; 2) improved capital planning, budgeting, and managing; 3) reduced subsidies to private investments; 4) project-specific cost-sharing arrangements with private firms; 5) user fees for public services to promote a more efficient use of public facilities; 6) improved bond financing mechanisms (e.g., through state bond banks); 7) increased state assistance to local governments; 8) increased public capital investment.

The two volumes are intended to help state and local officials to think strategically about public capital investment policies. Volume 1, **Planning and Managing Public Works in the 1980s**, analyzes the first three elements in the list presented above, with chapters on anticipating the future, the economics of planning, the capital planning process, assigning responsibilities, and timing public works investments. Volume 2, **Financing Public Works in the 1980s** [also published as part of **Rebuilding America's Infrastructure** (Duke U Press, 1984; **FS Annual 1984**, #6023)], addresses elements #4 to 8, above.

(rebuilding US infrastructure)

6785

Forget Today's Fleeting Fashions—We Really Need More Government, Not Less, Gar Alperovitz and Jeff Faux (Co-Directors, National Center for Economic Alternatives), *The Washington Post* (Outlook Section), Sunday, 7 Oct 1984, D1.

Unfashionable as it is to say in the midst of the "Reagan revolution," it is almost certain that we will one day look back at this current period of anti-government sentiment in the US as a brief interlude before a new era of efficient, enlightened, and expanded involvement of Federal, state, and local government in the economy. It is pure nostalgia to think that our post-industrial society will be run in the future as if it were a semi-developed agricultural nation in mid-19th century. There is a worldwide trend toward more government, and not even America under Reagan has been immune to it. In every nation in the world, governments have been deeply involved in planning, subsidizing, and in some cases operating major sectors of the economy. Such public-private cooperation helps countries compete internationally, avoids wasteful duplication, and maintains community stability. At present, the expansion of US government is carried on behind a smokescreen of free-enterprise rhetoric that makes rational decision-making impossible. A sensible economic policy for the US would recognize the need to build up a coherent planning capacity at both the national and local level. Planning does not do away with politics; it puts politics out in the open, forcing special interest groups to stand up and be counted.

(more government coming)

6786

Toward a New Public Philosophy, Robert B. Reich (Harvard U), *The Atlantic Monthly*, May 1985, 68-79.

Two public philosophies in the US have struggled for dominance in the 20th century: one termed "conservative," the other "liberal." American conservatives now have a clear and coherent public philosophy [NOTE: See #6779], whereas liberals do not. Reich explains why this is so, and addresses the need for a new and more coherent liberal public philosophy. Whatever form it takes, it must embrace a much more informed and strategic approach to global change. It would reject the notion—so deeply embedded in both liberal altruism and conservative pugnacity—that the central struggle of our age is over the division of a fixed quantity of global wealth. It would suggest instead the possibility of an enhanced quality of life for all, contingent upon mutual adaptation—a larger and more enlightened self-interest. A more adaptable world economy would help restore the long-term upward direction of American incomes, including those of poorer Americans. But a new public philosophy would also embody the recognition that we have a direct stake in the poor themselves; national economic competitiveness depends to an ever greater extent on the health and readiness of all of our people. Finally, a new public philosophy must be adequate to reality and emotionally compelling. If it is to be accepted, it must do so in a manner that simplifies and reassures.

(new liberal public philosophy needed)

6787

A Neoliberal's Manifesto, Charles Peters (Editor, *TWM*), *The Washington Monthly*, 15:3, May 1983, 8-18.

If neoconservatives are liberals who took a critical look at liberalism and decided to become conservatives, we are liberals who took the same look and decided to retain our goals while abandoning some of our prejudices. We still believe in liberty, justice, and a fair chance for all—but we no longer automatically favor unions and big government, or oppose the military and big business. Rather, we have come to distrust all automatic responses, liberal or conservative, especially in areas of crime and welfare. The primary concerns of neoliberals are community, democracy, and prosperity. [Also see **Neoliberalism: A Manifesto of the New Politics** by Charles Peters (Addison-Wesley, Aug 1984/224p/$16.95) and **The Neoliberals: Creating the New American Politics** by Randall Rothenberg (Simon & Schuster, June 1984/287p/$16.95), who describes neoliberals as concerned with economic growth, public-private cooperation, high-technology, and human capital investment.]

(neoliberalism)

D. Beyond Left and Right?

6788

Beyond Liberal and Conservative: Reassessing the Political Spectrum. William S. Maddox and Stuart A. Lilie (both Dept of Political Science, U of Central Florida). Foreword by David Boaz. Washington: Cato Institute, Fall 1984/203p/$8.95pb.

Our political language is not sufficient to describe political reality. The belief systems of Americans are more complex than acknowledged by the widely-used liberal-conservative dichotomy. The authors reject the single dimension analysis of American politics, arguing that mass belief systems are better understood if analyzed in terms of two separate dimensions: attitude toward government intervention in the economy and attitude toward the maintenance or expansion of personal freedoms. This makes possible a four-way description of US politics: 1) **Liberals** support government intervention and expansion of personal freedoms; 2) **Conservatives** oppose both; 3) **Libertarians** support expanded individual freedom but oppose government economic intervention; 4) **Populists** oppose expansion of individual freedom but support government intervention in the economy. These four basic categories are justified both theoretically and empirically; indeed, a reexamination of data suggests that the Libertarian and Populist categories actually included more Americans in the 1970s than did the liberal and conservative categories. One of the most important aspects of this study is generational: Populists (and to a lesser extent Conservatives) tend to be heavily concentrated in older generations, whereas Libertarians and Liberals tend to be younger, especially dominating the baby boom generation. [NOTE: A very important contribution to changing a fundamental paradigm of how we view ourselves politically—and well-supported by the Cato Institute, which would stand to further its aims by this new view of politics. For inadvertent "early warnings" and somewhat similar suggestions of two-axis politics, see Hazel Henderson, **The Politics of the Solar Age** (Anchor, 1981), p23; also Michael Marien in the *World Future Society Bulletin*, 16:3, May-June 1982, p20.]

(two-axis political analysis)

6789

Beyond Left Versus Right: Evolution of Political Economy in an Information Age, William E. Halal (Prof of Management, School of Government and Business Administration, GWU), *Futures*, 17:3, June 1985, 202-213.

As the worldwide economic crisis escalates, both capitalism and socialism are forced to search for new solutions, resulting in a proliferation of hybrid economies. If these trends continue, the outcome could be an international standard of political economy that synthesizes capitalist and socialist ideologies into a more powerful generic model that combines the best features of both while overcoming their disadvantages. This post-industrial paradigm of the New Capitalism, or Democratic Free Enterprise, is the indispensable course of action to handle the complexity of a knowledge-based society. Within the US, large corporations like IBM, GE, and AT&T are being transformed into flexible, decentralized systems of numerous small, self-managed enterprises. As the growth of information technology urges the development of such fluid structures, institutions should become organic networks of semi-autonomous units. Large institutions are thus moving closer to the ideal of the free enterprise system. At the same time, progressive corporations are slowly absorbing various business stakeholders into a democratic form of governance that serves multiple goals while enhancing profit. By 2000, modern business is likely to be characterized by such a myriad of small, innovative, constantly changing enterprises offering an endless variety of sophisticated goods and services, and governed by democratically elected representatives of their various constituencies. This powerful union of cooperation and competition should provide the necessary conditions for strong and equitable growth, lower taxes, rapid innovation, and collaborative working relations. [NOTE: An appealing ideal boosted into orbit by overstating good trends and ignoring bad trends.]

(New Capitalism: Democratic Free Enterprise)

6790

A Preface to Economic Democracy. Robert A. Dahl (Prof of Political Science, Yale U). Berkeley CA: U of California Press, March 1985/184p/$14.95.

The framers of the US Constitution could not fully foresee the way in which the agrarian society would be revolutionized by the development of the modern corporation as the main employer of most Americans and the driving force of the economy and the society. The older vision of a citizen body of free farmers, among whom an equality of resources seemed altogether possible, no longer fits the reality of an economic order in which large enterprises generate inequalities among citizens. Dahl explores the possibility of an alternative to this system of corporate capitalism: a system of economic enterprises collectively owned and democratically governed by all the people who work in them. Such systems are known as workers' cooperatives, self-management, or industrial democracy. Although these self-governing enterprises may prove to have economic advantages over the typical stockholder-owned and management-controlled corporation, the justification most relevant here is the contribution they might make to the values of justice and democracy. Such enterprises would give all citizens a more nearly equal stake in maintaining political equality and democratic institutions in the government of the state, and facilitate a stronger consensus on standards of fairness. If democracy is justified in governing the state, then it must also be justified in governing economic enterprises. Dahl addresses the

main objections, arguing that it is not true that: 1) self-governing enterprises would violate a superior right to private ownership; 2) the assumptions justifying the democratic process in government do not apply to economic enterprises; and 3) democracy in an economic enterprise would be a sham. A system of self-governing enterprises could be brought about by government facilitation of employees taking over firms in financial difficulty, and by experimentation with self-government in a few typical firms in several industries. If broader experience were to confirm the initial judgment, a country could proceed to move more boldly. In due time, it could bring about an economic order with wide distribution of authority and economic resources, and thus provide an appropriate foundation for a democratic order. In doing so, it could eliminate, or at least reduce, the contradiction between liberty and equality.

(self-governing enterprises and political democracy)

*6791

Strong Democracy: Participatory Politics for a New Age. Benjamin R. Barber (Prof of Political Science, Rutgers U). Berkeley CA: U of California Press, June 1984/320p/$16.95. (Brief version in *The Atlantic Monthly*, June 1984, 45-52.)

In the face of our era's manifold crises, we suffer not from too much democracy but from too little. This Jeffersonian conviction holds that strong democracy is the only viable form modern democratic politics can take. Liberal democracy, with its three dominant dispositions (anarchist, realist, minimalist) is a thin theory of democracy. Strong democracy tries to revitalize citizenship by encouraging participation of all the people in at least some public matters at least some of the time. To further this end, various reforms are proposed. 1) Neighborhood Assemblies: the first and most important reform is a national system of assemblies in every rural, suburban, and urban district in America, in that political consciousness begins in the neighborhood; assemblies would meet weekly at times when people could attend, and permit individuals to question their representatives on a regular basis; 2) A Civic Communications Cooperative: a national body to oversee the civic use of new telecommunications, and to promote televised forums for national and regional talk; 3) Civic Education: a civic videotex service and subsidized postal rates for civic education publishing so as to equalize access to information; 4) Supplementary Institutions: filling the great majority of local offices by lot, involving the community in the justice system; 5) A National Initiative and Referendum Process: to increase popular participation in and responsibility for government, and provide an instrument of civic education; 6) Electronic Balloting: encouraged in public places, rather than in the home; 7) Election by Lot: for selection of delegates to regional representative assemblies; 8) Voucher Systems: vesting individuals with the economic power to make public choices in housing, education, and transportation; 9) Universal Citizen Service: a program of general national service where young men and women would serve for one to two years in a military service or an Urban Projects Corps, a Rural Projects Corps, an International (Peace) Corps, or a Special Services Corps; 10) Local Volunteer Programs: blockwatchers in crime-watch organizations, sweat-equity programs, etc.; 11) Promoting Workplace Democracy: the possibility of using government-sponsored projects as models has been underexplored; 12) A New Architecture of Civic and Public Space: buildings that encourage talk and citizenship. **(encouraging civic participation)**

6792
Governance: Power, Process, and New Options.
Edited by Robert Gilman and Catherine Burton. *In Context: A Quarterly of Humane, Sustainable Culture* (Box 215, Sequim WA), No 7, Autumn 1984/64p/$4.00 single issue.

Based on the belief that the vast majority of people would choose to live in a humane sustainable culture if they could, these essays are grouped in two parts: 1) **Power and Process**: Andrew Schmookler on the parable of the tribes (#6475), Jane Mansbridge on unitary and adversary democracy (**FS Annual 1980-81**, #3006), Anne and Hank Maiden on holistic governance, Caroline Estes on decision-making by consensus, Corinne McLaughlin and Gordon Davidson on leadership and power in intentional communities, Elaine and David Lee Myers on lessons about energy decision-making learned from the Washington Public Power Supply System fiasco; 2) **New Options**: Catherine Burton on governance in the planetary age and the need to translate the natural law of the planet into human activities, an interview with Ted Becker on tele-democracy (electronic communications enabling direct democracy on a larger scale), David Heinke reporting on the first convening of the North American Bioregional Conference in May 1984, Charlene Spretnak describing the global promise of green politics, and Robert Gilman on how lessons from old cultures—the wisdom of the tribe—may help us overcome the reign of raw power that we now call civilization. **(governance for sustainability)**

6793
Community Is Possible: Repairing America's Roots.
Harry C. Boyte (Minneapolis, MN). NY: Harper & Row/Colophon Books, 1984/243p/$6.95pb.

Author of **The Backyard Revolution: Understanding the New Citizen Movement** (Temple U Press, 1980; **FS Annual 1981-82**, #3982) warns that the search for democratic, vital community animates the efforts of enormous numbers of people, but there is simultaneously a kind of conspiracy of silence about such a search. As noted by C. Wright Mills, the basic dilemma of a mass society is that people are gripped by personal troubles which they are not able to turn into social issues. We must learn how to talk to each other and discover how to share spaces, solve common problems, and discern the common values in different heritages. The widespread call for a return of power to ordinary people—the defining project of populism—has emerged from all parts of the political spectrum in recent years. If experts and distant problem-solvers seem perplexed and impotent, the appropriate solution is to devolve authority to those closer to home and to institutions grounded in the life of actual communities. Community action represents the stirrings of a different way—a commonwealth way—of looking at things in a society. The spirit of democratic populism charts another direction, away from conventional notions of progress, success, and unbridled individualism. How fully it might prevail, in the face of enormous forces that move against it in the modern world, is an open question. [NOTE: Most of the book is devoted to anecdotes of bake sales, barn raisings, and other forms of empowerment and self-help.]
(populism emerging?)

6794
Seeing Green: The Politics of Ecology Explained.
Jonathon Porritt (Director, Friends of the Earth-England). Foreword by Petra Kelly. NY: Basil Blackwell, May 1985/252p/$24.95;$6.95pb.

A passionate and personalized overview of eco-decentralist worldviews and the resulting green politics, ar-

ranged in four parts: 1) green politics in Europe; 2) why industrial societies have gotten themselves into a mess (global ecological problems, the arms race, the collapse of economics, alienation, systems without a soul, mindless materialism); 3) what we must do (ecologics and enlightened self-interest, long-term economic security by local production for local needs, non-nuclear defense, a sustainable society of human scale, a self-sustaining permaculture, reclaiming the feminine, voluntary simplicity; 4) recent stirrings of green politics in America. [NOTE: Possibly of use as an introduction to recent thinking; for anyone with a modicum of sophistication, this book is likely to be seen as glib, superficial, overly generalized, and politically naive. For somewhat greater specificity, see **Programme of the German Green Party** (Preface by Jonathon Porritt), Long River Books, March 1983/54p/$3.50 from Inland Book Co, 22 Hemingway Ave, East Haven CT 06512. Also see **Green Politics** by Fritjof Capra and Charlene Spretnak (**FS Annual 1984** #5623), for a very similar argument. The most astute view is provided in *The Green Party Comes of Age* by Horst Mewes (Dept of Political Science, U. of Colorado), *Environment*, 27:5, June 1985, 13-17ff.] **(green politics)**

6795
Bioregionalism—A New Way to Treat the Land,
Kirkpatrick Sale (NYC), *The Ecologist*, 14:4, 1984, 167-173.

The author of **Human Scale** (Coward, McCann & Geoghegan, 1980; **FS Annual 1980-81**, #2269) describes a bioregion as naturally defined by its location, geology, soils, wildlife, and human communities. Bioregionalism is the modern version of a very old perception of the world held not merely by the Greeks but by virtually every preliterate society. Much today goes against the grain of regionalism, forcing the nation away from its natural contours toward the artificial unanimity of a monolithic plasticised government. Political principles on a bioregional scale are grounded in the dictates presented by nature: scale, decentralization, division, and diversity. The economy that comes into being within a bioregion also derives its character from the conditions and laws of nature. The first law is that conservation and sustenance is the central goal: human systems would minimize resource use, emphasize preservation and recycling, and avoid pollution and waste. They would be self-sufficient, and not at the mercy of distant and uncontrollable national bureaucracies. Bioregionalism has the potential to join (or ignore) right and left: many kinds of people can be allied by the concern for place, the preservation of nature, and the return to such traditional American values as self-reliance, local control, and town meeting democracy. Whether we speak of bioregion, ecoregion, georegion, or vitaregion, once this essential archetype is comprehended on any significant scale, the matter of creating human institutions to match it can be safely left to the dwellers on the land who will always know best. Bioregionalism has the virtue of gradualism, suggesting that the processes of change toward recreating a continent are continuous, regular, and inevitable. Only by the long and steady tenor of evolution will people ease themselves into the bioregional future, as the alternative futures gradually come to seem senseless. [NOTE: Wishful thinking, or the "third future of mankind" as suggested by Wagar (#6466)?]

(the bioregional future)

6796

The Future Is Not What It Used to Be: Returning to Traditional Values in an Age of Scarcity. Warren Johnson (Prof of Geography, San Diego State U). NY: Dodd, Mead & Co, Jan 1985/246p/$16.95.

Author of **Muddling Toward Frugality** (Sierra Club, 1978; **FS Annual 1979** #763) continues his argument against industrial society and for a sustainable way of life. The power and wealth created by modern society overwhelmed traditional ways, but something was lost in the process. If affluence is inexorably eroded by higher prices for resources, capital shortages, budget deficits, and declines in world trade, we will experience the darker side of modern ways: unemployment and powerlessness, without the old supports of community and extended family. But as we slowly realize that our economic problems are part of a long-term deterioration of industrial society, people will begin to search for more satisfying ways to live than by the values of the marketplace (strident individualism, competitiveness, and accumulation). Scarcity is, after all, the more universal condition of human existence, and because of this the universal values are ones such as loyalty, generosity, and cooperation. As we move toward scarcity, we too will learn to appreciate these values once again. To argue that the time-tested ways of the past will be valuable in the future is not to say that the future will be like the past, but only that they are shaped by the same force—scarcity. In all likelihood, we can look forward to the evolution of a dual economy: the familiar industrial economy and the sustainable economy, which will increasingly be the only alternative as jobs are lost. Johnson argues against various false solutions: reindustrialization, the electronic revolution, deregulation (using government as a scapegoat for economic stagnation), reduced government spending, and more government. All of these options are everywhere restricted. It is better that the task of building a sustainable way of life begin now, rather than trying to delay it. If we fail to see that the season is turning, and recklessly plant seeds only to see them killed by the winter of industrial civilization, then spring will be cruel, afflicted by privation and strife. There is a time for everything, and wisdom is to know what is appropriate for our times: what to take forward and what to leave behind. We have had our time of affluence, and now the individuals who are fortunate are those who will not miss it. These people will be richer in the more important ways, and can look forward to the future with confidence and hope. [NOTE: One of the best contributions to the "simple life" genre (now somewhat out of fashion in the mid-1980s), and an excellent contrast to champions of modernity.]

(values for the coming sustainable society)

6797

The Simple Life: Plain Living and High Thinking in American Culture. David E. Shi (Davidson College). NY: Oxford U Press, Jan 1985/332p/$19.95;$8.95pb.

Those who say that "less is more" and "small is beautiful" have helped sustain a rich tradition of enlightened material restraint in the American experience, dating back to the colonial era. This intellectual history describes the shifting cluster of ideas, sentiments, and activities that have included a hostility toward luxury and riches, a reverence for nature, a preference for rural over urban ways of life and work, a desire for personal self-reliance, a nostalgia for the past and a skepticism toward the claims of modernity, conscientious rather than conspicuous consumption, and an aesthetic taste for the plain and functional. Such a philosophy of living is of course by no means distinctively American, for the primacy of the spiritual or intellectual life has been a central emphasis of most of the world's major religions and philosophies, and characterizes the lives of such figures as Thomas More, William Blake, Prince Kropotkin, Albert Schweitzer, Mahatma Gandhi, E.F. Schumacher, and Mother Teresa. For them, simplicity entailed what the English poet William Wordsworth called "plain living and high thinking." The simple life, as an ideal mode of living in an American society preoccupied with material standards of value, has been both a myth of social aspiration and a guide for individual living. In both respects it has experienced frustrating failures. Yet it has displayed considerable resiliency over the years: no sooner do advocates in one era declare it dead, than members of the next proclaim its revival. The much-ballyhooed "frugality phenomenon" of the 1970s was overstated, and the myth of ever-increasing material abundance and consumption guides the aspirations of many Americans in the mid-1980s. Yet the trend to simpler and more ecologically sensitive ways of living did not die, and continues to represent a significant alternative to the consumer culture. The simple life, though destined to be a minority ethic, can nevertheless be more than an anachronism or an eccentricity. [NOTE: A valuable historical background for understanding a significant part of recent futurist thought.]

("simple life" thinking in US history)

E. Politics and Administration

6798

In Search of the Rules of the New Games: Social Experiments in Scandinavia and North America. Edited by Scandinavian Seminar College (Holte, Denmark). Copenhagen: The Danish Institute, Nov 1984/178p (English language).

Contributions to a June 1984 Nordic-North American conference sponsored by the college in cooperation with the Danish Society for Futures Studies, Nordplan Association, and the Nordic Institute of Planning. The purpose of the conference was to search for guidelines for necessary changes in the governmental process of Western democracies—the rules of the new games. One of the keynote addresses is provided by Walt W. Rostow, who describes the emerging Fourth Industrial Revolution (embracing microelectronics, genetic engineering, robots, new materials, etc.) and suggests that the new rules will involve a higher priority on education and retraining, a catering to tastes in a more flexible way, and smaller and more creative firms. Other contributions consider entrepreneurial experiments, energy cooperatives in the US, a municipal labor market, the Highlander Folk School, self-help groups, nine homes and a glass-covered courtyard, and the antagonism between equality before the law and societal experimentation. [NOTE: Great theme, little follow-through.]

(new rules for new games)

6799

The New Directions in American Politics. Edited by John E. Chubb and Paul E. Peterson. Washington: Brookings Institution, June 1985/409p/$26.95;$9.95pb.

Analyzes the principal components of the political system with essays in two parts: 1) **Voters and Elections**: the new two-party system, the economic basis of Reagan's appeal, realignment in Congressional elections, the Republican advantage in campaign finance, the rise of national parties; 2) **Institutions and Policy**: new patterns of decision making in Congress, the politicized presidency,

Federalism and the bias for centralization, controlling entitlements, security policy, the new politics of deficits. Each essay compares developments during the 1980s to trends that were in place before Reagan took office. Changes have been most evident in voter loyalties, party organization, campaign finance, senatorial elections, and presidential politics. With the increasing capacity of the executive branch to dominate the policy agenda, and with a President and a governing party holding a clear vision of what goals and policies to place on that agenda, the changes have been extensive. Together, they represent a new direction in American politics, substantially different from that established during the New Deal. But it would be incorrect to predict that the Republican party will necessarily rise to a position of national dominance. An economic downturn or a foreign policy reverse may rejuvenate the Democrats, but the policies they once espoused will not be as resilient. Big deficits, strong defense commitments, and doubts about the welfare state will shape the political and policy future, whatever the fate of parties or presidents in particular elections. **(new direction in US politics)**

6800

The Personal President: Power Invested, Promise Unfulfilled. Theodore J. Lowi (Prof of American Institutions, Cornell U). Ithaca NY: Cornell U Press, April 1985/221p/$19.95.

In the last 25 years, the institution of the presidency has been redefined to reflect and legitimize the large national state that gradually emerged after the New Deal and WWII. The result is a "plebiscitary presidency," entailing a direct but no-win relationship of President and people. With both Congress and political parties in eclipse, the presidency is now the center of a political system that is the result of a pathological adjustment to big government. Inherent in the plebiscitary presidency are contradictory tasks and expectations that make success a virtual impossibility. Placing more power in the hands of an individual than can or should be wielded, the plebiscitary presidency removes all remnants of collective responsibility from the political system. With mass expectations invested entirely in the President, it leads to a cycle of extravagant promises followed by disappointing performances. Concludes with suggestions to "build down" the presidency and restore a constitutional balance to American democracy. **(plebiscitary presidency)**

6801

The Election and After, Edmund G. Brown Jr, Walter Dean Burnham (MIT), Kevin Phillips, and Arthur Schlesinger Jr (CUNY), *New York Review of Books*, 31:13, 16 Aug 1984, 33-38.

Excerpts from a June 1984 discussion on the future of US politics, sponsored by the Institute for National Strategy. **Burnham** predicts that Reagan will probably win by a decisive margin, and will attempt to complete as much of his revolution as possible by 1989. There will be an active promotion of a budget-balancing amendment designed to eliminate future efforts at reviving the liberal-activist state, and Reagan will probably be able to appoint five new conservative members of the Supreme Court. But it is hard to see how a consensus around Reagan policies can survive the bursts of adversity that may be coming, and the almost certain polarization of the US into a two-class society. **Phillips** views the US to be in a period of

enormous upheaval as it moves forward to a postindustrial, high-tech era. For at least another 5 to 10 years, the conservative-to-rightest tone of the major populist movement of recent times will continue. The major development in foreign policy might be called "a new nationalism," which may be preferable to the weak internationalism of the Carter administration. **Schlesinger** warns that if Reagan is re-elected, the next four years will very likely be years of unrelieved disaster for him. The larger the margin by which Reagan wins, the more trouble he will be in, because triumphant re-election diminishes a President's sense of reality. Somewhere in the late 1980s or early 1990s, the failures of the Reagan Administration, combined with American political cycles, will bring a new activist generation into salience, and a very significant change in the direction of American life. **Brown** argues that eventually we will have to divert more skills and intelligence away from the military and toward the international commercial struggle. Winning this struggle will require improved education and retraining, and coherent economic strategies—quite a difference from what the Republicans now offer.

(after the 1984 election)

6802

Huge Campaign Borrowing Is Corrupting Elections, Edward Roeder (Sunshine News Services), *The Washington Post*, Sunday, 14 April 1985, B1.

Senators and representatives elected in 1984 spent some $18 million more on their campaigns than they raised in contributions before Election Day. This deficit financing trend can shift power from the voters and candidates to creditors—banks and companies providing campaign services on credit. In a routine that is becoming increasingly common in US politics, office holders seek contributions from interest groups and lobbies to help them repay banks or replenish personal fortunes into which they dipped to pay their electioneering costs. This practice raises a number of serious questions about the effectiveness of the campaign spending reforms enacted in the early 1970s.

(deficit financing of political candidates)

6803

Fraud, Waste and Abuse in Government: Causes, Consequences and Cures. Edited by Jerome B. McKinney and Michael Johnston. Philadelphia PA: Institute for the Study of Human Issues, Fall 1984/c280p/$35.00.

The widespread concern over government fraud, waste, and abuse has not always produced careful analysis. These essays discuss the scope of the problem, types of practices frequently encountered, the origins of fraud and waste in organizations and society, and possible strategies for reform. Topics include risk analysis for combating fraud and abuse, mandatory international control systems in the public sector, zero-base budgeting in government, auditing as a political instrument, civil rights reform, and reform of Congressional oversight. [Also, for a steamy journalistic treatment, see **Washington—City of Scandals: Investigating Congress and Other Big Spenders**, by Donald Lambro (Little, Brown, Oct 1984/299p/$18.95), who views the government as a jumble of conflicting laws and programs exploited by lawmakers, bureaucrats, and special interest groups.] **(fraud and waste in government)**

6804

Innovation in the Public Sector. Edited by Richard L. Merritt and Anna J. Merritt (U of Illinois-Champaign). Beverly Hills CA: Sage Publications, Jan 1985 / 312p/ $25.00.

Papers from a conference sponsored by the International Political Science Association and the International Institute for Comparative Social Research in Berlin, based on the perceptions that Western governments are facing a complex of issues crucial for their future existence, and that static policies could lead to disaster. The ability of governments to surmount the current crisis depends on their learning capacity: the adoption of new ideas and practices and their diffusion. Contributions include Karl W. Deutsch on a generative model of innovation that can contribute to mankind's ability to control its fate, individual creativity and political leadership, groups and the innovative process, diffusion of innovations in public organizations, innovations in West Germany's public sector, West German technology policy, the politics of educational reform, legal culture and the chances for legal innovation, large-scale policy innovation in East and West European agriculture, trends and perspectives in innovation policies, and optimal organizing and managing of policy-making groups. The conclusions of the conference are that: 1) even in crises, traditional methods of problem-solving are usually applied because the known is viewed as preferable to an uncertain search for truly new ways; 2) understanding the process of innovation requires a greater understanding of the motivation of individuals; 3) the more industrialized a state is, the greater the need for an innovative capacity to meet expected and unexpected demands on the system.

(public sector innovation)

6805

Public Sector Performance: A Conceptual Turning Point. Edited by Trudi C. Miller (Decision and Management Science Program, NSF). Baltimore MD: Johns Hopkins U Press, Oct 1984/288p/$24.75;$11.75pb.

Provides a critical overview of the theories and realities of contemporary US government at the Federal, state, and local levels. Chapters cover intergovernmental change, why government grows, information systems and intergovernmental relations, the effect of demographic trends on government expenditures, a new framework for evaluating public sector performance (focusing on government's choice-making role), public finance as a resource for understanding and controlling public sector performance, and management and accountability models. The overall portrait is one of failure of prevailing approaches to political science and public administration. The root of the problem lies in treating social systems as if they were physical, biological, or mechanical systems, with behavior governed by immutable laws. The natural science model encourages standardization and centralization in government. The design sciences, which deal with manmade objects of inquiry, offer a more promising paradigm for political systems.

(design science perspective needed)

VIII. THE ECONOMY

A. Forecasts and Forecasters

6806

Why World May Be Near Another Economic Boom,
Alfred Zanker, *U.S. News & World Report*, 20 Aug 1984,
54-57.

After more than a decade of instability and uncertainty,
the US and the free world appear to be headed for long-last-
ing recovery—if governments don't mess things up. New
setbacks cannot be ruled out, but on balance the good news
outweighs the bad: inflation is fairly well under control,
profits are improving, and business investments are picking up. Output in Western industrial nations is likely to
grow at more than 4% in 1984, and world trade may expand
by nearly 6%. According to some long-wave economists in
Europe and the US, this signals the beginning of a long
upswing that will set the stage of the next era of prosperity
in the 1990s. [An accompanying chart shows five long-
waves (or Kondratieff waves) over the past 200 years, with
1985 marking the beginning of the fifth wave upturn,
spearheaded by microelectronics, telecommunications,
biotechnology, and nuclear energy.] The next long wave is
expected to start in the US, closely followed by Japan and
Southeast Asia, but with Europe lagging. Once started,
innovation and growth cycles will spread around the world.
Experts cited are Gerhart Bruckmann (U of Vienna), Herbert Giersch (Kiel Institute), Jacob J. van Duijn (Rotter-
dam), and Cesare Marchetti (Italy).

(world economic boom in 1990s?)

6807

Economic Conditions Ahead: Understanding the Kon-
dratieff Wave, Jay W. Forrester (Director, Systems
Dynamics Program, MIT), *The Futurist*, 19:3, June 1985,
16-20.

The Kondratieff cycle or economic long wave with peaks
of 45-60 years apart is the phenomenon responsible for the
great depressions of the 1830s, the 1890s, and the 1930s.
Present worldwide economic crosscurrents suggest that we
are entering another such downturn of the long wave.
Throughout the economy, there have been replays of what
went on before the 1930s. Defaults, unmanageable debt
on agricultural land, and inflation turning into deflation
are all part of working out the imbalances that have accumulated by the peak of long-wave expansion of production capacity. If the US deficit is not brought under control,
it will rapidly get out of hand, with no solution available
except for the US to default on its debt. If we had an
awareness of the economic long wave through use of the
System Dynamics National Model, we could have prevented some of the overshoot from which we must now
recover. [Also see pro and con arguments for the Kondratieff Wave in *The Futurist*, Feb 1985 (pp23-27), and a
technical discussion of the System Dynamics National
Model: ***An Integrated Theory of the Economic Long***
Wave by John D. Sterman of MIT (*Futures*, April 1985,
104-131).] **(long wave depression ahead?)**

6808

Fearless Forecast: Economists Don't See Threats to
Economy Portending Depression, Lindley H. Clark Jr
and Alfred L. Malabre Jr, *The Wall Street Journal*, Friday,
12 Oct 1984, p1.

The question of whether a Great Depression can happen
again has been nagging for about a decade. Since the late
1970s, *The Wall Street Journal* has polled ten eminent
analysts (including three Nobel Laureates and two former
Federal Reserve Board Chairmen). These experts have
always unanimously discounted the likelihood of an
economic collapse, and they persist in that view in 1984.
Paul Samuelson, for example, thinks that the current expansion could well give way to another recession, perhaps
by 1986, but "another depression on the order of the 1930s
just doesn't seem possible." The general conviction is that
history won't repeat itself because of changes in attitudes
about government action, the expanding role of the FDIC,
the structure of employment (jobs in the service sector are
more stable), and the closer monitoring of business activity.
As Arthur Burns notes, "I still see no new Great Depression
in the cards for the simple reason that the government
can prevent collapse, and the government will prevent it."
The economists did express worry about the deficit (Martin
Feldstein, Robert Hall), worsening inflation (J. K. Galbraith), protectionism (Charles P. Kindleberger) and having gone too far with deregulation of financial institutions
(William McChesney Martin, Lawrence Klein). [NOTE:
What do these optimists see that the pessimists (e.g. Frank,
#6541) do not see—and vice versa? Is the major difference
one of national vs. global worldviews?]

(depression prospect dismissed by experts)

6809

Half Speed Ahead for the Long Haul, *Fortune*, 21 Jan
1985, 34-44.

The *Fortune* economic forecast for the next 18 months
sees no recession likely before mid-1986 at least. But
growth will be slow enough to kick the deficit upward, and
unemployment will rise from 7.5% to more than 8%. Interest rates may not go up as much, but inflation (now at
about 4%) will rise to 4.7% in 1985 and over 5% in the
first half of 1986. The economy is expanding slowly to
accommodate Washington's failure to narrow the budget
gap. But overall performance may not be so bad: a
peacetime expansion lasting through mid-1986 would be
the third longest of the last century. Forecasts are provided
for 16 basic industries. [The analysis by *U.S.News & World
Report* (8 April 1985, p29) forecasts the US economy as
dropping "into lower gear," with growth for 1985 as a whole
at 3.4% after inflation adjustment, in contrast to 6.8% in
1984.] **(US economy in 1985-86)**

6810

Economic Chill Seen in 2nd Term, James Sterngold,
The New York Times, Monday, 12 Nov 1984, D1.

Most economic analysts doubt that the economic performance during President Reagan's first term will continue
in the next four years. Most of them view a slowdown in
economic growth, but little prospect for a renewed surge
in inflation (most see consumer prices rising less than 6%
annually). Nine major forecasters are consulted. Forecasts
for real GNP growth in 1987 range from 0.2% (Evans) to
4.8% (Wharton). Forecasts for consumer price increases in
1987 range from 3.5% (Claremont) to 6.5% (Citicorp). Forecasts for average unemployment rate in 1987 range from
5.6% (Claremont) to 9.2% (Evans).

(economic forecasts for 1987)

6811

Are Economic Forecasters Worth Listening To? Peter L. Bernstein (Editor, *Journal of Portfolio Management*) and Theodore H. Silbert (Chairman, Sterling National Bank, NYC), *Harvard Business Review*, 84:5, Sept-Oct 1984, 32-40.

At one time or another, every professional economic forecaster is wrong. Taken as a group, however, they have a good record. Reliance on a consensus outlook can at least keep one aware of signs that current trends are changing. Economic forecasts deserve to be taken seriously because they are much more useful than having no forecasts at all.

(value of economic forecasts)

6812

Economists Missing the Mark: More Tools, Bigger Errors, Robert A. Bennett, *The New York Times*, Wed, 12 Dec 1984, D1.

Always an inexact science, economic forecasting seems to have been deteriorating in accuracy in recent years, raising serious questions about the degree to which government and business should depend on economic forecasts. In early 1984, as the economy continued to boom, most economists revised their projections once again, predicting economic growth would be excessively strong. They were wrong again, as real growth plunged from 10.1% in the first quarter to 1.9% in the third quarter. Geoffrey H. Moore (Columbia U) has calculated that the US government's projection for GNP growth in the last three years was wrong by 2.9% on average, or almost three times the average error for the previous 13 years. Private forecasters did somewhat better: their GNP projections were off by 1.8%, more than twice the average error of 0.8% in the previous 13 years. Moore's studies show, however, that if the government had resorted to its former method of mere extrapolation, the accuracy of the forecasts would have been considerably worse, averaging an error of 4.1% for the past three years. Alan Greenspan, former chairman of the Council of Economic Advisors, points out that "Even though we've had an extraordinary increase in our tools, such as computers, we have not been able to keep pace with the growing complexity of economic relationships, both domestic and international." Economic models are based on past performance, and structural changes in the way the economy operates make old models obsolete. Wider use of computers, for example, allows many companies to hold much lower levels of inventory than in the past, creating new relationships between retail sales and the ordering of goods from factories. As inventories are reduced, corporate borrowing requirements also decline. The article concludes that more than 1000 savings institutions have been forced out of business in recent years because of failure to foresee interest-rate trends.

(decline in economic forecasting accuracy)

6813

Business Forecasters Find Demand Is Weak In Their Own Business, Lindley H. Clark, Jr and Alfred L. Malabre, Jr, *The Wall Street Journal*, Friday, 7 Sept 1984, p1.

The US economy is proving far stronger than most economists anticipated—and far peppier than the economic consulting business itself. The major reason for the problems in the "business-prophecy business" result from "an epidemic of wide-of-the-mark forecasts" which looked particularly bad because many economists probably oversold their forecasting abilities. Other reasons for the slump include corporate and government cost-cutting and the spread of do-it-yourself analysis by means of personal computers. A particularly glum assessment is offered by Michael K. Evans, a Washington consultant, who says "We're a declining industry." Deepening skepticism about the usefulness of economic advice is leading some companies to drop in-house forecasting. On the other hand, the Cleveland-based National Association of Business Economists is still growing, with a record 3800 members in 1984, up from 2575 members in 1978.

(economic forecasting in decline?)

6814

The Poverty of Economics, Robert Kuttner, *The Atlantic Monthly*, Feb 1985, 74-84.

During the 1970s, the world's industrial economies faltered in ways that confounded the received theory of economics. Business and governments found economic advice to be wanting. Yet the teaching and research of economics shows deep resistance to change. Kuttner critiques the neoclassical model, econometric techniques and overmathematization, and the lack of commitment to observation and disputation. Indeed, economists have become the least worldly of social scientists. The handful of brilliant dissenting eclectics such as John Kenneth Galbraith, Herbert Simon, Wassily Leontief, and Lester Thurow does not add up to a contending school, and no dissenting paradigm seems able to gain a foothold. Concludes that in the economics profession, the free marketplace of ideas is one more market that doesn't work like the model. [Also see *What Good Are Economists?* (*Newsweek*, 4 Feb 1985, 60-63), which comments on fractious squabbles, intellectual paralysis, prediction failures, and the growing tendency of economists to devise elegant mathematical theories while neglecting the real world. *It's Back to Doghouse for Economists* (*U.S. News & World Report*, 4 Feb 1985, p55) echoes this theme, viewing the profession as being devalued in the market of public opinion.]

(economists questioned)

6815

The Future of Economics: A Delphi Study, James Cicarelli (Dean, School of Business Administration, St. Bonaventure U), *Technological Forecasting and Social Change*, 25:2, April 1984, 139-157.

An expansion of an earlier Delphi on the future of economics (*Journal of Post-Keynesian Economics*, Fall 1980; **FS Annual 1980-81**, #2364), confined to 24 New York State economists. The current study involves 206 economists in 18 countries, resulting in a list of 28 breakthroughs in thought likely to occur in the next 20 years. **Consensus breakthroughs** (those thought achievable by two-thirds or more of the panelists) include a new paradigm for the study of labor market adjustments, modeling of optimal exploitation of non-renewable resources, integration of micro- and macrotheory, and an explicit merger of economic theory with aspects of political science, psychology, sociology, sociobiology, and law. **Majority breakthroughs** (those thought achievable by more than 50% but less than 66% of the panelists) include general equilibrium modeling of energy in the economy, insights into the sources and remedies of unemployment, improved policies for dealing with stagflation, and dynamic modeling of anticipated behavior of policymakers. **Minority breakthroughs** (those thought achievable by less than half of the panelists) include analysis of voting that will allow estimation of consumer preferences for publicly produced goods, a general methodological revolution (possibly in the direction of Austrian economics), models of the processes of technological change and the economics of invention, and integration of decision theory, administrative science, and the principles of accounting into a new theory of the firm. Concludes that the philosophical basis of Western economics is cyclical: the current mobilization of bias in economics is conservative, but the study suggests that liberal economics will be on the ascendancy again by the 1990s. **(future of economics Delphi)**

6816

Energy and the U.S. Economy: A Biophysical Perspective, Cutler J. Cleveland (U of Illinois) *et al.*, *Science*, Vol 225, 31 Aug 1984, 890-897.

The concept of energy return on investment is introduced as a major driving force in the economy, and data are provided which show a marked decline in energy return on investment for all our principal fuels in recent decades. Future economic growth will depend largely on the net energy yield of alternative fuel sources, and some standard economic models may require modification to account for the biophysical constraints on human economic activity.

(biophysical constraints on economy)

B. Deficits and Taxes

*6817

The Trillion Dollar Budget: How to Stop the Bankrupting of America. Glenn Pascall (Institute of Public Policy, U of Washington). Seattle WA: U of Washington Press, Feb 1985/400p/$19.95;$9.95pb.

Updating of a 1980 study by the Washington State Research Council on ways to reduce Federal spending. Pascall warns that Federal revenues are stuck at about 19% of GNP and spending is stuck at about 24% of GNP, and the gap will increase over time. The total Federal debt at the end of 1985 will have doubled from its 1980 level—$1.8 trillion versus $900 billion—and a recession in 1986 or 1987 could easily balloon a single year's deficit to $300 billion. Vast savings are possible and urgently needed in defense, and huge future costs can and must be avoided in Medicare and Social Security. Chapters are devoted to the problems of defense procurement and the permanent war economy, and the problems of transfer payments resulting in subsidies for the strong. Concludes with a chapter calling for a new American social contract, in which demands are moderated and sacrifices shared so that we do not mortgage the future. This includes a list of proposals, integrating suggestions from ten other sources, that would reduce the deficit by $144 billion per year, including $45 billion in defense, $24 billion in Medicare, $20 billion in Social Security, $4 billion in Federal employee benefits, $6 billion in economy measures for the Federal bureaucracy, $32 billion in subsidies to agriculture and transportation, etc. **(reducing Federal spending)**

6818

Economic Choices 1984. Edited by Alice M. Rivlin. Washington: The Brookings Institution, Fall 1984/171p/ $8.95pb.

Sustained economic growth should be a high priority of public policy, for in a growing economy public choices are less agonizing and divisive. The US economy would greatly benefit from a major switch in monetary and fiscal policies, turning away from high deficits and high interest rates. A plan is offered here by a group of Brookings economists to bring the Federal budget close to balance by 1989. A short-run freeze on domestic spending would be followed by more basic restructuring of domestic programs. Defense spending proposals call for immediate cuts in weapons systems deemed duplicative or related to questionable objectives. The tax system could bring in more than $100 billion of new revenues by 1989 by broadening the tax base and taxing spending rather than income. Individual and corporate income taxes would be replaced by a cash flow tax. Changes in domestic spending include steps to reduce somewhat the automatic growth in Social Security, changes in civil service and military retirement systems, and a restructuring of agricultural programs. But even if the economy grows and unemployment declines, recent increases in poverty will be reversed very slowly unless policy is changed. In the short run, the most direct approach is to increase benefits going directly to poor people; over the long term, we should concentrate on improving the education and training of low-income youth.

(plan to end deficit by 1989)

6819

Budget Cuts Now; Then Tax Reform, Bipartisan Budget Appeal, *The New York Times*, Sun, 23 June 1985, E6-E7.

A full-page appeal to Congress by a group of 500 government, business, and academic leaders, led by six former Cabinet Secretaries (Blumenthal, Connally, Dillon, Fowler, Peterson, and Simon). The President and the Congress have at last acknowledged the scale of the budgetary imbalance, and have discarded the notion that we can "grow our way out." But action is incomplete, the hour late, and the damage mounting fast. Economic warning signs are flashing. Real interest rates remain at unprecedented levels that strain and destabilize our financial system. The dollar remains massively overvalued as a result of unprecedented capital inflows needed to balance our national accounts. The spiraling Federal debt held by the public now towers at $1.5 trillion—nearly double its level five years ago. It will rise by a third or another $500 billion by 1988—even with full implementation of current budget resolutions. Current budget plans fail to come fully to grips with the excessive long-term costs of middle-class entitlements. After five years of defense real growth averaging nearly 9% annually, we have reached the point where military and foreign policy gains from defense spending would be more than offset by faltering US economic performance and weakened world economic leadership. Issues of defense priorities which have been avoided since 1980 must now be seriously addressed. And it must be acknowledged that tax reform and tax increases will both be necessary. [For previous statements by this group, see **FS Annual 1984** #6031 and **FS Annual 1983** #4743 and #5008.] **(US debt: more action needed)**

6820

A Deficit Disaster Isn't Imminent, Isabel V. Sawhill (The Urban Institute), *The New York Times* (Op-Ed), Thurs, 7 Feb 1985, A27.

The dire consequences of the deficit are not short-term. Deficits do not cause recession, and they need not be inflationary. The damage is mostly long-term: 1) Less Capital Formation: high interest rates curb capital spending; 2) Interest Costs: at an interest rate of 10%, the cost of financing the debt is rising by about $20 billion a year; 3) Loss of Strategic Advantage: deficits push up the value of the dollar and reshuffle the growth of jobs and output away from industries that compete in international markets.

(long-term damage from deficit)

6821

How To Make Sense of the Deficit, Robert Eisner (Northwestern U) and Paul J. Pieper (U of Illinois-Chicago), *The Public Interest*, No 78, Winter 1985, 101-118.

Debt and deficits do matter, but they must be measured correctly. When done so, the US debt can be seen as declining substantially until a few years ago, and the official deficits were really surpluses. These surpluses contributed greatly to the stagnation of the economy in the last decade, and to the 1981-82 recession. Despite their loud rejections of the "old" Keynesian policies, the Reagan Administration's massive move to budget deficits contributed significantly to the recovery of 1983-84. The deficit is less than it seems because the Federal government does not have a separate capital budget (investment in hard assets accounts for about one-third of recent deficits), and because government debt figures reflect the par or face value of government obligations, most of which are medium- or long-term. Under conditions of high interest rates, the market value of these obligations falls; thus the market value of total US government liabilities in 1980 was $1,154 billion, or $66 billion less than its par value. [NOTE: An interesting but technical argument, based on an even more technical analysis in *The American Economic Review*, March 1984.] **(deficit less than it seems)**

6822

Going Into Hock: Soaring Levels of Debt, National and Private, Cause Rising Worries, Randall Smith, *The Wall Street Journal*, Thursday, 9 May 1985, p1.

While all eyes are on the Federal deficit, both business and household debts have grown at an even faster rate. The 1984 total growth rate of all types of debt—public, corporate, and personal—and the ratio of total debt to GNP are at their highest levels since WWII. One money manager (William Gross of Newport Beach CA) calls it the "Roaring '80s." Businesses have been borrowing more than ever to finance takeovers and increase the return on their equity. Consumers, particularly baby boomers unscarred by Depression memories, have borrowed to buy homes, furniture, and cars. Both have been encouraged by aggressive deregulated lenders. Chances that all corporate debt will be repaid have declined: between 1980 and 1984, Standard & Poor (which rates corporate credit) downgraded 789 debt issues while upgrading 496; the percentage of issues rated AAA (highest) fell from 5.2% to 2.7%, while the percentage rated B (speculative) grew from 14.4% to 19.2%. The 192 bank failures from 1982-1984 were more than the total of 190 in the 1953-1981 period. Business failure rates were higher in the past three years than at any time since 1932. Farm debt has quadrupled from 1970 to 1982. Mortgage delinquency rates of homeowners have risen steadily since the mid-1950s. Total household debt stands at a record 83% of disposable income. At a minimum, current debt levels raise the question of how long the present recovery can last. **(soaring private debt)**

6823

Feeding the Card Habit, *Newsweek*, 8 July 1985, 52-53.

The US is on a credit-card spending spree. In 1985, Americans will charge $331 billion on their credit cards—up from $293 billion in 1984—and two-thirds of them will pay only a portion of their monthly bills, incurring an average interest rate of 19.2% on the remainder. The growing appetite of Credit Card Man has helped consumer indebtedness reach a historic high, and touched off a frantic scramble to sign up new Visa and MasterCard customers.

Surprisingly, this competition has not led to lower prices. Consumers have become addicted to credit, and like other addicts they don't seem to care about the cost of a fix. Total installment debt now stands at a historic peak relative to disposable income. This indebtedness may force consumers to cut their spending sharply at the first signs of an economic slump, which in turn could hasten the onset of a recession. **(credit card boom)**

6824

A Sales Tax but No Income Tax, Peter Fong (Emory U), *The New York Times* (Op-Ed), Thurs, 10 Jan 1985, A23.

The crucial issue of tax reform is not so much the tax rate or the distribution of the tax burden, but the mode of collection. A sales tax is simple, fixed, and indisputable, and it cannot be evaded. It taxes what one takes from society (consumption) and not what one contributes (earnings). The major argument against a national sales tax is that it would be regressive, with the poor paying more of their income than the rich. But this can be corrected with excise and value-added taxes for luxury items, and by exempting necessities from any sales tax. A 13% national sales tax with exemptions for food, health care, transportation, and housing would be enough to replace the $328 billion now raised through income taxes. Another 8% would close the current $200 billion budget deficit. The total of 21% would still be lower than the current average income tax rate, because of the elimination of evasion and loopholes. And the demoralizing and ineffective relationship between the IRS and citizens would be eliminated. [A less radical version of a national sales tax is proposed by Charls E. Walker (*The New York Times*, 29 Nov 1984, A31), who advocates a 10% sales tax to raise some $300 billion per year in additional revenues by 1990, with some of the revenue paying for an income tax credit to ease the burden on low-income individuals.]

(national sales tax proposals)

6825

Tax Gasoline a Dollar a Gallon, Stewart L. Udall, *The New York Times* (Op-Ed), Thurs, 27 Dec 1984.

Former US Secretary of the Interior points out that gasoline prices are $2.50 to $3.00 a gallon in Europe. A simple gas tax of $1.00 a gallon at the pump could be quickly enacted and would raise $100 billion, thus halving the annual US deficit. Such a tax would also end our borrowing binge, protect millions of jobs, help reduce the trade deficits, and encourage conservation of oil. [A related proposal is made by S. Fred Singer (*The Wall Street Journal*, 18 Jan 1985, p22), who warns of a possible price war that could drive oil prices down toward pre-1974 levels, and advocates a variable import fee to stabilize domestic prices for all fuels.] **(gas tax to halve deficit)**

6826

Disarm the Deficit: End Corporate Tax Dodges, Robert S. McIntyre (Citizens for Tax Justice), *The Washington Post* (Outlook Section), Sunday, 24 March 1985, C1.

In the 1960s, taxes paid by US corporations covered the cost of about one-fourth of Federal spending other than Social Security. By 1984, corporate taxes financed only 8.8% of Federal spending. If every corporation again paid taxes at the level they paid in the 1960s, the budget deficit would be cut in half, interest rates would fall, the dollar would return to a more sensible value, and the economy would prosper without the dangerous imbalances that threaten our future. Corporate taxes have declined from

4.3% of GNP in 1960 to 1.6% in 1984 largely because of two megaloopholes: the Accelerated Cost Recovery System enacted in 1981 (allowing depreciation of machinery and buildings far faster than they wear out) and the investment tax credit. As a result, for every dollar paid in taxes, loopholes allowed firms to avoid $1.42.

(corporate tax loopholes)

6827

The Tide Shifts Toward Tax Reform, Albert R. Hunt (*WSJ* Washington Bureau), *The Wall Street Journal*, Friday, 22 March 1985, p24.

The conventional wisdom in Wall Street and in Washington has been that any tax-overhaul scheme won't fly. But the odds are improving for some combination of a revised Treasury plan with the Democratic Bradley-Gephardt and GOP Kemp-Kasten bills. Despite the vehement protest from affected interests, public support favors a fairer system with fewer deductions, lower rates, and a broader base. The similarities between the Treasury proposals and the two major Congressional initiatives are far more striking than the differences, and this will facilitate any compromise.

(tax reform odds improving)

C. Economic Renewal

6828

To Promote Prosperity: U.S. Domestic Policy in the Mid-1980s. Edited by John H. Moore. Stanford CA: Hoover Institution Press (Publication 295), 1984/429p/$19.95.

Companion of **To Promote Peace** (#6516) and a sequel to **The United States in the 1980s** (Hoover, 1980; **FS Annual 1980-81**, #2232). Martin Anderson proposes an economic bill of rights as a constitutional amendment, restricting governmental powers in the economic sphere and thus ensuring responsible economic policy. To avoid a monetary crisis, Milton Friedman seeks to end the power of the Federal Reserve to issue money. Robert Hall disagrees, recommending that the Federal Reserve adopt a rule of keeping nominal GNP on a steady growth path. Paul Craig Roberts argues against high tax rates. Rita Ricardo-Campbell questions the Social Security Administration forecast projecting a deficit in the 21st century and warns that a deficit may recur by the late 1980s. Patricia Danzon views the control of health care costs as requiring modification of the incentives facing patients and providers. John C. Goodman examines disincentives in the welfare system. Stuart B. Hardy points out the financial problems of US agriculture and advocates increased reliance on market forces in a program including phased reduction or elimination of most price supports and an emphasis on expanding exports. Annelise Anderson asserts that sustained economic growth is the best tonic for the deficit problem. Robert Hessen holds that the reconstitution of corporate boards so that they are dominated by outsiders would seriously damage corporate efficiency. Long-run prosperity depends significantly on the educational system of the nation, and Roger Freeman shows that the problem is not inadequate funding or increasing class sizes, but the decline of standards and the lack of discipline. Other chapters are devoted to controlling the Federal budget, bank regulation, transportation policy, the corporate income tax, the Reagan record on civil rights, and demographic changes and problems. [NOTE: Typical of the conservative

worldview, military spending and public works spending are not considered significant enough to deserve chapters in this volume on promoting prosperity. To others, the excess of one and paucity of the other are instrumental to prosperity. Also absent is any concern for natural resources (#6845).]

(Hoover Institution on prosperity)

6829

The Second Industrial Divide: Possibilities for Prosperity. Michael J. Piore and Charles F. Sabel (both MIT). NY: Basic Books, Oct 1984/355p/$21.95.

An economist and a political scientist argue that the present deterioration in economic performance results from the limits of the model of industrial development founded on mass production. The first industrial divide came in the 19th century with the emergence of mass-production technologies. We are now living through the second industrial divide, where strategies for relaunching growth can build on the dominant principles of mass-production technology (requiring a dramatic extension of regulatory institutions), or lead back to those craft methods of production that lost out at the first industrial divide. The alternative to multinational Keynesianism as a new economic regime is flexible specialization, which has four forms: regional conglomerations, federated enterprises, solar firms with orbiting suppliers, and the workshop factory. Flexible specialization, which is predicated on collaboration, opens up long-term prospects for improving conditions of working life. The ideal of yeoman democracy can catalyze American efforts to rebuild the economy on a model of flexible specialization: an economy of craft communities (some organized in large corporations; many regionally based) speaks to the American tradition of localism; an economy based on skilled workers appeals to American individualism and entrepreneurship. The vision of an alternative past can inspire the vision of an alternative future, with yeoman democracy becoming another form of American capitalism. [NOTE: Opaque and narrow, with some resemblance to Alvin Toffler's **The Third Wave** and Paul Hawken's **The Next Economy**, neither of which is cited.]

(flexible specialization)

6830

The Economic Illusion: False Choices Between Prosperity and Social Justice. Robert Kuttner (Contributing Editor, *The New Republic*). Boston MA: Houghton Mifflin, Sept 1984/308p/$19.95.

The economic illusion is the belief that social justice is bad for economic growth. A wide range of matters are discussed where equity and efficiency are thought to come into conflict—social security, protectionism, income taxation, welfare—and it is demonstrated, based on the economic experiences of the European social democracies, that the conventional wisdom is exaggerated or wrong. While some inequality of economic status may be required as a stimulus to effort in the economic arena, an efficient and expanding economy does not require the extreme inequalities of income and wealth present in the US today. Although Kuttner agrees with conservatives that welfare capitalism has failed, he argues that too little redistribution of income has occurred despite the activity of a large public sector. Economic policies are advocated that increase intervention in private markets to equalize the distribution of incomes, rather than relying on redistribution after the fact.

(greater equality advocated)

6831

Rebuilding America: The Case for Economic Regulation. Frederick C. Thayer (U of Pittsburgh). NY: Praeger Publishers, Jan 1984/168p/$27.95.

Minor upturns in indicators may make it appear that things are getting better, but any real recovery is impossible without a massive change in our beliefs about market systems and tackling head-on the global crisis of industrial overcapacity and/or overproduction. Two tasks are necessary: 1) industry should be reorganized across the board in the US and perhaps the rest of the world as well to check the destructive forces of unrestrained competition (economic regulation is shown to be the normal state of affairs); 2) the crumbling public works structure should be rebuilt (contrary to the popular view of the textbooks,the private sector creates some wealth but much more waste, while government creates some waste but could create much more wealth). Truly giant mega-projects are in order if the world is to manage the delivery of what is needed to where it is needed. The most recent US project of significant magnitude was the interstate highway system. Such projects are needed to replace war as the focus of the most intensive form of human dedication. If economic theory turns to the concept of voluntary cooperation, it can lead to non-violent and non-authoritarian revolution on a global scale. [NOTE: A feisty challenge to the "intellectual fraud of free-market thought."]

(need for regulation and public works)

6832

Rebuilding America. Gar Alperovitz and Jeff Faux (Co-Directors, National Center for Economic Alternatives). NY: Pantheon Books, April 1984/319p/$20.00;$10.95pb.

The US economy is rudderless, and cannot recover its health unless the Federal government becomes a more competent manager of the economy. Hamstrung by obsolete ideologies, mainstream economic strategies cannot offer a program providing sustainable benefits to a majority. The dominant realities of today require us consciously to accept planning, but in ways that support freedom, decentralization, locality, and individual responsibility. The state will not wither away, but must be hollowed out, making it strong, but lean. Democracy and planning must be anchored in local communities, allowing national planning goals to be set at least in part directly by citizens. Hard choices confront us, but we can resolve the seeming incompatibility between full employment and stable prices by a strategy of regionally balanced full employment stimulated by increases in domestic public investment, and an anti-inflation program built around assuring access to the basic necessities of life.   **(decentralized planning needed)**

*6833

Unexplored America: Economic Rebirth in a Post-Industrial World, Fred Branfman (Director, The Policy Center), *World Policy Journal*, 2:1, Fall 1984, 33-62.

The Director of Research for Governor Jerry Brown in California (1980-1983) observes that we are in the early stages of a transformation to a global civilization. As the world's leading technological power, the US has the most to gain from the information revolution, but as the world's leading industrial power it also has the most to lose. This slowness to adjust to the post-industrial revolution has caused the US economy to decline by every postwar measure during the past decade. The present recovery is a sign more of continued weakness than of resurgent strength, in that it is due to massive and unsustainable borrowing. Over the coming decade, as these debts come due, the US economy is likely to continue ratcheting downward. We have reached a watershed where we must shift from today's high-consumption, high-debt economy to one that places its highest priority on savings and investment. Post-industrial growth will require investment of trillions to diffuse new technologies throughout the economy, improve education and training, build the infrastructure for a 21st century economy, create more effective environmental and health-care systems, and redesign the social structure to cope with the growing underclass of the unemployed and underpaid. National modernization must replace short-term growth as the organizing principle of American politics. America can modernize only if it adopts a comprehensive strategy that combines all of the following: 1) fiscal policies that reduce the budget deficit by two-thirds, requiring at least a 20% cut in military spending; 2) monetary policies that tie monetary growth to interest rate reduction and specific economic growth targets; 3) policies that resolve the international debt crisis and allow Third World nations to resume development; 4) private sector policies to promote entrepreneurialism and competitiveness and discourage misdirection of resources; 5) investments in modernization by public sector institutions; 6) economic democracy policies. As the US moves into a new recession, today's conservative neo-Darwinism will be discredited, and an option that promises long-term prosperity through short-term sacrifice could well attract far more support than now seems likely. [NOTE: Some glimmerings here of a viable post-Reagan strategy for the Democratic Party.]

(US modernization needed)

6834

The Peterson Prescription, Peter G. Peterson (Chairman, Peterson, Jacobs & Co), *Harvard Business Review*, 84:3, May-June 1984, 66-77.

An interview with the former US Secretary of Commerce and one of six founding members of the Bipartisan Budget Appeal (**FS Annual 1984**, #6031), who views US economic decline to be a result of uncritical choices we have made. We chose to sacrifice financial stability by printing too much money, to divert our national income from productive investment to immediate consumption, to give a low priority to R&D, and to impose an array of costly government regulations. Our worst problem is the phenomenon of nearly zero growth in real income per worker in the long term. Output of our economy has deteriorated because we refused to provide the requisite inputs. The political prescription has been to look for wonder drugs, e.g.: industrial policy. We need to draw down the Federal deficit, promote saving and long-term investment, and develop an honest public accounting system that indicates our unfunded liabilities (Social Security and Federal pensions) and net capital stock (depreciating public infrastructure). We are a crisis-activated society, and we may need a major external event (e.g., a big stock market drop and a significant rise in interest rates) to provide a window of opportunity leading to a national consensus behind tough-minded policies that focus on the fundamentals of long-term growth.   **(Peterson on economic policy)**

6835

Regaining the Lead: Policies for Economic Growth. Herbert E. Striner (Prof of Economics, American U). NY: Praeger Publishers, Feb 1984/205p/$22.95.

Unless we develop an industrial policy with new relationships between government, industry, and labor, the economic recovery of 1983 will prematurely abort and develop a two-track society of a majority sharing in the benefits of recovering industries and a very large minority remaining unemployed. Capitalism need not be wedded to the laissez-faire system; American ideals call for a form of capitalism that can coexist in a larger context of values. The success of Japan and West Germany results from their blending of private and public goals in a model of shared capitalism. The fantasies of supply-side economics and the equally illusory visions of easy solutions by Keynesian models have all gone their way. We are in a new world, requiring new approaches and new coalitions. Key aspects of the new perspective include: 1) a new coalition of industry and labor; 2) partnerships of government, industry, and labor; 3) integration and articulation of fiscal, monetary, and human resource policies; 4) adequate investment in human resources; 5) new government agencies for new functions and elimination of old ones as their utility disappears.　　**(shared capitalism)**

6836

The Case for a Share Economy, Martin L. Weitzman (Prof of Economics, MIT), *Challenge*, 27:5, Nov-Dec 1984, 34-40.

Author of **The Share Economy: Conquering Stagflation** (Harvard U Press, 1984, 167p/$15.00) argues that instead of paying workers a fixed wage, firms should pay a share of their revenues, correcting the underlying structural flaw of modern capitalism. Under a share contract, a profit-maximizing firm would offset any pay increase above the competitive rate by hiring more labor; in contrast, a traditional wage firm forced to pay a higher wage would decrease employment. A share system encourages resistance to unwarranted demands that initiate a wage-price spiral, and can soak up unemployment. Such a system can provide a lasting solution to the problem of stagflation, unlike the conventional tools of macroeconomic management.　　**(share economy proposed)**

6837

Revitalizing American Industry: Managing in a Competitive World Economy, Lester Thurow (Prof of Economics and Management, MIT), *California Management Review*, 27:1, Fall 1984, 9-41.

The huge technological edge enjoyed by Americans in the 1950s and 1960s has disappeared. The US is now faced with competitors who have matched our achievements and may be moving ahead of us. Moreover, as the US economy is absorbed into a world economy, it faces the task of learning how to compete in this world economy. Few industries are now safe from this international competition. Compared with their foreign competitors, American managers have been unable to generate an environment where the labor force takes a direct interest in raising productivity. The place to start is by altering the present structure of salaries and wages, so that part of the income of each worker and manager comes in the form of a bonus based upon increases in value added per hour of work. During the transition, all normal wage increases should be allocated to bonuses until they account for about one-third of total income. American managers must also stimulate "bubble-up" productivity, creating an environment where workers are interested in improving their performance. Finally, US firms must learn how to design products for foreign markets.　　**(improving US competitiveness)**

6838

Strategy for U.S. Industrial Competitiveness. Committee for Economic Development. NY: CED (477 Madison Ave), April 1984/$9.50 (6-page Executive Summary free).

The Committee, composed of major corporate leaders, opposes a more coordinated strategy of increased government intervention in managing economic change. Rather, they feel, the most effective strategy for improving US competitiveness is through placing significantly more reliance on market forces, and reforming necessary government interventions to provide an environment that stimulates innovation. Various public policies are suggested for the economic and strategic environment (reduce Federal budget deficits, reduce consumption bias in the tax system), encouraging adjustment to economic change, regulation of economic activity, and improving international trade arrangements.　　**(improving US competitiveness)**

6839

Restoring Our Competitive Edge: Competing Through Manufacturing. Robert H. Hayes (Harvard Business School) and Steven C. Wheelwright (Stanford Business School). NY: John Wiley & Sons, July 1984/$19.95.

America has allowed its manufacturing capability to slip into serious decline. Preoccupied with marketing and short-term financial results, we have lost sight of the actual products we are promoting. But the elements needed to regain our supremacy are still in place: experienced management, willing labor, and innovative technology. America does not need to look to Japan for the solution; the most successful US corporations found their answers at home.　　**(making US manufacturing competitive)**

6840

Staying on Top: The Business Case for a National Industrial Strategy. Kevin P. Phillips (Bethesda MD). NY: Random House, May 1984/171p/$15.95.

Much of the dislocation of the US economy and its soaring trade deficit stem from the macroeconomic policies of the Reagan Administration. But America's trade problems are due to its industrial decay, especially in manufacturing. A more aggressive economic nationalism is needed, channeling popular fears and frustrations into a crusade for a resurgence of the economy. A 15-plank platform is offered, included the establishment of a Federal Department of International Trade and Industry to foster US competitiveness, a revised tax code, greater regulation of foreign lobbying in the US, a revision of antitrust laws to allow corporate collaboration on R&D, and an expanded national program for sci/tech education.

(new economic nationalism)

6841

The Industrial Policy Debate. Edited by Chalmers Johnson (U of California-Berkeley). San Francisco CA: ICS Press (Institute for Contemporary Studies), June 1984/ 275p/$21.95;$8.95pb.

Industrial policy is a complex and controversial subject, especially because it has many meanings. In this volume, it is defined as the government's explicit attempt to coordinate and reform its activities and expenditures so as to attain a dynamic comparative advantage for the US economy. Essays are devoted to how Japanese industrial policy works, the European experience, problems of implementing an industrial policy, the problems of the Midwest "rust belt," sustaining the innovation process in America, trade policy and the dangers of protectionism, financial markets and the cost of capital in Japan and the US, industrial policy and national defense, and possibilities for tax reform. The contributors agree, Johnson concludes, that there is no such thing as not having an industrial policy: we have an implicit one in America, and it is not a good one. A good industrial policy must bring down the costs of capital for industry, help to commercialize inventions, and eliminate such root causes of inflation as protectionism. Attaining these goals requires tax simplification, curbing adversarial relationships between business and government, and perhaps some industrial targeting.

(US industrial policy)

6842

Technology, Innovation, and Regional Economic Development. U.S. Congress, Office of Technology Assessment. Washington DC: USGPO, July 1984/$5.50 (S/N 052-003-00959-5).

High-tech industries are expected to grow somewhat faster than overall employment over the next 10 years. But their relatively small employment base will directly account for only a small fraction of total employment growth. The growing competition for high-tech industries has generated hundred of initiatives by state and local governments, universities, and private sector organizations. These initiatives are more likely to succeed if they build on existing industries and available resources. For most communities, the greatest opportunities may lie in encouraging innovation from within, rather than trying to attract high-tech businesses from other regions. There is no compelling evidence that an extensive Federal effort targeted on this aspect of economic development will be necessary to promote regional high-tech development.

(high-tech and regional development)

6843

Economic Policy for the Eighties and Beyond. *Journal of Economic Issues*, 18:1, March 1984, 1-314.

Essays by members of the Association for Evolutionary Economics, an international organization of institutional economists. The institutional approach to economic policy is values-driven, process-oriented, activist, fact-based, holistic, non-dogmatic, and democratic. Essays are devoted to social reform and economic policy, the role of the public sector, economic stabilization and inflation, domestic monetary policy, employment programs, income maintenance and welfare, a geobased national agricultural policy, environmental protection, foreign economic policy, and the implementation of economic development.

(institutional approach to economic policy)

6844

Deindustrialization: Restructuring the Economy. Edited by Gene F. Summers (U of Wisconsin-Madison). *The Annals of the American Academy of Political and Social Science*, Vol 475, Sept 1984/174p/$15.00;$7.95pb.

Essays on the magnitude of job loss from plant closings, the generation of replacement jobs, capital mobility in the US economy, the human response to plant closures, private sector and community-based responses to plant closures, policy response to factory closings (the US, Sweden, and France compared), the British experience with economic restructuring, the Ford-UAW management-labor approach to plant closings and worker retraining, and public policies for investment (in which a new national framework is proposed that includes greater community involvement and increased worker control).

(plant closures)

*6845

America's Economic Future: Environmentalists Broaden the Industrial Policy Debate. A Report of the Project on Industrial Policy and the Environment (Robert D. Hamrin, Coordinator). Washington DC: Natural Resources Defense Council, June 1984/67p (8x11")/$5.00.

Environmentalists are deeply concerned about the economic future of the US. Broadly viewed, the shape of the economy will influence significantly the character of American society and the quality of American life. And the quality of life is the most fundamental concern of the environmental movement. The current industrial policy debate, however, is far too narrow. It focuses almost exclusively on heavy manufacturing industries, while neglecting the natural resource base and the global context. The greatest flaw in the debate is that it offers no goals and no overall vision of America's economic future. A vision is offered that encompasses five principal goals: a sustainable global economy (essential for economic, environmental, and moral reasons), a healthy US economy aimed at increasing the quality of life for all, sustaining the US environmental and resource base, total employment (to get people into jobs and free up people on the job), and widespread participation in economic and political decisions. Actions to achieve this vision are needed in each of the three parts of America's capital stock: 1) **Natural Resources**: establishing least-cost energy planning, removing Federal subsidies for nuclear power, farmland preservation initiatives, efforts to preserve and restore topsoil, introducing water charges, minimizing water loss in irrigation; 2) **Industrial Resources**: rejection of protectionist measures as a long-run solution, a redefinition of national security, a broadly representative Economic Cooperation Council to forge a broad consensus on needed change; 3) **Human Resources**: new education and retraining initiatives, periodic sabbaticals for workers, greater opportunities for part-time work, broader ownership of capital. Concludes by recommending establishment of foresight capability in the Federal government: as long as the government remains captive to the tyranny of the urgent, matters of fundamental long-range importance will get lost in the shuffle of day-to-day business. [NOTE: A much broader view of economic policy than any of the visions reviewed below.]

(environmentalist vision of economic future)

*6846

Revitalizing Western Economies. Russell L. Ackoff, Paul Broholm, and Roberta Snow (all The Wharton School, U of Pennsylvania). San Francisco CA: Jossey-Bass, Dec 1984/208p/$17.95.

The prolonged recession prevailing in most Western nations has led to many proposals for revitalizing their economies. These proposals are generally directed at reindustrialization, attempting to resurrect the economic conditions of the 1960s, and make no effort to solve the most serious aspect of the current economic malaise: unemployment. The developed economies have been moving into a new economic era, with more employment in the service sector. This postindustrial transformation involves a fundamental change in a society's focus and priorities, shifting attention to improving the quality of life and increasing the amount and variety of services offered. The objective of redesigning society should thus be societal development, not economic growth. If jobs are to be created, they must be created in the service sector. But much of the growing desire for services has not been translated into demand because of their high cost, low quality, and offensive manner of delivery. These defects in services derive from the fact that most are provided by bureaucratic monopolies either within government or the private sector. Solving the unemployment problem thus lies in debureaucratizing and de-monopolizing public and private services.

Governments can create an efficient and wealth-producing service sector by enabling the private sector to compete wherever possible, requiring consumers to pay directly for as many services as possible, subsidizing consumers who cannot pay for necessary services (rather than subsidizing suppliers), and assuring competitive sources of as many services as possible. Governments can also improve the productivity and quality of service work by initiating quality of work life programs in all public agencies. Governments are not likely to take these actions, however, unless considerable public pressure is applied, converting government to participative democracy. Corporations should also diversify into services and increase their productivity. Chapters are devoted to why current strategies are failing, shortcomings of proposed solutions, making government responsive and efficient, new corporate strategies, and examples of successful transformations in business and government. Concludes that the old ideas, however they may be repackaged, are not revitalizing our economies. Decreasing the cost and increasing the quality of services would create a large number of jobs that would significantly reduce, if not eliminate, the unemployment problem. [NOTE: A fresh and persuasive analysis.]

(more services to reduce unemployment)

6847

Out of the Depression Cycle, Peter F. Drucker (Prof of Social Sciences, Claremont Graduate School), *The Wall Street Journal*, Wed, 9 Jan 1985, p26.

The relationship between the primary economy and the industrial economy was once considered a proven law. A prolonged slump in the prices of primary commodities (agricultural and forest products, metals and minerals), the "law" asserted, would trigger a world-wide slump in the industrial economies within two or three years. Primary-producing economies such as the US farm belt have all been in a severe depression for almost five years. It is there that the problem loans of the world's big banks are concentrated. And yet the industrial economies of the free world seem to be unaffected, and the two biggest—the US and Japan—are enjoying near-boom conditions. This cannot be explained away as a time lag; rather, we may be witnessing a historic change and the first major impact of the shift from an energy economy to an information economy. We reached the limits of the mechanical model some 40 years ago, when we started switching with increasing momentum to a biological model based on information. "Progress" in a biological process does not mean more energy or more materials, but substituting information for both. The industries that exemplify the old model are the industries in trouble today. If there is anything to this hypothesis, it would render absurd all the forecasts of the past 10 or 20 years in respect to demand for energy, raw materials, and food, which all assume that materials input must go up faster than output. We may soon have to rethink the way we look at economics and at economies. Information is now classed as a "service," but it is the primary material of an information-based economy. In such an economy, the schools are as much primary producers as the farmer, and much of what we now consider as social overhead is actually capital investment. Only such an hypothesis can explain the failure so far of the primary-products depression to trigger an equally severe slump in the industrial world. **(shift to information economy)**

D. Banks and Financial Services

6848

The Emerging Financial Industry: Implications for Insurance Products, Portfolios, and Planning. Edited by Arnold W. Sametz (Salomon Brothers Center, NYU). Lexington MA: Lexington Books, 1984/136p/$21.50.

Since the mid-1970s, the combined impacts of unpredictable inflation, headlong technological change, and waves of deregulation have been revolutionizing the structure and functions of the financial industry. First the financial markets and the depository institutions were heavily affected; now it is the turn of the contractual financial institutions—notably the insurance industry—to adjust to cumulative changes in the economic and financial environment. These papers from a 1982 conference at NYU describe the new financial environment, the volatile financial markets, the evolving life insurance industry, marketing financial services, evolving insurance products and services, the emerging regulatory structure for banks, implications for investment and portfolio management, and implications for strategic planning.

(emerging financial industry)

6849

Banks, Thrifts, and Insurance Companies: Surviving the 1980s. Alan Gart (Alan Gart Inc, Huntingdon Valley PA). Lexington MA: Lexington Books, April 1985/136p/$19.95.

Former bank vice-president and professor of finance describes the many changes facing financial institutions as a result of deregulation and the blurring of functions, technological change, and the changing financial structure of major firms such as Merrill Lynch, Sears, American Express, Citicorp, Prudential, ITT, Transamerica, etc. Concludes with a discussion of 44 major trends, including: 1) banks will likely account for a respectable percentage of personal insurance by 2000; 2) the number of independent insurance agents may thus decline dramatically by 2000; 3) banking at home by computer is expected to increase in popularity over the next decade; 4) some form of interstate banking will probably be instituted by 2000, which should substantially reduce the total number of banks; 5) the insurance industry will move toward greater fee and consultation income as companies act increasingly as risk management advisors; 6) some observers expect a rapid nationalization of the mortgage market; 7) thrifts and real estate brokers may operate from desks in each other's offices as a natural alliance; 8) the trend toward forming financial conglomerates is likely to continue, although there will still be room for the financial boutique; 9) major consolidation is expected among banks and thrifts (the number of banks is expected to decline by one-third by 1990); 10) the number of foreign financial institutions in the US market will continue to grow; 11) by 1990, 41% of all small life insurance companies are expected to merge or be acquired by larger companies; 12) there will be at least three large power bases after the consolidation of the financial services industry: established banks, established insurers, and customer-oriented organizations that have access to large numbers of potential clients, such as Sears, Kroger, and JC Penney. [NOTE: Lacks sparkle in style, but otherwise a clearly presented overview of the tumult in financial services.] **(emerging financial industry)**

6850

The 20-Year Strategic Outlook for the U.S. Life and Health Insurance Industry. Norma L. Nielson, Selwyn Enzer, and Manolete V. Gonzalez. Los Angeles CA: USC Center for Futures Research, Report R-13, Dec 1984/160p. A 31-page Executive Summary (Paper F-58, Feb 1985) is also available.

A two-year inquiry into the life and health insurance industry, including the annuity and asset management functions vital to pension plans. In addition to a baseline surprise-free scenario (the economy continues into a steady prosperous period and government involvement increases on almost all fronts), six alternative scenarios are provided: technology leads the way (resulting in an aging US population), higher interest rates and a stagnant GNP, a collapse of the financial system around 2000, consumer and employer coalitions joining forces to reduce the price of insurance products, a rich-poor division of society, and deregulation of financial services. In general, the responsibility for risk-bearing in society will shift away from the public sector to the private sector, and increasingly the individual. Pushing this shift is concern for the stability of the Social Security system and high interest rates. Insurers face increasing competition from their own customers, as large corporate and institutional buyers extend the practice of self-insurance in search of cost savings and improved cash flow management.   **(insurance industry outlook)**

6851

The Savings and Loan Industry: Current Problems and Possible Solutions. Walter J. Woerhide. Westport CT: Greenwood Press, 1984/216p/$35.00.

Observers of the S&L industry are nearly unanimous in their opinion that it is in danger of failing. Three major developments in the industry are discussed: the growth of alternative mortgage instruments, the expansion of authority to trade in financial futures contracts, and the growth in consumer lending authority. The negative effect of the elimination of interest rate ceilings and the introduction of NOW accounts is examined, as well as the industry's basic problem: interest rate risk exposure. Concludes with a view of the thrift of the future and the role of the small thrift. [Also see **The Structural Transformation of the Savings and Loan Industry** by Frederick E. Balderston (Ballinger, Dec 1984/c244p/$29.95).]

(savings and loan industry)

6852

The Financial Services Explosion: Forecasting the Fallout, Lynn N. Hesselroth, _Futurics_, 9:2, 1985, 19-24.

Deregulation has resulted in a more creative and competitive marketplace in financial services. More than half of the largest US banks expect to diversify into related financial services within the next five years. Full-service financial institutions geared toward total financial planning (Prudential-Bache is the forerunner) are entering the market at a rapid rate, adding services through acquisition. Two scenarios are offered, depending on whether deregulation continues. 1) A Highly Deregulated Financial Service Environment: intense competition results in lower costs and more options for consumers, roles continue to blur as banks and financial service companies become more like each other, everyone claims to be a financial planner, consumers will be confused by the amount of information and options, more business will be transacted through computers and over the phone; 2) Deregulation Slows: competition grows in a more structured manner, personal investments will be better protected by government regulation, requirements for certification as a financial planner will

be clearly defined, roles of distributors will be clarified, the number and rate of mergers will slow (resulting in a greater number of competitors). By 1990, the explosion in the financial services industry will probably have subsided; the firms that will dominate the industry during the 1990s will emerge within the next three years. Concludes with the forecast that, by 1995, a system capable of reporting all an individual's assets will be in place, accessed by one universal credit card. Tomorrow's consumer will be able to determine his or her actual net worth at any moment, and the universal card will be used to buy services as well as make investments.   **(emerging financial industry)**

6853

Effects of Information Technology on Financial Service Systems. U.S. Congress, Office of Technology Assessment. Washington: USGPO, Sept 1984/$7.50 (S/N 052-003-00961-7). Summary copies free from OTA.

Today's financial services industry and its competitive structure differs markedly from that of the 1970s, and should continue its rapid change at least through the 1980s. Reliance on advancing technologies to deliver products and services such as credit, deposit-taking, investment, and insurance has increased rapidly. Providers of financial services have become so heavily dependent on information processing and telecommunications technologies that the failure of automated systems under some circumstances could be very serious. In the future, banks, savings and loans associations, and credit unions will concentrate on processing transactions, and place less emphasis on gathering deposits and providing financing. Branches will be dominated by a variety of machines, with personnel serving more of an advisory role than actually handling transactions. Changes in the financial services industry will both benefit customers and create problems for them. For example, consumers will have to be better informed to choose among the wider range of available options and services. And despite broader options for most, some consumers may find their options more constrained. Increasing use of electronic systems will heighten potential threats to individual privacy for all. The rapid transformation of the financial service industry raises many public policy issues involving access to services, system security, privacy, consumer protection, and fostering institutional stability.   **(financial services transformation)**

6854

Financial Institutions Are Showing the Strain Of a Decade of Turmoil, Tim Carrington and Daniel Hertzberg, _The Wall Street Journal_, 5 Sept 1984, p1.

Cracks in the financial services industry are showing, and more may come. For example, bank failures total 54 so far in 1984, already exceeding the post-Depression record of 48 for an entire year. The strains stem from high and unpredictable interest rates, a sudden end to steep inflation, and deregulation. They have been exacerbated by merger mania, reckless lending, and a proliferation of new financial products. As financial institutions become more interdependent, the strains cut across the entire financial services industry, causing a steady procession of financial scares in many businesses. Nobody knows where the turmoil will lead. At the least, analysts expect more mergers and forced liquidations. Further strains could weigh heavily on US taxpayers, as government bears the costs of protecting against major financial losses of banks, thrift institutions, brokerage firms (many of which are posting record deficits), and insurance companies. Many institutions and regulators are suffering from an overdose of change, and managerial responses to the shocks have often made things worse, e.g.: banks make riskier loans and insurance companies lower their premiums.

(US financial institutions in turmoil)

6855

Banking Deregulation and the New Competition in Financial Services. Kerry Cooper and Donald R. Fraser (both Texas A&M University). Cambridge MA: Ballinger Publishing Co, 1984/210p/$32.00.

On domestic and international trends in regulating financial institutions, causes of financial deregulation, the incidence of failure among depository institutions, the availability of credit, and future trends in financial deregulation and the role of depository institutions. [Also see Donald R. Fraser and James W. Kolari, **The Future of Small Banks in a Deregulated Environment** (Ballinger, 1985/c200p/c$25.00), which discusses the radical changes sweeping the financial services industry, major deregulation legislation, growing competition by non-banking organizations such as Sears and Merrill Lynch, and strategies that small banks can use to adjust to the new environment.] **(banking deregulation)**

6856

Interstate Banking's Difficult Birth, Robert A. Bennett, *The New York Times*, Sunday, 2 June 1985, F1.

Interstate banking in America is advancing in haphazard, almost accidental steps. Throughout the US, dealing with the inevitable appears to be the driving force in breaking down the decades-old barriers to interstate banks. The foundation of a national banking system is coming into view, involving regional and national banks. Within regions, banks are arranging mergers with partners in neighboring states, pooling their capital to be in a better position than the giant banks to make further acquisitions. In addition to this regional process, the largest banks increasingly are being called upon to leap across the country to rescue failing banks and savings and loans associations. Concludes by outlining the strategies of the biggest banks: Citicorp (California, Florida, Illinois, and Texas are primary targets), BankAmerica, Chase Manhattan (which would like to operate in almost every state), Manufactuers Hanover, Chemical, Security Pacific, and Marine Midland. **(interstate banking emerging)**

6857

Banking Will Be Dominated by a Handful of Giants, Arthur Burck (Arthur Burck Associates, Palm Beach), *Vital Speeches of the Day*, 50:21, 15 August 1984, 656-660.

Burck, an expert in corporate mergers who has worked with about one-third of the *Fortune* 500, has warned for years that mergermania was getting out of hand and causing extensive damage to our economy. Banking is the only major industry to have thus far escaped consolidation, largely because banks do not have to be big to be efficient. Huge, big city banks are usually in no position to cope with the financing needs of small business. Yet, it is only a matter of time before the US banking industry will be concentrated in a handful of gargantuan big-city banks. Another parallel trend is the concentration of stock ownership by institutions, especially the trust holdings of banks. If interstate banking comes, we will see even more concentrated ownership. In time, we will face the spectre of an industrial and financial economy owned by a few supergiants, and the controlling stock of these huge companies in turn owned by a few gigantic financial institutions. The orgies of corporate cannibalism could easily be stopped by

Congress withdrawing the tax breaks that fuel giant mergers, but this is not likely. At some point, government will intervene by more overregulation, at the least, or by takeover of supergiant companies, as in Western Europe. [NOTE: In the same issue of *Vital Speeches* (pp670-672), the President of Chase Manhattan Bank, Thomas G. Labrecque, argues that US banking laws are repressive, antiquated, and anti-competitive; allowing Chase Manhattan to cross state lines would result in a broader range of credit services, increased quality of services, and more jobs.]

(bank concentration growing)

6858

The Perils of Unrestricted Interstate Ownership of Banks, Arthur Burck (Arthur Burck Associates, Palm Beach), *Vital Speeches of the Day*, 51:15, 15 May 1985, 473-477.

With over 14,000 independent banks, the banking industry is the last bulwark of the Jeffersonian ideal that the nation is best served by a multiplicity of small businesses. Unlike most other industries where economies of scale prevail, banks do not have to be big to be efficient. But we are brainwashed by buzzwords that the big banks are better, safer, and the inevitable wave of the future. Our banking system will be hurt or imperiled if time-honored interstate restrictions are repealed: 1) banking will be dominated by a handful of giants; 2) our national economy will thus be imperiled, because the ripples from failure of a major bank can create havoc; 3) our loophole "non-bank" banks pose threats to economic stability since their depositors lack Federal deposit guarantees; 4) the small business sector and the farm economy will be hurt; 5) the big banks entering new states will be positioned to crush small independent banks through predatory practices; 6) communities will be hurt, because independent bankers are community leaders; 7) within a few decades, the US economy will be dominated by a few score supergiant industrial and commercial companies; the US will face multiple harms when trust departments of a few banks hold the stocks of most of our increasingly concentrated industry. [NOTE: Another dimension, not mentioned here, is that this process will by no means stop at national borders.]

(interstate banking questioned)

6859

Consumer Electronic Banking. International Resource Development Inc. Norwalk CT: IRD (6 Prowitt St), July 1985/171p/$1285.00.

Three forms of automation have the potential to replace all the activities of today's bank tellers and to foster growth of the home banking market: 1) personal computers in the home are becoming a substitute for branch banking, offering the potential of one-stop financial service including stock brokerage and insurance; 2) automated teller machines are increasingly accepted by consumers, especially in urban markets; they offer even more potential if deployed across the country by a single bank, in effect creating a nationwide bank; 3) point-of-sale terminals, located in retail outlets, allow the direct transfer of funds between accounts. Market forecasts suggest growing automation of banking, as "nonbank banks" take charge, users become more comfortable with electronic banking, national networks are established, and regulations become clearer. Banks have discovered that customers using electronic home services tend to be more profitable (only 20% of all bank customers are profitable), and that home banking encourages them to subscribe to a wider range of services. This pricey report forecasts the home banking market through 1995. **(automated banking)**

6860

Wall Street Is Finding Its Trusty Computers Have Their Dark Side, Linda Sandler, *The Wall Street Journal*, Tuesday, 4 Dec 1984, p1.

The advantages of computers in the security business are obvious: they link dealers across the nation and perform analyses in minutes that once took hours or days. They make possible the high-volume trading on the New York Stock Exchange, but this makes the market more volatile and unpredictable. A more subtle problem is that computers promote a blind faith, allowing brokers to make errors with more confidence.   (**computers & Wall Street**)

6861

Will Money Managers Wreck the Economy? (Cover Story), *Business Week*, 13 August 1984, 86-93.

Some 60% of all company shares are controlled by pension-fund and mutual-fund managers who focus on short-term returns. The power of the money managers acts as a Damoclean sword over companies today, forcing chief executives to keep earnings on a consistently upward track, quarter by quarter, even if it means frustrating their long-term plans. Ultimately, all but the largest and richest companies will be discouraged from taking risks. Short-term survival tactics of corporations include: 1) less money going into startup ventures and more into acquiring existing assets; 2) less research money to develop new products and more to improve existing processes; 3) shifting investment from businesses with high capital needs to service businesses with low capital needs; 4) less equity and fewer bonds underpinning business activity. The long-term implications of these decisions could add up to the slow deindustrialization of the US and the concentration of corporate power in fewer hands.

(money manager impact on economy)

6862

Takeover Abuses Mortgage the Future, Martin Lipton (Senior Partner, Wachtell, Lipton, Rosen & Katz, NYC), *The Wall Street Journal*, Friday, 5 April 1985, p16.

A specialist in takeover law warns that takeover abuses have become a pressing national problem. During the past three years, there have been growing instances of "greenmail"—where shareholders threaten to buy up a company and so force management to buy out their shares at a premium price. Also on the increase are highly leveraged takeovers, bust-up liquidations, and forced "white knight" transactions. All these financial transfers benefit takeover entrepreneurs, but do not add to the national wealth. Reagan Administration officials and some economists argue that hostile takeovers are economically desirable because they move assets into the hands of more efficient management. This can be true, but the new takeovers take place at the expense of R&D and capital improvements. Similar to the policy resulting in huge deficits in the national budget, the Federal policy favoring bust-up takeovers is one that favors the present at the expense of the future. The stock market also prefers projects with immediate results to those that would provide long-term growth and future profits to shareholders. Current accounting conventions and tax laws encourage the same view. Institutional investors exacerbate the situation because they also prefer short-term gains to long-term growth, and thus have joined with takeover entrepreneurs to pressure companies into new deals that will produce a premium over the current market. The extreme leverage that is being built into American business, while different in form, is no different in substance from what happened

in 1928 and 1929 before the crash. We need new laws that will eliminate both greenmail and speculative bust-up takeovers, while not restricting healthy mergers and acquisitions, and creative financing. [Also see ***Greenmail: New Form Of an Old Cynicism***, by Michael M. Thomas (*New York Times*, 24 June 1984, E23), who also warns that this "indecent recklessness" is pretty much like the years before 1929, and advocates some revision in tax policy to encourage long-term investing.]

(takeover abuse a national problem)

E. Poverty and Welfare

6863

Poverty in America: Trends and New Patterns. William P. O'Hare (Joint Center for Political Studies, Washington). *Population Bulletin*, 40:3, June 1985/43p/ $4.00 single copy.

In 1983, 35.3 million Americans—or 15.2% of the population—were defined as officially poor. Some attribute continued poverty to government social welfare spending, while others blame the 1981 Reagan budget cuts. But poverty among the nonelderly is linked much more to economic trends. The proportion of the US population in poverty dropped from 22.4% in 1959 to 11.1% in 1973, fluctuated with the economy to 1978, and then rose sharply. With the recent economic recovery, the 1984 poverty rate should be lower than that of 1983. The bulk of increased Federal social spending since the mid-1960s has gone to the elderly, aged 65 and over, whose poverty rate plunged from 35.2% in 1959 to 14.1% in 1983. Concludes by discussing basic measures to reduce poverty: 1) eliminate taxes paid by the poor; 2) standardize AFDC (Aid to Families with Dependent Children) payments from state to state, and link payments to inflation; 3) expand programs such as Head Start that reduce government expenditures in the long run.

(trends in US poverty)

6864

The Welfare State in America: Trends and Prospects. Edited by Yeheskel Hasenfeld and Mayer N. Zald (both Dept of Sociology, U of Michigan). *The ANNALS of The American Academy of Political and Social Science*, Vol 479, May 1985/155p.

Eight essays divided in two sections: 1) The Societal Context: flagging economic growth in modern welfare states, the changing nature of family composition and poverty (especially the feminization of poverty), expansion of citizen rights and the welfare state, changes in the funding and administration of human services in recent decades; 2) Policy Arenas and Issues: the future of Social Security as it attempts to balance the conflicting goals of efficacy and adequacy, employee welfare and the growth of private benefit packages, the role of child support insurance and problems of enforcing support from absent parents, welfare and deinstitutionalization (which in many cases has made the vulnerable population more vulnerable).

(welfare trends and issues)

6865

The State and the Poor in the 1980s. Edited by Manuel Carballo (Secretary, Massachusetts Office of Human Services) and Mary Jo Bane (Public Policy Program, Harvard U). Foreword by Samuel H. Beer. Boston MA: Auburn House, 1984/328p/$24.95;$16.00pb.

The depressed economy and the new federalism have combined to enlarge the state's responsibility toward the poor, and state officials and planners should take a new look at this old problem. Contributions are organized in three sections: 1) **Policies to Prevent Poverty**: helping those who can become self-sufficient to do so, health care programs for the poor, educational services and school finance; 2) **Policies to Ameliorate Poverty**: income transfers, transportation programs for the elderly and the poor, public housing, anti-displacement policy; 3) **Implementing and Financing Programs for the Poor**: taxation and the poor, policy planning and the poor, benefits of state planning, and governance. Overall conclusions are that there are many different causes and remedies for poverty, that a state can play a major role in reducing poverty, that state efforts can be most effective with a strategy embracing a comprehensive view of what needs to be done, and that state efforts must be complemented and supported by Federal, local, and private actions.

(**state anti-poverty policy**)

6866

Bishops' Pastoral Letter on Catholic Social Teaching and the U.S. Economy (First Draft). National Conference of Catholic Bishops. *Origins*, NC Documentary Service, 14: 22/23, 15 Nov 1984/46p/$3.00. [Order from National Catholic News Service, 1312 Massachusetts Ave NW, Washington DC 20005. Full page of excerpts in *The New York Times*, 12 Nov 1984, B10.]

The level of inequality in income and wealth in the US, and even more so on the world scale, must be judged morally unacceptable. The one fundamental criterion for economic decisions, policies, and institutions is that they must be at the service of human beings. The time has come for creating an order that guarantees the minimum conditions of human dignity in the economic sphere for every person. Meeting human needs and increasing participation should be priority targets in the investment of wealth, talent, and human energy. Among the proposals: 1) a major new policy commitment to achieve full employment, which can reasonably be defined as 3% or 4% unemployment; 2) increased support by the government for direct job creation programs targeted on the structurally unemployed; 3) public assistance programs that encourage rather than penalize gainful employment; 4) an economic safety net designed to serve the needs of the poor in a manner that respects their human dignity; 5) renewed dialogue between countries of the North and South, aimed at more equitable economic relations; 6) a campaign for an international agreement to reduce the arms trade.

(**Catholic Bishops on the economy**)

6867

End Results: The Impact of Federal Policies Since 1980 on Low Income Americans. Interfaith Action for Economic Justice, Center on Budget and Policy Priorities. Washington: IAEJ (110 Maryland Ave NE), Sept 1984/41p(8x11")/$2.00.

Budget reductions of the 1980s have been concentrated heavily on programs for poor people: overall, such programs bore nearly one-third of all cuts made anywhere in the Federal government, even though they constitute less than one-tenth of the budget. Consequently, in the 1979-1983 period, the number of Americans living below the poverty line increased by over nine million, or 35%. More than one of every seven Americans is now poor; one in every four American children under age six is poor; one of every two black children under six is poor. But budget cuts are only part of the story. The 1981 tax act gave major tax benefits to high income taxpayers and large corporations, while the minuscule tax cuts given to low income working families were more than wiped out by inflation (which pushed them into higher tax brackets) and by rising Social Security taxes. Today, the Federal tax burdens of families at the poverty line are typically double or triple what they were only six years ago. At the same time, the budget and tax policies have not produced promised increases in savings and capital investment, while generating record increases in the US deficit.

Decisive action to lower the deficit will be needed. But it is unnecessary and fundamentally unfair to push those who are poorest—and who have already made the largest sacrifices—deeper into poverty as part of this effort. Other ways of dealing with the deficit are vastly preferable: 1) **Military Spending**: defense has been a prime contributor to the growing deficit, and should now be a prime contributor to reducing it; little or no further growth in military spending is necessary, and many new weapons systems are not useful and even counter-productive to national security; 2) **Taxes**: those at or near the poverty line need tax relief, and ample revenue can be raised in other areas such as broadening the tax base and curbing tax shelters, corporate tax reforms, increasing tax rates for those in higher brackets (e.g., through a surcharge to reduce the gains received from the 1981 act), and tougher programs to reduce the $90 billion in taxes evaded each year; 3) **Entitlements and Pensions**: military retirement is the most lavish pension system in America and changes in this program since 1980 have been relatively minor; new cost control measures for Medicare are also needed. [NOTE: A well-documented eyebrow-raiser. Read it.] (**cutting US deficit without more harm to poor**)

6868

Losing Ground: American Social Policy, 1950-1980. Charles Murray (Manhattan Institute for Policy Research). NY: Basic Books, Sept 1984/323p/$23.95.

Challenges popular notions that Great Society programs of the 1960s marked the beginning of improvement in the situation of the poor. Substantial declines in poverty are shown to have occurred prior to 1964. During the Great Society period, many poor people escaped poverty, but a great number become mired even more deeply in welfarism and other social programs, or turned to crime. The proliferation of social programs in the mid-1960s changed the rules that governed the poor, making it profitable for them to behave in the short term in ways that were destructive in the long term, e.g., to choose welfare over work. At the same time, the decline of standards in urban schools took away incentives to learn, and lenient law enforcement reduced the penalties for crime. Improving this situation requires stiffer standards in the schools, and a voucher system to make them competitive. All preferential treatment for minorities should be eliminated, as well as virtually all welfare for adults. There is no way to untie the knot, so cut it. (**negative result of Great Society**)

6869

Helping the Poor: A Few Modest Proposals, Charles Murray (Manhattan Institute for Policy Research), *Commentary*, 79:5, May 1985, 27-34.

Author of **Losing Ground** (#6868 above) reiterates his startling argument that the Great Society reforms of the mid-1960s are largely to blame for the decline in the fortunes of the poor. The US is faced with some critical social pathologies that are not going to be solved or even much changed by continuing present policies. The single most important element of the poverty problem is poor single young women, often in their teens, who have babies and keep them. In 1965, there were about 155,000 13-year olds who were children of single mothers. In 1975, there were

240,000 of these new adolescents, and in 1985 there are about 394,000. In 1995, there will be about 700,000. These children of single mothers tend to have abnormally high incidences of mental and physical handicaps and bad employment records. They make schools hard to learn in and neighborhoods hard to live in.

Murray explores a variety of positive inducements (carrots) and negative inducements (sticks) that might reduce this problem: 1) Child Allowances: a monthly payment to all families with children that might encourage two-parent families (thus a woman does not lose AFDC benefits if she marries, as is presently the case); 2) Bribes: paying, say, $1000 per year to each single woman aged 15 to 34 who has not had a baby in the preceding year; 3) Residential Facilities: a sort of halfway house providing a good standard of living and a professional program for children; 4) Age Discrimination: prohibiting any kind of direct welfare assistance to people under 21 years old (thus deterring teenagers from using the welfare system to set up a household); 5) Making the Father Take Responsibility: requiring mothers to identify the father of the child as a condition of qualifying for welfare benefits; 6) Making the Mother Get a Job: the experience of various workfare programs indicates that such plans are very difficult to carry out; 7) Stigma: advertising campaigns to make unmarried pregnancy disreputable or taking away the right to vote from anyone who exists solely on welfare. The feasibility of each of these options is explored, as are possible backfire effects. Concludes that the present state of affairs is not acceptable, and there are no painless ways to rectify it. [NOTE: A thoughtful exploration of a limited range of alternatives; curiously, no mention is made of options involving job creation, training programs, day care, and public service for youth.]   (**discouraging single teen parenthood**)

6870

How Welfare Reform Finally Happened (Once Upon a Future Time), Ralph Segalman and Alfred Himelson (both Profs of Sociology, California State U-Northridge), *The Futurist*, 18:5, Oct 1984, 14-19.

Once upon a time in the future, the newly elected US President and Congress decided to put politics aside and start from scratch to build a rational welfare system. To clear the ground for new programs, they temporarily suspended Aid to Families with Dependent Children, substituting aid through a voucher system for such items as food, housing, medical care, and transportation. Researchers undertook an extensive study of the effects of AFDC suspension, finding: 1) significantly fewer pregnancies among women who already had dependent children; 2) more marriages resulting from lessened concern about loss of welfare benefits, and far fewer men deserting their families in fact or official fiction; 3) job training taking on new importance because trainees were motivated to learn; 4) the extended family once again serving as an important resource for support, subsistence, and job placement information; 5) a reduction in the public welfare bureaucracy and a renewed importance of private agencies.

(**welfare reform**)

6871

Investing in Poor Families and Their Children (Policy Statement), National Council of State Human Service Administrators, *Public Welfare* (American Public Welfare Association), Summer 1985, 4-9.

After steadily declining for most of the past two decades, poverty among children has recently begun to climb. Cutbacks in Federal aid to low-income families have combined with inflation and limited economic opportunities to increase the number of poor children to more than one in every five. A reinvigorated effort to help poor children and their families is in the self-interest of all Americans. The states today are testing a variety of new programs, but poverty is a national problem that requires a national effort involving all levels of government and the private sector. It is unrealistic and cruel to advocate moving people to maximum self-sufficiency while ignoring the fact that they are hungry, homeless, unhealthy, unskilled, or uneducated. In the short-term, the chief human service officials of the states support a Federal budget that does not further reduce resources or restrict eligibility in any of the basic programs that sustain human life, Federal efforts to prevent adolescent pregnancy, increased emphasis on preventing family violence and child abuse, and greater access of welfare recipients to job training and job placement programs. A long-term effort to help the poor should include: 1) a full reexamination of existing human service programs compared with other means of assuring basic life support; 2) an assessment of the effects of tax policies on the capacity of low-income families to support themselves; 3) a structured and continuous exchange of information on successful human service programs, to better determine what works at what cost, with a strategy for sharing such information with the public.

(**policy statement by state welfare officials**)

6872

Economic Growth Won't End Poverty, Michael Novak and Leslie Lenkowsky (American Enterprise Institute), *The New York Times* (Op-Ed), Wed, 24 July 1985, A19.

A large proportion of today's poor are people who get little or no help by economic change. Life is no longer what it was in the 1960s, when we could expect that "a rising tide will lift all boats." The elderly live longer, and the morals of family life and childhood have changed. To bring about a sizable drop in the poverty rate, we need policies that re-attach the poor (especially the elderly and the young in female-headed households) to the rest of society. This may take the form of improved job training, neighborhood development efforts, and changes in the workplace that increase flexibility or encourage longevity in employment. It will surely require moral and cultural leadership, largely from outside government.

(**reattaching the poor to society**)

*6873

Time to Care. A Report Prepared for the Swedish Secretariat for Futures Studies. Marten Lagergren (Project Leader) *et al*. Translated by Roger G. Tanner. Elmsford NY: Pergamon Press, Jan 1984/286p/$40.00.

The final report of the Care in Society project, addressing the difficult problems of the Swedish welfare state that are much the same for all advanced countries. To continue the old way will soon lead to economically disastrous consequences. The state is now borrowing money at home and abroad to finance its own activities and a mounting flow of pensions and benefits. Politicians are afraid to jeopardize their electoral following by demanding full payment for services they dare not reduce. Growing costs in a shrinking economy make citizens unwilling to pay the bill, even though they support the policy pursued. To this are added doubts about the actual achievements of public care and welfare, and questions about the real aim of social development. Growth has led to a "care apparatus" that employs one-sixth of the work force and has taken over duties once performed by families, relatives, and others. Care will always be needed because there will always be children, sick and disabled persons, and elderly who need support and assistance. But is there an alternative which can make people healthier, happier, and more contented? The project group suggests three principles of future welfare and good care in a democratic society: 1) Welfare problems must be solved nearer the source, which means activating people's innate resources instead of rendering them passive through overprotection; 2) Citizens must assume more responsibility in caring for each other, which means both men and women playing an active part in welfare tasks suitable for non-professionals (this does not mean abolishing society's fundamental responsibility for care and welfare); 3) Civic influence on professional care must be strengthened: persons providing care must not take over all responsibility for problems, and organized care must be subject to such political control as to be governed by the values of citizens, not those of professionals.

Concludes with a future picture of "Sweden with care" in 2006, which suggests how it may be possible to offer both better social care and a generally improved quality of life within the framework of relatively limited resources expected for the next 20 to 30 years. The public sector was allowed to continue expanding, but at a rate far slower than in the 1970s, and with a reduction of statutory working hours by 30% over a 25-year period. Many people are only employed part-time, while others have temporary leaves of absence to study or care for children or the elderly. Many people are involved in various communal bodies such as neighborhood committees and school boards, and there are flourishing voluntary organizations and cooperatives parallel to public agencies. A Care and Welfare Commmission made a number of recommendations that have gradually been implemented: increased tax equalization between regions and municipalities to prevent decentralization from accentuating inequalities, the conversion of compulsory military service to a year's community service for all young men and women, publically guaranteed employment for young persons ("the youth guarantee"), legislative amendments to facilitate the formation of cooperatives for social and other purposes, revised rules of taxation to facilitate economic activity by retired people, and more scope for voluntary organizations in the care and welfare services sector. The school system of 2006 encourages parents and other non-teacher adults to serve as supportive teachers, and pupils from the age of 11 are required to help look after the very young, to help with cleaning and making repairs at school, and to help adults who have difficulty in coping by themselves.(As a result, petty theft and vandalism have diminished because young people feel more a part of things.) Neighborhood care centers serving 5,000 to 10,000 persons have assumed general responsibility for health, welfare, and environmental questions in their area. Preventive work constitutes an important sector of care center duties. Small nursing homes are attached to the care center, pursuing the principle of developing the client's own resources as far as possible. Another type of dwelling arrangement is the senior collective. [NOTE: A significant rethinking of social design that is applicable to all developed/overdeveloped nations.]

(welfare state reexamined)

6874

The Aging: A Guide to Public Policy. Bennett M. Rich and Martha Baum (both U of Pittsburgh). Pittsburgh PA: U of Pittsburgh Press (127 N Bellefield Ave), Dec 1984/ 275p/$24.95; $8.95pb.

The percentage of Americans aged 65 and over grew from 4.1% in 1900 to 8.2% in 1950 and 11.3% in 1980, with projections for further expansion in the future. More than

any other population group, the elderly have become dependent on publicly funded resources in many areas of their lives. Efforts on behalf of the elderly have increased markedly over the last decades, and many programs have been developed in a piecemeal fashion. This book describes the major Federal programs for older Americans, their degree of fit and consistency with each other, and the extent of coverage they offer to aged groups. Chapters are devoted to discussing the politics of aging (describing various Congressional committees and interest groups representing the aging), the 1965 Older Americans Act and the machinery to carry out its objectives (often referred to as the Aging Network), general retirement and economic programs, the numerous retirement programs directed at special groups, health programs for the elderly, transportation and housing for the elderly, government and the older worker (programs to protect against discrimination and to provide opportunities), and programs for the aging veteran. Concludes that there is a vast array of resources and services available to older persons, but they do not cohere into a national policy. This fragmentation and lack of coordination is a result of the complex structure and incremental process of US policymaking. In the US Congress, about a dozen committees in the Senate and another dozen committees in the House have legislative responsibilities for particular programs. There is little promise in the near future of any increased policy coherence. Indeed, in the current climate of austerity, a number of existing programs for the elderly may disappear or undergo cutbacks or modifications.

(Federal programs for the elderly)

6875

The Oldest Old. Edited by Richard Suzman and Matilda White Riley (both National Institute on Aging). *Milbank Memorial Fund Quarterly: Health and Society*, 63:2, Spring 1985, 177-451.

The mounting numbers of the very old is so new a phenomenon that there is little historical experience to help in interpreting it. Numbering less than a million in 1960, there are now 2.6 million Americans age 85 or over, or 1% of the population; this proportion is projected to increase to 1.9% by 2000 and 5.2% by 2050. The oldest of the old is the most rapidly growing group in the US population. They have striking differences from other Americans: a unique sex ratio (only 44 males per 100 females in 1980), higher rates of institutionalization, and lower family income. Essays in this special issue explore recent demographic trends, qualitative changes in aging, changes in the service needs of the oldest old (efficient planning for those aged 85 and over requires early identification of those most in need), interactions of age and disease in this increasingly diverse population, epidemiology of disability in the oldest old, the increasing costs and declining income of the very old, and the economic status of the oldest old (proposals to shift more Medicare costs to beneficiaries raise the question of whether the oldest old—the heaviest users—have the resources to bear these costs).

(very old Americans)

6876

Technology and Aging in America. U.S. Congress, Office of Technology Assessment. Washington: USGPO, July 1985/496p/$17.00 (S/N 052-003-00970-6).

Effective use of both "high-tech" and "low-tech" can improve the health and functional ability of older Americans, and possibly reduce health care expenditures. 1) **Biomedical Research**: expanded support will hasten progress toward new treatments, cures, or even preventive measures for chronic debilitating diseases that are not well understood (osteoarthritis, dementia, osteoporosis, hearing impairments, and urinary incontinence); 2) **Health Promotion**: low-tech applications such as exercise regimens, smoking cessation, and improved diets can have short- and long-term benefits; 3) **Computer-Based Technologies**: the severely disabled can be assisted by programmable wheelchairs, voice-activated robots, and a variety of prosthetic devices; 4) **Telecommunications Applications**: video cassette players and personal computers could provide information on healthy behavior; videotex could link patient homes and physician offices for two-way communication and monitoring of medications and vital signs; 5) **Appropriate Design in the Home**: relatively inexpensive adjustments of the living environment can greatly enhance the safety of older persons; new housing options could reduce isolation and provide more supportive living environments; 6) **Work**: opportunities for home-based work through the "electronic cottage" may evolve for older persons.

(aging Americans and technology)

6877

Social/Health Maintenance Organizations: New Policy Options for the Aged, Blind, and Disabled, Charlene Harrington and Robert J. Newcomer (both Aging Health Policy Center, U of California-San Francisco), *Journal of Public Health Policy*, 6:2, June 1985, 204-222.

One of the most crucial issues facing Americans is how to reduce costs and improve care for the elderly. The most troublesome aspects of current long-term care systems are barriers to access, high costs, questionable quality, and lack of continuity in care. An innovative and viable alternative to present systems is the Social/Health Maintenance Organization. The S/HMO model is designed to cover long-term care on a prepaid basis, thereby controlling costs with a fixed budget while providing a full range of health care and supportive services from a single organizational system. Instead of institutionalization, the model stresses continuous case management, home care, and appropriate social services. Four S/HMO demonstration projects have been established nationwide and they show great promise, although they will not be formally evaluated for at least two more years. The authors describe S/HMO benefits and how to remove barriers to S/HMO development for consumers, providers, and public policymakers.

(S/HMO: a new system for long-term care)

6878

Social Security: Prospects for Real Reform. Edited by Peter J. Ferrara. Washington: The Cato Institute, July 1985/220p/$20.00;$8.95pb.

Despite the 1983 tax increases in Social Security, the system still faces real financial problems. Virtually all young workers today will receive returns of 1% or less on their Social Security "investment," while they could receive several times as much if they were allowed to invest their retirement savings in a private plan. Such a plan is proposed by Ferrara, author of **Social Security: The Inherent Contradiction** (Cato, 1980; **FS Annual 1980-81** #2419), who would modify today's Individual Retirement Account system to create a "Super IRA." Under this plan, workers would be allowed to contribute to their IRAs an amount up to a certain percentage of their Social Security taxes each year. Instead of the usual IRA income tax deduction, they would receive a dollar-for-dollar income tax credit for these contributions. The program could be phased in over a period of years, and eventually workers would have the option to direct the entire amount of their Social

Security contribution to their Super IRAs. Benefits of such a reform: 1) the elderly would be more securely guaranteed than they are today; 2) workers who opt for the Super IRA could expect much higher retirement benefits; 3) the Super IRA would allow workers much greater freedom of choice over their retirement investments and more freedom to choose their retirement age; 4) major inequities of the Social Security system would be alleviated (because of the difference in life expectancies of blacks and whites, the average black male receives 50% less from Social Security than the average white male); 5) the Super IRA would help to break the poverty cycle by spreading new wealth into the hands of millions. [NOTE: Sound too good to be true? Reviewing Ferrara's book in *The Washington Post* (4 August 1985), Robert Kuttner sees little prospect of the Super IRA being enacted; as a universal program, Social Security is too popular to tamper with, let alone replace with Ferrara's $50 billion tax loophole. Moreover, thanks to recent reforms, Kuttner thinks that Social Security seems to be in good financial order, at least for the next few decades.]

("Super IRA" alternative to Social Security)

6879

Civil Rights: Rhetoric or Reality? Thomas Sowell (Hoover Institution). NY: William Morrow & Co, June 1984/164p/$11.95.

Reconsiders actions taken in the name of "civil rights" since 1954, arguing that the major premises of the civil rights vision oversimplify and often distort cause-and-effect relationships. The trend of minority movement into higher paying occupations began many years before the Civil Rights Act of 1964, and was not accelerated by the Act or by mandatory quotas. With the advent of affirmative action, the most disadvantaged segments of the minority population have fallen behind their white counterparts, while the more advantaged minority members have improved their positions vis-a-vis comparable whites in both relative and absolute terms. In sum, although affirmative action invokes the name of the disadvantaged, these are precisely the people who have fallen further behind under its auspices.   **(affirmative action questioned)**

6880

Blacks and Whites: Narrowing the Gap? Reynolds Farley (Prof of Sociology, U of Michigan). Cambridge MA: Harvard U Press, Nov 1984/304p/$22.50.

Are blacks catching up to whites economically and socially? Techniques of demographic measurement are applied to Census Bureau data, with mixed conclusions. On many measures, blacks have made progress toward equality with whites. But there are some disturbing trends, such as the increasing proportion of poor black families headed by single women. In spite of an overall picture of progress, it is too early to assume that blacks will soon catch up with whites, and an active policy aimed at correcting racial inequality must continue.   **(black-white gap)**

6881

Contemporary Public Policy Perspectives and Black Americans: Issues in an Era of Retrenchment Politics. Edited by Mitchell F. Rice and Woodrow Jones, Jr. Westport CT: Greenwood Press, Dec 1984/c256p/$29.95.

Provides a synopsis of contemporary public policies and their resultant benefits and burdens to the black community. Issues examined include the urban crisis, Reaganomics, public employment, minority business enterprise, energy, the military, police, affirmative action, health, the economy, and ethics policies.   **(blacks and public policy)**

6882

Hispanics in the United States: A New Social Agenda.
Edited by Pastora San Juan Cafferty and William
McCready (National Opinion Research Center, U of
Chicago). New Brunswick NJ: Transaction Books, Sept
1984/330p/$29.95;$12.95pb.

Provides a basic foundation in the information available,
research performed, and policy agendas of Hispanics, emphasizing the diversity of the Hispanic experience in
America. Themes include immigration patterns and history, demographics and fertility, education, jobs and employment, social services and health, safety and crime, and
political participation.

(social agenda of US Hispanics)

*6883

The Self-Help Revolution. Edited by Alan Gartner and
Frank Riessman (Co-Directors, National Self-Help Clearing
house, CUNY Graduate Center). Volume X, Community
Psychology Series. NY: Human Sciences Press (72 Fifth
Ave), Aug 1984/266p/$29.95.

Essays arranged in three parts: 1) **The Groups**:
women's self-help groups, lesbian and gay groups, the De-
lancy Street foundation for the "Hard-Core Helpless," Parents Anonymous for the treatment and prevention of family
violence, overeaters anonymous, mutual help groups for
the physically disabled, self-help groups for caregivers of
the aged, 2) **Professionals and Self-Help**: the professional's role as sponsor, a collaborative model for professionals and self-help groups, cooperation vs. co-optation;
3) **Evaluation and Assessment**: research issues, health-
related outcomes of self-help participation, therapeutic
groups for the elderly, and an international perspective by
Alfred Katz (who notes that self-help groups in some European countries commonly receive public funding).

Gartner and Riessman conclude that it is becoming recognized that the need for services is, in a way, a bottomless
pit. There is no end to it, and professionals cannot possibly
meet the need.The human services must be reconstructed,
shifting emphasis from the professional service giver to
the consumer. Services are too big and bureaucratized, too
costly and ineffective, and producing iatrogenic dependency and a deep malaise among human service workers.
Mutual aid groups are inexpensive, highly responsive, and
accessible to consumers. They do not encourage dependency or emphasize a pathology model. A new trend in the
self-help movement is to involve professionals in various
ways: initiating and facilitating self-help groups, providing
consultation and training, offering resources and publicity,
and conducting research. Professionals and their agencies
need these groups to revitalize themselves and to win a
new constituency. Self-help groups generate an enormous
power, and supply an infusion of inner strength. Along
with competition and criticism of professional practice, this
fortifies against the dangers of co-optation. In sum, the
self-help/mutual aid phenomenon is too important to be
allowed to grow in isolation from the professional care-giv-
ing system, and too strong to be endangered by such inter-
fusion. Concludes with an unannotated bibliography of
about 250 items. [Also see **Rediscovering Self Help**
(Sage, 1983; **FS Annual 1984** # 6051).]

(self-help groups and professionals)

6884

New Dimensions in Self-Help. Edited by Frank
Riessman. *Social Policy*, 15:3, Winter 1985, 2-46.

Seven contributions on the following: the complementary
character of self-help and social services provided by government (arguing against the simplistic formulation that self-
help groups substitute for necessary large-scale services),
a major ongoing longitudinal study of an important self-help
group of former mental patients, a conceptualization of how
women's various roles are reflected in a wide range of
mutual support groups, how social work curricula would be
greatly strengthened by including an understanding of natural support systems and mutual aid groups, an organizational theory of self-help groups, organizing for neighborhood development, and support groups for the rehabilitation
of crime victims. **(self-help)**

IX. WORK

A. Unemployment and Jobs

6885

The Underbelly of the U.S. Economy: Joblessness and Pauperization of Work in America. Ward Morehouse and David Dembo. Special Report No 3. NY: Council on International and Public Affairs (777 UN Plaza), May 1985/28p/$6.00.

In March 1985, 8.2 million Americans were considered by the US Bureau of Labor Statistics to be unemployed. But this did not include 5.5 million persons who wanted full-time jobs while working only part-time (although counted by the government as working full-time), and another 6.1 million persons who wanted jobs but had stopped looking (and thus were defined out of the labor force). Taken together, these and other categories of jobless persons, calculated on a full-time equivalent basis, add up to a Jobless Rate in March of 14.8%, in contrast to the official unemployment rate of 7.3%. These adjustments give a more meaningful picture of the extent of joblessness in the US than does the narrowly defined official unemployment rate. They indicate that the dislocations of the 1981-83 recession—the most severe since the Great Depression—were far more widespread than is generally perceived, and that many of these dislocations are persisting during the current recovery. The true jobless rate is only part of the "underbelly" of the US economy. Also important is the pauperization of work: replacement of higher paid jobs with jobs at or close to the minimum wage—and often part-time. A high proportion of the new jobs created in the last decade have been relatively low wage, increasingly part-time service sector jobs held more and more by women. This trend appears to have accelerated sharply during the recent recession. Feminization of the labor force and pauperization of wage employment has been enhanced by increasing joblessness among both white and black male workers. Concludes that the formal economy is less and less effective in meeting essential needs of a growing number of US workers, and measures of it such as the official unemployment rate are increasingly less significant as indicators of the true state of work in America. If the informal economy is assuming an increasingly important role, we need to know more about it and to encourage its development as an alternative way to enable people to meet their needs. [NOTE: An important reassessment of official data. For a diametrically opposed view, see John Naisbitt's cheery but dataless vision of forthcoming labor shortages and "full" employment (#6755).]

(US Jobless Rate at 14.8%)

6886

Conceptions of the Dual Economy, Joseph Huber (Free University of West Berlin), *Technological Forecasting and Social Change*, 27:1, Feb 1985, 63-73.

In the last ten years, interest has increased in the other half of the "dual economy"—unpaid labor as opposed to paid labor. The concept has a variety of meanings, though, including domestic and do-it-yourself work, leisure-time activities, black labor, tax evasion, smuggling, self-help, etc. Huber attempts to clarify the various distinctions, since the concept of the "dual economy" may well become as important in the

future as the concept of the "mixed economy" was from the 1920s to the 1970s. To do so, he presents a chart of 19 English-language terms (such as informal sector, shadow economy, counter-economy, voluntary sector, vernacular sphere, etc.) with equivalent terms in French and German. He discusses 12 dimensions of economic dualism and regroups them into four basic categories.

("dual economy" clarification)

6887

Overcoming Unemployment: Some Radical Proposals, David Macarov (School of Social Work, Hebrew U, Jerusalem), *The Futurist*, 19:2, April 1985, 19-24.

The likelihood of permanent and widespread unemployment is becoming more accepted as a reality among social planners. Various options to deal with unemployment are briefly mentioned—job creation, subsidized jobs, work relief, public works, work sharing, universal service, and reducing retirement age—and all are seen as lacking. Rather, what is needed is a goal of full unemployment: a planned movement toward the highest technology possible, replacing as much human effort as possible. Once unemployment is widespread, work will be dethroned from its central position in the pantheon of values, and more radical proposals can then be considered such as guaranteed incomes, paying people to engage in activities such as housework that are currently unpaid, ever-widening circles of cooperatives in which income is divided among members, and collectives to provide for all member needs. [A well-known Canadian futurist, John Kettle, observes that the average worker a century ago worked 3,600 hours a year, while today's worker puts in only 1,800 hours. This process of dethroning work and replacing it with other preoccupations is expected to continue, with average weekly hours of work dropping by about 1% per year (*John Kettle's FutureLetter*, 31 Aug 1984, p5).]

(full unemployment goal?)

6888

Employment Security in a Free Economy. Work in America Institute (Scarsdale NY). Elmsford NY: Pergamon Press, Sept 1984/192p/$15.00.

Discusses the need for planning ahead, lean staffing, responding to temporary economic declines, responding to permanent declines, alliances, a supportive role for government, and the importance of making employment security an integral part of corporate strategy. Measures are recommended that can be adopted to deal with internal and external threats to employment security. Also recommended are specific external measures in aid of employer and union initiatives.

(enhancing employment security)

6889

High Technology: Narrow Sector of the Economy That Affects Many American Industries, David E. Sanger, *The New York Times* National Employment Report (Section 12), Sunday, 14 Oct 1984, p1.

Jobs associated with high technology—in computers, software, defense, electronics, and biotechnology—account for only a tiny fraction of total US employment. While growing fast, the number will probably never be large. Between 1984 and 1995, even the most optimistic projections show that only one new job in 25 will be technology-oriented—involving engineering, the sciences, or the computer industry. But if high tech has not saved the US economy, neither has it destroyed it. Fears that automation would threaten the jobs of millions of workers in traditional industries now seem somewhat overstated, or at least premature. Automation has come slowly to a variety of industries, but the results are hard to measure. High tech's biggest contribution to the job market may prove to be indirect, in the service sector. Efforts by states and cities to attract the glamor industries of high technology are thus misplaced, because high tech manufacturing is highly automated, job growth in high tech fields is not very large and will be slowing down, and high-tech jobs will likely never be evenly distributed throughout the US; new Silicon Valleys cannot be created.   (**high tech and jobs**)

6890

Jobs Increase in Number, but Trends Are Said to Be Leaving Many Behind, William Serrin, *The New York Times*, Monday, 15 Oct 1984, B4.

The US is experiencing a rapid growth in jobs. Under the Reagan Administration, civilian employment has risen 7.7% to 105.2 million in September 1984 (under the Carter Administration, however, it increased by 12.5%). From late 1979 to late 1984, employment in the service-producing part of the economy increased by 8.6%, while employment in the production of goods declined by 5.5%. The largest employment increases have come in business services (up 35.1%), health services (up 19.2%), eating and drinking establishments (up 13.8%), and in finance, insurance, and real estate (up 12.2%). Employment in all governments has dropped by 1%. Since December 1979, two-thirds of the jobs created in the US have been taken by women. Many of the nation's new jobs are attractive and offer good pay: 48% of the employment growth from 1972 to 1983 was in professional, technical, and managerial jobs. But many of the new jobs pay comparatively low wages and some are part-time. Many are in rural and suburban areas, rather than in large cities where unemployment rates are highest. Thierry J. Noyelle (Conservation of Human Resources, Columbia U) warns that the transformation of the work force is producing a stratum of managers, professionals, and other highly skilled employees living in a relatively well-protected and well-paying economic world, and a large stratum of assembly workers, clericals, and service workers who find it increasingly difficult to make ends meet and to deal with the stress associated with unrewarding and somewhat insecure work.   (**job creation since 1979**)

6891

Career Prospects for the Next Decade, *The New York Times* National Employment Report (Section 12), Sunday, 14 Oct 1984, p8.

Job prospects in all career categories, based on projections by the U.S. Department of Labor's **Occupational Outlook Handbook**. Top gainers in the 1982-1995 period include increases in computer-systems analysts by 85%, electrical engineers by 65%, health-service administrators by 58%, registered nurses by 49%, guards by 47%, accountants and auditors by 40%, and lawyers and physicians by 34% each. Top losers in the same period involve decreases in postal clerks by -18%, college and university teachers by -15%, and stenographers by -7%, and increases in both typists and bookkeepers by only 16% each. [NOTE: A rough conclusion from these projections is that certain types of information handlers will not prosper in the emerging information society, notably college faculty—seemingly one of the most important occupations. An alternative presentation of the job outlook projections, arranged by occupations with better-than-average, average, and below-average prospects is available in *U.S. News & World Report*, 13 Aug 1984, 62-63. A selection of promising jobs is provided by Cetron, below.]   (**career prospects to 1995**)

6892

Jobs of the Future: The 500 Best Jobs—Where They'll Be and How to Get Them. Marvin J. Cetron (President, Forecasting International, Arlington VA), with Marcia Appel. NY: McGraw-Hill, 1984/258p/$15.95.

A breezy overview oriented toward young job-seekers, with promising new positions organized into six chapters: the office of the future, servicing and educating America, health-related jobs, engineering, communication and the arts, and factories and manufacturing. Each chapter has introductory comments, and for listed jobs a brief description, the projected number of workers required by 1990, and starting and mid-career salaries.   (**guide to jobs**)

B. The Changing World of Work

*6893

The Future of Work: A Guide to a Changing Society. Charles Handy (Visiting Professor, London Business School). Oxford UK and NY: Basil Blackwell, July 1984/201p/$19.95;$6.95pb.

Many analysts see present employment difficulties as but a stage in history's self-correcting cycle of adjustment; we have only to endure and the old patterns will come into their own again. Handy's central argument is that work will not be the same again, and that we are experiencing more than just a cyclical adjustment. New patterns of work are on their way whether we welcome them or not: the full-employment society is becoming the part-employment society, muscle jobs are yielding to finger and brain jobs, industry is declining and services are growing, hierarchies and bureaucracies are going out and networks and partnerships are coming in, the one-organization career is becoming rarer, the third age of life (beyond the ages of growing up and of employment) is becoming important to more people, sexual stereotypes are being challenged at work and in the home, and work is shifting southwards inside countries and between countries. If trends and portents turn out to be significant, we are likely in the future to find many more people than at present not working for an organization, shorter working lives for many people, fewer mammoth bureaucracies and more tiny businesses, more requirements for specialists and professionals in organizations, more importance given to the informal economy, a smaller earning population and a bigger dependent population, a greatly increased demand for education, and new forms of social organization to complement the employment organization. This raises some big new questions: Who gets the jobs and what counts as a job? How do we pay ourselves, and how will money be collected and distributed? What do we use for wealth, and what needs to be done, by whom, to make more of it? Who will protect consumers and workers in the new, more dispersed world of work? Concludes that full employment as we used to know it is not feasible in the foreseeable future. Four scenarios are discussed as a way of focusing the options: 1) accepting unemployment as the necessary price for bringing down inflation (a convenient scenario for those with work); 2) the leisure scenario where a few people aided by many machines will do the work for the many; 3) the employment scenario where more jobs are created by infrastructure spending and beefing up the state service sector; 4) the work scenario (advocated by Handy) where the employment economy is seen as only part of the whole economy and money is only one of the rewards for work. We shall probably, in the end, muddle towards a compromise blend of all four scenarios. [NOTE: Well-written and provocative; perhaps the best overview to date on rethinking and reorganizing work.]   (**new patterns of work**)

6894
New Technology and the Future of Work and Skills.
Edited by Pauline Marstrand. London UK and Dover NH:
Frances Pinter Publishers, May 1984/260p/$25.00.

Proceedings of a 1983 symposium at the British Association for the Advancement of Science meeting. Includes
such topics as creating a new context for work in Europe
by promoting an "open model" that revaluates nonpaid
work and encourages greater diversity and flexibility of
regulations, the social consequences of mass unemployment, changes in time spent at work, engineering skills
in the robot age, long-term trends in automation, microelectronics and the quality of employment in services, the
effects of technical change on employment opportunities
for women, the future of service employment, and the program of research at the Science Policy Research Unit (U of
Sussex). About half of the contributors are associated with
SPRU, including J.I. Gershuny, Ian Miles, Christopher
Freeman, and Marie Jahoda.   (**technology and work**)

6895
**Beyond Mechanization: Work and Technology in a
Postindustrial Age**. Larry Hirschhorn (Management and
Behavioral Science Center, U of Pennsylvania). Cambridge
MA: MIT Press, Oct 1984/187p/$17.50.

Robots can't run factories. The common notion that computers eliminate the need for human skill and judgment
is wrong. Postindustrial machine systems fail in unexpected ways—Three Mile Island is a major example. Workers are now required to solve problems and uncover patterns presented by the new technology. They increasingly
face unstructured and open-ended problems. Working and
learning have become progressively integrated, demanding new methods of management and new relationships
among workers. The new technologies do not reduce everything to a formula; on the contrary, they demand that we
develop a culture of learning, an appreciation of emergent
phenomena, an understanding of tacit knowledge, a feeling
for interpersonal processes, and an appreciation of organizational design choices. Current failures are indicators of
the unique problems we face in managing the transition
to a postindustrial work system and developing policies to
take us beyond mechanization.   (**technology and work**)

6896
Is Your Friendly Computer Rating You on the Job?
U.S. News & World Report, 18 Feb 1985, p66.

Computer monitoring connects work stations in offices,
factories, and other settings to computers that keep a close
watch on an individual worker's production by counting
such functions as keystrokes per hour. Variations of the
monitoring technique are being applied increasingly in offices, supermarkets, airlines, mail-sorting centers, restaurants, hotels, and long-haul trucking (where on-board computers track a driver's average speed and number of stops).
At least one-third of the more than 7 million workers now
linked to computers through video display terminals are
thought to be subject to some form of monitoring. Experts
think that share will grow to more than half of the 40
million workers expected to be using VDTs by 1990. Despite enthusiasm for the system among employers, critics
contend that such constant surveillance is counterproductive, leading to increased stress, fatigue, and turnover
among workers. Legislation regulating VDT use is expected to be introduced in 24 states in 1985, with half the
bills confronting the issue of monitoring.

(**computer monitoring**)

6897
The Changing Workplace, Sar A. Levitan (Director,
Center for Social Policy Studies, GWU), *Society*, 21:6, Sept-
Oct 1984, 41-48.

Various forecasts on the future of work over the next
decade. Female participation in the labor force will continue to climb, accounting for about 3 in 5 additions to the
work force; if recent trends continue, women will constitute
47% of the work force by 1995. Poverty, however, has been
increasing in the US since 1978 and is becoming feminized.
As long as women are concentrated in low-paying occupations, female-headed families will face serious economic
problems. As for the workplace, there is no reason to believe
that it will be radically transformed. Worker participation
in corporate decision-making is allowed only insofar as it
does not infringe on management prerogatives. Because
both managers and workers are accustomed to hierarchical
structures, they continue to be reluctant to embrace participative values. Computer technology will generate a
wide variety of service jobs, but mostly for lower skills and
lower pay. Within the next dozen years, the economy is
not going to generate any extraordinary demand for new
skills. Higher educational attainment and greater affluence among employees, however, will require greater sensitivity by management to the concerns of their work force.

(**no radical change in work expected**)

6898
**Economics, Work, and Human Values: New Phil-
osophies of Productivity**. *ReVISION: The Journal of
Consciousness and Change* (PO Box 316, Cambridge MA
02238), 7:2, Winter 1984-Spring 1985/123p/$8.95.

Hazel Henderson explains why macro-economic theory
is dangerously out of sync with reality, and is unsuitable
as a policy tool for managing society. Werner Erhard, the
founder of est, is interviewed about transformation in the
workplace. Peter Vaill describes process wisdom and organizational transformation as a liberating spirit. Peter
Senge is interviewed about the philosophical underpinnings of system dynamics, empowerment, and corporate
vision. William Mingin wonders whether the increasing
complexity of the information age will push us to more
profound simplicity. Clement L. Russo reviews influential
thinkers and trends in the philosophy of work. Aristide H.
Esser, Clive Simmonds, and Keith Wilde criticize current
economic analysis and propose broader and more diverse
measures of productivity. Ian Mitroff proposes that
machine-age metaphors as the model for contemporary
organizations should be replaced by a complex hologram.

Accompanying this issue of *ReVISION* is a 40x15" special
map insert by Philip Mirvis, entitled ***Work in the 20th
Century: America's Trends & Tracts, Visions &
Values, Economic & Human Developments***. The vertical axis covers the time span from 1900 to 1984. The horizontal axis is divided into thematic groupings: trends in
management thinking, the better thinking formulas, assumptions about people, the better management formulas,
trends in the work force, trends in the economy and politics,
trends in industry and organization, trends in labor, and
choices to be made. The mid-1980s is characterized as a
clash between a technocratic vs. a people-oriented approach to management and organizational excellence. A
12-page booklet of commentary explains the entries on the
map. [NOTE: The over-simplifications of the map are more
than compensated for by its ambitious originality.]

(**new views of work and productivity**)

6899

Alternative Modes of Co-operative Production, Tom Clarke (Trent Polytechnic, Nottingham UK), *Economic and Industrial Democracy* (Sage), 5:1, Feb 1984, 97-129.

Although producer cooperatives still account for less than 1% of total industrial and commercial activity in all western economies (with the possible exception of Italy), their theoretical potential for growth is generally held to be enormous, due to the widespread desire for secure and meaningful work. Clarke outlines different possibilities for cooperative production, ranging from commercial viability to democratic control, from capital intensive to labor intensive, from bureaucratic control to autonomous groups, and from national self-managed systems to local worker takeover and radical cooperatives. Concludes that a range of cooperative philosophies, forms, and activities will continue to be attempted, and that there will be conflicts between the cooperatives as well as within them over the direction of future development. [NOTE: A useful inventory, especially if contrasted with Mintzberg's inventory on forms of corporate control, #6921.]

(forms of cooperative production)

6900

Worker Cooperatives in America. Edited by Robert Jackall (Williams College) and Henry M. Levin (Stanford U). Berkeley CA: U of California Press, Nov 1984/300p/ $24.95.

Examines the history, dynamics, challenges, and potential of this form of enterprise that is owned and managed democratically by workers. Particular attention is devoted to the continuous need to balance internal demands for democratic organization with the external exigencies of a market system. If the potential for worker cooperatives is realized, they could do much to save and create jobs, while engaging workers more productively and with a greater sense of job satisfaction. **(worker cooperatives)**

6901

Quality Circles After the Fad, Edward E. Lawler III and Susan A. Mohrman (Both Center for Effective Organizations, USC Business School), *Harvard Business Review*, 63:1, Jan-Feb 1985, 64-71.

A quality circle is a group of employees that meets regularly to solve problems affecting its work area. In the past five years, QC activity has increased dramatically. A 1982 study showed that 44% of companies with more than 500 employees had QC programs; nearly three-quarters of these had started after 1980. It might now be estimated that over 90% of the Fortune 500 companies have QC programs in their structures. After having studied many QCs in different organizations, the authors conclude that they have their distinct advantages, but they also tend to self-destruct. The QCs initially pick the easiest problems to solve, and then some groups run out of problems and the groups meet less often. Initial success may also lead participants to ask for financial rewards. Despite these problems, companies can use QCs in three sensible ways: as group suggestion programs, as special projects dealing with critical or temporary organizational issues, or as an interim or transitional device in moving toward a more participative management system and culture. **(quality circles)**

6902

Sabbaticals Spread From Campus to Business, U.S. News & World Report, 28 Jan 1985, 79-80.

After gaining some initial acceptance in the 1960s, the expansion of extended-leave programs stalled. But the concept of job absences for a month to a year is spreading again, especially in newer companies. Today, about 1 in every 10 companies has some form of sabbatical. At McDonald's, for example, the leave consists of an eight-week period at full pay for every 10 years of full-time service. Employers who offer sabbaticals say that the expense is small compared with the improved productivity, creativity, and morale that they get in return. But some consultants caution that employees can lose touch with their work during sabbaticals, or that time off can be used to explore other employment opportunities.

(sabbaticals increasing)

6903

The New Achievers: Creating a Modern Work Ethic. Perry Pascarella (Executive Editor, *Industry Week*). NY: Free Press, 1984/210p/$17.95.

Too few people have had an opportunity to invest themselves in the world's work in ways that are of full human value to themselves and others. This book is written in the hope that people will become aware of their own potential, their fundamental need to work, and the possibility that the workplace can be a source of fulfillment. Business corporations are now making the first significant moves toward helping workers to come alive at work, acquire life skills, and proceed toward personal growth. Corporations are beginning to realize that the values leading to personal growth are the very ones that generate economic growth at this point in US evolution. We are at a stage where efforts to integrate economic and human considerations will be intensified. Concludes with a 36-point agenda for management action to help people develop their full human potential, including: 1) establish non-economic as well as economic objectives for the organization and make them widely known; 2) set standards of excellence and make them known internally and externally; 3) help people attain a feeling of significance; 4) lead people to teamwork by helping them to realize their interdependencies; 5) establish corporate training programs enabling employees to explore their potential for growth; 6) encourage all workers to participate in problem solving; 7) share corporate financial information and plans, so employees at all levels will know how they can contribute more effectively; 8) teach consensus-building skills; 9) evaluate managers on their contribution to long-term objectives and people development. [NOTE: Hortatory rather than empirical.] **(human potential in corporations)**

6904

Transforming Work: A Collection of Organizational Transformation Readings. Edited by John D. Adams (Resources for Human Systems Development, Arlington VA). Alexandria VA: Miles River Press (1009 Duke St), 1984/278p/$16.50pb.

Organizational Development (OD) emerged from applied social psychology and adult education in the 1960s, as a process for helping organizations to solve problems and more fully realize their potentials. Organizational Transformation (OT) now appears to be emerging as a new paradigm that emphasizes an expanded sense of personal identity and an awareness of the interconnectedness of people in their organizational cultures. In contrast to OD, the focus of OT is to establish a vision of what is desired, working to create that vision from the perspective of a clearly articulated set of humanistic values. These readings (most of which were written specifically for this book) stress six themes: the importance of a clear vision, questioning the basic assumptions and beliefs which are taken for granted in organizations, the power of collective belief and myth, leadership to create and sustain a vision, performance excellence, and human empowerment. The 18 essays are arranged in four sections. 1) **The Realm of Organization Transformation**: a new paradigm for lives on a human scale, process wisdom for a new age, a cultural approach to transformations that last, managing the complexity of OT, metanoic-organizations; 2) **Leadership in Transforming Organizations**: changing authority patterns, a new age view of leadership and strategic thinking, managing in a flow state to help energy flow (contrasted to managing in a fear state or a solid state), spirituality in the workplace; 3) **Working with Transformational Dynamics**: consulting for paradigm change, characteristics of organizations capable of inspired performance, myth and the change agent; 4) **Transformational Technologies**: achieving and maintaining personal peak performance, the uses of myth and ritual in managing organizations, high-performance programming, fast-tracking the transformative process, the fusion team as a model of organic and shared leadership, the goal of corporate fitness. **(organizational transformation)**

C. Corporate Innovation and Organization

6905

The Adaptive Corporation. Alvin Toffler. NY: McGraw-Hill, Oct 1984/217p/$15.95.

Presents the basic text of a 1972 report, "Social Dynamics and the Bell System," that Toffler was commissioned to prepare for AT&T. New introductory comments are added to chapters on yesterday's assumptions, destandardization in the super-industrial (Third Wave) communications market, the management of surprise, and shaping a super-industrial corporation. In the introduction written for this volume, Toffler asserts that many non-adaptive corporations will disappear between now and 2000. Many firms were successful in the 1955-1970 years of straight-line growth in an equilibrial environment, but the corporate environment has grown increasingly unstable, accelerative, and revolutionary. Technological breakthroughs, deregulation, stagflation, volatile interest rates, and other erratic forces subvert the strategic assumptions of even the best-run firms. The managers of adaptation must be equipped with a whole new set of non-linear skills. They must deconstruct their companies to maximize maneuverability and to coordinate ad-hocracy. They must be willing to think beyond the unthinkable: to reconceptualize products, procedures, programs, and purposes before crisis makes drastic change inescapable. Companies must ruthlessly review their basic premises, or they will become exhibits in the Museum of Corporate Dinosaurs.

(managers of adaptation)

6906

Reinventing the American Corporation: Megatrends of '85, John Naisbitt (The Naisbitt Group, Washington), *The New York Times*, Sunday, 23 Dec 1984, F2.

We are not in a recovery and we were not in a recession; rather, we are changing economies. The US is experiencing an entrepreneurial boom unmatched since the last time we changed economies, from an agricultural to an industrial society. To survive in the new information-electronics economy, American corporations must reinvent themselves. They must be reconstituted as confederations of entrepreneurs, developing new management systems that exchange the old hierarchical style for an environment in which every employee participates in decision-making. The new networking style of management will witness a shift from manager-as-order-giver to manager-as-facilitator. The manager's role will be to create a nourishing environment for personal growth. As we change the way we view corporations and management style, we are changing our job outlook. The nation is moving from widespead unemployment toward full employment and even toward labor shortages. New jobs are being created at a phenomenal pace: if continued at the current rate, there will be more jobs created than workers to fill them. Although high-tech will not create many jobs, the intelligent application of technology will generate hundreds of thousands of positions. While most new jobs tend to fall on the no-skill, low-pay side, many service jobs are being upgraded to higher pay and skills. [NOTE: A concise assemblage of trendy phrases and upbeat, Panglossian angles.]

(new management style and more jobs)

6907

Playing in the Information-Based "Orchestra," Peter F. Drucker (Claremont Graduate School), *The Wall Street Journal*, Tuesday, 4 June 1985, p32.

The organization of the future is rapidly becoming reality, with a structure in which information serves as an axis. The information-based structure is relatively flat, requiring fewer levels of management than before. These levels are not levels of authority, but relays for information, similar to the boosters on a telephone cable which collect, amplify, repackage, and send on information. This new structure makes irrelevant the famous principle of the span of control, replacing it with a new principle of "span of communications." The information-based structure permits and indeed requires far more "soloists" with far more specializations. The conventional business organization was originally modeled after the military; the information-based system more closely resembles the symphony orchestra. All instruments play the same score, but each plays a different part. They play together, but rarely in unison. Unlike the orchestra, the score in business is being written as it is being played, which requires high self-discipline, management by objectives, and strong decisive leadership. **(information-based organization)**

*6908

Innovation and Entrepreneurship: Practice and Principles. Peter F. Drucker (Claremont Graduate School). NY: Harper & Row, June 1985/277p/$19.95.

Innovation and entrepreneurship are purposeful tasks that can be organized as systematic work; they are part of the executive's job. Chapters are grouped into three parts: 1) The Practice of Innovation: where and how the entrepreneur searches for innovative opportunities, and the do's and don'ts of developing an innovative idea into a viable business or service; 2) The Practice of Entrepreneurship: entrepreneurial management in the existing business, the public service institution, and the new venture; 3) Four Entrepreneurial Strategies: being "fustest with the mostest," "hitting them where they ain't," finding and occupying a specialized ecological niche, and changing the economic characteristics of a product, a market, or an industry.

The Introduction relates innovation and entrepreneurship to the economy, claiming that the emergence of a truly entrepreneurial economy in the US during the last 10 to 15 years is "the most significant and hopeful event to have occurred in recent economic and social history." In no other peacetime period has the US created as many new jobs:

40 million-plus since 1965. The Kondratieff theory of economic long waves fails totally to account for this job creation. "We are indeed in the early stages of a major technological transformation, one that is far more sweeping than the most ecstatic of the 'futurologists' yet realize, greater even than **Megatrends** or **Future Shock**." Drucker's conclusion, tying these developments to society, is equally exuberant: "The emergence of the entrepreneurial society may be a major turning point in history." Innovation and entrepreneurship are needed in society as much as in the economy, in public-service institutions as much as in businesses. There are two areas in which an entrepreneurial society requires substantial innovation: a policy to take care of redundant workers, and some way to systematically abandon outworn social policies and obsolete public-service institutions, e.g. a tax system that encourages moving capital from yesterday to tomorrow. Underlying these needed policies is the need to encourage habits of flexibility and continuous learning for institutions as well as individuals. [NOTE: For a contrasting pessimistic view that favors Kondratieff long waves, see Forrester, #6807. For an earlier pronouncement by Drucker on the entrepreneurial economy, see **FS Annual 1984** #6065.]

(entrepreneurial economy emerging)

6909

The Innovators: Rediscovering America's Creative Energy. James Botkin, Dan Dimancescu, and Ray Stata. NY: Harper & Row, Nov 1984/312p/$16.95.

The co-authors of **Global Stakes** find the stereotype of the innovator far too limiting. Innovators not only make new products, but, equally if not more importantly, they create new production processes, management styles, policies, and educational systems. Most recent industrial policy proposals call for a centralized top-down approach, but this cannot work. Instead, the authors advocate a wide array of decentralized initiatives to boost the visibility of innovation in the economy. The emphasis in the book is on four major aspects of innovation: R&D, education, management, and capital. The picture of the new emerging America is portrayed by case studies of three US companies undergoing rapid transformation (Ford, Emhart, and Aetna), three states in different stages of economic transition (Massachusetts, Michigan, and Mississippi), and changes in several educational institutions (especially Carnegie-Mellon University and Worcester Polytechnic Institute). One of the most promising new responses is the recent emergence of "centers of innovation" at many US universities: industry-university consortia organized to create new knowledge and to transfer it effectively to the commercial environment. Few leaders in government, industry, or academia have yet recognized these centers as the cores for high-leverage economic-development policy, and a new source of inspiration and leadership for America's future.   **(innovation centers)**

6910

Making the Future Work: Unleashing Our Powers of Innovation for the Decades Ahead. John Diebold (The Diebold Group, Inc-NYC). NY: Simon & Schuster, Oct 1984/466p/$18.95.

Chapters on why things don't work anymore, short time horizons, the misrule of law, unleashing innovation in public services, talent as capital, managing for sociopolitical change, facilitating change in jobs, the information age, and the bio-revolution. Concludes that reshaping the future will require new relationships and new roles in many of our fundamental institutions. Examples include new business-government relationships, new prospects in public services made possible by privatization experiments, alternative legal institutions to end obstacles and delay in the judicial process, organizational inventions such as the Public Agenda foundation, and Diebold's proposal for a series of publicly-funded Institutes of the Future, using a diversity of forecasting techniques to provide constantly updated independent views of the future for use by policymakers. [NOTE: Perhaps a few gems of wisdom from this famous consultant, but hard to find in the poorly-organized swamp of rambling, hortatory, cliches.]

(promoting innovation)

*6911

Leaders: The Strategies for Taking Charge. Warren Bennis (Prof of Management, USC) and Burt Nanus (Director, Center for Futures Research, USC). NY: Harper & Row, May 1985/244p/$19.95.

Leadership is the pivotal force behind successful organizations. It is necessary to help organizations develop a vision of what they can be, and to mobilize change toward this vision. The need for men and women of vision has never been so great, for a chronic crisis of governance is now an overwhelming factor worldwide. Decades of academic analysis have given us more than 350 definitions of leadership, but no clear understanding of what distinguishes leaders from non-leaders, effective leaders from ineffective leaders, and effective organizations from ineffective organizations. All of the current paradigms of organizational life, whether "new age" or conventional, have failed to consider the essential element of power. Power is the reciprocal of leadership. It is the basic energy needed to initiate and sustain action—the capacity to translate intention into reality and sustain it. Leadership is the wise use of this power. Such "transformative leadership" achieves significant change that reflects the community of interests of both leaders and followers; it frees up and pools collective energies in pursuit of a common goal.

The authors conducted 60 depth interviews with successful CEOs and 30 with outstanding leaders from the public sector. All of the leaders embodied four major strategies (or areas of competency, or types of human handling skills): 1) Attention Through Vision: the creating of focus, an agenda, a fixation on outcome; 2) Meaning Through Communication: capturing imagination, communicating the vision, getting people to recognize and accept an idea, creating a commonwealth of learning; 3) Trust Through Positioning: we trust people who are predictable—whose positions are known and who keep at it—people who make their positions clear; positioning is the implementation of the leader's vision; 4) Deployment of Self: enabled by positive self-regard (knowledge of one's strengths, the capacity to nurture these strengths, and the ability to discern the fit between one's strengths and weaknesses and organization needs) and the Wallenda factor (the capacity to embrace positive goals—to put energies in walking the tightrope rather than into not falling, which was the downfall of tightrope walker Karl Wallenda in 1978).

For successful leadership to occur, there has to be a fusion between positive self-regard and optimism about a desired outcome. All of the leaders interviewed here appeared to be masters at selecting, synthesizing, and articulating an appropriate vision of the future. Leaders require foresight, hindsight, a world view, depth perception, peripheral vision, and a process of revision so that all visions previously synthesized are constantly reviewed as the environment changes. Learning is the essential fuel for the leader; it is absolutely indispensable under today's conditions of rapid change and complexity. Those who do not learn do not long survive as leaders. Leaders can provide the proper setting for innovative learning by designing open organizations in which participation and anticipation work together to extend the time horizons of decision-makers. The great leader, like the great orchestra conductor, calls forth the best that is in the organization; each performance is a learning experience enabling the next undertaking to be much more effective.

Concludes by dispelling various myths that discourage potential leaders from "taking charge" of their organizations: leadership is a rare skill (rather, everyone has leadership potential); leaders are born and not made (rather, we are all educable, and whatever natural endowments we have can be enhanced, similar to learning to be a parent or a lover); leaders are charismatic (some are, some aren't); leadership exists only at the top of an organization (rather, the larger the organization, the more leadership roles it is likely to have); the leader controls, directs, prods, manipulates (rather, leadership is not so much the exercise of power itself as the empowerment of others). Once these five myths are cleared away, the question becomes not one of how to become a leader, but of improving one's effectiveness at leadership. Our present crisis calls out for leadership at every level of society and in all organizations that compose it.   (**need for effective leaders**)

6912

A Passion for Excellence: The Leadership Difference. Tom Peters and Nancy Austin (The Tom Peters Group, Palo Alto CA). NY: Random House, May 1985/437p/$19.95.

A sequel to the extraordinarily successful **In Search of Excellence** (**FS Annual 1984** #6463), which has sold about five million copies. The authors assert that a revolution is underway—that managers in every field are rethinking the tried and not-so-true principles that have often served their institutions poorly. In large measure it is a "back to the basics" revolution. We have been so tied up in our techniques, devices, and programs that we forgot about the people who produce the product or service and the people who consume it. In the public or the private sector, in big business or small, the basic model for creating and sustaining superior performance over the long haul involves taking exceptional care of one's customers, constant innovation, and turned on people who are proud of their organization. The critical element that connects these three is leadership. Leadership means vision, cheerleading, enthusiasm, love, trust, verve, passion, obsession, consistency, the use of symbols, and effectively wandering around. In this book, there is no litany of external forces than can affect the enterprise; the management practices advocated here ensure that the organization is always externally focused, always sensing change before it sneaks up. The brand of leadership proposed here has a simple base of MBWA (Managing By Wandering Around). To "wander" with customers, vendors, and one's own people is to be in touch with the first vibrations of the new. The surviving organization is the adaptive organization—one that is in touch with the outside world via living data.

Chapters are devoted to MBWA as the technology of the obvious, integrity, common courtesy with customers, the mythology of innovation, skunks and skunkworks (small innovative groups), the "smell" of innovation (23 ways listed, such as tolerating failure, invention with customers, bootleg products), ownership, awards, small wins and de-bureaucratizing, coaching, doing MBWA, excellence in school leadership, and the price of excellence (time, energy, attention, and focus). [NOTE: A jumble of repetitious exhortations, lists, and anecdotes—but nonetheless inspiring. And not only for corporations and schools; e.g., think of *Future Survey* as Thinking By Wandering Around.]
    (**excellence, leadership, skunkworks, MBWA**)

6913

Who's Excellent Now? (Cover Story), *Business Week*, 5 Nov 1984, 76-88.

At least 14 of the 43 "excellent" companies highlighted by Peters and Waterman in their 1982 bestseller, **In Search of Excellence** (**FS Annual 1984**, #6463) have now lost their luster. Such companies as Delta Airlines, Eastman Kodak, Texas Instruments, 3M, Atari, and Revlon have suffered significant earnings declines arising from serious business problems, management problems, or both. In many instances, the transgressors walked away from the principles that had been key to their earlier successes. A major lesson from this is that the excellent companies of today will not necessarily be those of tomorrow. The more important lesson is that good management requires much more than following any one set of rules.
    (**changing list of excellent companies**)

6914

Loyalty Ebbs at Many Companies As Employees Grow Disillusioned, Thomas F. O'Boyle, *The Wall Street Journal*, Thursday, 11 July 1985, p27.

The intangible yet indispensable asset of loyalty is waning at a growing number of corporations. An average of annual surveys by the Opinion Research Corp. shows a declining proportion of managers who rate their company favorably (from 82% in the early 1970s to 70% in the early 1980s) and a declining proportion of managers who rate management favorably (from 70% to 47% in the same periods). The proportion of clericals who rate management favorably fell from 53% to 38%; among hourly workers the rating fell from 36% to 22%. Anecdotal evidence and interviews across the country confirm this declining devotion. Two reasons are given for this change: 1) younger workers, who are generally better educated, have higher expectations about their jobs, and are more likely to feel dissatisfied when ambitions aren't met; 2) a wave of mergers and corporate cutbacks has resulted in a net reduction of nearly 500,000 managerial and professional jobs since 1979, convincing many workers that companies won't return their loyalty. Some industries have almost epidemic defection: in Silicon Valley, employee turnover at 231 electronics companies averaged 27% in 1984—more than five times the departure rate of all US manufacturing. According to one testing expert, nearly one-third of all prospective employees are now judged "high risk," up from 13% in 1964. [NOTE: A sobering view of the dark side of the organizational moon, raising questions about the "excellence revolution" proclaimed by Peters and Austin. In fact, this "revolution" may merely reflect the growing need and desire for effective management, rather than any actual growth of this laudable practice. Also see below.]
    (**employee loyalty declining**)

6915

Corporate America's Little Secret, Barry A. Stein (President, Goodmeasure, Inc), *New Management*, 2:4, Spring 1985, 28-33.

A consultant to hundreds of (primarily) blue-chip companies for 25 years asserts that most corporations are riddled with massive problems, dysfunctional practices, and counterproductive arrangements. The "little secret" is that large corporations more or less universally are not effective. Even the best—so-called "excellent" organizations—are only moderately effective when judged by their capacity to use their resources, especially people. Three particularly wrong premises have captured the mind of many executives: that all organizational outcomes can be traced to the efforts of individuals (rather, outcomes mainly reflect joint effort), that people cannot be trusted (rather, people are interested in and capable of doing better and being more effective), and that executives are largely responsible for their organization's successes and failures (rather, the key task for managers is to create a system that enables others to act in appropriate ways). Concludes with a list of ways to address these issues: 1) understand and accept reality (there is great reluctance to recognize just how fundamentally screwed-up our organizations are); 2) realize that most of an organization's problems are not unique errors, but recurring problems reflecting underlying organization patterns; 3) design any change strategy to involve and empower people throughout the organization and to be tied operationally to the organization's critical goals.

(most corporations not effective)

6916
The Greatest Management Principle in the World. Michael LeBoeuf (U of New Orleans). NY: Putnam, May 1985/$14.95.

Author of **The Productivity Challenge** (McGraw-Hill, 1982; **FS Annual 1983** #5001) argues that US business is bogged down in encrusted organizational habits and red tape that penalize enterprise, stifle originality, and actually reward people who lie low. Managers must set up specific employee incentives for higher productivity: money, freedom to grow, public recognition. Employees can also establish rewards to motivate their bosses. The Magical Question is who is being rewarded for what?

(rewards for productivity)

6917
Beyond Human Scale: The Large Corporation at Risk. Eli Ginzberg (Director, Conservation of Human Resources, Columbia U) and George Vojta (Executive VP, Bankers Trust Co). NY: Basic Books, April 1985/242p/$16.95.

The large corporation, because of the way it is organized, forces managers to spend much of their time and energy preparing reports for supervisors, coordinating with other managers, and protecting their turf so that in countless ways they are constrained from using their own initiative. Scale has resulted in an organizational structure that limits the effective utilization of managerial talent, thereby placing the large corporation at risk. Five basic elements contribute to the underutilization of human resources: 1) the cushion of retained profits that helps to establish and maintain the atmosphere of security; 2) the management information system; 3) the performance appraisal system; 4) divisionalization (the decentralization of authority and responsibility transforms the large corporation into an association of cooperating but also competing units); 5) the role of the chief executive officer, whose duties have become inordinately complex. The "unequivocal" conclusion is that only those large corporations that learn to use their managerial personnel effectively in the increasingly competitive world economy will survive and prosper.

(managerial resources underutilized)

6918
The M Form Society: How American Teamwork Can Capture the Competitive Edge. William Ouchi (Prof of Management, UCLA). Reading MA: Addison-Wesley, April 1984/256p/$19.95.

Author of **Theory Z** announces that the strongest companies are M Form—multi-divisional companies—where middle managers may compete with each other but work together to iron out their differences before approaching top management with unified proposals. This idea of management teamwork can be successfully applied to American society. Three basic interacting elements are needed: 1) strong interlocking trade associations to push for new business initiatives and support basic R&D that benefits everyone; 2) a responsive governmental organization; 3) the active participation of banks. The US can move ahead significantly if we throw off our addiction to adversarial competition and emphasize teamwork.

(teamwork needed)

6919
The Management Challenge: Japanese Views. Edited by Lester C. Thurow (Prof of Economics and Management, MIT). Cambridge MA: MIT Press, June 1985/256p/$14.95.

Original essays on Japanese management as the Japanese see it, with the aim of sparking new American solutions to old economic problems. The American focus on improving capital rather than labor markets, short-term financial objectives, and large bonuses based on current profits have not resulted in an optimal corporate environment. Key practices that seem to enhance Japanese effectiveness include seniority promotions, lifetime employment, a wage structure heavily conditioned by bonuses, a culture that emphasizes the group rather than the individual, attention to good people management, and an efficient labor market.

(lessons from Japanese management)

6920
Status Un-Quo. Change: The Agenda for Survival. Marion S. Kellogg *et al*. Hartford CT: Emhart Corporation, Fall 1984/84p. (Free on letterhead from Emhart External Relations Dept, Box 2730, Hartford CT 06101.)

Presentations on contemporary trends from the 1984 Emhart transnational conference for its senior executives: Marion S. Kellogg on people management, T. Mitchell Ford on people as the pivotal asset, Glenn E. Watts on the future of work, J. Alistair Graham on the new realism in labor (seeking balance between the manager and the managed, jobs and technology, the head and the heart), Sidney Harman on designing jobs in accord with the new model of participative democracy, Daniel Yankelovich on a new social contract in the workplace (organized around shared meanings of success, pleasure, autonomy, harmony with nature, and competition), John Diebold on automation and computers, C. Fred Bergsten on the disruption of world society by the costly dollar, and Daniel J. Boorstin on the wisdom of history (man's great capacity is not as a problem solver, but as a problem inventor).

(change and corporations)

6921
Who Should Control the Corporation? Henry Mintzberg (Prof of Management, McGill U), *California Management Review*, 27:1, Fall 1984, 90-115.

The major debate revolving around the private sector is: Who should control large corporations, how, and for pursuit of what goals? The answers that are accepted will determine what kind of society we shall live in. Eight positions are identified that form a spectrum: 1) Nationalize It (a taboo subject in the US); 2) Democratize It (the use of formal devices to broaden governance); 3) Regulate It (a clumsy instrument, but not useless); 4) Pressure It (try to do what regulation fails to do); 5) Trust It (hope for responsible and ethical people in important places); 6) Ignore It (hope for enlightened self-interest); 7) Induce It (reward corporations for doing what they might not otherwise do—the opposite of regulation); 8) Restore It (return power to the rightful owners—the shareholders). This spectrum of positions, however, is folded around in the shape of a horseshoe, in that the two extremes both call for direct control of corporate managers, either by the government in pursuit of social goals (#1) or the shareholders in pursuit of economic goals (#8). The moderate positions—trusting the corporation to the social responsibility of its managers—is farthest from the extremes. Concludes that we must treat this "conceptual horseshoe" as a portfolio of positions from which we can draw, depending on circumstances. Conversely, exclusive reliance on one position will lead to a narrow and dogmatic society with an excess concentration of power. [NOTE: A fascinating and illuminating synthesis.] (**8 forms of corporate control**)

D. Special Groups in the Labor Force

6922

The Future of American Unionism. Edited by Louis A. Ferman (Prof of Social Work, U of Michigan). *The ANNALS of the American Academy of Political and Social Science*, Vol 473, May 1984/189p/$15.00;$7.95pb.

Includes essays on the following: programs to increase worker participation, changes in union organizing, the future demographics of unionism (slow growth in jobs, aging of the labor force and more concern for retirement, more women and minorities in the labor force, declining opportunities for upward mobility in the baby-boom generation), changing concepts of worker rights, the changing workplace, the growing trend toward employee ownership and involvement of unions, changes in the industrial relations system, the new American labor leader (a trend toward less charismatic bureaucrats, and a probable increase of women and minorities in top leadership positions), the potential of local labor-management committees to improve the power of unions at the community level, the next 20 years for collective bargaining (job security will be a central issue, with increased emphasis on reducing work time to create more jobs), trade unions and productivity (short version of Freeman/Medoff book, #6923), and the future of public employee unionism (bargaining will become more widespread in the public sector because of less management resistance). [NOTE: New data from the U.S. Bureau of Labor Statistics show that union membership has continued to decline from 23% of all wage and salary workers in 1980 to 18.8% in 1984 (*New York Times*, 8 Feb 1985, D5).] (**future of unions**)

6923

What Do Unions Do? Richard B. Freeman and James L. Medoff (both Dept of Economics, Harvard U). NY: Basic Books, April 1984/293p/$22.95.

Trade unionism has two faces. If one looks only at the monopoly face, most of what unions do is socially harmful; if one looks only at the voice/response face, most of what

unions do is socially beneficial. The authors apply statistical techniques to data files on thousands of workers and establishments, comparing what happens under trade unions with what happens in comparable settings. In doing so, they arrive at a generally positive assessment. 1) Efficiency: unionism reduces employment, but it permits labor to create valuable workplace practices and in many settings it is associated with increased productivity (thus conflicting with the traditional monopoly interpretation of what unions do to efficiency); 2) Distribution of Income: unions reduce wage inequality and lower profits which generally go to higher-income persons (unions are thus good if one favors greater economic equality); 3) Social Organization: unions generally provide political voice to all labor. Concludes that, in most but not all circumstances, American unionism is a plus on the overall social balance sheet and a minus on the corporate balance sheet. This paradox underlies the national ambivalence toward unions. Policies are suggested that might enable society to benefit from the pluses and to reduce the minuses of unionism. Current labor law should be substantially revised to limit the power of management to oppose unionization, because continued decline in unionization is bad not only for unions but for the entire society. The "union-free" economy desired by some business groups would be a disaster. (**enhancing benefits of unionism**)

6924

Challenges and Choices Facing American Labor. Edited by Thomas A. Kochan (Prof of Industrial Relations, MIT). Cambridge MA: MIT Press, Feb 1985/368p/ $30.00;$15.00pb.

After decades of stability, labor-management relations are undergoing dramatic changes. These essays, from a three-year study of US industrial relations in transition sponsored by the Sloan Foundation, discuss challenges to union organizing, employer strategies for union avoidance, corporate investment and decision-making, labor market and technological developments, changes in collective bargaining, unions and quality-of-work-life programs, and a comparison of labor movements in the US and Canada.

(**industrial relations in transition**)

6925

Working Class Hero: A New Strategy for Labor. Stanley Aronowitz (Prof of Sociology, CUNY Graduate Center). NY: Pilgrim Press, July 1984/229p/$18.95.

Argues that labor organizations have been good for all Americans other than corporate executives and investors. Since the 1960s, however, the social contract has become fragile, as global economic shifts have encouraged transnational corporations to deindustrialize America. Labor laws must be reformed to inhibit the blatantly coercive tactics now routinely used by employers during union representation campaigns. The labor movement must organize with new techniques in unfamiliar settings, devoting special attention to both the impoverished underclass and highly educated professional and technical employees. A new political bloc is needed, allying unions with feminists, minority groups, peace activists and others who challenge the mismanagement of corporate America.

(**strategy for labor**)

6926
The Paraprofessional Movement: An Update, Anna Lou Pickett (National Resource Center for Paraprofessionals in Special Education, CUNY Graduate School), *Social Policy*, 15:1, Winter 1984, 40-43.

Over the past 20 years, efforts have been made to provide status to a new group of workers to serve alongside professionals: instructional assistants, mental health technicians, social worker assistants, physical and speech therapy aides, vocational trainers, and paralegals. Various reports indicate that roles and responsibilities of paraprofessionals are expanding in all areas of the human services. But they also show that opportunities for training, career advancement, and continuing education are not keeping pace. Despite efforts to establish career ladders, few exist. Training is sporadic, fragmented, and based on highly parochial needs. Disadvantaged youth, women, the disabled, and others able to contribute to the helping professions are consigned to dead-end jobs, or remain unemployed. Yet, human service programs are still confronted with personnel shortages, and there is new evidence to show that paraprofessionals can improve the quality of a variety of human services in a cost-effective fashion.
(**paraprofessional movement**)

6927
The Coming Opportunity to Work Until You're 75, Jarold A. Kieffer (former Deputy Commissioner of Social Security), *The Washington Post* (Outlook Section), Sunday, 9 Sept 1984, D1.

In the near future, we will have to radically alter our traditional views of a "working life," as the majority of us probably find it desirable and perhaps necessary to delay retirement. Before the end of the century, many people will want or need to continue working to age 70, or even 75 and beyond. A 1981 Harris poll found that most working Americans in all age groups do not look forward to retiring. And this is fortunate, for the burdens on the Social Security system will rise drastically after the year 2000 if people retire at the ages that workers do today. Longer work lives would keep people paying Social Security payroll taxes, while delaying the time at which workers claim benefits. Leaders in both the private and the public sector should act quickly to tap the social and financial dividends that could accrue to the nation from longer work lives. Doing so, however, will not keep younger people out of the work force, for employment is not a zero-sum game. It is possible to preserve existing jobs while creating new ones for older persons that are cost-effective in the long run. Some of the possibilities are in home health care and home help (saving health and welfare costs), employment services, community work, day care, paralegal services, and part-time help for small businesses. (**new jobs for older workers**)

6928
Comparable Worth: The Myth and the Movement. Elaine Johansen (Dept of Political Science, U of Connecticut). Boulder CO: Westview, Sept 1984/c175p/$24.50.

"Comparable worth" has superseded "equal pay for equal work" as the equal opportunity issue of the 1980s—a social doctrine that portends sweeping changes in defining the value of paid work traditionally performed by women. Johansen looks at who desires comparable worth and who does not, its standing in law and legal precedents, its diffusion through interest group strategies, and its probable consequences. (**comparable worth doctrine**)

6929
Youth Is Maturing Later, Kenneth L. Woodward and Arthur Kornaber, *The New York Times* (Op-Ed), Friday, 10 May 1985, A31.

As the life expectancy of Americans has increased, so has preparation for adulthood. In a society that is taking longer to grow old, the young are taking longer to grow up. In matters of emotional development—abilities to set goals, postpone gratification, take responsibility for others—today's students are significantly less mature than their parents and grandparents were at the same age. Serious college study requires motivation, self-discipline, enthusiasm for learning, and a capacity for sustained attention; most 18-year olds lack this maturity. It is time to change our institutions to fit the real needs of the young. One way to do so would be through a year or two of mandatory public service in the military, domestic volunteer programs, or overseas programs. This would help adolescents to grow up by working cooperatively for others, learning self-management, and becoming involved with people of other classes and backgrounds. Colleges could then become places of intellectual excitement, rather than expensive preserves for the young. [Also see ***National Service for Jobless Youth*** by Franklin Thomas (President, The Ford Foundation), *The New York Times* (Op-Ed), 6 June 1985, A27, who advocates the same sort of youth service programs for the added reasons that young people are a vastly underused resource, and youth service might help dampen the incidence of crime and drug abuse.]
(**national service needed for today's youth**)

6930
The Job Market for College Graduates, 1960-90, Russell W. Rumberger (Stanford U), *Journal of Higher Education*, 55:4, July-August 1984, 433-454.

Employment opportunities for inexperienced college graduates improved during the 1960s, but declined in the 1970s. Projections of educational attainment and employment suggest that labor market opportunities for college graduates will continue to decline in the 1980s. Whereas 36% of employment growth between 1960 and 1970 took place in professional and managerial occupations and 45% between 1970 and 1980, only 28% of employment growth is projected to take place in these two areas between 1980 and 1990. Contrary to conventional beliefs, employment growth in the 1980s will not produce widespread opportunities in high-level, high-tech fields. College graduates may continue to hold an advantage in the labor market, but an increasing number will be forced to accept jobs incommensurate with their training.
(**declining opportunities for college graduates**)

6931
The Illegals, Courtenay Slater (Washington DC), *American Demographics*, 7:1, Jan 1985, 26-29.

The size of the illegal population in the US has been a great demographic mystery. The 1980 census provides some clues and shows that the number of illegals is not as large or as threatening as believed. Roughly two million illegal aliens can be estimated from the 1980 census. About 50% come from Mexico, with another 25% from Central and South America and the Caribbean. Roughly half of all illegals live in California, with 11% in New York, 9% in Texas, 7% in Illinois, and 4% in Florida. The preponderance of young adults among illegal aliens, and the high ratio of males to females, indicates that these immigrants are workers. Various studies have shown that illegals can have a positive impact on local economies and that they do not steal jobs from American workers, although they do hold down wages. If the job threat posed by immigrants has been exaggerated, so too have been estimates of their costs in government programs. As workers, illegals tend to pay more in taxes than they claim in program benefits, although an exception may be education costs. Concludes that no form of legislation will halt the flow of migrants across US borders as long as economic disparities persist between the US and other countries.

(illegals no threat to jobs)

6932

Immigration Policy and the American Labor Force. Vernon M. Briggs, Jr (NYS School of Industrial and Labor Relations, Cornell U). Baltimore MD: Johns Hopkins U Press, Dec 1984/304p/$26.50.

Since the late 1970s, the US has been in the midst of the largest influx of immigrants in its history. In 1980 alone, more people immigrated to the US, legally and illegally, than in any previous single year. But contemporary immigration policy has been dominated by political considerations rather than labor market implications. Briggs charts the evolution of US immigration policies toward all types of immigrants, and analyzes the impact of these policies on US labor practices. After noting the experiences and policies of other nations, alternative policy options are proposed, including ceilings on immigration that are flexible and responsive to US employment trends, and a return to occupational (rather than family) preferences as the basis for allowing immigrants to enter the US. Such changes would provide more job opportunities to citizen workers. **(immigrants and US labor force)**

X. SPATIAL AFFAIRS

A. World Cities

6933

The World Cities. Third Edition. Peter Hall (Prof of Geography, U of Reading). NY: St. Martin's Press, 1984/ 276p/$27.50.

A comparative view of New York, Paris, Moscow, Tokyo, Hong Kong, and Mexico City, analyzing the forces behind their growth and, in some cases, decline. Solutions that planners have designed for the major problems of each city are also examined. A new and disturbing paradox of urban development is highlighted: while the great cities of the developed world begin to contract, those of the poorer countries show explosive and apparently uncontrollable growth. [Also see **Have Cities a Future?** by Peter Hall (*Futures*, 16:4, Aug 1984, 344-350), and **World Capitals**, edited by H. Wentworth Eldredge (Anchor Press/Doubleday, 1975/642p).]   **(world cities)**

6934

The Growth of Core Regions in the Third World, Daniel R. Vining Jr (Population Studies Center, U of Pennsylvania), *Scientific American*, 252:4, April 1985, 42-49.

The most pressing demographic problem in the Third World is not rapid population growth, but the increasing concentration of population in major cities. These core regions may cover a considerable portion of the national territory, and serve as the nerve center of the nation, the hub of transportation, and the seat of national government. Some of the large cities in developing nations are so crowded and polluted that it appears they have reached the limit of the carrying capacity of their environment. Vining surveyed 46 Third World countries to find out if the movement toward the core, which was quite rapid in the 1950s and 1960s, had slackened during the 1970s. Most of these great metropolitan regions continued to attract population during the 1970s at the same high rates of preceding decades. There are some countries where the pace of concentration has slowed, as a result of economic depression (Peru, Chile), stringent measures imposed by a powerful state (Vietnam, Kampuchea), or measures to improve the life of those who live in the periphery (Sri Lanka). Concludes that population concentration appears to be an almost inevitable concomitant of economic growth in the non-Communist world. Some of the adverse effects of rapid concentration can be relieved by a government that pays attention to the countryside, but the choices are by no means easy or without costs.

                                    (Third World urban growth)

6935

Project Ecoville and the Urban Crisis, Rodney R. White (Institute for Environmental Studies, U of Toronto; Coordinator, Project Ecoville), *Mazingira*, 8:3, July 1984, 36-39.

The growth of Third World settlements has shown remarkable constancy in the post-WWII period: the larger the initial settlement size, the faster the settlement has grown. This sustained high rate of growth has produced recurrent crises in virtually all the major Third World cities: high rates of unemployment, poor housing conditions, overburdened social services, and the threat of political instability. Efforts to decentralize—e.g., by shifting the national capital to an interior location—have met with very limited success. It seems most likely that the large cities will continue to grow, at least until the end of this century, at a 5% annual rate or more—thus doubling size in 14 years. Project Ecoville was established with a grant from the International Federation of Institutes for Advanced Study, as part of their larger program entitled Analyzing Biospheric Change. The three goals of the Project are: 1) measuring the urban quality of life to provide a database for policy reform; comparative experience will be assessed on such reforms as self-help housing, squatter upgrading, informal public transport, etc.; 2) examining the relationship between urban growth and rural decline; 3) linking urban and regional scale effects to global scale problems. Concludes that unless development takes place as eco-development—sustainable within the local environment—then it will not take place at all.

                                    (Third World urban growth)

6936

Report on a New Technological Community: The Making of a Technopolis in an International Context, Magoroh Maruyama (Visiting Prof of International Business, U of Hawaii), *Technological Forecasting and Social Change*, 27:1, Feb 1985, 75-98.

In 1980, the concept of "technopolis" was first used by the Japanese government, to indicate a healthy living environment with cultural amenities, combined with high technology industries, adapted to local characteristics, and located away from existing overcrowded industrial centers. In 1981, some 19 locations were designated for further feasibility study, with various themes such as technology for northern living, pastoral city, futuristic city of sound and light, health technology, life science community, innovation city, and coexistence of people and ocean. In March 1984, nine locations received a green light from the national government to begin development. Maruyama reports on the most advanced of these new communities: Kumamoto Prefecture on the "silicon island" of Kyushu. It is described as a fascinating place in a beautiful environment, with frontier industries and hard-working people. Kumamoto is contrasted with high-technology zones in the US, such as California's Silicon Valley and Boston's Route 128. In the US, where land is not as scarce, the high technology industries have gone to where brainpower is available. In Japan, the initiative and sustaining efforts for technopolises come from local governments seeking to develop a new economic base, with an auxiliary role played by the national government (in the form of incentive measures and preferential treatments, to be limited to a five-year period). The concept of technopolis is spreading to other countries, and the first meeting of the International Technopolis Association was held in France in July 1984. A second meeting will be held in Kumamoto in October 1986. [NOTE: A stark contrast to Third World cities, described above!]   **(technopolis communities in Japan)**

6937

Hailed at Its Birth, Brasilia Is Snubbed On Its 25th Birthday, Everett G. Martin, *The Wall Street Journal*, Monday, 29 April 1985, p1.

When President Kubitschek built Brasilia in 1960, he believed Brazil was setting the pattern for cities of the 21st century. Brazil's futuristic capital stands out like a moon station on a rolling savanna 550 miles northwest of Rio de Janeiro. But its great promise has all but vanished. Some critics blame Brazil's triple-digit inflation on

Brasilia. Others simply think the city is sterile and boring—an isolated settlement of half a million civil servants and politicians subsidized by the rest of the country (the million or so shopkeepers and workers who serve them live outside the capital in unplanned shantytowns). Brasilia's architect and city planner were disciples of Le Corbusier, then the dominent voice in city planning, who believed that cities should be redesigned to accommodate the automobile. Sectors are set aside for each city function: a monument sector, a hotel sector, a banking sector, a publishing sector, a recreation sector, etc. To get from sector to sector one must have a car, using an intricate network of superhighways and cloverleafs. Empty spaces by law must be covered by green lawns, which uses more than a third of the municipality's budget to keep the grass green. A lake that was to have been a center for aquatic sports has been polluted beyond use by seepage from cesspools. [NOTE: Appears to be an obvious candidate for Peter Hall's **Great Planning Disasters (FS Annual 1983**, #5512), and a sobering reminder of fad and fashion in images of the future. Indeed, are there images being taken seriously today that, 25 years from now, will seem as silly as Brasilia does today?]   (**Brasilia's faded promise**)

6938

The Death of the Urban Vision? John R. Gold (Dept of Social Studies, Oxford Polytechnic), *Futures*, 16:4, August 1984, 372-381.

Debate on the future city has changed greatly in the last 20 years. In the heady years of the late 1960s, the typical product stressed possibilities rather than constraints. The potential of technology would be actively embraced, producing radically changed urban forms. Inhabitants of such cities would enjoy a leisured, sophisticated, and mobile life-style, made comfortable by the fruits of economic growth. In marked contrast, equivalent literature of the early 1980s is imbued with a scepticism, even hostility, toward many of the cherished notions of earlier urban futurists, and is distinctly more pessimistic about standards of living. Greater emphasis is placed on the local scale, and conserving the physical and social fabric of the city. These changes may be welcomed for indicating the need to reestablish a human scale in urban futures. But this powerful critique has effectively undermined modernist notions of the future city without offering replacements. There are now few coherent ideas about what the future city will be like, and even less consensus about what the future city should be like. To stumble into the future without such forethought is to abandon any real prospect of meeting the potential needs of urban society. [NOTE: An astute comment on worrisome trends toward fragmentation in futures thinking.]   (**urban vision dissipated?**)

*6939

The Future of Urban Form: The Impact of New Technology. Edited by John Brotchie (Victoria, Australia), Peter Newton (Victoria, Australia), Peter Hall (U of Reading, UK), and Peter Nijkamp (Free U, Amsterdam). London: Croom Helm; New York: Nichols Publishing Co, May 1985/374p/$43.50.

Essays from a workshop held at the University of Waterloo (Canada) in July 1983, on the new information technologies and their likely impact on urban form (defined as the pattern of residential and non-residential urban activities and their interactions). In general, the post-industrial society will be characterized by non-routine employment in information-based activities, informality and flexi-time, mixed zones, private transport, more working

at home, diversity, and dispersion. The 26 chapters are divided into nine parts: 1) International and Regional Perspectives: changes in industrial and living patterns in Europe and North America; 2) Future Impacts on Industry: the transition to consumer-led development patterns, the continued increase in capital substitution, the quaternary sector in California; 3) The Role of Innovation in Development: the dynamics of urban change, spatial patterns of biotechnology industries; 4) Communication/Transport Interactions: information technology in the urban system, information-related transport innovations in the development pipeline, the impacts of energy price changes; 5) Information Systems Impacts: trends in high-tech and low-tech service industries, teleshopping systems and their impacts on shopping-center development, infotech and urban planning, the reaction to perceived threats from high-technology; 6) Institutional Influences: the state as a facilitator of technological change, the role of the state as a safety net for the unemployed, the increasing roles of the informal sector and self-help networks; 7) Modelling Urban Systems: metropolitan implications of technological change, energy impacts for a metro region, new techniques for modelling urban dynamics; 8) The Future Urban System: emerging socio-technical trends and impacts, criteria for a desirable urban system; 9) Implications for Planning: forces which operate to increase or decrease the concentration of activities (dispersal and decentralization are expected), reasons for short-term pessimism and cautious optimism. [NOTE: A broad range of future-oriented essays addressed to planning professionals.]

(**infotech and urban form**)

B. U.S. Cities

6940

America's Cities: A Report on the Myth of Urban Renaissance. Michael C.D. MacDonald (Asst to the Commissioner of Housing-NYC). NY: Simon & Schuster, Sept 1984/428p/$16.95.

More than 70% of America lives in metro areas, but US cities are dying because too many people have ignored them. Federal neglect, state tax revolts, and passive mayors are among the forces contributing to the downward spiral. MacDonald examines 12 cities in the Sunbelt states and 10 cities in the Snowbelt states. Most of them are suffering from service cuts, taxpayer flight, and revenue loss, and no major American city is truly safe from this decline. All the shiny new office towers, luxury hotels, and downtown pedestrian malls cannot hide the growing abandonment behind Potemkin village facades. Five cities are viewed as notable disasters: Philadelphia, Baltimore, Detroit, St. Louis, and Newark (our worst city). Four cities are selected as paragons—Minneapolis, Milwaukee, Kansas City, and Wichita—illustrating the law that diversified economies succeed. Concludes that we can begin to restore fairness and purpose, as well as equity and stability, by a military draft (or some kind of required national service for all young citizens), an all-out attack on drugs, real tax reform, and a thorough public works program complemented by a Federal guarantee to train or relocate workers who need such aid.

(**urban renaissance questioned**)

6941

Metropolitan Areas Dominate Growth Again, Richard A. Engels and Richard L. Forstall (both US Bureau of the Census), *American Demographics*, 7:4, April 1985, 23-25.

In the 1970s, nonmetropolitan population growth (1.3% per year) outpaced growth of metropolitan areas (1.0% per year) for the first time in US history. This turnaround is over, according to the latest set of county population estimates, reversing the reversal of the 1970s. Metro population in America grew 3.5% between 1980 and 1983, while nonmetro population grew only 2.7%. Today, 76% of Americans live in metro areas. These areas dominate US growth again largely because nonmetro growth has slowed. Nearly 30% of the nonmetro countries that experienced a resurgence of population growth in the 1970s are losing population again. There is mounting evidence, too, that the housing development, industrial expansion, capital investment, and plant outlays of the recovery have been concentrated in metro areas, rather than in the small plant openings typical of the nonmetro expansion of the 1970s.

(**metro areas again lead US growth**)

6942

The Metropolitan Midwest: Policy Problems and Prospects for Change. Edited by Barry Checkoway (U of Michigan) and Carl V. Patton (U of Wisconsin-Milwaukee). Urbana, Ill: U of Illinois Press, April 1985/328p/ $21.95.

Examines such topics as population, redistribution, economic development, energy costs, land use, housing patterns, Federal aid, and transportation in Chicago, Detroit, Cleveland, St. Louis, Milwaukee, and other major urban centers. The studies point to new directions for policy and planning for the metropolitan Midwest, and show how other parts of the US might learn from this region's plight.

(**Midwest cities**)

6943

Setting Municipal Priorities: American Cities and the New York Experience. Edited by Charles Brecher and Raymond D. Horton (Co-Directors, Setting Municipal Priorities Project, NYU and Columbia U). NY: New York University Press (dist. by Columbia U Press), Dec 1984/ 560p/$50.00.

For the past five years, the Setting Municipal Priorities project prepared annual volumes analyzing the public and private sectors of NYC in order to provide understanding and policy guidance to New Yorkers and a broader understanding of where American cities are headed. This volume addresses a national audience on the most important lessons from five years of intense study of NYC during its recent recovery from a serious fiscal crisis. Contributions are arranged in four parts: 1) The Setting: population, the local economy, local revenues; 2) Financial Resources: taxes, state aid, Federal aid, financing policy; 3) Budgeting and Management: financial planning, expenditures, debt and capital management, labor relations; 4) Service Delivery: expenditures and services, police, sanitation, housing, health care, aiding the poor. Concludes that the future of NYC is far from secure. Its past teaches that growth is neither continuous or inevitable, but the most recent experience also demonstrates that the same is true of urban decline. Prevailing frameworks of social science inquiry reinforce pessimistic views. But in NYC there is recurring evidence of vitality, and the pattern of urban decline has been reversed, at least temporarily. [NOTE: A gloomier view is taken in **The Rise and Fall of New York City** by Roger Starr (Basic Books, April 1985/246p/$17.95), who laments that NYC once was a place of civil peace and moral order of more controlled lives.] (**NYC decline reversed?**)

*6944

The Future of State and Local Government as Seen in the Futures Literature. Henry H. Hitchcock and Joseph F. Coates (J.F. Coates Inc, Washington). Washington: Academy for State and Local Government (400 N Capitol St NW), March 1985/122p.

The Academy for State and Local Government is reexamining its agenda of research, looking for topics which will help state and local governments to understand and better manage their futures. This report, summarizing a variety of trends and issues, is an early step in the Academy's agenda setting. Brief sections are devoted to 17 topics: energy, environment, natural resources, agriculture, housing, land use and planning, transportation, infrastructure, health, population, services, government and organization, management, education and training, the arts, tax and finance, and economic development. Under each topic is a listing of trends, issues, neglected trends and issues, and bibliographic notes. The executive summary provides an overview: 1) Ten Recurring Trends: steadily rising costs, more aggressive demands for resources, growing citizen demands for services, declining and vacillating Federal support, more state and local innovation, an aging and more diverse population of growing numbers, the rise of the sunbelt and decline of the snowbelt, a cascade of infrastructure and environmental problems, change and disruption from new technologies, integration of the US and global economy; 2) Eight Recurring Conflicts or Issues: development vs. environmental protection, Federal vs. state/local responsibilities, elderly/poor/ minorities vs. other priorities, who pays vs. who gains, efficiency vs. expanding needs, integration vs. local control, regulation vs. deregulation, new problems vs. continuing problems; 3) Neglected Trends and Issues in the Literature: national systems in a local setting (growing air traffic, nuclear power), newly emerging environmental problems (declining rangeland quality, wetlands degradation, fisheries), opportunities for innovation (alternative work schedules, new housing arrangements, etc.), needs of the elderly/poor/minorities, implications of technology. Concludes with a bibliography listing 57 state and city future studies and about 100 general books and articles of special relevance. (**state/local trends and issues guide**)

6945

More Cities Paying Industry To Provide Public Services, Martin Tolchin, *The New York Times*, Tuesday, 28 May 1985, p31.

Mayors and county officials are increasingly paying private industry to provide a wide range of services, in a move that has redefined the role of local government. As Gov. Mario Cuomo has noted, "It is not government's obligation to provide services but to see that they're provided." According to a 1984 survey by the International City Management Association, the following percentages of public services have been turned over to private industry by cities and counties: garbage collection (34%), street repair (26%), street light operation (38%), vehicle towing and storage (78%), hospital operation (25%), legal services (48%), data processing (22%), tax assessing (6%), secretarial services (4%). The trend is so new that no comparable data exists for earlier periods; nor is there any conclusive evidence in most areas as to whether private industry is performing public services better or cheaper than governments (as claimed by those who support the trend), or whether governments are turning to private contractors in an effort to curtail services (as some critics maintain).

(**urban services privatized**)

6946

A Breath of Free Markets in Zoning, Robert H. Nelson, *The Wall Street Journal*, Wed, 22 May 1985, p32.

The author of **Zoning and Property Rights** (MIT Press, 1977) argues that land use planning has turned out to be much more art than science. The progressive idea that politics could be separated from the zoning process has been discredited. Because zoning does not allow for market transactions, it makes many beneficial changes in land use difficult or impossible. A wave of scholarly criticism, however, has recently brought into focus the outlines of a new system that would preserve the protective functions already well served through zoning, while introducing greater flexibility by allowing market transactions. The resulting reality of "private neighborhoods" would offer wider options in the types of controls over existing structures. Some neighbors might prefer a minimum of control; others might wish strict guidelines on architectural changes, landscaping, and other features. While adoption of such a system might seem a remote possibility, in the past year homeowners in Atlanta and Northern Virginia have managed to double or triple the value of their property by unanimously deciding to sell their entire neighborhood as a single package so more intensive development could occur. The lure of such gains makes it likely that many more neighborhoods will follow, thereby significantly reasserting the role of market forces in US land use. The ultimate decision-making power would rest where it properly belongs—with property owners, rather than political entities. **(private neighborhhods?)**

6947

Citizen Censorship: Threats from Libel Suits, Eugene L. Roberts Jr (Executive Editor, *The Philadelphia Inquirer*), *Vital Speeches of the Day*, 51:16, 1 June 1985, 490-493.

The same series of court decisions that has opened the American press to intimidating libel suits by public officials has also opened average people to legal harassment by those who govern them. It started 21 years ago with the *Times* vs. Sullivan decision by the US Supreme Court, when a city commissioner in Montgomery, Alabama, was awarded $500,000 for an advertisement in *The New York Times* outlining a wave of terror against blacks. There is no clearinghouse to keep count of public official libel cases against the press or slander suits against private citizens, but there are powerful indications that the movement toward them has gathered such momentum that it threatens to become an avalanche. One First Amendment lawyer estimates the number of cases as a few hundred in the 1970s, increasing to about a thousand today. In the Philadelphia area alone, 15 public officials have sued or are now suing in 20 separate libel cases against newpapers, magazines, TV stations, and at least one private citizen. Libel suits by public officials do not promote diversity and dissent, but enforce the power of those who govern while reducing the power of those who are governed. The only remedy is strict adherence to the First Amendment guaranteeing free speech. [NOTE: For the other side of the worrisome trend to litigiousness, see below.]
(right to criticize government at risk?)

6948

Lawsuits' Surge Strains Budgets of Many Cities, Robert Lindsey, *The New York Times*, Sunday, 12 May 1985, p1.

Officials of cities around the US say they are being swamped by a surge of multi-million dollar court judgments that are straining their budgets, forcing cutbacks in services and in some cases threatening bankruptcy. Specialists on municipal law estimate that the cost to taxpayers for settling such claims has tripled over the past five years. They attribute the increase to court decisions and legislation in the 1970s broadening city liability in suits involving antitrust, civil rights, and personal injury. New York City has been especially affected by these soaring costs, which rose from $23 million in 1978 to an estimate of $110 million in 1985. In California, local governments are closing libraries and recreation facilities and cutting back on police and fire services to pay the cost of this litigation explosion. Despite complaints about the surge of big judgments against cities, trial lawyers are said to be unlikely to surrender the broader latitude granted them by courts and legislators. There is heavy lobbying by the well-financed trial lawyers, who represent plaintiffs on a contingency basis, frequently getting one-third to one-half of a settlement.   **(rising lawsuits against cities)**

6949

Neighborhood Revitalization and the Postindustrial City: A Multinational Perspective. Dennis E. Gale (School of Government and Business Administration, George Washington U). Lexington MA: Lexington Books, Dec 1984/183p/$22.00.

Neighborhood revitalization in this study refers to the processes by which older, residential urban enclaves are transformed by gentrification and/or apartment conversion. In contrast to the heavy emphasis on public funding of urban renewal programs in the 1950s and 1960s, neighborhood revitalization is a significant departure because it is brought about largely by investing private capital. Typically in the US, UK, Canada, and Australia, gentrification involves the purchase of an older single-family house and its renovation or restoration. Once residential rehabilitation has progressed to the point that a certain critical mass of "gentry" have located there, renovation of commercial buildings usually proceeds. The processes of apartment conversion, although similar, seldom bring the sharp transitions in population or neighborhood environment characteristic of gentrification. Concludes that, at least among the major metro areas, a kind of quadripartite system of central cities will characterize urban America in the early 21st century: 1) cities whose economies have successfully adapted to a white-collar employment base, with residential emphasis remaining in the surrounding suburbs; 2) cities adapting successfully to the postindustrial economy, with revitalization of large areas of their central cores; 3) cities struggling to adapt successfully to the postindustrial economy, while experiencing varying degrees of gentrification and apartment conversion (the large majority of US metro areas); 4) cities that continue to deteriorate and suffer from disinvestment. The benefits of revitalization are likely to be met with more enthusiasm in the US, because neighborhood deterioration has advanced further in many US cities. In every nation in which gentrification and apartment conversion occur, these processes are likely to parallel the continuing shift to a white-collar, postindustrial economy. Political systems will wrestle continuously with the social and economic friction resulting from this class competition for urban space.
(gentrification; apartment conversion)

C. Housing

*6950

No Place to Hide: Crisis and Future of American Habitats. Manuel Marti Jr. Westport CT: Greenwood Press, Sept 1984/245p/$29.95.

Habitats bridge a gap between technology and human nature, reflecting man as an individual and within society. Human shelter was once a refuge from an uncontrollable and hostile world. As mankind started to understand and take advantage of the world's natural components, the concept of shelter changed from temporary refuge to permanent dwellings that eventually expanded in large settlements. The increased integration of techno-scientific elements and conditions within edifices in recent decades has caused a relative dehumanization of built environments. In the future, it is quite possible that there may be no place left for man to retreat to.

Marti discusses the conditions that define interactions of social, economic, and technical factors, and considers the basic factors likely to structure the future evolution of buildings and communities. In a flourishing economy, habitats would improve in quality and durability, and households would increase their use of appliances and electronic equipment. A declining economy would reduce the proportion of detached single family dwellings, delay building improvements and urban renewal projects, and increase the number of do-it-yourself features in habitats. Economic decline might also force an upswing in shared ownership arrangements and cause the gradual disappearance of small builders, while giving birth to corporate mega-builders and standardized building types. Some other possibilities: 1) the gradual abandonment of existing utility systems as electric toilets and efficient water recirculating systems are developed; 2) a worldwide land crisis sometime in the early 21st century, forcing vertical urban growth, above and underground; 3) a probable boom in home entertainment centers, facilitated by the widespread use of computers and other electronic devices; 4) bathrooms are likely to evolve into complex health and hygiene support units; 5) as shelters diminish in size, beds may be stored vertically or evolve into sleep capsules with environmental, sleep/awakening, and therapeutic controls; 6) increased work-at-home patterns could encourage mobile "work module" units that "plug" into dwellings for indefinite periods of time; 7) new building materials such as electrolysis processes that "grow" underwater structures and sprayed plastic molecules that solidify in contact with light. It is cautioned, however, that building construction reality rarely follows long-range forecasts, as many attractive innovations encounter various forms of resistance. Wall-size video screens are possible, for example, but may not be found desirable. [NOTE: A wide-ranging but sometimes rambling overview of habitats in time and space, blending empirical fact with visionary promise. Useful companion to the WFS anthology, below.]

(future of habitats)

6951

Habitats Tomorrow: Homes and Communities in an Exciting New Era. Edited by Edward Cornish (President, WFS). Bethesda MD: World Future Society, 1984/160p(8x11")/$6.95pb.

Selections from *The Futurist* on the computerized home, videotex in the electronic household, electronic money and home banking, the declining size of new houses, a new

type of city for an energy-short world, human-scale technology to solve urban problems (options for waste management, personal rapid transit), the future of older central cities, characteristics of a low-waste society, the Meadowcreek Project (Fox, Arkansas) as a model sustainable community, appropriate technologies for a small city (Winona, Minnesota), the "Ark" of the New Alchemy Institute (a solar-heated, wind-powered greenhouse and fish pond complex), self-help housing in the US and the Third World, new materials and structural forms, megastructures (gigantic underground complexes, floating cities, massive domes), underground architecture, designing a space village to house 100 workers, and ocean platforms. [NOTE: Grand and exciting visions, a few of which are being slowly realized. A useful contrast to the more sobering survey of what is actually happening, below.]

(futuristic homes and communities)

6952

The Homelessness Problem, Ellen L. Bassuk (Harvard Medical School), *Scientific American*, 251:1, July 1984, 40-45.

More Americans were homeless in the winter of 1983-84 than at any time since the Great Depression. The Department of Housing and Urban Development estimates that 250,000 to 350,000 are homeless nationwide, but the National Coalition for the Homeless estimated 2.5 million homeless in 1983, an increase of 500,000 over 1982. Government officials and private groups have responded by opening emergency shelters, but only a fraction of those in need are provided for. There are no reliable national data on the homeless, but the population appears to be getting progressively younger, and an increasing number—perhaps a large majority—suffer from mental illness. Factors contributing to the recent swelling of the homeless population include: 1) long-term policy changes in dealing with the mentally ill (deinstitutionalization has led to a patient population at state and county hospitals that is less than one-quarter of its 1955 peak of 559,000); 2) the lack of community mental health centers, halfway houses, and group homes for discharged mental patients (shelters save lives, but the mentally ill need more than just a meal and protection); 3) the dearth of low-cost housing; 4) the recession and unemployment; 5) recent cuts in government benefit payments. The best solution to homelessness is to carry out the aborted plans of the 1963 community mental health law, providing a spectrum of housing options and related health and social services. [NOTE: *U.S. News & World Report* (14 Jan 1985, p55) reports that, by some estimates, the ranks of the homeless are swelling at a rate as high as 10% annually.]

(factors affecting homelessness)

6953

Mobility for the Poor Sought in Housing Plan, John Herbers, *The New York Times*, Sat, 1 June 1985, p1.

The Reagan Administration has sharply reduced Federal aid to restore the cities and all but halted construction of Federally subsidized housing. It is now instituting the first subsidy to be used by the chronically unemployed to move to where the jobs are. The subsidy, in the form of a housing voucher, would help to pay family rent anywhere in the US. A five-year, $1 billion demonstration program began in San Antonio this spring, and is expected to be operating by August 1985 in 20 cities and states. Administration officials hope that in the 1990s, vouchers will replace virtually all Federally assisted housing programs, which now cost about $10 billion a year. The subsidy is tied to people, rather than buildings or places, and is expected to be economical because they use existing housing stock. Some possible problems already being raised by skeptics include: 1) the breakup of black communities and a threat to the political influence of black leaders; 2) the poor cannot afford to buy or rent housing that is vacant; 3) widespread use of vouchers would increase rents; 4) moving the poor into better housing would not do much good in areas that have few entry-level jobs. (**housing vouchers experiment**)

6954

Housing Problems, American Style. *Society*, 21:3, March-April 1984, 18-70.

Eight articles, of which the following are noteworthy. 1) **Chester Hartman** (Institute for Policy Studies) describes a growing percentage of both renters and owners paying an increasing proportion of their incomes for housing, aggravated by low levels of new construction, high rates of new household formation, and increasing investment and speculation in housing as a hedge against inflation. We are rapidly falling behind in our ability to house people decently in satisfying environments at affordable costs. An alternative approach is recommended, involving a "de-commodification" of housing. 2) **George Sternlieb** and **James W. Hughes** (Rutgers U) warn that home ownership in America is beginning to decline as a result of implicit public policies that are altering the shape of the shelter industry. 3) **Richard F. Muth** (Emory U), a member of the President's Commission on Housing in 1981-82, comments on the Commission Report, suggesting that, if poor-quality housing is the result of poverty, we should seek to provide more income rather than better housing for the poor. 4) **Philip L. Clay** and **Bernard J. Frieden** (MIT) also comment on the 1982 Housing Commission Report, and advocate less regulation in the housing industry. The most serious of liberal misconceptions is the belief that new local regulations are important to environmental protection. The net result of protecting the private environment is to make environmental conditions worse for the public at large. (**US housing problems**)

6955

Affordable Housing: New Policies for the Housing and Mortgage Markets. Kenneth T. Rosen (Center for Real Estate and Urban Economics, U of California-Berkeley). A Twentieth Century Fund Report. Cambridge MA: Ballinger, Sept 1984/c168p/$25.00.

Shows how current problems in housing emerged from government policies, why our long-standing national housing goals are obsolete, and how the Federal macropolicy on housing is mismanaged. Proposals concern the efficient use of housing subsidy funds, how to heal the ailing home construction industry, and the proper role of Federal mortgage subsidy programs, tax incentives, and low-interest and long-term mortgage loans.
(**Federal housing and mortgage policy**)

6956

The $100,000 House: Getting Smaller Every Year, David E. Rosenbaum, *The New York Times*, Wed, 1 Aug 1984, A8.

In the past decade, housing prices have increased much faster than incomes. The Commerce Department reported that the average price of a new house was $103,600 in May 1984—the first time ever in six digits. A more significant measure (in that the average price is distorted by a few very expensive homes) is that of the median price for a single-family home, which was $73,300 in May 1984, a rise of more than 6% over the previous year. Ten years ago, the median price was $32,000.

Another *New York Times* article commemorating the $100,000 house (30 June 1984, p1) states that the median price of a new home in May 1984 was $80,900, up from $64,600 in 1980. In 1976, the average American family's monthly home payment came to a quarter of its income; by 1982, it had reached one-third—and it is still rising. [NOTE: Crude but significant indicators, regardless of which price is chosen.] (**fast rise of housing prices**)

6957

The American House, Philip Langdon, *The Atlantic Monthly*, Sept 1984, 45-73.

A survey of how housing has changed in America and ways in which it is getting better and worse. There has been an explosion of variety in housing to correspond with the growing heterogeneity of the population. Home builders are increasingly reverting to historical styles, and a revival of Victorian taste has occurred all over the US—a new picturesque movement quite the opposite of futuristic styles such as Xanadu (**FS Annual 1984**, #6161), which Langdon sees as an outdated vision of the house of the future. Enthusiasm for novel space-age or even organic shapes is virtually dead now, e.g., the failure of the geodesic dome. There are only perhaps 5,000 to 10,000 earth-sheltered or underground homes. At least half a million houses in the US now depend partly on solar energy, and pockets of solar home-building have become well-established. One expert on the future of housing sees the homes of the 1980s focusing on amenities such as intercoms, translucent panels, hot water taps, and spa baths. Some disappointments: there is much discontent about the quality of construction, and new mobile homes—a major source of low income housing—have declined from 576,000 in 1972 to 295,000 in 1983. (**new US housing surveyed**)

6958

Redesigning the American Dream: The Future of Housing, Work and Family Life. Dolores Hayden (Dept of Architecture and Urban Planning, UCLA). NY: W. W. Norton, March 1984/270p/$17.95.

The dream house is a uniquely American form. For the first time in history, a civilization has created a utopian ideal based on the house, rather than the city or the nation. The dream house was designed around a full-time housewife who would provide her man with a haven from the cold public world—but only 12% of households now duplicate this family. The trend in US housing still moves toward the dream, while the trend in population moves steadily away from the breadwinner-housewife couple. The American housing problem is not that average wage earners cannot afford a suburban home, but that they still want this private suburban house—miles from work, day care, and public life—even though it no longer suits their needs. (**dream house as American utopia**)

6959

Condominiums Fade As the Life Style Sours and Deflation Sets in, William Celis III, *The Wall Street Journal*, Tuesday, 16 April 1985, p1.

Many condo owners across the US are now complaining about disappointments with their condo life styles: shabby construction of their homes, lack of privacy, and fights with neighbors and condo associations. Many condos are physically deteriorating, turning into "yuppie tenements." Deflation in condo prices is widespread, and developers and lenders have lost money. (**yuppie tenements?**)

6960

Women and Abandoned Buildings: A Feminist Approach to Housing, Jacqueline Leavitt (UCLA) and Susan Saegert (CUNY Graduate School), *Social Policy*, 15:1, Summer 1984, 32-39.

Increasingly, more women and female-headed households are to be found in the lowest income groups, and thus are dependent on subsidized housing. Low-income cooperative housing, however, offers the possibility of home ownership, reduced costs of construction, and control over the living environment. Based on recent feminist theory and research, the authors believe that low-income women should seize upon tenant cooperatives not only to preserve their own homes, but to make a more homelike world. Women interviewed in the NYC Tenant Interim Lease Program were shown to extend their care outward to the building and its residents, and often the community. The personal and intensive nature of their approach contrasts with the impersonal, standardized, and efficiency-oriented strategies embedded in most housing policies.

(cooperative housing for poor women)

6961

Home Security Sales Are Surging, Despite Concern Over Effectiveness, Edwin A. Finn Jr, *The Wall Street Journal*, Wed, 24 Oct 1984, p35.

One out of 11 US households had a professionally installed burglar alarm in 1984, up from one household in 83 in 1978. By 1990, nearly one out of five households will own a burglar alarm. Despite questions about effectiveness, and the bevy of false alarms that drive cops and neighbors crazy, residential security is becoming a big business. Technical innovations including smoke and fire detectors may bring sophisticated systems within the price range of middle-class families (less than $1000). But this booming industry also points to a worrisome fortress mentality in many homes. **(burglar alarm sales up)**

D. Transportation

*6962

The Future of the Automobile: The Report of MIT's International Automobile Program. Alan Altshuler (NYU), Daniel Roos (Center for Transportation Studies, MIT), *et al.* Cambridge MA: MIT Press, Sept 1984/321p/ $16.95.

An intensive four-year study involving researchers and industry experts in the seven auto-producing nations in an examination of the industry over the next 20 years and the demand for its product. It appears that no energy shortages or environmental threats will halt automobility in the time frame under study—if automotive technology continues to address problems in a timely manner. Fuel prices may well rise over the next 20 years, but the auto industry has had ample warning and stands well prepared to deal with this situation, primarily through new technologies to reduce fuel consumption. The world demand for new automobiles and commercial vehicles is expected to grow from 41.3 million in 1979 to 51.2 million in 1990 and 66.7 million in 2000, with total vehicle ownership rising from 396 million to 679 million in the 21 year period. This 62% increase in total output means that the motor vehicle industry "is almost certain to continue as the world's largest manufacturing enterprise." The auto industry has evolved over the past 100 years through a series of dramatic transformations. The first of these was the breakthrough by US producers around 1910 from custom building to a mass-volume industry. The second occurred in Europe in the 1950s, when producers emphasized product differentiation to challenge US production. The third commenced in the late 1960s, when Japanese auto producers made dramatic breakthroughs in production organization that yielded a lower-cost product of high quality. A fourth transformation may take place in the late 1980s, as the world outside the three auto-producing regions accounts for a growing share of the total world auto market, while insisting on local production for its markets.

Only a few years ago, the conventional wisdom about the future of the auto industry was that intense pressure for energy conservation and environmental protection would make the small "world car" the standard-size vehicle in all world auto markets, that six "mega-producers" would coalesce out of the 20 final assemblers in the Western world (leading to a world oligopoly), and that manufacturing would shift from the developed countries to the LDCs. The MIT Auto Program found these beliefs to be far from the mark because of four important factors: 1) the introduction of micro-processor controlled production methods, enabling increasingly smaller economies of scale for individual product lines; 2) new product technologies enabling a wider range of "sensible" vehicles; 3) the perfection of a new system of social organization of the production process (in response to Japanese innovations on the shop floor, the supplier chain, and the financial system); 4) the failure of the world's auto purchasers to demand a single size and type of car. These four factors create a new shape for the auto industry that is quite different from the one widely forecasted. Because of strong restraints on entry and exit, there are likely to be as many automakers 20 years from now as today. Indeed, the declining minimum efficient scale in manufacturing will give the medium-size and specialist producers a more level field on which to compete. Few if any new names will be added to the end-of-century list of assemblers because of the very large initial investment. All companies will have competitive strengths (in some instances because of nationality and production location), and all will have competitive weaknesses. The world system of auto production will be highly dynamic for decades to come, with tendencies toward copying, collaboration, and labor-force contraction.

(evolution of world auto industry)

6963

Technological Trends in Automobiles, Emmett J. Horton and W. Dale Compton (Ford Motor Co, Dearborn MI), *Science*, Vol 225, 10 Aug 1984, 587-593.

Current technological trends in the automotive industry reflect many high-technology disciplines involving electronics and microprocessors, new engine transmission concepts, composite and ceramic materials, and computer-aided design and manufacture. An "average" vehicle of the late 1990s could be a four- or five-passenger model in the 2000-pound inertia weight class, with an aerodynamic drag coefficient of 0.20 or less. Its fiber and plastic composite body panels, assembled by adhesive bonding, would ride on an electronically controlled suspension system, with the driver selecting either a boulevard ride or a stiffer ride more appropriate for freeway cruising. Electronics would control a turbocharged, ceramic, diesel engine and continuously variable transmission to provide smooth, effortless performance and fuel economy in excess of 100 miles per gallon on the highway. (The appearance of such a vehicle, however, will depend strongly on the price of fuel, and increased vehicle costs should be weighed against savings in fuel cost.) The vehicle's fully electronic instrument panel will provide the driver with constant monitoring of all vehicle and power train operating conditions, and the on-board diagnostic system would warn of impending or actual malfunctioning. A push of the button would pinpoint the vehicle's position on the highway, and provide guidance instructions and suggestions for safe, quick, and economical operation. **(100 mpg car by late 1990s?)**

6964

An Inside Look At Cars of the '90s, U.S. News & World Report, 10 Sept 1984, 49-50.

The automobiles of the 1990s will be sleeker, smarter, safer, and sexier than anything on the road today. Some of the new features include aerodynamic styling, retractable headlights, the disappearance of chrome, navigation sensors that show a car's position on computerized maps displayed on a dashboard screen, electronically controlled suspension systems, four-wheel steering (allowing far tighter turning in parking and improved stability in high-speed turns), brake systems governed by computers, dent-resistant body panels made from polyurethane, fuel cells (gas tanks composed of honeycomb-like compartments) that could reduce crash fires, keyless door and ignition locks that respond to computerized passwords, more comfortable seats made of foam and plastics, and sensors that warn of impending brake failure or worn engine belts. By 2000, acceptance of high-tech electronics and aerodynamic styling will be as commonplace as automatic transmissions today. **(auto technologies of the 1990s)**

6965

Why Motorists Won't Buckle Up, Stephen Engelberg, *The New York Times,* Wed, 26 Sept 1984, C1.

For many American motorists, the decision not to wear seat belts is a way to deny the risks of driving. Self-deception takes many forms, including faulty perceptions of vulnerability, poor assessments of accident risks, and belief in the false notion that being belted is dangerous in the aftermath of a crash (in fact, the chances of being killed in a crash increase 25 times if an occupant flies from a vehicle). Despite a two-year campaign by the Federal government and an independent effort by auto manufacturers, fewer than 15% of Americans wear seat belts when they drive. This is a slight increase from the all-time low of 11% in 1980-81, but far from the 90% rates in countries such as Britain, whose laws require seat belt use. Voluntary programs will probably never get higher than 25% compliance in the US. Transportation Secretary Elizabeth Dole is now urging states to enact mandatory seat belt laws, but recent Canadian experience offers only modest support for this action. Since the late 1970s, when four provinces mandated belting up, usage more than doubled, reaching 50% in Ontario and Saskatchewan, 55% in British Columbia, and 68% in Quebec. But fatalities fell only 11%, with injuries dropping only 6%. [NOTE: Any connection between the proclivity of Americans to deny individual auto accidents and "It can't happen here" denial of major collective dangers such as earthquake, nuclear war, and economic collapse?] **(mandatory seat belt laws in US?)**

6966

Flights of Imagination, William D. Marbach, *Newsweek,* 10 Sept 1984, 72-74.

Virtually all of today's front-line military and civilian aircraft are based on technologies developed several decades ago. Faced with new demands for high performance

at low cost, aircraft designers are now taking major risks to make spectacular advances. Grumman is developing the X-29 fighter with wings swept forward in a radically new design. The tilt-rotor JVX, being developed for the Navy and Marine Corps, will look and work like a cross between a helicopter and a plane. Sikorsky is working on an X-wing aircraft that would lift off like a helicopter and then freeze the rotor in place, forming an X-shaped wing. The Air Force is exploring the concept of a transatmospheric vehicle: a 21st century plane that would enter space briefly for transcontinental flight at hypersonic speeds; if successful, it would cut the 17-hour trip from Los Angeles to Australia to under 90 minutes. Many designs now on the drawing boards depend on advances in materials, electronics, and computer technologies. Composites (epoxy resins reinforced with Kevlar or glass fibers) are likely to be crucial in the next generation of airframes: they are as much as 25% lighter than aluminum and seven times as strong as steel, and they are more aerodynamically efficient because they can be made without rivets and joints. Today's integrated circuits make it possible to build "fly-by-wire" controls, allowing flight in ways not allowed by conventional controls. Researchers are also working on computerized controls that will vary the shape of an airplane's wings to suit maneuvering requirements. **(new aircraft technology)**

6967

The Shape of Wings to Come, Sandy Burns (British Aerospace), *New Scientist,* 12 April 1984, 32-35.

On wing design of future aircraft, which should result in better cruising economy for commercial airlines. Concludes that supersonic transports will be revived again, taking advantage of recent advances in aerodynamic design and structural materials. The new supersonics will probably cruise at Mach 2.5, carry 250 to 300 passengers, and bring about a steep increase in productivity resulting in lower transglobal fares. **(new supersonic aircraft)**

6968

Deregulation and the New Airline Entrepreneurs. John R. Meyer (Harvard U) and Clinton V. Oster, Jr (Indiana U). Cambridge MA: MIT Press, Nov 1984/256p/ $22.50.

Deregulation in the airline industry has spurred a major growth in entrepreneurs competing with established carriers. Developments in two areas are examined: commuter airlines using small prop-driven aircraft for short-haul service in low density markets, and jet-equipped carriers (e.g., PEOPLExpress, New York Air, Southwest Airlines) offering no-frills services and low fares in short to medium hauls. These carriers have played significant roles in rationalizing service to small communities, broadening the range of fare and service offerings, improving productivity, and lowering cost structures. Chapters cover such topics as commuter airline safety, financial and competitive strategies, the role of Federal subsidy in small community service, and airline industry structure and public policy. **(new air carriers)**

6969

Airport System Development. U.S. Congress, Office of Technology Assessment. Washington DC: USGPO, Aug 1984/$7.50 (S/N 052-003-00960-9). Summary copies free from OTA.

Lack of capacity at major US airports, notably during peak travel periods and adverse weather, is a significant cause of delay and rising costs. In most cities, it is impractical to build new airports to absorb growing demand, due to scarcity of land, high development costs, and community concern about noise and land use. It is unlikely that more than one or two major new airports will be built before 2000. This study examines possible approaches to increase capacity and reduce delay at existing airports. Technological methods include more accurate radar use, more precise guidance for landing, improved air traffic control systems, and methods to detect wind shear. If coupled with reduced aircraft separation standards and revised rules for use of multiple runways, these technologies could increase capacity by as much as 30% at some airports during adverse weather, but, on average, only by 5% to 10%. Other approaches include: 1) separate small runways for small aircraft at major airports; 2) setting landing fees according to time of day or level of demand; 3) regulatory action to limit the number or type of flights; 4) retargeting Federal funds to shift responsibilities to state and local levels. The major finding with regard to planning is the need to look at airports from a regional and multi-modal perspective, seeking ways to weld them into the overall transportation network. [NOTE: In the long run, growing airport congestion may force serious consideration of a transnational maglev rail system, described below.]

(airport system capacity)

6970

Propelling Passengers Faster Than a Speeding Bullet, Hans Alscher (West Germany), Ion F. Boldea (Rumania), Anthony R. Eastham (Queens U, Ontario), and Mazakasu Iguchi (U of Tokyo), *IEEE Spectrum,* 21:8, Aug 1984, 57-64.

In May 1984, magnetic-levitation cars began carrying passengers between the Birmingham (England) airport and the city's railway station. The short (625 meter) route is the first of several urban maglev railways that will begin commercial service in the next few years. (A chart depicts 13 maglev projects worldwide: 6 in Japan, 4 in West Germany, and one each in Rumania, England, and the US.) The technology for faster maglev trains that could travel between cities at 180 to 300mph has been researched in many countries and is in an advanced stage of development in West Germany and Japan. Canadian officials are considering the Toronto-Montreal corridor for a 450km/h system that could be commercially successful early in the 21st century. A 1978 Rand study (*Futures,* Oct 1978; **FS Annual 1979,** #1079) suggests the possibility of transcontinental travel across the US in less than an hour, and global systems that would enable passengers to travel cheaply and conveniently between any two major cities in the world in 90 minutes or less. The big advantage of magnetic levitation is that it overcomes a major limitation of wheels: loss of traction at high speed. Maglev vehicles are quiet, dependable, safe (they cannot derail or topple from a guideway), and economical to operate. A trip on a maglev vehicle could consume about one-quarter of the energy per passenger-mile of a trip on an airplane. Despite these advantages, maglev has not been implemented before now because of the huge capital investment. But as conventional rail, auto, and air links become saturated in their passenger-carrying capacity, and as fuel costs rise, many countries will begin planning for maglev systems.   **(maglev railways)**

6971

Rolling Nowhere, David M. Stewart, *Inquiry: A Libertarian Review,* 7:7, July 1984, 18-23.

The current boom in public mass-transit depends on gold-plated, high-tech versions of antique transportation systems. Nearly 30 US cities have new rail systems or bus tunnels in construction or in planning. Yet, ridership has declined from 19 billion passenger trips in 1945 to 5 to 6 billion trips in recent years. New rail systems face construction cost overruns and immense operating losses. The benefits of mass transit are either negligible or wholly illusory, and cardinal tenets of transit orthodoxy are examined in areas of energy, urban population density, urban development, ridership, and traffic congestion and pollution. Concludes that it would be better to allow transportation markets to develop freely. A wide variety of vehicles and routes would seem chaotic from a planner's Godlike point of view, but it would serve consumers better than the superficial "rationality" and "efficiency" of collective transit. [Also see ***Mass Transit: The Expensive Dream*** (cover story), *Business Week*, 27 Aug 1984, 62-69, on chronic cost overruns and giant operating deficits.]

(mass transit criticized)

XI. JUSTICE

A. Criminal Justice Overviews

6972

Law and Disorder: Criminal Justice in America. Bruce Jackson (Director, Center for Studies in American Culture, SUNY-Buffalo). Urbana, IL: U of Illinois Press, Dec 1984/324p/$19.95.

Describes how criminal justice agencies really work and how they make their decisions about what work to do. These decisions have little to do with the efficiency of the organizations at catching, convicting, or punishing criminals. They have even less to do with how well or badly the public is protected. Criminal justice workers select the discretionary options that simplify their bureaucratic functioning. Justice is seldom a basic concern; rather, getting through the workload exhausts the imagination and consumes the days. Justice is a time-consuming luxury, so the system floats on a swamp of compromise. Perhaps of all agencies in society, criminal justice is least capable of dealing with the causes of crime, because the roots of crime lie almost entirely beyond the areas of activity of any criminal justice agency. Some crime will always occur, but much crime can be obliterated by abolishing the conditions that make it necessary or reasonable. Our criminal justice machinery must, of course, be as efficient and as decent as possible. But using it to fight the war against crime commits us to fighting the wrong war in the wrong place. Until we understand that these institutions at best help us cope marginally, they will continue to seem to betray us, and we will continue to be crippled by and with them.

(criminal justice system examined)

6973

A Capacity to Punish: The Ecology of Crime and Punishment. Henry N. Pontell (U of California-Irvine). Bloomington IN: Indiana U Press, March 1984 / 140p/ $19.50;$9.95pb.

The control of crime is one of the most important social issues of our time. Our society is marked by increasing suspicion, anxiety, and paranoia over the fear of being criminally victimized—especially among the elderly and poor. But when the criminal justice system grows, so does the crime problem. A larger system allows greater opportunities for crime to be officially recorded; in turn, we react by further enlarging the system. We typically rely on the criminal justice system to do more than it is capable of doing. Creating more laws and legislating harsher punishments have not solved the crime problem. Crime is more a function of diverse social-psychological and social-structural phenomena than it is of legal sanctions. Punishment is most likely to be effective in deterring crime when it is needed the least—where crime rates are already low. Current criminal justice practices, especially the extremely low probability of certain and severe punishment, indicate that the deterrent efficacy of punishment is likely to be minimal. Increasing the state's capacity to punish is an expensive and negative strategy that will fail unless concomitant efforts are made to improve social conditions. [NOTE: A similar opinion is offered by Richard Moran (Mt. Holyoke College), who suggests that the more crime there is the less we are able to punish it, and that prolonged incarceration is not cost-effective (*Newsweek*, 7 May 1984, p22).]

(crime and punishment)

6974

Myths That Cause Crime. Harold E. Pepinsky and Paul Jesilow (both Dept of Forensic Studies, Indiana U). Cabin John MD: Seven Locks Press (7425 MacArthur Blvd), Sept 1984/170p/$13.95.

If it is the government's business to reduce crime, it must concentrate not so much on law enforcement but on action to strengthen communities and make them secure. To do this, Americans have to overcome some basic myths about crime. Criminal justice policy and practice is built on a centuries-old body of assumptions—much of it nonsense—that many leading criminologists still propagate. The major myths discussed are: 1) Crime is increasing—crime statistics only indicate the willingness of people to have incidents managed by criminal justice officials; 2) Most crime is committed by the poor—the poor get into trouble with the law far more than the rich, but it appears that the rich unlawfully hurt their fellow citizens far more than the poor do; 3) Some groups are more law-abiding than others—no group is immune, and the criminality encouraged by the structure of medical care is discussed; 4) White-collar crime is non-violent—it turns out that white-collar and organizational crimes kill far more people than street criminals through legal drugs, unnecessary surgery, unsafe working conditions, etc.; 5) Regulatory agencies prevent white-collar crime—even when victims and agencies are aware of criminality (which most often they are not), regulatory effectiveness is impaired by numerous factors; 6) Rich and poor are equal before the law—rather, the wealthy have the capacity to protect themselves against prosecution, and the invisibility of their crimes prevents detection; 7) Drug addiction causes crime—the criminalization of the addict does more harm than good; 8) Community corrections is a viable alternative; 9) The punishment can fit the crime—punishment cannot be made to do so, and societies that generate punishment generate crime; 10) Law makes people behave—greater resort to criminal justice is a sign that social ties are unreliable. Concludes that the single most important contribution American government can make to domestic peace and security is the creation of meaningful and responsible jobs: opportunity to do work that others appreciate is the social control measure best suited to making people behave civilly toward one another. Government should also change its pattern of investment away from protection of wealthy vested interests toward increasing the security and welfare of the general populace.

(myths causing crime)

*6975

Sense and Nonsense About Crime: A Policy Guide. Samuel Walker (U of Nebraska-Omaha). Monterey CA: Brooks/Cole Publishing Co, Jan 1985/229p/$10.50pb.

Crime overwhelms us, and affects how we think, how we act, and how we behave toward one another. The crime problem overwhelms our thinking as well. Our crime policy is intellectually bankrupt—at present, we have no credible set of policies to reduce our persistently high levels of crime. Instead we are offered a series of desperate nostrums promising quick and easy solutions; virtually all of them will not work and many are positively dangerous. This book is about what we can do to reduce crime, focusing on the simple question of what works. Over the past 15 years, the "research revolution" in criminal justice offers a substantial and growing body of literature on how the criminal justice system works, as well as the effectiveness of various alternatives. Walker examines various conservative proposals to "get tough," as well as liberal prescriptions for system reform and individual rehabilitation, and sets forth his conclusions in light of the evidence in the form of various propositions, e.g.: 1) most current crime control proposals are nonsense; 2) both liberals and conservatives are guilty of peddling nonsense about crime (conservative ideas appear fresh today partly because they have not been fully tested); 3) most crime control proposals rest on faith rather than facts (thinking of crime control policy as theology helps us to explain the dogged tenacity of various ideas); 4) preventive detention will not reduce violent crime; 5) selective incapacitation is not a realistic policy for reducing serious crime; 6) mandatory sentencing has no significant impact on serious crime; 7) more use of the death penalty will not reduce crime; 8) adding more police will not reduce crime; 9) career criminal prosecution programs will not produce lower crime rates (we are already tough on so-called career criminals); 10) abolishing or restricting the use of the insanity defense will have absolutely no effect on serious crime; 11) current gun control proposals do not offer realistic hope for significantly reducing violent crime in the near future; 12) neither the improvement nor the abolition of parole will reduce serious crime; 13) social tinkering (i.e., the programs of the 1960s) will not reduce the level of serious crime.

Concludes that we are at a loss for an effective crime reduction program, and the best criminological minds of our time do not have anything practical to offer. We already punish rather severely those major offenders whom we succeed in catching. There do not appear to be any realistic prospects for improving the rate of apprehension. All of our criminal justice institutions resist dramatic change. And criminal offenders do not respond to our attempts to manipulate their behavior by adjusting various penalties and opportunities. But this discouraging picture does not mean that we are completely helpless in the face of our seemingly high level of serious crime. Some fundamental and long-held insights still remain as valid as ever, i.e. that serious delinquency and adult criminality are overly concentrated among the poor. A genuine anticrime program can thus begin only by creating real economic opportunity. Direct assaults to change the criminal justice system are futile. We can only strike back at crime indirectly, by attacking economic opportunity directly. People are capable of taking care of themselves if they have an opportunity to do so. All we have to do is act on it. [NOTE: Fresh, feisty, authoritative—and quite readable. A useful companion to the Violence Commission update (#6976), with similar conclusions.] **(bankruptcy of crime policy)**

*6976
American Violence and Public Policy: An Update of the National Commission on the Causes and Prevention of Violence. Edited by Lynn A. Curtis (President, The Eisenhower Foundation). New Haven CT: Yale U Press, March 1985/263p/$23.00.

Shortly after the assassination of Senator Robert Kennedy in 1968, a National Commission on the Causes and Prevention of Violence was established. Chaired by Milton S. Eisenhower, it issued its final report in 1969. The Violence Commission followed closely on the heels of two other presidential commissions that overlapped in scope and had similar philosophies: the 1966-67 President's Commission on Law Enforcement and the Administration of Justice (chaired by Nicholas deB. Katzenbach), and the 1967-68 National Advisory Commission on Civil Disorders (chaired by Governor Otto Kerner). This volume seeks to update the main policy conclusions of the Violence Commission, as well as consonant recommendations of the Katzenbach and Kerner Commissions.

In 1969, the Violence Commission concluded that the US was the clear leader among modern democratic nations in its rates of homicide, assault, rape, and robbery. Violent crime has continued to increase, reaching its highest levels in 1981 and 1982. In 1981, there were 3,461 seriously violent offenders for every 100,000 Americans, compared to 1,972 such offenders in 1969. And the level of crime in the US remains astronomical when compared to that in other democratic nations. Moreover, the level of fear of crime remains at least as high today as in the 1960s. Minorities are disproportionately involved as both offenders and victims. Today, the chance of becoming a victim of violent crime is greater than the risk of being in an automobile accident or of dying from cancer. As for political violence, the threat remains; what has changed since the Violence Commission reports is the frequency of terrorism, which is expected to continue.   The core statement of the 1969 Violence Commission concluded that: "To be a young, poor male; to be undereducated and without means of escape from an oppressive urban environment; to want what the society claims is available (but mostly to others); to see around oneself illegitimate and often violent methods being used to achieve material success; and to observe others using these means with impunity—all this is to be burdened with an enormous set of influences that pull many toward crime and delinquency." A similar observation lay behind the Kerner Commission's conclusion that we consist of two societies, black and white, separate and unequal. The central message of this volume is that the criminal justice system merely reacts to crime and cannot do much to prevent it. We need to continue improving the equity and efficiency of the criminal justice system. But massive new investments will not reduce our historically high levels of crime. Rather, the consensus recommendation, based on two decades of empirical research, program evaluations, practical experience, and political feasibility, can be summarized as "neighborhood, family, and employment." Or, as phrased by one of the contributors to this volume, "we will never be able to mop the water off the floor unless we turn off the faucet that is causing the tub to overflow."

A framework of "neighborhood, family, and employment" promises a new departure that avoids the limitations of deterrence, the shortcomings of incapacitation, and the naivete of past social reform. It is also politically feasible, offering some common ground among those who would mobilize youth or create community action, and those who want people to pull themselves up by their bootstraps. More specifically, we must demonstrate ways in which indigenous inner-city organizations can take the lead in reducing crime and fear, how extended families and other personal support networks can be a crucial source of support for minority youth, and how the employment of minority youth can lead to the reduction of crime. But to have any significant impact on crime and fear, neighborhood-based crime prevention, and the employment and family programs that can be integrated with it, need a nationally coordinated policy for both public and private sectors. [NOTE: An important rethinking of official recommendations, but will our leaders get the message?]

(1969 Violence Commission updated)

6977

Fighting Violent Crime in America. Ronald S. Lauder (Deputy Assistant Secretary of Defense). NY: Dodd, Mead & Co, May 1985/241p/$16.95.

A businessman (former Chairman, Estee Lauder International) advocates applying to the fight against crime the same successful business techniques and advanced technology used by the best-run American corporations, combined with entrepreneurial sense and decency. Chapters are devoted to the subteen criminal, juvenile predators, juveniles and the courts, the adult criminal, prisons and other options, women criminals, victims and restitution, and the role of volunteers. Proposals include a "computer czar" to oversee the US fight against crime, computer profiles to predict and identify criminal patterns in repeat offenders, computers to locate policemen and civilian crime watchers, facilities to keep juveniles out of prisons inhabited by hardened criminals, ending most probation for juveniles and putting released manpower and money into family counseling, removing from the streets the minuscule number of young predator criminals from 13 to 17 who commit much of our violent crime, more halfway houses and intensive job programs as a less expensive alternative to building new prisons, releasing most women prisoners to free up space for males warranting incarceration, more Federal funding for state plans to compensate victims of crime, restitution by criminals to their victims in every case where it is practical (if a crime is serious enough, everything an offender has when he goes to prison should be put into a restitution or compensation fund), and financial support to local efforts such as neighborhood watches and the Guardian Angels.

(reducing violent crime)

6978

Crime: How It Destroys, What Can Be Done, Roger Starr (Editorial Board, *NYT*), *The New York Times Magazine*, 27 Jan 1985, 18ff.

Author of **The Rise and Fall of New York City** (Basic Books, 1985) reports that a siege mentality has changed the pattern of lives of many city dwellers and has raised new problems for the cities themselves. The criminals involved in today's random violence are themselves different, with far greater resources than their predecessors. The new elements of modern random crime threaten the very principle of city life, for nothing is more dangerous to the web of urban living than the fear that prevents people from assembling. Fighting back and saving the cities involves at least nine priorities: 1) each city must concentrate anti-crime efforts on its most strategic target (in the case of NYC, the subways); 2) the public must see that in the prime target area, no breach of law is so trivial that it can be ignored (in NYC, subway tribunals would hear cases against turnstile jumpers, graffiti writers, litterers, etc.); 3) new ways must be found to coordinate the various kinds of police forces, even if they must each give up some autonomy; 4) civic leadership should organize across race and ethnic lines in support of a crime fight; 5) a sentencing procedure is needed to deter young delinquents from becoming career criminals, and crimes should be punished in relation to the criminal's past record; 6) the criminal court system must be expanded and its procedures simplified; 7) new incentives must be found to recruit good candidates for police work (e.g., a police corps of young people who would sign up for a limited period of police or corrections work); 8) civic organizations to observe judges in action and evaluate them for the general public; 9) support by all for efforts of leaders in the current crime-prone

population (blacks and Hispanics) to strengthen family structure and educate the young. [NOTE: Curiously, nothing is said about providing opportunities for youth employment (see #85-383).]   **(saving cities from crime)**

6979

Money and Justice: Who Owns the Courts? Judge Lois G. Forer (Court of Common Pleas, Philadelphia). NY: W.W. Norton & Co, June 1984/244p/$16.95.

There are two separate and unequal systems of justice in the US: one for the rich in which the courts take limitless time to examine an abundance of evidence; the other for the poor, in which hasty guilty pleas and brief hearings are the rule and appeals are the exception. These two spheres are reinforced by a de facto divison of the legal profession into two tracks: the fast-track corporation lawyer is typically drawn from a private liberal arts college and a prestige law school; the slow-track solo lawyers come from low-status families and are graduates of the less prestigious law schools. Federal judges are largely appointed from the first group; state judges from the latter. Although the American system provides more safeguards for accused persons than the legal system of any other country, these carefully enunciated rights are a cruel hoax for most poor people. The situation is worsening with the widening disparity between the systems of justice accorded rich and poor (in part aggravated by Reagan Administration curbs to the Legal Services Corporation, a chief source of legal support for poor people). Possible remedies include abolishing all court filing fees, requiring litigants to reimburse court costs if a claim or defense is frivolous, enabling every poor litigant the right to counsel of choice at government expense, and alternative and cheaper forms of dispute resolution. [Also see "Lawyers for the Poor" by Ronald F. Pollack, *The New York Times* (Op-Ed), 17 June 1983, which points to a similar widening disparity and proposes a loan forgiveness program for low-income law school students who commit themselves to working 2 to 3 years with legal services programs.]   **(dual justice system)**

6980

Juvenile Justice Policy: Analyzing Trends and Outcomes. Edited by Scott H. Decker. Beverly Hills CA: Sage Publications, Jan 1984/168p/$20.00;$8.95pb.

Major policy revisions of the past two decades—characterized by jurisdiction shifts and various diversion programs—have added layers of confusion onto an already complex juvenile justice system. These essays consider an historical analysis of policy formulation, the utility of multi-goal evaluation, the effect of proposed changes in court jurisdiction, likely consequences of removing status offender jurisdiction, and whether or not diversion produces an unintended expansion of the number of youths under judicial control. [Also see **Western Systems of Juvenile Justice,** edited by Malcolm W. Klein (Sage, Jan 1984/240p/$25.00), which describes policies of eight Western nations.] **(juvenile justice)**

6981

New Crime Act A Vast Change, Experts Assert, Stuart Taylor Jr, *The New York Times*, Monday, 15 Oct 1984, p1.

A package of anti-crime legislation with more than 50 provisions was signed into law by President Reagan on October 12. Attorney General William French Smith called the package "the most far-reaching and substantial reform of the criminal justice system in our history." Many experts agree, also noting that the bail and sentencing provisions will probably have a greater effect than all the rest combined. The new bail law marks the first time in peacetime history that Federal law has explicitly authorized detention without bail of allegedly dangerous defendants in cases other than murder. Such preventive detention is already allowed in about half the states, but is invoked sporadically. Civil libertarians contend that this will result in imprisonment of innocent people without reducing crime. The sentencing provisions seek standard penalties or determinate sentencing for each offense, with the elimination of early releases on parole. The anti-crime package also includes curbs on the insanity defense, wider authority to seize the property of convicted drug dealers, outlawing the unauthorized use of computers in gaining access to national security data, and a $100 million fund to aid victims of Federal offenses. These provisions affect only Federal law, not the state laws under which 95% of all crimes are prosecuted. (**new Federal anti-crime legislation**)

6982

Visions of Social Control: Crime, Punishment and Classification. Stanley Cohen (Hebrew U of Jerusalem). Cambridge UK: Polity Press (dist by Basil Blackwell), April 1985/325p/$39.95;$11.95pb.

There have been two transformations—one transparent, the other opaque, one real, the other eventually illusory— in the master patterns and strategies for controlling deviance in Western industrial societies. The response appears under such terms as punishment, deterrence, treatment, prevention; the people to whom the response is directed are seen variously as villains, fools, rebels, monsters, victims; those who respond are known as judges, police, social workers, psychologists, etc. The first transformation, beginning in the late 18th century, encompasses growing involvement of the state in deviancy control, growing differentiation and classification of deviant and dependent groups into separate types and categories, increasing segregation of deviants into various institutions, and decline of punishment involving public infliction of physical pain. Beginning in the 1960s, the massively entrenched transformations of the 19th century began to be attacked, taking the form of a profound destructuring impulse: away from the state (decentralization, deformalization, diversion), away from the expert (deprofessionalization, demedicalization, delegalization), away from the institution (toward open institutions and more community control), and away from the mind (an impatience with individual treatment or rehabilitation). But there is a major gap between the rhetoric of the destructuring movement and the reality of the emerging deviancy control system. Rather than any destructuring, the original structures have become stronger, the reach and intensity of state control has been increased, centralization and bureaucracy remain, and professions and experts are proliferating dramatically. The new methods are not always much cheaper and not necessarily any more humane. The alternatives have merely left us with wider, stronger, and different nets.

(**deviancy control: the real changes**)

B. Counting and Watching Crime

6983

Justice for All: Why Crime Rates Are Falling for the Third Straight Year, Lisa Schiffren (*The Detroit News*), *Policy Review*, No. 32, Spring 1985, 56-57.

Crime in America is the single greatest domestic threat to life, liberty, and the pursuit of happiness. Although crime increased over 300% between 1960 and 1980, the good news is that it has gone down some and should continue to do so. There are three main reasons for the recent decline in crime rates: 1) the demographic explanation that much serious crime is committed by the shrinking age cohort of young males (but we will see a resurgence of crime in the early 1990s when the "echo-boom" generation hits their mid-teens); 2) twice as many people are in prison today as ten years ago, thus keeping career criminals from victimizing the public; 3) public attitudes toward crime and the police have changed, and at least 20% of the US is currently covered by some type of neighborhood crime watch program. But the demographic downturn won't last, and economic resources are finite. A long-term strategy will thus require some innovation. The most promising new idea among professionals is "selective incapacitation": the early prediction of high-rate offenders so that the criminal justice system can effectively isolate them from society. (**crime rate decline explained**)

6984

Robbers Keep Hitting 6,000 Banks Each Year Despite Few Successes, Barry Schiffman, *The Wall Streeet Journal*, Friday, 26 April 1985, p1.

Bank robberies have soared in the past decade, partly because of increased drug abuse. After peaking at 7,000 in 1981, the number has leveled off at about 6,000 a year (nearly a quarter of these robberies taking place in Los Angeles). Before this surge in robberies, the annual figure was about 2,500 in the early 1970s and in the hundreds in the 1950s. The typical perpetrator in the 1980s is younger and more likely to be black than the robbers of the 1960s. Robbers are apt to be narcotics users looking for big scores, with their judgment clouded by drug use. About 75% to 80% of robbers are apprehended, and the odds against successful bank robberies widen as security precautions improve. [NOTE: White-collar robbery is, of course, another category!]

(**bank robberies more than doubled since 1970s**)

6985

Stealing $200 Billion 'The Respectable Way', U.S. *News & World Report*, 20 May 1985, 83-85.

Experts estimate that white-collar criminals rake in a minimum of $200 billion annually, far overshadowing the $11 billion cost of violent crimes. Many offenses go undetected, while others are swept under the rug by corporations or consumers too embarassed to report their losses. Economic crime is rife because the rewards are high and the risks of detection (as well as penalties when caught) are low. While white-collar crime is proliferating, Federal authorities are spending less time investigating it than they did five years ago, emphasizing drugs and organized crime instead. State and local law enforcers, overburdened with street crime, don't have the resources to pursue complex offenses. (**white-collar robbery widespread**)

6986

Crime That Pays, August Bequai (Washington DC), *The New York Times* (Op-Ed), Wed, 9 May 1984, A27.

Talk about getting tough with criminals refers to street crime; almost nothing is said about the more than $40 billion that the US Chamber of Commerce says is stolen each year by white-collar criminals. This includes some $15 billion in commercial counterfeiting of goods [also see *A Plague of Counterfeit Goods*, *Newsweek*, 17 Dec 1984, 68-70], $4 billion of securities-related frauds, $3 billion in embezzlement and pilferage, $3 billion in insurance frauds, and the growing area of computer crime. White-collar crime pays because our criminal justice system is ill-equipped to deal with it. The handful of white-collar criminals who are prosecuted are often given only a slap on the wrist. [NOTE: Not mentioned may be the biggest category of all: fraud in defense contracting.]   (**white-collar crime**)

6987

Offshore Haven Banks, Trusts, and Companies: The Business of Crime in the Euromarket. Richard H. Blum (Stanford U). NY: Praeger Publishers, May 1984/ 334p/$29.95.

Prepared for a special US Senate Committee investigation, this volume explores the functions and characteristics of offshore bank and company havens, especially those uses which facilitate or constitute violations of US criminal law. Emphasis is also given to violations that offer protection from detection and prosecution for US offenders. Blum describes the expanding offshore criminal market and applies this information on a country-by-country basis. Concludes by recommending critical intervention points in the system.   (**offshore crime**)

6988

Technology and Crime Reduction: New Approaches to Controlling Dangerous Behavior, Charles J. Brown (Birmingham, AL), *The Futurist*, 18:6, Dec 1984, 27-30.

Improvements in electronics and wider use of computers will decrease the cost of burglar alarms while improving accuracy, thus leading to their greater use in protecting property from crime (also see #6961). Electronic devices in automobiles might make car theft more difficult, and may prohibit operation by would-be drivers who are incapacitated by alcohol or drugs. Special monitoring devices attached to convicted offenders could determine the wearer's location at any time, enabling greater use of probation and parole. Such devices would be especially useful to keep young offenders out of institutions. Even in a prison setting, they could be used to reduce violence, drug use, and escape. Monitoring devices can also be programmed to activate other monitoring devices, enabling separation of individuals who persistently fight with each other or commit crimes together. Concludes that monitoring may well permit less expensive or demeaning punishment of criminals, while at the same time better protecting society.

(**technology to reduce crime?**)

6989

It's Sidney, A New Foe Of Scofflaw, David W. Dunlap, *The New York Times*, Monday, 25 June 1984, B1.

Sidney—the Summons Issuing Device for New York—is a handheld computer that weighs less than five pounds. A traffic agent coming across an illegally parked vehicle would enter the license plate number, color, make, and model, and the time, place, and nature of the violation. Besides emitting a machine-printed waterproof ticket, Sidney would match the license plate and car description with its 10,000-plate memory of scofflaws and stolen vehicles. If a match is made, a message would flash on the screen

and the traffic agent would get a tow truck (in the case of scofflaws) or summon the police (in the case of stolen cars). These computers will be ready for use in 1986, and if successful might eventually be used by all NYC traffic agents.

(**computerized traffic summons coming**)

6990

The Electronic Informer, Michael Rogers, *Newsweek*, 15 April 1985, 88-89.

A fledgling technology called biometrics is now in operation, identifying people through their unique physical characteristics: 1) Safeguarding Buildings—the most familiar use is door locks linked to scanners, in turn linked to computers in which authorized entrants have enrolled their palm or fingerprints; 2) Fingerprint Computers—the most dramatic use is for fingerprint matching in police work; 27 police departments worldwide now have fingerprint computers, and an additional 100 or so are planning to buy them at a price of $1 million or more (such computers not only solve crimes, but trip up criminals who give false identities during booking); 3) Signature Dynamics—banks and other credit-issuing agencies will soon use biometrics to discourage credit-card fraud through electronic measurement of the act of signing one's signature. Other potential targets for biometrics include ear shape, facial profile, and footsteps.   (**biometrics; fingerprint computers**)

6991

I'll Be Watching You: Reflections on the New Surveillance, Gary T. Marx (Dept of Sociology, MIT), *Dissent*, 32:1, Winter 1985, 26-34. (Also in *Technology Review* 88:4, May-June 1985, 42-49.)

The rationalization of crime control has crossed a critical threshold as a result of broad changes in technology and social organization. Surveillance has become penetrating and intrusive in ways that previously were imagined only in fiction. Some of the major types of this new surveillance include the 2,000 staffed interception posts of the National Security Agency, the interception of information transmitted in digital microwave form (much computer information and half of all long-distance telephone calls), the expansion of hot lines for anonymous reporting, mobile robot guards, telemetric devices attached to offenders on parole (see #6988), electronic systems for monitoring where and when a car is driven [being tested in Hong Kong as a means to apply a road tax—see **FS Annual 1984**, #6168], and monitoring employees and customers. These new forms and methods differ from traditional surveillance in the following ways: 1) they transcend distance, darkness, and physical barriers; 2) they transcend time, enabling surveillance information to be "socially freeze-dried" for many years after the fact; 3) they are capital- rather than labor-intensive, allowing a few persons to monitor a great many things; 4) they trigger a shift from targeting a specific suspect to categorical suspicion; everyone is assumed to be guilty until proven innocent; 5) they seek to prevent violations or make apprehension easier; 6) they are decentralized and trigger self-policing; 7) they are invisible or have low visiblity, making surveillance increasingly depersonalized; 8) they are ever more intensive, discovering previously inaccessible information; 9) they grow ever more extensive, covering deeper and larger areas and weaving previously unconnected threads into gigantic tapestries of information. The new surveillance does have many attractive features, and has been generally welcomed in business, government, and law enforcement. But in our eagerness to innovate and our infatuation with technological progress, it is easy to miss embedded time bombs. The new surveillance goes beyond merely invading privacy—it makes many of the constraints that made privacy possible irrelevant, eliminating certain physical, spatial, or temporal barriers. In the face of these changes, we must rethink the nature of privacy and create new supports such as coded or scrambled communication devices and binding standards for the collection, maintenance, and dissemination of personal information. Otherwise, as records become ever more important in administering society, persons may decline needed services (e.g., mental health), avoid conflictual or controversial action (e.g., filing a grievance against a boss or a landlord), and shun taking risks and experimenting for fear of what it will look like on the record. This in turn can lead to a degree of inhibition, fear, and anxiety unbecoming a democratic society. And with a more repressive government and a more intolerant public—perhaps upset over severe economic downturns—the new surveillance could easily be used against those with the "wrong" political beliefs.

(traits of the new surveillance)

6992

The Surveillance Society: The Threat of 1984-Style Techniques, Gary T. Marx (Dept of Sociology, MIT), *The Futurist*, 19:3, June 1985, 21-26.

Over the last decade, undercover practices in the US have expanded in scale and changed in form. Informing, a related but less costly investigative means of surveillance, has also expanded significantly. And there are many recent developments in technology that permit new intrusions, e.g. heat-sensing imaging devices that can tell if a house is occupied, a subminiature spy camera that permits one to unobtrusively snap photos, and a palm-sized voice stress computer that can fit inside a desk drawer and listen to micro-tremors in the voice. The categorical monitoring associated with video cameras, metal detectors, computers, and electronic markers on consumer goods are creating a society in which everyone—not just a few suspects—is a target for surveillance. With a different government and a more intolerant public, the new surveillance devices and practices could easily be used against political, religious, ethnic, or cultural minorities. Even without this danger, the low visibility of surveillance technology makes privacy much more difficult to protect. And with computer technology, one of the final barriers to total control is crumbling—the inability to retrieve, aggregate, and analyze vast amounts of data. Inefficiency is losing its role as the unplanned protector of liberty. **(new surveillance)**

C. Punishment

6993

Punishment and Restitution: A Restitutionary Approach to Crime and the Criminal. Charles F. Abel and Frank H. March. Westport CT: Greenwood Press, Sept 1984/c232p/$29.95.

The criminal justice system is a political institution created by public demands and values. An effective criminal justice system must be remedial and faciliatory, and attempt to heal both victims and criminals. To do so, the scope of what is legally relevant in criminal law must be broadened, and courts and penal institutions must be made flexible enough to help correct the effects of crime and the roots of recidivism. A restitutionary approach that draws attention to the victim is more viable and ethical than our existing system. **(restitutionary approach)**

6994

Minitrials: Scaling Down the Costs of Justice to Business, James F. Henry (President, Center for Public Resources, NYC), *across the board*, 21:10, Oct 1984, 45-49.

The minitrial is a nonbinding settlement procedure for converting a legal dispute back into a business problem. Lawyers make abbreviated presentations to business executives from both sides, and also (often) to a presiding neutral advisor—a retired judge or an authority on technical issues who may offer opinions. With this information, executives are equipped to negotiate a settlement. The costs of such a minitrial are about 10% of ordinary litigation. It also provides confidentiality not afforded by formal litigation. The Center for Public Resources(founded by Henry) has developed a model for resolving complex issues out of court, and distributes The Alternative Dispute Resolution Pledge, now endorsed by more than 60 major companies such as AT&T, Xerox, and Chrysler. The pledge commits signatory companies to explore ADR techniques early on in a dispute with another company that adheres to the pledge.

A related article follows: ***Justice Begins at Home*** by Alan F. Westin (pp50-54), which describes the growing number of employers who are creating internal adjudicative mechanisms, as an alternative to intervention by courts and regulatory agencies, for handling the growing number of complaints from non-unionized employees.

(alternative dispute resolution)

6995

Our Crowded Prisons. Edited by National Institute of Corrections (US Dept of Justice). *The Annals of the American Academy of Political and Social Science*, Vol 478, March 1985/182p/$10.00;$6.95pb.

Prison populations have reached an historic peak in the US, and are likely to continue to grow, albeit more slowly, as a result of sentencing reforms aimed at increasing prison terms. These essays address the evolution of public policy (prison crowding has been a persistent feature of US prisons), local jails and state prisons, the human impact of congested prisons, the true costs of prisons, the history of prison-crowding litigation, sentencing reform to reduce overcrowding (by Senator Kennedy), elements of a coherent imprisonment policy, selective incapacitation (setting prison terms on the amount of crime an offender is predicted to commit if not in prison), the National Prison Overcrowding Project, and effective prison resource management. **(crowded US prisons)**

6996

As Privately Owned Prisons Increase, So Do Their Critics, Martin Tolchin, *The New York Times*, Monday, 11 Feb 1985, p1.

About two dozen major correction facilities are owned or operated by private groups, and the American Correctional Association estimates that the number will double in the next 18 months. These are in additional to several hundred adult halfway houses and juvenile centers that private groups began operating in the 1970s. The trend toward private correction operations was born of overcrowded and antiquated institutions, as well as the entrepreneurial spirit. Supporters see a new efficiency, greater vitality, flexibility, and lower costs. They say that private businesses and nonprofit agencies do a better job because they are insulated from public pressures and free from political interference, patronage obligations, and the high salaries and pensions of public employees. Critics attack the concept of making a profit on incarceration, raise questions of accountability, and fear an assault on prisoners' rights to due process of law. They also fear that private corporations may develop a vested interest in having their facilities filled, and that emphasis on profits could lead to cutting corners on staff, salaries, training, and rehabilitation. **(private prisons pro and con)**

6997

Pace of Executions in U.S. Quickens, Walter Goodman, *The New York Times*, Thursday, 13 Dec 1984, A18.

In 1984, nearly twice as many Americans were executed as in the previous 20 years. The sharp increase grew out of a Supreme Court ruling in 1976 permitting capital punishment under certain conditions. This decision ended a moratorium that lasted a decade, and Gary Gilmore, who went before a Utah firing squad in 1977, was the first person executed after the hiatus. With some 1,450 convicted murderers—a record number—now on death rows in the 38 states that permit capital punishment, and with the figure growing by about 250 a year, the rate of executions is expected to keep accelerating for several years at least. The debate continues to rage as to whether the threat of death is more of a deterrent to murder than other penalities. [NOTE: Support for the death penalty, according to the Gallup Poll, has risen to 72% in 1985--the highest percentage since 1936--up from 66% in 1981 and 42% in 1966 (*New York Times*, 3 Feb 1985, p 23).]
(accelerating rate of executions)

6998

The Public Health Effects of the Death Penalty, Jonathan B. Weisbuch (President, The Foundation for Health and Fitness), *Journal of Public Health Policy*, 5:3, Sept 1984, 305-311.

A state policy supporting the death penalty is a policy against the public's health. Contrary to the widespread notion of the death penalty as a deterrent, evidence indicates that legal homicide is associated with an increase in subsequent illegal homicide, and that other forms of social disorder occur with increased frequency following executions. And, contrary to the notion that it is cheaper to kill an offender so as to forego incarceration costs of $20,000 a year, capital cases are inordinately more expensive for the public—at the expense of other programs in education and public health. Executing an offender in modern America while assuring all the rights of due process costs nearly $2.0 million for the average case. This includes $1.5 million for trial costs to establish guilt and define the penalty, some $300,000 to move the case through state and Federal appellate processes, and $100,000 to $200,000 for the execution itself.

(death penalty detracts from public health)

XII. HEALTH

A. World Issues

*6999
Improving World Health: A Least Cost Strategy.
William U. Chandler. Worldwatch Paper 59. Washington
DC: Worldwatch Institute, July 1984/66p/$4.00.

World health leaders have set a goal of "health for all
by the year 2000" [**FS Annual 1981-82**, #4038], which
has led to a global effort to define health and devise ways
to achieve it. Though their health care needs differ drastically, the rich and the poor have one thing in common:
both die unnecessarily. The rich die of heart disease and
cancer; the poor die of diarrhea, pneumonia, and measles.
Modern medicine can vastly reduce the mortality caused
by these illnesses. Yet, half the developing world lacks
medical care of any kind, while the rich have had to begin
to ration health care in the face of rising costs. A policy of
"health for all" can thus succeed only if limited resources
are used in the most efficient way possible. Major improvements in world health can be made with cost-effective preventive and primary care measures. The most important
of these are providing maternal and child care for the
world's poorest people, clean drinking water and sanitation
facilities to the third of the world's population that lacks
them, diet education for populations at high risk of heart
disease and cancer, control of tobacco products, and basic
research for low-cost cures. But even the largest opportunities for improving the human condition continue to be
neglected, e.g.: primary health care is tragically under-
funded, diet education is haphazard at best, and anti-smok-
ing efforts are sporadic. Recent advances in biotechnology
may revolutionize medicine, but applying this potential
for the good of humanity is a challenge that may not be
met, for along with the maldistribution of wealth goes the
maldistribution of science. Rich countries and their scientists have an ethical responsibility to allocate a share of
this good fortune to solving the problems of the poor.

(low-cost "health for all")

7000
**Health Promotion: A Discussion Document on the
Concept and Principles**. World Health Organization,
Regional Office for Europe. Copenhagen, Denmark: WHO
(8, Scherfigsvej), Sept 1984/8p/free (ICP/HSR 602m01).

Health promotion has come to represent a unifying concept for those who recognize the need for change in the
ways and conditions of living in order to promote health.
It represents a mediating strategy between people and
their environments, synthesizing personal choice and social responsibility to create a healthier future. Supporters
of health promotion within governments need to be aware
of the role of social movements, self-help, and self-care,
and the need for continuous cooperation with the public
on all health promotion issues. Four possible conflicts of
interest are noted: 1) the ideology of healthism—viewing
health as the ultimate goal incorporating all of life—is
contrary to the principles of health promotion; 2) health
promotion programs may be inappropriately directed to
individuals at the expense of tackling economic and social
problems; 3) resources, including information, may not be
accessible to people in ways which are sensitive to their
beliefs, preferences, or skills (thus increasing social inequalities); 4) there is a danger that health promotion will
be appropriated by one professional group and made a field
of specialization to the exclusion of other professionals and
lay people. **(health promotion principles)**

*7001
**Beyond Health Care: Proceedings of a Conference
on Healthy Public Policy** (Special Issue). *Canadian
Journal of Public Health*, Vol 76, Supplement 1, May-June
1985, 104p. (Available for $10.00 plus $1.50 postage &
handling from CPHA, 1335 Carling Ave, #210, Ottawa
K1Z 8N8.)

Papers from an October 1984 conference in Toronto.
Trevor Hancock (Conference Chairman) reviews the
principles of a healthy public policy: holistic, future-
oriented, and dominated by the soft health path [described
in *The Futurist*, Aug 1982; **FS Annual 1983** #5205].
James Robertson outlines basic paradigms in three possible futures: business-as-usual, hyper-expansionist, and
sane, humane, and ecological. **Carol Buck** (U of Western
Ontario) lists various social obstacles to health such as
dangerous environments, lack of necessities, stressful
work, isolation and alienation, and poverty. **Rick Carlson**
presents a list of 16 health megatrends and forcing events,
such as demographic change, healthier elders, wellness
movements, holism, the rise of self-care and consumer competence, disintermediation (eliminating the middleman),
the toxification of our environment, the notion of biochem-
ical individuality, and greater emphasis on nutrition.
Hakan Hellberg (Director, Health for All Strategy Coordination, World Health Organization) describes basic
concepts in moving toward the WHO goal of health for all
by the year 2000 (participation by people, multisectoral
action, appropriate technology, health education and communication, and policy changes in the global self-interest).
Briefer papers consider education for lifelong learning,
families and health, health and empowerment, developing
human potential, healthy workplaces, reducing unemployment, healthy communities, health-promoting economic
policy, and healthy nations.

Concludes with a variety of recommendations for action
by the Canadian Public Health Association, such as:
1) establishing formal links with non-health groups to discuss public policy and health; 2) monitoring public policy
for its health implications; 3) publishing an annual report
on the state of Canadian health; 4) commissioning a curriculum review of health science schools to see that healthy
public policy is being taught; 5) awarding annual prizes
for those who contribute to and those who detract from
healthy public policy; 6) encouraging community groups
to undertake healthy public policy initiatives at the local
level. **(healthy public policy)**

7002
The Health Planning Predicament. Victor G. Rodwin
(Institute for Health Policy Studies, U of California-San
Francisco).Berkeley CA: U of California Press, March 1984/
320p/$24.50.

Examines the evolution of health planning efforts in
France, Quebec, and England, comparing these experiences with those of the US. In the non-US cases, health
planners have challenged the model of hospital-centered
medical care. But attempts to redistribute health resources
have been hobbled by the failure to effectively link health
care budgeting and the financial incentives that influence
hospitals and physicians. Whether health planning
strategies rely on regulation or competition, the critical
policy issue is the design of a reimbursement system that
encourages hospitals and physicians to pursue society's
interest and their own. **(health planning compared)**

7003

Transformation of Health Care in China (Special Report), William C. Hsiao (Harvard School of Public Health), *The New England Journal of Medicine*, 310:14, 5 April 1984, 932-936.

China's recent shift from a collective agricultural production system to one that rewards peasants according to their individual output has inadvertently caused major changes in its highly acclaimed rural cooperative medical system. The economic reforms have altered peasant incentives, weakened community organization, and lessened the central government's influence over local communities. Consequences of these changes include: a decreased supply of primary health care personnel or "barefoot doctors" from 1.8 million in 1978 to 1.2 million in 1982, disintegration of organized primary care, a decline in cooperative health insurance, reduced primary health care, and an increased demand for higher-quality medical care among peasants with rising incomes. The Chinese example vividly demonstrates the inextricable relation between economic structure and health care.

(Chinese medical system transformed)

7004

Public Health and Agricultural Practice, Linda Marks (St. Thomas's Hospital, London), *Food Policy*, 9:2, May 1984, 131-138.

Health, ecological, and social aspects of agricultural policy are beginning to supplement traditional concerns of productivity and profitability, underlining the interdependence of agricultural policy with other policy areas. Marks reviews various health-related aspects of agriculture: chemicals used in agricultural production, pollution from sewage, pesticide residues, hormones and antibiotics, increased nitrate levels in drinking water as a result of massive increases in the use of nitrogen fertilizers, and nutritional quality of plants. Concludes that the health and environmental advantages of combining the best practices of organic farming with some of the advances of modern farming techniques have yet to be reflected in policies and practices. Many related research questions remain unanswered, such as quantifying the environmental costs of agriculture, understanding interactions between nitrates and pesticide residues, and improving the nutritional quality of modern food.   **(agriculture and public health)**

7005

The New Age of Vaccines, Harold M. Schmeck Jr, *The New York Times Magazine*, 29 April 1984, 58ff.

The new techniques of genetic engineering allow vaccine designers to do things with precision that they used to do almost blindly. Many scientists see a new era ahead in which vaccines unimaginable just a decade ago make a major contribution to world health. In Asia, for example, some 200 million people have liver disease caused by hepatitus B virus; new vaccines might prevent much of this illness and death. Experts foresee greatly improved vaccines against flu, cholera, malaria, herpes, and infections that may be linked to cancer. [Also see "Scientists in U.S. Say Malaria Vaccine Is Near," (*The New York Times*, 3 Aug 1984, A8), which reports that a vaccine against malaria will be ready for trial in humans in late 1985, and widely available throughout the world within five years. The World Health Organization estimates that there are at least 150 million new cases of malarial disease each year, and tens of millions more chronically afflicted.]

(new vaccines; an end to malaria?)

*7006

Alternative Medicines: Popular and Policy Perspectives. Edited by J. Warren Salmon (Prof of Health Planning, U of Illinois-Chicago). NY and London: Tavistock Publications (dist by Methuen, Inc., 29 W 35th St, NYC 10001), Nov 1984/302p/$12.95pb.

Scientific medicine is the term commonly used to define the theoretical framework and medical procedures of Western society, which have become officially sanctioned by the organized medical profession. A specter of alternative approaches to health and healing is haunting scientific medicine, through a popular resurgence of interest and activity in a wide variety of new and age-old therapeutic modalities. A grab-bag of therapeutic interventions have been called "holistic," even while they may not address all three aspects of the "whole" person (body, mind, and spirit) in either theory or practice. This book explores some of these unorthodox systems, offering a variety of viewpoints on their public acceptance and related policy issues. Chapters are devoted to scientific medicine since the late 19th century, homeopathy (a Western system that is quite popular worldwide, especially outside the US), chiropractic (the major "hands-on" body therapy, originating in America around the turn of the century), traditional Chinese medicine, indigenous systems of healing (advocates of these methods of folk healing often idolize their practices), psychic healing, the social dimensions to the flourishing interest in alternative forms of healing (the rising demand for participation, the deterioration of the medical encounter), and holistic health centers in the US (model holistic programs are needed in a variety of communities, with assessment as to how they can mesh with Western medicine and meet people's needs). Salmon concludes by noting the likelihood that the new medical industrial complex of nationwide providers will, over time, exploit popular sentiments for a broader range of services, but only for those in the population able to pay. [NOTE: A welcome scholarly overview of various streams that someday may merge into a variegated "world medicine," in turn part of a world science. Also see **The Other Medicines**, by Richard Grossman (Doubleday, Nov 1985, $17.95; $10.95pb).]   **(holistic health alternatives)**

B. U.S. Issues

7007

Visions of the Year 2000, James O. Mason (Director, Centers for Disease Control, Atlanta) *et al.*, *American Journal of Preventive Medicine*, 1:1, Spring 1985, 4-10.

Examines some of the major demographic and social trends that will influence health in 2000, and proposes ten health goals for the 21st century: 1) adequate nutrition for all children and reduced infant mortality from 80/1000 live births to below 50/1000; 2) all children should be free of vaccine-preventable diseases; 3) safe drinking water and adequate sanitary facilities should be available; 4) heart disease death rates in the US should continue to decline at about 2% per year; 5) cancer mortality in the US should be reduced by 50%; 6) injuries in motor vehicles, at home, and in the workplace should be reduced by 50%; 7) deaths from homicide and suicide should be prevented; 8) the quality of life for older adults should be enhanced; 9) the benefits of prevention should be shared among all socioeconomic subgroups in the US and in other nations; 10) humankind should be at peace, lest we incur the "final epidemic" of nuclear war. State and local authorities are urged to develop comparable priorities and objectives for their jurisdictions.   **(health goals for 2000)**

7008

U.S. National Health Policy: An Analysis of the Federal Role. Jennie J. Kronenfeld and Marcia Lynn Whicker (both U of South Carolina). NY: Praeger Publishers, July 1984/288p/$29.95.

Analyzes the US health care system, with special emphasis on the Federal role in establishing health policy and how the diverse pieces of the system come together. The authors consider supply and demand for health functions, health and income equity, preventive vs. morbidity services, national health policies in other countries, and alternatives to US national health policy.

(Federal role in US health care)

7009

Another Health-Care Changeover—at What Cost? Victor R. Fuchs (Prof of Economics, Stanford U), *The Wall Street Journal*, Friday, 28 June 1985, p22.

The US is in the midst of the third revolution in health-care finance since the end of WWII. The first revolution entailed the rapid diffusion of private health insurance between 1945 and 1960. The second occurred in 1965 with the creation of Medicare and Medicaid, providing coverage to the elderly and poor. This widespread private and public insurance contributed to the explosion of health care costs; the current revolution seeks to contain these costs. The first two revolutions increased the demand for medical care, promoted greater equality of access, and posed no threat to the traditional organization and delivery of care. The current changes in finance and reimbursement will have revolutionary effects on hospitals, medical practice, and medical education. The need to compete through price and service may lead hospitals and physicians to abandon the open, collaborative behavior of the past. Fragmentation of insurance markets will mean very high premiums for some groups, and abandonment of collective responsibility for health care. The new revolution in financing may result in new efficiencies, but may also lead to erosion of professional ethics, loss of trust between physicians and patients, a decline in medical research, and inadequate insurance coverage for millions.

(third revolution in health care finance)

7010

The Corporate Prescription for Medical Costs (Cover Story), *Business Week*, 15 Oct 1984, 138-146.

Escalation of health care costs stems from third party payment mechanisms: employees with company health insurance and the elderly with government Medicare see no reason to question medical bills. In 1983, the Federal government launched the first major attack in the battle against rising health care costs by establishing a new pricing system for Medicare that pays set amounts for each of 468 ailments. Now employers are making it clear to hospitals that they want efficient care at the lowest price, because medical care is their fastest-rising cost. Companies are now taking such unprecedented steps as touching off hospital price wars, negotiating fixed fees for medical services, building their own clinics, forming local business coalitions to monitor health care costs, and pressing for employee cost-sharing. [Also see *Companies Pour Millions Into Programs Aimed at Keeping Workers Well* (*The New York Times*, 14 Oct 1984, p36) and *Fitness, Corporate Style* (*Newsweek*, 5 Nov 1984, 96-97), which both describe various corporate wellness programs.]

(corporate health programs)

7011

Public Health in a Retrenchment Era: An Alternative to Managerialism. Helen J. Muller (U of New Mexico) and Curtis Ventriss (Johns Hopkins U). Albany NY: State U of New York Press, July 1985/162p/$32.50; $10.95pb.

We have all entered a new era that is forcing us to rethink what we are doing and why. Fiscal cutbacks can be used to legitimize government disengagement from commitments to the disadvantaged. But these cutbacks can also be used to shatter traditional methods of bureaucratic management and control, and to consider new service delivery alternatives that would otherwise be unthinkable. Public health was historically based on a participatory relationship between the client, the community, and the professional. These relationships have been eroded by the emphasis on managerialism: the overarching utilitarian belief system that insists on orthodox techniques and strategies. To reforge links between government and citizens, the authors focus on the process of joint power sharing, or "co-possibility strategies" in health and social services. The displacement of democratic values by managerialism is illustrated in the book's case study of the Los Angeles County Department of Health Services, which never considered the possibility of citizen involvement in the coproduction of health services. Co-possibility strategies stress knowledge transfer to citizens and the community, a policy and social learning approach, enabling citizens to effectively communicate their concerns to human service organizations, and a client-oriented approach to health planning. Such strategies bring people together to invest their shared efforts in improving their health and their environment.

(co-possibility strategies in public health)

7012

Hospitals: A Sick Industry, *U.S. News & World Report*, 18 March 1985, 39-40.

As government agencies and corporations clamp down on health care costs, hospitals are competing against each other to survive in a radically changed medical marketplace. Americans are going to the hospital less often and staying for shorter periods; the overall occupancy rate of US hospitals dropped from 73% in 1983 to 67% in 1984. To find additional sources of revenue, hospitals are offering new services such as alcohol-and-drug-abuse units, a catering service, a dry-cleaning and laundry business, health insurance, and converting empty beds to motel rooms at discount rates for relatives of patients. Competition is forcing many hospitals into multisystems or for-profit chains: today, more than 35% of hospitals are part of some system, with nearly 15% owned by corporations.

(effects of hospital competition)

7013

Private Hospitals Are Now Offering Health Insurance, Martin Tolchin, *The New York Times*, Friday, 5 July 1985, p1.

Several large private hospital chains have expanded into health insurance, a move that many experts predict will significantly alter the health care industry. Barely a year old, hospital chain insurance already has about a million subscribers. Unlike the locally-based Blue Cross-Blue Shield programs, insurance offered by such chains as Humana and Hospital Corporation of America is nationally oriented. Many observers view the new trend as a direct result of the recent change in Federal health reimbursement policies. Some of these experts estimate that chain insurance costs 10% to 15% less than Blue Cross-Blue

Shield, if patients use the chain hospitals. One expert, Dr. Paul Elwood, forecasts that this "industrialization of medicine" will result in the majority of US medical care being delivered by 10 to 15 corporations, with these "super-meds" replacing individual physicians, hospitals, clinics, and insurance companies.

(hospital chains offer health insurance)

7014

Ownership and Mental-Health Services: A Reapprais-al of the Shift Toward Privately Owned Facilities, Mark Schlesinger and Robert Dorwart (Mental Health Policy Working Group, Harvard U), *The New England Journal of Medicine*, 311:15, 11 Oct 1984, 959-969.

The system of mental-health care in the US is undergoing a marked privatization. Analyzing data from several surveys, it is argued that the type of ownership is definitely linked to several aspects of institutional performance: 1) private facilities are more likely to screen out nonpaying patients than are government-owned providers; 2) there is no evidence that the profit motive leads to more efficient delivery of mental-health care; 3) for-profit providers devote fewer staff resources to patient care and offer fewer services with community-wide benefits.

(privatization of mental health service)

7015

Mental Health and Social Policy: Initiatives for the 1980s, David Mechanic (University Professor, Rutgers U), *Health Affairs*, 4:1, Spring 1985, 75-88.

In 1980, mental illness was the third most expensive class of disorders, accounting for more than $20 billion of health care expenditures. Those with chronic mental illnesses make up less than 1% of the total US population, but these persons constitute an enormous burden on the community and a serious challenge to social policy—especially in light of cost-containment pressures on the health care system. It seems unlikely that much new funding will be available. Patterns of care continue to be fragmented and poorly organized, and the range and complexity of existing entitlements requires ingenuity and energy to negotiate. The most important contribution that we could make to patient care is to consolidate funding sources at the local level, allowing rational calculation and choosing among alternatives. **(mental health care policy)**

7016

Longer Life But Worsening Health? Trends in Health and Mortality of Middle-Aged and Older Persons, Lois M. Verbrugge (U of Michigan), *Milbank Memorial Fund Quarterly: Health and Society*, 62:3, Summer 1984, 475-518.

Over the past decade, the US population has enjoyed rapidly declining mortality rates at all ages and for both sexes. But for the rest of this century, some health statistics will continue to show increasing morbidity or relative incidence of disease, especially for non-killer conditions. Medical research and care will continue to focus on diagnosis and control of killer diseases. But as advances for them slow and as non-killers assume prominence, medicine will gradually shift emphasis toward musculoskeletal diseases and symptoms, sensory impairments, allergies, and skin problems. As a result, middle-aged and older people in the future will probably have more years of healthful life than current cohorts. Work environments will probably pose fewer hazards for chronic disease development, and medical diagnosis and treatment will be more efficacious. Mortality rates will thus continue to fall as fast or faster than in the 1970s. **(mortality and morbidity)**

7017

Infant Mortality in the U.S., C. Arden Miller (Prof of Public Health, U of North Carolina), *Scientific American*, 253:1, July 1985, 31-37.

The infant mortality rate in the US has been declining steadily, from 124 per 1000 live births in 1910 to 47 in 1940 and 11.5 in 1982 (in contrast, world leaders in 1982 were Finland at 6.0 and Japan with 6.6). In 1979, the US Public Health Service established 9 infant deaths per 1000 births as a goal to be met by 1990. In recent years, though, the rate of decline in the US has diminished markedly, coinciding with cutbacks in programs for mothers and children, and it does not seem likely that this PHS goal will be reached. The means to reach the goal require certain public policies that are not being seriously considered: assured access to comprehensive prenatal care, guaranteed maternity leaves for all working pregnant women and recent mothers, and adequate cash benefits. These measures can be promoted on the basis of humanitarian concern, social equity, cost-effectiveness, and national security.

(US infant mortality rate)

7018

Checking for Symptoms of Declining Health Care, David E. Rogers and Robert J. Blendon (Robert Wood Johnson Foundation, Princeton NJ), *The Wall Street Journal*, Thursday, 15 Nov 1984, p32.

The past 15 years have seen extraordinary progress in improving the health of Americans, with life expectancy growing by four years and reductions in deaths from 10 of the 15 leading killers. But the good news of the past does not guarantee continued progress in the future, and there is reason to worry that the tremendous strides in securing access to care may be undone. Expensive and competing national needs, coupled with deficits and double-digit health care inflation, have led virtually all parts of the US to consider restrictions on health care spending (e.g., the share of employers requiring employees to pay deductibles for in-patient hospital care has gone from 30% in 1982 to 63% in 1984). There are several reasonably sensitive warning signals that might tell us whether arrangements for medical care are holding up: 1) how often people are seeing doctors (if visits to the doctor by the poor begin regressing toward past levels, it would signal a reversal of progress); 2) where people go for care (a rising rate in emergency room visits suggests difficult access to personal physician services); 3) maternal mortality rates, and whether the wide gap between white and black infant mortality continues to narrow; 4) any rise in the incidence of certain diseases such as rheumatic fever or measles. Keeping track of such indicators is likely to be of critical importance in the years ahead, for only by doing so can proper decisions be made about where medical care is vital and where it is not. A dramatic restructuring of health care is underway (involving for-profit hospital chains, HMOs, restructured employer insurance programs, and a surfeit of physicians), and health indicators are needed to understand the resulting impacts. **(key indicators of health care)**

7019

Health Service Funding Cuts and the Declining Health of the Poor, Mary O'Neil Mundinger (Columbia U College of Physicians and Surgeons), *The New England Journal of Medicine*, 313:1, 4 July 1985, 44-47.

The health of poor Americans is getting worse, and there is reason to suspect that health funding cuts are at least partly responsible for this decline. Studies have shown that insurance coverage is the key factor that determines the use of health care services, and increased use of such services is associated with increased health. The 1981 Federal cuts were targeted at those on the margin of poverty and at providers. But the combined effect has been to force hundreds of thousands of the working poor and the elderly below the poverty line and to restrict their access to health care. As a result, 35 million Americans—15% of the population—are without health insurance today, an increase of 10 million since 1977. Some 5 million people annually report that they do not seek medical care because they are unable to pay for it. Medicaid today covers only 52% of the poor, compared with 65% in 1976; in some states, fewer than 20% of the poor are covered. There has been a nationwide increase in the number and percentage of women who do not receive any prenatal care. The women who receive the least care are the ones without insurance coverage. The incidence of low birth weight is increasing, and preventable childhood diseases are also on the rise in certain populations. [Also in the same issue of *NEJM* see ***Medical Care of the Poor—A Growing Problem***, by John K. Iglehart, pp59-63.]

(15% of US without health insurance)

7020

Care of the Poor Revisited, David M. Kinzer (President, Massachusetts Hospital Association), *Inquiry* (Blue Cross/Blue Shield), 21:1, Spring 1984, 5-16.

The Chairman of a 1982 committee of the American Hospital Association that issued a report on health care and government financial cuts warns that the health "safety net" for the poor has deteriorated significantly since the report was issued. The main burden of meeting health care needs of dependent groups in the US seems to be falling on an ever-narrowing group of institutions that generally are not in good financial shape. The health services situation for the poor will get worse before it gets better. The new form of payment for Medicare by diagnosis-related groups is likely to force more hospital retrenchment. The American public has always tolerated a certain amount of poverty, including the dual standard in health care, but there are limits to how much more it will allow.

(health care for poor in decline)

7021

The Best Medicine: Organizing Local Health Care Campaigns. Geraldine Dallek, Will Collette, and Jeff Kirsch. Washington: The Villers Foundation (1334 G St. NW), Oct 1984/204p(8x11 notebook)/$7.00 ($5.00 each for six or more copies).

By exercising their strength of numbers—and using the right tactics—consumers can change the way decisions are made in the health care industry. This workbook explains how to organize for changing health care. Chapters are devoted to getting doctors to accept Medicare payment as full charge for services, expanding Medicaid eligibles, getting doctors to provide free care and to accept Medicaid patients, getting hospitals to provide free or reduced-cost care, insuring the health of public and non-profit hospitals, getting drug discounts from stores and suppliers, getting good generic drug laws, and cost containment measures.

(local health care campaigns)

7022

After Years of Cancer Alarms, Progress Amid the Mistakes, Philip M. Boffey, *The New York Times*, Tuesday, 20 March 1984, C1.

In the 1970s, a decade of great environmental sensitivity, scientists and government officials emphasized the role of manmade chemicals in consumer products or the workplace as a major cause of disease, including cancer. There has since been a striking shift of opinion as to the importance attached to chemical carcinogens: they are now seen to cause only a small proportion of the 450,000 annual cancer deaths in the US—probably less than 10% by the most widely accepted estimates. Far more significant are tobacco (estimated to cause 30% of all cancer deaths) and a diet with too much fat and not enough fiber (estimated to cause 35% of cancer deaths). Even so, such chemicals remain a significant health problem, causing thousands of cancer deaths each year that could be prevented. Some other generalizations, derived from recent interviews with more than two dozen cancer and health experts: 1) substantial progress has been made in assessing the carcinogen problem, but an enormous amount of work remains, and there are many gaps in regulatory surveillance; 2) the impression that carcinogens are cropping up everywhere results in part from major advances in analytic instruments that can detect chemicals in food or the environment in minute quantities; 3) some scientists warn that cancer deaths from chemicals could surge in the future, because there has been a sharp increase since the 1960s in the production of cancer-causing chemicals, and it usually takes 15 to 40 years for cancer to develop after first exposure to a carcinogen (a group of scientists at Johns Hopkins University contends that "epidemic increases" in certain cancers can already be detected among elderly whites).

(new views on carcinogens)

7023

The Apocalyptics: Cancer and the Big Lie. Edith Efron (School of Management, U of Rochester). NY: Simon & Schuster, May 1984/589p/$19.95. (Excerpt in *Reason*, 16:1, May 1984, 22-30.)

Rachel Carson's 1962 **Silent Spring** set off an "apocalyptic" movement with such doomsayers as Barry Commoner, Paul Ehrlich, Rene Dubos, and the Club of Rome, based on the scientifically unproven premise that American industry has poisoned our environment with carcinogens. The apocalyptics, committed to a blind assault on industrial civilization, have dominated both the media and key government agencies. The cancer prevention establishment wallows in a morass of scientific contradictions, false assumptions, and distortions—irrationalities so numerous that they add up to "a cultural crime." The most fundamental controversy revolves around the "no threshold" theory, which holds that the most minute amount of a carcinogen, even a single molecule, might give someone cancer, and that the only safe exposure is zero. This has been the basis of the stringent Federal regulatory effort of the past 10 years, yet we regularly ingest much larger amounts of natural carcinogens with every meal. The most obvious fact about cancer in the US is that it is not increasing, and that America ranks far down on the scale of industrial nations in cancer incidence. Moreover, cancer prevention by means of animal data alone is a science that is still unborn—a moral illusion created by the apocalyptic paradigm. [NOTE: A **"Silent Spring"** for the conservatives?]   **(cancer establishment questioned)**

7024

AIDS (Special Report), *Newsweek*, 12 August 1985, 20-29.

Acquired immune deficiency syndrome, or AIDS, was not identified and named until 1981. Since then, it has at least doubled the number of its victims each year. More than 6,000 Americans have died as a result of AIDS, and no one has ever been known to recover. Because of the long period when AIDS lies latent, thousands of people may be infected and infectious without knowing it. Thus the standard public health measure of quarantine is impossible as a means of controlling AIDS. It is now clearly seen that the disease is not restricted to homosexual or bisexual men (40% of AIDS patients at Walter Reed Hospital are men and women who appear to have contacted the disease through heterosexual activity). Apprehension about AIDS is already having an effect on both straight and gay sexual behavior, and some experts think it may change forever the freewheeling attitudes of the '60s and '70s. More important, what was once dismissed as the "gay plague" has assumed the proportions of a worldwide public health disaster. It could dramatically sweep the general population, just as it burst out among gay men a few years ago. It could, according to some experts, become one of those infectious diseases that change history. According to Dr. Ward Cates (US Centers for Disease Control), "Anyone who has the least ability to look into the future can already see the potential for this disease being much worse than anything mankind has seen before." [NOTE: AIDS is an outstanding example of the uncertainties in thinking about the future. The dire forebodings suggested above could be realized in the next 5 or 10 years. But development of some means to prevent, detect, and/or treat the disease, before it alters the course of history, would seem more likely—or is it? It would also seem that "the final epidemic" of nuclear weapons is even more likely to menace public health, and that a remedy—an effective Star Wars scheme and/or disarmament—is much less likely than any cure for AIDS.]

(**AIDS: world health disaster?**)

C. Physicians, Patients and Prevention

7025

Medicine and the Management of Living: Taming the Last Great Beast. William Ray Arney (Evergreen State College) and Bernard J. Bergen (Dartmouth Medical School). Chicago, Ill: U of Chicago Press, Nov 1984/202p/ $19.95.

In recent years, relations between patients and physicians in America have undergone a dramatic change. The growing acceptance of natural childbirth, support groups for patients, HMOs, and hospices for a "happy death" is part of a redefinition of medical practice and reformulation of medical power. No longer is medical practice confined to "taming the beast" of death and fighting the diseases observable in the human body. The modern practitioner is now a manager of the living, taking an ecological view of the patient as a whole person in a network of relationships. Whereas the taxonomic approach of medicine narrowed its field of vision, the ecological model and systems-theoretic logic are expanding it. The health care team extends medicine's reach into many dimensions of life. Epidemiology extends the scope of surveillance out into the community. Lay education makes people monitors of their own health and the first line in detection. But medicine is not "medicalizing" more aspects of life; rather, the new field of medical power has become incorporative and rapidly responsive to developments around it. Everything must now be noted, recorded, and made the object

of analysis. [NOTE: See #7148 on the growing need for information management in medicine, which is the driving force for introducing computers, in turn encouraging the recording of still more information.] Concludes that, as an alternative to the tyranny of harmony, we might begin to consider medicine in a free and humane society.

(**physician/patient relationships changed**)

7026

Women and Medicalization: A New Perspective, Catherine Kohler Riessman (Smith College), *Social Policy*, 14:1, Summer 1983, 3-18.

Both physicians and women have contributed to the redefining of women's experience into medical categories. Physicians seek to medicalize experience because of their specific beliefs and economic interests, while women collaborate because of their own needs growing out of the class-specific nature of their subordination. This framework is used to explore five areas relevant to women's experience: childbirth (now considered a medical event, which was not always the case), reproductive freedom (abortion, too, is now considered a medical event), premenstrual syndrome, weight, and psychological distress. Concludes that demedicalization is necessary for some problems; the challenge will be to differentiate beneficial treatments from those that are useless and harmful.

(**medicalized experience of women**)

7027

Matters of Life & Death: Risks vs. Benefits of Medical Care. Eugene D. Robin (Prof of Medicine, Stanford U). NY: W.H. Freeman, Dec 1984/205p/$18.95;$10.95pb.

The past 20 years have seen an unprecedented accumulation of medical knowledge, accompanied by a growing disillusion with the applications of this knowledge to patient care. This book, written primarily for the general public, challenges the system whereby medical knowledge is applied to patient care. There are major but reversible flaws in the present system, and these flaws can be understood by most patients. We need more, not less, science in medicine, but it has to be better science and more closely linked to patient welfare than it is today. The potential for both harm and good has increased as medical science and technology has progressed. The number of things that doctors can do has multiplied enormously. But this growth has occurred without corresponding changes in the processes by which medical practices are established and by which doctors are trained. Most medical interventions currently employed in normal subjects appear to have little favorable influence on health; many are untested, and some are either harmful or have unacceptably high risks. Patients have the right and the responsibility to ask doctors about the risks and benefits of tests and treatments. If patients' lack of medical expertise makes them feel insecure, they should use an intermediary as their representative and advocate—an "ombudsdoctor" with no ego investment or financial stake in the treatment. To change the medical system, a substantial part of the medical curriculum should be devoted to an in-depth analysis of the limits of medicine and doctors, and how to apply risk-benefit analysis to every aspect of patient care. A frank recognition of the deficiencies in medical knowledge would create an atmosphere of essential humility, weaken the hierarchical structure that is still the rule in medicine, and allow a greater closeness among all members of the medical team. Two accurate statements that doctors could frequently make are "I don't know" and "I was wrong." They seldom make these statements to each other, and almost never to a patient. [NOTE: Simply-written, wise, and non-flamboyant. An excellent example of the first two elements of "the new competence" advocated by Donald Michael: acknowledging uncertainty and embracing error (see #7101).]   (**doctors need more humility**)

7028

The High Cost of Healing: Physicians and the Health Care System. J.H.U. Brown (Prof of Biology, U of Houston). NY: Human Sciences Press, Mar 1985/213p/$26.95.

Blame for the high costs of medical care is often placed on the hospitals and the increasing cost of technology, but in the ultimate analysis it is the physician who is to blame. Physicians tend to prescribe too much hospital care, too much high technology of dubious value, and too many drugs of dubious efficiency, in concert with too little concern for the overall costs of care to the patient. The third party reimbursement system aggravates this problem by separating the consumer from the costs of care. Medical schools and their emphasis on high technology are a major influence on the physician; few of them teach courses in such necessary topics as office management, the economics of medical care, and the elements of preventive medicine. Physicians believe that the use of more resources will improve service, where the contrary may actually be true. The medical profession uses resources to protect itself against malpractice, to satisfy patient demand for service, and to make more money. The most logical ways to stem these costs would be to publish the fees and costs of care, to refuse to pay for unnecessary tests, and to pay all physicians the same for equal work.
          (**physicians at root of high medical costs**)

7029

Moving and Shaking American Medicine: The Structure of a Socioeconomic Transformation. Betty Leyerle (Fort Lewis College, CO). Westport CT: Greenwood Press, Aug 1984/218p/$27.95.

Since the early 1970s, qualitative changes have occurred in the US health care system that have been both a cause and a consequence of the transformation in occupational authority enjoyed by physicians. The image and ideology of the independent, free professional are giving way to the intrusion into medicine of managerial accountability and control. These changes have been facilitated by US corporations intent on restructuring and rationalizing health care delivery in an attempt to cut costs. Two new kinds of delivery systems function to enforce peer and utilization review procedures and increase cost-efficiency: alternative treatment settings such as out-patient clinics, and HMOs.
          (**physician authority transformed**)

7030

Handbook of Health Professions Education. Edited by Christine H. McGuire *et al* (U of Chicago Health Sciences Center). San Francisco CA: Jossey-Bass, Nov 1983/c600p/$35.00.

Examines recent trends in educating professionals for medicine, dentistry, pharmacy, nursing, allied health, and public health. Chapters are devoted to each of the following forces for change: social values, economic trends, political influences, financial constraints, demographic change, environmental problems, technological innovations, and international needs. Concludes with chapters on new goals for health professions reform and challenges to academic health centers. [Also see **Physicians in the Making: Personal, Academic, and Socioeconomic Characteristics of Medical Students from 1950 to 2000** by Davis

G. Johnson (Jossey-Bass, 1983/297p/$22.95; summary in *The Futurist*, June 1984, 58-59), which reports on a Delphi study conducted by the Association of American Medical Colleges.]   (**trends in health professions education**)

7031

Of Foxes and Hen Houses: Licensing and the Health Professions. Stanley J. Gross. Westport CT: Greenwood Press, 1984/204p/$35.00.

Professionals ignore the substantial amount of evidence discounting the assumptions that self-regulation safeguards the public. Gross details the history of licensing, outlines the definition and measurement of competency, and explores alternatives to licensure and the possibility of using nongovernmental resources as avenues of change. Concludes that a phased deregulation of the professions can enhance both competition and accountability, and result in increased quality, reduced cost, and improved public self-protection.   (**deregulate professions?**)

7032

Why Not Try Preventing Illness as a Way of Controlling Medicare Costs? Anne R. Somers (Rutgers Medical School), *The New England Journal of Medicine*, 311:13, 27 Sept 1984, 853-856.

Now that health-care costs have reached 10.5% of GNP and Medicare alone is approaching 2%, the search for cost-control strategies has also escalated. But there is a continued lack of attention to what is potentially the most effective of all cost-control strategies: the prevention or minimization of disease and disability. Four modest measures are proposed to promote greater knowledge and responsibility among Medicare enrollees and encourage greater professional interest in prevention: 1) Consumer Information: pamphlets issued free or at nominal cost with information about symptom recognition, self-care, when to see the doctor, etc.; 2) Financial Incentives: for example, raising Federal cigarette and alcohol excise taxes and earmarking the revenue for the Medicare Trust Fund; 3) Preventive Procedures to be Covered by Medicare; 4) Encouraging Prevention-Oriented Primary Care: early detection of suspected illness is now discouraged by Medicare's exclusion of preventive services and by general disincentives to primary care. In sum, ignoring the challenge of prevention is not only poor health policy but poor insurance policy.   (**control Medicare cost by prevention**)

7033

Prevention, the Aged, and the Costs of Medical Care (Editorial), Milton Terris (Editor), *Journal of Public Health Policy*, 5:2, June 1984, 157-164.

The enormous escalation of medical care costs is forcing a reexamination of priorities; the primacy of prevention is no longer a concept, but an inescapable necessity. Major savings in medical care costs are now possible as a result of research over the past 30 years that has laid the groundwork for a "second epidemiologic revolution" to conquer major noninfectious diseases such as cancer, heart disease, and injuries. Considerable progress has already been made, but much more needs to be done. Expanded public health control programs could, for example, bring the death rate from cerebrovascular disease down to a third of the 1978 rate of 80 per 100,000 population. Effective implementation of this revolution will result in a significant decline in the need and expenditures for medical care. It will also create a demographic revolution, with a greater proportion of older people and of the healthy aged.
          (**a second epidemiologic revolution?**)

7034

Preventing Illness and Injury in the Workplace. U.S. Congress, Office of Technology Assessment. Washington: USGPO, April 1985/$15.00 (S/N 052-003-00978-1). Summary copies free from OTA.

Each year, about 6,000 Americans die from workplace injuries. Depending on what kinds of injuries are counted, non-fatal injuries total between 2.5 and 11.3 million annually. Congressional action could promote occupational health and safety in the following areas: 1) more and better efforts to enhance hazard identification; 2) enhancing the development of controls for safety hazards (machine guarding, process redesign, work practices, personal protective equipment); 3) changing incentives that affect employer decisions to control workplace hazards (providing information to workers and employers, changes in business taxes, providing financial assistance or loans); 4) increasing OSHA and NIOSH consultation (most studies on injury rates have shown that OSHA has had little or no effect).
(workplace injury prevention)

7035

No Limits to Health: Creating a New Strategy for Health, Robert Rodale (Editor, *Prevention*), *The Futurist*, 19:3, June 1985, 40-42.

Our disease-handling structure is not sustainable in its present form. Costs are too high, and continue to rise. The number of older people who need great amounts of care is increasing dramatically. Only by learning to think beyond sickness will we be able to break out of the present frustrating pattern. The potential to create far greater health exists, if we concentrate on fitness, wellness, and other more positive visions of what health is. Everyone can begin to feel better and be healthier because institutions are learning to separate the production of health from the strategies used to deal with disease, accidents, and other maladies. The current treatment system gets 96% to 98% of all health resources. The scattered efforts at prevention of disease and accidents get the rest. Prevention has been undervalued because it is usually thought of as preventive medicine—another medical strategy—and because the acts of prevention are diffuse and hard to pin down. To stimulate recognition of the unrealized potential for prevention, Rodale Press has established a Prevention Research Center, which in turn has devised a Prevention Index based on annual surveys by Louis Harris and Associates. [NOTE: These views are compatible with the advocacy of "health promotion" and "healthy public policy," #7000/7001]   **(better health by more prevention)**

7036

Mind, Body, and Health: Toward an Integral Medicine. Edited by James S. Gordon (Georgetown U Medical Center), Dennis T. Jaffe (UCLA School of Medicine), and David E. Bresler (Center for Integral Medicine, Los Angeles). NY: Human Sciences Press, 1984/ 269p/$39.95;$16.95pb.

Within the health care community today, a new focus is emerging, characterized by an integrated or holistic approach to treating the whole person. It emphasizes the psychological aspects of the healing process, and stresses the maintenance of health rather than the treatment of disease. These essays consider conditioned relaxation, mind-body harmony, guided imagery, biofeedback, a historical view of nutrition (by Robert Rodale), therapeutic touch and the metaphysics of nursing, acupuncture, pain control, a whole-person approach to cancer treatment, overcoming self-defeating behavior, wellness education,

the integral birth model, family therapy and physical illness, creative aging, and alternative mental health services.[NOTE: A more specific (i.e. reductionist, or less holistic) and more polemical (i.e., less scholarly) guide to holistic alternatives than that offered by Salmon, #7006. Also see **Health and Healing: Understanding Conventional and Alternative Medicine** by Andrew Weil (Houghton Mifflin, Nov 1983/296p/$13.95), which falls somewhere between these two anthologies in breadth and style.]
(holistic health alternatives)

7037

Cashing in on Fitness Foods, Winston Williams, *The New York Times*, Sunday, 4 Nov 1984, F1.

Once an underground movement isolated on the nation's coasts, the fitness phenomenon has exploded across the US and turned into big business. Lighter and healthier foods are the largest part of the fitness market and the fastest growing segment of the retail food industry, now accounting for 9% of sales. Sales of "healthy" products are growing at about 6% per year, in contrast to growth of less than 1% for the entire food industry, and this pace is likely to continue through 1990. Companies are engaged in a huge research effort, with recent successes such as removing caffeine and sugar from soft drinks. The best promise of a revolutionary breakthrough is at Procter & Gamble, where a synthetic fat (sucrose polyester) is being tested that lines the stomach and prevents absorption of fats and cholesterol. Many food executives regard the health and fitness movement as the most significant shift in the food industry in nearly 40 years. But nutritionists and consumer groups question many "healthy products"; some are seen as "nouveau junk food."   **(fitness foods booming)**

7038

Flood of Health Kits Widens Home Tests For Early Symptoms, N. R. Kleinfield, *The New York Times*, Monday, 1 Oct 1984, p1.

Home medical testing is riding the rising wave of attention to physical well-being, as a result of a better-educated population more alert to how the body works, rising costs of conventional medical care, and new technology (especially smaller and cheaper computer chips) allowing medical devices to be transferred from the doctor's office to the patient's home. The $0.8 billion health-care products market in 1984 is expected to swell to $1.8 billion by 1988. The biggest-selling items are blood pressure and blood glucose monitors, fever thermometers and biofeedback equipment, and the home pregnancy test. Products to arrive in the next few years include test kits for diabetes and urinary tract infections, a test for hidden blood in the stool, a device that detects breast diseases, and a test measuring enzymes in the saliva that alerts a woman at least five days ahead of her peak fertility period.   **(home medical testing)**

D. Drugs

*7039

Pharmacy in the 21st Century: Planning for an Uncertain Future. Edited by Clement Bezold (IAF) *et al*. Published by Institute for Alternative Futures and Project HOPE. Bethesda MD: American Association of Colleges of Pharmacy (4720 Montgomery Ave), April 1985 / 291p/ $18.50. Executive Summary, $1.00.

Proceedings from a March 1984 conference in Millwood, Virginia, on the future environment for pharmacy within an evolving health care delivery system. **Clement Bezold** sketches a range of four alternative futures for society and the health care system—continued growth, decline and stagnation, an Orwellian reaction leading to a disciplined society, and a transformation to a more decentralized and participatory society—which are considered in most of the subsequent papers. **Rick Carlson** describes trends that are reshaping the health care system: an aging population, health promotion and wellness movements, the shift from mechanistic to biological metaphors for health, the rise of "holistic" approaches to health care, etc. **Jack Meyer** worries that new technology and the increasing percentage of the aged will drive health care costs ever upward to 14% or 15% of GNP by the early 21st century, and that physicians may start to dispense drugs to enhance their income. **Gail Wilensky** reviews the Federal role in health care, suggesting that marketplace forces will be given greater freedom by providing vouchers for health care to the non-aged poor. **Ken Dychtwald** notes recent changes in the health care system that are generally consistent with the transformation scenario, and identifies prospects and potential techniques for extending life expectancy to 120-140 years. **Daniel Callahan** argues that we are entering an era of recognizing the limits of our ability to pay for everything we might be able to do in health care, and forecasts a greater sensitivity to the full costs and benefits of new technology. **Keith Weikel** sees for-profit and non-profit hospital management companies emerging as super-corporations of the 1980s and 1990s, diversifying beyond acute inpatient care to a variety of medical, health, and personal services delivered through a variety of settings. **Willis Goldbeck** explores the nature of employee benefits in 2035, and views the emergence of associations of individuals and small employers pressing for negotiated care and bulk purchase of drugs. He also forecasts ready access to information on the values and risks associated with the full range of drug and non-drug therapies. **Lawrence Lutz** observes that, in the future, many chronic medical problems will be handled by computerized systems, with physicians left to handle urgent and acute problems. **J. Richard Crout** foresees ever more sophisticated pharmaceuticals and pharmacists (many requiring a doctorate in pharmacy after 2005), with the communications revolution enabling consumers to bypass pharmacists as a counseling and information source. **William Check** reports on a survey of leading researchers in industry and universities on new drugs and drug delivery systems. **Lawrence Hoff** reviews the factors that will shape pharmaceutical marketing and distribution. **Louis Rossiter** and **Luann Dodini** examine the supply and roles of pharmacists: more physicians and nurses will be dispensing drugs, a greater number of pharmacists will be women, and future pharmacopeias may include herbal remedies. The editors conclude by noting two areas of disagreement: whether or not the role of health promotion would have a significant effect on health care, and whether health costs would continue to rise or decline to levels of 20 years ago. One area of consensus was the prediction of an increase in the over-the-counter share of the drug market. [NOTE: Although this volume covers a broad range of concerns and possibilities, it must be noted that very little or no attention is given to the topics of illegal and black market drugs, drug abuse, various chemicals in the environment, and misuse of drugs in the Third World.]   **(future of drugs and health care)**

7040

Orphan Drugs: Medical vs. Market Value. Carolyn H. Asbury (Robert Wood Johnson Foundation, Princeton NJ). Lexington MA: Lexington Books, Jan 1985/219p/$27.00.

Orphan drugs—the drugs nobody wants to manufacture—are the only effective treatment for some rare and chronic diseases. But they are often unavailable because they have a small market, require costly testing, have high liability risks, lack patent protection, or are appropriate only for diseases indigenous to poor countries. A new drug now costs an estimated $50 million, on average, to develop and bring to the market. As a consequence, drugs with a low anticipated return on investment often do not undergo development. Orphan drugs are market losers because of the changing processes by which new drugs are discovered, developed, approved, and distributed in the US. Chapters discuss the changing drug system, the Federal role, patents and publishing, efforts to legislate orphan drugs, the Orphan Drug Act signed by President Reagan in January 1983, and new plans and vistas for orphan drugs.

(low volume/high risk drugs)

7041

Soon Drugs May Make Us Smarter, Michael Schrage, *The Washington Post*, Sunday, 3 Feb 1985, C1.

Puritan notions of drugs as a way to escape reality are collapsing in a society where people are looking for virtually any edge they can find to succeed. Yesterday's searches for personal pleasure may be superseded by tomorrow's quest for improved personal productivity. The present controversy surrounding athletes who use drugs to sharpen their competitive edge offers a disquieting vision of the future for people who live by their wits. Several scientists are now predicting that, by 2000, the revolution in understanding the chemistry of the brain will result in pills that are the brain's equivalent of the steroids now taken by athletes. They will alter mental competition as radically as steroids and other chemicals have altered sports. Just as we seek an edge in computer technology, we may seek pharmacological tools to yield productivity gains. Will students who take exams then have to take urine tests? Will Nobel laureates of two or three decades hence be using drugs to enhance their research abilities? Is that bad?

("brain steroids"?)

7042

Man's Addictions and How to Deal with Them. *impact of science on society* (Unesco, Paris), 34:1, No 133, 1984/170p/20 Francs.

Essays on the global problem of drug abuse (concluding that progress in drug control will depend on the coordinated activities of national authorities), an overview of research on cannibis stressing both its dangers and its promise in various therapies, preventing use of drugs through education and improving the quality of life, fighting drug dependence, the harmful effect of commercializing alcoholic beverages in developing countries, and efforts at control and treatment in Thailand, Pakistan, Spain, The Philippines, China, and Austria.   **(world drug abuse)**

7043

Rampant Drug Abuse Brings Call for Move Against Source Nations, Joel Brinkley, *The New York Times*, Sunday, 9 Sept 1984, p1.

The first of six articles on how almost every strategy to control drug abuse has failed. Federal estimates show that more marijuana, cocaine, and heroin are being produced than ever before, and far more of the world's supply goes to the US than to any other country. At least one million Americans are addicted to cocaine, and many Federal officials say that it has become the most serious drug problem the US has ever faced. With the tens of billions of dollars Americans spend on these illicit drugs each year, the world's drug traffickers are corrupting Third World governments and disrupting their economies. Many in Congress are saying that the US must try more drastic approaches, such as revoking foreign aid to drug-producing countries. But when one country manages to reduce or eliminate narcotics production, other countries start growing the plants instead. The US State Department estimates that since 1980, worldwide production of opium poppies has increased more than 50%, while coca production has increased by 40% and cannibis by 20%. Other articles in this series (September 10-14) explore drug trafficking in Jamaica, Columbia, Bolivia, Thailand, and Mexico, and how traffickers evade attempts to stem the flow of drugs.

(US drug abuse worst ever)

7044

Drug Use Down, Lloyd Johnston *et al* (Institute for Social Research), *ISR Newsletter* (U of Michigan), 12:3, Winter 1984-85, 4-5.

Results from the latest of ISR's annual studies of some 17,000 high school seniors continue to reveal a gradual but steady decline in illicit drug use since 1980. Marijuana use reached a peak in 1978, with 37% reporting they had smoked it at least once during the previous month, and some 11% reporting daily or near-daily use. The 1984 survey shows the proportion of seniors smoking marijuana daily dropping to 5%, while occasionial use has dropped to 25%. Parallel to this decline is a rise of student disapproval of the drug, with the proportion of seniors disapproving of regular marijuana use rising from 65% in 1977 to 85% in 1984. The use of alcohol and cigarettes has also continued to decline, suggesting a trend toward healthier behavior among young people. In 1979, 72% of seniors reported alcohol use in the past month, with the proportion dropping to 67% by 1984. Daily cigarette smoking fell by nearly a third between 1977 and 1980, but then leveled off through 1983, before falling again in 1984, from 21.2% to 18.7%. The use of cocaine, however, increased sharply among high school students between 1976 and 1979, but has now leveled off as a growing number of students see its use as dangerous. Further details are provided in a series of annual ISR volumes entitled **Monitoring the Future: Questionnaire Responses from the Nation's High School Seniors**. [NOTE: On the other hand, *Newsweek* (1 April 1985, 84-87) reports that various studies have shown that young people's performance levels on various tests of physical endurance have declined over the past decade.]   **(high school senior's drug use decline)**

7045

Toward a Global Strategy to Combat Smoking: The 5th World Conference on Smoking and Health, Kenneth E. Warner (Prof of Health Planning, U of Michigan), *Journal of Public Health Policy*, 5:1, March 1984, 28-39.

Some 1100 people from 80 countries gathered in Winnipeg, Canada, in July 1983 to discuss the scientific, social, and political aspects of smoking. The main themes of the plenary sessions are summarized. 1) Smoking and Women: the popularity of smoking has grown enormously among women worldwide, exacting a substantial health toll (a recent study suggests that virtually all of women's life expectancy superiority to men is attributable to differences in male-female smoking behaviors); 2) Smoking and Children: the general downward trend in the prevalence of teenage smoking since the mid-1970s, pervading all age groups of both boys and girls, is a source of encouragement; 3) Smoking in the Third World: smoking rates have leveled off or are falling in the developed world, but are increasing rapidly in the LDCs, where people often have little awareness of the health consequences of smoking (in many countries, tobacco provides a substantial proportion of government revenues). The conference concluded with 20 recommendations, such as urging all governments to adopt regular increases in cigarette taxation, reduce the upper limit of nicotine and other substances in cigarettes, and place health warnings on all tobacco products. UN agencies are urged to cease supporting tobacco growing and initiate programs to develop alternative crops.

(World Conference on Smoking and Health)

7046

The Smoke Ring: Tobacco, Money, and Multinational Politics. Peter Taylor (BBC). NY: Pantheon, Oct 1984/ $18.95.

Smoking has wiped out more people than all the wars of this century. But the tobacco industry, as documented by Taylor, has a powerful influence on the British and American governments, the news media, and consumers. It has created a "smoke ring" that encourages smoking, and it provides other political and economic benefits such as jobs and revenues from cigarette sales taxes. Cigarettes should not be banned, but governments should ban all cigarette advertising and promotion, while launching extensive education programs.   **(tobacco industry)**

XIII. FAMILIES AND EDUCATION

A. Children and Families

*7047

Marriage and the Family in the Year 2020. Edited by Lester A. Kirkendall and Arthur E. Gravett (both Oregon State U). Buffalo NY: Prometheus Books, 1984/320p/ $19.95.

Essays intended to stimulate thinking about the future of marriage and the family and the forces which are certain to produce marked alterations in family form and interaction. Topics include social forces and the changing family, new marriage styles and family forms, mate selection in 2020, transformations in human reproduction (in 2020, every pregnancy is carefully planned and thoroughly monitored from fertilization to delivery), children in the information age, parenting in the 21st century (helped by more leisure time, parent training, and return of work to the home), the blending of male and female value systems (although certain differences remain), the transition from sex to sensuality and intimacy, moral concepts in 2020 (interrelated trends toward decriminalizing, demaritalizing, degenderizing, degenitalizing, deprocreating, deisolating, and deindividualizing), work and family connections (flexible interspersing of work, family time, education, and leisure), physical settings for families in space and on earth, more acceptance of options for families by governments, greater tolerance and cultural heterogeneity, and the social consequences of life extension.

(sex and families in 2020)

7048

Abortion and the Politics of Motherhood. Kristin Luker (Associate Prof of Sociology, U of California-San Diego). Berkeley CA: U of California Press, April 1984/ 309p/$14.95.

On the issues, people, and beliefs on both sides of the abortion conflict, showing that moral positions on abortion are intimately tied to views on sexual behavior, child care, family life, and technology. The overwhelming majority of pro-life activists are pious, full-time housewives who have built their lives around a worldview emphasizing differences rather than similarities between the sexes, viewing homemaking and motherhood as a woman's highest calling. For pro-choice women, paid work figures importantly in personal identity, and sex is for intimacy and pleasure as much as for making babies. Pro-life and pro-choice people talk past each other because they live in different worlds; what advances one group's social interests threatens those of the other. Both movements are remarkably ineffective in changing people's minds on the abortion question because activists from the two sides are deeply committed and seem unable to agree on fundamental premises or even to find a common vocabulary. Continued bitter polarization is expected.

(polarization on abortion and lifestyle)

7049

Family, Self, and Society: Emerging Issues, Alternatives, and Interventions. Edited by Douglas B. Gutknecht *et al.* (Chapman College, Orange CA). Lanham MD: University Press of America, July 1983 / 592p/ $37.25;$23.00 pb.

Essays on such topics as individual and family well-being over the life course, supports for the dual-career couple, fathers-to-be in transition, family social problems and the future, issues in modern divorce, choices in the American family of the future, issues in family policy, the decline of the middle-class family, shrinking households, alternative lifestyles, and ramifications for clinical social work.

(family and society essays)

7050

Parents, Children, and Change. Edited by L. Eugene Arnold (Ohio State U). Lexington MA: Lexington Books, Jan 1985/204p/$21.00;$9.95pb.

Essays on future shock and the parent/child relationship: Jessie Bernard on changing family lifestyles, Urie Bronfenbrenner on the effects of social change (single parenthood, maternal employment, poverty) on child development, and others on high technology and the family, feeding patterns and the changing family, the workplace and the family, divorce law and custody, and alternative parent/child support systems. **(families and change)**

7051

Families and Change: Social Needs and Public Policies. Edited by Rosalie G. Genovese (Center for the Study of Women and Sex Roles, CUNY Graduate Center). Foreword by Jessie Bernard. South Hadley MA: Bergin & Garvey (in association with Praeger, New York), May 1984/ 344p/$27.95;$14.95pb.

Government documents and original essays arranged in five areas: 1) Needs and Rights of Children and Youth: minority children, Federal involvement in child rearing, child care and family benefits, youth problems; 2) Work and Family: women vs. protective labor legislation, equal opportunity and the need for child care, working mothers and family life, unemployment among family men, teenage unemployment; 3) The Economic Status of Families: the President's Commission for a National Agenda for the Eighties on promoting the welfare of Americans, women and children alone in poverty, policy options for older women, changing male/female roles and Social Security; 4) Housing and Community: policy and research options for housing families, community care policies in Britain, developing a community response to a plant closing; 5) Policy Issues for the 1980s: report of the New York State Task Force on Domestic Violence, never-married Americans and public policy, the cooperative "family" as an alternative lifestyle for the elderly, self-help networks for meeting family needs. **(families and public policy)**

7052

Prevention in Family Services: Approaches to Family Wellness. Edited by David R. Mace (Bowman Gray Medical School). Beverly Hills CA: Sage Publications, Dec 1983/c232p/$25.00;$12.50.

Family problems can be prevented, as well as remedied. In this new approach to family services, figures in the "family wellness" movement write on such matters as prevention as a profession, marriage enrichment, whole family enrichment, preparing for parenthood during pregnancy, preventing parent-adolescent crises, promoting effective communication in families, training families to deal with conflict, promoting family wellness through the churches and the educational system, and growth-promoting family therapy. **(preventing family problems)**

7053

Child Development Research and Social Policy. Volume 1. Edited by Harold W. Stevenson (U of Michigan) and Alberta E. Siegel (Stanford U). Chicago, Ill.: U of Chicago Press, 1984/c520p/$30.00;$15.00.

The first in a series commissioned by the Committee on Social Policy of the Society for Research in Child Development, applying recent findings in child development research to various social issues: 1) policies toward various ethnic, racial, and language groups in the US; 2) child health policy; 3) social policies affecting children of divorced parents; 4) institutionalization of mentally retarded children; 5) cross-national political socialization.

(social policy for children)

7054

Children, Mental Health, and the Law. Edited by N. Dickon Reppucci *et al*. Beverly Hills CA: Sage Publications, Jan 1984/312p/$28.00;$14.00pb.

Who should be the final authority in determining the mental health needs of a child: parents, psychologists, judges, or children themselves? This collection of essays offers a broad view of the relationship between families, schools, courts, and the health care system, examining such topics as child custody, maltreatment, reproductive rights, juvenile justice, education for the handicapped, what children need, and what parents want.

(children and mental health needs)

7055

In the Interests of Children: Advocacy, Law Reform, and Public Policy. Robert H. Mnookin (Prof of Law, Stanford U). NY: W.H. Freeman, Jan 1985/572p/$27.95; $14.95pb.

Case studies on crucial areas of policy concern relating to children—foster care, teenage pregnancy and abortion, school discipline, institutions for the mentally retarded, and the welfare system—with an emphasis on the strengths and weaknesses of litigation as a means of achieving reform. Children need advocates because, in most instances, they cannot speak for and defend their own interests. Child advocates in the Progressive Era (roughly the first two decades of this century) sought to ameliorate social conditions by enacting protective laws and creating new institutions. They believed in state paternalism and the efficacy of professional help. Today's child advocates have much less faith in state power, and often fight to protect parental autonomy against state intrusion. The earlier generation of child advocates achieved their greatest success in state legislatures; modern advocates typically shun state legislatures in favor of Federal courts. Litigation has several attractions compared with legislation: 1) courts are open as a matter of right, whereas legislatures can be a procedural labyrinth; 2) courts appear to be more receptive to arguments based on principle, and costs are not explicitly considered in most circumstances; 3) courtroom advocacy may create fewer ethical and political problems for its partisans, in contrast to lobbying; 4) by casting a policy change in the form of a lawsuit, child advocates may substantially reduce the power of organized interest groups to frustrate action; 5) lawsuits may require much less time and expense to obtain reform. Mnookin concludes by stressing the profound difficulties of making policy for children, no matter what the forum.

(child advocacy trend to litigation)

7056

Employer-Supported Child Care: Investing in Human Resources. National Employer-Supported Child Care Project. Dover MA: Auburn House (14 Dedham St), 1984/362p/$24.95;$15.00pb.

Given the rise in female-headed families, one of the most important aspects of the new work situation is the critical need of employees for child care while they work. The number of companies that provide such care has increased dramatically. In a recent Harris Poll, 67% of corporate human resource executives reported that they expect to provide child care services within the next five years. This book reports on the experience of 425 employer-supported programs, and the benefits to employers such as improved recruitment and retention of workers and reduced absenteeism. **(employer-supported child care)**

7057

More Corporations Are Offering Child Care, Glenn Collins, *The New York Times*, Friday, 21 June 1985.

A new study by The Conference Board (Research Bulletin No. 177/39p/$15.00) found more than 1,800 companies providing some form of child-care assistance to workers, up from only 600 in 1982. An estimated 120 companies and 400 hospitals and public agencies sponsor day-care centers at or near their facilities. Some companies provide child care information and referral services to their employees, after-school care, or nursing services for sick children so their parents can work. About 30 companies have undertaken to train and license family day-care providers who care for children in their homes. Many companies provide direct financial assistance to employees through a variety of programs: 1) voucher programs that add money to employee paychecks to pay for child care or that pay providers directly; 2) negotiated discounts with local child-care centers; 3) child care as an option in employee benefit plans, or 4) reducing employees' taxable salaries to establish tax-free spending accounts for child care. Corporate child-care programs are most commonly found among high-tech companies, banks, insurance companies, and hospitals. **(corporate child-care assistance)**

7058

All Grown Up & No Place to Go: Teenagers in Crisis. David Elkind (Prof of Child Study, Tufts U). Reading MA: Addison-Wesley, June 1984/232p/$17.95;$8.95pb.

Author of **The Hurried Child** (Addison-Wesley, 1981; **FS Annual 1981-82**, #4159) finds that many "hurried children" who were pushed to grow up are now teenagers. But there is no protected place for teenagers in today's hurried society. A decade ago, teenagers had a clearly defined position in the social structure.   They have now lost their privileged position, and are expected to confront life and its challenges with the maturity once expected only of the middle-aged. The result is a staggering number of teenagers who have not made a healthy transition to adulthood, and may never be productive and responsible citizens, much less lead happy and rewarding lives. When 50% of our youth are at one or another time abusing alcohol or drugs, something is seriously wrong. Concludes with a chapter on what can be done by parents (learn to say no), schools (reduce class size to 18 or fewer students so teachers can devote more time to each student), and the media (a concerted effort to stem the flow of trash for kids—a lessening of violence and sex on the small and large screen).

(hurried teenagers in crisis)

B. Learning Needs

7059
The World Educational Crisis Revisited. Philip H. Coombs (International Council for Education Development). NY: Oxford U Press, Dec 1984 / 384p / $19.95; $10.95pb.

Author of **The World Educational Crisis: A Systems Analysis** (Oxford, 1968) concentrates on critical issues that will confront the family of nations in the years to come: the worldwide growth of learning needs and how to meet them through formal and nonformal education, the growing financial squeeze and inequalities that exist between and within countries, the growing imbalance between rising educational output and limited employment opportunities, the potential for educational reforms, innovations and new technologies, and possible ways of coping with these issues.

(world educational crisis)

7060
Education and Development: The Recovery of Commons, Ivan Illich (Cuernavaca, Mexico), *Resurgence*, No 106, Sept-Oct 1984, 26-28.

Author of the highly controversial **De-Schooling Society** (Harper & Row, 1971) argues that education and development are notions that have been harnessed as the draught animals of so-called progress. Education advertised enlightened and productive citizenship and in fact delivered certification; development promised paychecks for all, and so changed the environment that the penniless lost much of their ability to survive by muddling through. Education is the most direct threat to those conditions under which meaningful learning can take place, while economic growth is the most direct challenge to commons and customs on which vernacular subsistence is built. Education is a means to make people adjuncts to economic growth. Once, everywhere, almost everything that people needed for everyday life was learned because it was meaningful and had proven useful. Now we are constantly taught what is meaningful, from a perspective that is not yet ours, and we are taught only as much as we are able to pay for, or society is rich enough to give us. By creating an inner void, education blights the commons of sense. Both education and development are based on the assumption of scarcity, and both tend to propagate the assumption, the experience, and the organization of scarcity. E&D thus act as self-fulfilling prophecies about man. The desirable counterfoil to E&D is more informal and non-programmed learning, and reducing the need for commodities. This project can be called the recovery of commons—the porous cultural space that is used for different purposes by different people. It is not possible to recreate the old commons, but the notion of "recovery" can at least help us, conceptually, to move beyond our notions of E&D.

(education as threat to meaningful learning)

7061
Theory and Resistance in Education: A Pedagogy for the Opposition. Henry A. Giroux (Miami U, Oxford, Ohio). Foreword by Paulo Freire. South Hadley MA: Bergin & Garvey, 1983/280p/pb.

The spirit of radical pedagogy is its aversion to all forms of domination. Its challenge centers around the need to develop modes of critique fashioned in a theoretical discourse that mediates the possibility for social action and emancipatory transformation. Radical pedagogy must be informed by a passionate faith in the necessity of struggling to create a better world. It needs a vision that celebrates not what is but what could be, linking struggle to a new set of human possibilities. It is a call for concrete utopianism, and for alternative modes of experience that affirm the possibilities of creative risk-taking. Chapters are devoted to exploring critical theory and educational practice, schooling and the politics of the hidden curriculum, resistance and accommodation, culture and schooling, rationality in citizenship education, literacy and ideology, and the need for a new public sphere.

(radical pedagogy)

7062
Global Stakes: The Future of High Technology in America. James Botkin, Dan Dimancescu (both Technology and Strategy Group, Cambridge MA), and Ray Stata. NY: Penguin Books, April 1984/235p/$7.95pb. (First published by Ballinger, Fall 1982.)

Economic leadership in the high-tech world of the coming decades will depend on a steady supply of brainpower. The US is losing out in the high-tech stakes to countries such as Japan and France because of a shortage of scientists, engineers, and mathematicians. America's leadership has failed to recognize the shift from a capital-intensive economy to a knowledge-intensive economy centering on electronics and computers. The solution should focus on higher education and be targeted specifically at improving engineering education. To this end, a "High Technology Morrill Act" is proposed, fashioned after the Land Grant Act 100 years earlier and named after its author, Justin Morrill. In the introduction to this paperbound edition, the authors note that this recommendation has been translated into a legislative proposal filed in the US Senate.

("High Technology Morrill Act" for engineering)

7063
Jobs: A Changing Workforce, A Changing Education? Henry M. Levin (Prof of Education, Stanford U), *Change*, 16:7, Oct 1984, 32-37.

The US is entering a new age in which high technology products and processes will play an increasingly significant role. The advent of high technology will expand the capabilities of the economy, reduce prices, and offer a large array of new products. But it is not likely to add large numbers of jobs for highly educated and trained persons. Many workers will likely be replaced by new technology, and skill requirements of broad classes of occupations will probably be reduced. The number and kind of jobs that will be available to any individual over a lifetime cannot be predicted. Accordingly, it is important to possess a broad array of fundamental skills in higher education for the vast majority of students, rather than narrow vocational preparation. These skills include written and oral expression, mathematics, sciences, fine and performing arts, analytical skills, social sciences, and foreign languages. Much more emphasis should be placed on the training of entrepreneurs and on fostering creativity. Virtually all students in higher education should be required to obtain proficiency in at least one foreign language and the study of another culture. Concludes that accepting the realities of high-tech societies and making conscious choices with both economics and education in mind can improve the future considerably. Ignoring the problem will lead to serious consequences for both the labor force and education.

(higher education in a high-tech society)

7064

Learning for Life: Overcoming the Separation of Work and Learning. The Report of the National Advisory Panel on Skill Development Leave to the Minister of Employment and Immigration. Ottawa: Employment and Immigration Canada (Public Affairs), March 1984/29p.

The earned right to leave for educational purposes is an idea whose time has come. The pace of technological change and international competition increases the value of flexibility and adaptability on the part of working Canadians. The existing pattern of learning, earning, and retirement must give way to an inter-weaving of working and learning spread over a lifetime. But self-reliance and productivity of many groups in Canada are handicapped by poor access to learning opportunities; among these groups, the most pressing priorities are educationally disadvantaged adults and those threatened with job loss and skill obsolescence. A number of significant barriers face adults who seek to upgrade their skills and capacities: situational barriers (lack of time, money, transportation, or child care), attitudes and dispositional barriers, institutional barriers (scheduling, red tape, discrimination against part-time students), and a "shocking lack" of relevant information. Recommendations include: 1) endorsement by the Federal government of the goal of "Canada as a Learning Society" and associated principles of a Right to Learn throughout life and an Earned Right to time to engage in learning; 2) a ten year program to combat illiteracy in Canada, with paid time off for those taking literacy leave; 3) a program for retraining employees threatened with job loss and skill obsolescence; 4) accelerated removal of barriers; 5) a program for Universal Educational Leave, whereby all Canadian workers would earn one day of leave for every 30 days worked, with costs covered by a surtax on individual and corporate income taxes; 6) a "Finish High School (or equivalent)" program made available at times and in locations suitable to the disadvantaged learner; 7) Local Training Councils to plan and coordinate programs to meet local needs (the Councils should include representatives from governments, industry, the voluntary sector, labor, and education—as well as users and potential users of the system); 8) a Federal-Provincial Council on Educational Leave to promote, coordinate, and report on the discussion, planning, and implementation of the recommendations in this report. [NOTE: A set of very interesting and ambitious ideas.]   **(educational leave proposed)**

7065

The Learning Enterprise: Adult Learning, Human Capital, and Economic Development. Lewis J. Perelman (Strategic Performance Services, Alexandria VA). Washington: The Council of State Planning Agencies, 1984/63p/$7.95pb.

Learning is the key capital-forming industry of the post-industrial economy. Education of children is important, but school reforms will have little impact on the immediate human capital crisis that will put the US at risk for the next 20 to 30 years. The emergence of a knowledge-based economy requires a new synthesis of the functions of training, education, and other forms of communication and learning under the single umbrella of "the learning enterprise." This enterprise is destined to become the keystone industry of the emerging fourth sector of the economy—the knowledge sector. The major barrier to creating the kind of learning enterprise needed by a new economy is the appalling lack of timely and accurate information about the entire system of adult learning in the US. In addition to developing better information on adult learning,

policymakers should consider the following options for action: 1) reduce emphasis on academic degrees, in that the proliferation of degree granting and the decline of standards tells an employer little about individual competence; 2) focus on evaluation of competency and achievement; 3) expand basic R&D on adult learning and development; 4) develop human capital investment advisory services; 5) focus telematics industry products and services on the adult learning market; 6) rethink the means for financing human capital development and the resulting distribution of costs and benefits. [NOTE: Broadly generalized; more specific proposals addressed to the same concern can be found in the Canadian report, above.]

(need to develop human capital)

7066

The Strategic Context of Education in America 1985-1995. David Pearce Snyder (Bethesda MD). Washington: National Education Assn Office of Planning (1201 16th St NW), Nov 1984/36p(8x11").

The principal legacy of the Baby Boom will be the "Baby Boom Echo," a new surge of births in the US expected to peak around 1990 at about 4 million a year, ultimately producing about the same number of children during the next ten years as did the first Baby Boom in the 1950s. At the same time, a central concern of public policy will be the effective recycling of 15 to 20 million skilled blue collar, technical, and professional employees who will lose their jobs due to improved productivity. (This will include 2 to 3 million middle managers who will lose their jobs due to the "delayering of management.") With this retraining of workers, the new Baby Boom, and remedial education for sub-standard entry-level workers, the expenditures for education should grow by 20% to 25% from 1981 to 1990, so that education surpasses health care to become the largest industry in America. The compelling necessity to upgrade our human resources will clearly elicit significant increases in both public and private sector funding for education and training during the coming decade. But there will also be equally compelling demands on the limited supplies of discretionary capital for equally essential national purposes, and a worldwide capital shortage will sustain double-digit interest rates beyond 2000. This basic reality suggests that all proposals for both post-industrial educational reform and for trans-industrial retraining should be rigorously assessed in terms of cost-effectiveness, in order to assure adoption of the most productive initiatives. Concludes by suggesting major initiatives for NEA: a commitment to intellectual rearmament, creating an educational innovators network, re-skilling America's teachers, and quality circles for quality education. Concludes that what is at stake in educational adaptation and innovation during the coming decade is not the future of education but the future of the nation.

(education as largest US industry by 1990)

7067

Illiterate America. Jonathan Kozol. NY: Anchor/Doubleday, March 1985/270p/$15.95.

At least one-third of all adults now living in America are illiterate or nearly so, and thus cannot function competently in our society. This means that 60 million American adults, conservatively estimated, are substantially excluded from the democratic process and the ordinary commerce of a print society. The US ranks 49th in literacy levels among 158 UN countries. Moreover, the problem is getting worse. As our society edges away from print as its primary means of communication, the reading level required to get a job increases. Why should we be concerned?

The moral reason is to promote equity and justice, respite from grief, and relief from needless fear. The economic reason is that illiteracy costs us some $20 billion a year in industrial and tax expenditures. Our prison population represents the largest concentration of adult illiterates, and requires an investment of $6.6 billion a year to maintain. Illiteracy is not a result of genetic deficiency; rather, it is self-perpetuating because illiterate parents cannot prepare their children for schools or argue for reform of schools which fail to educate their children. An all-out literacy war is advocated. Given $10 billion a year for ten years, adult illiterates in the US could be reduced by half. Such funding will obviously not be forthcoming from the Reagan Administration, so we must begin with a grass-roots movement that will prove so successful the Federal government must repond. Volunteeers should live in communities where illiterates live, students and the elderly should get involved as teachers, and publishers should donate books. [Also see *Futuribles*, No 84-85, Jan-Feb 1985, 88-90, for a review of **Des illettres en France, rapport au Premier Ministre** by Veronique Esperandieu *et al*. Paris: La Documentation Francaise, 1984/158p.]

(60 million functional illiterates in US)

7068

Handbook for Achieving Sex Equity Through Education. Edited by Susan S. Klein (American Educational Research Assn). Baltimore MD: Johns Hopkins U Press, Jan 1985/512p/$25.95.

Essays seeking to aid in the achievement of sex equity in educational activities and to aid in achievement of sex equity in society through education. Topics include economic considerations for achieving sex equity, facts and assumptions about the nature of sex differences, administrative strategies for institutionalizing sex equity in education, the role of government, overcoming barriers to women in educational administration, sex equity in instructional materials and testing, sex equity in classroom organization and climate, sex equity strategies in content areas (reading and communication skills, social studies, visual arts education, physical education and athletics, career and vocational education), sex equity strategies for specific populations (minority women, gifted women and girls, rural women and girls, programs for adult women), and equity in early education environments. Concludes with a summary of proposals. **(sex equity and education)**

7069

Interest in Learning Foreign Languages Rises, Gene I. Maeroff, *The New York Times*, Monday, 29 Oct 1984, A1.

After an era of neglect, interest in foreign languages is reawakening in US schools and colleges. Responding to an outpouring of reports urging higher educational standards, colleges are reinstituting language requirements abandoned in the late 1960s. Despite some improvements, though, enrollments in such languages as Chinese, Japanese, and Russian remain extremely low compared with the numbers of students studying English in China, Japan, and the USSR. A 1984 study by the National Center of Educational Statistics showed that almost 80% of US high school students have access to the study of at least one foreign language, but fewer than half undertake such study. Only 6% of all students attend high schools that require more than two years of a foreign language.

(foreign language interest rising)

7070

On the Education of Policymakers, Israel Scheffler (Prof of Education and Philosophy, Harvard U), *Harvard Educational Review*, 54:2, May 1984, 152-165.

Offers a set of central guidelines and basic concepts that, ideally, should permeate a curriculum for makers of policy, especially educational decision-makers. Policy reflects and reacts upon the long-range time-binding of historical communities, possessed of common memories and shared dreams for the future. The policy role cannot be reduced to technical matters, but requires historical awareness and self-consciousness respecting values. The policymaker needs to be multilingual, to learn to speak and hear various disciplinary dialects (including the ordinary languages of the persons whose problems are to be addressed), and to employ them conjointly in understanding problems.

(ideal curriculum for policymakers)

7071

How To Make Leaders, Frank Pace Jr (Chairman, National Executive Service Corps), *The New York Times* (Op-Ed), Saturday, 28 July 1984, p23.

Strong leadership, both in quality and quantity, is needed in a successful democracy. We are not producing the number and quality of leaders needed to make our institutions function effectively. American high schools have been facing up to this situation better than higher education. More than 15,000 secondary schools now provide leadership development courses, including 1200 offered for credit. Leadership development will be taught this year at only 12 colleges and universities, but many others are now expressing interest in following suit. The purpose of these programs is to expose young people to the requirements of being a leader, and to show them that leadership skills can be developed.

(leadership development)

C. Schools

*7072

Teaching in Tomorrow's Classrooms, Richard F. Bowman Jr (School of Education, Moorhead State U), *The Educational Forum*, 49:2, Winter 1985, 241-248.

Given what we know about the nature of the learner, our evolving cultural values and beliefs, and our technological capabilities, what potential aims of education should we consider? Bowman suggests: 1) development of skills and behaviors appropriate for interdependent roles and relationships; 2) to cope with the demands of global interdependence, students should be immersed in a diversity of thoughts, values, beliefs, and cultures; 3) an evolving tolerance of ambiguity, reflecting the transition of society to greater pluralism and ambiguity of roles; 4) opportunities for discovering that all of life must be open to question, rather than the recitation of facts or demonstration of techniques; 5) an awareness of the applicability of the concept of "fixability"—opportunities to mend and heal in an era of scarce resources; 6) an appreciation for stating things tentatively, rather than definitively and magisterially. **(learning for the future)**

7073

The Schools We Deserve: Reflections on the Educational Crises of Our Times. Diane Ravitch (Teachers College, Columbia U). NY: Basic Books, April 1985/337p/ $19.95.

A collection of Ravitch's essays over the past decade on such topics as the problem of educational reform, the dilemma of what kind of schooling is most appropriate for a democratic society, fashions in education, scapegoating teachers, past and present criticisms of the high school curriculum, tuition tax credits, uses and misuses of tests, the history of minority group education in the US, desegregation, bilingual education, and a case study of an effective high school in Brooklyn. The common theme throughout is that what happens in the schools and to the schools is determined by our assumptions, ideals, and policies; the effort to improve schools depends on the quality of our ideas. Ravitch's preferences are not for differentiation, but for a strengthening of the academic program for every child. All children should meet real standards of achievement in history, literature, science, math, and foreign language. This is not an argument for a homogeneous curriculum, but for a sense of commitment to intellectual development for all children, not just the gifted. The nature of work is changing, and we cannot predict with any accuracy what kinds of job skills will be needed; therefore, the best preparation for any young person is a general education, a sense of responsibility, and the capacity to keep on learning.   **(improve academic program for all)**

7074

Challenges to American Schools: The Case for Standards and Values. Edited by John H. Bunzel (Hoover Institution, Stanford U). NY: Oxford U Press, March 1985/ 248p/$19.95.

Essays on some of the problems facing US education today that have led to a marked decline in public esteem for the schools. **Joseph Adelson** cautions that widespread enthusiasm for reform of the schools may not bear fruit, due to entrenched bureaucracy and ideological interests. **Robert B. Hawkins, Jr** laments that the elements of diversity, competition, and parental choice have been nearly eliminated in public education; what is needed is a variety of institutions responding to diverse communities of interests and needs. **Diane Ravitch** explores the historical roots of the curriculum debate. **Brigette Berger** argues that educational reform cannot succeed without the help of the family. **Chester E. Finn, Jr** describes how unions can be constructive partners in the quest for educational excellence. **Gerald Grant** focuses on outstanding schools that make an imprint; the leaders of such schools ground their daily decisions in a strong, positive, and shared ethos. **Denis P. Doyle** views the quality of private schools as frequently higher than that of comparable public schools, and argues for a means-tested voucher system designed to extend the benefits of choice to the poor. **Barbara Lerner** shows how Federal judges make educational policy. **Martin Trow** addresses the old problems of unprepared students who enter colleges and universities. **Nathan Glazer** asserts that the problem of raising standards in education is exacerbated by ethnic and racial factors, and discusses strategies to deal with the problem.

(standards and values in schooling)

7075

Choosing Equality: The Case for Democratic Schooling, Ann Bastian, Norm Fruchter, Marilyn Gittell, Colin Greer, and Kenneth Haskins, *Social Policy*, 15:4, Spring 1985, 34-51.

A lengthy excerpt from a longer report with the same title, available from the New World Foundation (100 E 85th St, NYC 10028). The authors contend that the new neo-conservative consensus has identified excellence with an elitist concept of meritocracy, thus reinforcing competitive structures of achievement modeled on and serving the economic marketplace.This perspective misconstrues the real crisis in education: 1) school failure in the bottom tiers (50% to 80% of low income students do not graduate from high school); and 2) narrow achievement throughout the system (the chronic failure to provide citizenship and reasoning skills for all students). The crisis in public schools will not be effectively or fairly addressed without constituent participation in the change process, particularly the empowerment of parents, teachers, and communities. New forces must be added to the institutional politics of schooling, to make those politics more participatory and more directed by the needs of the entire community. School efforts to tap community resources and develop supportive constituents should be matched by efforts to use school resources for the community.

(expanding participation in school change)

7076

School Effectiveness (Special Issue). Edited by Alan Gartner. *Social Policy*, 15:2, Fall 1984, 1-64.

Essays in honor of the late Ronald Edmonds, a black social scientist who served as the chief instructional officer of the NYC public schools from 1978 to 1983 and is regarded as the father of the effective schools movement. Edmonds challenged the accepted view in the early 1970s that "schools don't make a difference" because family background and social class are more important. Even inner city schools can be effective. The effective school has five traits: strong leadership at the school level, high expectations that no child will fall below minimal levels of achievement, an orderly school atmosphere conducive to teaching and learning, acquisition of basic and higher order skills taking precedence over all other school activities, and frequent and consistent evaluation of student progress. These essays deal with the topics of effective schooling for black children, the roots of the present "excellence" movement, the NYC School Improvement Project, effective inner-city elementary schools, advocacy by school administrators, the role of parent participation, building a good school of education, the corporate role in public education, effective schools research, and the proposed Effective Schools Development Act of 1984 to give Federal matching grants to state and local agencies for improving effective schools programs. [Also see **The Good High School: Portraits of Character and Culture** by Sarah Lawrence Lightfoot. NY: Basic Books, Oct 1983/$17.95.]

(promoting effective schools)

7077

Concern Over Schools Spurs Extensive Efforts at Reform, Edward B. Fiske, *The New York Times*, Sunday, 9 Sept 1984, p1.

Educators across the country are turning to the task of carrying out one of the most widespread attempts ever to improve American public education. The current reform movement is often compared to a similar outpouring of concern about educational quality after the Soviet launch of Sputnik in 1957. In both cases, the efforts were spurred by a perceived threat to the nation: the first military, the current one economic. But post-Sputnik initiatives focused primarily on producing a scientific elite through teacher training and new Federally-sponsored curricula, whereas current efforts have been aimed at all students and at the entire spectrum of academic subjects. Chris Pipho (Education Commission of the States) has identified the following developments: 1) at least 240 state-level commissions and study groups have offered suggestions on how to improve schools; 2) numerous governors, especially in the South, have made educational improvement a keystone of their programs; 3) at least 40 states have increased the number of courses required for a high school diploma; 4) 32 states have changed curriculum standards or adopted new procedures for choosing textbooks; 5) 23 states have lengthened the school day or year, or taken other steps to increase the amount of time students spend learning; 6) 42 states have moved to improve the training or raise the certification standards of new teachers; 7) at least 17 states have taken steps to increase teacher salaries; in some of these states, increased pay is being tied to merit pay or master teacher programs. These changes have also created problems: the magnitude of the changes poses considerable administrative difficulties, policies such as "educational bankruptcy" (allowing a state to assume operating control of local school districts in which student achievement is lagging) may shift power from the local to the state level, and teachers are reluctant to carry out the new policies since much of the reform initiative came from non-educators. [A similar article on state reforms, *The Fourth 'R' Is for Reform* by Sharon Johnson, appears in *The New York Times Education Survey, Spring 1985,* 14 April 1985, Section 12, 17-18.]   (**school reforms widespread**)

7078
As States Take Charge Of Schools: A New Plan, Chester E. Finn Jr (Vanderbilt U) and Denis T. Doyle (American Enterprise Institute), *The New York Times Education Survey, Winter 1984-85*, 6 Jan 1985, Section 12, p69.

Local control of public education is on the way out, as the states take charge of school standard-setting, prescribe curriculum content and teacher qualifications, impose elaborate mechanisms of pupil testing and school accountability, equalize resources and offerings throughout their borders, and furnish the major portions of the school dollar. One consequence is that local school boards and superintendents are becoming obsolete. Another consequence is the threat of homogenization and centralized control. A way to gain the advantages of educational equity and enhanced quality without taking on this handicap is to revive the idea of education vouchers—a system in which parents receive certificates equal in value to the cost of their children's education, to be used for the schools they like best. The state would prescribe minimum standards for schools and develop multiple indicators of school performance. Within these limits, each school would run itself, and try to attract students by providing offerings that they and their parents want. Local school boards and superintendents' offices, as we now know them, would vanish. [Also see *States Gain Wider Influence on School Policy*, by Edward B. Fiske (*The New York Times*, 2 Dec 1984, p1), who notes that the growing role of the states has found considerable support from the Reagan Administration, which has worked for reduction of the Federal role in education, but not for a further decentralization of authority from the state to the local level.]

(**state control of education growing**)

7079
The Paideia Program: An Educational Syllabus. Essays by the Paideia Group. Preface and Introduction by Mortimer J. Adler (Chairman, Encyclopaedia Britannica). NY: Macmillan, Nov 1984/238p/$8.95;$4.95pb.

The completion of a trilogy on the reform of basic schooling in the US. **The Paideia Proposal** (1982; **FS Annual 1983**, #5318) advocated a democratic system of public schooling, giving the same quality of schooling to all children: a general, liberal, and humanistic curriculum that includes all three kinds of learning and teaching (seminars, coaching, and didactic instruction), thoroughly integrated with each other. **Paideia Problems and Possibilities** (1983; **FS Annual 1984,** #6253) clarified misconceptions about the first book and elaborated on methods of implementation. This third volume is concerned with what is to be learned, why, and how. Chapters are devoted to each of the three kinds of teaching and learning, how a Paideia school should be structured, and subject matters to be taught and learned: English language and literature, mathematics, science, history, social studies, a foreign language, the fine arts, the manual arts, the world of work, and physical education. Adler concludes with a brief chapter on how to recognize a Paideia school: 1) the three kinds of teaching and learning would be found in reverse to present proportions (about 80% to 85% of classroom time is now occupied by didactic instruction; instead, active Socratic interchanges between teachers and students should occupy 60% to 70% of classroom time); 2) most important, such a school would provide all its students with educational opportunities equal in quality and quantity—one track and the same objectives for all; 3) the principal would be seen as the educational leader of the teaching staff and as the principal teacher; 4) the most striking sign of a Paideia school would be the absence of present methods of educational score-keeping—of testing, examining, and grading students; a different mode of teaching and learning requires a far more comprehensive and accurate type of score-keeping.   (**general education for all**)

7080
The High School and The University: What Went Wrong in America, Burton R. Clark (Prof of Higher Education and Sociology, UCLA), *Phi Delta Kappan*, 66:6, Feb 1985 and 66:7, Mar 1985.

A two-part essay on five features that work to bias the upper level of US secondary education against excellence in preparing students for higher education: universal education, comprehensive schools, downward coupling, local control, and local monopoly. In turn, US higher education is biased against serving effectively in the selection and training of high school teachers. If competence is the long-range goal of education, Americans may have to be willing to differentiate among students and to allow schools to drift into hierarchies. Clearly we need a strategy for injecting some variety into our system of secondary education. A long-term strategy of fundamental structural change would involve greater choice for upper-secondary students, teachers, and school administrators. Methods of increasing choice include schools-within-schools, specialized schools, private schools, networks of schools that share special programs, and competitive comprehensive schools. Greater variety in the types of school units would end the sameness, rigidity, boredom and alienation that are the end products of structural uniformity. [NOTE: A very different approach to the goal of excellence than that set forth by the Paideia group, #7079 above.]

(**variety needed in US secondary education**)

7081

The Great School Reform Hoax, George Leonard, *Esquire*, April 1984, 47-56.

A Nation at Risk and eight other major reports, all released in 1983 and all urging reform, have drawn attention to the schools. But despite the good intentions of the reports, schools will not emerge transformed. If all of these proposals were put into effect, the resulting school would still be pretty much the same as that of 100 years ago, with teachers standing or sitting in front of some 20 to 35 mostly passive students of the same age, giving out the same information at the same time to all of them. Our schools need a thorough restructuring. Leonard's proposals include: 1) individualize education in every responsible way possible; 2) initiate a large-scale curriculum design program, with new material designed to exploit the computer's potential for interaction and individualization; 3) pay teachers more, treat them as masters, and expect them to live up to that assumption; 4) improve education in integrative, nonacademic subjects such as interpersonal communication and physical education; 5) initiate tough, consistent rules concerning dangerous or disruptive behavior (such as bringing drugs or weapons to school, or committing any act of violence); 6) get parents and the community involved in schools; 7) most important, make school exciting, challenging, and vivid.

(proposals to truly reform schools)

7082

Horace's Compromise: The Dilemma of the American High School. Theodore R. Sizer (former Dean, Graduate School of Education, Harvard U). Boston MA: Houghton Mifflin, March 1984/241p/$16.95.

"Horace" is a combination of hundreds of teachers, from urban and rural, rich and poor high schools across America who were interviewed by Sizer for this study sponsored by the National Association of Secondary School Principals. Horace is an excellent teacher who believes in his work, cares about his students, and spends hours after class in extracurricular activities. But he knows that he will never be able to do an adequate job, and this is his compromise. Sizer points out how the entire system works to stifle good will, sap energy, and flatten the hopes of the best of teachers. Everything works against good teaching, including interruptions, the demands of too many pupils on too little time, and financial needs encouraging moonlighting. Schools are friendly and orderly, but they are places of wasteful triviality, rather than serious learning. Students do not learn from teaching, but from coaching. Teachers must be able to prod, encourage, and criticize. Schools must break out of the rigid grade progression, and promote students only when they master subject matter. Other recommendations are made to personalize high schools without ruinously increasing the cost of education.

(dilemma of high school teachers)

7083

Twenty Teachers. Ken Macrorie (Emeritus Prof of English, Western Michigan U). NY: Oxford U Press, Nov 1984/ $17.95.

Identifies characteristics that outstanding teachers have in common, from elementary schools to research universities. The profiles show that the most vital qualities may stem more from personality than from the teaching training process. The best teachers are "enablers"—people whose openness, encouragement, and dedication allow students to rise to their potential, whether they are in remedial classes or programs for the gifted.

(excellent teachers are enablers)

7084

An ROTC of Teachers, Frank Newman (President, Education Commission of the States), *The New York Times Education Survey*, 14 April 1985, Section 12, p73.

Three important social forces have come together to create an opportunity for a new form of student aid: 1) the growing concern over helping the young to develop a greater responsibility for serving their community and country; 2) a growing concern over attracting capable young people into the teaching profession; 3) the need to help students to finance their college education. All these needs could be met by taking a new look at an old American concept—the model that works for the Reserve Officers Training Corps. Applied to teaching, such a proposal would give fellowships to carefully selected college sophomores, who would spend their summers with low-performing elementary or secondary school pupils, helping them to reach grade level or beyond. Upon graduation, the student would be assigned to a school at the regular beginning teacher's salary, with the obligation to serve for a limited period of time, similar to lieutenants in the military, but not necessarily making a career choice. Such a program could be initiated nationally, or by states, cities, or individual school districts. Indeed, one school district in Colorado has already established such a program.

(ROTC for teachers proposed)

7085

Huck Finn Is Dead; Long Live Year-Round School, Denis P. Doyle (American Enterprise Institute) and Chester E. Finn, Jr (Vanderbilt U), *The Washington Post*, Sunday, 30 Dec 1984, C1.

The present school year is an anachronism, designed for a 19th century nation that needed young people to help with the crops and did not have air-conditioned school buildings in the hot months. A 48-week school year would bring the US education system more into line with our major economic competitors (Japanese children attend school for 240 days, compared to 180 days for American children). All US youngsters should be required to attend school for three quarters, and allowed to attend a fourth. A longer school year would help reformers achieve many of their objectives, such as opportunities for disadvantaged and slow-learning youngsters. The costs of such a change would be considerable, but Americans will be willing to pay for it because it would provide dramatic, tangible benefits.   **(year-round school proposed)**

7086

The New American Dilemma: Liberal Democracy and School Desegregation. Jennifer L. Hochschild (Dept of Politics, Princeton U). New Haven CT: Yale U Press, Jan 1985/279p/$27.00;$8.95pb.

Conventional wisdom and democratic theory hold that the best way to achieve controversial policy changes is in small, cautious steps. America's 30 years of experience with school desegregation shows this belief to be false. When incremental and participatory methods are used to desegregate schools, both blacks and whites end up worse off. However, school desegregation can succeed for everyone when rapid and extensive change is imposed by nonelected officials, at a centralized level, and without citizen involvement. The real American dilemma is between superficial "safe" changes that benefit a few at the expense of the many, and profound and deeply unpopular changes that in the long run will liberate most.

(successful school desegregation)

7087

School Desegregation Plans That Work. Charles Vert Willie (Prof of Sociology, Harvard U). Westport CT: Greenwood Press, 1984/239p/$29.95.

Presents a series of court-ordered and community initiated school desegregation plans that have been tested and proven in cities such as Atlanta, Boston, Milwaukee, and Seattle. Willie reviews the recent history of school desegregation planning, state and local responsibilities, the implications of various plans, how cities can prevent violence and foster a sense of community, and the lack of correlation between white flight from the cities and the kind of plan adopted.　　　**(desegregation of schools)**

7088

The Measurement of Equity in School Finance: Conceptual, Methodological, and Empirical Dimensions. Robert Berne and Leanna Stiefel (both NYU Graduate School of Public Administration). Baltimore MD: Johns Hopkins U Press, Sept 1984/320p/$35.00.

Who are the students entitled to an equitable share of school finances? Which taxpayers should share the financial responsibilities? What resources and services are to be equitably distributed? At least three distinct models are under public consideration: 1) equal opportunity, requiring that no discrimination be made on the basis of property wealth or other arbitrary categories in the funding of school districts; 2) vertical equity, considering that the differential needs of students must be taken into account (thus allotting more resources to the handicapped); 3) horizontal equity, demanding equal expenditure for all students of equal status. A model is provided of alternative ways to calculate the consequences to equity of changes in Federal, state, and local policies in a fiscally restrictive period.　　　**(school finance equity)**

7089

Efforts Are Failing to Close Gaps Separating Rich and Poor Schools, Jonathan Friendly, *The New York Times*, Tues, 19 Feb 1985, A1.

Efforts by states to equalize the financial resources of school districts—a major goal of educational reformers in the 1970s—have not significantly reduced the gap. In some states, the disparities of wealth and spending have increased. For example, according to one critic, the richest school districts in New Jersey spent about $1100 more for each pupil in 1984 than the poorer districts; in 1980, the gap was $600.　　　**(rich-poor school gap increasing?)**

7090

School Finance and School Improvement: Linkages for the 1980s. Edited by Allan Odden (Education Commission of the States) and L. Dean Webb (Arizona State U). Cambridge MA: Ballinger Publishing Co, Nov 1983/248p/$28.00.

Polls have suggested that taxpayers will support increases in school aid only if they are linked to programs designed to improve education quality. This volume presents research results showing how these programs can be designed fund suggesting strategies for financing and implementation. Essays cover such topics as recent insights into characteristics of effective schooling and implications for finance and governance, state and local strategies to improve schools, the role technology can play in both school finances and school improvement, and improving the quality of the education workforce.

　　　(linking school improvement and finance)

D. Higher and Continuing Education

7091

The American University: Problems, Prospects, and Trends. Edited by Jan H. Blits (U of Delaware). Buffalo NY: Prometheus Books, June 1985/180p/$18.95.

Essays written to mark the University of Delaware's 150th anniversary, addressing science and liberal education, university research, private industry and university research, the impact of computer technology on higher education (incorporation is expected into nearly every facet of campus operations), liberal education in transition, managing the university for excellence, and productivity in the university. [NOTE: A dull summation of the guiding conventional wisdoms, fully immunized to considering any new societal conditions, new learners, or new research needs.]　　　**(essays on US universities)**

7092

Trying Higher Education: An Eight Count Indictment, Chester E. Finn, Jr (Institute for Public Policy Studies, Vanderbilt U), *Change: The Magazine of Higher Learning*, 16:4, May-June 1984, 28-33ff.

It is only a matter of time before citizen groups, legislators, and critics begin to complain about the standards and performance of colleges and universities. Searching national scrutiny of the quality of higher education is a necessary complement to the examination of elementary and secondary schooling now underway. Based on his visits to about two dozen institutions, and talks with faculty and administrators from about 100 others, Finn suggests an agenda for inquiry. 1) Unqualified students: many colleges will do practically anything to lure warm, tuition-paying bodies into their classrooms; 2) diluted standards: once a student has enrolled, institutions will do practically anything to keep him; 3) coddled faculty: many faculty members do very little work, at least for the institutions that pay their salaries; 4) low quantity and quality of scholarly research; 5) low standards by which the faculty evaluates itself; 6) inadequate measures of institutional performance; 7) declining academic freedom; 8) self-righteousness: the smugness that the world owes colleges and universities a living. Finn shared his impressions with several groups of college presidents, finding many smiles and grimaces of familiarity, and only a few mild rejoinders. If these symptoms are as widespread as suspected, some painful therapies will be needed.

　　　(higher education standards)

7093

Integrity in the College Curriculum. Association of American Colleges. Washington: AAC (1818 R St NW), Feb 1985/$3.00. (Reprinted in *The Chronicle of Higher Education*, 29:22, 13 Feb 1985, 12-30.)

A report addressing the crisis in US education as revealed in the decay of the college course of study and in the role of college faculties in creating and nurturing that decay. Evidence of the decline and devaluation of the undergraduate degree is everywhere. For example, foreign language incompetence is not only a national embarassment, but threatens to be an enfeebling disadvantage in the conduct of US business and diplomacy. Developments in science and technology have outpaced the understanding of science provided by most college programs. As for what passes as a college course, almost anything goes. The collapse of structure and control has invited the intrusion of programs of ephemeral knowledge and a marketplace philosophy. A minimum required curriculum is proposed, consisting of nine basic intellectual, aesthetic, and philosophic experiences: 1) inquiry, abstract logical thinking, critical analysis; 2) literacy—reading, writing, speaking, listening; 3) understanding numerical data; 4) historical consciousness, enabling the recognition of complexity, ambiguity, and uncertainty as intractable conditions of human society; 5) scientific method and the human implications of scientific research; 6) values—to assume responsibility for decision and to embody the values of a democratic society; 7) art—appreciation and experience of the fine and performing arts; 8) international and multicultural experiences; 9) study in depth—building on blocks of knowledge that lead to more sophisticated understanding. Concludes that all efforts to improve college teaching will be to no avail unless the reward system in higher education measures teaching performance as well as research. **(basic college curriculum needed)**

7094

Wave of Curriculum Change Sweeping American Colleges, Edward B. Fiske, *The New York Times*, Sunday, 10 March 1985, p1.

In the last few years, hundreds of colleges, including virtually every major liberal arts institution, have stepped up the number of mandated courses, redesigned their general education programs, and proclaimed that graduates must now possess skills ranging from mathematical proficiency to computer literacy. In essence, according to the President of Skidmore College, we have redefined our concept of what constitutes an educated person. Other college officials, however, view the flurry of curriculum changes as the higher education equivalent of the "back to basics" movement at the elementary and secondary level. [*The Chronicle of Higher Education* (13 March 1985, p1) reports a recent survey by the American Council on Education (**Campus Trends, 1984**, not mentioned in the *NYT* article) indicating that curriculum reviews are underway at 58% of 413 responding colleges and universities, with an additional 29% having completed such a review in the last five years.] **(curriculum change widespread)**

7095

Liberating Education. Zelda F. Gamson (Prof of Higher Education, U of Michigan) and Associates. San Francisco CA: Jossey-Bass, March 1984/$16.95.

Because of increasing specialization and vocationalism, liberal education as traditionally understood has disappeared from some campuses, and many fear that US colleges and universities may become glorified vocational institutions. What is needed is not simply a return to the traditional goals of a liberal education—passing on our intellectual and cultural heritage—but a redefinition of goals to meet today's needs and circumstances, and a new strategy for revitalizing higher education. Gamson and her associates discuss ways to improve teaching practices, course content, student development, and program evaluation to foster a liberating education—one that develops critical awareness, sharpens skills of inquiry and analysis, and promotes self-assurance and independence. Both experimental and well-established programs are discussed in a range of colleges and universities, and two model programs are described: a core program of required courses and a mentor program for external degree students. **(liberating education)**

7096

Against the Current: Reform and Experimentation in Higher Education. Edited by Richard M. Jones and Barbara Leigh Smith (both Evergreen State College). Introduction by Ernest Boyer. Cambridge MA: Schenkman Publishing Co, 1984/389p/$22.95;$11.95pb.

Essays from a conference commemorating the 10th anniversary of The Evergreen State College, one of a handful of institutional innovations from the late 60s/early 70s to survive into the 1980s. Topics include the problems of disciplinary professionalism (the dominant mode of academic organization), alternative education at the college level, innovation in very large universities, and roots of contemporary experimentation. Chapters are devoted to the experiences of the University of California at Santa Cruz, Hampshire College, San Jose State College, The University of Nebraska, Goddard College, and The Evergreen State College. Concludes with a bibliography of about 200 items and a list of 77 alternative colleges and programs. **(alternative higher education)**

7097

Retrofitting Colleges, M. Garrett Bauman (Human Ecology Program, Monroe Community College, Rochester NY), *In Context: A Quarterly of Humane, Sustainable Culture* (Sequim WA), No 6, Summer 1984, 28-31.

Several dozen US colleges and universities (listed at the end of the article) have programs that seek to promote a humane, sustainable society. A variety of names are used: "Agroecology," "Science, Technology, and Society," "Global Studies," "Appropriate Technology," "Environmental Design." All can be seen as a new paradigm for liberal arts education—liberal arts for the 21st century. This paradigm may replace the antiquated liberal arts degree based on such outdated assumptions as specialization, an expanding industrial base, and unlimited energy and resources. Bauman goes on to describe the MCC program involving 20 faculty members from 18 departments. The curriculum includes such courses as "Global Interdependence," "The Self-Reliant Lifestyle," "Health for Life" (holistic self-care replacing a physical education requirement), "Applied Energy Systems," "Energy-Efficient Home Design," and a "Human Ecology Practicum" in which students work for a semester as interns. **(liberal arts for the 21st century?)**

7098

Retooling Colleges for the 21st Century, Harold T. Shapiro (President, U of Michigan), *The New York Times* (Education Section), 15 April 1984, p67.

Unless we find the determination and means to rebuild and modernize the inventories of scientific equipment and library material in our colleges and universities, we will seriously undermine US capacity to train the next generation of students, maintain our leadership in science and technology, and preserve our cultural heritage. To properly equip teaching laboratories alone will require a capital investment of about $3 billion, with additional annual expenditures of $500 million a year. [NOTE: This infrastructure problem parallels that of the wider society,e.g., *FS* 6:4, #84-238.]
(need to modernize college labs and libraries)

7099

Community Colleges, The Future, and SPOD. Edited by Richard J. Brass (Future Trends Commission, American Assn of Community and Junior Colleges). Stillwater OK: New Forums Press (PO Box 876), Fall 1984/162p/$6.95.

Essays related to Staff, Program, and Organizational Development (SPOD), including questions about the future, excellence from a SPOD perspective, the community college as a future-oriented community learning system, developing a college/community futures network to help focus on objectives, designing organizational structures to match changing missions, rethinking student services programs, the impact of educational technology on staff development programs, educators as futurists and advocates, and institutionalizing SPOD.

(community college planning)

7100
Strategic Management in the Community College. Edited by Gunder A. Myran (President, Washtenaw Community College). New Directions for Community Colleges, #44. San Francisco CA: Jossey-Bass, Dec 1983 / 120p/ $8.95pb.

There is a growing sense that a transformation is taking place in community college management, from operational to strategic management, or from running a smooth ship to steering the ship. To function in a turbulent environment, the colleges have begun to emphasize a more systematic approach to the external environment, and charting out definite courses of action to shape fundamental character and direction. Essays in this volume consider choosing the community college future, strategic elements of external relationships, the strategy of internal communications and working relationships, the strategic planning process, strategic elements of financial management, translating plans into programs, and the role of the CEO in strategic staff development.

(community college strategic planning)

7101
The New Competence: Management Skills for the Future, Donald N. Michael (San Francisco CA; Emeritus Prof of Planning, U of Michigan), in **Leadership and Institutional Renewal**, edited by R. M. Davis. New Directions for Higher Education, No 49. San Francisco: Jossey-Bass, March 1985, 91-104.

Most organizational cultures are drastically unfit for meeting the challenges confronting them as they move toward the 21st century, especially organizations such as universities that must operate at high levels of uncertainty. To cope constructively, the university culture must perform as a learning organization, continuously asking the questions: Where do we want to go? How do we get there? Are we getting there? The broadest overriding observation about the societal context is that the dominant myth systems are facing multiple challenges, and growing amounts of information are increasing these uncertainties. The contentious and information-rich societal context is certain to confront the university with multiple claims regarding priorities, services, opportunities, and claimant legitimacy. The new competence for performing resiliently in the turbulent environment has five attributes: 1) the ability to live with and acknowledge high degrees of uncertainty; 2) embracing error: discovering what is not going as anticipated, and using these discoveries to learn, revise, and experiment anew; 3) being future-responsive: considering multiple futures and their consequences, to confront us with the ethical issues abiding in what we aspire to and what we avoid; 4) the ability to span information and normative boundaries; 5) interpersonal competence: the ability to listen, support and empower others, and cope with value conflicts.   **(new competence for universities)**

7102
Lifelong Learning and Higher Education. Christopher K. Knapper (U of Waterloo, Ontario) and Arthur J. Cropley (U of Hamberg). London and Dover NH: Croom Helm, Jan 1985/201p/$27.50.

The idea of lifelong education should be adopted as the guiding principle for reforming education at all levels and in all countries. When viewed as a unifying principle linking existing trends and tendencies, lifelong education is a useful device for bringing together a number of ideas and practices which would otherwise have continued to be treated separately. Higher education merits special study because of its particular importance in helping to develop a system of lifelong education. In such a system, education would lead to the systematic renewal and upgrading of knowledge and skills, be dependent on people's increasing ability to engage in self-directed learning activities, and acknowledge the contribution of all educational influences, formal and non-formal. Chapters are devoted to lifelong education as a system, learners and learning processes, transforming existing institutions of higher learning, instructional methods, and a framework for evaluation.

(lifelong learning as reform principle)

7103
Post-Education Society: Recognising Adults as Learners. Norman Evans (Policy Studies Institute, London). London and Dover NH: Croom Helm, Nov 1984/157p/ $26.00;$11.95pb.

"Post-industrial society" is a slogan, serving as a metaphor for fundamental changes in employment. "Post-education society" is also a useful slogan, drawing attention to equally dramatic changes taking place in the world of formal education. A learning society has developed outside the formal education system, and is only casually related to it. To talk of post-education does not mean a society without education, any more than a post-industrial society means doing without industry. It only points to the need to change some of the means whereby we have arrived at the present, in order to more effectively deal with the future. The fundamental purpose of any education is how best to enable people to learn. It is monstrous but sadly true that most people are discouraged by their years of compulsory education. The task for any improved arrangements must be to reverse the general experience and expectation of most people that the education system will not help them. The theme for dealing with the future is recognition. Feeling recognized by someone is an enriching and enlivening experience. It is precisely this experience that so many young people do not get from their schooling. Recognizing what someone knows and can do means respecting the knowledge that belongs to the other person, however they come to own it. And a respect for ownership is the essence of recognition. A teacher who recognizes knowledge in a pupil draws things out rather than putting things in, leading pupils into additional knowledge and skills. Working from concepts of recognition and ownership as effective ways of facilitating learning means abandoning the ways in which schools are presently organized. Four main groups of changes are needed to bring opportunities for adult learning into a better relationship with the lives adults live: 1) accepting that sources of academic learning are diverse, and that institutions should accord such learning official recognition; 2) acknowledging the psychological roots of readiness for learning; 3) designing modes and patterns of study such as learning contracts as variations from present practice; 4) developing appropriate funding of institutions and students. To empower individuals to take charge of their own study through basing facilities for learning on the principles of recognition, accumulation, and progression means assuring individual choice and creating a democracy of learners. If education can work out the learning equivalent of a post-industrial society, ministering to each person's learning needs, we can move toward an adult society. [NOTE: Murky, but important. Amply cites Alvin Toffler, E. F. Schumacher, Gail Sheehy, Erik Erikson, and A.H. Maslow.] (**post-education society**)

7104

Adult Learners: Key to the Nation's Future. Commission on Higher Education and the Adult Learner. Columbia MD: The Commission (10598 Marble Faun Court), Nov 1984/19p/free.

The Commission was established by the American Council on Education in 1981 to recommend public policy and institutional arrangements to increase opportunities for adult learners. The Commission believes that the ongoing pursuit of learning by adults throughout their years of competence is no longer a luxury, but is essential to three critical public needs: economic strength, social equity in the interest of political stability, and enhancing the quality of life for all. We face five major tasks in fully developing our human resources: developing or renewing employability for the unemployed, maintaining and enhancing occupational skills, re-education for functional illiterates (estimated to range from 25 to 45 million Americans), providing equal access to education for all adults, and developing knowledgeable citizens in a technological information society. The impediments to meeting this need are institutional barriers (most university units dedicated to continuing education have limited curricular scope and restricted scheduling), inadequate funding, and lack of awareness among adults of opportunities open to them. Components of the solution include: 1) a public commitment to adult learning by governments, corporations, and educational institutions; 2) a Federal program for adult learners to stimulate innovative adult learning services and programs; 3) among the states, comprehensive planning and initiatives for lifelong learning; 4) enhancing the capacity of institutions to deliver services by a program of multi-year challenge grants; 5) financial assistance for needy adult learners; 6) eliminating tax disincentives to serious adult learning; 7) a Federal grant program to the states to enable them to establish comprehensive adult learning information and counseling services.

(**adult learning now a necessity**)

7105

Patterns of Learning: New Perspectives on Life Span Education. Cyril O. Houle (Prof Emeritus of Education, U of Chicago). San Francisco CA: Jossey-Bass, July 1984/243p/$16.95.

The belief that learning should extend during the whole span of life was accepted throughout all earlier history, but gradually forgotten by most people as education came to be thought of as a youth-related or even a youth-bound activity. A monolithic educational system has been created which can be understood by everyone. Adult education has not freed itself from the dominance of the formal school system and the use of the mode of instruction as virtually the only way by which education can occur. Individuals have continued to find other ways to change themselves, often self-directed, but these countless private ventures seldom challenge the orthodoxy of the system. The purposes of this book are to explore several ways by which learning processes are provided, in the hope that, in light of illustrations presented, life-span learning can be consid-

ered in a broader framework. The bulk of the book is devoted to illustrative cases of Michel de Montaigne (a 16th century Frenchman who enlarged his horizon by scholarly companionship and reading), Henry David Thoreau's self-directed patterns of learning, the art of Billy Graham's oratory, the educational value of travel, the educational principles of Edward Everett, and William Osler's thoughts on lifelong learning for professionals. Concludes with a discussion of the major patterns by which education can best be woven into an entire design of life: education as the entire purpose of life, education as a way of examining life, education as an inherent part of a complex pattern of life, education as mastery of all knowledge, and education as a way of preserving or protecting the state. The most widely-used processes are also discussed: self-directed study, tutorial teaching, scholarly companionship, voluntary groups, disputation, masters and teachers, spoken discourse, separate communities based on study, and education by experience.

(**toward a broader view of adult learning**)

7106

Synergogy: A New Strategy for Education, Training, and Development. Jane Srygley Mouton and Robert R. Blake (both of Scientific Methods, Inc, Austin TX). San Francisco CA: Jossey-Bass, April 1984/188p/$17.95.

Pedagogy is the standard classroom model, where an instructor lectures, gives assignments, and tests achievement. Its chief disadvantage is that students are often passive and unmotivated. Andragogy (adults teaching other adults) allows the teacher to serve as a facilitator or catalyst. Its disadvantage is that it cannot be applied to codify or standardize information for mass use. Synergogy builds on the best features of pedagogy and andragogy while avoiding the limitations associated with each. It differs from other approaches by 1) replacing authority figures with learning designs and instruments managed by a learning administrator; 2) enabling learners to become proactive participants; 3) applying synergy to education; 4) relying on teamwork, and using colleague affiliations to **provide** motivation for learning. Unlike other learner-centered methodologies, synergogy offers meaningful direction for learners. Potentially, it can accelerate the rate at which true learning occurs, enabling us to move toward excellence through effective participation. Chapters are devoted to describing applications in schools, colleges, and business. (**"synergogy" as new learning method**)

7107

Beyond Schools: Education for Economic, Social and Personal Development. Edited by Horace B. Reed and Elizabeth Lee Loughran. Amherst MA: U of Massachusetts School of Education (Furcolo Hall #225), 1984 / 253p / $12.00.

Jointly published by the Citizen Involvement Training Program and the Community Education Resource Center, this book is based on the belief that the education occurring after graduation is as important to both individuals and society as is schooling. Chapters discuss non-formal education, education for community development, appropriate technology and education, educational innovation in the workplace, human services as education, community legal education, self-help groups as education, museum education, community eduction in context, and adult basic and continuing education. (**nonformal education**)

XIV. COMMUNICATIONS

A. Information Societies

*7108

The Uneasy Eighties: The Transition to an Information Society. Arthur J. Cordell (Science Council of Canada). Background Study 53. Ottawa: Science Council of Canada, March 1985/150p/$7.00 (other countries, $8.40). Bilingual Summary available free from Science Council Publications Office, 100 Metcalfe St, Ottawa.

A series of connected essays examining some of the consequences for our working, public, and private lives of the widespread use of computers and related technologies. Chapters are devoted to the information infrastructure (the computer is central, but it also includes various transmission and carrier technologies), products and processes, work and income, new industries and new ways of doing things (information as the primary commodity in an information economy), concerns about privacy, some solutions for the privacy issue (legislation, professional self-regulation, individual action), the psychological dimension to the privacy issue, and applications and implications of artificial intelligence. Concludes that the advent of an information society will bring about widely divergent changes in the kinds and range of goods and services, requiring a major reorientation of workers, institutions, and production technologies. Although the transition to an information society will make the management of information more efficient, it will also present very serious threats to personal and corporate privacy, requiring increasingly sophisticated safeguards. In the early 20th century, when goods were scarce, governments ensured that all citizens would have free and equal access to information in public libraries. In the future, the situation may turn around completely: goods will be in great supply and may therefore be virtually given away (e.g., food stamps), whereas it will increasingly make sense to charge for the use of information, the real source of value. The uneasy eighties are a time of transition and uncertainty. A large part of the unease is due to knowing that change is taking place, but not knowing what it all means. The industrialized nations are experiencing change in the very underpinnings of society, but we have not yet developed an adequate theory of change, or tools for measuring its extent and potential. The meaning of productivity, growth, innovation, value, and wealth are known and understood in an industrial context; in the new context of an information economy, new terms will have to be developed, and terms no longer relevant will have to be discarded.

(transition to information society)

7109

Meeting the Challenges of the World Information Economy, Geza Feketekuty (Senior Asst Trade Representative, Executive Office of the President of the US) and Jonathan D. Aronson (Associate Prof of International Relations, USC), *The World Economy* (Basil Blackwell), 7:1, March 1984, 63-86.

The computer chip and the communication satellite are creating a new world information economy that is carrying interdependence of national economies to a new level. The international system of rules and procedures created 35 years ago to bring some order to the exchange of goods did not envisage a world economy increasingly driven by flows of information. The authors seek to clarify the issues involved: restrictions on international trade in telecommunication hardware, procurement of services such as computer software, regulation of communications by individual national governments, policies affecting competition in value-added communication services such as teletex and videotex, transborder data flows, and international sale of information and data-processing services. The critical question that governments must resolve is whether they will accommodate change by extending the liberal international economic order established after WWII. A similar liberal order for information services is in every country's interests. In a world where information is of central economic importance, a country will suffer by closing itself off from global sources. **(world information economy)**

7110

Communications With and Without Technology. Edited by Mit Mitropoulos and P. Psomopoulos. *Ekistics*, 50:302, Sept-Oct 1983, 320-421.

Essays on communications interconnections and the need for both global and local planning, future prospects and options for the satellite program of the European Space Agency, the social functions of the telephone, the role of telecommunications networks as a measure of the quality of life in the past and future metropolis (by Richard L. Meier), urban and regional impacts of the new information and communications technologies, balancing rational and participatory processes in communications planning, participation in community affairs by two-way cable TV, the construction of a center for international communication in Paris (soon to become a link in an extensive international network of communications centers), designing a prototype space colony to maintain 1000 people, and the new reorienting of human networking (by R. Buckminster Fuller).

(communications and planning)

7111

The Global Challenge of the Chip, Zavis P. Zeman (ZZ International, Toronto), *World Futures*, 20:1/2, May 1984, 23-36.

The power of the microchip has increased a hundredfold over the past decade, while its costs have dropped a thousandfold. Its diffusion rate through the global economy is claimed to be seven to ten times faster than that of any previous technology. Any country that desires to participate fully in the life of the international community must become active in the new microelectronic technologies. Those countries left behind now will be second-class global citizens of tomorrow. The brave new world of information technologies is emerging as a duopoly dominated by the US and Japan. It is most likely that the gap between the technological leaders and those who merely follow will increase. **(microchip to increase technological gap?)**

7112
Communism vs. the Computer: Can the Soviet Union Survive Information Technology? Rex Malik (*The Times*, London), *InterMedia*, 12:3, May 1984, 10-23.

The mass production of digital electronics and the software that goes with it pose a fundamental challenge to the Soviet system. Western countries have organizations and a general ethos to encourage adaptation of the new technology; the USSR does not have this infrastructure. The Soviet system has the industrial society at its heart, and the growth of information technology is inimical to the industrial society. Soviet leaders can choose to reject the information society and to hope that the fort can be held, or adapt to the external realities of the world. Initially, information technology will strengthen the grip of the elites. But it is hard to control information resources, and access will eventually become widespread, undermining the power of the traditional special interests in the USSR.   (**Soviet system and information society**)

7113
The Twilight of Hierarchy: Speculations on the Global Information Society, Harlan Cleveland (U of Minnesota), *Public Administration Review*, 45:1, Jan-Feb 1985, 185-195.

Information is becoming the crucial resource of our society. Its inherent characteristics provide some clues to the vigorous rethinking that lies ahead for all of us: information is expandable, substitutable, transportable, diffusive, sharable—and it is not resource hungry. The inherent characteristics of physical resources, natural and man-made, made possible the development of hierarchies of power based on control, secrecy, ownership, access, and geography. Each of these five bases for discrimination and unfairness is crumbling today: the old means of control are of dwindling efficacy, secrets are harder to keep, and ownership, access, and geography are of diminishing significance in getting access to knowledge. Openness is the buzzword of modernization. The state is not withering away, but power is leaking out of sovereign national governments in three directions at once: 1) at the top, as more international functions require the pooling of sovereignty; 2) sideways, as MNCs conduct more of the world's commerce across political frontiers; 3) from the bottom, as communities take control of their destinies.
(**information erodes hierarchy**)

*7114
Information and the Crisis Economy. Herbert I. Schiller (Prof of Communication, U of California-San Diego). Norwood NJ: Ablex Publishing Co, Sept 1984/133p/$22.50.

Multiplying informational activities and the growing stock of instrumentation around us are attributable, in large part, to the economic, political, and cultural strains produced by the general crisis of the world market system. Information and information technologies have been seized upon as the means to alleviate and overcome the crisis. At the same time, they offer increased returns to information controllers and powerful users. An enormous technico-social transformation is underway, promoted by two central and interactive forces: the emergence of the transnational corporation and the new information technologies. The scale of activity of the transnational corporation is unthinkable without the new technologies; at the same time, these technologies have found their main application and utilization in the operations of large-scale firms. Governments and the military are also heavy users, and both have as their primary task the protection of the transnational corporation.

The emerging information age is viewed as a set of paradoxes or contradictory developments. 1) The renewal of dynamism alongside increased system vulnerability: the new technologies have provided a tremendous stimulus to capitalism, but the dependence on unimpeded international communication requires a relatively secure world system—the least likely outcome of the forces now in motion. 2) Consumerism and the temporary withering of radical consciousness: the new information technologies substantially increase the penetrative power of the marketing system; carried into the world, the consumerist model is a radicalizing force that diminishes political stability. 3) The new information technologies confront national sovereignty. 4) Information impoverishment accompanies information abundance: the present situation is one of unprecedented abundance of information, but information is also being privatized and commoditized at an accelerating rate, dividing society into information-rich and information-poor. 5) Short-run economic decisions to encourage the new communications technologies have long-run cultural consequences: already the center of the global information system, US informational goods cannot fail to gain still greater advantage in the world market. 6) Growing separation of American thinking from international realities: in the midst of information abundance, Americans may be among the globe's least knowledgeable in comprehending recent changes in the international arena. Concludes that there are still grounds for cautious hope of more democratic communication; despite the gigantic concentration of capital and informational control, there are vulnerabilities in the system that allow popular expression, and significant numbers of people in the new professions who seek a human application of the new technologies.   (**information and transnational corporations**)

7115
Managing Information: The Challenge and the Opportunity. John Diebold (Chairman, The Diebold Group, Inc). NY: AMACOM/American Management Associations, Jan 1985/131p/$14.95.

Six speeches given in 1980 and one given in 1979, on the meaning of the information age for business (the most important benefit is enhanced decision-making), information as an executive resource (a revitalized information strategy requires a revitalized information architecture), effective information resource management, corporate information policy to shape a unified outlook for dealing with information of every kind, the revolutionary promise of interactive videotex to increase business productivity and enrich the quality of life, information service opportunities, and the need for a US information policy in the context of a global perspective.   (**Diebold on information**)

7116
Business in the Age of Information. John Diebold (Chairman, The Diebold Group, Inc). NY: AMACOM/American Management Association, July 1985/145p/$14.95.

Another collection of speeches to complement **Managing Information** (#7115 above). ***Six Issues for the Future*** (1983) explores organizational issues associated with computers and communications, staffing and human development questions, the problem of accounting conventions used with respect to information systems, information technology as an agent of human change, future technology, and information technology as a key determinant of international economic competitiveness. ***National Information Policy and Economic Consequences*** (1982) discusses policy in the US, Japan, and France, and proposes a coherent and well-integrated policy for the US. *International Business in the Information Age*(1980) suggests that any international enterprise must seek the ability to move information quickly, at reasonable cost, and in a stable regulatory climate. *Seventeen Possible Future States* (1979) briefly explores possibilities such as an entrepreneurial work force, the rapidly deteriorating value of a worker's knowledge due to new discoveries, business communication and training in the home, home purchasing of goods and services, and the emergence of national universities. *Information Technology: Unleashing a New Era of Competition* (1984) touches on incorporating information technology into products and services, changes in business relationships, and new definitions of the mission of business. **(Diebold speeches)**

7117
IBM: More Worlds to Conquer (Cover Story), Marilyn A. Harris, *Business Week*, 18 Feb 1985, 84-98.

With 395,000 employees and 1984 sales of $46 billion, IBM plans to more than double its revenues by 1990 to $100 billion annually. Barring global economic crises, revenues should nearly double again by 1994 to at least $185 billion. The company has its plant in place to back its ambitions to be the largest company in history. In the past five years, IBM spent $13 billion on land, buildings, and equipment, and an additional $15 billion on R&D. And their pace of capital investment is accelerating: in the next five years, IBM will invest at least $56 billion.

(IBM to quadruple by 1994?)

7118
Information, Ideology and Communication: The New Nations' Perspectives on an Intellectual Revolution. Arnold Gibbons (Dept of Communications, CUNY-Hunter College). Lanham MD: University Press of America, April 1985/219p/$23.50;$11.75pb.

Slowly but inexorably, the Third World is being deluged and strangled by a movement of men and machines from rich countries, peddling hard- and software in the name of progress. The peddlers of technology assume that they are indeed welcome and will always be so. Rich countries believe that the rest of the world should emulate their approach toward the entire paraphernalia of technology and communication. The imperatives of an industrial culture promote the development and growth of international information structures. Gibbons explores the relations between rich and poor countries which have come about as a result of the enormous gap in information technology, with chapters on the emerging debate over international news, communication and development issues, the litany of Third World complaints, the culture of technogy, internationalism and information, and the New International Information Order and other Third World initiatives.

(Third World view of communications)

7119
The Missing Link. Report of the Independent Commission for World Wide Telecommunications Development. Geneva, Switzerland: International Telecommunications Union, 1985. (Executive Summary reprinted in *Telecommunications Policy*, 9:1, March 1985, 84-87.)

Of the 600 million telephones in the world, three-quarters are concentrated in nine countries. While telecommunication is taken for granted in developed countries, the telecommunications system in most developing countries is not adequate to sustain even essential services. Over half of the world's population lives in countries with less than one telephone for every 100 persons. By the early part of the 21st century, virtually the whole of mankind should be brought within easy reach of a telephone and, in due course, the other services telecommunications can provide. Such an expanded world telecommunications network would benefit both developing and developed countries. A joint effort of all governments is needed to improve this network, in turn making the world a better and safer place. **(telecommunications need in Third World)**

7120
The Social Impacts of Information Technologies in Rural North America, Don A. Dillman (Prof of Rural Sociology, Washington State U), *Rural Sociology*, 50:1, 1985, 1-26.

Presidential address presented at the 1984 meeting of the Rural Sociological Society, noting that the essence of the information age is massive increases in the speed of communication, the amount of information transmitted, the fidelity of long-distance communication, miniaturization of technology, capabilities to send and receive information, and the relative importance of information vs. labor and energy in producing goods and services. The sociological implication of the information age is the plausibility of a new structure of social interaction not based significantly on locality, with such geographically unbounded interaction becoming a dominant influence on individual behavior. This raises the questions of who will live in rural places, and whether the electronic workplaces will encourage a resurgence of growth in rural places. In the information age, who will interact with whom and what institutional structures will serve rural people?

(information age and rural society)

7121
No Sense of Place: The Impact of Electronic Media on Social Behavior. Joshua Meyrowitz (U of New Hampshire). NY: Oxford U Press, March 1985/416p/$22.50.

The electronic media have radically altered social roles by changing who knows what about whom. Because of TV, children today know much more about adult behavior, men and women are exposed to each other's strategies and domains, and all of us can now see the fallibility of politicians. The result has been a shattering of roles that once were mystified, and of barriers that once kept things in their place. The evolution of media has decreased the significance of physical presence in the experience of people and events. The physical structures that once divided our society into many distinct spatial settings for interaction have been greatly reduced in social significance. The walls of the family home no longer isolate the family from the larger community. Even within the home, media have reshaped the social significance of individual rooms. Physically bounded space is less significant, as information is increasingly able to flow through walls and rush across great distances. As a result, where one is has less and less to do with what one knows and experiences. The thesis of this book is that this change in behavioral settings is a common element linking many of the trends, events, and movements of the last three decades. To the extent that electronic media tend to reunite many formerly distinct spheres of interaction, we may be returning to a world that is similar to primitive social forms. As nomadic peoples, hunters and gatherers had no loyal relationship to territory, or little sense of place. Sex roles were not as sharply divided as in agricultural societies, and work and play often took place in the same sphere. In today's information age, we hunt and gather information rather than food. **(diminishing sense of place)**

7122

McLuhan: It's All Going According to Marshall's Plan, Mark Edmundson, *Channels of Communications*, 4:2, May-June 1984, 49-54.

Much of what Marshall McLuhan predicted in the 1960s has come to pass, and his observations are now more pertinent than ever. McLuhan saw the "media explosion" not as an isolated blast, but as one of a series of detonations that will probably last through and beyond our lifetimes. He helped us to see how "perceptual numbing"—insensitivity to all but the most extreme experiences of life—is related to the new media environment. This numbness, endemic to large segments of contemporary character and culture, is substantially encouraged if not created by the "depth experience of media." This experience may be transforming our inner lives, giving new, mass-produced forms to our fantasies and imaginings. Depth involvement in the media may be undermining our confidence in the possibilities for first-hand individual experience and reliable knowledge about events in the world.

(McLuhan "perceptual numbing" forecast)

7123

War of the Words: Advertising in the Year 2010, Leo Bogart (Executive VP, Newspaper Advertising Bureau), *Across the Board*, 22:1, Jan 1985, 21-28.

Results from a Delphi-like survey involving 250 senior advertising and marketing executives. Between 1967 and 1982, the number of ads disseminated doubled. A majority of the respondents expect the total number of ads disseminated annually to double again by 1997. Accordingly, they expect that a typical individual will be within sight or hearing of twice as many advertising messages each day as at present. The proliferation of advertising messages in the past 25 years reflects the growth in the number of advertised products and services, growth in the number of publications and broadcast stations, and a shift from 60-second to 30-second commercials on TV. Most agency executives expect the 15-second commercial to become the standard television advertising unit within the next eight years. According to the consensus, new media such as videotex and VCRs will by 1995 cut at least 10% from the time people spend with present communications media. By 1997, there will be twice as many specialized media vehicles as there are today, aimed at narrowly defined markets; the major network share of the prime-time TV audience will be less than half of its present 78% (before the spread of cable increased viewing options, it was 93%). By 1997, the experts think that ten international superagencies will place 25% of all ad agency billings worldwide. Marketers will think and practice in an international arena. Direct broadcasting by satellite to the home will make worldwide TV advertising possible using commercials without language. World trade is expected to double its present level by 2001. Industrialization in China and India, raising living standards to levels already achieved in South Korea and Taiwan, will open a vast consumer market, significantly stimulating worldwide advertising. But to be more productive, advertising will have to be more informative and more localized. Bogart concludes that US marketing executives seem to resist confronting the consequences of major problems that are clearly in our path, and they have a marvelously optimistic confidence that advertising will grow with an eternally expanding market for consumer goods.   **(advertising to double by 1997?)**

7124

Science, Computers, and the Information Onslaught: A Collection of Essays. Edited by Donald M. Kerr *et al*. (Los Alamos National Laboratory). NY: Academic Press, Sept 1984/276p.

The current information onslaught, triggered by the computer revolution, has catapulted the needs of information science into a foremost national priority. These essays from a meeting held at Los Alamos in 1981 bring together representatives from the physical sciences with leaders in national security and government. Topics include technological innovation as the key to national security, the human possession and transfer of information, computers and control, the information onslaught in geoscience (resulting in the need for "middlemen" with a broad perspective to translate scientific data into the kinds of information usable by society), libraries in the year 2000 (the need for a better system of service will result in the amalgamation of libraries into larger systems, with increased emphasis on access techniques to provide the user with faster and more effective service), future large-scale parallel computers, implications of long-term advances in human ability to deal with the information onslaught (we may as a race be so altered that taxonomists a century hence will declare *Homo sapiens* to be extinct), speech-related chips, natural language based information management systems, science and national security decisions, the irrelevance of information to much government decision-making (or "Gonzo decision-making," where decisions are made without reference to facts or analysis), and the steady loss of ground by science education to the information onslaught (requiring broad-based incentive programs for students and teachers).

(information onslaught and science)

7125

The Biomedical Information Crisis: A User's Viewpoint, W. Curtis Worthington, Jr (Prof of Anatomy, Medical U of South Carolina), *Perspectives in Biology and Medicine*, 27:2, Winter 1984, 251-258.

Scholars in biomedical science and in information science are concerned with the growing quantity of information, the increasing cost of journals, fragmentation as interdisciplinary needs increase, and pressures which increase questionable publication. Worthington proposes: 1) continuous development of bibliographic data bases and highly efficient computer systems for their access; 2) support and development of libraries in the classical sense, while making their operation more efficient; 3) encouraging a publication network in which abstracts of research are made available by computer transfer; 4) eliminating weaker journals; 5) reducing pressures to publish by reducing rewards for doing so [NOTE: Worthington expresses "only faint hope for this one"]; 6) most important, incorporating the values of brevity, precision, and grace in the written word into the education of scientists.

(coping with infoglut in biomedicine)

7126

Torrent of Print Strains the Fabric of Libraries, Colin Campbell, *The New York Times*, Monday, 25 Feb 1985, A10.

In self-defense against torrents of information, the most comprehensive libraries (mainly at universities) are being forced to pool their resources in an international network—a kind of superlibrary whose collections, catalogues, computers, and lending practices are increasingly integrated.

The Research Libraries Group, which now links three dozen major libraries through a computer at Stanford University, has taken steps to coordinate its members' acquisitions, so that each library collects books in its fields of special strength. Member libraries agree to assume primary responsibility in fields that either produce too much literature for most libraries to handle, or that are highly specialized. The new system aims at creating a gigantic "bibliographic utility," comparable to a national telephone system. But the unfinished utility is already so heavily used that libraries have to compete for the attention of the central computer. Moreover, the system depends increasingly on interlibrary loans—each costing about $15. Warren J. Haas (President, Council on Library Resources, Washington) worries that this development may lead to an inequitable and unwise new system of handling knowledge, with poor students and colleges in danger of becoming an informational Third World. Rutherford D. Rogers (former University Librarian, Yale U), worries that there are too many books, and that the entire US library system is suffering from overload. He laments that "We're drowning in information and starving for knowledge."

(information flood and research libraries)

7127

Yellow Snow Drifting to the Floor, Carlton C. Rochell (Dean of Libraries, NYU), *The New York Times* (Op-Ed), Saturday, 26 Nov 1983, p23.

About one-third of all books in US libraries are seriously deteriorated. Every day, library staffers at institutions across the country sweep from the floor not just a handful of pages, but fragments from disintegrating books. The problem is increasing in magnitude, for most books published since 1850 have a life expectancy of only 50 to 100 years, and many are now reaching the end of their allotted days. To limit these losses, librarians now must devote a substantial amount of their budgets to preservation. Despite these attempts, they are losing the battle. Several libraries are studying ways to remove acid from paper and the possibility of transferring fragile materials onto video disks.   **(1/3 of US library books deteriorated)**

7128

Books in an Age of Post-Literacy, George Steiner, *Publishers Weekly*, 24 May 1985, 44-48.

Excerpts from the R.R.Bowker Memorial Lecture, delivered by a leading cultural historian who suspects that we are now seeing the gradual end of the classical age of reading. From the end of the 18th century to WWI, books became a mass medium for the first time. The best that was being thought and written in this unique period received a very large popularity. Since then, there has been a deepening disassociation between the semi- and sub-literacies of the modern mass media and the ideals of literacy in the old sense. Bookstores are closing and consolidating into chains (in the US, 52% of books are sold by four large chains). There has been a "catastrophic decline" in the space and quality given to serious reviewing of books of specialized interest. There has been a decline in the skills of the middle-class reader, and an unwillingness to afford those spaces of silence, time, and concentration that surround the classic act of reading. The Gutenberg revolution took a long time; what now seems to lie ahead of us is far more dramatic: the information revolution will touch every facet of composition, publication, distribution, and reading. It may be that the privately owned book will become a luxury object—an article for special use, as were the hand-copied manuscripts which appeared after Gutenberg. It looks as if the arts of reading will undergo fundamental changes, falling into three sharply distinct categories: 1) a vast amorphous mass of reading for distraction and momentary entertainment, increasingly taking place via cable transmission to the home screen; 2) information, knowledge, education—the Library of Babel—in which the library of all possible libraries can be summoned up on the screen for personal or institutional use; 3) reading in the old, archaic, private, silent sense—which may once more become the practice of an elite, of a mandarinate of silences. But this elite of lovers of the text, unlike those of the past, will not have the power, political reach, and prestige which it had in the Renaissance or during the Enlightenment. That power almost inevitably will belong to the aliterate and the numerate. It will belong increasingly to those who are technically almost unable to read a serious book, and who are mostly unwilling to do so. [NOTE: For earlier intimations of this profoundly gloomy view, see **In Bluebeard's Castle: Some Notes Towards the Redefinition of Culture** (Yale, 1971), in which Steiner muses about a Post-Culture which eliminates certain vital futures from the spectrum of possibility, a general retreat from the word, and a global sound-sphere replacing the traditional ideals of literate speech by the musicalization of culture. We shall open the last of the successive doors in Bluebeard's castle, he warns, because opening doors is the tragic merit of our identity.]

(three types of future reading)

7129

The Brave New World of Electronic Publishing, Herbert R. Brinberg (President, Aspen Systems Corp, NYC), *Publishers Weekly*, 23 Nov 1984, 32-35.

Electronic publishing is the delivery of information via computer from a publisher to a user, directly or over a communications network. It is more than faster and cheaper typesetting: it represents a quantum leap that will drastically alter the creation, organization, and transfer of knowledge. Electronic publishing makes it possible to organize the vast store of accumulated data, documents, and literature, providing a capability to bring this vast store of knowledge directly to the user—by-passing in-place distribution channels and minimizing the role of traditional libraries. Electronic publishing is essentially classified into two principal forms: on-line systems that deliver information from a host computer over a communications network [NOTE: generically known as "videotex"—see below], and the on-disk delivery system that is now being developed along with the proliferation of personal computers. It is expected that updatable materials, reference services, etc. will be increasingly offered on floppy disks. Electronic publishing is not merely a revolution in technology; the dramatic change is that the power of the new technology is forcing the integration of human resources into the publishing process in previously unknown ways. Users for the first time can interact directly with authors and with publishers. User-driven or "on-demand" publishing shifts the focus of information packaging, so that the end user is an integral player. However, the printed word is not about to vanish, and most print products will not go electronic. But future growth in publishing will come from the electronic medium, while print products will remain relatively stable, especially in the 1990s.

Five other articles in this special *PW* section on "Electronic Publishing" (pp 32-58) focus on the wealth of new choices in information storage and retrieval, PC software and online databases, the new economics of publishing, social goals vs private interests, and "A Vision of the Future" by Theodor H. Nelson, who views an overall 21st century publishing system with a million documents an hour added to the system and a billion simultaneous users in a world population of 13 billion. **(electronic publishing)**

7130

The Future of Copyright, David Ladd (U.S. Register of Copyrights), *Publishers Weekly*, 1 June 1984, 24-26.

A vast new array of technological innovations is testing our understanding of authorship and copyright, and our will to vindicate their values. These rights have become difficult to enforce as we move away from print culture toward broad-based dissemination. The new technologies—photocopying, cable TV, satellite transmissions, computers, and videotaping—result in widespread consumer ownership of instruments for display, performance, and copying. The unchecked spread of unauthorized use raises doubts about the very applicability of copyright control. This will be especially true if optical disks are used to organize library collections and reference to them. These disks would enable display and print-out at remote stations, and could be cheaply replicated. Such a system promises untold efficiencies in providing library services to remote corners of the globe, with obvious benefits for developing countries. But if copyright is not somehow provided for, it can be grievously hurt. Minimal international standards of protection, or an international treaty, will be needed. Without copyright, the liberty of speech and the freedom of expression in literature and the arts would be in danger. Copyright sustains both authors and publishers, and supports a varied cultural marketplace. These arguments are not as obvious as the opposing populist argument of cheap access to copyright works by the general public. To preserve copyright, the case for it must be continually made. Government should abstain as much as possible from intervention in the copyright world, and willingly forbear from setting or affecting the price of works of authorship. **(new technology challenges copyright)**

B. Computer Impacts

*7131

The Information Technology Revolution. Edited by Tom Forester (London UK). Cambridge MA: MIT Press, April 1985/696p/$30.00;$14.95pb.

A sequel volume to an earlier Forester anthology, **The Microelectronics Revolution** (MIT Press, 1980/589p), consisting entirely of new material published in the 1980-1984 period. The 48 contributions (33 are of US origin and most of the rest are British) are arranged in four sections. 1) **The Computer Revolution**: the anatomy of computing, artificial intelligence and the fifth generation, the telecommunications explosion, cellular radio, videotex; 2) **The Human Interface**: computers in the home, computers in schools, factory automation, the office of the future, new technology in banking and commerce, micros in medicine; 3) **The Impact on Work**: the future quantity of work, the vulnerability of women workers, the quality of work, robots and labor; 4) **Implications for Society**: social problems, infotech and the Third World, smart weapons, computopia, and questions for the information society. Each sub-section is accompanied by a guide to further reading, with about 400 items listed in all.

In the introduction, Forester notes four major developments since his first collection of readings: 1) computer software gaining in importance relative to hardware, and setting the pace of the infotech revolution; 2) the remarkable rise of the personal computer, coupled with IBM's entry into the market (the personal computer has unexpectedly become the basic building block of the infotech revolution); 3) the race to build the fifth generation of computers (see #7237); 4) an explosion of innovation in telecommunications. Concludes that the debate on the future of industrial society has become somewhat sterile, but we are certainly headed somewhere, and the future shape of society is still, to some extent, negotiable. [NOTE: A broad and even-handed selection of writings.]

(information technology)

7132

The Social and Economic Impact of New Technology 1978-84: A Select Bibliography. Compiled by Lesley Grayson (Environmental Abstracts Services, Chandlers Ford, UK). London and NY: IFI/Plenum, 1984/80p(8x11")/$85.00.

Some 700 briefly annotated references on microelectronic technology from US, British, and European literature. Categories include general books and articles on the information society and information technology, bibliographies, national and international policies and initiatives, social impacts (education, employment, female employment, data protection and security, quality of working life, health and safety, homeworking), economic structure and policy, impact on business and industry, and administrative impact and industrial relations. [NOTE: The lack of an author or subject index adds to the irritation of the vague title and high cost.]

(impacts of microelectronics bibliography)

7133

The Macro- and Microeconomic Social Impact of Advanced Computer Technology, Gunda Schumann (Berlin, FRG), *Futures*, 16:3, June 1984, 260-285.

Computers and information technologies under control of transnational corporations tend to provide concentration of power in headquarters. They increase the rate of unemployment, alienate employees from their work environment, reinforce traditional economic and social roles of women, and widen the gap between developed countries and LDCs. Strategies to enable all human beings to participate in the benefits of computers have been outlined in a report submitted by the author to the UN Centre on Transnational Corporations, on which this article is based.

(computers concentrate corporate power)

7134

Social Science and the Social Impacts of Computer Technology, James N. Danziger (U of California-Irvine), *Social Science Quarterly*, 66:1, March 1985, 3-21.

Social science research on the impacts of computing is a young area of inquiry, still short on theory and on empirical findings that are systematic and consistent. These shortcomings are exacerbated by the absence of a network of scholars, the growth of the domain of inquiry to nearly unmanageable proportions, and a rapidly changing technology. Nevertheless, eight tentative generalizations or tendency statements, suggestive of the kinds of insights that are emerging, can be noted briefly: 1) in most settings, the short-run social impacts of computing have been far less pervasive and dramatic than were forecast by many sources; 2) most individuals perceive the direct impacts of computing to have been mildly benign, to the extent that any impact is perceived; 3) computing has become a major source of productivity gain for individuals and organizations (some, however, dispute the validity of the productivity measures or argue that the costs of the total computer package are greatly underestimated); 4) computing tends to increase the importance of quantitative and technical criteria for making decisions; 5) computing use tends to isolate individuals, reducing their interaction with other people in both work and leisure settings; 6) computers have substantially increased the capacity of central managers and resource controllers to monitor how resources are allocated and used (computing may facilitate decentralization of operations, but it centralizes or maintains control, especially of funds and personnel); 7) computing increases social control and monitoring, reducing the privacy of individuals and small groups (microcomputers may, however, personalize the computing activities of users, if they are used as independent and unmonitored systems); 8) the current impacts of computing tend primarily to serve the interests of the more dominant groups in a given setting, thus reinforcing existing power distributions. Concludes by reiterating that our knowledge of the social impacts of computing remains seriously inadequate in relation to the significance of the subject, in part because such research receives minimal infrastructure support within academia. [NOTE: A valuable overview of research, pointing to both positive (#1-#3) and negative (#4-#8) tendencies, the sum of which could dampen some current acritical enthusiasms about computopia. Unfortunately, the aloof social science style may be off-putting to some readers.]   (**computer impacts: research overview**)

*7135

The Intimate Machine: Close Encounters with Computers and Robots. Neil Frude (University College, Cardiff, Wales). NY: NAL Books/ New American Library, Sept 1983/244p/$15.50;$3.95 Mentor pb.

Vast new horizons are opening up via microtechnology. There are already computers that speak, that understand words spoken by humans, and that are programmed to converse in a friendly way. We may soon have systems that, to a degree, counterfeit a person: computers and robots programmed to interact socially with people. The age-old fascination with the simulation of human characteristics now promises—or threatens—to produce powerful results, leading to intense social relations between people and machines. These artificial systems will invite us to enter a fiction that they are people with personalities and feelings. There is every indication that many people will readily accept this fiction, accepting mere machines as their companions. The manufacture of companion machines will very soon be an area of intense marketing activity. They are technologically and economically feasible, and costs are falling. We are irretrievably set on a course of technological expansion, and a future world with a constant barrage of diversions and devices, many of them computer-based. The companion machine will be just one aspect of the change, supplementing the current image of the computer as calculator with those of counselor, colleague, and friend. This raises a distinct threat that in the process of "humanizing" machines, we will come to "dehumanize" people. A concluding chapter suggests some of the possible delights and plausible horrors in medicine (computer-based psychotherapy), education (tutorial opportunities for interactive learning), social welfare (computerized information and advice systems), politics (an automated propagandist that dials the telephone numbers of voters and enters into discussion and debate), justice (systems capable of making judicial decisions), trade (automated selling based on an intimate knowledge of a

consumer's needs and preferences), religion (a Pastoral Counseling Program that could provide aid in accordance with an established religion), sex (machines programmed in seduction and giving satisfaction; sex-counseling programs), personal relations (companion machines to enhance human relationships by arranging interpersonal contacts and helping to develop social skills), and immortality (a life-sized, moving replica made in the physical image of the departed, speaking with the same voice and able to "carry on the relationship" indefinitely). A longer-term prospect is that machines will evolve to a level of intellect far beyond that of the species which brought them into being. Machines will design, build, and program other machines, and the offspring may show allegiance to their "next of kin," rather than to alien human masters. [NOTE: A thoughtful and imaginative exploration of a significant matter.]   (**future humanized computers**)

7136

The Second Self: Computers and the Human Spirit. Sherry Turkle (Program in Science, Technology, and Society, MIT). NY: Simon & Schuster, July 1984/362p/$17.95.

A sociologist/psychologist reports on a six-year field trip through all levels of the rapidly emerging "computer culture," including children with computer toys and computers in the classroom, video game players, home computer amateurs, virtuoso "hackers" who love the machine for itself, professional programmers, and the new philosophers of artificial intelligence.   The focus is on the "subjective computer"—the machine as it enters into social life and psychological development, and how it affects the way we think, especially about ourselves. We live in a culture that invites us to interact with computers in ways that permit us to become intimate with them. As this happens, the relationships between people and machines, as illustrated in the various computer sub-cultures, become harbingers of new tensions and the search for new resolutions that will mark our culture.   The 19th century Romantics looked for perfect friendship and perfect love. Today, instead of a quest for an idealized person, there is the computer as a second self. Before the computer, the animals seemed our nearest neighbors in the known universe; computers now bid for this place. Where we once were rational animals, now we are feeling computers, emotional machines. Under pressure from the computer, the question of mind in relation to machine is becoming a central cultural preoccupation. It is becoming for us what sex was to the Victorians—threat and obsession, taboo and fascination.   (**computer cultures as harbingers**)

7137

The Micro Revolution Revisited. Peter Large (Technology Correspondent, *The Guardian*). Totawa NJ: Rowman & Allanheld, June 1984/216p/$17.95.

A much-extended updating of **The Micro Revolution** (1980), with chapters on the nature of the microchip, how it all began, why information is power, the reinvention of TV, satellites and laser light, the cashless society, jobs that have gone and are going, personal computers, the keyboard generation, industrial robots, the threat to privacy, fifth generation computers, and the five deadly dangers of commitment to the computer (crime, inefficiency, ignorance, unemployment, and totalitarianism) which extend our already apparent failure to grasp and control the complexities of the societies we have created. The case for concern is that many jobs are disappearing—not only jobs that are distasteful and dangerous, but middleman jobs, thus reducing the human intervention between the originator of a product or service and the customer who uses it. We are tending toward a world in which we no longer work to live, and only live to work if we want to, which might destroy every power base. [NOTE: A balanced view, but poorly summarized.] **(computers, overview)**

7138

Transportation for the Mind: Computers in the World of 1985, Lane Jennings (Research Director, World Future Society), *American Educator*, 8:1, Spring 1984, 42-46.

The fear and mistrust of computers still common today owes a great deal to Orwell's **1984**, even though he never mentioned them. The connection between computers and tyranny seems to have grown in the 1950s and 1960s, when the awesome size and mysterious power of the machines was made to seem even more inhuman by the bureaucratic ways in which they were used. But the computer is not only a centralizing force, but also an independence tool, particularly in the form of the small, portable personal computer—computers we can love. Human scale in size, easy to talk to and work with, and as versatile as our ingenuity can make them, the computers of the mid-1980s will be extensions of our bodies and our imaginations— transportation for the mind.   Computers are becoming an accepted part of the environment, like central heating, plumbing, and the telephone. They promise to make the world of 1985 a better one for humans and machines.   Like transportation systems, computers take many different forms; tomorrow's computer users, like the travelers and car buyers of today, must be able to select appropriate programs from the many varieties offered. "Computer literacy" will involve knowing how to use systems and programs; "computer wisdom" will require knowing when to use a particular program or system, and to recognize situations in which no computer is needed. Perhaps within this decade, these two skills will emerge as the mark of the well-educated individual. [Also see **Electronic Life: How to Think About Computers**, by Michael Crichton (NY: Knopf, Sept 1983/209p/$12.95), who argues that the dawning computer age will not rob us of our human uniqueness and create a technocracy; rather, computers are giving power to people.]

(computers as enabling mind transport)

7139

Cohabiting with Computers. Edited by Joseph F. Traub (Prof of Computer Science, Columbia U). Los Altos CA: William Kaufmann, Inc (95 First St), April 1985/185p/ $15.00.

Addresses from an October 1983 convocation at Columbia University. **William R. Miller** (SRI International) lists nine perspectives on the future environment of a high-tech society, concluding that if we can capture the energy of the new individualism, we will be headed for a new Golden Economic Era. **Gordon Bell** (Encore Computer Corp) addresses challenges in creating the next generation of computers. **Robert Spinrad** (Xerox-Palo Alto) sketches a scenario of the electronic university. **Edward E. David, Jr** (Exxon Research and Engineering Co) states that modern computing is a prime mover toward decentralization [NOTE: see social science research, #7134, suggesting that this is not true], and that computing need not be a force for unimaginative conformity in science and technology. **Joel S. Birnbaum** (Hewlett-Packard) shows how the taming of computers can enrich our daily lives and enhance our opportunities for personal creativity and effective communication. **Lewis W. Branscomb** (IBM) surveys university-industry partnership in computer science. **Arno Penzias** (Bell Laboratories) asserts that ever-larger numbers of computers with ever-greater computing power

promise to bring enhanced capabilities for solving large-scale human problems. **Herbert A. Simon** (Carnegie-Mellon U) cautions that we should avoid deifying computers, but concludes that when human intelligence is generously augmented with machine intelligence, in the world ahead of myriads of interlinked computers, we will have the means for enlarging the space of our thoughts, our hopes, and our actions; on balance, our new intelligence will bring some measure of improvement in the human condition. [NOTE: A handsomely-produced array of Panglossian sentiment, appropriate for the occasion of dedicating a new computer science building at Columbia, but not to be confused with serious thinking about the proper use of computers.]   **(living with computers: addresses)**

7140

Silicon Shock: The Menace of the Computer Invasion. Geoff Simons. NY: Basil Blackwell, Aug 1985/191p/ $19.95.

Six chapters on negative aspects of computers: 1) computer phobia at home and in the workplace, from various uses that generate anxiety and apprehension; 2) the threat of machines to displace employment; 3) dehumanizing aspects, as the computer destroys a whole range of human activity, de-skills remaining tasks, unwholesomely distorts personalities (the hacker phenomenon), and encourages the viewing of people as components in mechanized systems; 4) the alternative love-object: another dehumanizing aspect, as humans develop relationships (sexual and other) with computers and robots; 5) increased reliance on computer systems in the military, with possibilities of greater instability and insecurity (e.g., faulty silicon chips could cause a war); 6) the omnipotent machine: increasing human reliance on artifical systems that we cannot comprehend—indeed, the evolution of free-will capabilities in computers. Concludes that, as people begin to notice the lengthening shadow cast by the computer on the future of human society, fear will be replaced by more disabling psychological conditions: perhaps computer phobia will be the epidemic of tomorrow. [NOTE: A pessimistic jumble of anecdotes and shrill alarms—but no more irresponsible than the "good ol' boy" platitudes of the computer establishment (above).   **(negative aspects of computers)**

7141

Technostress: The Human Cost of the Computer Revolution. Craig Brod (Berkeley CA). Reading MA: Addison-Wesley, Feb 1984/242p/$16.95.

A psychoanalyst reports on his interviews with people in organizational contexts at all levels and in all phases of computer adaptation—from clerical workers and computer programmers to CEOs. He found widespread evidence of technostress—a modern disease of adaptation caused by an inability to cope with the new computer technologies in a healthy manner. It manifests itself in two distinct but related ways: the struggle to accept computer technology, and the more specialized form of over-identification with computer technology (adopting the computer's standards as our own, and beginning to speak like machines, e.g. "interfacing" with people). Widespread symptoms of technostress were also found among children who have been socialized by the computer and isolated from their families. As a society, we are in danger of moving farther and farther away from the bright and productive people we hope to be, proliferating our workload and cutting ourselves off from the outside world. The appealing "high tech/high touch" imagery of John Naisbitt is the opposite of reality: the computer world is symbol-intensive, not sensual, and constricts our abilities to interpret and create in a manner that reflects our unique human sensibilities. We are facing the mechanization of the mind, and the loss of our inner selves and the quality of our thinking. A new, uncritical faith is developing, seeing computer technology as the harbinger of a brighter future. But, love being blind, our devotion to the new machine inhibits us from asking significant questions about the changes in ourselves and our children. Concludes with chapters on appropriate corporate policies for humane use of computers, the pivotal role of teachers and school systems, and the role of psychologists in treating and preventing technostress.   **(technostress from computers)**

7142
Six Grave Doubts About Computers, Jerry Mander (Public Media Center, San Francisco), *Whole Earth Review* (formerly *Co-Evolution Quarterly*), No 44, Jan 1985, 10-20.

Author of **Four Arguments for the Elimination of Television** (Morrow, 1978) argues that the first waves of news about a technology are invariably positive, even utopian, because the information comes from corporations and scientists who stand to gain from a favorable view. By the time we begin to notice problems, the technologies have advanced to a point where it is difficult to do anything about them. Some perspectives are offered that are not found in the computer ads. 1) The computer industry has a high incidence of occupational illness (more than three times the average for the manufacturing industry), and it produces environmental side effects. 2) "Information" is increasingly defined in terms of what can be collected and processed through machines; thus a certain sort of knowledge will dominate, while other more subtle forms recede. As computer programs replace teachers, a great degree of uniformity will likely emerge. 3) Automation and computation will eliminate many jobs, especially among the middle class. 4) Computers make possible a high degree of military centralization and enhance the possibility of annihilating the world by minimizing the time available for human decision-making at critical moments. 5) Slow is beautiful, and computers speed up processes and accelerate our nervous systems. 6) Computers help large institutions and work against small, decentralized institutions.   **(computers questioned)**

7143
Mythinformation, Langdon Winner (U of California-Santa Cruz), *Whole Earth Review*, No 44, Jan 1985, 22-28.

According to some visionaries, industrial society is being supplanted by a society in which information services will enable all the people of the world to satisfy their economic and social needs. According to Winner, author of **Autonomous Technology** (MIT Press, 1977), these beliefs taken as a whole are "mythinformation": the almost religious conviction that a widespread adoption of computers and communications systems, along with broad access to electronic information, will produce a better world. It is common for the advent of a new technology to provide occasion for flights of utopian fancy. But even within the great tradition of optimistic technophilia, current dreams of a computer age stand out as exaggerated. The arguments of computer romantics draw on four false assumptions: 1) people are bereft of information; 2) information is knowledge, and speed conquers quantity; 3) knowledge is power; 4) increased access to information enhances democracy and equalizes social power. The long-term consequences of computerization will be quite different, and will require

rethinking of many fundamental conditions and institutions. Three areas of concern seem paramount: the growing technical ability to monitor various human activities, the elimination of social layers that were previously needed, and the basic structure of the political order. Concludes that, rather than being guided by new wonders in artificial intelligence, the present course of the computer revolution is influenced by something much more familiar: the absent mind.   **(computer romanticism questioned)**

7144
Computer Is Leaving a Wide Imprint on Congress, David Burnham, *The New York Times*, Friday, 13 April 1984, B10.

The computer has become essential to the functioning of virtually every aspect of Congress. It appears to be contributing to subtle but far-reaching changes such as: 1) increasing the advantages that Congressional incumbents enjoy over challengers by enabling greater use of the free mailing privilege; 2) enhancing the ability of Congressional committees to collect and organize information about the performance of individual agencies or the potential impact of proposed changes in policy, possibly augmenting the power of the legislative branch relative to the executive branch (e.g., the computerized budget enables far more specific detail than before, as well as swifter analysis); 3) increasing the pressure on members of Congress to provide quick responses to complex social issues, thus reducing time for thoughtful reflection; 4) increasing the number of roll-call votes, thus making it much easier for constitutents and lobbies to keep track of positions taken by House and Senate members.

(computer impacts on Congress)

7145
Experts Fear Computers' Use Imperils Government History, David Burnham, *The New York Times*, Sunday, 26 August 1984, p1.

A number of administrators, archivists and historians have become concerned that the rapidly growing use of computers and word processors may be undermining the government's administrative and historical record. Documents such as the drafts of speeches and preliminary memos outlining policy options can offer essential information to a new agency head attempting to understand the reasoning behind a predecessor's decisions. When these documents are written on paper, the bureaucracy tends to save them systematically. But when a computer or word processor is used, there is sometimes pressure to erase the electronic copy and use the storage space for fresh material. In addition, the very accuracy of information on computer tapes can deteriorate over a long period, or information recorded in one form can be difficult to retrieve if the technology it was recorded on becomes obsolete and the machines needed to make the information available have been dropped from government inventories. Three national scholarly organizations have formed a privately supported Committee on the Records of Government to explore this threat. None of the problems are considered insoluble, and some preliminary steps are being taken to deal with them. For example, senior White House officials using computerized work stations will now have them equipped with a new "Archives" key that will automatically send historical material to an electronic file. Indeed, some experts acknowledge scattered developments that could ultimately lead to better record-keeping.

(computer a threat to official records?)

7146

Computer Called Peril to U.S. Record Keeping, David Burnham, *The New York Times*, Wed, 6 March 1985, A11.

A committee of historians and former government officials, chaired by Ernest R. May (Prof of History, Harvard U), has warned that the government's shift from paper to computerized records has increased the possibility that historically valuable documents will be lost forever. This can happen by 1) changes in the record (policy statements, memoranda, and letters are rewritten with previous versions automatically erased); 2) the gradual disappearance of machines developed to read earlier forms of computerized information; 3) deterioration of computer tapes used to store data (which can begin in 15 years), as well as computer disks (5 years). The study warned that without records, there is no history; and without history, there is no understanding of continuity and change.

(information loss by computerized records?)

7147

Brave New City Government, Desmond Smith, *New York*, 14 May 1984, 56-64.

The electronic dragnet enabled by the new computers in New York City's government tracks the lights on the street, the Mayor's correspondence, babies born in city hospitals, the homeless in need of shelter, parking violations, welfare checks, bond repayments, potholes, heat complaints, garbage disposal, department expenditures, tax arrears, and the tax records of virtually every business. In the past few years, NYC has collected $60 million in delinquent taxes and penalties—all located through computer detective work. Costs are less than five cents for every dollar collected, and one official estimates $1 billion in back taxes to be collected. Behind the good news about management, though, a new civil liberties issue is taking shape regarding the safeguarding of citizens.

(computers in NYC government)

7148

The Application of Computer-Based Medical-Record Systems in Ambulatory Practice, G. Octo Barnett (Laboratory of Computer Science, Mass. General Hospital, Boston), *The New England Journal of Medicine*, 310:25, 21 June 1984, 1643-1650.

It is no longer possible to continue the information-recording practices developed under simpler conditions of medical care, because: 1) today's medical records carry longer notes from more health personnel, together with results from more examinations and lab tests; 2) an increasing proportion of care is concerned with the management of chronic disease and the greater emphasis on screening, early detection of disease, and preventive medicine; 3) government agencies increasingly impose reporting requirements; 4) the legal system demands documentation and justification of prescribed treatments. This need for radically improved computer management, rather than the power of the computer, is the driving force introducing computer technology into medicine. As administrative costs increase, and costs of computer-based systems decrease, there will be more use of automated systems in office practice. Such systems will provide improved data retrieval and analytical capability, allowing study of aggregate patterns of care in large populations and assisting in diagnosis. It may also be possible to gain a greater appreciation of the economic implications of different diseases in different populations, and the costs of different therapies. Communication between remote computers will enable access to national systems with drug information, library information-retrieval, and continuing medical education programs. Computers can be used to monitor inappropriate prescription of drugs, potential patient-specific allergic reactions, and drug-drug interactions. Computer-based systems will be used to prepare patient-specific educational materials, including information about the nature of a patient's disease, drugs being taken, and specific instructions.

(computers in medical practice)

7149

Computers and Research (Special Issue). *Science*, Vol 228, 26 April 1985, 403-470.

Eleven articles on electronic databases (there are now more than 2800 databases available online), personal computers on campus, intelligent tutoring systems, mul⁺is (a new class of computers based on multiple microprocessors), workstations in science, and the uses of computers for numerical computations, organic synthesis, economic analysis, production agriculture, sociology (simulating social processes and collecting data), and the humanities (compiling concordances).   **(computers and research)**

7150

The Electronic Scholar: A Guide to Academic Microcomputing. John Shelton Lawrence (Morningside College, Sioux City, Iowa). Norwood NJ: Ablex Publishing Corp, Nov 1984/181p/$26.50;$14.95pb.

The microcomputer offers assistance to research, instruction, and administration; by extending powers through microprocessor technology, academics become "electronic" scholars. Chapters cover word processing, cooperative writing and revision, electronic filing, electronic searches for information, publication, and the computer as helper in clerical, instructional, and analytical tasks. A final chapter discusses key legal and social issues related to the computer and scholarship: 1) software copyright and infringement (users are strongly attracted to copying commercial program disks); 2) canonical texts, intellectual priority, and online publication (an overall system of scholarship less exclusively dedicated to permanent print will lead to revision of policies for university promotion and tenure); 3) regulation of ideas and surveillance; 4) computerization and public resources for scholarship (some schools or individuals may be priced out of the scholarly system, exacerbating divisions between academic haves and have-nots). Concludes that computer technology has not saved us from complexity, but is adding to a growing number of difficult social and economic choices. These issues will continue to be troublesome as computers move toward a central place in scholarship and in education generally.   **(computers and scholarship)**

7151

The Burgeoning Data Base Business. Patricia Munson (Project Analyst). Business Opportunity Report G-068. Stamford CT: Business Communications Co, June 1985/ 230p/$1500.00.

The online database industry has survived tough economic times, growing at the very healthy rate of between 20% and 30% annually during the past decade. Rather than slowing down, the industry is optimistically expected to continue to grow through 1990 at an average annual rate of 23%. A more conservative forecast projects an 11% annual growth rate. The number of online users is expected to increase from 0.5 million in 1984 to 2.35 million in 1990. A mass consumer market of database users in every home, however, will not be a real force until 2000, at least. Three factors will account for the industry's continued growth: 1) more microcomputers (17 million are now in place in US homes and offices) and more home computer modems (expected to grow at perhaps 30% per year over the next five years); 2) the innovation and flexibility of the database industry, making their systems easier to use; 3) new technology such as laser/optic disk storage and developments in software. [Also see **The Electronic Messaging / Mail Revolution** (BCC Report G-049R, May 1985/125p/$1500.00), which projects an increase in the number of electronic mail transactions from 0.36 billion in 1985 to 65 billion in 1995—an average annual growth rate of 67%.]

(**database industry: continued growth expected**)

7152
Electronic Information—Impact of the Database, James Ducker (Datasolve Ltd, Sunbury-on-Thames, UK), *Futures*, 17:2, April 1985, 164-169.

The arrival of the computer for general use in the 1960s made possible a new advance in the organization of information. Electronic information services have grown rapidly in recent years, from 300 databases available worldwide in 1978 to 2,020 databases in 1983. Of this number, 1,140 were located in the US and 528 in Europe; 1,120 were devoted to science and technology and 240 to the social sciences. By 1983, over 50% of online databases consisted of primary material rather than references, compared with only 3% in 1978. This change makes databases independent of librarians and information specialists. Indeed, the connection to an electronic library gives users access to more indexes and source material than a single physical library could contain. In the future, users will see material on the electronic library before it is available in the physical library. Five key issues arising out of these developments are discussed: the treatment of information as a tradeable commodity, the nature of the home market for private users, the impact of electronic information on political and economic power, applications of electronic library technology in education, and the advent of intelligent terminals to facilitate connections with appropriate services. Concludes that the availability of the world's information through computer-based electronic library services could give the same advantage to developing countries as well as developed, to small companies as well as large, and to individuals as well as organizations. [NOTE: The sanguine conclusion implicitly assumes that the information is relevant and acquired at low cost, and that the currently disadvantaged are capable of using it.]

(**growth of electronic library**)

7153
Save That Road Map, It May Soon Become a Collector's Item, Bill Richards, *The Wall Street Journal*, 18 April 1985, p1.

The science of map making is being revolutionized by the computer. Old-fashioned service station road maps may soon be replaced by computer mapping. A Massachusetts company hopes to install computer terminals at roadside locations so motorists can make their own maps: for a small fee, they will be able to punch in their destination and get a printout of a made-to-order map. Auto makers in the US, Europe, and Japan are working on more advanced systems installed in their cars, which will be ready for market by 1990. The Chrysler Corporation prototype, for example, has 13,000 maps of various sections of the US programmed into the car's computer, which

tracks the car's progress across the maps as they flash on a dashboard-mounted screen. A California company hopes to market its own $1400 computerized dashboard map system in late 1985, to be marketed to salesmen, package-delivery services, and car-rental companies. In other realms of map-making, the US Geological Survey has 1400 cartographers computerizing its collection of 55,000 maps, and it is computerizing data for some 300,000 maps to be given to census enumerators in 1990. Military mappers are using computers to devise elaborate guidance systems for low-flying missiles, and it will soon be possible for infantry units in tactical situations to receive computer-generated intelligence on demand for most of the earth's surface.

(**computerized mapping**)

7154
Hyperintelligence: The Next Evolutionary Step, George Bugliarello (President, Polytechnic Institute of New York-Brooklyn), *The Futurist*, 18:6, Dec 1984, 6-11.

Emerging computer networks interconnecting millions of computers and their users are the most recent step in the development of the human ability to sense and reason. This development started within our own bodies, and is now being accelerated by societal and mechanical devices. These global networks offer the possibility of expanding our biological intelligence to form a hyperintelligence, representing a major evolutionary step for our society and our species. The extended symbiosis of telecommunications and computers will make the global village truly possible in a technical sense, endowing it with global intelligence. Expert networks can enable improvement in the quality of health care and in teaching through an electronic classroom. The biosomic amplification of our brains will make possible more complex and significant activities bound to propel our society to higher levels of achievement. Global computer networks will be greatly enriched by terms and concepts from many languages, ultimately leading to a world language (probably a new hybrid English). Hyperintelligence and hyperlanguage should lead to a new morality, transforming global computer networks into global action networks. [NOTE: A bit giddy for a college president!]

(**computer networks and hyperintelligence**)

C. <u>Telecommunications</u>

7155
Space, Earth and Communication. Edward W. Ploman (Vice-Rector, United Nations U, Tokyo). Westport CT: Greenwood Press / Quorum Books, Sept 1984/237p/$27.50.

Communication satellites raise many questions both of opportunity and risk. Ploman attempts to put the advent of satellite communications in the context of the space age, the information age, and changes in international relations. Increasing demands on the radio frequency spectrum and the geo-stationary orbit can only strengthen the trend toward politicization of issues relating to satellite communications. Concludes with three items for the planet's agenda: 1) safeguarding the global commons of the earth, which includes the resource realms of knowledge and information; 2) the need for learning how to manage complexity caused by the interdependence of countries and issues; 3) the need to increase our individual, institutional, and societal learning capacities.

(**satellite communications issues**)

7156

The Future Role of International Telecommunications Institutions, Jonathan Solomon (UK Dept of Trade and Industry, London), *Telecommunications Policy*, 8:3, Sept 1984, 213-221.

International telecommunications institutions such as INTELSAT and the International Telecommunications Union were founded in times when technological trends were more stable and national regulation was more homogeneous. In an era of increasing heterogeneity, these institutions will have to initiate change or face a loss of authority to other institutions such as OECD and EEC.

(world telecommunications institutions)

7157

A Global Information Utility, Robert S. Block (President, Telease Inc, Los Angeles), *The Futurist*, 18:6, Dec 1984, 31-34.

An information utility using direct broadcast satellites could be launched in the US in a few years, and the utility could operate worldwide by 1990. Such a utility would be a distribution center for information. Users would receive it directly from the satellite, or it might be redistributed by cable, broadcast, or microwave. To control access, a utility would encrypt the information and assign it an identification number; terminals would accumulate a record of usage and print out a monthly bill for subscribers. There are no technical, political, regulatory, or economic roadblocks to establishing such a service in the US; it is merely an extension of existing services. But creating a World Information Utility requires the solution of complex non-technical problems such as cultural and political censorship, cross-border data flow, copyright and patent protection, and language barriers. Even so, a flexible system could operate almost within any established government policy. [Also see two earlier visions of the information utility ideal. Edwin B. Parker and Donald A. Dunn (***Information Technology: Its Social Potential***, *Science*, 30 June 1972, 1392-1399) proposed an information utility made available to every home by 1985 as a national goal for the US. Harold Sackman (**Mass Information Utilities and Social Excellence**. Princeton NJ: Auerbach, 1971/284p) described alternative information utilities of the future that might enhance democratic participation and lifelong learning for all.] **(an information utility?)**

7158

Appropriate Telecommunications for Economic Development, Edwin B. Parker (VP, Equatorial Communications Co, Mountain View CA), *Telecommunications Policy*, 8:3, Sept 1984, 173-177.

A widely distributed telecommunications infrastructure can be a catalyst for the release and organization of the human brainpower that all countries have in abundance. Communication satellite networks are most likely to meet the criteria for this infrastructure, if earth stations are made small, low-cost, highly reliable, and easily transportable. With small earth stations costing under $10,000, a national telecommunications infrastructure can serve every community, however remote. [NOTE: Mythinformation? See #7143. Parker was also an early supporter of a national information utility, #7157 above.]

(satellite networks for development)

7159

Whatever Happened to Cable? Les Brown (Editor-in-Chief), *Channels of Communications*, 4:2, May-June, 1984, 21-22.

The golden age of cable TV lasted for two or three years and ended in 1983. As modern cable arrived in millions of homes, it promptly exploded its own myth. It turned out not to be the medium that was more than TV, but merely one offering more TV. Cable was not wide open to new ideas or new practitioners, but kept to the conventional forms and the mass-interest mentality. Cable made the mistake of playing to the habitual viewer, already "owned" by conventional television, when its natural audience—the intelligentsia—was among people with other things to do much of the time who watch TV occasionally.

(decline of cable TV)

7160

Satellite Dish Vies With Cable, Hans Fantel, *The New York Times*, Thursday, 9 August 1984, C18.

The hottest item in video is not the video cassette recorder but the satellite dish. The first private satellite dishes were installed around 1980. Today roughly 400,000 such backyard space stations operate in the US, with sales growing at a 300% annual rate. Reasons for this rapid growth include 1) rural access: some 5 to 7 million Americans live beyond the reach of normal TV broadcasts, while another 15 million live in areas where stations are few and reception is poor; 2) better urban access: city dwellers often get erratic reception because TV signals bounce off the steel skeletons of tall buildings creating "ghosts;" 3) the picture from a dish is far superior to that from regular TV or cable; 4) viewers with a dish receive pay programs for free by taking the signal directly from the satellite, bypassing the cable company and its scrambler. Cable and pay program operators seek legislation to "evict" dish owners, but will likely have to scramble their signals before sending them to satellites. Dish owners are also being challenged on aesthetic grounds by local governments, but the issue of ugliness may be made moot by a new technology—Direct Broadcasting Satellite—that shrinks the size of the dish to that of a generous salad bowl. The DBS minidishes have received scant support from established broadcasters, for the new technology could make conventional TV stations obsolete.   **(300% annual growth of satellite dish)**

7161

Direct Broadcast Satellites: Proximity, Sovereignty and National Identity, David Webster (British Broadcasting Corp), *Foreign Affairs*, 62:5, Summer 1984, 1161-1174.

We are passing from the era of the low-powered distribution satellite, which transmits programs through the filter of a broadcaster or a cable system, into the era of the Direct Broadcast Satellite, with a higher-powered signal that can go into homes. DBS will, in effect, create proximity between far-flung points; thus, all countries could become as Canada to the US and as Ireland to Britain, as the economics of communication satellites destroy geography. With a working DBS, we could all become each other's neighbors, to be enriched and irritated by each other (and, in this sense, we may all become Canadians). The emergence of unregulated TV access poses problems of law, politics, and economics far more profound than any of the familiar conflicts over radio, e.g.: possibilities for direct or indirect propaganda are immense. This revolution in transnational TV will be speeded by technological feasibility (which creates its own kind of imperative), the drive for markets, and a defensive need to occupy territory before it is inhabited by others. Slowing down the revolution are different national technical standards, some newly erected for defensive reasons.   **(transnational TV issues)**

7162

Coping with Transborder Penetration: The Politics of Television, George H. Quester (Prof of Government, U of Maryland), *Journal of Policy Analysis and Management,* 3:4, Summer 1984, 532-543.

International conflicts are brewing over the transmission of TV signals across national boundaries, illustrative of an increasing range of cases in which the actions of one national economy penetrate deeply into another. The US government defends such transmissions on the basis of strongly held American values of free choice and fear of government censorship. When other governments complain of "externalities" or "media imperialism," many Americans hear a defense of censorship and jamming. The prerequisites of a serious international disagreement are thus in place. Satellite broadcasts beamed to other countries may be regarded as a deliberately hostile act, justifying the destruction of the threatening satellite. Would there be a better occasion for the Soviets to employ their antisatellite weaponry?　　**(transnational TV issues)**

7163

Foreign 'Piracy' of TV Signals Stirs Concern, Peter Kerr, *The New York Times,* Thursday, 13 Oct 1983, A1.

In the last two years, US satellite signals carrying entertainment and news programs intended for US cable TV viewers have been intercepted by a growing number of TV stations in the Caribbean and Central America and broadcast without authorization. In Belize, for example, there are seven privately run TV channels that depend on US satellites for their programming. Officials in the film industry call the practice "piracy," and worry that the practice will spread to other continents as nations such as Brazil, France, Germany, Japan, and Saudi Arabia launch more than 25 transmitting satellites in the next 3 to 4 years. The theft of satellite transmissions could seriously damage the overseas markets for US films, and have a critical impact on film companies. At the heart of the problem are international laws that have not kept pace with rapid changes in communications technology.

(theft of US satellite signals)

7164

Policy Issues Raised by Direct Broadcast Satellites, Joseph P. Martino (U of Dayton Research Institute), *Technological Forecasting and Social Change,* 26:1, August 1984, 81-92.

Direct Broadcast Satellites are intended to transmit TV signals from the satellite in geosynchronous orbit to individual households. They have been used experimentally in Europe and Japan, and appear to offer a low-cost means for wide distribution of TV signals. At this point, it is not clear whether DBS is a new way of doing old things or a way of doing something new. In either case, it raises a number of policy issues for the US, each briefly discussed. 1) Issues Transcending DBS: property rights in spectrum, First Amendment protection, antitrust; 2) Producer Issues: the nature of DBS, piracy; 3) Viewer Issues: regulation by local governments, privacy; 4) Technology Issues:improved signals, flat antennas instead of dishes. Concludes that it is important at this point to recognize that unwise policy choices can halt or warp the growth of this new medium of telecommunications. Policy choices should especially take into account the certainty of technological change, and make allowances for beneficial change.

(DBS policy issues)

7165

Misregulating Television: Network Dominance and the FCC. Stanley M. Besen (Rand Corp) *et al.* Chicago, Ill: U of Chicago Press, Jan 1985/c160p/$19.00.

More than 85% of Americans' television viewing time is spent watching programs of the Big Three networks. The Federal Communications Commission has regulated the practices of these networks for over 40 years, in an effort to minimize the dangers of monopoly. The authors, key participants in a recent FCC inquiry into TV regulation, move beyond the official report to analyze the ill-conceived premises underlying FCC actions. By standards of competition, programming diversity, and localism, the FCC restraints have been ineffective or harmful. Indeed, the FCC regulations themselves, rather than the networks, have been mainly responsible for shaping and limiting the viewing options of the public. A less intrusive regulatory model is proposed that encourages new networks by lowering entry barriers.　　**(FCC regulations questioned)**

7166

The New Television: Looking Behind the Tube (Special Report), Trudy E. Bell (Senior Associate Editor), *IEEE Spectrum,* 21:8, Aug 1984, 48-56, and 21:9, Sept 1984, 52-62.

In the August article, Bell reviews new developments in improving the quality of both the transmitted and the received image, audio improvements by adding stereo sound, low-power television enabling mini-TV stations similar to FM radio, and multichannel multipoint distribution service (MMDS). The September article examines cable TV and the possibility of blending it with the telephone for two-way communication, direct broadcast satellites, and the possibility of hybrids among the various TV techlogies. [NOTE: An authoritative overview.]

(television developments)

7167

How the Chip Spurs TV Growth, Barbara Aarsteinsen, *The New York Times,* Sunday, 20 May 1984, F4.

A revolution in digital circuitry—television through a chip—promises an explosion in available TV options in the next few years. New picture clarity will show the beads of sweat on a linebacker's face. A button on a TV command module will freeze an image; another button will start a stock ticker running along the bottom of the screen. TV sets will have telephone circuits will allow the homeowner to call in with instructions that activate various functions. Industry experts predict that by 1990, consumers will buy TV sets the way they purchase cars, picking various digital-based options according to individual tastes. A TV with all the options may cost $2000 or more. The US companies that stand to gain the most from the new technology and the expected surge in sales are RCA, Zenith, and GE, which make nearly 50% of the sets sold in the US and are leaders in developing the new technology.

(more options with new digital TV)

7168

The Promises and Perils of Videotex, Paul Hurly (Canadian Centre for Occupational Health and Safety, Hamilton, Ontario), *The Futurist,* 19:2, April 1985, 7-13.

Videotex is a generic term for systems that provide easy-to-use, low-cost, computer-based services via communication facilities. Videotex usage is growing rapidly thoughout Europe and North America, with a variety of applications in the broad areas of information retrieval, instruction, commercial transactions (teleshopping, telebanking), messaging, and downline loading (transmitting telesoftware programs to terminals). Various issues concerning the use and regulation of videotex are briefly discussed: rate-setting (high costs may exclude access by the poor), billing (centralized billing systems can expose users to a possible breach of privacy), system ownership in the face of increasing concentration of the private ownership of information distribution systems, system compatibility, transborder data flow, the elimination of white-collar and middle-management jobs, measures to ensure personal data privacy, the possible reduction of public participation in live events, and human seclusion as a consequence of the electronic cottage. Concludes with reservations about the present laissez faire strategy in determining the course of videotex; rather, some measure of government regulation is needed to ensure that videotex will benefit the majority, and that personal privacy will not be infringed upon.

(videotex issues)

D. New Ways to Communicate

7169

The New Media: Communication, Research, and Technology. Edited by Ronald E. Rice (Annenberg School of Communications, USC). Foreword by Robert Johansen (IFF). Beverly Hills CA: Sage Publications, May 1984/352p/ $28.00;$14.00pb.

State-of-the-art summaries of recent research on new media technology, new methods and data for the study of media, electronic newspapers, computer conferencing, organizational teleconferencing, productivity impacts of new organizational media, word processing, libraries as communicators of information, television and computers in the lives of children, and competitive displacement in the communication industry. Concludes with a bibliography of about 800 items. [NOTE: Highly academic; probably of interest only to specialists.] **(research on new media)**

7170

Cellular Radio: First Step in the Personal Communications Revolution, Stuart Crump Jr (Publisher, *Cellular Radio News*, Fairfax VA), *The Futurist*, 18:5, Oct 1984, 25-28.

The cellular radio telephone reduces the high cost of mobile telephones. It can operate without wires throughout an entire metro area, and it can make long-distance calls through the existing telephone network. More than two dozen cities will have fully operating cellular systems by the end of 1984. The first cellular phones will be expensive (about $150-$200 a month, excluding equipment), but the price is expected to drop dramatically within a few years. Lighter and more portable cellular phones that can be carried everywhere (not unlike the Dick Tracy two-way wrist radio) are expected to eventually replace the bulkier car phones. **(cellular radio telephone)**

7171

Now, Pay Phones on Jetliners, Stuart Diamond, *The New York Times*, Monday, 15 Oct 1984, p1.

Pay telephones have been installed on 20 wide-body jets owned by six airlines. The service, costing $7.50 for the first three minutes, is expected to be greatly expanded in coming months, since market studies have found that 20% to 30% of all long-distance airline travelers would use such phones. Calls initially can be made only from the air, but the new system, which uses radio waves, is also capable of receiving phone calls to the plane from the ground. The Airfone system was established by the founder of MCI Communications. **(pay phones on big jets)**

7172

F.C.C. Moves Toward National Paging System, *The New York Times* Monday, 20 August 1984, D1.

The Federal Communications Commission is taking the first steps to permit a nationwide paging network that allows people with beepers to receive signals anywhere in the US. The FCC has allocated three radio frequencies for the interstate paging network, each to be assigned to a company which will operate a system using either satellites or existing phone systems. The systems, which will probably begin in 1985, will operate as current local systems do. The Telelocator Network of America, the industry trade association, estimates 3 million people using beepers in 1984 (a sevenfold increase from 1976), and as many as 10 million people carrying beepers by 1990.

(national paging system by 1985)

7173

Speak, Master: Typewriters That Take Dictation, Peter Petre, *Fortune*, 7 Jan 1985, 74-78.

Talkwriters—machines that transcribe speech—already work in the laboratory. An IBM experimental device can understand 5000 words (enough for composing routine business correspondence). Talkwriters promise to make computers accessible to millions of people who can't type, and to speed the journey of ideas to paper. It is too early to forecast their full potential, but industry people think the market for talkwriters could grow as quickly as that for word processors. One expert, Prof Victor Zue (MIT), estimates that 10 to 20 years will be required before talkwriters are perfected. [Zavis P. Zeman (ZZ International, Toronto) reports that a 15,000-word talkwriter costing $20,000 will be on the market in 1985, but that a fully-developed system still seems to be a decade away (*John Kettle's FutureLetter*, 31 March 1985).]

(talkwriters in 10-20 years?)

7174

VCR's Bring Big Changes in Use of Leisure, Robert Lindsey, *The New York Times*, Sunday, 3 March 1985, p1.

The video cassette recorder is changing the way that millions of Americans use their leisure time—the most fundamental change in the enjoyment of filmed entertainment since the postwar expansion of television. More than 17 million VCRs are now in American homes, following sales in 1984 of 7.6 million units. Sales of more than 9.5 million VCRs are expected for 1985, thus increasing the market for home film rentals by more than 50%. The number of tapes rented by Americans has risen from 26 million in 1980 to 304 million in 1984; in the same period, rental prices have fallen from an average of almost $8 to $3. Attendance at movie theaters has yet to fall: the number of movie tickets sold in 1984 remained at 1.2 billion for the third year in a row. Some theater owners predict that a large audience of Americans will continue to prefer seeing the latest movies on a full-size screen. [NOTE: Per capita ownership of VCRs in Canada is now decisively ahead of US ownership. VCRs per 1000 people in Canada rose from 3.3 in 1980 to an estimated 110 in 1984 with a forecast of 358 in 1988. In the US, VCRs per 1000 people rose from 6.6 in 1980 to an estimated 67 in 1984 with a forecast of 249 in 1988 (*John Kettle's FutureLetter*, 31 March 1985).] **(growth of VCR use)**

7175

Hollywood Thriving on Video-Cassette Boom, Aljean Harmetz, *The New York Times*, Monday, 7 May 1984, A1.

In 1978, video-cassettes did not exist as a source of revenue for Hollywood film studios. By 1982, a typical movie earned 8% of its revenues from cassettes and disks, and the figure jumped to 13% in 1983 (pay cable accounted for 24% of revenues, and theatrical film rentals for 63%). In 1983, 4.1 million video-cassette recorders were sold in the US. By the end of 1984, there will be 17 to 18 million machines in US homes, three times more than the highest estimate of two years ago. Jack Valenti (President, Motion Picture Assn) predicts as many as 60 million VCRs in US homes by 1990. The video-cassette has already triumphed over the videodisk (which cannot tape TV programs off the air), and may win out in the long-run over pay-cable TV as a way of showing movies at home. [Also see *Wave of Videocassettes Sweeps Into U.S. Homes, U.S. News & World Report*, 23 July 1984, 45-46, which reports that there are now 40 million VCR owners outside of the US. Video-cassettes are especially popular in countries where moral or political censorship is strong. In some Middle East countries, nearly every home has a VCR; in Moscow, a black market for foreign video equipment and tapes has sprung up. The effect of this tiny hole in the Iron Curtain could eventually be far-reaching.]   **(video-cassette boom)**

7176

Invasion of the Compact Disks, John Rockwell, *The New York Times*, Sunday, 10 March 1985, H1.

Digital laser compact disks—four and three/quarters inches in diameter and able to reproduce sounds with an astonishing clarity and precision—have become a revolutionary force in the music business in the past few months. Sales have mushroomed in the US from 0.8 million CDs in 1983 to 4.3 million in 1984, with projected sales of 9.9 million in 1985. Worldwide, 16.4 million CDs were sold in 1984, with a projected doubling in sales to 32.5 million in 1985. Compact disks appeal to people for their sound, their durability (they are virtually indestructible), and their convenience (they require no dexterity at all, unlike conventional turntables). Will the conventional LP or vinyl disk be quickly outmoded? At present, there are some 2,600 CD titles available in the US, compared with 50,000 in-print LP titles. (Of these CDs, about one-third are classical, in that a new and sophisticated technology appeals to sophisticated consumers.) In 1983, Americans bought 210 million LPs and 237 million cassettes, so CDs still have a long way to go before they replace conventional forms of recording. Most industry spokesmen predict a coexistence of the CD and the LP for many years, due to the current abundance of music on LPs and the unwillingness of consumers to abandon their investment in record players. But the gradual domination by the CD of the home sound reproduction market seems nearly inevitable.

(compact disks vs. LPs)

7177

Photography's New Bag of Tricks, Fred Ritchin, *The New York Times Magazine*, 4 Nov 1984, 42-56.

Photography has long been thought of as a generally trustworthy transcriber of reality, a primary and virtually omnipresent form of communication in our culture. But the computer is now creating a revolution in image making. It is now possible to make almost seamless composites of existing photographs, to alter images in such a way that changes cannot be detected, and to create images that are nearly photographic in their realism. To illustrate, a photograph of Midtown Manhattan is displayed, which includes the Eiffel Tower, the Statue of Liberty, the Transamerica Building, and other modifications. The advantages of this computerized image-making are that one sees the results of each step almost immediately, and computer modification is more precise than manual retouching (NASA regularly employs these techniques to clarify images transmit-

ted from outer space). What is disquieting about the new technology is that its effectiveness may lead to dangerous deceptions. Bogus but convincing images could be a powerful weapon in the hands of political opponents, the KGB, or the CIA. Terrorists could use these doctored images for international blackmail or to create confusion with "news" announcements about impending disasters. In the not-too-distant future, realistic-looking images will probably have to be labeled like words as fiction or non-fiction. Compounding this problem, a new type of electronic camera from Japan will soon appear on the market that records light as a series of digital impulses on a magnetic disk. Such cameras will eliminate the need for a darkroom, enabling almost immediate transmission of a photograph to a newspaper or magazine. The danger is that this digital information can be easily altered, and there may be no permanent record such as the original negative that is now used.

Outside of journalism and politics, the ability of computers to manipulate imagery is less ominous. Artists have developed a number of imaginative uses. A process has been patented to show what someone might look like as he or she ages, which could be used by families of missing children and the FBI. Film makers will be able to simulate deceased movie stars, such as Clark Gable, and put them into new movies. They may also be able to portray environments that no one has ever seen and where cameras cannot go, such as prehistoric Earth or distant galaxies. Full-length computer-generated movies, using special-purpose supercomputers, may be possible in the next few years. An architect can design a house, encode the information into a computer, and have the machine construct it on the screen. Designers, automotive engineers, military officers, and medical researchers are all using a variety of image-making techniques on the computer to envision solutions to problems.   **(computers and photography)**

7178

How U.S. Newspaper Content Is Changing, Leo Bogart (Executive VP, Newspaper Advertising Bureau), *Journal of Communication*, 35:2, Spring 1985, 82-90.

Results from a survey of 1,310 US daily newspapers (representing 77% of all newspapers and 90% of all circulation) conducted in 1983, asking about major changes since 1979 in editorial content and format. In this period, 71% made substantial changes in format, and 64% made substantial changes in content. Many papers reported a decrease in the ratio of international and national news to state and local news. The ratio of hard news to features has also declined.   **(changing newspaper content)**

7179

Free Distribution 'Shoppers' Are Posing Serious Threat to Local Daily Newspapers, Gregory Stricharchuk, *The Wall Street Journal*, Tuesday, 19 June 1984, p31.

An estimated 3000 "shoppers" and "pennysavers" are being published in the US, attracting advertisers with their guarantee of blanket door-to-door circulation. In contrast, daily newspapers often reach no more than one out of three suburban homes. At the other end of the scale, newspapers like *The Wall Street Journal, USA Today*, and *The New York Times* are stepping up their efforts to reach national audiences. By 2000, predicts Hal Lister (Prof of Journalism, U of Missouri), there will not be any metro dailies as we know them today. To compete with the neighborhood news in the shoppers and the national scope of the bigger dailies, local papers will have to carve out new niches as regional newspapers.   **(metro newspapers vs. shoppers)**

XV. SCIENCE AND TECHNOLOGY

A. Social and Political Issues

7180

Order Out of Chaos: Man's New Dialogue with Nature. Ilya Prigogine (Brussels) and Isabelle Stengers (Paris). Foreword by Alvin Toffler. NY: Bantam Books, April 1984/349p/$8.95pb. (First published in France in 1979.)

Our vision of nature is undergoing a radical change toward the multiple, the temporal, and the complex. For a long time a mechanistic world view dominated Western science, in which the world appeared as a vast automaton. In the classical view, the basic processes of nature were considered to be deterministic and reversible. Processes involving randomness or irreversibility were considered only exceptions. Today we see everywhere the role of irreversible processes, of fluctuations. We now understand that we live in a pluralistic world. On all levels, from elementary particles to cosmology, randomness and irreversibility play an ever-increasing role. Science is rediscovering time, and this book seeks to describe this conceptual revolution. Contents are ordered in three parts: The Delusion of the Universal (on the triumph of classical science and the cultural consequences), The Science of Complexity (chapters on energy and the industrial age, the three stages of thermodynamics, and evolutionary feedback), and From Being to Becoming (chapters on rediscovering time, the entropy barrier, and the reenchantment of nature).

In his 16-page foreword, Alvin Toffler asserts that this book is important because it is a lever for changing science itself, compelling us to reexamine its goals, methods, and epistemology. The decline of the industrial age forces us to confront the limitations of the machine model of reality, and the notion that all systems operate deterministically in equilibrium.This book not only challenges the Newtonian model, but shows how the limited claims of Newtonianism might fit compatibly into a larger scientific image of reality. It argues that the old universal laws are not universal at all, but apply only to local regions of reality that happen to be the ones to which science has devoted the most effort. The Prigoginian paradigm shifts attention to those aspects of reality that characterize today's accelerated social change: disorder, instability, diversity, nonlinear relationships, and temporality—a heightened sensitivity to the flows of time. The work of Nobel Prize winner Prigogine and his colleagues in the "Brussels school," Toffler suggests, may well represent the next revolution in science as it enters into a new dialogue not merely with nature, but with society itself.

(a new scientific worldview?)

7181

The Touch of Midas: Science, Values and Environment in Islam and the West. Edited by Ziauddin Sardar (London, UK). Manchester UK and Dover NH: Manchester U Press, Sept 1984/253p/$35.00.

Contemporary science has the touch of Midas. It has brought mankind riches beyond dreams and freedom from disease. But, like Midas, mankind is discovering that the golden touch has serious shortcomings. Science's ability to do good now seems to be overshadowed by an even greater capacity to do evil. This book, based on two seminars held in Stockholm in 1981 and Granada in 1982, examines whether a synthesis can be achieved between the growing awareness of a crisis in science in the West, and various attempts to rediscover the spirit of Islamic science in the Muslim world. Essays focus on the rebirth of Islamic science, the underlying value system of sci/tech in Islam, science and values, the emergence of environmental awareness in the West, an Islamic perspective on environment and values, a framework for synthesizing knowledge and worldviews, and approaches to synthesis.

(a synthesis of Islamic and Western science?)

7182

A Strategic Analysis of Science and Technology Policy. Harvey A. Averch (NSF). Baltimore MD: Johns Hopkins U Press, Dec 1984/224p/$20.00.

A systematic study of US sci/tech policy from the Eisenhower to the Reagan administrations. Over the past 30 years, critical issues have included the apportionment of resources for R&D, the design of market incentives or government programs for technological innovation, the delivery of science and engineering education, sci/tech information services provided by government, and the use of science and technology in trade, aid, and diplomacy. Sci/tech decisions influence economic growth, productivity, and international trade. Yet, the policy models that have been used to guide these decisions are for the most part weak, lacking precision in language and rigor in causal connections. Despite the marked rise of interest in science policy, increased Federal funding of the sciences, and the growing sophistication of analytic methods, the logic of science policy remains informal, qualitative, and intuitive. Averch calls for applying the quantitative testing and systems analytic thinking that have become common in the domains of economics and operations research.

(logic of sci/tech policy questioned)

7183

Rethinking Our Approach to Science and Technology Policy, Christopher T. Hill (Congressional Research Service), *Technology Review*, 88:3, April 1985, 11-15.

There is reason to ask whether US science policy, guided by the same premises since WWII, is adequate for today's challenges. Physicists have had enormous influence on sci/tech policy during the last few decades—an influence promoting their view of what constitutes good research (quantification, elegant experimentation, uniqueness of explanation) as the touchstone of quality in other fields. But other fields do not work this way. Moreover, priorities have been set largely by government officials and the scientific elite, whereas national needs might be better served by a process that more openly considers the views of policymakers and a wider range of scientists. Nurturing multiple approaches to the same goal appears to be more effective than selecting one approach early on. We may also wish to consider a system of competitive support for insitutions or investigators, rather than for projects, and one with relatively long-term funding commitments. Finally, we should change the current emphasis on combining graduate education and basic research at US universities—a system that diverts faculty from teaching undergraduates and improperly trains graduate students as research entrepreneurs. By contrast, the Japanese try to ensure that all students perform at an acceptable level, and they focus less on catering to the excellent few.

(US science policy questioned)

7184

Lost at the Frontier: U.S. Science and Technology Policy Adrift. Deborah Shapley (CSIS, Georgetown U) and Rustum Roy (Director, Materials Research Laboratory, Penn State U). Philadelphia PA: ISI Press/Institute for Scientific Information (3501 Market St), March 1985/223p/$19.95;$13.95pb.

An important 1945 report to President Roosevelt by Vannevar Bush, **Science—The Endless Frontier**, has become sanctified as the charter for Federal support of basic research. But contrary to the mythology that later grew up around the report, Bush did not treat basic research in a vacuum, but as one of the steps in a chain of endeavor that leads to industrial advance, better public health, and stronger national defense. The since-neglected passages of the Bush report still ring true, and explain why US science today seems lost at the endless frontier Bush spoke of. The authors argue that US science should be reorganized to give equal weight to undirected basic research, purposive basic research, applied science, engineering, and technology. Instead of invoking undirected basic research as the central jewel in the research system's crown, the unique value of each separate jewel should be stressed, as well as their essential interdependence. Moreover, there should be a change in the values of scientists to stress the interconnections among disciplines and institutions, and across various artificial barriers. A synergistic model of science/engineering/technology relations is not only more accurate historically, but more useful in policy design. The broad vision of Bush should characterize the profession of science; instead, this vision has been betrayed.

Various proposals are made to remedy the divorce between basic science and its applications. They include an independent advisory board attached to the US Office of Management and Budget to articulate national sci/tech policy, a greater concentration of basic science in the US university science system, scientists and their students devoting some part of their time to pro bono general education in the sciences, an expanded commitment to internationalism, judging scientists by the usefulness of their papers rather than by the quantity of published work, and longer-term grants of funds (perhaps 3 to 5 years) so as to free up some energies now devoted to the funding process. The volume is concluded with invited reponses from William O. Baker, Rep. George E. Brown Jr, Pat Choate, Harry C. Gatos, James R. Killian Jr, Edwin H. Land, F. James Rutherford, Eric A. Walker, and Walter A. Hahn, who proposes a new study, **Science—The Endless Frontier, II**, to be prepared by all parties to the science-and-society contract. **(US science policy questioned)**

7185

Planning Science and Technology Policy, Ann L. Hollick (Visiting Prof of Political Science, MIT), *Journal of Policy Analysis and Management*, 3:4, Summer 1984, 516-531.

The importance of sci/tech in foreign affairs is growing rapidly. As a sci/tech leader, the US is in a position to use its capabilities to further its foreign policy objectives. But the government must first develop the ability to think systematically about the medium- and long-range implications of sci/tech developments. Such planning has been hindered by the crisis-response nature of foreign policy and the difficulty of developing technical information needed for sound forecasts. An effective planning staff should combine the skills of both foreign policy specialists and scientists. **(sci/tech policy in foreign affairs)**

7186

Planning for National Technology Policy. Edited by Richard Alan Goodman (UCLA) and Julian Pavon (Center for Technological Development of Industry). NY: Praeger Publishers, Jan 1984/460p/$32.95.

Offers a detailed planning process for developing a sectoral and national policy for the technological development of a nation. Such development is seen as a process in service of larger national objectives and not an end in itself; thus a comprehensive process with rudimentary techniques is preferable to sophisticated development of techniques for only part of the overall problem. Chapters are addressed to such topics as innovation in developing countries, the diffusion process and public policy, the planning process for R&D, a comparison of industrial policies in five nations (Brazil, France, Germany, Israel, and The Netherlands), and a lengthy case study of technological development in Spain. **(national technological development)**

*7187

Citizen Participation in Science Policy. Edited by James C. Peterson (Dept of Sociology, Western Michigan U). Amherst MA: U of Massachusetts Press, Aug 1984/241p/$23.50;$9.95pb.

Few values in American society are held more deeply than the right of citizens to participate in decisions on matters that directly affect them. Yet effective public participation on toxic waste disposal, nuclear plant building, energy conservation, drug regulation, and many other concerns is difficult due to the sci/tech content of such issues. Specialized knowledge and impenetrable jargon are barriers to meaningful participation. The public is often excluded because issues are defined as technical questions. But the issues at stake are too critical to permit any but the most thorough of debates. These essays and case studies place citizen involvement in science policy in the context of larger participatory movements, and explore the forms that citizen participation may take. Topics include new routes for citizen involvement in social risk assessment, public participation and professionalism in impact assessment, institutionalizing public service science, lessons from people's participation in India, consumers and health planning, the impact of public participation in biomedical policy, solving problems of nuclear technology, and nonviolent anti-nuclear protest. [NOTE: An excellent anthology on an important topic.]

(citizen participation in science policy)

7188

The New Politics of Science. David Dickson. NY: Pantheon Books, May 1984/404p/$22.95.

A British science journalist and author of **The Politics of Alternative Technology** (Universe, 1975) argues that a new politics of science has used tax, patent, and regulatory policy to spur technological innovation and reduce social controls over new technologies. The result is that planning for science is now almost exclusively based on the needs of the military and the marketplace, while broader social benefits (health, nutrition, safety, a clean environment) are largely neglected. The technology assessment movement, which seeks to define the hazards in new technologies, is antidemocratic because it reduces political conflicts to technical terms. Control of scientific knowledge is crucial to control of the economy. The need to democratize the practice and application of science can be divided into three principal stages: 1) reforming the procedures and work practices of the scientific community; 2) democratizing the institutions that decide how research funds should be allocated; and 3) maintaining public access to the fruits of publically funded research.

(**democratizing science**)

7189

Science, the Greatest Experiment: An Essential Role for the Humanities, E. E. David, Jr (President, Exxon Research and Engineering Co), *Vital Speeches of the Day*, 51:5, 15 Dec 1984, 142-146.

Former President of AAAS views science and technology in the US as entering what may be its most buoyant period in history. In contrast to the anti-technology mood of the 1970s, there is now heightened public enthusiasm for the major role that science and technology play in creating new jobs and fostering economic growth. But science and technology are not self-contained. They spring from a culture, they survive as part of a culture, and they are responsible to their culture. They thrive only if the surrounding culture continuously refreshes their assumptions and goals. A vibrant humanistic tradition will insure that our culture assimilates the changes resulting from science and technology, while preserving and enhancing our values. **Science remains perhaps humanity's greatest experiment, but its place in the modern world is far from secure. Its future depends on reconciliation at the interface between the values necessary for promoting its progress and the values necessary for holding a society together.** In a break with past patterns, technological and economic progress now depends closely and directly upon scientific progress. This means that in the long run, a world that does not cherish science will be a world without material progress, and perhaps without spiritual progress as well. We hear much of the need for scientific and technological literacy; we must also pay close attention to humanistic literacy, especially for those who will create the technologies that shape the future.

The potential rewards are very great. The coming century promises to be one of astonishing achievement, in that 90% of all scientists who have ever lived are alive today. In the next 30 years, both the pool of working scientists and the pool of knowledge are expected to double, as they have over the past 30 years. Perhaps the most profound insights will come in molecular biology; the potential rewards promise to be so immense that it will almost inevitably cause a metamorphosis in values—if science retains its place in our culture. The fields of molecular science and chemical reactivity to energy supply are creating the knowledge needed to synthesize all manner of material resources with properties precisely tailored to human needs. Such science will transform utterly the dour Malthusian vision of a world with sharp limits to growth because of depleting resources. [NOTE: A splendid companion to the less sanguine views, below.]

(**science and culture**)

7190

Progress or Catastrophe: The Nature of Biological Science and Its Impact on Human Society. Bentley Glass (Director, History of Genetics Program, American Philosophical Society). Convergence Series, edited by Ruth Nanda Anshen. NY: Praeger Special Studies, June 1985/253p/$9.95pb.

Essays by the past president of AAAS and AAUP on the brave new world of genetic engineering (and the insepara-

bility of Prometheus and Pandora), the goals of human evolution, liberal education in a scientific age, developing countries and scientific knowledge, and the biology of nuclear war. (**science and society essays**)

7191

Hope, Fear, and Technology: Changing Prospects in the 1980's, Michael Marien (Editor, *Future Survey*), *Vital Speeches of the Day*, 51:5, 15 Dec 1984, 137-142.

The US and the world are in the midst of multiple technological revolutions that generate much to hope for— and much to fear. But the public interest appears to be suffering from a polarization between naive optimists and naive pessimists, especially regarding technological prospects, even as we experience a cultural shift from pessimism to optimism and from needs-centered appropriate technology to high-tech. The Pollyannas and Cassandras seem to thrive on each other: one offers foolish hope, the other gloomy exaggerations. Rather, we need a more adult perspective of tough-minded optimism: one that encourages both intelligent hopes and fears. High-tech may bring some high-touch, as the high-cheer Panglosses tell us, but it also brings high risk. To illustrate, hopes and fears are listed in each of four broad clusters of modern technology. 1) The Information Revolution: advances in computers and telecommunications, balanced by "infoglut" or information overload; 2) Biotechnologies: innumerable possibilities in medicine and agriculture, offset by a multitude of new and old questions; 3) Energy Technologies: many possibilities for abundant power, matched by the likelihood that we will stumble a few more times before acquiring an energy system that is cheap, safe, and reliable; 4) Nuclear Weapons: the possibility that we might still avoid a holocaust or nuclear winter vs. the possibility that many people will be hurt or killed before we somehow come to our senses. Concludes that, to encourage more tough-minded optimists to mediate between the wildly conflicting views of the Pollyannas and Cassandras, we need far more technology assessment (and far more dissemination of the findings), forums for serious and sustained dialogue and debate, and more courses and programs in institutions of higher learning that address these matters. [NOTE: *Future Survey* in a nutshell, to the degree that such can be done!] (**balancing hopes and fears about technology**)

7192

Technology and the Character of Contemporary Life: A Philosophical Inquiry. Albert Borgmann (Prof of Philosophy, U of Montana). Chicago, Ill: U of Chicago Press, Dec 1984/c342p/$26.00.

The problems of modern society are usually blamed not on technology, but on political indecision, social injustice, or environmental constraint. Borgmann offers an alternative to this optimistic view, arguing that technology creates a controlling pattern in our lives. This pattern sharply divides life into labor and leisure, sustains the industrial democracies, and fosters the view that the earth itself is a technological device. A "device paradigm," in which objects satisfy our needs, has served us well in conquering hunger and disease. But when we turn to it for richer experiences, it leads to a life dominated by thoughtless consumption. We should not reject technology, but we do need a public conversation about the nature of the good life.

(**technology controls our lives**)

7193

Wayward Technology. Ernst Braun (former Head, Technology Policy Unit, U of Aston). Westport CT: Greenwood Press, Feb 1984/224p/$27.50.

There is now an overwhelming impression that society has come to be at the mercy of its technology, irrespective of whether it is socially good or evil. Yet never before has society made such strenuous efforts not so much to control technology as to advance it. Despite the fear of technology and the feelings of being overrun and perhaps destroyed by it, societies feel that technology is their best weapon in gaining competitive advantages over rival societies. Perhaps we still live the Promethean myth—we want the fire yet fear punishment for using it. Perhaps also the immediate economic interest of any social entity militates against the wider long-term interests of human society at large. Braun attempts to shed some light on this dilemma, and the related twin questions of the forces that shape technology and how society can and does control these forces. Chapters are devoted to the rise of industrial society, technological innovation, contemporary fears about technology, technology assessment (which was to be the answer to all fears about technology), government policies for technology, market control of technology, and technology and social goals. Concludes that technology must be allowed considerable freedom to develop in its own wayward way. Yet it must be subject to certain rules of social intercourse, for total freedom is in the end self-destructive. Technology can be steered a little, and if the steering is done with sensitivity, wisdom, and knowledge it can greatly enhance the value of technology while curbing its excesses. Technology policy is part of the body politic and therefore full of controversy, but valuable consensus can be obtained on many of its aspects, and this should be actively sought. **(technology policy)**

7194

Perilous Progress: Managing the Hazards of Technology. Edited by Robert W. Kates *et al.*(Clark U). Boulder CO: Westview, April 1985/c460p/$32.50.

A comprehensive and comparative perspective on a broad range of technological risks confronting contemporary society, providing a framework for thinking about hazards and hazard management. Chapters cover causal taxonomy, characterizing perceived risk, human and nonhuman mortality, economic costs and losses, automobile accidents, regulating automobile safety, nuclear power, controlling PCBs, the Consumer Product Safety Commission, the hazards of contraceptives, television as a social hazard, Congress as hazard manager, and the art, science, and ideology of hazard assessment.

(technological hazards)

7195

The Snare of Specialization, Rogers Hollingsworth (Prof of History, U of Wisconsin-Madison), *Bulletin of the Atomic Scientists*, 40:6, June-July 1984, 34-37.

Although US science today is strong, some of its contradictions must be addressed to protect its strength. Increasing specialization and fragmentation of knowledge have led most scientists to narrow their field of concern, resulting in poor communication both within and across academic disciplines. As the sciences pursue the logic of their own disciplines and become even more specialized, they risk becoming remote from the needs of society. Alternative structures are needed to facilitate interdisciplinary communication: 1) truly interdisciplinary centers in our universities where scientists may come from a variety of academic disciplines and engage in basic research; 2) some structural arrangement within universities to assist scholars in periodically changing their research specialties; 3) a restructuring of curricula so that students can better comprehend relationships among different branches of knowledge before the rigidities of specialization begin to kill their curiosity about a complex world.

(problems of scientific specialization)

7196

Feminists Look at Science, Catherine Manthorpe (U of Leeds), *New Scientist*, 7 March 1985, 29-31.

Feminist interest in, and criticism of, science is making an important contribution towards a new understanding of the operations of science within contemporary Western culture. Attention is centered in three areas: 1) the question of access of women to science education and science-related careers; 2) a challenge to the power that science has over women's lives (especially in the biological and medical sciences, and to the ideological content of theories used to support sexist assumptions); 3) a challenge to the neutral objectivity of science, with charges that masculine concepts are imbedded in the categories of scientific thought, and that science has developed only from the male half of human experience. **(feminists question science)**

7197

Dissident Science in West Germany, Helmut Hirsch (Gruppe Ökologie, Hannover FRG), *The Ecologist*, 14:1, 1984, 15-20.

Many ecologically-oriented scientists became critical of established science when they realized that science plays a considerable part in the conceptualization, justification, and realization of large industrial projects. A number of dissident West German institutes and groups are members of an umbrella organization, the AGOF, which has been in existence since 1980. These ecologically-oriented scientists strongly reject the corruption of establishment science and its claim for absolute truth. AGOF members view truth as relative and existing in multiple forms, and they argue that this problem of relative truth must always be considered openly and publically. AGOF scientists recognize the limited validity of scientific results, and are willing to consider everyday knowledge (that which has not been gained by a scientific process) in their studies. Accordingly, ecologically-oriented science closely cooperates with concerned citizens. It is also organized non-hierarchically, in contrast to the high division of labor in establishment science. Ecologically-oriented scientists also explicitly consider questions of a political nature which are ignored by establishment scientists.

(ecological vs. established science)

B. Biotechnology

*7198

Biotechnology: A New Industrial Revolution. Steve Prentis (Editor, *Trends in Biotechnology*). NY: George Braziller, Inc (One Park Ave), 1984/192p/$18.50. (First published in London by Orbis Publishing Ltd in 1984.)

Traces the scientific and technological discoveries that have led us to the brink of a new industrial revolution. The myriad prospects of biotechnology are even more far-reaching that that of the silicon microchip, because biotechnology can produce materials. The crucial feature of biotechnology, as defined here, is that it makes use of microbes or cells obtained from plants and animals. Most of the new biotechnological processes aim to harvest certain valuable materials manufactured by the microbes, such as antibiotics, fuels, and chemicals. The following list suggests a few of the benefits biotechnology can bring: 1) **Medicine**: new and improved treatments for the three major killers in developed countries (heart disease, cancer, diabetes), better and cheaper antibiotics, vaccines to protect aginst viral and parasitic diseases, rapid tests to aid doctors in making accurate diagnoses of many diseases, techniques for correcting body chemistry to cure hereditary diseases; 2) **Agriculture and Food Production**: creating crops which make their own fertilizers, new plants that can thrive on land that presently lacks water or is too salty, substances to speed the growth of farm animals, vaccines to protect cattle, cheaper forms of animal feed from microbes grown on waste materials; 3) **Energy Production**: renewable fuels such as methane and hydrogen gases for domestic and industrial use, substances manufactured by microbes to extract oil locked underground; 4) **Industry**: microbes to extract metals from solid rock, new systems for controlling pollution, and new sources of raw materials for the manufacture of plastics, paints, artificial fibers, and adhesives. The inflated claims of "biohype" are foolish and unnecessary, for the realistic expectations of the bioindustrial revolution are impressive enough to command the attention of anyone who wants to know how our world will change in the next few years.

Chapters are devoted to the chemistry of life, reweaving the threads of life through genetic engineering, fermentation and selection, biotechnology and disease, the new green revolution, biotechnology from farm to supermarket, bioenergy and fuels for the future, biotransformations as the way ahead for industry, and who will benefit from biotechnology. The economic advantages of being among the first to capitalize on new technologies are enormous. The US and Japan are in the best position now, with the US having a clear lead in genetic engineering, and Japan having an edge in the kind of technology needed for large-scale fermentations (with about 80% of the patents in this area). But it is certainly not too late for Western European countries to seize a large slice of the pie. And, given the necessary commitment, a number of developing countries could become more involved in the lower-technology, less capital-intensive areas of biotechnology. [NOTE: Perhaps the best overview yet on this critically important area.]

(biotechnology revolution)

*7199
Broken Code: The Exploitation of DNA. Marc Lappé (U of California-Berkeley). San Francisco CA: Sierra Club Books, July 1985/368p/$17.95.

Biologists have decoded the secret language of the gene and are fast learning to control it. In breaking the code of life, we have opened up a previously closed system. We can now add or subtract genetic information to the flow of life on earth.The new science of recombinant DNA promises humankind the ability to control what genetic information is carried into the future. Today's venture is different from past interventions with plants and livestock, because we now have the power to systematically select genetic properties without waiting for the laborious and time-consuming propagation of the species in question. But who will control the fruits of this new scientific knowledge, and who will direct the ends to which new techniques will be applied? The words "broken code" thus carry a double meaning: breaking the genetic code made the DNA revolution possible, but the moral code of scientific inquiry may be in jeopardy. This book seeks to defuse fears where they

appear unwarranted, to highlight previously unrecognized perils, and to investigate the potential of genetic engineering to do good. Worldwide, nearly 2500 companies are exploring genetic engineering techniques to produce feedstuffs, energy products, drugs, fragrances, and any other biological substance with sufficient value to warrant commercialization. This growth should be viewed cautiously because it is occurring without direct regulation. Lappé argues for some sort of oversight and priority-setting. Continuing public involvement is necessary to insure that the industry is responsive to public needs, and that its evolution occurs in public view. To protect the environment, we should require simulation tests before releasing genetically engineered organisms, ensure that newly introduced species contain devices for limited survival, and incorporate in an organism specific sensitivities to known therapeutic or other antagonistic agents so that any unanticipated spread could be contained.

(need to control DNA revolution)

7200
The Double-Edged Helix: Genetic Engineering in the Real World. Liebe F. Cavalieri (Sloan Kettering Institute for Cancer Research). Convergence Series, edited by Ruth Nanda Anshen. NY: Praeger Special Studies, Jan 1985/ 213p/$9.95pb.

This new edition adds a brief preface and a six-page epilogue on the moral dilemma of genetic engineering to a discussion of advances in science and technology, the nature of gene splicing, the hazards of success, and the need for an active social conscience in the scientific community. Since the first edition of this book (Columbia University Press, 1981), Cavalieri sees virtually no serious effort made to explore this area. There is still time, however, for rigorous forethought and selection of what recombinant DNA technology has to offer. For once let us not do everything simply because we can.   **(genetic engineering)**

7201
Human Gene Therapy. U.S. Congress, Office of Technology Assessment. Washington DC: USGPO, Dec 1984/$5.50 (S/N 052-003-00983-8).

Using human genes to cure serious genetic diseases may raise ethical questions if the changes can be inherited, but such therapy is not practical at present. Gene therapy affecting only individual patients, not their offspring, is similar enough to other medical treatments, such as vaccination or drug administration, that it does not raise fundamental new ethical issues. Non-inheritable gene therapy is likely to be attempted soon to help patients whose defective genes cause devastating diseases for which no better treatment is available. There are some 2000 to 3000 genetic diseases (such as Tay-Sachs disease and sickle-cell anemia), and only a few can be treated using present technologies. Human gene therapy will probably involve taking cells from a patient's bone marrow, treating them with new genes prepared by recombinant DNA, and restoring the cells to the patient. Reproductive cells are unlikely to be affected. Gene therapy that would make inheritable changes should not proceed without further public discussion and evaluation.   **(human gene therapy)**

7202
Prospects for Human Gene Therapy, W. French Anderson (National Heart, Lung, and Blood Institute, Bethesda MD), *Science*, Vol 226, 26 Oct 1984, 401-409.

Gene therapy—the insertion into an organism of a normal gene which then corrects a genetic defect—has been carried out in fruit flies and mice. Somatic gene cell therapy techniques are becoming increasingly efficient, and their future application in humans should result in at least partial correction of a number of genetic disorders. However, the safety of the procedures must still be established by further animal studies before human clinical trials would be ethical. The issues of enhancement engineering need to be debated. But arguments that genetic engineering might someday be misused do not justify the perpetuation of human suffering that would result from delay in the application of this potentially powerful therapy.

(human gene therapy)

7203

Human Genetic Engineering, Alexander Morgan Capron (Prof of Law, Georgetown U), *Technology in Society*, 6:1, 1984, 23-35.

The extension of gene-splicing techniques to human beings will soon be brought about because of advances in biomedical knowledge, raising new sets of questions not previously encountered in the recombinant DNA debate. Four potentially troublesome consequences especially deserve attention: 1) effects on human genetic makeup; 2) intergenerational responsibilities (prenatal diagnosis upsets the traditional norm of accepting children unconditionally; should responsible parents then be expected to correct or augment certain genes?); 3) the distribution of social benefits (should everyone have the same genetic alterations?); 4) the concept of being human. [Also see ***Will We Still Be 'Human' If We Have Engineered Genes and Animal Organs?*** Samuel Gorovitz (Prof of Philosophy, U of Maryland), *The Washington Post*, 9 Dec 1984, C1.] **(human gene therapy)**

7204

Safety Concerns and Genetic Engineering in Agriculture, Winston J. Brill (VP of R&D, Agricetus, Middleton WI), *Science*, Vol 227, 25 Jan 1985, 381-384.

Predictions about the safety of a recombinant plant or microorganism for agricultural use should be based on the vast experience with traditional practices such as plant breeding and the use of microbial inoculants. Traditional agricultural practices continually improve useful crops and microbes by taking advantage of new genetic modifications. An introduced plant with foreign genes should be no greater environmental threat than such organisms without recombinant genes. [Also see ***Greening the Gene: Biotechnology Is Sowing a Crop of Brave New Plants***, *Newsweek*, 12 Nov 1984, 103-105.]

(biotechnology safety)

7205

How Brave a New World? Dilemmas in Bioethics. Richard A. McCormick, S.J. (Georgetown U). Washington DC: Georgetown U Press, Jan 1985/459p/$12.95pb.

Collected essays by a Catholic moral theologian, on such topics as the teaching of medical ethics, some neglected aspects of the moral responsiblity for health, proxy consent in the experimentation situation, public policy and fetal research, public policy on abortion, contraceptive interventions, ethics and reproductive interventions, saving defective infants, the moral right to privacy, the dilemma of modern medicine to save or let die, and the living will.

(Catholic view of bioethics)

7206

Making Babies: The State of the Art, Robert H. Blank (Prof of Political Science, U of Idaho), *The Futurist*, 19:1, Feb 1985, 11-17.

Author of **The Political Implications of Human Genetic Technology** (Westview, 1981) and **Redefining**

Human Life: Reproductive Technologies and Social Policy (Westview, 1984/270p/$25.00) surveys the reproduction-aiding technologies that enable childless couples to have children: artificial insemination (the most widely-used technology), in-vitro fertilization (a procedure by which a woman's egg is fertilized outside her body and reimplanted in her uterus), the possibility of cloning and egg fusion in the future, artificial embryonation (where a childless husband and wife pay a fertile woman to be inseminated with the husband's sperm, after which the embryo is flushed out and implanted in the wife), embryo adoption (the same procedure, using sperm from a donor rather than the husband), surrogate motherhood, fetal transfer, reversing sterilization, and prenatal intervention (amniocentesis, ultrasound, fetoscopy). These technologies may be increasingly demanded as a result of what some experts call an "epidemic of infertility" in the US, whereby the sperm count of American males has fallen more than 30% in the last 50 years, probably due to environmental pollution. Whatever the cause, nearly 25% of American men now have sperm counts so low as to be considered functionally sterile. The proportion of American women finding it difficult to conceive is also on the rise. Concludes that diligent and cautious policymaking will be required to ensure that potential benefits are realized, while undesirable "brave new world" consequences are minimized.

(reproduction technology and rising infertility)

7207

What Should We Do With Surplus Potential Humans?
George J. Annas (Prof of Health Law, Boston U), *The Washington Post*, Sunday, 31 March 1985, K1.

We could be close to a future in which prefabricated human embryos are frozen and sold in supermarkets and through mail-order catalogs. Such embryos may be used not for reproduction, but purely for experimental purposes, such as testing the toxicity of new drugs, chemicals, and cosmetics. Such techniques for creating children without sex close a circle opened by effective contraception, which made sex without reproduction dependable. Research on embryos will likely cheapen our view of human life. Like babies from surrogate mothers, embryos will be bought and sold in the belief that they will produce a healthy child. It seems reasonable legally to assign rearing rights to the gestational as opposed to the genetic mother. Doing so will permit the donation of eggs and even embryos from one woman or couple to another, but does not necessarily permit commerce in human embryos. A model state law should be drafted and enacted now, designed to clarify the identity of the gestational mother as the legal mother, while outlawing the sale of human embryos.

(prefabricated human embryos)

7208

The Biotechnology of Sex Preselection: Social Issues in a Public Policy Context, Thomas C. Wiegle (Program for Biosocial Research, Northern Illinois U), *Policy Studies Review*, 4:3, Feb 1985, 445-460.

The ability to select the sex of one's offspring could be diffused through many societies in the near future. If such use takes place on a broad scale, the natural sex ratios in those societies will become unbalanced in favor of males. Likely social effects are explored, as are five broad major policy choices that governments could make: prohibition, regulation, encouragement, coercive mandating, and no action. Concludes that it is likely that governments will make some type of policy response, but not until sex preselection technologies are widely available and sex imbalances begin to appear. **(sex preselection policy)**

7209

Human Sterilization: Emerging Technologies and Reemerging Social Issues, Robert H. Blank (Prof of Political Science, U of Idaho), *Science, Technology & Human Values*, 9:3, Summer 1984, 8-20.

One of the most volatile of contemporary social issues is the development and use of reproductive technologies. New technological developments in human sterilization promise to complicate the constitutional, political, and social problems surrounding the termination of fertility. The technique that may drastically revise concepts of sterilization and contraception is the removable silicone plug, a method involving occlusion of the fallopian tubes that is presently undergoing clinical trials for the Food and Drug Administration. The availability of such a technique that is safe and reversible will heighten pressures for voluntary and involuntary sterilization. Given current negative public attitudes toward those on welfare and the scarcity of public funds for welfare programs, it would not be surprising to see pressures for widespread use of incentives (or coercion) to encourage (or force) sterilization of the poor, retarded, and those otherwise deemed unfit. It seems certain that public controversy surrounding sterilization will intensify. **(human sterilization technology)**

7210

To Clone a Dinosaur, Mike Benton (Queens U, Belfast), *New Scientist*, 17 Jan 1985, 41-43.

Paleontologists have long known that organic material can survive in fossilized bones. Recent research now suggests that an extinct animal may eventually be cloned. Small quantities of collagen, a protein in bone and skin, probably exist in fossils of Mesozoic age, including dinosaurs. It may be possible to concentrate tiny quantities of collagen by grinding up fossil bones. Much more speculative is the idea that the DNA of extinct organisms could be cloned to reconstruct all of its genetic materials. The DNA from, say, a quagga (an African animal hunted to extinction by 1883) could then be inserted into an early embryo of a zebra, in the hopes that it would take over the processes of development. But the chances of such a success seem remote at present. As for cloning a dinosaur, what could serve as a surrogate mother?

(cloning extinct animals?)

*7211

Future Man. Brian Stableford (U of Reading,UK). NY: Crown Publishers, Nov 1984/192p (8x11") / $17.95; $12.95pb.

The human race is on the verge of the most profound revolution in its history, as a result of the new biotechnology. The first phase of human evolution, in which "human nature" was slowly shaped by natural selection, lasted for more than a million years. The second phase began when man freed himself from his dependence on nature. In this final phase of human evolution, man will be able to control the evolution of his own race through genetic engineering. In the future we may be able to transform any species, including our own, adding or subtracting characteristics at will. This will not be easy, but in a matter of centuries flesh will become a medium in which our descendents can work as artists and craftsmen.

Chapters are devoted to the foundations of the biological revolution, the potential for mastering our environment (biological factories, ecological streamlining, cultivation of algae for food on vast expanses of ocean, battery chickens without heads and wings as a biological production line), new ways to combat disease, spare parts for people (artificial organs, biosensors, regeneration), controlling the lifespan, engineering people (eliminating imperfections such as our vulnerable backbones, a new metabolism, man modified to live underwater and in space), control of the mind, and extensions of man such as computers and robots. A concluding chapter sketches some largely unpleasant scenarios for the future of mankind, such as a new viral plague resulting from a genetic engineering accident, biological warfare, and various forms of tyrannical control such as implanted devices in brains. [NOTE: A broad and fascinating survey of possibilities, accompanied by more than 150 striking photos, drawings, and charts which are well worth the price of the book alone. Highly recommended!] **(bioengineering as a new phase of evolution)**

7212

Bionic Human Is No Longer a Pipe Dream, *U.S. News & World Report*, 4 March 1985, p12.

Researchers around the US are busy enlarging the inventory of replaceable human parts, and more than one million people annually receive bionic parts ranging from joints to lenses in the eye. Some new devices being tested and refined include: 1) a polyurethane blood vessel that could benefit 500,000 patients annually who need heart bypasses; 2) artificial skin to treat 100,000 burn victims each year; 3) an artificial pancreas that could benefit millions of diabetics; 4) ear implants that could offer partial hearing to 200,000 profoundly deaf Americans; 5) an "artificial eye" consisting of a grid of 64 electrodes implanted in the brain, enabling the blind to discern simple images.

(artificial parts for humans)

7213

New Bodies for Sale (Cover Story), *Newsweek*, 27 May 1985, 64-71.

Plastic or cosmetic surgery, for decades regarded as an indulgence of vain women, is one of the fastest-growing medical specialties in the US, up 61% between 1981 and 1984. An estimated 477,000 operations were performed in 1984 in this "esthetic" surgery—optional procedures to make essentially normal people look better. There were also 1.3 million procedures in "reconstructive" surgery, such as burn treatment or the rebuilding of breasts following a mastectomy. These figures exclude surgery by specialists in other fields, such as dermatologists, who increasingly perform many of the same operations as plastic surgeons, such as using lasers to get rid of birthmarks. Major clinical breakthroughs have been developed, such as "suction lipectomy" to reduce fat thighs. A 1979 Federal ruling allowing doctors to advertise has affected plastic surgery more than any other branch of medicine, by attracting patients who never in the past would have considered such bodily changes. Rising demand also reflects the decline in occupations for which appearance is largely irrelevant, such as farming, and a rise in jobs where the primary qualification is to look attractive and competent. [NOTE: Also see *Plastic Surgery Wooing Patients Hoping to Move Up Career Ladder*, *The Wall Street Journal*, 6 Aug 1985, p31, which describes how looking good helps people to feel good and be competitive. This trend seems to aptly parallel the powers of genetic engineering to make all sorts of changes in plants and animals.]

(cosmetic surgery boom)

7214

Laser Is Designed To Clean Arteries, Sandra Blakeslee, *The New York Times*, Tuesday, 29 Jan 1985, C1.

Millions of Americans have clogged arteries that leads to serious heart disease and requires coronary bypass surgery. But important progress has been made on an experimental technique that could, without surgery, ream out clogged arteries as a plumber's snake clears blocked pipes. The technique uses a laser attached to flexible glass fibers, encased in a catheter, that is threaded through arteries to reach the plaque that blocks blood flow. The laser's energy obliterates the plaque, but without the usual heat that can damage surrounding tissues. Tests on human patients are expected in 1986; if successful, the procedure could revolutionize the treatment of cardiovascular disease—and save money. A patient could have his arteries reamed out in minutes, possibly without an overnight hospital stay. **(laser to clean arteries)**

C. Outer Space and Planet Earth

*7215

Out Of The Cradle: Exploring the Frontiers Beyond Earth. William K. Hartmann (Tucson, Ariz.), Ron Miller, and Pamela Lee. NY: Workman Publishing Co, Dec 1984/ 190p(10x8")/$19.95;$11.95pb.

A small "coffee-table" book by an astronomer and two artists, with 120 photos and paintings. Chapters are devoted to the need for space exploration (both as an adventure and as a possible way to revitalize Earth and it economy), the evolution of shuttles to space cities, robot astronauts, future goals of lunar exploration and the first lunar industry (oxygen production), asteroids and comets as the first landfalls beyond the Moon, the exploration of Mars and its moons, the cold realm of the outer solar system, and the search for extraterrestrial life. Concludes that the most important next step in space exploration is not a particular mission, but adapting a critical golden rule: "Space exploration must be carried out in a way so as to reduce, not aggravate, tensions in human society." Each future decision must be tested against this principle. In doing so, we can encourage a sense of world participation in the space venture. The book title is derived from an 1899 statement by Russian rocket pioneer Konstantin Tsiolkovsky: "Earth is the cradle of humanity, but one cannot live in the cradle forever." [NOTE: An excellent overview and introduction to space exploration, with stunning illustrations. Quite similar in glossy presentation and quality to **Future Man** (#7211).]

(space exploration)

7216

The New Race for Space: The U.S. and Russia Leap to the Challenge for Unlimited Rewards. James E. Oberg (NASA Johnson Space Center). Harrisburg PA: Stackpole Books, Sept 1984/210p/$14.95.

The current round of the space race is no longer for glory or curiosity, but for wealth and power. Both the US and the USSR bring their own capabilities and shortcomings into this competition. The immediate Soviet advantage is a prototype permanent sunned space station: the Salyut complex (which, however, is small and inflexible). The US advantage lies with the space shuttle. The space applications paths of the US and the USSR may start to converge. At the same time, the bilateral nature of the space race is fading into a multilateral effort, as the space programs of both superpowers begin to allow other nations to actively participate. There may also be opportunities for significant joint endeavors by the US and USSR, such as spacelab modules attached to both Soviet and American space platforms. Oberg devotes chapters to describing the questions of utilizing astronauts vs. robots, spaceflight geography, space fleets, human maladies in space (weightlessness, space adaptation syndrome), the Soviet space shuttle programs, the possibility of an American shuttle and Soviet Salyut joint mission, Soviet paranoia and anti-US propaganda, new orbits for spacecraft, exploring the asteroid belt, spaceships of the future (which could reach the Moon in 4 hours and Mars in 55 hours), and the potential of space tethers (long lines connecting two or more space vehicles, thus reducing costs of various operations). [NOTE: Authoritative and non-technical coverage of a melange of space-related topics; far broader than the title suggests.] **(US and Soviet space programs)**

7217

Mars: A Great Planet, But It Needs a Little Work, Eugene F. Mallove, *The Washington Post*, Sunday, 16 Dec 1984, F1.

Manned exploration of Mars will probably be attempted in the next 20 years by Americans, Russians, or both, commencing after or in parallel with a manned lunar base. Once there, the yearning to remake Mars in Earth's image may become irresistible. "Terraforming" planets to be habitable, a word first used by Jack Williamson in two 1940s science fiction novels, has acquired new respectability among planetary scientists and engineers. Mallove explores several suggestions for transforming Mars. [Also see James E. Oberg, **New Earths: Transforming Other Planets for Humanity** (Stackpole, 1981; **FS Annual 1983**, #5449) and James Lovelock and Michael Allaby, **The Greening of Mars** (St. Martin's/Marek, Oct 1984/ 166p/$11.95), a fictional scenario of how Mars was made habitable.] **(terraforming Mars)**

7218

Scientists Chart a Return To Moon for New Exploits, Walter Sullivan, *The New York Times*, Tuesday, 4 Dec 1984, C1.

Twelve years after the last Apollo astronauts walked on the Moon, scientists and space agency officials are calling for a return to the scene of earlier glories. They envision establishing observatories able to penetrate the universe far better than the space telescope to be launched in 1986, and lunar bases to provide materials needed to build space colonies. Some see the lunar base as a national facility; others would have it international or multinational, as on the Antarctic continent, with an international sharing of risks and benefits. As with the Antarctic, there is a move within the UN to treat the Moon as the property of all mankind, to be exploited only under global auspices.

(lunar bases and observatories?)

7219

The Future for Space Technology. Geoffrey K. C. Pardoe (UK). Dover NH: Frances Pinter Publishers, July 1984/206p/$18.75.

A British aerospace expert discusses the future scope for unmanned scientific satellites and probes, applications of space technology for communication and Earth observation, manned space stations and large structures in Earth orbit, space colonization, space transportation systems, benefits of space technology for the developing countries (energy supply, better resource management, communication satellites), military space systems, the organization of space programs, and practical implications for management. Concludes that by the mid-21st century, we will surely see major manned stations in Earth orbit and regular visits to the Moon and the near planets. One speculative development might be major space stations built of lightweight reflectors and aligned by control systems to reflect sunlight into concentrated beams to illuminate cities and larger areas. [NOTE: This volume is the first in The Future for Science and Technology Series, edited by Prof Bernard Taylor of Henley Management College. Other titles in the series include the future for automotive technology, transport technology, robotics and automation, energy technologies, construction technology, and use of the ocean.]   **(space technology)**

7220

Civilian Space Stations and the U.S. Future in Space. U.S. Congress, Office of Technology Assessment. Washington: USGPO, Nov 1984/$7.50 (S/N 052-003-00969-2). Summary copies free from OTA.

After 25 years of experience, the US has the capability to succeed in virtually any civilian space venture it chooses. America is now poised to make a major decision on the future direction of its publically funded civilian space program: whether or not—and how—to proceed with the acquisition of a space station. Such a decision can only be made in the context of agreed upon long-term goals. Although there are important reasons for acquiring advanced space infrastructure elements, the lack of clearly defined goals argues against committing at this time to the specific space station concept proposed by NASA. Some potential broad goals might involve reduction of the unit cost of space activities, direct involvement of the public, increased international cooperation and collaboration, and exploration of the solar system and the universe. Specific objectives to address these larger goals might include a global natural hazard warning service, a lunar settlement, medical studies of potential direct benefit to the public, direct investigation of asteroids, large numbers of the public visiting space each year, and a global direct audio broadcasting service. All could be attained within the next decade or two, and within currently anticipated appropriations.   **(US space program alternatives)**

7221

The Next Step—Space Stations, Roy Gibson (former Director, European Space Agency), *Futures*, 16:6, Dec 1984, 610-626.

A permanently manned orbital station is clearly the next major step in man's investigation and exploitation of space. Gibson describes space station programs in the USSR, US, and Europe. He warns that the sheer size of the space station expenditure may damage other space activities, and that it may be forgotten that the space station is only the infrastructure to be used for other activities.

(space stations)

7222

Technology Forecast of Space Robots to the Year 2000, Kan Chen (U of Michigan) and Nicholas Chang (Shanghai Jiao Tong U), *Technological Forecasting and Social Change*, 26:1, Aug 1984, 47-57.

On the technological capabilities of robotics systems to perform assembly and maintenance functions of the space station program. Concludes that space robots in 1995-2000 are likely to use limited artificial intelligence in a simple form of computer vision, but are not likely to be able to do more than simple spatial reasoning. The core technologies used by space robots of this period are likely to be similar to those for industrial robots in the late 1980s.

(space robots)

7223

Astrobusiness: A Guide to the Commerce and Law of Outer Space. Edward Ridley Finch Jr (Chairman, Aerospace Law Committee, American Bar Association) and Amanda Lee Moore (US Advisory Committee on 1985 ITU Conference). NY: Praeger Publishers, Jan 1985/141p/ $29.95.

On the commercialization of outer space and the growth of space-related opportunities for the private sector in communications, remote sensing, materials processing, transportation, and support services and structures. Chapters discuss the commercial uses of space, space structures and transportation services, risks and liabilities (insurance for satellites and space personnel), financing business in space, US and international space law, and the militarization of space. Concludes that commercial space business is a new sunrise sector of the economy, poised for a new phase of growth. Over 350 companies (listed in an appendix) are exploring the possibility of commercial manufacturing in outer space. The success of these enterprises should promote longer missions in space, and thereby support the market for space platforms and structures. Further into the future, there will be the development of lunar and asteroidal resources, and electric power to be sold as energy to earth. [Also see ***Starship 'Free Enterprise'*** (*Newsweek*,17 Sept 1984, 62-64) which describes such commercial attractions of space as communications satellites, manufacturing in gravity-free environments, and remote sensing.]   **(space commercialization)**

7224

They're Getting Better About Predicting the Weather (Even Though You Don't Believe It), James Gleick (*NYT*), *The New York Times Magazine*, 27 Jan 1985, 30-45.

More scientists and more industries are committing more time and money than ever before to the weather game. Predictions are getting better, as a result of the rapid evolution of global computer forecasts. Improbable as it seems to people betrayed by daily local predictions, the global forecasts have now gained an accuracy at five or six days into the future that matches the two-day forecasts of a decade ago. Improved forecasts would save vast sums of money, enabling gas and electric companies to anticipate consumer demand, construction companies to know when to pour concrete, farmers to time harvests, truckers to plan the fastest and safest routes, etc. The next great improvement will not come from the global models, but from short-range forecasts of 0 to 12 hours for local conditions. But improvements in both local and global forecasting will only widen the gap between what meteorologists know and what they tell the public, unless the new forecasts are matched by new ideas in delivery. Computers in the home are certain to be a key; perhaps people will soon get graphic displays of up-to-the-minute local weather over the telephone line. Despite these improvements, the expectations of a generation ago about modifying weather and predicting it far into the future seem farther away than ever. Rather than creating a society free of the weather, our complex and interdependent societies may have made us more vulnerable.

(weather forecasts improving)

7225

Favourable Outlook for Weather Forecasts, William Burroughs, *New Scientist*, 24 Jan 1985, 31-33.

Steady progress has been achieved over the past three years in 3- to 7-day weather forecasts for Europe. Forecasts are expected to continue improving, although progress will be slow, as a result of still faster computers, better global models of climatic processes, and improved satellite data. Even with these advances, the quality of forecasts will still be bounded by the essential unpredictability of weather.

(weather forecasts improving)

7226

An Inquiry into the State of the Earth, M. Mitchell Waldrop, *Science*, Vol 226, 5 Oct 1984, 33-35.

Humans are beginning to perturb the climate and the biosphere on a planetary scale, but there are still enormous gaps in knowledge of the global system, and governments have been faced with making expensive and controversial decisions on the basis of scientific guesswork. Momentum is thus building for the largest cooperative endeavor in the history of science: a study of the earth and its environs as an integrated whole. The proposed International Geosphere-Biosphere Program (IGBP) would encompass the global climate, the biosphere, and the biogeochemical cycles of all major nutrients. It would take data from satellites in orbit and instruments on the ground, perhaps including pulsations of the sun and the tectonic processes in the core of the earth. It would involve a sharing of effort among scientists from every part of the world, and would have to be sustained for decades. The International Council of Scientific Unions has just endorsed a two-year study to draw up a plan for the IGBP. In the US, the National Academy of Sciences is formulating a detailed plan in conjunction with NASA, NSF, NOAA, and other agencies. By 1986, the IGBP could be ready to move. In addition to the practical need for this information, the IGBP has only recently been made possible by advances in computers and the relative maturity of remote sensing. A final reason for the interest and support for IGBP is the desire of many to revive the international cooperation and communication that resulted from the International Geophysical Year of 1957-1958.

(largest scientific study ever?)

7227

Polar Flip-Flop: A Reversal of the Earth's Magnetic Field Is Long Overdue, Subir K. Banerjee (Prof of Geology, U of Minnesota), *The Sciences* (NY Academy of Sciences), 24:6, Nov-Dec 1984, 24-30.

Dating studies have indicated that the earth's poles have flipped as many as 25 times over the past five million years, averaging once every 200,000 years. The last such flip happened 730,000 years ago, so it seems that we are long overdue for a magnetic reversal. But the poles will probably not reverse themselves for another 2000 years or so, and such a reversal would be the culmination of centuries of change. If such a reversal does happen, it would disrupt magnetic guidance systems of ships and spacecraft, disorient the magnetic field that fish and birds use for guides, and perhaps change world climate.

(polar reversal in 2000 years?)

7228

Terra Non Firma: Understanding and Preparing for Earthquakes.James M. Gere and Haresh C. Shah (both Stanford U). NY: W. H. Freeman, June 1984/203p/ $19.95;$11.95pb.

On a worldwide basis, about one person in 8000 will lose his life in an earthquake, and one in 800 will be injured by an earthquake sometime during their lives. This illustrated non-technical guide devotes chapters to why we have earthquakes, landslides and other earthquake

hazards, tsunamis, measuring earthquakes and their effects, safe engineering design, community and individual planning, earthquake prediction, and preparing for an earthquake. The best way to reduce losses from earthquakes is to prepare for them, which can be done in many ways, such as improving disaster facilities, educating the public, and improving the quality of construction. The single most important step in preparation is to strengthen old buildings so they will not collapse or suffer extensive damage. As Charles Richter has said: "I regret the pervasive emphasis on prediction. It directs attention away from the known risks and the known measures that could be taken to remove them." In other words, earthquakes do not kill people; buildings do.

(preparing for earthquakes)

7229

Little by Little, California Prepares for the Big One, Robert Lindsey, *The New York Times*, Sunday, 2 Sept 1984, E2.

California is starting to take seriously the warnings by scientists that a catastrophic earthquake lurks somewhere in the state's future. Cities have begun making plans to coordinate communications and emergency procedures. Computers are especially vulnerable to a major earthquake, and banks and other concerns are trying to find ways to continue functioning after a big quake. Some newspapers and television stations are developing contingency plans. But despite the recently displayed concern, officials say the preparations are still inadequate. Federal and state governments spend only about $65 million a year on earthquake research and planning, compared with $1.7 billion committed in Japan to a five-year plan to prepare an area half the size of Southern California for an earthquake. [NOTE: US earthquake planners might do better fiscally if they labeled their activities as "national defense."]

(earthquake planning)

7230

Predicting the Next Great Earthquake in California, Robert L. Wesson and Robert E. Wallace (both Office of Earthquakes, US Geological Survey), *Scientific American*, 252:2, Feb 1985, 35-43.

California is the most populous state in the US and a center for many critical technology-oriented industries. About 85% of its population and technical industry is located in a strip of 21 counties along the continental margin that are well within the seismic domain of the San Andreas fault. The likelihood of a major earthquake of magnitude 8 occurring sometime in the next 30 years is estimated to be about 50%. [Also see *Big California Quake Within 50 Years Is Forecast* (*New York Times*, 7 Oct 1984, p34), which quotes Kerry Sieh (California Institute of Technology) as estimating a 50% to 90% probability of a devastating earthquake within 50 years along the southernmost 200 miles of the San Andreas fault, running from near the Mexican border to Los Angeles. Predictions of an upheaval along the entire length of the fault may be unfounded.]

A major US quake might also reappear in the Midwest, where three powerful earthquakes were centered on New Madrid, Missouri, in the winter of 1811-1812. Otto Nuttli (St. Louis U) warns that there is a high potential for a big shock in this area, which could cause the worst natural disaster in US history—"a disaster whose magnitude would only be eclipsed by an all-out nuclear war." (*Newsweek*, 30 April 1984, p62.) A seven-state consortium is now trying to predict and prepare for such a shock.

(big quakes in California or Midwest)

D. Other Frontiers

*7231

Project Outlook: Scientific and Technical Events,
Selwyn Enzer (Project Director), *New Management* (USC),
2:3, Winter 1985, 33-37.

Once a year, the USC Center for Futures Research polls
a large panel of planners and futurists concerned with the
future environment of business. This "Club of 1000" shares
its forecasts of 150 possible social, political, economic, and
technological events. Each panelist selects those few future
events on which he or she has the most information. For
each item selected panelists forecast the probability of its
occurrence over the next 20 years. The following developments are considered possible:

1) Feasible commercial use of nuclear fusion (50% median estimate by 2004; 20% to 65% Inter-Quartile range
of estimates);

2) Super Battery developed with 10 + times the energy/
density ratio of the present lead/acid battery (60% median;
45%-80% I-Q);

3) Hydrogen produced by cost-effective solar energy processes amenable to large-scale production (40% median;
18%-60% I-Q);

4) Salt-tolerant grains that can be irrigated with sea
water and grown in sandy soils (60% median; 25%-75%
I-Q);

5) Drugs developed that can treat most mood and behavior disorders effectively (75% median; 50%-90% I-Q);

6) A medical cure for alcoholism that permanently eliminates addiction (30% median; 10%-60% I-Q);

7) Obesity cure developed enabling safe and permanent
loss of significant weight without discomfort (40% median;
18%-65% I-Q);

8) A cure for most forms of cancer when detected in the
early stages (58% median; 50%-90% I-Q);

9) Most cancer prevented by a vaccine (40% median;
10%-70% I-Q);

10) 100-year average life expectancy of a newborn child
in the industrialized world (30% median; 10%-50% I-Q);

11) Treatment of senility enabling lifetime retention of
at least 90% of mental capacity (63% median; 20%-80%
I-Q);

12) Computers accepting voice inputs become commercially available (90% median; 70%-90% I-Q);

13) Complete artificial intelligence capability developed,
with units speaking several languages (70% median; 35%-
88% I-Q);

14) Limited versions of artificial intelligence used widely
in retail stores and public transport (80% median; 60%-
90% I-Q);

15) Computer use in public schools to a point where stu-
dent/teacher ratios are double that of 1983 (60% median;
30%-80% I-Q);

16) Pocket-size computers with capability of current IBM
PC in widespread use (80% median; 70%-90% I-Q);

17) Wristwatch telephones widely used (70% median;
50%-90% I-Q);

18) Computer language translators developed, capable
of translating simple sentences (80% median; 60%-95%
I-Q);

19) A foolproof personal ID system based on fingerprint
or voiceprint (80% median; 55%-90% I-Q);

20) A desalinization process, cost-effectively producing
large quantities of fresh water from oceans (50% median;
25%-75% I-Q);

21) A large, permanently manned US space station is
launched (90% median; 60%-99% I-Q);

22) Commercial TV via direct satellite transmission
available to any US home (90% median; 60%-99% I-Q);

23) Prefabricated housing sections widely used, so that
on-site construction hours reduced by half (75% median;
55%-90% I-Q);

24) Solar and cogenerated electricity produce at least
10% of US residential electricity (50% median; 20%-73%
I-Q). **(sci/tech developments by 2004)**

7232

**The Robotics Revolution: The Complete Guide for
Managers and Engineers**. Peter B. Scott (Center for
Robotics and Automated Systems, U of London). Oxford
UK and NY: Basil Blackwell, Dec 1984/345p/$24.95.

Chapters on the evolution of robotics, robot mechanics,
control systems, external-state sensors, workplace man-
ipulation, wrist-mounted devices, optimal robotic assembly, mobile devices (land, sea, space), robotics and jobs,
managing with robots, safety and reliability, and economic
justification for robots. A concluding chapter briefly surveys a variety of research areas and applications: arm
designs, artificial intelligence, robotic assembly, automated guided vehicles, automated factories, farm work
(robotized milking, driverless tractors), flexible manufacturing systems, helping the disabled (robots to assist in
eating, turning pages), work in chemistry laboratories,
submersible robots operating independently of the surface
ship, deboning meat in packinghouses, nursing care, micro-
surgery, military applications, mining, work in breeder
reactors, security patrolling, sheep shearing, and ware-
housing. The final chapter speculates on developments in
three time periods. **1984-1990**: many conventional designs
will be upgraded, and robot tasks will become more complex; by 1990, third-generation "intelligent" robots will
start to appear. **1990-2000**: robots employed for handling
flexible materials such as textiles and rubber; occasional
use in some surgical operations; robotic automated guided
vehicles experimentally introduced. **2000-2050**: a wide
spectrum of robot types, and large numbers of truly integrated robotic systems (factories largely); a few of these
robots will be able to mimic humans to some extent if so
designed, but the vast majority are unlikely to be humanoid
in shape. [Also see ***Robots and the Economy***, by James
S. Albus (*The Futurist*, 18:6, Dec 1984, 38-44), for an upbeat
view of how robots could make us all rich.]

(robotics guide)

7233

The Future for Automotive Technology. Ulrich Seif-
fert and Peter Walzer (both Research Division, Volks-
wagenwerk, Wolfsburg FRG). The Future for Science and
Technology Series. London and Dover NH: Frances Pinter
Publishers, June 1984/197p/$22.50.

The passenger car of the future will have to meet demands for lower energy consumption, lower exhaust emissions and noise levels, better safety, and improved performance and reliability without increased expense. By 2000,
our cars will give twice as many miles per gallon (about
70 to 80 mpg) as today, and steel content will be reduced
to 50% compared with 70% today. The engine may be a
gas turbine or a gas/electric hybrid. It will probably have
a continuously variable transmission, and it may have a
start-stop system that switches off the engine when power
is not required. The car's shape will be similar to those of
today, but more aerodynamic. Chapters are devoted to describing the influence of legislation on auto development,
the development of the car body and the suspension, engines and transmissions, the trend toward more electronic
components, alternative materials for the car body and the
engine, integrated research vehicles (including VW's "Auto

2000"), liquified gas and alcohol as fuels, alternative types of engines, traffic and transportation systems, and energy, environment, economics, and politics as influential factors. [Also see *The High Tech Car Hits the Road*, by Peter Petre, *Fortune*, 29 April 1985.] (**future auto technology**)

7234
Superchip Heralds A Revolution, William J. Broad, *The New York Times*, Tuesday, 3 July 1984, C1.

Scientists at dozens of laboratories in Europe, Japan, and the U.S. are racing toward another revolution in the speed, size, cost, and reliability of computers. They are on the verge of shrinking the present generation of room-sized supercomputers down to the size of a baseball through a new technology—wafer-scale integration—that will allow the complex circuitry of hundreds of silicon chips to be etched on a single, thin wafer. While many of today's chips carry thousands of transisters, a single wafer could hold millions. It is believed that the wafer and its supporting hardware will result in computers hundreds of times faster and more powerful than anything now in existence. Small desk-top computers based on a wafer will easily outperform large mainframes that now occupy whole rooms. The more powerful computers will lead to improvements in weather forecasting, aircraft design, building weapons, breaking codes, and developing new sources of energy.

(**wafer-scale integration: a computer revolution**)

7235
Macro Wonders from the Latest Micros, Peter Petre, *Fortune*, 10 Dec 1984, 115-128.

The microprocessor—a silicon chip that acts as the brain of a computer—has created many revolutions in the past 15 years. Now a new generation of 32-bit microprocessors is emerging that will give low-cost desktop work stations and personal computers the capacity to tackle big jobs formerly reserved for expensive minicomputers and mainframes. The term "32-bit chip" comes from its ability to process the binary code computers understand in great gulps of 32 ones and zeros at a time—a natural unit for data that is enough to handle most chores. The earliest microprocessors could nibble only 4 bits of information at a time; today's chips handle 16 bits. The new 32-bit microprocessors are likely to appear in personal computers within three years. The 32-bit chip will likely be the basic building block of the computer industry at the turn of the 21st century. A 64-bit chip will surely come, but computer engineers can barely imagine tasks for which it will be necessary, so great is the power of the 32-bit chip.

(**new 32-bit computer capability**)

7236
Japan Falters On Next Step In Computers, Andrew Pollack, *The New York Times*, Monday, 13 August 1984, p1.

The Japanese goal to become the world leader in creating computers that think like human beings, announced in 1981 as the Fifth Generation Project, is running into stumbling blocks. The first four generations of computers were marked by improvements in components—from vacuum tubes in the first generation to very-large-scale integrated circuits in the fourth. The Fifth Generation computer, perhaps more aptly called the second generation computer, is intended to handle symbols, not numbers, and will do many things at once, much like the human brain. But the project's original goals were imprecise and overly ambitious, and budget and staffing problems now pose a threat. The project has drastically cut back on some highly publicized goals, such as the development of technology to allow computers to "see," to understand human speech,

and to translate from one language to another. But the core program has been preserved: to develop technology enabling computers to "think."

(**goals reduced for Fifth Generation computer**)

7237
The Race for Computer Supremacy: Who's Ahead? Philip M. Boffey, *The New York Times*, Tuesday, 23 Oct 1984, C1.

An international race for computer supremacy is underway, touched off by Japanese announcements in 1980 and 1981 of major new national programs to develop a supercomputer and a radically new "fifth generation" or artificial intelligence computer. Interviews with some 20 technical experts and computer analysts in government, industry, and universities, as well as a series of Federal evaluations completed over the past year, suggest that the US is facing a serious challenge where no challenge existed before. Virtually all experts acknowledge that faster and smarter computers hold great potential to affect a wide range of civilian and military activities. But the US is still judged the world leader in computers, artificial intelligence, and related scientific fields, while Japanese efforts look less fearsome than originally thought. The Western Europeans and Russians are believed to be lagging behind. And virtually all of the announced programs around the world are having startup problems.

The full dimensions of the international race are still only partly discernible. The official national programs are roughly comparable in size. For example, the Japanese "fifth generation" budget is $430 million in the first five years, roughly comparable to the Defense Department's "strategic computing" budget of $600 million over five years. (This program seeks to develop a driverless vehicle that uses visual sensors to avoid barriers, a computerized "pilot's assistant" that responds to spoken language and helps make split-second decisions in dogfights, and a battle management system for naval commanders.) These public programs are moderate, however, compared to the $3 billion or more that IBM spends on R&D in a single year. A panel of experts assembled by the National Academy of Sciences recently concluded that the US is well-positioned to retain its computing lead. The panel found that Japan's much publicized "fifth generation" effort (potentially far more important than the supercomputer effort) lacked a persuasive technical explanation of how the ambitious goals can be reached.   (**US maintains computer lead**)

7238
Can U.S. Hold Its Lead Over Soviets In Science Race? *U.S. News & World Report*, 1 Oct 1984, 51-54.

On every count, both American and Soviet experts agree that the US is ahead of the Soviet Union in scientific and technical achievement. American science produces more Nobel prizes (only five have gone to the USSR), more innovative genius, and more commercial successes in fields from microchips to microbiology than the USSR and Western Europe combined. Yet the Soviet Union invests more to develop scientific brainpower than any other nation: it supports some 1500 science centers (including vast complexes in "academic cities") and employs 1.5 million scientists—one-fourth of the global total. The reasons for poor Soviet performance are various bureaucratic obstacles (e.g., frequent shortages of paper to publish scientific journals), outdated approaches to science, and systematic persecution of Jewish and dissident scientists. For the foreseeable future, it is clear that the Soviets will remain close to the US in their theoretical grasp of many technologies, but far behind in application. [Also see Malik, #7122.]

(**US leads Soviet science**)

7239

Science and Politicians Both See Opportunity in Big Atom-Smasher, Arlen J. Large and Hal Lancaster, *The Wall Street Journal*, Wed, 10 Oct 1984, p1.

The Superconducting Super Collider, an atom smasher now at the planning stage, may cost $4 billion or more and would be the world's most expensive scientific instrument. The proposed machine would take the form of a circular tunnel perhaps 70 miles long and lined by powerful magnets that would accelerate two beams of atomic particles on a collision course. The machine would open a frontier in the study of fundamental matter. It should also open new frontiers in pork barrel politics, as physicists build a constituency by ensuring that enough pieces of the machine are manufactured in enough congressional districts around the country. Illinois and Texas are already scrambling to be chosen as the site of the Super Collider. If the project proceeds, construction will start around 1989, and the machine will be ready in 1994.

(largest scientific instrument ever?)

7240

At Home with High Technology (Special Issue). *IEEE Spectrum*, 22:5, May 1985, 34-112.

Articles grouped in three parts: 1) Basic House Systems: heating and cooling, electronic watchdogs, communications, lighting, robots in the home; 2) Case Studies: three high-tech homes in Dallas, suburban Boston (sponsored by Boston Edison as an energy-conservation experiment), and the foothills of the Sierra Nevada in California; 3) A Room-by-Room Tour: living room/entertainment center, audio in the living room, kitchen, study, bedroom, electronic babysitters in the nursery, an electronic bathtub for $11,500, hobby room, and laundry and sewing. Concludes with a brief scenario of what can happen if the systems do not perform as they should. **(high-tech homes)**

7241

What's Become of Alternative Technology? Godfrey Boyle (The Open U), *Resurgence*, No 108, Jan-Feb 1985, 34-36.

A brief survey of conventional or "right-wing" alternative technology (photovoltaics and wind power), and the more radical stream of AT that stresses the need for an accompanying change in the social and political context (community-based technologies). Concludes that the "alternative technology" phrase has acquired such a variety of meanings as to become almost meaningless. "Ecotechnics" is proposed as a preferable term to represent those tools and techniques, items of hardware and software, equipment and related knowledge, which can help create a more ecological society. **("ecotechnics")**

7242

Appropriate Technology: Choice and Development. Edited by Mathew J. Betz *et al.* (Arizona State U). Durham NC: Duke U Press, Aug 1984/c330p/$32.50.

An analysis with case studies of high, intermediate, and labor-intensive technology appropriate for developing countries. Chapters cover intermediate technology and development, political problems of technology transfer to Third World countries, the political economy of appropriate technology, nuclear power in the Philippines, China's experience with technology transfer, and direct satellite broadcasting. **(appropriate technology in LDCs)**

7243

Printing Technology, 1995: Evolution not Revolution, Nelson Eldred (Manager of Techno-Economic Forecasting, Graphic Arts Technical Foundation), *Printing Impressions* (North American Publishing Co, Philadelphia), June 1984, 21-23.

A technical survey for managers in the printing industry, viewing continuing growth of printing and lithography over the next decade, with lithography increasing its market share of commercial and publication printing, along with a rapidly increasing growth of color printing. However, no simple solution is seen for bindery problems before 1995. And despite forecasts of new printing processes, it seems quite likely that web offset will still be the major printing process in 1995. **(printing technology in 1995)**

7244

Powerful Ceramics Ready for Major Technology Role, William J. Broad, *The New York Times*, Tuesday, 13 Nov 1984, C1.

Over the past decade, chemists have learned how to blend, beat, and bake different kinds of ceramic compounds into materials that are stronger than steel, hard as diamonds, tough enough to take the heat of a blast furnace, able to resist wear and rust, and characterized by unusual electrical properties. Their manufacture involves extremely pure and ultra-fine particles of alumina, titania, sand, feldspar and other minerals and chemicals that are carefully mixed and then fired and treated under closely regulated conditions. High-tech ceramics have already started to show up in such products as batteries, bearings, fuel cells, solar cells, electronic chips, cutting tools, stoves, artificial bones, and dental implants. A future possibility is creating tiny computers of ceramic material that would run on light instead of electricity. Another future device under study is a ceramic automobile engine that would be smaller, lighter, cheaper, and able to run hotter than engines made of metal, thus boosting fuel efficiency by as much as 30%. An economist with the National Bureau of Standards estimates that the revolution in high-tech ceramics is only just beginning, and that sales of advanced ceramics from the US alone might grow more than five-fold to $10 billion by 2000. **(new ceramics)**

7245

Breakthrough in Problem Solving, James Gleick, *The New York Times*, Monday, 19 Nov 1984, A1.

Narendra Karmarkar (AT&T Bell Laboratories), a 28-year old mathematician, has made a startling theoretical breakthrough in solving systems of equations, often with thousands of variables, that are too vast and complex for the most powerful computers. These problems arise in a variety of commercial and government applications, such as allocating time on a communications satellite, routing millions of telephone calls over long distances, efficient allocation of time among competing users, and devising investment portfolios with the best mix of stocks and bonds. The Karmarkar algorithm, replacing the simplex method-devised in 1947, may speed the routine handling of such problems, and make it possible to tackle problems that are now far out of reach. American Airlines, for example, is investigating applications of the new technique to speed their handling of scheduling flight crews and planning fuel loads. In 1979, a group of Soviet mathematicians also devised a new algorithm, the ellipsoid method. This theoretical advance stimulated a burst of activity on the problem that led to Karmarkar's breakthrough.

(new problem solving technique)

7246
Award Papers From Honeywell Futures Contest
(Special Issue). *Futurics* (Minnesota Futurists), 8:3, 1984,
1-26.

Award-winning essays by ten college students in the
Honeywell Futurist Awards Competition, held in late 1983.
The ten were among 750 students from 282 colleges and
universities who submitted essays on technology advances
and their societal impacts by 2008. Topics address biomedical technology, computers, aerospace, energy, marine systems, and electronic communications. [NOTE: Young
people should be encouraged to think about the future in
many ways, and Honeywell deserves recognition for spon-
soring this limited contest for college students. Ideally,
such a contest should be expanded not only to more college
undergraduates, but also to graduate students and high
school students. Unfortunately, these essays are confined
to the future of non-weapons technology, tend to employ
conventional upbeat cliches, and were rewarded with a
summer internship at Honeywell. A more neutral, public-
interest oriented source of funding and basis of award
would be most welcome in this sadly neglected area.]
(college student essays on technology)

XVI. METHODS TO SHAPE THE FUTURE

A. New Thinking

7247
Models of Reality: Shaping Thought and Action.
Edited by Jacques Richardson (UNESCO). Mt. Airy MD:
Lomond Publications (PO Box 88), July 1984/328p/$22.95.

Essays that seek to provide a definitive understanding
of the nature of models (verbal, graphic, mathematical,
physical) as representations of reality and as tools for description, analysis, interpretation, forecasting, planning,
and policy-making. Contributions include **Jacques
Richardson** on a primer of model systems, **James Grier
Miller** and **Jessie L. Miller** (Center for the Study of
Democratic Institutions) on the earth as a system (a general theory of systems within the context of our planet,
and the relationship of this theory to policy-making),
J.N.R. Jeffers (Institute of Terrestrial Ecology, UK) on
the development of models in urban and regional planning,
John M. Richardson, Jr (American U) on an agenda for
global modeling in the 1980s, **Kenneth L. Kraemer** (U
of California-Irvine) on the politics of model implementation (a case study of a computerized fiscal-impact model
for urban planning), **Dennis Meadows** (Dartmouth College) on the validity and usefulness of large economic models, **Jay W. Forrester** (MIT) on his Systems Dynamics
National Model and its usefulness for learning about
economic dynamics, **Veronica Stolte-Heiskanen** (U of
Tampere, Finland) on the use of models for directing scientific and technical research toward solutions of social and
environmental problems, **Rahat Nabi Khan** (India) on
uses and limitations of models in policy planning and
evaluation, **James Clayson** (The American College, Paris)
on micro-operational research as the design of simple models (not necessarily mathematical) for use by managers,
and **Ilya Prigogine** and **Isabelle Stengers** (U of Brussels) on the transition to new models of interrogation rather
than certainties in physics, and the impacts of these models. **(models for policy-making)**

7248
**Modeling As Negotiating: The Political Dynamics of
Computer Models in the Policy Process**. William H.
Dutton (USC) and Kenneth L. Kraemer (U of California-
Irvine). Norwood NJ: Ablex Publishing Corp, May 1985/
261p/$39.50.

Models can be influential in the policy process by struc-
turing problems, informing and involving participants, setting agendas, and legitimating decisions and nondecisions.
Modeling tends to facilitate conflict resolution and consensus building in policy making—a conclusion that differs
from previous research. But in the process of helping to
resolve conflict and build consensus, models almost inevitably bias the outcomes of policy-making. Models are not
apolitical: their structure, their forecasts, and their policy
implications all tend to support and legitimate the interests of those who are most influential in the modeling
process. Such a potentially powerful technology is seldom
left in the hands of the modelers—the technical experts.
To the contrary, model implementation is a labyrinthine

process that must be sensitively negotiated by the modelers
who anticipate the reactions of multiple participants with
sometimes shifting and conflicting agendas. In this way,
policy modeling tends to become a process of negotiation
and bargaining. [NOTE: The focus of this book is on the
utilization of computer-based fiscal impact models in US
cities, but the insights should have broader applications.]
(politics of modeling)

7249
Systems Analysis in Public Policy: A Critique. Revised Edition. Ida R. Hoos (Space Sciences Laboratory, U
of California-Berkeley). Berkeley CA: U of California
Press, Dec 1983/327p/$35.00;$7.95pb.

Reprint of the 1972 edition, which reviews the ways in
which systems analysis and the family of techniques to
which it is related has created a management syndrome:
the notion that all human affairs could be managed, and
that using the tools of management science would solve
society's problems "rationally." Chapters cover the systems
approach in theoretical perspective, the systems approach
in practical perspective, systems analysis as technological
transfer, the techniques at work (in waste management,
supersonic transport, education, and health), management
information systems, futurology and the future of systems
analysis [at that time, the mystique of futurism was seen
as purporting "to study the future scientifically, explore
alternative futures rationally, and thus design the best of
all possible futures"], and the imprint and implications of
systems methodology.

In the new introduction, Hoos argues that her criticisms
are valid and have been substantiated by time. Welcomed
because of the semblance of methodical rigor, the techniques brought an aura of respectability in an era of computerized models. Paradoxically, the techniques that have
been bought and sold as "scientific" continue to blatantly
ignore the rudimentary precepts of scientific procedure.
Independent verification and validation are virtually
nonexistent, while huge expenditure continues to flow into
systems studies, risk analyses, and technology assessments. Yet there is very little difference between systems
studies performed a decade ago and those performed
today—nor does there seem to be any appreciable improvement in the quality of management decisions. The crown-
ing irony is that, while the military was the original model,
the Department of Defense continues as a prime example
of managerial ineptness. It is not the misuse of the
techniques that is culpable—the standard excuse—but
their use that leads to grave blunders. Indeed, the technico-
economic management model may be the root cause of
America's fiscal malaise, rather than its remedy. But there
are huge vested interests that prevent the wholesale rejection of these techniques. Systems analysis has assured
longevity because its principles, for all their fancy electronic trappings, are simple, easy to apply, and consistent
with the quick fix, plug-in modularity of a technical era.
By now, experience should have taught us that we have
turned to the wrong experts, who define problems to fit
their narrow aptitude and desired solutions.

(systems analysis re-critiqued)

7250
**Filters Against Folly: How to Survive Despite
Economists, Ecologists, and the Merely Eloquent**.
Garrett Hardin (Prof Emeritus of Human Ecology, U of
California-Santa Barbara). NY: Viking, July 1985/240p/
$15.95.

Author of **Exploring New Ethics for Survival** (Viking, 1972), which expands on his classic *The Tragedy of
the Commons* essay (*Science*, 13 Dec 1968), argues that

we need specialists in our complex world, but we must filter the data and arguments that come into us so that we can protect ourselves against the assumptions and biases (conscious and unconscious) of our experts. Three intellectual filters are described that will enable anyone to assess the rhetoric of experts: 1) the "literate filter" calls for an understanding of the precise meaning of words, standing for skill in written or spoken language; 2) the "numerate filter" asks how much and how many, emphasizing ratios and proportions which are often more important than actual numbers alone; 3) the "ecolate filter" refers to the needs to evaluate the consequences of an action over time ("ecolacy" is a term coined by Hardin). No one filter by itself is adequate for understanding the world and predicting the consequences of our actions. By focusing on these three intellectual filters, rather than C.P. Snow's "two cultures" (science and literature), we have a better chance of keeping our attention directed toward substantive issues. After discussing the strengths and weaknesses of each of these filters, Hardin goes on to introduce the notion of the CC-PP Game, or the hidden rules of the free enterprise system that seeks to Commonize Costs and Privatize Profits. Pure research offers a new distribution system of Privatized Costs and Commonized Profits, with the commonized information extending over the whole world. Concludes that to be a conservative is to want to conserve, save, or maintain something. Continuity is at the heart of conservatism, and ecology serves that heart, for an ecoconservative is profoundly concerned for the survival of the real wealth of the biological world. [NOTE: As always, a feisty jumble of original ideas, including an attack on the unattainable ideal of zero pollution and how the noble "One World" ideal can easily lead to disaster.]

(literacy, numeracy, and "ecolacy")

7251

Big Structures, Large Processes, Huge Comparisons. Charles Tilly (Center for Studies of Social Change, New School for Social Research). NY: Russell Sage Foundation (dist. by Basic Books), Dec 1984/176p/$14.50.

How can we improve our understanding of the large-scale structures and processes that transformed the world of the 19th century and are transforming our world today? Tilly explores how comparisons of times, places, populations, structures, and processes can aid this understanding. He contends that 20th century social theories have been encumbered by a 19th century heritage of eight "pernicious postulates," such as the belief in societies as distinct entities, social change as a coherent phenomenon, stage theories, and differentiation (the drive toward ever-greater complexity) as the master principle of social change. As an alternative to timeless and placeless models of social change, Tilly advocates historically grounded analysis and systematic comparison. [NOTE: Heavy analysis for would-be rigorous megathinkers.]

(understanding large-scale social change)

7252

Strategies for Cultural Change. Edited by Robert Gilman (Sequim WA) and Robert Theobald (Wickenberg AZ). *In Context: A Quarterly of Humane Sustainable Culture*, No 9, Spring 1985/64p/$4.50.

Articles on the process of cultural change, "The Hundredth Monkey" story, leadership and group process for cultural midwives, the stages in group development, the many forms of leadership and participation, facilitating meetings, conflict resolution, practical steps for enabling fundamental positive change (by Robert Theobald), videotapes as a transforming tool, developing community leadership, building non-governmental person-to-person links with the people of the USSR, how to be an effective "David" in the world of "Goliaths," transforming the health care system. [NOTE: Thinking big and acting small...very small.]

(leadership, cultural change)

*7253

Mobilizing the Ultimate Resource: A Discussion of Critical Problems (Special Issue). Edited by Harold A. Linstone (Futures Research Institute, Portland State U; Editor, *TF&SC*). *Technological Forecasting and Social Change*, 26:2, Sept 1984, 107-226.

Papers responding to a "Manifesto to Mankind" from C. West Churchman (U of California-Berkeley), who asks how we can better apply the resource of the human intellect to the crisis of the human species. **Edward Wenk Jr** (U of Washington) proposes greater citizen involvement in the steering of technology as the contemporary form of patriotism. **Yehezkel Dror** (Hebrew U of Jerusalem) argues that more must be done to upgrade capacities of human thinking to handle grand issues. **Arnold J. Meltsner** (U of California-Berkeley) warns that we lack built-in devices to counter the biases of the tunnel-visioned expert. **Donald N. Michael** (San Francisco CA) highlights "reason's shadow," or the psychodynamics of obstruction: alternative rationalities such as political expedience, nonrational norms and commitments, and unconscious psychodynamic processes. **Joseph P. Martino** (U of Dayton) scorns engineered fascism and cybernetic socialism, concluding that we must abandon any idea of centralized management of the ultimate resource. **Clive Simmonds** (Ottawa) asserts that the critical step is to make fuller use of the human brain. **Ian I.Mitroff** (USC) charges that the modern university is designed for an outmoded conception of the world. **Frederick A. Rossini** (Georgia Institute of Technology) also agrees that the university is intellectually obsolescent, and proposes EARTHNET—a network, rather than a place—as the university of the future. **Robert U Ayres** (Carnegie-Mellon U) focuses on three methodological problems of a fundamental nature that continue to afflict decision-making at all levels: the failure to allow for adequate uncertainty, the myopic failure to recognize low-probability events and changing rules of the game, and the failure to allow sufficiently for market externalities in calculating costs and benefits of programs. **Olaf Helmer** (Carmel CA) stresses the need to reorder our national priorities, and to construct a framework for making public decisions in compliance with them. **Ida R. Hoos** (U of California-Berkeley) deplores our trained incapacity: the iatrogenic decision-making methodology promulgated by management science. **Harold A. Linstone** concludes that analysts must stop playing games and rediscover the real world, recognize that ill-structured problems require multiple perspectives, deal explicitly with the discounting dilemma (declining interest in a problem or opportunity as its horizon in the future lengthens), gain deeper insight on social system behavior, prepare for the next cluster of technological innovations, and provide better access to information for the Third World.

(mobilizing human resources)

7254

Putting Knowledge to Use: Facilitating the Diffusion of Knowledge and the Implementation of Planned Change. Edward M. Glaser, Harold H. Abelson, and Kathalee N. Garrison (Human Interaction Research Institute). San Francisco CA: Jossey-Bass, Dec 1983/636p/ $29.95.

Many promising new ideas and programs are never implemented, and programs and practices that have been successful in one organization often fail to reach others that could benefit. The authors bring together research on the application of knowledge for planned change from such fields as psychology, organizational behavior, sociology, economics, education, and evaluation research. Chapters cover factors influencing knowledge utilization and change (personal and social influences, organizational factors), stages in problem solving and planned change, and linking knowledge with potential users (roles of change agents, means of communication, relating R&D to practice, international transfer of technical knowledge, models and systems for facilitating planned change). Concludes with an unannotated and uncategorized bibliography of about 2200 items. **(applying knowledge for planned change)**

7255

Basic Dilemmas in the Social Sciences. Hubert M. Blalock, Jr (Prof of Sociology, U of Washington). Beverly Hills CA: Sage Publications, Feb 1984/184p/$17.95.

The past president of the American Sociological Association attempts to assess what is wrong with the social sciences and steps to improve the situation. Some of the "real-world" complications are that: 1) virtually all social processes are far more complex than we often realize, and our explanatory laws must therefore be multivariate and probabilistic; 2) measurement problems in the social sciences are formidable; 3) rates of change in social phenomena are sometimes far too rapid to be studied with present resources; 4) the reality we must deal with is often fuzzy and imprecise; 5) there is no obvious way to divide up the labor among the separate social science disciplines or within any one of them: multiple explanatory variables spill across the domains of each of the social sciences; 6) most social research is very expensive and time consuming. Blalock cautions professional associations against wishy-washy endorsement of virtually every new activity, subgroup, or subfield that receives the support of a dozen or so members. At minimum, it is necessary to develop a set of priorities and reasonably general guidelines for achieving them, finding ways to reward scholars for valuable behaviors. Far greater attention needs to be given to problems of measurement and conceptualization, focusing on a core set of questions and a reasonably small number of important variables. A set of scholarly norms is needed to improve communication across the several social sciences—norms that stress the importance of intellectual honesty, completeness, and open-mindedness.

(problems of the social sciences)

7256

Socio-Economic Accounting. Ahmed Belkaoui. Westport CT: Greenwood Press, 1984/324p/$39.95.

Examines the various social science paradigms and avenues that define the emerging field of socio-economic accounting: the measurement of the total performance of economic and governmental units, and their contributions to the quality of life. These perspectives include the new sociological environmental paradigm, the ecosystem perspective, ethical paradigms, and the commitment to social welfare. **(socio-economic accounting)**

7257

Projection, Forecast, and Plan: On the Future of Population Forecasting, Andrew M. Isserman (U of Iowa), *Journal of the American Planning Association*, 50:2, Spring 1984, 208-221.

Projections are conditional statements about the future resulting from calculations of numerical consequences of underlying assumptions. A forecast is a statement of the most likely future. Planners tend to use the terms interchangeably, and to use projections when they should be using forecasts. The misuse and uncritical reliance on projections of current trends should end, with more attention devoted to the systematic analysis of factors not considered by today's formal models. Reasons for the widespread use of projections are discussed: demographers do not like to forecast, many smaller agencies do not have the capability of making projections or forecasts (and are thus grateful to obtain any future numbers from a respected source), analysts do not know how to forecast, preparation of projections is safer, projections appear professional and scientific, projections appear apolitical and not self-serving, and projections can be prepared mechanically and quickly.

(misuse of projections)

7258

Human Resource Forecasting: A Survey of Practice and Potential, Michael J. Feuer (Drexel U) *et al.*, *Human Resources Planning*, 7:2, June 1984, 85-93.

Reviews the literature of forecasting for human resource planning and reports on a survey of about 100 corporations. Of this group, about 60% indicated that they were doing human resource forecasting, although most do not use complicated techniques. The literature indicates that the state of the art is pushing toward integrated systems of supply and demand models that have the ability to simulate various economic scenarios. The outputs of such systems are then linked to business planning systems. Concludes that, ten years from now, most companies will have forecasting systems in place and be able to perform alternative scenario analysis of work flows and skill mixes. [Other articles in this issue of *Human Resources Planning* deal with the same topic.] **(human resource forecasting)**

7259

Social Impact Assessment and Monitoring: A Cross-Disciplinary Guide to the Literature. Michael J. Carley (Policy Studies Institute, London) and Eduardo Bustelo (UNICEF, Brazil). Boulder CO: Westview, Oct 1984/c250p/ $32.50.

A critical review of more than 600 recent publications in social impact assessment (SIA) and related fields, based on the view that SIA is more than an analytical technique, but a logical and timely response to the ever-growing need for more and better information for decision-making in an increasingly complex world. Topics covered include social forecasting, SIA methodologies, socio-cultural effects, SIA in developing countries, public participation, community vs. expert preferences, energy developments, risk, environmental impact assessment, monitoring, cost-benefit analysis, and decision analysis.

(social impact assessment guide)

7260

Improving Impact Assessment: Increasing the Relevance and Utilization of Scientific and Technical Information. Edited by Stuart L. Hart (U of Michigan) *et al.* Boulder CO: Westview, Sept 1984/c410p/$30.00.

On ways in which the development and evaluation of scientific and technical information for environmental impact statements can be improved. Authors consider such topics as the role of human values and attitudes in environmental assessment, assessing human concerns, improving predictive performance of biological impact assessment, closing the gap between analysis and the decisionmaker, and assessment methods and costs.

(environmental impact statements)

7261

Socioeconomic Impact Management: Design and Implementation. John M. Halstead (North Dakota State U) *et al.* Boulder CO: Westview, Sept 1984/c250p/$32.50.

On impact management for such large-scale resource and industrial development projects as power plants, mines, and nuclear waste disposal facilities. An overall framework for designing an impact management program is presented, enabling a choice among alternatives in designing a management system, and recommendations are made for implementing management measures.

(impact analysis of large projects)

7262

Social Impact Analysis and Development Planning in the Third World. Edited by William Derman (Michigan State U) and Scott Whiteford (School of American Research, New Mexico). Boulder CO: Westview, Nov 1984/c250p/$26.00.

National governments and international agencies have committed vast sums of money to development projects over the past three decades. Many projects, however, have not only failed to help the people they were intended to help, but have created more social and economic problems than they resolved. The failure of many of the projects can be traced to an inadequate understanding of the socio-cultural reality of the people they most directly affect, and to a lack of participation of these people in project planning, implementation, and evaluation. Drawing on case material from socialist and capitalist countries, primarily in Africa and Latin America, the authors of these original essays show how socio-cultural factors should be incorporated into planning processes.   **(impact analysis in Third World)**

7263

Looking Ahead with Confidence (Special Report), Joseph P. Martino (U of Dayton), *IEEE Spectrum*, 22:3, March 1985, 76-81.

Technological forecasting, despite occasional embarassing failures, is a needed and heavily used technique. The proper use of forecasting methods will lead to reasonably accurate R&D planning—even if some initial errors are made. To plan an R&D product, two questions must be answered: what types of technology are needed, and when will the technology be developed? Two complementary types of forecasting are required to answer these questions: normative forecasting and exploratory forecasting. Normative forecasting develops the road map for the projects, determining what the objectives are and the ways to meet them. Techniques commonly used in normative forecasting are relevance trees, morphological models, and scissors-flow diagrams. Once objectives are expressed, the R&D manager can use exploratory forecasting to estimate dates for reaching project milestones. The three most common methods of exploratory forecasting are trends, growth curves, and the Delphi technique. Each technique is briefly described. [NOTE: A good introduction to tech forecasting by a leading expert and author of **Technological Forecasting for Decision Making** (FS Annual 1983 #5498).]

(tech forecasting introduction)

7264

The IDEAL Problem Solver: A Guide for Improving Thinking, Learning, and Creativity. John D. Bransford (Vanderbilt U) and Barry S. Stein (Tennessee Tech U). NY: W.H. Freeman, Oct 1984/150p/$15.95;$6.95pb.

The IDEAL approach to problem-solving is simple but powerful, based on five components: Identifying potential problems, Defining the problem, Exploring possible strategies, Acting on the strategies, and Looking back and evaluating the effects of one's activities. After explaining the IDEAL model, the authors devote chapters to improving memory skills, learning with understanding, intelligent criticism (focusing on factual accuracy, demonstrating that one's reasoning is not logical, questioning basic assumptions), approaching problems in more creative ways, and effective communication. [NOTE: Although aimed at college students, going back to some of these basics might benefit a good number of adults.]

(basics of problem-solving)

B. Public Planning

7265

Thinking Strategically: A Primer for Public Leaders. Susan Walter (Manager for State Government Issues, General Electric Co) and Pat Choate (Senior Policy Analyst, TRW Inc). Washington DC: Council of State Planning Agencies, 1984/101p/$9.95pb.

The authors of the seminal work on the crumbling US infrastructure, **America in Ruins** (CSPA, 1981; **FS Annual 1981-82,** #3705), describe the principles that leading public and private organizations employ to create a strategic vision, examine specific techniques they are using, and explain how these techniques can be replicated. Systematic foresight, coupled with the creation of clear, long-term goals and strategic plans, motivates and guides these organizations, enabling them to minimize uncertainties, maximize opportunities, and provide greater organizational stability in these unsettled times. The consequences of limited vision are disordered management, pork-barrel politics dominating public spending, favoring short-term payoffs over long-term goals, and imposing limits on joint public-private action. The five interrelated components of strategic management are: 1) **foresight**: systematic efforts to identify and analyze long-term trends and issues likely to affect the institution's future environment; 2) **goal setting**: explicit definition of the institution's basic aims; 3) **strategic planning**: identifying policies and resources to be used in attaining goals; 4) **operational management**: translating goals and strategies into ongoing operations; 5) **evaluation**: a systematic review, resulting in recommendations for needed adjustments.   **(strategic management primer)**

7266

Required Breakthroughs in Think Tanks, Yehezkel Dror (Hebrew U of Jerusalem), *Policy Sciences,* 16:3, Feb 1984, 199-225.

An analysis of Think Tanks—enclaves of putative excellence in which multidisciplinary scholars and professionals work full-time on main policy problems—based on Dror's two years of work at a major US Think Tank, one year involvement in establishing a Think Tank, visits and interviewing at about 50 research institutes in the US and elsewhere, and interviews with 35 offices of heads of governments in most OECD countries and a number of Third World countries. The most striking finding of all is the relative scarcity of Think Tanks on a global scale, with the exception of the US. The vast majority of countries have no Think Tanks, and most existing ones outside the US have a very limited scope of activity. Futures studies units in some countries fulfill some Think Tank functions, but such units are usually closed down or made harmless. Other organizations operating at least in part as Think Tanks include special planning units, political party research organizations, units located at universities (which have generally failed), and public commissions of inquiry. Reasons for the difficulties of Think Tanks include: 1) pressures to cut budget items with little political cost (Think Tanks have small constituencies); 2) growing public doubts about the contributions of science and scientific methodology; 3) the political-ideological nature of many policy problems, which reduces the importance of the quasi-rationalistic contributions of Think Tanks; 4) an image of negative correlation between the great number of US Think Tanks and the lack of public policy wisdom in the US; 5) Think Tank outputs falling short of policymaking needs (paradigm reconsideration only done in limited domains, limited diagnosis of problem causes, naive handling of uncertainty, little work on crisis management); 6) endogenous causes (lack of self-evaluation and capacity-development strategy, shortcomings in methodology, inadequate diffusion of findings, inadequate mission conception).

Recommendations for improving Think Tanks include 1) continuous support and adequate resources; 2) establishing suitable liaison with government rulers; 3) personal tutoring of rulers in modern policy planning and analysis; 4) more diversified staff in Think Tanks, with staff members familiarized in alternative modes of thinking; 5) conscious efforts to overcome methodological narrowness and to build up innovative methods; 6) cooperation between Think Tanks.   **(building Think Tank capability)**

7267

Facing Momentous Choices, Yehezkel Dror (Hebrew U of Jerusalem), *International Review of Administrative Sciences* (International Institute of Administrative Sciences, Brussels), 50:2, 1984, 97-106.

Many countries are facing momentous choices which may well have very significant impacts on their future. When momentous choices are posed, the building of government capacities to develop, select, and implement preferable options must receive top priority. Far-going improvements in the "central mind of government" are needed. Some improvement principles include: selective radicalism (radical transformation of a small number of key factors), a short-range breakthrough orientation, and debunking of common reform errors such as preoccupation with formal structures. Five proposals are made for upgrading momentous choice capacities: 1) policy planning and policy analysis units near heads of government, to introduce some heterodoxy into the central mind of government; 2) Think Tanks for central minds of government, with direct channels to top-level decision-making [also see Dror essay, above]; 3) national policy colleges to provide learning experiences for senior policy-makers (none exist outside the domain of national security); 4) ad hoc implementation agencies to carry out innovative options—the more innovative the option pursued, the more radical the changes required in implementation agencies; 5) a small unit of top-quality professionals to devote all their efforts to major improvements in momentous choice capacities.

(building momentous choice capacity)

7268

Future Studies and Policy Studies: Complementary Multi-Fields in Public Affairs, Michael Marien (Editor, *Future Survey*), *World Future Society Bulletin,* 18:5, Sept-Oct 1984, 2-10. Also published without listing of 275 journals in *Policy Studies Review,* 4:1, Aug 1984, 35-42.

A comparison of the overlapping concerns of future studies and policy studies: fuzzy, multi-disciplinary fields (or multi-fields) with distinctly different cores. Both share a vast amount of literature, as illustrated by a single indicator of 275 English-language futures-relevant and policy-relevant journals arranged chronologically in three broad categories and 15 sub-categories. Of the 248 journals still being published, the median date of initial publication is 1975; thus, the journal literature has doubled in the past nine years, leading to ever-greater fragmentation of perspectives. The fragmentation is such that no single journal or cluster of journals comes close to illuminating all of the important perspectives for any broad policy area. Bridge-building is necessary to overcome this fragmentation, and one place to start is between the realms of future studies and policy studies, which have largely ignored each other. Distinctive differences between the two multi-fields are summarized by five traits: 1) **Background**: futurists are more diverse; policy analysts are largely PhD social scientists; 2) **Affiliation**: most policy analysts are affiliated with large universities or think tanks; 3) **Values**: futurists tend to be idealists; policy analysts are "realists"; 4) **Focus**: futurists tend to be generalists and global in perspective; policy analysts tend to be nation-bound specialists; 5) **Functions**: futurists are catalysts, intellectual leaders, innovators. Both sets of traits are valuable to society; ideally, the two should work together. [NOTE: An updated and expanded list of about 300 journals was included in **FS Annual 1984,** and has been further updated and refined for the present volume, **FS Annual 1985.**]

(futures/policy journals doubled since 1975)

7269

Contemporary Public Policy Analysis. Stuart S. Nagel (Prof of Political Science, U of Illinois). University, Ala: U of Alabama Press, March 1984/174p/$17.75;$7.50pb.

A series of lectures at the University of Alabama in 1982, offering an introductory survey of trends in policy analysis. Public policy analysis is defined as evaluation of alternative government policies or decisions in order to arrive at the best (or a good) decision in light of given goals, constraints, and conditions. It is an important part of the larger field of policy studies, which deals with the nature, causes, and effects of alternative public policies. In the first chapter, Nagel states that systematic policy evaluation is increasingly being used in government at the Federal, state, and local levels, and in the executive, legislative, and judicial branches. Policy analysis research also seems to be thriving as a sub-discipline of various social sciences, as a discipline in itself, and as an interdiscipline. Although the academic marketplace is in bad shape, the percentage of policy-relevant positions in social science fields seems to be high and not decreasing. Because of the Reagan administration interest in showing that many government programs produce greater costs than benefits, cost/benefit analysis may become for this Administration what zero-based budgeting, etc. were to previous administrations. And there may be substantial opportunities for policy analysts at state and local levels. Other chapters explore policy analysis with non-monetary and unknown variables, policy analysis and productivity improvement, and ethical dilemmas in policy analysis. [NOTE: No attempt is made to suggest whether government decisions, with or without policy analysis tools, are better serving the public interest today.]

(trends in public policy analysis)

7270

Initiating Change in Organizations and Communities: A Macro Practice Model. Peter M. Kettner, John M. Daley, and Ann Weaver Nichols (all at Arizona State U). Monterey CA: Brooks/Cole Publishing Co, Feb 1985/321p/$20.00.

Presents an integrated model for human service professionals to initiate and carry out a change process in human service organizations and in communitywide, human service efforts. The model provides an orderly, systematic process for change that incorporates broad participation. Implementation requires the efforts of many organizations and people, but is coordinated and facilitated by a change agent. The model places heavy emphasis on analysis, planning, monitoring, and evaluation, and lends itself well to demands for accountability by consumers and funding sources. The change process entails nine separate phases: identifying the change opportunity, analyzing the opportunity, setting goals and objectives, designing the change effort, resource planning, implementing the change effort, monitoring the effort, evaluating the effort, and reassessing and stabilizing the situation. Chapters are devoted to each of these phases. **(changing human services)**

7271

Social Experimentation. Edited by Jerry A. Hausman (MIT) and David A. Wise (Harvard U). Chicago: U of Chicago Press, May 1985/292p/$33.00.

Since 1970, the US government has spent over half a billion dollars on social experiments intended to assess the effect of various policies. These contributions from a 1981 conference sponsored by the National Bureau of Economic Research ask whether the effort was worth it. The first four chapters look at four types of experiments: the negative income tax experiments (finding that a great deal was learned, but that the results were broadly consistent with nonexperimental analyses), experiments with electricity pricing based on time of use (finding that the experimentation period was too short to allow consumers to adjust to altered rates), housing allowance experiments, and health experiments. The next four chapters address experimental design and analysis. Hausman and Wise highlight the absence of random selection of participants in social experiments, and suggest improvements in design even when voluntary participation is necessary. Concludes that, while experimental data are of uneven quality and tend not to be used in a consistent manner, they have been helpful. **(social experiments by US government)**

C. Business Planning

7272

The Truth About Corporate Planning: International Research into the Practice of Planning. Edited by D. E. Hussey (Harbridge House Europe, London). Elmsford NY: Pergamon, 1983/c388p/$35.00.

The 30 papers deal with such topics as organized planning in major US corporations, a survey of how planning works in 48 UK companies, the accuracy of long-range planning, pitfalls in multinational long-range planning, the state of the art in environmental scanning and forecasting, computer models for corporate planning, and a comparative study of long-range planning in Japan and the US.

(corporate planning)

7273

Long-Range Planning in Large Corporations: A Cross-National Survey, Christopher Orpen (Prof of Management, Deakin U, Australia), *Managerial Planning*, Nov-Dec 1984, 33:3, 18-22.

A systematic comparison of the extent to which comparable firms in a developed country (the US) and an undeveloped country (India) employ long-range planning to improve their corporate performance. Questionnaires were returned by senior planning managers in 72 US and 64 Indian corporations. The results suggest that long-range planning has become an integral part of the decision-making process in both countries. But US firms involved more managers in the planning process, projected their plans further into the future, subjected their planning assumptions more often to review, updated their plans more regularly, and required managers to spend more time on planning than did the Indian firms. These differences suggest that planning is done more thoroughly in US firms than Indian firms, and this difference may be a partial reason for the different economic performance of the two countries. **(long-range planning in US and India)**

7274

Maintaining Momentum in Long-Range Planning. Merritt L. Kastens (Hamilton NY). NY: AMACOM/American Management Association, Dec 1984/178p/$17.95.

A sequel to **Long-Range Planning for Your Business** (AMACOM, 1976), addressed to managers who have had four or five years of experience with long-range planning. The objective of planning is to gain full control over the future of the enterprise. But it is likely that frustration will arise from a growing awareness that planning is not coming to grips with the "really important issues"—which probably means that planning has spotlighted the really important issues and will not let the managers sweep them under the carpet. Topics covered include planning for change, maintaining concentration, policing policies, analyzing the business environment, setting up strategic business units, assessing corporate strengths and weaknesses, action planning, the hierarchy of objectives, and cost/benefit analysis. Concludes that the primary reasons why plans fail to get implemented are inappropriate management style, inadequate delegation, awkward organization, lack of credibility, and incompetence.

(long-range business planning)

7275

Eight Half-Truths of Strategic Planning: A Fresh Look, Vasudevan Ramanujam (Case Western Reserve U) and N. Venkatraman (U of Pittsburgh), *Planning Review*, 13:1, Jan 1985, 22-27.

Examines some widely accepted propositions that form the design priciples of good planning, arguing for purposes of stimulating discussion that they are half-truths rather than myths. 1) Effective planning should be future-oriented—but many planning systems fail as a result of excessive obsession with the future; 2) Effective planning should be flexible—but overly flexible systems threaten organization-wide commitment and encourage premature bail-out; 3) Top management involvement insures planning success—yes, but the commitment of the entire organization, especially lower level management, is now of paramount importance; 4) Effectiveness results from top-down planning and bottom-up implementation—the reverse formula might better use the creative energy that pervades all levels of the organization; 5) Effectiveness requires integration of strategic planning and issues management—rather, the two are more or less self-contained parts of strategic management; 6) Planning is a line function—the role of the staff planner is probably diminishing, but they are still important as coordinators and as devil's advocates; 7) Planning should be an ongoing activity—rather, it is a periodic process, driven by the calendar or by events; 8) Effective planning will increase organizational performance—rather, it is naive to expect any causal relationship between planning and performance. Concludes that planners must evaluate the appropriateness of each "truth" in its specific context.

(half-truths of planning)

7276

Using Scenarios in Strategic Decision-Making, Robert E. Linneman and Harold E. Klein (both Temple U), *Business Horizons* (Indiana U), 28:1, Jan-Feb 1985, 64-74.

The authors surveyed US corporations in 1977-78 and again in 1981-82 as to their use of scenarios (**FS Annual 1984** #6451). This article focuses on the use of environmental scenarios in strategic planning at the corporate level, assuming a time horizon of at least three years. Five basic types of scenarios can be used to portray environmental assessment: global (external) scenarios, industry-specific scenarios, exploration scenarios (broader than industry but more focused than global), issue-oriented scenarios, and external assumption scenarios. Also discussed are differences between simplicity and complexity, proactive vs. reactive, format, length, and number of scenarios (most firms should develop no more than 2-3). Concludes that many trends point toward titanic changes, resulting in six trends in company planning itself: more distant planning horizons, formalization of the environmental assessment process, more formal involvement by top management in environmental assessment, greater use of the multiple-scenario approach, and greater emphasis on adaptive strategies. [Also see ***Using Scenarios to Develop Strategies***, by J. P. Leemhuis (Shell Nederland), *Long Range Planning*, 18:2, April 1985, 30-37.]

(scenarios and decision-making)

7277

Environmental Assessment: An International Study of Corporate Practice, Harold E. Klein and Robert E. Linneman (both School of Business Admin., Temple U), *Journal of Business Strategy*, 5:1, Summer 1984, 66-75.

Environmental scanning or assessment has emerged as an explicit task in corporate planning processes, due to the emerging interest in formalized strategic planning and the increasing complexity of the external environment. The authors conducted a survey in 1981-82, receiving about 500 responses from the world's largest corporations, divided into US industrials, US non-industrials, and foreign corporations. Between 92% and 95% of respondents in each of the three groups had formal planning departments, and between 45% and 64% had a formal environmental assessment task in the planning process. The most common long-range planning horizon has been and continues to be five years, although 38% of foreign industrials and 21% of US industrials have a time horizon of 10+ years. The overwhelming majority of corporate planners in all three groups appears to have recognized the severe limitations of conventional analytical/statistical techniques for forecasts of three or more years. Respondents were asked about their use of forecasting techniques, with the finding that trend extrapolation is still the most widely practiced, perhaps because of its relative simplicity. Scenarios appear to be the most widely employed conjectural technique. [Also see ***Scenarios in Europe—Who Uses Them and Why?*** by P. Maleska *et al.*, (*Long Range Planning*, 17:5, Oct 1984,

45-49), describing results from 166 responses to a 1981 questionnaire, in which 36% of European corporations were found to use scenarios, in contrast to 51% of US corporations as determined in a 1981 study by Linneman and Klein (*LRP*, Dec 1983; **FS Annual 1984**, #6451).]

(corporate use of scanning and scenarios)

7278

Future Search: Innovative Business Conference, Marvin R. Weisbord (Senior VP, Block-Petrella-Weisbord), *Planning Review*, 12:4, July 1984, 16-20.

The future search conference is a planning meeting designed for high participation, interaction, and productivity in a relatively short time. Still largely unknown in the US, it was developed nearly 25 years ago by social scientists Eric Trist and Fred Emery. Such a conference—a technique that can be used by any organization—sorts through a firm's past, present, and future to find the events and aspirations that have shaped its values and may determine its future course. It is designed to produce new insights, and to build a sense of common values and purpose. Although it could become an annual event, most companies use it at critical turning points, when significant new data are needed quickly and when it is important for every class of stakeholder to be heard. The search conference is a supplement to strategic planning, based on three assumptions: 1) change has become so rapid and unpredictable that more face-to-face discussion is needed to make intelligent strategic decisions; 2) successful new strategies will be based increasingly on envisioning preferred futures; 3) when people participate in developing plans, they are much more committed to carrying them out. Search conferences differ from traditional business meetings, which tend to get clogged with numbers and to focus too narrowly on symptoms rather than bedrock issues.

(future search conference technique)

7279

A Spreadsheet Way of Knowledge: How the Computer Is Reshaping American Business—For Better and For Worse, Steven Levy, *Harper's*, Nov 1984, 58-64.

Author of **Hackers: Heroes of the Computer Revolution** (Doubleday, Nov 1984) describes the potential revolution of the electronic spreadsheet. Beginning with the introduction of the VisiCalc program in late 1979, and continuing with more powerful programs such as Lotus 1-2-3, fundamental changes are underway. For the first time, businessmen have at their fingertips a flexible means to chart all the variables that make and break enterprises. This allows them to calculate the effects of sudden changes in the corporate environment and to experiment with scenarios (anything from the expansion of a product line to a merger) with an ease inconceivable five years ago. More than a million computer spreadsheet programs were purchased in the US in 1984, and both corporate executives and small business owners cite prodigious gains in productivity. The spreadsheet has redefined the nature of some jobs, enabling decentralization and diminishing the power of data processing. It encourages businesses to keep track of things that were previously unquantified or overlooked. Executives are no longer satisfied with quarterly updates, for it is now easy to compile monthly, weekly, and even daily updates. Rather than taking guesses, people now feel obligated to run the numbers. It may well be that the electronic spreadsheet will have an effect like that brought about during the Renaissance by the introduction of double-entry bookkeeping, which also gave merchants a more accurate picture of their businesses. But spreadsheets can also be used in the drive for paper profits, and as a tool of

takeover architects. The flexibility of spreadsheets can enable experimentation with insidious scenarios. Perhaps most importantly, there is a danger that users will accept these hypothetical models as gospel, forgetting the oft-repeated "garbage in, garbage out" truism about computers. The accuracy of a spreadsheet model depends on the accuracy of the formulas and their underlying assumptions that govern the relationship between various figures. The benefits of the spreadsheet metaphor will be meaningless if it is taken too much to heart.
(**electronic spreadsheets revolutionizing business?**)

7280
Corporate Tragedies: Product Tampering, Sabotage, and Other Catastrophes. Ian I. Mitroff (Distinguished Prof of Business Policy, USC) and Ralph H. Kilmann (Prof of Business Administration, U of Pittsburgh). NY: Praeger Publishers, July 1984/140p/$23.95.

What was once unimaginable and unthinkable seems to be increasingly happening to executives and organizations. Products and services produced and provided under the best intentions of doing good become sabotaged or converted into agents of evil. This book seeks to help those connected with organizations of all kinds to face up to tragedies, to think about them, and to cope more effectively—how to survive future shock. Five basic kinds of tragedies are discussed: 1) Tampering: the evil from without (e.g., the Tylenol case); 2) Unplanned and Unwanted Defects: the evil from within (e.g., the Rely tampons case and Toxic Shock Syndrome); 3) Unwanted Compatibility: the evil of the parasite (e.g. pornographic uses of Atari video games); 4) Projection: the evil in the mind's eye (e.g., the Procter and Gamble logo); 5) Collapse of a Belief System: the evil of blindness to change (e.g., basic assumptions of the US auto industry). The authors warn that we have bred a nation of certainty-junkies, training people in highly structured and bounded exercises at a time when the problems of organizations and society have become highly unstructured and unbounded. The world is no longer a simple machine, but a complex, highly interdependent system. Organizations must thus develop cultures that encourage and reward individuals who think about the unthinkable within the context of strategic thinking about the whole organization. The strong resistance to thinking about the unthinkable, so as to avoid blame and pain, must be systematically organized against. We cannot prevent all tragedies from occurring, but this does not relieve us from the basic responsibility of thinking about them. [NOTE: Obviously a timely warning, prefiguring the Union Carbide tragedy in Bhopal, India. Industrial accidents such as Bhopal surely deserve addition to the five basic kinds of tragedies discussed in the text. Also see Charles Perrow, **Normal Accidents: Living with High-Risk Technologies** (Basic Books, 1984; **FS Annual 1984**, #6360).]   (**organization tragedies**)

D. Guidebooks

*7281
Ideas About the Future: A History of Futurism, 1794-1982. Burnham P. Beckwith. Palo Alto CA: B. P. Beckwith (656 Lytton Ave, C430), 1984/307p/$10.00.

One of the best ways to prepare to make scientific predictions about the future is to review the predictions made by the most able and/or stimulating earlier futurists, and their reasons for making them. This book is largely devoted to critical essays on 25 writers on the future, each concluded with an assessment of strong points and weak points: Condorcet, Saint-Simon, Comte, de Tocqueville, J.S. Mill, Marx and Engels (the great majority of their predictions have been substantially or largely verified by history), Edward Bellamy (failed to see many important trends because he allowed his hopes to determine his predictions), H.G. Wells, J.M. Keynes (made his worst predictions in the field of economics), J.B.S. Haldane, C.C. Furnas, James Burnham, Joseph A. Schumpeter, Morris L. Ernst, Gunnar Myrdal, Ferdinand Lundberg, Arnold Toynbee, Stuart Chase, Daniel Bell (plausible, original, and stimulating, although failing to discuss many major trends), R. L. Heilbroner, Herman Kahn (his picture of the future is very incomplete), Alvin Toffler (in many areas of social thought a pure reactionary; also an apologist for many counter-culture fads), John Naisbitt (on the whole, has contributed very little to our knowledge of the future), Gerard O'Neill (consistently minimizes the need for and probability of social change, while maximizing the probability of technological change), and Adrian Berry.

In the introduction, futurism is defined as all forecasts of future events, covering naive prophecies as well as scientific predictions. A scientific futurist does not predict what may or can happen, but what probably will happen. A good scientific futurist does not prescribe what he believes ought to happen. Scientific prediction of the future will become more accurate, detailed, and respectable, as a profession of well-trained, full-time, professional scientific futurists is created during the next century. Beckwith concludes with his own summary of major US social trends through 2100 (most of which were discussed in his 1967 book, **The Next 500 Years**): 1) Social Trends: US population between 400-500 million, 15% of GNP invested in education, continued technological progress, more socialization of health care, more group child care, declining religious faith, less crime; 2) Economic Trends: rising real wages, unemployment less than 2%, more specialization and monopoly, the elimination of commercial banking, rationalization of water supply; 3) Political Trends: more government control of business, more free distribution, more public ownership, taxes above 50% of GNP, more government by experts, a US-USSR condominium agreement dividing the world into two zones of control, etc. [NOTE: Despite Beckwith's own collectivist and positivist views, which many readers may find quaintly naive in light of contemporary sensibilities, his sketches of the 25 futurist thinkers are quite good and the comments generally astute. Such restrospective assessment of who was largely right and who was way off base is a much-needed exercise. And as an introduction to the great futurist thinkers (most of whom should be in any Futurist Hall of Fame) this book should prove useful.]

(**critique of 25 major futurist writers**)

7282
Contemporary Issues Criticism. Volume Two. Edited by Robert L. Brubaker. Detroit MI: Gale Research Co, Feb 1984/632p/$78.00.

Covers 39 leaders of contemporary thought. For each writer, there is a biographical introduction, followed by excerpts from principal works and critical commentary from other writers who discuss, clarify, and criticize the thought leader's point of view. Writers in Volume Two who have also appeared in *Future Survey* include Richard J. Barnet, Daniel Bell, Helen Caldicott, Jerome Deshusses, Amitai Etzioni, Betty Friedan, Marvin Harris, John Holt, Carl Sagan, B.F. Skinner, Thomas Sowell, Edward Teller, and William Appleman Williams. Noteworthy writers in Volume One of **CIC** (Gale, 1982; **FS Annual 1983** #5590) include Murray Bookchin, Barry Commoner, Richard A.

Falk, Herman Kahn, Margaret Mead, E.F. Schumacher, and Alvin Toffler. A listing of some 350 writers to appear in subsequent volumes of **CIC** includes Isaac Asimov, Kenneth E. Boulding, Victor Ferkiss, Buckminster Fuller, Bertram Gross, Robert L. Heilbroner, Ivan Illich, Robert Theobald, and Ben J. Wattenberg. [NOTE: A useful companion to Beckwith's historical survey #7281 above.]
(critiques of contemporary thinkers)

7283
Futurecasting: Charting a Way to Your Future. Joel Kurtzman. Palm Springs CA: ETC Publications, Nov 1984/94p(8x11")/$9.95pb.

An introduction to the use of futures research methods to generate alternative futures for one's personal and organizational life. Chapters on clues to looking for the future, imagining or visioning the future, the systems approach, trees of impact, scenarios for the future, systematizing intuition through the Delphi method, trend analysis, and setting new goals. [NOTE: A useful survey for high school students, although perhaps the most important method of all is omitted: widespread reading.]
(futures research primer for high school students)

7284
Slogans. First Edition. Edited by Laurence Urdang and Ceila Dame Robbins. Detroit MI: Gale Research Co, Sept 1984/556p/$65.00.

A collection of more than 6000 slogans and rallying cries, arranged in 126 categories such as Aerospace, Broadcasting, Health and Fitness, and Presidential Campaigns (423 entries). Slogans are arranged alphabetically in each category, with information on their source. [NOTE: An excellent idea to collect the phrases that "urge people to take action," but the vast bulk of the slogans in this guide are from the world of advertising, and social issue slogans such as "Small is Beautiful" are virtually absent.]
(advertising slogans)

7285
Economics Information Resource Directory. First Edition. Detroit MI: Gale Research Co, 1983-84 (3 parts)/c750p/$85.00.

A guide to about 2000 organizations in the economic sphere, including government agencies, trade and professional groups, state and regional departments, key international bodies (e.g., OECD), research centers, databases, statistical data collecting institutions, consulting firms, associations and societies, and selected reference works and periodicals. **(economics-related organizations)**

7286
Basic Literature in Policy Studies: A Comprehensive Bibliography. Edited by Stuart S. Nagel (Prof of Political Science, U of Illinois). Greenwich CT: JAI Press (36 Sherwood Place), Feb 1984/453p/c$75.00.

Seeks to bring together, update, and supplement various bibliographies that have appeared in *Policy Studies Journal*.The 37 chapters by various experts are arranged in two parts: 1) **General Aspects of Policy Studies:** basic concepts, social values in public policy, methods of policy analysis, social indicators data, utilization of policy research, policy formation, administering public policy, cross-national public policy, international dimensions of policy studies, interdisciplinary public policy, state policy, urban policy; 2) **Specific Policy Problems:** foreign policy, defense and arms control, electoral policy, legislative reform, civil liberties, economic regulation, labor policy, communication policy, taxing and spending policy, agriculture, racial discrimination, women and public policy, criminal justice, higher education, population, aging, poverty

and welfare, land use, housing, transportation, environmental protection, science, health, biomedical policy, energy. In all, there are about 4000 unannotated but well-categorized entries. Concludes with a list of over 250 bibliographic syllabi for various policy studies courses, which are available from the authors. [NOTE: A valuable compilation, although not the "comprehensive" work that it claims to be, since the great majority of items date from the 1970s, and certain topics are not touched on, e.g.: family policy, elementary and secondary education, natural resources, trade policy, international monetary policy, and general societal directions. The jumbled effect from 37 chapters with finely categorized entries is aggravated by the lack of an author index. Also see Nagel's gargantuan 914-page **Encyclopedia of Policy Studies** (Dekker, 1983; **FS Annual 1983,** #5515), a useful companion to the above, with a generally parallel organization of contents.] **(literature of policy studies)**

7287
The Analysis of Public Policy: A Bibliography of Dissertations, 1977-1982. Compiled by John S. Robey. Westport CT: Greenwood Press, 1984/225p/$35.00.

A guide to over 1000 recent English-language dissertations, divided into 16 fields of concentration: policy analysis, policy-making at the state level, public administration, agricultural policy, civil rights and the status of women, domestic taxing and economic policy, educational policy, US foreign policy, government regulation of morality (sex, drugs, abortion), housing, energy and the environment, international trade and economics, judicial policy making, military policy, and health and welfare.
(public policy dissertations)

7288
Encyclopedia of Governmental Advisory Organizations. Fourth Edition. Edited by Denise Allard Adzigian. Detroit MI: Gale Research Co, Nov 1983/964p/$350.00.

Covers nearly 4000 groups, on-going and defunct, assigned to advise the President, Congress, and departments and bureaus of the Federal government. The ten broad subject categories, with sample advisory organizations in parentheses, are: 1) **Agriculture**: Agricultural Policy Committee (1976-1980), Agricultural Research Policy Advisory Committee (1969-1977); 2) **Business, Economics, Industry**: Cost of Living Council (1971-1974), Council of Economic Advisors (1946...); 3) **Defense and Military Science**: Military Manpower Task Force (1981...), President's Commission on Strategic Forces (1983-1984); 4) **Education and Social Welfare**: President's Council on Aging (1962-1982), Commission on Civil Rights (1957...); 5) **Environment and Natural Resources**: Acid Rain Coordination Committee (1979...), EPA Sludge Task Force (1982...); 6) **Health and Medicine**: National Advisory Council on Drug Abuse (1972...), National Advisory Council on Health Professions Education (1971...); 7) **History and Culture**: Federal Architecture Task Force (1973-1975), Museum Advisory Panel (1970...); 8) **Government, Law, and International Affairs**: Presidential Task Force on Management Reform (1982...), Presidential Task Force on International Development (1969-1970); 9) **Engineering, Science and Technology**: Aerospace Safety Advisory Panel (1967...), President's Task Force on Science Policy (1969-1970); 10) **Transportation**: Commission on Highway Beautification (1970-1973), National Transportation Policy Study Commission (1976-1979). [NOTE: A fascinating glimpse at the wide world of government advising, then and now.] **(government advisory organizations)**

7289

Surveys, Polls, Censuses, and Forecasts Directory.
First Edition. Detroit MI: Gale Research Co, Oct 1983/
c300p in three issues/$175.00pb.

About 400 entries in each of three softbound issues, providing access to organizations that conduct surveys and
polls. Issue # 1 includes such entries as Dow Theory Forecasts, the Economic Outlook of the U.S. Chamber of Commerce, Frost & Sullivan's Future Office Systems Market,
Forecast Associates' ten-year forecast of NATO Tactical
Missile Systems, the National Travel Survey, Techno-
Economic Forecasts of the printing and publishing industry, Predicasts' Technology Update, the American Council
of Life Insurance Trend Analysis Program Report, the
World Missile Forecast, and World Population Data. [NOTE:
Information for each entry tends to be skimpy, relative to
other, more developed Gale guides.]   **(surveys and polls)**

7290

International Research Centers Directory 1984.
2nd Edition. Edited by Kay Gill and Anthony T. Kruzas.
Detroit MI: Gale Research Co, Feb 1984/739p/$250.00.

Contains almost 3000 entries for research centers located in numerous countries of the world, excluding the
US. Also see **Research Centers Directory 1984-85**
(Ninth Edition), edited by Mary Michelle Watkins and
James A. Ruffner (Gale, Sept 1984/1308p/$275.00), which
provides some 7500 entries of research centers in the US
and Canada conducting programs in agriculture, business,
education, government, social sciences, etc.

(research centers)

7291

The New Book of World Rankings. George Thomas
Kurian. NY: Facts on File, 1984/490p/$29.95.

An international scorecard that compares and ranks over
190 nations of the world according to performance in 343
areas, divided into 23 chapters: geography and climate,
vital statistics, population dynamics, race and religion,
politics (registered voters, civil disorder index, age of
nations, index of democratization, political executions, refugees), foreign aid, military power, economy, finance and
banking, trade, agriculture, industry and mining, energy,
labor, transportation and communications, consumption,
housing (the US ranks 52nd in home ownership!), health,
food, education, crime, media, cities (including estimated
population in the year 2000) and culture. Concludes with
profiles summarizing highs and lows for each country.
[NOTE: Lacks the flash and dazzle of the Kidron/Segal
maps (#6468), but provides much data in an accessible
fashion, including odd but interesting tables on such topics
as users of contraceptives, deaths from political violence,
farm ownership, children in the labor force, cinema seats,
age of cities, and public library use.]

(rankings of nations in 343 areas)

7292

**Peace and World Order Studies: A Curriculum
Guide**. Fourth Edition. Edited by Barbara J. Wien. NY:
World Policy Institute (777 UN Plaza), Nov 1984/741p/
$16.00.

The bulk of this guide is devoted to reproducing syllabi
of college courses in the following areas: overview of global
problems (9 syllabi), peacemaking and nonviolence (11),
women and world order (5), teacher training for world
order education (9), hunger and the politics of food distribution (9), ecological balance (7), international law and
organizations (6), human rights and social justice (8), world
political economy and economic justice (12), militarism and

the arms race (12), religious perspectives on peace and
justice (7), culture and change (7), regional studies (6), and
alternative futures (8). Also offered is an introductory
essay on the need to be interdisciplinary and to consider
values, case studies of peace studies programs at 31 colleges and universities, a "sampling" of 55 funding organizations which may consider requests for supporting peace
and social justice education, a filmography of about 220
items, lists of about 140 periodicals and journals and 170
organizations, and a categorized bibliography of about 500
items. [NOTE: A very useful guide for teachers and independent learners.]   **(world order curriculum guide)**

7293

Yearbook of International Organizations. 20th
Edition (Three Volumes). Edited by Union of International
Associations (Brussels). Detroit MI: Gale Research Co (US
distributor), Dec 1983.

Volume 1, **Main Volume** (1500p/$168.00), covers some
20,000 international organizations, centers, institutes, etc.
concerned with international issues. Volume 2, **Geographic Volume** (1000p/$168.00), classifies organizations
by country of secretariat. Volume 3, **Subject Volume**
(500p/$98.00), arranges organizations by subjects such as
science and technology, social sciences, commerce and industry, education and youth, development, etc.

(international associations)

7294

Alternative America. 1984 Edition. Compiled by Richard
Gardner. Cambridge MA: Resources (Box 134, Harvard
Square), 1984/$19.95.

First published in 1976 with a listing of 5000 groups,
this new edition lists 13,000 alternative, progressive, innovative, and experimental groups and organizations—
geographically, alphabetically, and by keyword. Included
are members of the alternative press, intentional communities and communes, ecology groups, film/video
groups, health care organizations, alternative radio stations, anti-nuclear groups, alternative technology groups,
women's groups, and groups in the human potential movement. This edition includes about 1000 non-US entries.
[NOTE: A growth in the counter-culture—or an expansion
of categories and the data collection effort? A major cultural
development, or inflated data on miniscule, unimportant,
and evanescent groups? In any event, the raw number
reported on here is far greater than the 1526 groups of
"Another America" listed in **Networking** (Doubleday,
1982; **FS Annual 1983**, #5586).]

(US counter-culture groups)

7295

Encyclopedia of Associations 1985. 19th Edition (Four
Volumes). Edited by Denise S. Akey. Detroit MI: Gale
Research Co, 1984.

Volume 1, **National Organizations of the U.S.**
(c2000p/$185.00) has over 18,100 entries arranged in 17
subject categories: business and commercial, governmental and public administration, educational, cultural, social
welfare, health and medical, public affairs, labor unions,
etc. Volume 2 (c1050p/$165.00) provides geographic and
executive indexes. Volume 3 ($180.00) provides a between-
editions supplement of new associations and projects.
Volume 4, **International Organizations** (Nov 1984/
508p/$160.00), offers information on about 2000 nonprofit
organizations that are international in scope, membership,
or interest, and are headquartered outside the US.

(US and international associations)

7296

The Encyclopedia of Community Planning and Environmental Management. Marilyn Spigel Schultz and Vivian Loeb Kasen. NY: Facts on File (460 Park Ave South), Oct 1984/$45.00.

Over 2000 listings on concepts and terms used in the field of community planning and environmental protection (e.g., acid rain, garden cities, urban sprawl). Major subject areas include land use regulation, transportation, housing, planning techniques, recreation, urban design, economic development, history of planning, Federal programs, energy conservation, air and water pollution, and solid waste management.

(community/environmental planning)

7297

Guidelines for Preparing Proposals. Roy Meador (Ann Arbor MI). Chelsea MI: Lewis Publishers (121 S Main St), Jan 1985/116p/$19.95.

Billions of dollars are distributed annually in R&D grants and in funding responses to other proposals. The proposal game is wide open for anyone who wants to play, even a lone individual with one idea. But many proposals, perhaps the majority of those submitted, fail because the work is done hurriedly or carelessly. This manual describes how to organize winning proposals for grants, venture capital, R&D projects, and other good ideas. Chapters are devoted to elements of a proposal, submitting a proposal, do's and don'ts of government and foundation grantsmanship, business plans, and a sample grant proposal. Some recommendations for more convincing proposals: keep up-to-date on current literature, use the names of recognized authorities to validate a proposal, learn from the experience of grant winners by interviewing them, persist despite rejection, study the activities and needs of the government agency or foundation which will receive your proposal, read instructions and follow them, and make sure that you have an original idea or true innovation.

(writing good proposals)

7298

The Directory of Directories 1985. Third Edition. Edited by James M. Ethridge. Detroit MI: Gale Research Co, Oct 1984/c1250p/$125.00.

Over 8200 listings in such sections as public affairs and social concerns, general business directories, specific industries and lines of business, banking/finance/insurance/real estate, law and government, science and engineering, education, health and medicine, etc.   **(directories)**

7299

Encyclopedia of Information Systems and Services 1985-86. Sixth Edition (Two Volumes). Detroit MI: Gale Research Co, Oct 1984/669p/$165.00 (International Volume); Dec 1984/c1400p/$190.00 (United States Volume).

A comprehensive guide to computer-based information systems and services. The International Volume covers more than 1100 organizations, systems, and services located in some 65 countries; The United States Volume covers about 2200 systems and services located in the US.

(info systems and services)

Appendix 1

100 Impacts of New Information Technologies

Many writers have stated that the new information technologies—computers, robots, satellites, cable TV, videotex, VCRs, etc.—are having a profound impact on society. To give some greater definition to this generalization about the emerging information society (also called the microelectronics revolution, the telematic transformation, etc.), the following specific ideas have been gleaned from various books and articles abstracted in **Future Survey Annual 1985** and the two previous annuals. Items with numbers ranging from #5616 to #6464 are in **FS Annual 1984**; items from #4458 to #5615 are in **FS Annual 1983**.

The "final word" on impacts of computers and other information technologies will not be written for decades; perhaps it will never be written, because of differences of opinion and ever-changing technology. Many of the ideas listed below are speculative. Other statements about impacts conflict with each other, notably whether computers lead to more or fewer jobs (54,55), centralization or decentralization (57,59), and to humanization or dehumanization (99,100). These arguments will surely continue as this awesome, many-faceted technological transformation continues to unfold. The best that can be done in such a dynamic and opaque situation is to look as clearly as we can at the full range of possible impacts. As demonstrated here, there are far more impacts—for better and for worse—than any one writer has yet described.

Similar appendices to this one include "60 Paths to US and Global Security" and "75 Paths to Economic Health" in **Future Survey Annual 1984** (pp. 185-188), and "55 Ways to End the Energy Crunch" in **Future Survey Annual 1980-81** (p.vii).

I. International Relations

1. Increased rich-poor gap between nations (7111,7118, 5328,5352)
2. Power leaking out of sovereign nation-states (7113, 7114,7161/7162)
3. Threat to cultural autonomy in Third World (6290)
4. Aid to Third World development (6291/6293, 5346)
5. Computerized language translation by year 2000 enabling better international understanding (7231)
6. Undermining of industrial society interests in USSR (7112)
7. Destabilizing military balance of power by possible false alerts, etc. (7140,7142,5772)

II. Economics and Finance

8. New meaning of poverty, wealth, and growth (7108)
9. Productivity gains from computers; better models for business decisions (7134,7279)
10. Computer enables large-scale transnational corporations and reinforces existing power distribution (7114, 7134)
11. Computer enables lower inventories for manufacturers (6812)
12. Ability to clone talent creates superrich superstars (6336)
13. Loss of industry boundary lines (6346)
14. Financial deregulation encouraged (6524,6849,6852)
15. Home banking encourages use of more services (6859)
16. Stock trading globalized and accelerated (6553, 6755, 6860,6324)
17. Increased vulnerability of international financial system (6853,7114)
18. Advertising messages proliferating (7123)
19. Consumers have increased choices available (5369, 6346)

III. Government

20. New decision-making models available (7247)
21. More information makes decision-making more difficult (6298/6299)
22. Historical record eroded (7145/7146)
23. Tax collection facilitated (7147)
24. Increased advantage to incumbent Congressmen (7144)
25. Possible increase of legislative branch power (7144)
26. Congress better informed and democratized (6322)
27. Potential to enhance democratic participation (6321, 7157)
28. Widespread TV changes presentation of politics and intensifies system fragmentation (6338)
29. New technologies undermine rationale for airwave regulation (6340/6341)
30. Urban planning facilitated (6939)
31. Auto traffic monitoring enabling road-use fees (6168)
32. VCR use evades government censors (7175)

IV. Crime and Justice

33. Computer crime more extensive than bank robbery (6906,6180,5172)
34. Computerized parking tickets (6989)
35. Better surveillance technologies (6991/6992)
36. Better property protection (6988,6990)
37. National computerized criminal history system (5190)
38. Computerized files interconnected (5362)
39. Fingerprint computers for foolproof ID (6990,7231)
40. Smart cards for better ID (6349)
41. Robots as prison guards and for security (FS 8:4, #86-241)
42. Electronic devices to monitor parolees (6988; FS 8:4, #86-241, 86-245)
43. Computers to ease caseloads in courts (FS 8:4, #86-245)

V. Health and Health Care

44. Telemedicine enabling patient examination at a distance (6332)
45. Computers to handle increased health information demand (7148)
46. Computers to prepare patient-specific educational materials (7148)
47. Computers to assist in diagnosis and cost analysis (7148)
48. Smart card health records carry full medical history (5250)
49. Home computer health adviser (7039,5250)
50. "Hospital on the Wrist" to administer drugs and monitor response (5250,5252)
51. Phobia of computers among some workers (7140)
52. Technostress (7141/7142)
53. High occupational illness in the computer industry (7142)

VI. Work

54. Job displacement (7133,7137,7142,6115)
55. Job creation (6117)
56. Computer monitoring of employees (6896,7134)
57. Increased capability of central managers (7133/7134, 7142,5353/5354)
58. Middle managers: shrinking ranks and changing roles (6115,5072)
59. Decentralization of operations (7139,7279,5353)
60. Women's work more tedious and specialized (6112)
61. Work at home enabled by computer (6950,6113)
62. Impact on work spaces and offices (6090,6344)
63. Mechanization of agriculture; better marketing information for farmers (5937/5938)
64. "Gods and Clods": work divided into smart jobs and dumb jobs (6084,6114,5070/5071)
65. Conspicuous consumption of computers leads to waste and abuse (5366)

VII. Education

66. New literacy required; need educated and flexible workforce (6089,6115,6258,5295)
67. Information overload (infoglut) results in overinformed and underenlightened (6296/6299)
68. Capability for global tele-education (6264/6265)
69. Computer potential for tutoring and improved learning (6319, 7149)
70. Possible central data facility with wide public access (5979)
71. Computers to displace teachers, doubling student/teacher ratio by 2003 (7231)
72. Decline of reading (7128)
73. Computerization results in growing division between academic haves and have-nots (7150)

VIII. Knowledge

74. Computers facilitate scholarly research and coordinate library acquisitions (7126,7149/7150)
75. Weather forecasting improved by computers (7234)
76. Mapmaking greatly improved, and computerized maps soon in automobiles (7153,6391)
77. Knowledge engineering demystifies expertise (6400)
78. Databases and electronic publishing enable independence of users from librarians and interaction with authors and publishers (7129,7152)
79. Technologies have improved TV newscasting (6334)
80. New microchips to improve TV sets (7167)
81. Computerized photo composites may create dangerous deceptions (7177)
82. Blind faith encouraged in computer decisions (6860, 7279)
83. Fragmentation of knowledge as information increases (7123/7125)
84. Continuous modification of electronic record makes referencing more ambiguous (5371)
85. "Meaning lag"—growing gap between information and meaning (5347)
86. More uncertainty created (5350)
87. Certain types of knowledge valued less; quantitative criteria more important for decisions (7134,7142)
88. Electronic pollution of too many signals creates false readings on instruments (6300)
89. Erosion of copyright control (7130,7150)

IX. Individual and Society

90. New definition of man as information processor (6317)
91. Living patterns dispersed; travel demand increased (6167)
92. Electronic devices encroach on commons of speech (6304)
93. New structure of societal interaction not based on locality; no sense of place (7120/7121)
94. Changed roles of men, women, and children (7121)
95. Perceptual numbing (7122)
96. Privatization of information results in information-rich and information-poor (7126,7134,7168)
97. Applications in the home: electronic hearth and house brains (6161)
98. Monitoring and decreased privacy (7134,7137,7143)
99. Humanized machines to liberate people, amplify the brain (7138/7139,7154,7158,7177,7211)
100. Human-machine interactions as dehumanizing and isolating (7134/7136,7140/7141)

Appendix 2

Futures-Relevant and Policy-Relevant Periodicals 1985
A Chronological and Categorized Listing

This Appendix illustrates the problem of profound intellectual fragmentation, by listing 330 active and defunct periodicals that purport to have some relevance to the overlapping multi-fields of future studies and policy studies. All of the following are in English, except for #4, *Futuribles*, a French-language monthly that exemplifies good futures thinking. Most of these periodicals are scholarly journals. Newsletters, which come and go, and number in the hundreds if not thousands, are not included here.

This listing has been designed not only to demonstrate the problems of fragmentation, but to assist researchers who may wish access to specialized journals that are presently beyond the scope of *Future Survey* coverage. Complete addresses of selected periodicals regularly assessed for *Future Survey* are listed in Appendix 3. Addresses for journals that are listed below, but are not in Appendix 3, can be found in **Ulrich's International Periodicals Directory** or by sending inquiries to the World Future Society (c/o Editor, *Future Survey*).

Periodicals are arranged in three broad categories: 82 General Periodicals (which consider a variety of special problem areas), 218 Special Focus Periodicals (largely parallel to the chapters in this annual), and 30 Defunct Periodicals (many of which, notably, were broadly interdisciplinary and futures-focused). Periodicals that have been merged into or succeeded by other periodicals are preceeded by [x] instead of a number.

This is the most comprehensive listing of futures- and policy-relevant periodicals available anywhere. An updated listing will be a regular feature of **Future Survey Annual**. Readers are encouraged to suggest titles that are not listed below so that the most comprehensive inventory is made available.

I. GENERAL PERIODICALS

A. General Futures Research

1. *The Futurist* (World Future Society, 1967)
[x] *World Future Society Bulletin* (WFS, 1967-1984; succeeded by *Futures Research Quarterly*, #12)
2. *Futures: The Journal of Planning and Forecasting* (Butterworths-UK, 1969)
3. *Technological Forecasting and Social Change* (Elsevier, 1969)
4. *Futuribles* (Association Internationale Futuribles-Paris, 1975)
5. *Futurics: A Quarterly Journal of Futures Research* (Minnesota Futurists-Minneapolis, 1977)
6. *Cultural Futures Research* (Dept of Anthropology, Northern Arizona U, 1977)
7. *Futures Canada* (Canadian Association for Futures Studies, 3764 Côtes-des-Neiges, Montreal, 1977)
8. *Future Survey/FS Annual* (World Future Society, 1979)
9. *World Futures* (Gordon & Breach, 1981; successor to *The Philosophy Forum*)
10. *Impact Assessment Bulletin* (International Association for Impact Assessment, Georgia Institute of Technology, 1981)
11. *Journal of Forecasting* (Wiley, 1983)
12. *Futures Research Quarterly* (World Future Society, 1985; successor to *World Future Society Bulletin*)
13. *International Journal of Forecasting* (Elsevier, 1985)
14. *Project Appraisal* (Beech Tree Publishing, Guildford UK, March 1986; on consequences of social and techological projects)

B. General Policy Studies

[x] *Public Policy* (Harvard U, 1952-1980; succeeded by *J. of Policy Analysis and Management*, #24)
15. *Policy Sciences* (Elsevier, 1970)
16. *Policy Studies Journal* (Policy Studies Organization/Florida State U, 1972; also see #26)
17. *Philosophy and Public Affairs* (Princeton U Press, 1972)
18. *Policy and Politics* (U of Bristol, 1973)
19. *Canadian Public Policy* (1975)
[x] *Policy Analysis* (U of California-Berkeley, 1975-1980; succeeded by *J. of Policy Analysis and Management*, #24)

20. *International Journal of Policy Analysis and Information Systems* (Plenum, 1977)
21. *Policy Studies Review Annual* (Transaction Books, 1977)
22. *Journal of Policy Modeling* (Elsevier, 1978)
23. *Policy Options/Options Politiques* (Institute for Research in Public Policy-Toronto, 1980)
24. *Journal of Policy Analysis and Management* (Wiley, 1981; successor to *Public Policy* and *Policy Analysis*)
25. *Journal of Public Policy* (Cambridge U, 1981)
26. *Policy Studies Review* (Policy Studies Organization/Arizona State U, 1981)
27. *Report from the Center of Philosophy and Public Policy* (U of Maryland, 1981)
28. *Risk Analysis* (Society for Risk Analysis/Plenum, 1981)
29. *Options* (International Institute for Applied Systems Analysis, 1983)
30. *Systems Research* (International Federation for Systems Research/Pergamon, 1984)
31. *Social Philosophy and Policy* (Social Philosophy and Policy Center, Bowling Green State U / Basil Blackwell, 1984)

C. Social Science

32. *The Annals of the American Academy of Political and Social Science* (AAPSS-Philadelphia/Sage Publications, 1890)
33. *Population Bulletin* (Population Reference Bureau, 1946)
34. *International Social Science Journal* (UNESCO-Paris, 1949)
35. *Social Problems* (Society for the Study of Social Problems, 1953)
36. *American Behavioral Scientist* (Sage Publications, 1957)
37. *Society/Transaction* (Rutgers U, 1964)
38. *The Public Interest* (New York, 1965)
39. *The Center Magazine* (Center for the Study of Democratic Institutions, 1968)
40. *Social Policy* (New York, 1970)
41. *Social Indicators Research* (D. Reidel, 1971)
42. *Journal of Social Policy* (Cambridge U, 1972)
43. *Journal of the Institute for Socioeconomic Studies* (White Plains NY, 1976)

44. *Wilson Quarterly* (Woodrow Wilson International Center for Scholars-Washington, 1977)
45. *American Demographics* (Dow Jones, 1978)
46. *Human Resources Planning* (Human Resources Planning Society-NYC, 1978)
47. *Brookings Review* (Brookings Institution-Washington, 1982)
48. *Social Philosophy and Policy* (Basil Blackwell, 1983 biannual)

D. **Conservative / Libertarian**

49. *National Review* (New York, 1955)
50. *Reason: Free Minds and Free Markets* (Santa Barbara CA, 1969)
51. *Reason Papers: A Journal of Interdisciplinary Normative Studies* (Santa Barbara CA, 1975 annual)
52. *The Human Life Review* (Human Life Foundation-NYC, 1975)
53. *Journal of Libertarian Studies* (New York, 1976)
54. *Journal of Social, Political, and Economic Studies* (Council for Economic Studies-Washington, 1976)
55. *Journal of Contemporary Studies* (Institute for Contemporary Studies-San Francisco, 1978)
56. *Policy Review* (Heritage Foundation-Washington, 1978)
57. *Public Opinion* (American Enterprise Institute-Washington, 1978)
58. *Policy Report* (Cato Institute-Washington, 1979)
59. *Cato Journal* (Cato Institute-Washington, 1981)
60. *This World* (Institute for Educational Affairs/American Enterprise Institute, 1982)
61. *The National Interest* (Washington; Fall 1985)

E. **Radical / Socialist**

62. *Monthly Review* (New York, 1950)
63. *Dissent* (New York, 1953)

64. *Our Generation* (Montreal, 1961)
65. *Socialist Review* (Oakland CA, 1972)
66. *Critique: A Journal of Socialist Theory* (Glascow UK, 1973)
67. *In These Times: The Independent Socialist Newspaper* (Institute for Public Affairs-Chicago, 1976)
68. *Contemporary Crises* (Elsevier, 1977)
69. *New Political Science* (Columbia U, 1980)
70. *Critical Social Policy* (Pluto Press, 1981)

F. **Populist / Humanist / New Age / Decentralist**

71. *The Progressive* (Madison WI, 1909)
72. *The Humanist* (American Humanist Association-Buffalo, 1941)
73. *Journal of Humanistic Psychology* (Association for Humanistic Psychology/Sage Publications, 1961)
74. *Resurgence* (Devon UK, 1970)
[x] *Co-Evolution Quarterly* (Sausalito CA, 1974-1984; continued as *Whole Earth Review*, #82)
75. *New Age Journal* (Brighton MA, 1975)
76. *ReVision: The Journal of Consciousness and Change* (Heldref Publications, Washington,1978)
77. *In Context: A Quarterly of Humane, Sustainable Culture* (Sequim WA, 1982)
78. *Harbinger: The Journal of Social Ecology* (Plainfield VT, 1983)
79. *Utne Reader: The Best of the Alternative Press* (LENS Publishing Co-Minneapolis, 1983)
80. *Afkar Inquiry: Magazine of Events and Ideas* (Tropvale Ltd-London, 1984) [NOTE: Islamic perspective]
81. *New Options* (Box 19324, Washington 20036; 1984)
82. *Whole Earth Review* (Sausalito CA, 1985; continuation of *Co-Evolution Quarterly*)

II.   **SPECIAL FOCUS PERIODICALS**

A. **World Futures / International Relations**

83. *Foreign Affairs* (Council on Foreign Relations-New York, 1921)
84. *International Affairs* (Royal Institute of International Affairs-London, 1922)
85. *International Organization* (World Peace Foundation, 1946)
86. *International Perspectives: The Canadian Journal on World Affairs* (Ottawa, 1948)
87. *Journal of International Affairs* (Columbia U, 1948)
88. *World Politics* (Princeton U, 1948)
89. *Orbis: A Journal of World Affairs* (Foreign Policy Research Institute-Philadelphia, 1957)
90. *Survey: A Journal of East and West Studies* (1957)
91. *Atlantic Community Quarterly* (The Atlantic Council of the US-Washington, 1963)
92. *Co-Existence: A Review of East-West and Development Issues* (U of Glasgow/Nijhoff, 1964)
93. *Foreign Policy* (Carnegie Endowment for International Peace, 1970)
94. *Millenium: Journal of International Studies* (London School of Economics, 1972)
95. *Transnational Perspectives: An Independent Journal of World Concerns* (Geneva, 1974)
96. *Cultures: Dialogue between the Peoples of the World* (UNESCO-Paris, 1975)
97. *Alternatives: Social Transformation and Humane Governance* (World Order Models Project / Butterorths, 1976; formerly *Alternatives: A Journal of World Policy* until 1986)

98. *Trialogue* (Trilateral Commission, 1976)
99. *Fletcher Forum* (Tufts U, 1977)
100. *Washington Quarterly* (Georgetown U, 1978)
101. *Human Rights Quarterly* (Johns Hopkins U, 1979)
102. *World Policy Journal* (World Policy Institute-NYC, 1983)
103. *Global Perspectives: An Interdisciplinary Journal of International Relations* (Transnational Studies Association, Orlando, Fla., 1983)

B. **International Economics / Development**

104. *International Labour Review* (ILO-Geneva, 1921)
105. *Economic Development and Cultural Change* (U of Chicago Press, 1952)
106. *OECD Observer* (Organisation for Economic Co-operation and Development-Paris, 1963)
107. *Ceres: FAO Review on Agriculture and Development* (Rome, 1967)
108. *IDS Bulletin* (Institute of Development Studies, U of Sussex, 1970)
109. *Development and Change* (Institute of Social Studies, The Hague, 1970)
110. *Development Dialogue* (Dag Hammarskjold Centre, Sweden, 1972)
[x] *International Development Review* (Society for International Development, 1973-1982; continued as *Development:Seeds of Change*, #126)
111. *World Development* (Pergamon, 1973)
112. *Journal of Energy and Development* (U of Colorado, 1975)
113. *Population and Development Review* (Population Council-NYC, 1975)

114. *Cultural Survival Quarterly* (Cultural Survival Inc-Cambridge MA, 1976)
115. *Social Development Issues* (U of Iowa School of Social Work, 1977)
116. *IFDA Dossier* (International Foundation for Development Alternatives-Nyon, Switzerland, 1977)
117. *Review* (Fernand Braudel Center, SUNY-Binghamton/Sage Publications, 1977)
118. *The World Economy* (Basil Blackwell, 1978)
119. *Mazingira: The International Journal for Environment and Development* (Tycooly International-Ireland, 1979)
120. *Third World Planning Review* (Liverpool U, 1979)
121. *Third World Quarterly* (London, 1979)
122. *World Bank Research News* (Washington, 1980)
123. *Journal of Development Research and Policy* (Washington, 1981)
124. *Population Policy* (de Gruyter, 1981)
125. *Population Research and Policy Review* (Elsevier, 1982)
126. *Development Seeds of Change* (Society for International Development, 1983; continuation of *International Development Review*)
127. *Public Enterprise* (International Center for Public Enterprise/Kumarian Press, 1983?; on role of public sector in developing countries)
128. *OECD Economic Studies* (OECD-Paris, 1983 biannual)
129. *Development Policy Review* (Overseas Development Institute-London/Sage Publications, 1983)
130. *International Political Economy Yearbook* (International Studies Association/Westview, 1984)

C. **Defense and Disarmament**

131. *Bulletin of the Atomic Scientists* (Chicago, 1945)
132. *Survival* (International Institute for Strategic Studies-London, 1959)
133. *Peace Research Abstracts Journal* (International Peace Research Assn, Dundas, Ont., Canada, 1964)
134. *Journal of Peace Research* (International Peace Research Institute-Norway, 1964)
135. *Cooperation and Conflict: Nordic Journal of International Politics* (Universitetsforlaget-Oslo, 1965)
136. *Bulletin of Peace Proposals* (IPRI-Norway, 1970)
137. *Strategic Review* (US Strategic Institute-Washington, 1973)
 [x] *Journal of Peace Studies* (Peace Science Society, 1974; continued as *Conflict Management and Peace Science*, #146)
138. *Peace and Change: A Journal of Peace Research* (Kent State U, 1975)
139. *Armed Forces and Society* (Seven Locks Press-Cabin John MD, 1975)
140. *International Security* (Harvard/MIT-Cambridge MA, 1976)
141. *Comparative Strategy* (Crane, Russak-NYC, 1978)
142. *Conflict: An International Journal for Conflict and Policy Studies* (Crane, Russak-NYC, 1978)
143. *Terrorism* (Crane, Russak-NYC, 1978)
144. *AEI Foreign Policy and Defense Review* (American Enterprise Institute-Washington, 1979)
145. *Arms Control* (Frank Cass, 1980)
146. *Conflict Management and Peace Science* (Peace Science Society, SUNY-Binghamton, 1981; continuation of *Journal of Peace Studies*)
147. *Nuclear Times* (298 Fifth Ave, NYC 10001; 1983)
148. *The International Security Yearbook* (CSIS-Georgetown U/St. Martin's, 1984 annual)
149. *International Journal on World Peace* (Professors World Peace Academy, Box 1311, NYC 10116; 1984)

D. **Environment / Resources / Energy**

150. *Journal of Soil and Water Conservation* (1958)
151. *Environment* (Heldref Publications-Washington, 1959)
152. *Resources* (Resources for the Future-Washington, 1959)
153. *Alternatives: Perspectives on Society, Technology & Environment* (Faculty of Environmental Studies, U of Waterloo, Canada, 1971; formerly *Alternatives: Journal of Friends of the Earth, Canada*)
154. *The Ecologist: Journal of the Post Industrial Age* (Cornwall-UK, 1971)
155. *Ambio* (Royal Swedish Academy of Sciences/Pergamon, 1972)
156. *Boston College Environmental Affairs Law Review* (1972)
157. *Outlook on Agriculture* (Pergamon, 1972)
158. *Energy Policy* (Butterworths-UK, 1973)
159. *Ocean Development and International Law* (Crane, Russak-NYC, 1973)
160. *Energy Systems and Policy* (Crane, Russak-NYC, 1974)
161. *Environmental Policy and Law* (Elsevier Sequoia, 1974)
162. *Resources Policy* (Butterworths-UK, 1974)
163. *Environment International* (Pergamon, 1975)
164. *Food Policy* (Butterworths-UK, 1976)
165. *Natural Resources Forum* (United Nations/Graham & Trotman-London, 1976)
166. *Marine Policy* (Butterworths-UK, 1977)
167. *Materials and Society* (Pergamon, 1977)
168. *Forest Ecology and Management* (Elsevier, 1978)
169. *Conservation & Recycling* (Pergamon, 1978)
170. *Amicus Journal* (Natural Resources Defense Council-NYC, 1979)
171. *The Energy Journal* (International Assn of Energy Economists/Oelgeschlager, Gunn & Hain, 1980)
172. *Environmental Impact Assessment Review* (Plenum, 1980)
173. *The Environmentalist* (Elsevier Sequoia, 1981)
174. *The Environmental Forum* (Environmental Law Institute, Washington, 1982)
175. *Agriculture and Human Values* (U of Florida Humanities and Agriculture Program, 1984)
176. *Land Use Policy* (Butterworths-UK, 1984)
177. *Journal of the World Resources Institute* (Washington, 1984 annual)
178. *World Resources Report* (World Resources Institute/International Institute for Environment and Development, 1985 annual)
179. *Food, Agriculture, and Resource Policy Review* (Resources for the Future, Washington; 1985 annual)

E. **Economics and Business**

180. *Harvard Business Review* (Harvard U, 1922)
181. *Managerial Planning* (Planning Executives Institute, Oxford, Ohio; 1952)
182. *Challenge: The Magazine of Economic Affairs* (M.E. Sharpe-White Plains NY, 1958)
183. *Columbia Journal of World Business* (Columbia U, 1966)
184. *Journal of Economic Issues* (Association for Evolutionary Economics, California State U-Sacramento, 1967)
185. *Socio-Economic Planning Sciences* (Pergamon, 1967)
186. *Journal of Consumer Affairs* (American Council on Consumer Interests, 1968)
187. *Long-Range Planning* (Oxford U/Pergamon, 1968)

188. *Review of Radical Political Economics* (Union of Radical Political Economists, 1969)
189. *Business and Society Review* (Warren, Gorham & Lamont, 1972)
190. *Planning Review* (North American Society for Corporate Planning, 1973)
191. *The Review of Black Political Economy* (Transaction, 1973)
192. *Accounting, Organization, and Society* (Pergamon, 1976)
193. *Looking Ahead and Projection Highlights* (National Planning Association-Washington, 1976)
194. *AEI Economist* (American Enterprise Institute-Washington, 1978)
195. *Journal of Consumer Policy* (D. Reidel, 1978)
196. *Journal of Post-Keynesian Economics* (M.E. Sharpe, 1978)
197. *Economic and Industrial Democracy* (Sage, 1980)
198. *The Journal of Business Strategy* (Warren, Gorham & Lamont, 1981)
199. *Human Systems Management* (Elsevier, 1981)
200. *Journal of Macromarketing* (U of Colorado, 1981)
201. *Contemporary Policy Issues* (Western Economic Association International, 1982)
202. *Journal of Business Forecasting* (Graceway Publishing-Flushing NY, 1982)
203. *Indian Review of Management and Future* (Recorder Press-New Delhi, 1983)
204. *New Management* (USC Graduate School of Business Administration, 1983)
205. *The Journal of Product Innovation Management* (Elsevier/North-Holland, 1984)
206. *Information Strategy: The Executive's Journal* (Auerbach Publishers, Boston; 1984)
207. *Economic Modelling* (Butterworths-UK, 1985)

F. Government / Justice / Law

208. *Public Administration Review* (American Society for Public Administration, 1941)
209. *Public Choice* (Martinus Nijhoff, 1943)
210. *National Tax Journal* (National Tax Association/Tax Institute of America-Columbia OH, 1948)
211. *Crime and Delinquency* (National Council on Crime and Delinquency/Sage, 1955)
212. *The Howard Journal of Criminal Justice* (The Howard League-London/Basil Blackwell, 1962)
213. *The Washington Monthly* (Washington, 1969)
214. *Publius: The Journal of Federalism* (Temple U, 1971)
215. *Journal of Voluntary Action Research* (Transaction Periodicals Consortium, 1972)
216. *Public Finance Quarterly* (Sage, 1973)
217. *Regulation* (American Enterprise Institute, 1977)
218. *Journal of Crime and Justice* (Midwestern Criminal Justice Association/Anderson, 1978)
219. *Police Studies* (Anderson, 1978)
220. *Citizen Participation* (Tufts U, 1979)
221. *Law and Policy Quarterly* (Baldy Center for Law and Social Policy, SUNY-Buffalo/Basil Blackwell, 1979)
222. *Public Budgeting and Finance* (ASPA/Transaction, 1981)
223. *Yale Journal on Regulation* (Yale U, 1983)
224. *Justice Quarterly* (Academy of Criminal Justice Sciences, 1984)
225. *Negotiation Journal: On the Process of Dispute Settlement* (Harvard Program on Negotiation/Plenum, 1985)

G. Cities / Housing / Transport

226. *National Civic Review* (National Municipal League-NYC, 1911)
227. *State Government* (The Council of State Governments, Lexington KY, 1928)
228. *Journal of the American Planning Association* (Chicago, 1934)
229. *Planning* (American Planning Association-Chicago, 1935)
230. *Ekistics* (Athens Center of Ekistics, 1937)
[x] *Traffic Quarterly* (Eno Foundation-Westport CT, 1946-1982; continued as *Transportation Quarterly*, #240)
231. *Progress in Planning* (Pergamon, 1960)
232. *Urban Affairs Quarterly* (Sage, 1964)
233. *Growth and Change: A Journal of Public, Urban, and Regional Policy* (U of Kentucky, 1970)
234. *Urban Institute Policy and Research Report* (Washington, 1970)
235. *Habitat International* (Pergamon, 1977)
236. *Ways and Means* (Conference on Alternative State and Local Policies-Washington, 1978)
237. *The Urban Interest* (U of Kansas, 1979)
238. *Transportation Policy and Decision Making* (Nijhoff, 1980)
239. *Journal of Community Action* (Center for Responsive Governance-Washington, 1982)
240. *Transportation Quarterly* (Eno Foundation-Westport CT, 1983; continuation of *Traffic Quarterly*)
241. *Cities* (Butterworths-UK, 1983)
242. *Land Use Policy* (Butterworths-UK, 1984)

H. Health

243. *Milbank Memorial Fund Quarterly: Health and Society* (MIT Press, 1922)
244. *Perspectives in Biology and Medicine* (U of Chicago, 1957)
245. *Inquiry: The Journal of Health Organization, Provision and Financing* (Blue Cross Association-Chicago, 1964)
246. *Aging and Work* (National Council on Aging, 1969)
247. *Family Planning Perspectives* (Alan Guttmacher Institute, 1969)
248. *The Hastings Center Report* (Institute of Society, Ethics, and the Life Sciences, 1971)
249. *Journal of Health Policy, Politics, and Law* (Duke U, 1976)
250. *American Journal of Health Planning* (1976; discontinued??)
251. *Child Abuse and Neglect* (Pergamon, 1977)
252. *Holistic Health Review* (Human Sciences Press, 1977)
253. *Health Policy and Education* (Elsevier, 1979)
254. *Health Care for Women International* (Hemisphere Publishing Corp-Washington, 1980; formerly *Issues in Health Care for Women*)
255. *Journal of Public Health Policy* (South Burlington VT, 1980)
256. *Health and Medicine* (Health and Medicine Policy Research Group-Chicago, 1981)
257. *Health Policy Quarterly* (Human Sciences Press, 1981)
258. *Health Affairs* (Project HOPE-Millwood VA, 1982)
259. *"Psychology in the Public Forum" section of American Psychologist* (American Psychological Association-Washington, 1982; journal initiated in 1945)
260. *Politics and the Life Sciences* (Northern Illinois U, 1982)

I. **Education**

261. *Teachers College Record* (Columbia U, 1899)
262. *Phi Delta Kappan* (Bloomington IN, 1906)
263. *Journal of Higher Education* (1930)
264. *Educational Leadership* (Assn for Supervision and Curriculum Development, 1953)
265. *Change: The Magazine of Higher Learning* (Heldref Publications-Washington, 1969)
266. *Review of Higher Education* (Association for the Study of Higher Education, 1977)

J. **Communications**

267. *Journal of Communication* (Annenberg School-U of Pennsylvania, 1951)
268. *InterMedia* (International Institute of Communications-London, 1973)
269. *Telecommunications Policy* (Butterworths-UK, 1977)
270. *Journal of Community Communications* (Berkeley CA, 1978)
271. *Media, Culture & Society* (Sage Publications, London, 1979)
272. *Channels of Communications* (Media Commentary Council-NYC, 1981)
273. *The Information Society Journal* (Crane, Russak-NYC, 1981)
274. *Information Age* (Butterworths-UK, 1983)
275. *Information Economics and Policy* (North Holland, 1983)
276. *Telematics and Informatics* (Pergamon, 1984)

K. **Science and Technology**

277. *Science* (American Assn for the Advancement of Science, 1880)
278. *Technology Review* (MIT, 1899)
279. *BioScience* (American Institute of Biological Sciences-Arlington VA, 1951)

280. *Impact of Science on Society* (UNESCO-Paris, 1951)
281. *New Scientist* (London, 1956)
282. *The Sciences* (New York Academy of Sciences, 1961)
283. *IEEE Spectrum* (Institute of Electrical and Electronic Engineers-NYC, 1964)
284. *Zygon: Journal of Religion and Science* (1966)
285. *Research Policy* (North-Holland, 1972)
286. *Interdisciplinary Science Reviews* (Wiley Heyden, 1973)
287. *Science and Public Policy: The Journal of the Science Policy Foundation* (Beech Tree Publishing, Guildford UK; 1974)
288. *Science, Technology, and Human Values* (Harvard-MIT/Wiley, 1975)
289. *Interciencia: Journal of Science and Technology of the Americas* (Interciencia Assn/Pergamon, 1976)
290. *Journal of Technology Transfer* (Technology Transfer Society-Los Angeles CA, 1976 biannual)
291. *Outlook on Science Policy* (1979)
292. *Technology in Society* (Pergamon, 1979)
293. *Bulletin of Science, Technology, and Society* (STS Press, Materials Research Lab, Univ. Park PA; 1981)
294. *High Technology* (38 Commercial Wharf-Boston, 1981)
295. *Technovation: An International Journal of Technical Innovation and Entrepreneurship* (Elsevier, 1982)
296. *IEEE Technology and Society Magazine* (IEEE Society on Social Implications of Technology, 1982)
297. *Bio/Technology* (1983)
298. *Prometheus: Technological Change and Science Policy* (U of Queensland-Australia, 1983)
299. *Issues in Science and Technology* (National Academy of Sciences-Washington, 1984)
300. *Space Policy* (Butterworths-UK, 1985)

III. **DEFUNCT JOURNALS**

301. *World Unity Magazine* (New York, 1927-1935?)
302. *Free America* (New York, 1937-1947)
303. *Main Currents in Modern Thought* (Center for Integrative Education-New Rochelle NY, 1940-1974)
304. *The Land* (Friends of the Land-Baltimore MD, 1941-1948)
305. *Common Cause: A Journal of One World* (Committee to Frame a World Constitution, U of Chicago, 1947-1951?)
306. *War/Peace Report* (Gordon & Breach, 1960-1973?)
307. *World Union* (Pondicherry, India, 1961-19??)
308. *Systematics: The Journal of the Institute for the Comparative Study of History, Philosophy, and the Sciences* (Cheltenham UK, 1962-1974?)
309. *Technology + Society* (U of Bath-UK, 1963-1973)
310. *Human Potential* (Philadelphia, 1967-1970)
311. *Fields Within Fields* (World Institute Council-NYC, 1968-1974)
312. *Futurology and Philosophy of Technology* (Israel, 1968-1969?)
313. *Notes on the Future of Education* (Educational Policy Research Center, Syracuse U Research Corporation, 1969-1972)
314. *PHP: A Forum for a Better World* (PHP Institute-Tokyo, 1970-1975?)
315. *Social Forecasting Abstracts* (IRADES-Rome, 1970-1975)
316. *New Priorities* (Gordon & Breach, 1971-1972)

317. *Prometheus* (Archives of Institutional Change-Washington, 1971-1972)
318. *Technology Assessment* (International Society for Technology Assessment, 1972-1977)
319. *Working Papers for a New Society* (Cambridge MA, 1974-1983)
320. *Futurology* (Switzerland, c1975)
321. *Yearbook of World Problems and Human Development* (Union of International Associations-Brussels, 1975) [NOTE: Only one issue published, but new edition announced for 1985.]
322. *Alternative Futures: The Journal of Utopian Studies* (RPI/U of Michigan, 1977-1982)
323. *Canadian Futures: A Journal of Technological Forecasting and Applied Futures Research* (Institute for Canadian Futures-Mississauga, Ontario, 1978)
324. *The Ecologist Quarterly* (Cornwall UK, 1978)
325. *Inquiry: A Libertarian Review* (Washington, 1978-1984)
326. *Journal of Social Reconstruction* (Institute for Policy Studies/Earl M. Coleman, 1980)
327. *Next* (New York, 1980-1982)
328. *Man, Environment, Space & Time* (World Research Center, 1430 Mass. Ave., Cambridge MA; 1980-1981)
329. *democracy: A Journal of Political Renewal and Social Change* (New York, 1981-1983)
330. *Global Futures Digest* (Global Futures Network, Toronto; 1983-1984)

BOOK PUBLISHERS

The following publishers issued at least one futures-relevant book or report
abstracted in **Future Survey Annual 1985** or **Future Survey Annual 1984**:

Ablex Publishing Co, 355 Chestnut Street,
Norwood, NJ 07648.

Abt books, 55 Wheeler Street, Cambridge MA 02138.

Academic Press, 111 Fifth Ave, New York NY 10003.

Acropolis Books, 2400 17th Street NW,
Washington DC 20009.

Addison-Wesley, Jacob Way, Reading MA 01867.

Allanheld, Osmun & Co, 81 Adams Drive,
Totowa NJ 07511.

Allen & Unwin Inc, 9 Winchester Terrace,
Winchester MA 01890.

AMACOM, American Management Association,
135 50th Street, New York NY 10020.

American Enterprise Institute for Policy Research,
1150 17th Street NW, Washington DC 20036.

American Management Associations (see AMACOM)

Artech House Inc, 610 Washington Street,
Dedham MA 02026.

Aspen Systems Corp, PO Box 6018,
Gaithersburg MD 20760.

Atheneum Publishers, 597 Fifth Ave, New York NY 10017.

Auburn House Publishing Co, 14 Dedham Street,
Boston MA 02030.

Ballinger Publishing Co, 54 Church Street,
Cambridge MA 02138.

Bantam Books, 666 Fifth Ave, New York NY 10019.

Basic Books, 10 East 53rd Street, New York NY 10022.

Basil Blackwell, 432 Park Ave South, Suite 1505,
New York NY 10016.

Beacon Press, 25 Beacon Street, Boston MA 02108.

Beaufort Books, 9 East 40th Street, New York NY 10016.

Bergin & Garvey Publishers, 670 Amherst Road,
South Hadley MA 01075.

Black Rose Books, 3981 Blvd St Laurent,
Montreal, Quebec H2W 1Y5 Canada.

Books in Focus, 160 East 38th Street, Suite 31B,
New York NY 10016.

Bobbs-Merrill Co, 4300 West 62nd Street,
Indianapolis IN 46206.

Boyd & Fraser Publishing Co, 3627 Sacramento Street,
San Francisco CA 94118.

Brick House Publishing Co, 34 Essex Street,
Andover MA 01810.

Brookings Institution, 1775 Massachusetts Ave NW,
Washington DC 20036.

Butterworth Scientific Ltd, PO Box 63, Westbury House,
Bury Street, Guilford, Surrey GU2 5BH, England.

Cambridge University Press, 32 East 57th Street,
New York NY 10022.

Cato Institute, 224 Second Street SE,
Washington DC 20003.

Center for Urban Policy Research, Rutgers University,
PO Box 489, Piscataway NJ 08854.

Columbia University Press, 562 West 113th Street,
New York NY 10025. [Address orders to
136 S. Broadway, Irvington-on-Hudson NY 10533.]

Committee for Economic Development, 477 Madison Ave,
New York NY 10022.

Conference on Alternative State and Local Policies,
2000 Florida Ave NW, Washington DC 20009.

Congressional Quarterly Inc, 1414 22nd Street NW,
Washington DC 20037.

Conservation Foundation, 1255 23rd Street NW,
Washington DC 20037.

Cornell University Press, 124 Roberts Place,
Ithaca NY 14850.

Council of State Planning Agencies,
400 North Capitol Street, Washington DC 20001.

Council on Economic Priorities, 84 Fifth Ave,
New York NY 10011.

Council on Foreign Relations, 58 East 68th Street,
New York NY 10021. [Publications distributed by
McGraw-Hill.]

Crane, Russak & Co, 3 East 44th Street,
New York NY 10017.

Croom Helm, 51 Washington Street, Dover NH 03820.

Crown Publishers, 1 Park Ave, New York NY 10016.

David & Charles, North Pomfret VT 05053.

Dell Publishing Co/Delta Books, 1 Dag Hammarskjold
Plaza, New York NY 10017.

Devin-Adair Co, 6 North Water Street,
Greenwich CT 06830.

Marcel Dekker Inc, 270 Madison Ave,
New York NY 10016.

Dodd, Mead & Co, 79 Madison Avenue,
New York NY 10016.

Doubleday & Co, 501 Franklin Ave,
Garden City NY 11530.

Duke University Press, 6697 College Station,
Durham NC 27708.

E.P. Dutton, 2 Park Ave, New York NY 10016.

Earthscan (see International Institute for
Environment and Development)

Elsevier North Holland Inc, 52 Vanderbilt Ave,
New York NY 10017.

Facts on File, 460 Park Avenue South,
New York NY 10016.

Free Press, 866 Third Ave, New York NY 10022.

Freedom House, 20 West 40th Street,
New York NY 10018.

W.H. Freeman & Co, 41 Madison Ave,
New York NY 10010.

Gale Research Co, Book Tower, Detroit MI 48226.

Greenwood Press, 51 Riverside Ave, Westport CT 06880.

Halsted Press, c/o John Wiley & Sons, 605 Third Ave,
New York NY 10016.

Harcourt Brace Jovanovitch, 1250 Sixth Avenue,
San Diego CA 92101.

Harper & Row, 10 East 53rd Street, New York NY 10022.

Harvard University Press, 79 Garden Street,
Cambridge MA 02138.

Health Administration Press, M2240 School of Public
Health, University of Michigan, Ann Arbor MI 48109.

Heritage Foundation, 513 C Street NE,
Washington DC 20002.

Lawrence Hill & Co, 520 Riverside Ave, Westport CT 06880.

Holmes & Meier, 30 Irving Place, New York NY 10003.

Holt, Rinehart & Winston, 521 Fifth Ave,
New York NY 10175.

Hoover Institution Press, Stanford University,
Stanford CA 94305.

Houghton Mifflin Co, 2 Park Street, Boston MA 02107.

Human Sciences Press, 72 Fifth Ave, New York NY 10011.

Indiana University Press, Tenth & Morton Streets,
Bloomington IN 47401.

Institute for Contemporary Studies, 785 Market Street,
Suite 750, San Francisco CA 94103.

Institute for Food and Development Policy,
1885 Mission Street, San Francisco CA 94103.

Institute for Foreign Policy Analysis,
675 Massachusetts Ave, Cambridge MA 02139.

Institute for Local Self-Reliance, 1717 18th Street NW,
Washington DC 20009.

Institute for Policy Studies, 1901 Q Street NW,
Washington DC 20009.

Institute for Research On Public Policy, 3535 Queen Mary
Road, Montreal, Quebec H3V 1H8, Canada
(US distributors: Renouf USA, Brookfield VT 05036).

Institute for the Study of Human Issues, 3401 Market
Suite 252, Philadelphia PA 19104.

Intermediate Technology Development Group of North
America, PO Box 337, Croton-on-Hudon NY 10520.

International Institute for Environment and Development
(Earthscan), 1717 Massachusetts Avenue NW,
Washington DC 20036.

Iowa State University Press, 2121 South State Ave,
112C Press Office, Ames IA 50010.

IPC Science and Technology Press Ltd,
(see Butterworth Scientific, Ltd.)

JAI Press, 36 Sherwood Place, Greenwich CT 06836.

Johns Hopkins University Press, Baltimore MD 21218.

Jossey-Bass Publishers, 433 California Street,
San Francisco CA 94104.

William Kaufmann, Inc., 95 First Street,
Los Altos CA 94022.

Alfred A. Knopf, 201 E. 50th Street, New York NY 10022.

Knowledge Industry Publications, 701 Westchester Ave,
White Plains NY 10604.

Kumarian Press, 630 Oakwood Ave, Suite 119,
West Hartford CT 06110.

Lewis Publishers, 121 South Main Street,
Chelsea MI 48118.

Lexington Books, D.C. Heath & Co, 125 Spring Street,
Lexington MA 02173.

Little, Brown & Co, 34 Beacon Street, Boston MA 02106.

Lomond Publications, PO Box 88, Mt. Airy MD 21771.

Longman Inc, 19 West 44th Street, Suite 1012,
New York NY 10036.

Louisiana State University Press, Baton Rouge LA 70803.

Macmillan Publishing Co, 866 Third Ave,
New York NY 10022.

Manchester University Press, 51 Washington Street,
Dover NH 03820.

Mayfield Publishing, 285 Hamilton Ave,
Palo Alto CA 94301.

McGraw-Hill Book Co, 1221 Ave of the Americas,
New York NY 10020.

Methuen Inc, 29 West 35th Street, New York NY 10001.

MIT Press, 28 Carleton Street, Cambridge MA 02142.

Monthly Review Press, 62 West 14th Street,
New York NY 10011.

William Morrow & Co, 105 Madison Ave,
New York NY 10016.

National Academy of Sciences, Printing and
Publishing Office, 2101 Constitution Ave,
Washington DC 20418.

New American Library, Times Mirror Co,
1633 Broadway, New York NY 10019.

New Society Publications, 4722 Baltimore Ave,
Philadelphia PA 19143.

New York University Press, 21 West Fourth Street,
New York NY 10012.

Nichols Publishing Co, P.O. Box 96, New York NY 10024.

North Point Press, 850 Talbot Ave, Berkeley CA 94706.

W. W. Norton & Co, 500 Fifth Ave, New York NY 10036.

Oceana Publications, 75 Main Street,
Dobbs Ferry NY 10522.

OECD Publications, Organization for Economic Cooperation & Development, 1750-E Pennsylvania Ave NW,
Washington DC 20006.

Oelgeschlager, Gunn & Hain, 1278 Massachusetts Ave,
Cambridge MA 02138.

Oxford University Press, 200 Madison Ave,
New York NY 10016.

Pacific Institute for Public Policy Research,
177 Post Street, San Francisco CA 94108.

Pantheon Books, 201 East 50th Street,
New York NY 10022.

Penguin Books, 625 Madison Ave, New York NY 10022.

Pergamon Press, Maxwell House, Fairview Park,
Elmsford NY 10523.

Petrocelli Books, 1101 State Road, Princeton NJ 08540.

The Pilgrim Press, 132 West 31st Street,
New York NY 10001.

Planner's Press, American Planning Assn,
1313 East 60th Street, Chicago IL 60637.

Plenum Publishers, 233 Spring Street,
New York NY 10013.

Pocket Books, 1230 Avenue of the Americas,
New York NY 10020.

Policy Studies Organization, 361 Lincoln Hall,
University of Illinois, Urbana IL 61801.

Praeger Special Studies, 521 Fifth Ave,
New York NY 10017.

Prentice-Hall, Englewood Cliffs NJ 07632.

Princeton University Press, 41 William Street,
Princeton NJ 08540.

Prometheus Books, 700 East Amherst Street,
Buffalo NY 14215.

G. P. Putnam's, 200 Madison Ave, New York NY 10016.

Random House, 201 East 50th Street, New York NY 10022.

Rawson Associates, 597 Fifth Ave, New York NY 10017.

Lynne Rienner Publishers Inc., 948 North Street,
#8, Boulder CO 80302.

Rodale Press Inc, 33 East Minor Street, Emmaus PA 18049.

Routledge & Kegan Paul, 9 Park Street, Boston MA 02108.

Russell Sage Foundation, 112 East 64th Street,
New York NY 10021.

Rutgers University Press, 30 College Ave,
New Brunswick NJ 08903.

Sage Publications, 275 South Beverly Drive,
Beverly Hills CA 90212.

Schenkman Publishing Co, 190 Concord Avenue,
Cambridge MA 02138.

Schocken Books, 62 Cooper Square, New York NY 10003.

Charles Scribner's Sons, 597 Fifth Ave,
New York NY 10017.

Seabury Press, 815 Second Ave, New York NY 10017.

Seven Locks Press, PO Box 72, Cabin John MD 20818.

Shambhala Publications, Box 308, Boston MA 02117.

M.E. Sharpe, 80 Business Park Drive, Armonk NY 10504.

Sierra Club Books, 730 Polk Street,
San Francisco CA 94109.

Simon & Schuster, 1230 Sixth Ave, New York NY 10020.

South End Press, 116 St. Botolph Street,
Boston, MA 02115.

St. Martin's Press, 175 Fifth Ave, New York NY 10010.

Stackpole Books, Cammeron & Keller Streets,
Harrisburg PA 17105.

Stanford University Press, Stanford CA 94305.

Stanley Foundation, 420 East 3rd Street,
Muscatine IA 52761.

State University of New York Press,
State University Plaza, Albany NY 12246.

Stein & Day, Scarborough House,
Briarcliff Manor Ny 10510.

Syracuse University Press, 1011 East Water Street,
Syracuse NY 13210.

J.P. Tarcher Inc, 9110 Sunset Blvd,
Los Angeles CA 90069.

Taylor & Francis, Inc., 242 Cherry Street,
Philadelphia PA 19106.

Temple University Press, Philadelphia PA 19122.

Texas A & M University Press, Drawer "C",
College Station TX 77843.

Times Books, 201 East 50th Street, New York NY 10022.

Transaction Books, Rutgers University,
New Brunswick NJ 08903.

Tycooly International, 6 Crofton Terrace,
Dun Laoghaire, Dublin, Ireland.

Unipub, 345 Park Ave South, New York NY 10010.

United Nations Publications, Room DC2-853,
New York NY 10017.

United States Government Printing Office,
c/o Superintendent of Documents, USGPO,
Washington DC 20402.

Universe Books, 381 Park Ave South, New York NY 10016.

University of Alabama Press, Box 2877,
University AL 35486.

University of California Press, 2120 Berkeley Way,
Berkeley CA 94720.

University of Chicago Press, 5801 South Ellis Avenue,
Chicago IL 60637.

University of Illinois Press, 54 East Gregory Drive,
Champaign IL 61820.

University of Massachusetts Press, PO Box 429,
Amherst MA 01002.

University of Michigan Press, PO Box 1104,
Ann Arbor MI 48106.

University of Minnesota Press, 2037 University Ave SE,
Minneapolis MN 55455.

University of Nebraska Press, 901 N 17th Street,
Lincoln NE 68588.

University of North Carolina Press, PO Box 2288,
Chapel Hill NC 27514.

University of Notre Dame Press, Nortre Dame IN 46556.

University of Oklahoma Press, 1005 Asp Ave,
Norman OK 73019.

University of Pennsylvania Press, 3933 Walnut Street,
Philadelphia PA 19104.

University of Pittsburgh Press, 127 North
Bellefield Avenue, Pittsburgh PA 15260.

University of Texas Press, PO Box 7819,
University Station, Austin TX 78712.

University of Toronto Press, Toronto Ontario,
Canada (in US: 33 East Tupper Street,
Buffalo NY 14203).

University of Washington Press, Seattle WA 98105.

University Press of America, 4720 Boston Way,
Lanham MD 20706.

University Press of Hawaii, 2840 Kolowalu Street,
Honolulu HI 96822.

University Press of Kentucky, Lexington KY 40506.

University Press of New England, 3 Lebanon Street,
Hanover NH 03755.

W.E. Upjohn Institute, 300 S. Westnedge Ave,
Kalamazoo Mi 49007.

The Urban Institute, 2100 M Street NW,
Washington DC 20037.

Van Nostrand Reinhold, 135 West 59th Street,
New York NY 10020.

Vanier Institute of the Family, 151 Slater Street,
Ottawa, Ontario, Canada K1P 5H3.

Viking Press Inc, 40 West 23rd Street,
New York NY 10010.

Warner Books,, c/o Independent News Co,
75 Rockefeller Plaza, New York NY 10019.

Franklin Watts Inc, c/o Grolier Inc, 730 Fifth Ave,
New York NY 10019.

Westview Press, 5500 Central Ave, Boulder CO 80301.

John Wiley & Sons, 605 Third Ave, New York NY 10016.

Work in America Institute Inc, 700 White Plains Road,
Scarsdale NY 10583.

Workman Publishing Co., One West 39th Street,
New York NY 10018.

World Future Society, 4916 St. Elmo Ave,
Bethesda MD 20814.

World Priorities, Inc., PO Box 25140,
Washington DC 20007.

World Resources Institute Publications,
1735 New York Ave NW, Washington DC 20006.

Worldwatch Institute, 1776 Massachusetts Ave NW,
Washington DC 20036.

Yale University Press, 92A Yale Station,
New Haven CT 06520.

Selected Periodical Publishers

The following journals, magazines, and newspapers published at least one futures-relevant article abstracted in **Future Survey Annual 1985** or **Future Survey Annual 1984**.

Also see Appendix 2 for a chronological and categorized listing of 330 futures-relevant and policy-relevant journals. Most of the articles in most of the 300 active journals were too narrow in scope to be considered for abstracting in *Future Survey*, but access to these specialized journals may be of interest to some researchers.

Across the Board. The Conference Board, 845 Third Ave, New York NY 10022.

Alternatives: A Journal of World Policy. World Policy Institute, 777 UN Plaza, New York NY 10017.

Ambio: A Journal of the Human Environment. Royal Swedish Academy of Sciences/Pergamon Press, Fairview Park, Elmsford NY 10523.

American Behavioral Scientist. Sage Publications, 275 S. Beverly Drive, Beverly Hills CA 90212.

American Demographics. Dow Jones & Co, PO Box 68, Ithaca NY 14850.

American Planning Association Journal. American Planning Association, 1776 Massachusetts Ave NW, Washington DC 20036.

American Political Science Review. American Political Science Association, 1527 New Hampshire Ave NW, Washington DC 20036.

American Psychologist. American Psychological Association, 1200 17th Street NW, Washington DC 20036.

American Scholar. Phi Beta Kappa, 1811 Q Street NW, Washington DC 20009.

American Scientist. Sigma Xi, The Scientific Research Society, 345 Whitney Ave, New Haven CT 06511.

The Annals of the American Academy of Political and Social Science. AAPSS, Philadelphia/Sage Publications, 275 S. Beverly Drive, Beverly Hills CA 90212.

The Atlantic Monthly. 8 Arlington Street, Boston MA 02116.

Atlantic Community Quarterly. The Atlantic Council of the United States, 1616 H Street NW, Washington DC 20006.

BioScience. American Institute of Biological Sciences, 1401 Wilson Blvd, Arlington VA 22209.

Boston College Environmental Affairs Law Review. Boston College Law School, 885 Center Street, Newton Center MA 02159.

Bulletin of the Atomic Scientists. 1020-24 East 58th Street, Chicago IL 60637.

Business and Society Review. Warren, Gorham & Lamont, 870 Seventh Ave, New York NY 10019.

Business Horizons. Graduate School of Business, Indiana University, Bloomington IN 47405.

Business Week. McGraw-Hill, 1221 Ave of the Americas, New York NY 10020.

California Management Review. Graduate School of Business Administration, University of California, Berkeley CA 94720.

Canadian Public Policy. University of Guelph, Arts Bldg, Room 039, Guelph, Ontario N1G 2W1 Canada.

The Center Magazine. Center for the Study of Democratic Institutions, University of California, Box 4068, Santa Barbara CA 93103.

Ceres: FAO Review on Agriculture & Development. Food and Agriculture Organization, Via delle Terme di Caracalla, 00100 Rome, Italy.

Challenge: The Magazine of Economic Affairs. M.E. Sharpe Inc., 901 North Broadway, White Plains NY 10603.

Change: The Magazine of Higher Learning. Heldref Publications, 4000 Albemarle Street NW, Washington DC 20016.

Channels of Communications. Media Commentary Council, 1515 Broadway, New York NY 10036.

Commentary. American Jewish Committee, 165 East 65th Street, New York NY 10022.

Daedalus: Journal of the American Academy of Arts and Sciences. Harvard University, 7 Linden Street, Cambridge MA 02138.

Development: Seeds of Change, Village through Global Order. Society for International Development, Palazzo Civilta del Lavoro, 00144 Rome, Italy.

Dissent. 505 Fifth Ave, New York NY 10017.

The Ecologist: Journal of the Post Industrial Age. 73 Molesworth Street, Wadebridge, Cornwall PL27 7DS, England.

Ekistics. Athens Center of Ekistics, PO Box 471, Athens, Greece.

Encounter. 59 St. Martin's Lane, London WC2N 4JS, England.

Energy Policy. Butterworth Scientific Ltd, PO Box 63, Westbury House, Bury Street, Guildford, Surrey GU2 5BH, England.

Environment. Heldref Publications, 4000 Albemarle Street NW, Washington DC 20016.

Food Policy. Butterworth Scientific Ltd, PO Box 63, Westbury House, Bury Street, Guildford, Surrey GU2 5BH, England.

Foreign Affairs. Council on Foreign Relations, 58 East 68th Street, New York NY 10021.

Foreign Policy. Carnegie Endowment for International Peace, 11 Dupont Circle, Washington DC 20036.

Fortune. Rockefeller Center, New York NY 10020.

Futures: The Journal of Planning and Forecasting. Butterworth Scientific Ltd, PO Box 63, Westbury House, Bury Street, Guidford, Surrey GU2 5BH, England.

Futures Research Quarterly. World Future Society, 4916 St. Elmo Ave, Bethesda MD 20814.

Futurics. Minnesota Futurists, 365 Summit Ave, St. Paul MN 55102.

The Futurist. World Future Society, 4916 St. Elmo Ave, Bethesda MD 20814.

Harper's. 2 Park Ave, New York NY 10016.

Harvard Business Review. Harvard University, Graduate School of Business Administration, Boston MA 02163.

Hastings Center Report. Institute of Society, Ethics and the Life Sciences, 360 Broadway, Hastings-on-Hudson NY 10706.

Health Affairs. Project HOPE, Millwood VA.

High Technology. 38 Commercial Wharf, Boston MA 02110.

The Humanist. American Humanist Association,
7 Harwood Drive, Amherst NY 14226.

IEEE Spectrum. Institute of Electrical and Electronics
Engineers, 345 East 47th Street, New York NY 10017.

IFDA Dossier. International Foundation for Development
Alternatives, 2 Place du Marche, CH-1260,
Nyon, Switzerland.

Impact of Science on Society. UNESCO,
7 Place de Fontenoy, 75700 Paris, France.

In Context: A Quarterly of Humane Sustainable Culture.
Context Foundation, PO Box 215, Sequim WA 98382.

The Information Society Journal. Crane, Russak & Co,
3 East 44th Street, New York NY 10023.

Inquiry: A Libertarian Review. 1320 G Street SE,
Washington DC 20003. [NOTE: Discontinued after
July 1984.]

Interdisciplinary Science Reviews. Wiley Heyden,
Spectrum House, Hillview Gardens, London
NW4 2JQ England.

InterMedia. International Institute of Communications,
Tavistock House East, Tavistock Square, London
WC1 9LG England.

International Labour Review. International Labour Office,
CH-1211, Geneva 22, Switzerland.

International Organization. University of Wisconsin Press,
114 North Murray Street, Madison WI 53715.

International Security. Harvard Center for Science and
International Affairs/MIT Press, Cambridge MA 02142.

International Social Science Journal. UNESCO,
7 Place de Fontenoy, 75700 Paris, France.

Journal of Communication. The Annenberg School of
Communications, University of Pennsylvania,
Philadelphia PA 19104.

Journal of Health Politics, Policy and Law. Dept of Health
Administration, Duke University, Durham NC 27710.

Journal of Peace Research. International Peace Research
Institute, Radhusgt 4, N-Oslo l, Norway.

Journal of Policy Analysis and Management.
Wiley-Interscience Journals, 605 Third Ave,
New York NY 10016.

*Journal of Policy Modeling: A Social Science Forum of
World Issues*. Society for Policy Modeling,
c/o Elsevier/ North-Holland, 52 Vanderbilt Ave,
New York NY 10017.

Journal of Post-Keynesian Economics. M.E. Sharpe,
901 North Broadway, White Plains NY 10603.

The Journal of the Institute for Socioeconomic Studies.
Airport Road, White Plains NY 10604.

Knowledge: Creation, Diffusion, Utilization.
Sage Publications, 275 South Beverly Drive,
Beverly Hills CA 90212.

Long Range Planning. The Administrative Staff College,
Henley-on-Thames, Oxon UK; Pergamon Press,
Fairview Park, Elmsford NY 10523.

Looking Ahead & Projection Highlights. National
Planning Association, 1606 New Hampshire Ave NW,
Washington DC 20009.

Marine Policy. Butterworth Scientific Ltd,
Westbury House, Bury Street, Guidford,
Surrey GU2 5BH, England.

*Mazingira: The International Journal of Environment and
Development*. Tycooly International, 6 Crofton Terrace,
Dun Laoghaire, Dublin, Ireland.

Milbank Memorial Fund Quarterly: Health and Society.
Milbank Memorial Fund, 1 East 75th Street,
New York NY 10021; MIT Press, Cambridge MA 02142.

Mother Jones. Foundation for National Progress,
625 Third Street, San Francisco CA 94107.

The Nation. 72 Fifth Ave, New York NY 10011.

National Civic Review. National Municipal League,
47 East 68th Street, New York NY 10011.

National Review. 150 East 35th Street,
New York NY 10016.

Nature. 4 Little Essex Street,
London WC2R 3LF, England.

New England Journal of Medicine. 10 Shattuck Street,
Boston MA 02115.

New Options. PO Box 19324, Washington DC 20036.

The New Republic. 1220 19th Street NW,
Washington DC 20036.

New Scientist. King's Reach Tower, Stamford Street,
London SE1 9LS, England.

New York Review of Books. 250 West 57th Street,
New York NY 10019.

The New York Times Magazine. 229 West 43rd Street,
New York NY 10036.

Newsweek. 444 Madison Ave, New York NY 10022.

Oceanus. Woods Hole Oceanographic Institute,
Woods Hole MA 02543.

OECD Observer. Organisation for Economic Cooperation
and Development, 2 rue Andre-Pascal, F75775
Paris, France.

Orbis. Foreign Policy Research Institute,
3508 Market Street, Suite 350, Philadelphia PA 19104.

Our Generation. 3981 Blvd Saint-Laurent,
Montreal, Quebec H2W 1Y5, Canada.

Perspectives on Biology and Medicine. University of
Chicago Press, 5801 Ellis Ave, Chicago IL 60637.

Phi Delta Kappan. Phi Delta Kappa, 8th and Union,
Bloomington IN 47402.

Philosophy and Public Affairs. Princeton University
Press, Box 231, Princeton NJ 08540.

Planning. American Planning Association, 1313 East
60th Street, Chicago IL 60637.

Planning Review. North American Society for Corporate
Planning, Bell PubliCom, 1406 Third National Bldg,
Dayton OH 45402.

Policy Review. The Heritage Foundation,
513 C Street NE, Washington DC 20002.

Policy Sciences. Elsevier Scientific Publishing Co,
Box 211, Amsterdam, The Netherlands.

Policy Studies Journal. Policy Sciences Program,
Florida State University; Policy Studies Organization,
361 Lincoln Hall, University of Illinois, Urbana IL 61801.

Policy Studies Review. Center for Public Affairs,
Arizona State University; Policy Studies Organization,
361 Lincoln Hall, University of Illinois, Urbana IL 61801.

Political Science Quarterly. Academy of Political Science,
619 West 114th Street, Suite 500, New York NY 10025.

*Polity: Journal of the Northeastern Political Science
Association*. Thompson Hall, University of Massachusetts, Amherst MA 01003.

Population Bulletin. Population Reference Bureau,
1337 Connecticut Ave NW, Washington DC 20036.

The Progressive. 408 West Gorham Street,
Madison WI 53703.

Psychology Today. One Park Ave, New York NY 10016.

Public Administration Review. American Society for Public Administration, 1225 Connecticut Ave NW, Washington DC 20036.

The Public Interest. 10 East 53rd Street, New York NY 10022.

Rain: Resources for Building Community. 1135 S.E. Salmon, Portland OR 97214.

Reason. PO Box 40105, Santa Barbara CA 93103.

Resurgence. Ford House, Hartland, Devon, England.

Science. American Association for the Advancement of Science, 1515 Massachusetts Ave NW, Washington DC 20005.

The Sciences. New York Academy of Sciences, 2 East 63rd Street, New York NY 10021.

Scientific American. 415 Madison Ave, New York NY 10017.

Social Indicators Research. D. Reidel Publishing Co, PO Box 17, 3300 AA, Dordrecht, The Netherlands.

Social Policy. 33 West 42nd Street, Room 1212, New York NY 10036.

Social Problems. Society for the Study of Social Problems, State University College, 1300 Elmwood Ave, Buffalo NY 14222.

Socialist Review. Center for Social Research and Education, 4228 Telegraph Ave, Oakland CA 94609.

Society. Transaction Periodicals, Rutgers—The State University, New Brunswick NJ 08903.

State Government. The Council of State Governments, PO Box 11910, Lexington KY 40578.

Teacher's College Record. Columbia University, 525 West 120th Street, New York NY 10027.

Technological Forecasting and Social Change. Futures Research Institute, Portland State University; Elsevier North-Holland, 52 Vanderbilt Ave, New York NY 10017.

Technology in Society. Pergamon Press, Fairview Park, Elmsford NY 10523.

Technology Review. Massachusetts Institute of Technology, Room 10-140, Cambridge MA 02139.

Telecommunications Policy. Butterworth Scientific Ltd, Westbury House, Bury Street, Guildford, Surrey GU2 5BH, England.

Transportation Quarterly. Eno Foundation for Transportation, Box 55, Saugatuck Station, Westport CT 06880.

U.S. News & World Report. 2300 N Street NW, Washington DC 20037.

The Virginia Quarterly Review. University of Virginia, One West Range, Charlottesville VA 22903.

Vital Speeches of the Day. City News Publishing Co, Box 606, Southold NY 11971.

The Wall Street Journal. Dow Jones & Co, 22 Cortlandt Street, New York NY 10007.

Washington Monthly. 1525 18th Street NW, Washington DC 20036.

The Washington Post. 1150 15th Street NW, Washington DC 20071.

The Wharton Magazine. University of Pennsylvania, 3609 Locust Walk, Philadelphia PA 19104.

Whole Earth Review. Box 428, Sausalito CA 94965. [NOTE: Continuation of *Co-Evolution Quarterly* as of Jan 1985.]

World Development. Pergamon Press, Fairview Park, Elmsford NY 10523.

World Future Society Bulletin. World Future Society, 4916 St. Elmo Ave, Bethesda MD 20814. [NOTE: Final issue published Nov-Dec 1984; continued as *Futures Research Quarterly* in Spring 1985.]

World Futures. Program in Studies of the Future, University of Houston at Clear Lake City; Gordon and Breach Science Publishers, One Park Ave, New York NY 10016.

World Policy Journal. World Policy Institute, 777 UN Plaza, New York NY 10017.

World Politics. Center of International Studies, Princeton University, Princeton NJ 08540.

INSTITUTES AND ASSOCIATIONS PUBLISHING BOOKS OR JOURNALS RELEVANT TO *FUTURE SURVEY*
(For full address, see listing under
Book Publishers or Periodical Publishers)

Academy of Political Science. See *Political Science Quarterly*.

American Academy of Arts and Sciences. See *Daedalus*.

American Academy of Political and Social Science. See *The Annals*.

American Association for the Advancement of Science. See *Science*.

American Council on Education. See *Education Record*.

American Enterprise Institute for Public Policy Research. Publishes books, reports, *Public Opinion* and *Regulation*.

American Humanist Association. See *The Humanist*.

American Institute of Biological Sciences. See *BioScience*.

American Jewish Committee. See *Commentary*.

American Planning Association. See Planners Press and *American Planning Association Journal*.

American Psychological Association. See *American Psychologist*.

American Society for Public Administration. See *Public Administration Review*.

Athens Center for Ekistics. See *Ekistics*.

Atlantic Council of the United States. See *Atlantic Community Quarterly*.

Blue Cross Association. See *Inquiry*.

Brookings Institution. Publishes books.

California Institute for Public Affairs. Publishes guidebooks.

Canadian Association for Future Studies. See *Futures Canada*.

Cato Institute. Publishes books and *Cato Journal*.

Center for Social Research and Education. See *Socialist Review*.

Center for the Study of Democratic Institutions. See *The Center Magazine*.

Center for the Study of Public Policy. See *Working Papers for a New Society*.

Center for Urban Policy Research. Publishes books.

Committee for Economic Development. Publishes books and reports.

Conference Board. See *across the board*.

Conference on Alternative State and Local Policies. Publishes books.

Conservation Foundation. Publishes books.

Council of State Governments. See *State Government*.

Council of State Planning Agencies. Publishes reports.

Council on Foreign Relations. See *Foreign Affairs*.

Dag Hammarskjold Centre. See *Development Dialogue*.

Eno Foundation for Transportation. See *Transportation Quarterly*.

Foreign Policy Research Institute. See *Orbis*.

Foundation for National Progress. See *Mother Jones*.

Friends of the Earth. Publishes books and *Not Man Apart*.

Heritage Foundation. Publishes books and *Policy Review*.

Hoover Institution. Publishes books.

Institute for Ecological Priorities. Publishes books and reports.

Institute for Food and Development Policy. Publishes books.

Institute for Policy Studies. Publishes books.

Institute for Research on Public Policy. Publishes books and reports.

Institute for Socioeconomic Studies. See *The Journal of the Institute for Socioeconomic Studies*.

Institute for World Order (see World Policy Institute).

Institute of Electrical and Electronics Engineers. See *IEEE Spectrum*.

Institute of Society, Ethics, and Life Sciences. See *Hastings Center Report*.

International Foundation for Development Alternatives. See *IFDA Dossier*.

International Solar Energy Society. See *Sunworld*.

Milbank Memorial Fund. See *Milbank Memorial Fund Quarterly*.

Minnesota Futurists. See *Futurics*.

National Municipal League. See *National Civic Review*.

National Planning Association. See *Looking Ahead & Projection Highlights*.

New York Academy of Sciences. See *The Sciences*.

North American Society for Corporate Planning. See *Planning Review*.

Organisation for Economic Cooperation and Development (OECD). Publishes books and *OECD Observer*.

Phi Beta Kappa. See *American Scholar*.

Phi Delta Kappa. See *Phi Delta Kappan*.

Policy Studies Organization. See *Policy Studies Journal*.

Population Reference Bureau. Publishes pamphlets and *Population Bulletin*.

Resources for the Future. Publishes books and reports through Johns Hopkins University Press.

Sigma Xi, The Scientific Research Society. See *American Scientist*.

Society for International Development. See *International Development Review*.

Society for Policy Modeling. See *Journal of Policy Modeling*.

Society for the Study of Social Problems. See *Social Problems*.

Swedish Academy of Sciences. See *Ambio*.

UNESCO. See *Impact of Science and Society* and *International Social Science Journal*.

UN, FAO. See *Ceres*.

W.E. Upjohn Institute. Publishes books.

The Urban Institute. Publishes books.

Woods Hole Oceanographic Institute. See *Oceanus*.

Work in America Institute. Publishes books.

World Future Society. Publishes books, *The Futurist*, *Future Survey*, and *Futures Research Quarterly*.

World Policy Institute. Publishes papers, *Alternatives*, and *World Policy Journal*.

Worldwatch Institute. Publishes books and papers.

NOTE: Many of these institutes and associations, and many others as well, are described in the 270-item "Organizations" section of **The Future: A Guide to Information Sources**, Second Edition (World Future Society, Oct 1979/720p/$25.00pb).

SUBJECT INDEX

AUTHOR INDEX